WISDEN

History of the
Cricket World Cup

Edited by Tony Cozier • Photography by Patrick Eagar

Designed by 809 Design Associates Inc.

With special thanks to Keith Miller, of Miller Publishing Company, and to Christopher Lane and Steven Lynch, of Wisden, for their part in initiating and producing this book; also Gordon Brooks for the use of his two photographs on pages 168 and 169.

First published in 2006 by Wordsmith International Incorporated,
under licence from John Wisden & Co. Ltd., 13 Old Aylesfield, Froyle Road, Alton, Hampshire GU34 4BY, UK

www.wisden.com
www.cricinfo.com

Printed in Singapore

ISBN 1-905625-04-9
ISBN 978-1-905625-04-8

Distributed in the UK by Macmillan Distribution Ltd
Distributed in Australia by Hardie Grant Books, Melbourne
Distributed in the West Indies by Miller Publishing Company

Contents

Main Contributors

Tony Cozier, born and bred in the cricket-obsessed island of Barbados, has reported on more than 300 Tests and innumerable One-Day Internationals for press, radio and television in every major cricket country since 1963. He published the now defunct *West Indies Cricket Annual* and *Caribbean Cricket Quarterly.*

Stephen Thorpe is an English freelance writer whose articles on cricket have appeared in several international publications and whose assignments include several stints in the West Indies.

Dicky Rutnagur, a native of Mumbai, has covered cricket – as well as squash and table tennis – internationally for more than 50 years. In addition to a career on the staff of the *Daily Telegraph,* London, he has written extensively on cricket for publications the world over and been a commentator on All India Radio and West Indian radio.

Mike Coward, an Australian, is a freelance journalist and one of Australia's most experienced and travelled cricket writers. He has covered the game throughout the world for leading newspapers and magazines since 1972. He has been cricket columnist of *The Australian* newspaper since 1992, has written or edited several books and also worked as commentator on radio and television.

Osman Samiuddin is Pakistan editor of Cricinfo, the game's largest internet website. He has also written extensively for Pakistani and international publications, including *The Guardian* and *The Observer,* London.

Alan Lee was, for many years, cricket correspondent for *The Times* of London, reporting on England's fortunes the world over before becoming the newspaper's racing correspondent, a position he currently holds. He has authored or co-authored several books of both sports.

Matthew Engel is in his second stint as editor of *Wisden Cricketers' Almanack,* the established annual authority on the game. He has been a wide-ranging columnist on *The Guardian* newspaper for which he also once served as Washington correspondent.

Peter Roebuck captained Cambridge University and Somerset in a first-class career that yielded 17,558 runs and 33 hundreds. Since 1991, when his playing days ended, he has been one of the most prolific writers on the game. He is now a columnist with the *Sydney Morning Herald* in Australia, where he resides, and radio commentator for the Australian Broadcasting Corporation (ABC).

Patrick Eagar is recognised as cricket's pre-eminent photographer. In a career of more than 40 years, he has clicked his camera shutters at more than 300 Tests and every World Cup tournament. Son of the former Hampshire captain, Desmond, his interest in cricket is shared by that for wine, a subject which also benefits from his photographic talent.

Reports on the semi-finals and finals are taken from Wisden, Wisden Cricket Monthly, the West Indies Cricket Annual and Caribbean Cricket Quarterly.

Scoreboards and statistics are provided by Cricinfo (www.cricinfo.com).

Foreword

By Clive Lloyd

THE World Cup has become a significant feature of the cricketing calendar. Beginning in 1975, moving out of the confines of the English professional game and responding to the public desire for a shorter time-frame and a guaranteed result, the competition has become a global sporting spectacle, rivalled only by the Olympic Games and World Cup soccer.

The 1975 World Cup gave formal status to the one-day international (ODI). This is how it should be, since a World Cup competition represents a panorama of skills and a galaxy of talent. It is on these occasions that spectators around the world can see all the major teams and players competing against each other at one and the same time in similar conditions. It is an exhibition of technical and creative batting and bowling.

As a boy in Guyana, not unlike any other throughout the Caribbean, cricket was merely one of life's simple pleasures. It allowed us to display our natural athletic instincts, complemented with boundless, youthful energy and constantly under the searing heat of an unforgiving sun, a sort of endless summer. We often missed meals while flirting with the wrath of uncooperative parents.

It was not too long after those early days, having heard the West Indies team celebrated in song after their famous victory over England at Lord's in 1950, that I began to have a sense of not only the spirit of the game but the real meaning of that solitary, seminal triumph to the people of the Caribbean.

The catchy lyrics of that calypso, written more than half a century ago by Lord Beginner, said it all:
Cricket lovely cricket/At Lord's where I saw it/Yardley tried his best/But West Indies won the Test/With those little pals of mine, Ramadhin and Valentine.

As Frank Birbalsingh wrote in his book *The Rise of West Indies Cricket*, "it was a victory that brought more joy to descendants of former slaves and indentured labourers than any other, in the whole history of cricket."

It was remarkable that the extraordinary performance of two ordinary young men from the rustic playing fields of the country districts of Trinidad and Jamaica – Sonny Ramadhin and Alfred Valentine – defined the path of West Indies cricket for decades to follow and began to galvanise the Caribbean as a community. As I recall, in those days, whether we were playing cricket on the beaches, or in the backyards of our homes, or on the sidewalk, or on dusty fields, we would each take on the names of those heroes of 1950: Ram and Val, Everton Weekes, Frank Worrell, Clyde Walcott, Allan Rae, Jeffrey Stollmeyer and so on. The heroes of a later generation were Garfield Sobers and Rohan Kanhai.

Ironically, 25 years on, at the very same hallowed turf at Lord's in 1975, another famous West Indies triumph, over Australia in the inaugural World Cup final, catapulted the team to the top of international cricket and, in the true spirit of the game, changed the face of cricket forever. And, for the next decade and a half, the single-minded passion and pride of the Caribbean community soared with the dominance of their cricket team.

Having played in the first three World Cups, I have followed with close attention the evolution of the limited-overs version of the game. It would be fitting here to recognise that women have been in the forefront in this process, as they have been in so many others, for the 1975 World Cup was modelled on, and subsequent to, the women's World Cup of 1973.

The 1975 World Cup, sponsored by the Prudential Assurance Company, was a competition of only eight countries, with innings restricted to 60 overs. After that, the competition became more global in nature. It moved to the playing fields of India and Pakistan in 1987, to Australia and New Zealand in 1992, back to Pakistan and India, along with Sri Lanka, in 1996, to England again in 1999 and to South Africa for the first time four years later.

Now it is our turn, the turn of the West Indies to host this prestigious event with the pride and passion for which our people are well known.

The limitation on the number of overs in an innings has been standardised to 50, while the number of teams has doubled from the inaugural tournament, from eight to sixteen. There will be 51

matches in the Caribbean, spread over 54 days at eight different venues under the aegis of the International Cricket Council (ICC). The victorious West Indies team I had the honour to captain in 1975 played just five matches. Yes, the World Cup has truly grown in stature and extent.

In the beginning, the one-day game seemed tailor-made for the West Indies. Not many observers would have been too surprised that we notched the first triumphs in the Prudential Cup in 1975 and 1979. But for a painful loss to India in the final when we snatched defeat from the jaws of victory, we would have taken it back home to the Caribbean for good in 1983.

I will long remember my 102 off 85 balls in 1975 – the first century in a World Cup final – against the unrelenting Australian attack of Dennis Lillee and Jeff Thomson, Gary Gilmour and Max Walker – gathered with none of the fielding and bowling restrictions of today.

But ours was truly a team effort, with the great Rohan Kanhai, at 39 years old, grafting an invaluable half-century, and Viv Richards and Alvin Kallicharran putting on a fielding clinic as they garnered no fewer than five run-outs. There was no more exhilarating experience than holding the Prudential Cup aloft, with my team-mates around me, on the balcony at Lord's that night. And winning the World Cup for the second successive time in 1979, the only captain to have done so up till now, remains one of my greatest achievements.

Again it was a tribute to a great team. How could one forget the enthralling exhibition of batsmanship by Richards and Collis King in the 1979 final against England, or the awesome spectacle of our pacers, Joel Garner, Malcolm Marshall, Michael Holding and Andy Roberts, in full flight.

The shortened version of the game is now a permanent feature of international cricket. No Test series is complete without complementary ODIs. In my judgment this is a positive development as one-day – and, of course, night – cricket is compelling teams to bring greater creativity in their execution of the game. It serves as a laboratory for innovations and inventions relevant to cricket's further advance. In short, the ODI has not only fostered increased interest in the game on a global scale (China is among the latest members of the ICC) but has also had a positive impact on its longer, traditional version. It is not rare to see the reverse sweep played or novel field-placings employed in a Test match, all adapted from one-day cricket. Equally, it is doubtful whether the *doosra* would have been developed, or Test teams score at a notably faster rate, as they do these days, without the influence of the shorter game. Lastly, the ODIs, with large crowds and the attendant carnival atmosphere, are a sponsors' dream. They are a response to the need for more attractive cricket as well as the desires and deeply held feelings of the societies of those countries where cricket is entrenched.

As we welcome the world, not only to the legendary warmth and hospitality of the Caribbean, but to "the best Cricket World Cup ever", we must pay tribute to the sophisticated planning and organisation model so successfully executed by the 2007 West Indies World Cup Committee. Structurally, it is a model that should be emulated henceforth across the region as a formula for success.

If the short-term gain of a successful 2007 Cricket World Cup will be a financial windfall for the West Indies Cricket Board, the long-term benefits for the entire Caribbean and for West Indies cricket take on even greater proportions. Physically, new avenues of trade, tourism and technical assistance will develop to boost Caribbean economies, and the region will be the inheritors of much-needed world-class cricket infrastructure. Psychologically, a successfully staged World Cup tournament would cement Caribbean unity and validate a culture of confidence and an attitude of consistent achievement.

I am convinced that together we can create another first at the 2007 World Cup. At no time in the history of World Cup cricket has the host nation won the Cup. The power and support of the people of the Caribbean and the cohesion of the West Indies team could make this another first milestone.

The nature and scope of World Cup cricket and the drama and statistics that result from it, provide fertile soil for this unique book, the first to chronicle the previous eight tournaments in such detail and to preview the ninth. Well and lavishly illustrated, it takes the reader from the origins of the ODI to its evolution into a global spectacle and its mass appeal in a world driven by sponsorship and commercial considerations. The statistics which accompany the text are also fascinating and informative. Looking at them the West Indian fan, in particular, will note the glory years of their team. Versed as they are in the history and intricacies of the game, the West Indian cricket fans will also take careful note that the contents serve notice that there are global players at the top of international cricket whose excellence has been driven by their ability and capacity to harness technological innovation.

This book, edited by Tony Cozier, the West Indies' most experienced cricket writer and commentator, will add to the knowledge of those who are interested in cricket generally and to the future of West Indian cricket in particular.

Clive Lloyd captained the West Indies to victory in the first two World Cups in 1975 and 1979 and the final in 1983. He led the West Indies in 74 of his 110 Tests. He is now an ICC Match Referee and Chairman of the West Indies Cricket Board cricket committee.

Simply the **Best**

Patrick Eagar, the game's foremost photographer who has seen all eight World Cup finals, makes his personal choice and places them in order of excitement

1. **1975** In my opinion there have been only two great finals and this, the first, was the best of all. It had everything you could ask for. High drama, great cricket and suspense.

2. **1983** Just great for the twist in the tail. "What a boring one-sided final," we said at tea. How wrong we were as India humbled the mighty West Indies.

3. **1987** England's finest hour, looking to beat Australia at Calcutta – then Gatting's infamous reverse sweep which ruined everything.

4. **1996** Sri Lanka on a roll took the world by surprise. Their Lahore victory over Australia in the final was richly deserved.

5. **1992** England missed out to Pakistan in Melbourne and felt bitterly disappointed since they had already performed so well against them.

6. **2003** Ponting's innings was awesome but when Tendulkar was caught and bowled by McGrath in the first over, it was all over.

7. **1979** Chasing the West Indies total of 286, Brearley and Boycott batted as if it was a five-day Test. No contest.

8. **1999** It took Australia only 20 overs to get the runs after Pakistan were bowled out for 132.

The crowd in front of the Lord's pavilion after the 1975 final seem to agree with Patrick Eagar that it was the best.

Introduction

By Tony Cozier

It has evolved from a hopeful experiment into cricket's biggest, richest, most prestigious tournament.

Boldly initiated by the International Cricket Conference in 1975, at a time when limited-overs cricket was so much in its infancy that only 18 such international matches had ever been played (and then only in Australia, England and New Zealand), the World Cup has grown into an expensive, globally televised four-yearly extravaganza, organised with the detailed planning of a major military operation.

The inaugural tournament comprised eight teams and 15 matches. It was over in a fortnight. No upgrading of venues was needed, no additional investment required. But it was such a rousing success that its continuation and expansion were guaranteed.

As sponsors and television networks gradually recognised the value of such a wide-reaching sporting event, whose interest extended across diverse racial and cultural backgrounds and was strongest in the second-most populous nation on earth, the World Cup expanded, both financially and geographically.

The overall takings in 1975, from sponsorship of Britain's Prudential Assurance company, media rights and ticket sales were £100,000. In 2000, the Global Cricket Corporation (GCC), a subsidiary of Rupert Murdoch's Newscorp, negotiated a seven-year contract for commercial rights to all ICC tournaments worth US$550 million. It meant that the 2003 champions, Australia, pocketed US$2 million for their triumph. The 2007 edition, the first ever to come to the Caribbean, features 16 teams, 51 matches and occupies seven weeks. New stadiums are being constructed, others refurbished in the eight hosting countries.

Strict security measures have to be put in place and sponsors' rights must be protected by special legislation against so-called ambush marketing.

Governments have invested heavily in the expectation of a collective financial aftermath estimated by optimistic officials at US$500 million. The first three tournaments were hosted by England, cricket's ancestral home, before the potential for profit and promotion inevitably led to the spread across cricket's established, if limited, outposts and beyond.

In an affiliation that overrode the sharp political differences that led them three times to war, Pakistan and India twice combined to host the Cup, in 1987 and, with a third neighbour, Sri Lanka, in 1996. Australia and New Zealand were the shared venues in 1992. England held it once more in 1999 and South Africa in 2003, eleven years after the end of their ostracism from international sport for the apartheid policy of the government.

In 1999, England gave one match each to Holland and Ireland and two to Scotland. South Africa sought to make the 2003 tournament a celebration for the continent as a whole by allocating matches to Zimbabwe and Kenya, a noble gesture ultimately undermined by politics and its modern associate, terrorism.

The only two full members of the ICC (no longer Conference, but Council) yet to put on the Cup are the West Indies and Bangladesh. That is soon to be rectified. The Caribbean were awarded the 2007 event, Bangladesh a share in 2011 with sub-continental neighbours India, Pakistan and Sri Lanka. There are off-shoots that have rendered the Cup truly international. For the first tournament, the numbers were made up by teams from Canada and combined East Africa, the former supposedly representing

The obligatory fireworks display at opening and closing ceremonies have varied from Calcutta's spectacular climax in 1987 to the damp squibs at the Lord's launch in 1999 (inset).

North America, the latter the only entrant from that continent in the absence of the debarred South Africa.

They were chosen on an ad hoc basis, an unsatisfactory arrangement that was corrected when the ICC Trophy for the associates, those teams below Test level, was instituted in 1979 to determine the qualifiers. It was held in England in 1979, 1982 and 1986, Holland in 1990, Kenya in 1994, Malaysia in 1997, Canada in 2001 and Ireland in 2005, yet it is more than simply identifying those to proceed into the Cup proper.

The ICC Trophy is also an opportunity for the humble, yet zealous, amateurs of Argentina, Gibraltar, Hong Kong, Israel and the like to test their standards and enjoy the camaraderie cricket stimulates. Sri Lanka, Zimbabwe, Holland, Kenya, the United Arab Emirates, Scotland, Bangladesh and Namibia all won the right to compete alongside the powerhouses of world cricket through the tournament. Bermuda and Ireland make their first appearance at the top level in 2007. Sri Lanka, Zimbabwe and Bangladesh subsequently advanced to Test status.

Nor is the ICC Trophy the only derivative of the World Cup's success. The mini World Cup, as it was appropriately, if unofficially, dubbed because of its compressed schedule, was initiated in 1998 and held every two years since. The Champions Trophy, as it became, involved all the main teams along with two associates competing on a straight knockout basis.

Its purpose was ostensibly to raise funds for ICC projects in cricket's developing countries and to fly the flag in those not yet in the Test loop. The first was held in Bangladesh and the second in Kenya before it gravitated back to the main centres, to Sri Lanka in 2002, England in 2004 and India in 2006. It is not only the composition and financial structure of the World Cup that have changed over time.

The first three World Cups in England were little more than the traditional game abbreviated to one innings, each restricted to 60 overs. The clothing was white, the ball red, there were no additional limits on field placing and the hours were in daylight.

By the end of the 1970s, Kerry Packer's World Series Cricket in Australia had given one-day cricket its own special identity, with coloured uniforms, white balls (initially one from each end to avoid discoloration), field-restricting zones and floodlights. The world eventually, if not entirely willingly in some cases, was compelled to follow. The 1992 World Cup

The joyful multi-cultural, multi-national character of the World Cup has always been typified by the crowds – and there was no character more identifiable than Pakistani cheerleader Abdul Jalil or characters more motley than the England's Barmy Army in 1992 in Sydney.

How the Cup has **Grown**

Year	Hosts/Venues	Teams	Days	Matches
1975	England	8	15	15
1979	England	8	15	15
1983	England	8	17	27
1987	India/Pakistan	8	32	27
1992	Australia/New Zealand	9	33	39
1996	India/Pakistan/Sri Lanka	12	33	37
2000	England (Ireland/Holland)	12	38	42
2003	South Africa (Zimbabwe/Kenya)	14	43	54
2007	West Indies	16	49	51

was the first to adopt the Packer reforms, and they have become the norm since.

By then, the number of overs had been standardised to 50 an innings, initially to accommodate the shorter days in the 1987 event in India and Pakistan, and an international panel of umpires assembled, a precursor to the arrangement eventually introduced to Test cricket.

As with every sporting showpiece, politics has been an occasional, uninvited guest.

South Africa was disqualified from all international sport until the apartheid regime that ran the country was replaced in 1992, so one of the world's strongest teams missed the first four tournaments. In the first round in 1975, Tamil activists carried their placard-bearing protests against the Sri Lankan government on to the pitch at Old Trafford, delaying play in the match between Sri Lanka and the West Indies.

In 1986, the carnage created by a suicide bomber in Colombo so scared Australia and the West Indies that they forfeited their scheduled matches there a few weeks later rather than taking the minimal security risk.

A deadly terrorist attack in Nairobi prior to the 2003 tournament also persuaded New Zealand to sacrifice their match against Kenya. To the south, Andy Flower and Henry Olonga, two prominent Zimbabwe players, wore black armbands to draw attention to the deteriorating political situation in their country – for which they have not played since. England dithered over whether to fulfil their scheduled match in Zimbabwe, eventually deciding to stay away. They cited security concerns when it was clear the reason was more to do with the government's human-rights record.

Such distractions have been peripheral to the triumphs and the tribulations on the field. The wild national celebrations, and corresponding despair, that

have greeted famous upsets confirm the significance of sport to the human psyche.

There was spontaneous joy among the millions of passionate fans in India following the victory of Kapil Dev's team in the 1983 final over the seemingly invincible West Indies, champions of the first two tournaments. The people of Sri Lanka celebrated similarly in 1996 when Arjuna Ranatunga's self-confident, underestimated side beat Australia in the final at Lahore to dispel the depression of their prolonged civil war.

And, just as pertinent as winning the Cup itself, there were Kenya's defeat of the West Indies (all out 93) in their first Cup appearance in 1996, and Bangladesh's emphatic despatch of their Pakistani cousins in England in 1999, a result that fast-tracked Bangladesh to premature Test status but raised questions as to its authenticity.

Remarkably, no home captain has yet held the Cup aloft, while England remain the only hosts even to reach the final.

Australia, the most successful team with three titles, England and South Africa have all had the sinking feeling of departing after the first round in their own tournaments.

Yet, as recently as 40 years ago, a World Cup of cricket was inconceivable. International cricket was then limited to five-day Tests and a round-robin series, even among as few teams as the six with such status at the time, was plainly too time-consuming to contemplate.

Ironically, it was declining public interest in the attrition of the traditional game in England in the 1950s that persuaded generally conservative administrators to initiate the revolution of one-day cricket in their domestic season in 1963. It was 12 years before the first World Cup followed. Cricket has not been the same since.

World Cup **1975**

by Tony Cozier

Cricket's first World Cup was, I wrote at the time, the boldest and most ambitious innovation since the legalisation of overarm bowling. The hyperbole was not misplaced for its success, well beyond the expectations of even the most fervent optimist, instantly guaranteed its future.

Such an event was possible only through the formal, if measured, introduction of one-day limited-overs internationals a few years earlier, a natural progression from such tournaments introduced into English county cricket in the 1960s. England, as the birthplace of the game, and with its short travelling distances, its long summer days and its large emigrant populations from the cricket-playing Commonwealth, was the obvious venue.

There were as many as 60 overs an innings, with no additional restrictions on field placings, the players were dressed in customary white, and the ball was red. The exercise was viewed with scepticism by those who perceived trifling with the most traditional of all sports as an abomination but, for two weeks in England in June, it captured the wider public's imagination. The fans flocked to the 15 matches, with an aggregate attendance of 158,000 paying more than £200,000 to watch an enthralling competition.

The final at Lord's, a ground synonymous with the game itself, was a wonderful match in which the West Indies beat Australia by 17 runs. It drew a capacity, multinational crowd of 26,000 and gate receipts of £66,000, then a record for a single day's cricket in England.

There was a healthy profit derived from the sponsorship of £100,000 from the British insurance company, Prudential, television and radio rights, and ticket sales. It was split 10% to the hosts, England, 7.5% to the other seven participating teams, and the remainder to the inaugurators, the International Cricket Conference (ICC), for distribution to associate

The culmination of a long and happy day for Clive Lloyd as the West Indies captain and Man of the Match raises the Prudential Cup after receiving it from the admiring Prince Philip, the Duke of Edinburgh.

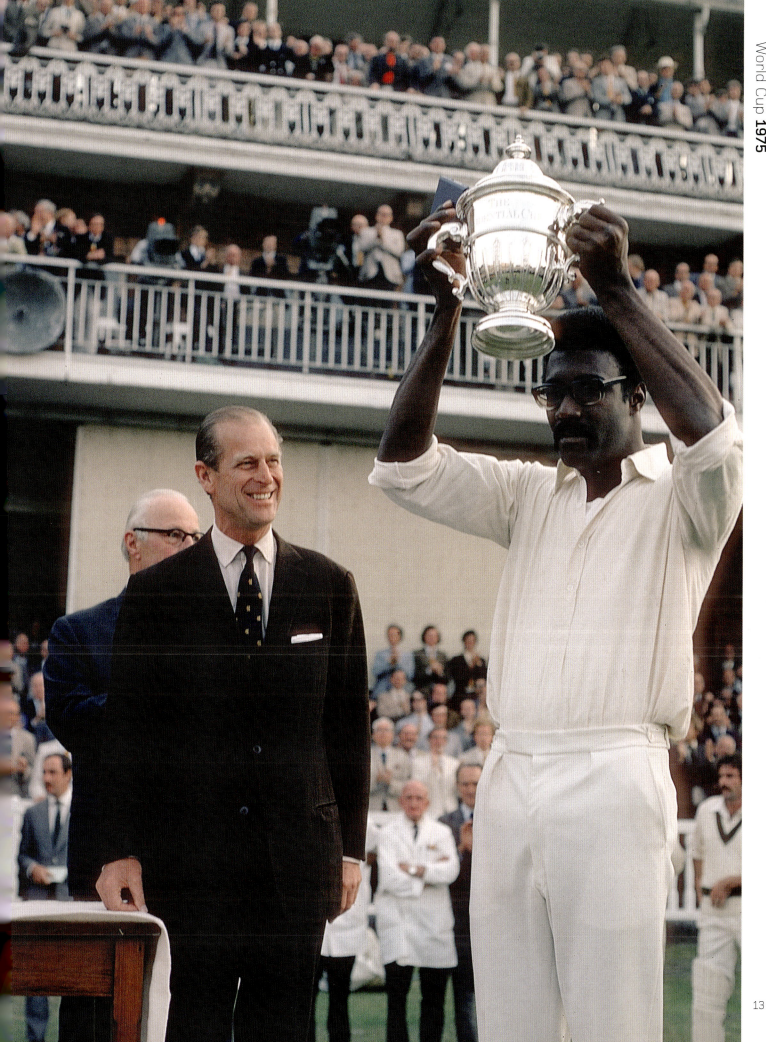

members, for its coaching programmes and for promotion of the next tournament.

One of the principal reasons for its triumphant run was the weather, as it needed to be. It remained glorious, if uncharacteristically British, all the way through. Not a ball was lost, and the final was able to run up to 8.41 p.m. in bright sunlight on the longest day of the year, June 21.

Such luck with the climate was complemented by the quality of the cricket. It is true that the two teams with little or no experience of international cricket – Sri Lanka, still six years away from Test status, and East Africa (a combination of Kenya, Tanzania and Uganda) – were out of their depth. Yet every round produced its fascination.

The West Indies were justifiable favourites, and lived up to the bookmakers' confidence. Their strength lay in their all-round depth, their fielding and the experience that 11 of their squad of 14 had of the special demands of the limited-overs format from their seasons of county cricket.

They did have one scare, in the first round against mercurial Pakistan, when they squeezed home by one wicket with two balls remaining. That apart, they showed themselves palpably the best team. Either side of the Pakistan thriller, they despatched Sri Lanka by nine wickets in 56 overs and, in a prelude to the final, beat Australia by seven wickets at The Oval, in the heart of London's pulsating West Indian population.

New Zealand proved no match in the semi-final, defeated by five wickets with as many as 19.5 overs remaining.

The West Indies captain, Clive Lloyd, a destroyer in spectacles, set up victory in the final – with significant help from Viv Richards, whose electrifying speed and throwing accuracy was responsible for undermining Australia's top order with three run-outs. It was immediate and conclusive confirmation of the enhanced value of fielding in the shortened game.

Lloyd's 102 from 85 balls was an exhilarating exhibition of power-hitting that saw the West Indies to 291 for eight from their 60 overs. He followed it with a containing spell of medium-pace bowling (12-1-38-1) that kept Australia in check as they were dismissed for 274.

The Australians were scheduled to play a series of four Tests against England following the Cup, and their captain, Ian Chappell, had made it plain that that was their main focus. With limited-overs cricket still in its infancy back home, they were reportedly not keen on it. But, being Australians, they were even less keen on losing.

The draw placed the West Indies, Australia and Pakistan in the same group that was completed by Sri Lanka. Only two could advance to the semi-final and Pakistan, also filled with county players, were the

unfortunate ones to miss out, even though they severely tested Australia and, by all that is logical, should have beaten the West Indies, whose last two wickets put on 110.

Sri Lanka might have fared better in the less-demanding group. Although they endured three heavy defeats on their way out, they won a host of fans with plucky batting that raised 276 for four against Australia at The Oval, even after two of their batsmen had to be hospitalised after taking blows from the fiery Jeff Thomson. Their time would come.

England had the advantage of a more favourable draw, and coasted into the semi-final after sweeping all three qualifying matches. They amassed 266 for six against New Zealand, 290 for five against East Africa and 334 for four against India, the tournament's highest total. The standard of their opponents only camouflaged England's known weaknesses, which were exposed in the semi-final against Australia when, on an appalling pitch at Headingley, they were routed for 93 by the left-arm swing and seam of Gary Gilmour (12-6-14-6) and lost by five wickets.

The second qualifier from the group, New Zealand, depended heavily on their captain, Glenn Turner, an established county pro with Worcestershire. He batted through the innings against both East Africa and India to become the only batsman to make two hundreds in the tournament. When he failed against England, and against the West Indies in the semi-final, his team couldn't muster 200 and lost comfortably.

India did run New Zealand close in their decisive first-round match, but a semi-final place would have been an undeserving honour after they reduced their match against England, the showpiece opener at Lord's, to a farce. They paid for the selectorial madness of omitting their left-arm spin wizard Bishan Bedi to be hammered around at 5.5 runs an over, and made little effort to compete. Sunil Gavaskar, their finest batsman, epitomised their cynical attitude by batting through the 60 overs for 36 not out. It took the sparkle of that ebullient cricketer, Abid Ali, to erase some of the shame with a thrilling, yet futile, all-round performance against New Zealand (70 and 12-2-35-2).

Africa's strongest team, South Africa, and its neighbour, Rhodesia, had both placed themselves beyond the pale of international sport by the racial policies of their governments. It would be another 17 years before the end of apartheid allowed South Africa's formal re-entry into international cricket, another six before the end of the illegal Ian Smith regime and the emergence of independent Zimbabwe. So it was left to the inadequate amalgamation of East Africa to represent the continent. Comprising weekend club cricketers never

before exposed to such standards, they were duly
outclassed.

The competition was an unqualified success even
before the final, but a remarkable match was a fitting
climax. "It might not be termed first-class," noted
Wisden, "but the game has never provided better
entertainment in one day."

The famous old ground had never seen anything
like it. It set a standard by which all subsequent finals
would be judged – and none has yet matched it.

*More trouble for Australia in the final as the predatory
Viv Richards prepares to effect his third run-out, beating
Ian Chappell with his spot-on throw to bowler Clive Lloyd.*

SEMI-FINALS
West Indies v New Zealand

At The Oval, June 18, 1975. West Indies won by five wickets.

The West Indies advanced to the final with few real worries. New Zealand were, as always, good, hard opponents but at no time did they genuinely threaten an upset.

Put in by Clive Lloyd, they went to lunch at 92 for one after 29 overs with their dangerous captain, Glenn Turner, still in occupation, and it appeared that the West Indies' batsmen would have a greater challenge than expected.

Andy Roberts soon ended such speculation with a spell of bowling as fast as any he had produced in the tournament. In the space of five overs, he disposed of Turner, to Rohan Kanhai's sharp, low catch at first slip, and Geoff Howarth, who played with great fluency for his half-century. Both edged outswingers and that, to all intents and purposes, was the end of the New Zealand effort.

Turner was the key to the New Zealand innings. He carried his bat for unbeaten centuries in first-round victories over East Africa and India and clearly set himself to repeat. Once Roberts removed him and Howarth, the Surrey pro on his home ground, and Lloyd's medium-pace found a way through John Parker's defence, New Zealand had declined to 106 for four. Bernard Julien's left-arm swing and Vanburn Holder's accurate seam swept aside the remaining six wickets, leaving No. 5 Brian Hastings stranded with 24.

New Zealand utilised only 52.2 of their allocated 60 overs, a vital shortfall that left the West Indies with a comfortable target. They initially approached it with the care and attention presumably prompted by the collapse after lunch of nine New Zealanders for 66 in 23.2 overs, the news of a similar clatter of wickets in the other semi-final at Headingley and the early loss of the cavalier left-hander Roy Fredericks.

Gordon Greenidge and Alvin Kallicharran, plunderer of Lillee, Thomson and the Australians at the same venue only a few days earlier, were so out of

character that the first 10 overs yielded only 21. Richard Collinge, the big left-arm fast bowler, was spelled after six overs that cost a mere seven runs. By tea, the two West Indians were travelling at a more familiar clip, carrying their partnership to 125 off 29 overs before Kallicharran, who had a six and seven fours in his 72, offered Collinge a low return catch.

New Zealand had the consolation of the wickets of Greenidge, Viv Richards and Lloyd, but the West Indies were winners with 19.5 overs to spare, to the satisfaction of their numerous supporters in a crowd of 15,000 that once more basked in the sunny, Caribbean-like weather.

(*Tony Cozier*)

Australia v England

At Headingley, June 18, 1975. Australia won by four wickets.

In recent years the Headingley pitch had been criticised as unsuitable for the big-match occasion. This surface was criticised by both captains as well. In

that a game, supposedly involving some of the finest batsmen in the world, could be finished in 65 overs, there was much to be said for their opinion. Yet there was no feeling of being cheated by anyone in the capacity crowd.

There was tremendous excitement, especially when Australia, in search of 94 runs needed to win, lost six wickets for 39. Gasps, groans or cheers followed every ball.

The strip was the same as that used ten days earlier in the Pakistan-Australia game, but the groundsman had watered it and it looked green and damp. Australia had no hesitation about putting England in

Above right: Another boundary for the prancing Clive Lloyd in his 102 in the final.

Above left: Too fast, too precise for Alan Turner, Viv Richards executes the first of his three decisive run-outs in the final.

to bat after winning the toss and, from the way the fieldsmen ran to change round at the end of each over, they were obviously trying to get in as many overs as possible before the greenness went or, if things went badly, they were concerned about batting in the faint light of late evening.

They need not have worried, for things went gloriously right for them. Their fast-medium, left-arm bowler Gary Gilmour ripped through the England batting. Bowling a full length, over the wicket, he not only swung the ball in the heavy atmosphere but moved it both ways after pitching. Bringing the ball back in, he had Dennis Amiss, Keith Fletcher, Frank Hayes and Alan Knott lbw, Fletcher without playing a shot, the others playing back. He bowled Barry Wood with a perfect yorker and had Tony Greig caught one-handed by the flying wicketkeeper, Rodney Marsh. In his 12 overs, bowled in one spell, Gilmour took six for 14. England came in for lunch at 52 for eight. Captain Mike Denness and the tail took the score to 93 in Gilmour's absence.

Not until the eighth over did England meet success

when Australia replied and then John Snow and Chris Old ripped into the Australian batsmen as dramatically as Gilmour had treated England. Then came Gilmour as a batsman. With Doug Walters, he shared an unbroken partnership of 55 that carried Australia to their goal. The huge crowd rose to him and the former West Indies captain, Jeffrey Stollmeyer, had no difficulty in naming him Man of the Match.
(Wisden Cricketers' Almanack, 1976)

The catch of the tournament as Australia's wicketkeeper Rodney Marsh clings on to Tony Greig's edge in the semi-final against England at Headingley, one of Gary Gilmour's six wickets for 14.

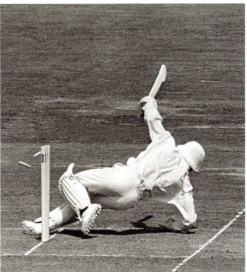

Left: Aged 39, a late replacement in the tournament for the injured Garry Sobers and in his last match at Lord's, the greying but evergreen Rohan Kanhai strokes leg-side runs during his critical 55 in the final.

Top: Australia's captain Ian Chappell swings high and hard over mid-wicket during his 62 in the final. But he was soon the third of Viv Richards' run-out victims.

Above: Six and out for West Indies' opener Roy Fredericks, who falls back onto his stumps after depositing Dennis Lillee's bouncer into the crowd at fine-leg in the final.

FINAL
West Indies v Australia

At Lord's, June 21, 1975. West Indies won by 17 runs.
Inspired by a magical performance by their captain, Clive Lloyd, the West Indies became the first World Cup champions with victory in a final that did the occasion proud.

The sun shone warmly throughout the longest day of the year, cricket's most famous ground was packed with a happy, colourful, multiracial crowd that spilled over to the edge of the roped boundary – and, for over nine hours, they watched international sport at its most competitive and its most entertaining. For the large West Indian section there was justifiable cause

for jubilation, for ringing their bells and for beating out Caribbean rhythms with used beer cans and recently consumed rum bottles.

The match was virtually decided by Lloyd's 102 off 85 balls, with two sixes and ten fours. From first ball to last, it was a brutal assault on the Australian bowling, of whom only the left-handed Gary Gilmour escaped unscathed.

A total of 291 for eight from 60 overs always seemed beyond Australia's capabilities – no team had ever made as many to win a limited-overs international – but there was an early threat that was checked by the accurate medium-pace of, who else, Lloyd, and the dynamic fielding of Viv Richards, whose anticipation, speed and pin-point throwing ran out three of the top four in the order, Alan Turner and the Chappell brothers.

The West Indies innings was not entirely a one-man show. While Lloyd was rampant, he was given quiet, reassuring support by the greying, yet evergreen, Rohan Kanhai, an opportune replacement drafted into the team at the last moment on the withdrawal, through injury, of Garry Sobers. His 55 was a highly significant contribution after the loss of three wickets for 50 in the first hour and 20 minutes. The partnership of 149 between the tall, power-hitting left-handed captain and his dapper, classical right-handed predecessor converted what might have been disaster into a position of command.

Australia chose to bowl on winning the toss and

claimed three early wickets, among them the unlucky Roy Fredericks who hooked Dennis Lillee into the stand at fine leg only to lose his footing and tumble back onto his stumps.

Lloyd, maroon cap jauntily perched on his head, strode to the middle earlier than he cared to and immediately stamped his authority on play, hooking Lillee for his first six, following with another off Max Walker whose last five overs went for 49 after his first seven cost 22.

Australia missed one chance to remove the rampaging Lloyd. He was 26 when Ross Edwards just failed to make a terrific catch low to his right at mid-wicket from a stroke off Lillee. He was eventually given out off a deflection down the leg side to wicket-keeper Rodney Marsh, waiting briefly for the umpires to confirm the catch was clean before departing to a standing ovation.

After Lloyd, Kanhai and Richards were dismissed in quick succession, the all-rounders Keith Boyce and Bernard Julien and the wicketkeeper Deryck Murray picked up the momentum again, contributing 82 for the last two wickets in the closing overs.

The Australians faced a considerable challenge, and it was clear they needed to take risks to meet it. As it turned out, they took a few too many. The first, in the 21st over, ended a growing stand of 56 between the left-handed Turner and Ian Chappell. Chappell turned a ball in Lloyd's first over to mid-wicket, there was a yes, a no and then a yes ... and just enough hesitation

to allow the sprinting Richards to find Turner short of his ground with a direct hit.

Two more run-outs by Richards and Lloyd's controlled medium-pace swung the balance decisively towards the West Indies on resumption. Richards again threw the stumps down to remove Greg Chappell, and when brother Ian hesitated for the last time, over a single, Richards, from wide of mid-on, returned to the bowler Lloyd and ran him out as well. There was no way a team composed largely of county professionals well versed in the demands of the shortened game would allow the Cup to slip from their grasp after Australia slipped to 170 for five, although their typically tenacious opponents carried the fight down to the very last wicket and the penultimate over amid mounting tension and unforgettable scenes.

When Lillee and Jeff Thomson came together for the last wicket, they needed to score 42 to clinch the Cup, an unlikely equation for a pair best known as fast-bowling partners. But there was a twist to the tale yet. Swinging effectively and scampering between wickets like a pair of Olympic sprinters, they ended the match with a fitting and exciting flurry.

When Thomson gave Fredericks a high catch at cover off Vanburn Holder, it was the signal for an invasion by hundreds of spectators who took it as the end of the contest. Umpire Dickie Bird's best efforts to have his no-ball shout heard were futile and, to add to the confusion, Fredericks's throw at the bowler's

end as the batsmen started to run, skidded into the outfield between stampeding legs. By the time the field was cleared, no one was sure how many the Australians had run. The umpires decided, in the circumstances, to award three.

Thomson and Lillee reduced the gap to 17, but only nine balls remained when Thomson charged down to Holder, missed, and was thrown out by Murray from 15 yards back, the fifth run-out of the innings.

At 8.41 precisely, a great tournament and a great match had finally ended. A few minutes later, in gathering darkness and before an ecstatic crowd, Lloyd received the Prudential World Cup, and his Man of the Match award, from Prince Philip.
(Tony Cozier)

Above left: It is a lengthier wait than anticipated for the police in front of the Taverner's Bar while Dennis Lillee and Jeff Thomson prolong the final with their pulsating last-wicket partnership. When Australia were finally beaten by 17 runs, they were powerless to prevent the inevitable human stampede anyhow.

Above right: The moment both captains were aware the final was all but decided. Seen off by his ice-cool counterpart Clive Lloyd, Ian Chappell heads for the pavilion after falling victim to another piece of Viv Richards' fielding magic.

"They said at the time"

West Indies captain Clive Lloyd on the final: *"We knew that, on that wicket, we had to make a fairly big score and that at least one of our batsmen had to really fire. Fortunately, I happened to be in good form but, although I would rank my innings as one of the best I've played, we would have been nowhere without the support of Rohan Kanhai and the thrust given at the end by the lower order."*

Clive Lloyd: *"The fielding, that was the outstanding feature. I'd told Viv Richards before the match that these Australians are very good runners between the wickets but that they do tend to take chances. I thought a run-out or two was on. It so happened, to our advantage, there were even more."*

Australia captain Ian Chappell on the final: *"The main difference between the teams was the fielding. Their fielding was tremendous and Richards was like a panther. Their throwing was right on the spot. On that good pitch and fast outfield, I thought we had a chance to get the runs but we had to take risks. I have to pay tribute to Clive Lloyd. His innings was magnificent and it was this that changed the game in the first place. He also bowled excellently. It was a superb all-round achievement."*

West Indies team manager Clyde Walcott: *"We won because we played well as a team and we fielded well throughout the competition. The latter, in my view, made the difference between the teams in the final."*

Former England captain Ted Dexter, in the Sunday Mirror: *"Cricket lovers will always remember the day when victorious West Indies skipper Clive Lloyd became King of Lord's with a majestic century in even time."*

Former England batsman Denis Compton: *"Lloyd deservedly took the Man of the Match award for his marvellous, all-round performance. His spectacular 102 was one of the greatest innings I have ever seen."*

Format

Two qualifying groups of four, playing each other once in 60-over matches; top two in each group progressed to semi-finals; 15 matches in all.

Innovations

Not many, apart from the concept itself (there had only been 18 ODIs worldwide before this). Most teams still treated the matches as if they were truncated Tests – especially India, who played for a draw in the first game, responding to England's 334 for four with 132 for three. Sunil Gavaskar batted through the 60 overs for 36 not out; a disgusted spectator dumped his lunch at the opener's feet.

World Cup 1975
Scoreboards

England v India, Group A
At Lord's, London, 7 June 1975 (60-overs)
Result: England won by 202 runs. Points: England 4, India 0.
Toss: England. Umpires: DJ Constant and JG Langridge.
Man of the Match: DL Amiss.

England innings (60 overs maximum)			R	B	4	6
JA Jameson	c Venkataraghavan	b Amarnath	21	42	2	0
DL Amiss		b Madan Lal	137	147	18	0
KWR Fletcher		b Abid Ali	68	107	4	0
AW Greig	lbw	b Abid Ali	4	8	0	0
*MH Denness	not out		37	31	2	1
CM Old	not out		51	30	4	2
Extras	(lb 12, w 2, nb 2)		16			
Total	(4 wickets, 60 overs)		334			

DNB: B Wood, +APE Knott, JA Snow, P Lever, GG Arnold.
Fall of wickets: 1-54 (Jameson), 2-230 (Fletcher), 3-237 (Greig), 4-245 (Amiss).

Bowling	O	M	R	W
Madan Lal	12	1	64	1
Amarnath	12	2	60	1
Abid Ali	12	0	58	2
Ghavri	11	1	83	0
Venkataraghavan	12	0	41	0
Solkar	1	0	12	0

India innings (target: 335 runs from 60 overs)			R	B	4	6
SM Gavaskar	not out		36	174	1	0
ED Solkar	c Lever	b Arnold	8	34	0	0
AD Gaekwad	c Knott	b Lever	22	46	2	0
GR Viswanath	c Fletcher	b Old	37	59	5	0
BP Patel	not out		16	57	0	0
Extras	(lb 3, w 1, nb 9)		13			
Total	(3 wickets, 60 overs)		132			

DNB: M Amarnath, +FM Engineer, S Abid Ali, S Madan Lal, *S Venkataraghavan, KD Ghavri.
Fall of wickets: 1-21 (Solkar), 2-50 (Gaekwad), 3-108 (Viswanath).

Bowling	O	M	R	W
Snow	12	2	24	0
Arnold	10	2	20	1
Old	12	4	26	1
Greig	9	1	26	0
Wood	5	2	4	0
Lever	10	0	16	1
Jameson	2	1	3	0

East Africa v New Zealand, Group A
At Edgbaston, Birmingham, 7 June 1975 (60-overs)
Result: New Zealand won by 181 runs. Points: New Zealand 4, East Africa 0.
Toss: New Zealand. Umpires: HD Bird and AE Fagg.
Man of the Match: GM Turner.

New Zealand innings (60 overs maximum)			R	B	4	6
*GM Turner	not out		171	201	16	2
JFM Morrison	c & b Nana		14	37	0	0
GP Howarth		b Mehmood Quaraishy	20	40	2	0
JM Parker	c Zulfiqar Ali	b Sethi	66	68	7	0
BF Hastings	c Sethi	b Zulfiqar Ali	8	7	1	0
+KJ Wadsworth		b Nagenda	10	7	0	1
RJ Hadlee	not out		6	4	0	0
Extras	(b 1, lb 8, w 5)		14			
Total	(5 wickets, 60 overs)		309			

DNB: BJ McKechnie, DR Hadlee, HJ Howarth, RO Collinge.
Fall of wickets: 1-51 (Morrison), 2-103 (GP Howarth), 3-252 (Parker), 4-278 (Hastings), 5-292 (Wadsworth).

Bowling	O	M	R	W
Nagenda	9	1	50	1
Frasat Ali	9	0	50	0
Nana	12	2	34	1
Sethi	10	1	51	1
Zulfiqar Ali	12	0	71	1
Mehmood Quaraishy	8	0	39	1

East Africa innings (target: 310 runs from 60 overs)			R	B	4	6
Frasat Ali	st Wadsworth	b HJ Howarth	45	123	1	1
S Walusimbi		b DR Hadlee	15	46	1	0
RK Sethi	run out		1	3	0	0
S Sumar		b DR Hadlee	4	11	0	0
Jawahir Shah		c & b HJ Howarth	5	17	0	0
*Harilal Shah	lbw	b HJ Howarth	0	1	0	0
Mehmood Quaraishy	not out		16	88	0	0
Zulfiqar Ali		b DR Hadlee	30	49	4	0
+H McLeod		b Collinge	5	8	0	0
PG Nana	not out		1	15	0	0
Extras	(lb 5, nb 1)		6			
Total	(8 wickets, 60 overs)		128			

DNB: J Nagenda.
Fall of wickets: 1-30 (Walusimbi), 2-32 (Sethi), 3-36 (Sumar), 4-59 (Jawahir Shah), 5-59 (Harilal Shah), 6-84 (Frasat Ali), 7-121 (Zulfiqar Ali), 8-126 (McLeod).

Bowling	O	M	R	W
Collinge	12	5	23	1
RJ Hadlee	12	6	10	0
McKechnie	12	2	39	0
DR Hadlee	12	1	21	3
HJ Howarth	12	3	29	3

Australia v Pakistan, Group B
At Headingley, Leeds, 7 June 1975 (60-overs)
Result: Australia won by 73 runs. Points: Australia 4, Pakistan 0.
Toss: Australia. Umpires: WE Alley and TW Spencer.
Man of the Match: DK Lillee.

Australia innings (60 overs maximum)			R	B	4	6
A Turner	c Mushtaq Mohammad b Asif Iqbal		46	54	4	0
RB McCosker	c Wasim Bari	b Naseer Malik	25	76	2	0
*IM Chappell	c Wasim Raja	b Sarfraz Nawaz	28	30	5	0
GS Chappell	c Asif Iqbal	b Imran Khan	45	56	5	0
KD Walters	c Sarfraz Nawaz	b Naseer Malik	2	13	0	0
R Edwards	not out		80	94	6	0
+RW Marsh	c Wasim Bari	b Imran Khan	1	5	0	0
MHN Walker		b Asif Masood	18	28	2	0
JR Thomson	not out		20	14	2	1
Extras	(lb 7, nb 6)		13			
Total	(7 wickets, 60 overs)		278			

DNB: AA Mallett, DK Lillee.
Fall of wickets: 1-63 (Turner), 2-99 (IM Chappell), 3-110 (McCosker), 4-124 (Walters), 5-184 (GS Chappell), 6-195 (Marsh), 7-243 (Walker).

Bowling	O	M	R	W
Naseer Malik	12	2	37	2
Asif Masood	12	0	50	1
Sarfraz Nawaz	12	0	63	1
Asif Iqbal	12	0	58	1
Imran Khan	10	0	44	2
Wasim Raja	2	0	13	0

Pakistan innings (target: 279 runs from 60 overs)			R	B	4	6
Sadiq Mohammad		b Lillee	4	12	0	0
Majid Khan	c Marsh	b Mallett	65	76	11	0
Zaheer Abbas	c Turner	b Thomson	8	10	2	0
Mushtaq Mohammad	c GS Chappell	b Walters	8	32	0	0
*Asif Iqbal		b Lillee	53	95	8	0
Wasim Raja	c Thomson	b Walker	31	57	4	0
Imran Khan	c Turner	b Walker	9	19	1	0
Sarfraz Nawaz	c Marsh	b Lillee	0	2	0	0
+Wasim Bari	c Marsh	b Lillee	2	18	0	0
Asif Masood	c Walker	b Lillee	6	7	1	0
Naseer Malik	not out		0	13	0	0
Extras	(lb 4, w 3, nb 12)		19			
Total	(all out, 53 overs)		205			

Fall of wickets: 1-15 (Sadiq Mohammad), 2-27 (Zaheer Abbas), 3-68 (Mushtaq Mohammad), 4-104 (Majid Khan), 5-181 (Asif Iqbal), 6-189 (Wasim Raja), 7-189 (Sarfraz Nawaz), 8-195 (Imran Khan), 9-203 (Asif Masood), 10-205 (Wasim Bari).

Bowling	O	M	R	W
Lillee	12	2	34	5
Thomson	8	2	25	1
Walker	12	3	32	2
Mallett	12	1	49	1
Walters	6	0	29	1
GS Chappell	3	0	17	0

Sri Lanka v West Indies, Group B
At Old Trafford, Manchester, 7 June 1975 (60-overs)
Result: West Indies won by 9 wickets. Points: West Indies 4, Sri Lanka 0.
Toss: West Indies. Umpires: WL Budd and A Jepson.
Man of the Match: BD Julien.

Sri Lanka innings (60 overs maximum)			R	B	4	6
+ER Fernando	c Murray	b Julien	4	6	0	0
B Warnapura	c Murray	b Boyce	8	54	1	0
*APB Tennekoon	c Murray	b Julien	0	4	0	0
PD Heyn	c Lloyd	b Roberts	2	12	0	0
MH Tissera	c Kallicharran	b Julien	14	35	1 0	
LRD Mendis	c Murray	b Boyce	8	13	1	0
AN Ranasinghe		b Boyce	0	2	0	0
HSM Pieris	c Lloyd	b Julien	3	12	0	0
ARM Opatha		b Roberts	11	18	1	0
DS de Silva	c Lloyd	b Holder	21	54	2	0
LWS Kaluperuma	not out		6	19	0	0
Extras	(b 3, lb 3, nb 3)		9			
Total	(all out, 37.2 overs)		86			

Fall of wickets: 1-5 (Fernando), 2-5 (Tennekoon), 3-16 (Heyn), 4-21 (Warnapura), 5-41 (Tissera), 6-41 (Mendis), 7-42 (Ranasinghe), 8-48 (Pieris), 9-58 (Opatha), 10-86 (de Silva).

Bowling	O	M	R	W
Roberts	12	5	16	2
Julien	12	3	20	4
Boyce	8	1	22	3
Gibbs	4	0	17	0
Holder	1.2	0	2	1

West Indies innings (target: 87 runs from 60 overs)			R	B	4	6
RC Fredericks	c Warnapura	b de Silva	33	38	4	0
+DL Murray	not out		30	50	2	1
AI Kallicharran	not out		19	37	2	0
Extras	(b 2, lb 1, w 1, nb 1)		5			
Total	(1 wicket, 20.4 overs)		87			

DNB: RB Kanhai, *CH Lloyd, IVA Richards, BD Julien, KD Boyce, VA Holder, AME Roberts, LR Gibbs.
Fall of wickets: 1-52 (Fredericks).

Bowling	O	M	R	W
Opatha	4	0	19	0
Pieris	2	0	13	0
de Silva	8	1	33	1
Kaluperuma	6.4	1	17	0

England v New Zealand, Group A
At Trent Bridge, Nottingham, 11 June 1975 (60-overs)
Result: England won by 80 runs. Points: England 4, New Zealand 0.
Toss: New Zealand. Umpires: WE Alley and TW Spencer.
Man of the Match: KWR Fletcher.

England innings (60 overs maximum)			R	B	4	6
DL Amiss		b Collinge	16	18	3	0
JA Jameson	c Wadsworth	b Collinge	11	31	0	0
KWR Fletcher	run out		131	147	13	0
FC Hayes	lbw	b RJ Hadlee	34	80	5	0
*MH Denness	c Morrison	b DR Hadlee	37	52	1	1
AW Greig		b DR Hadlee	9	19	0	0
CM Old	not out		20	16	0	1
Extras	(lb 6, w 1, nb 1)		8			
Total	(6 wickets, 60 overs)		266			

DNB: +APE Knott, DL Underwood, GG Arnold, P Lever.
Fall of wickets: 1-27 (Amiss), 2-28 (Jameson), 3-111 (Hayes), 4-177 (Denness), 5-200 (Greig), 6-266 (Fletcher).

Bowling	O	M	R	W
Collinge	12	2	43	2
RJ Hadlee	12	2	66	1
DR Hadlee	12	1	55	2
McKechnie	12	2	38	0
Howarth	12	2	56	0

New Zealand innings (target: 267 runs from 60 overs)			R	B	4	6
JFM Morrison	c Old	b Underwood	55	85	6	1
*GM Turne		b Lever	12	34	1	0
BG Hadlee		b Greig	19	77	1	0
JM Parker		b Greig	1	8	0	0
BF Hastings	c Underwood	b Old	10	26	1	0
+KJ Wadsworth		b Arnold	25	24	3	0
RJ Hadlee		b Old	0	6	0	0
BJ McKechnie	c Underwood	b Greig	27	50	4	0
DR Hadlee	c Arnold	b Greig	20	42	2	0
HJ Howarth	not out		1	7	0	0
RO Collinge		b Underwood	6	6	0	1
Extras	(b 1, lb 4, w 1, nb 4)		10			
Total	(all out, 60 overs)		186			

Fall of wickets: 1-30 (Turner), 2-83 (Morrison), 3-91 (Parker), 4-95 (BG Hadlee), 5-129 (Wadsworth), 6-129 (Hastings), 7-129 (RJ Hadlee), 8-177 (DR Hadlee), 9-180 (McKechnie), 10-186 (Collinge).

Bowling	O	M	R	W
Arnold	12	3	35	1
Lever	12	0	37	1
Old	12	2	29	2
Greig	12	0	45	4
Underwood	12	2	30	2

East Africa v India, Group A
At Headingley, Leeds, 11 June 1975 (60-overs)
Result: India won by 10 wickets. Points: India 4, East Africa 0.
Toss: East Africa. Umpires: HD Bird and A Jepson.
Man of the Match: FM Engineer.

East Africa innings (60 overs maximum)			R	B	4	6
Frasat Ali		b Abid Ali	12	36	1	0
S Walusimbi	lbw	b Abid Ali	16	50	1	0
+PS Mehta	run out		12	41	0	0
Yunus Badat		b Bedi	1	4	0	0
Jawahir Shah		b Amarnath	37	84	5	0
*Harilal Shah	c Engineer	b Amarnath	0	2	0	0
RK Sethi	c Gaekwad	b Madan Lal	23	80	2	0
Mehmood Quaraishy	run out		6	25	0	0
Zulfiqar Ali	not out		2	5	0	0
PG Nana	lbw	b Madan Lal	0	2	0	0
DJ Pringle		b Madan Lal	2	3	0	0
Extras	(lb 8, nb 1)		9			
Total	(all out, 55.3 overs)		120			

Fall of wickets: 1-26 (Frasat Ali), 2-36 (Walusimbi), 3-37 (Yunus Badat), 4-56 (Mehta), 5-56 (Harilal Shah), 6-98 (Jawahir Shah), 7-116 (Sethi), 8-116 (Mehmood Quaraishy), 9-116 (Nana), 10-120 (Pringle).

Bowling	O	M	R	W
Abid Ali	12	5	22	2
Madan Lal	9.3	2	15	3
Bedi	12	8	6	1
Venkataraghavan	12	4	29	0
Amarnath	10	0	39	2

India innings (target: 121 runs from 60 overs)			R	B	4	6
SM Gavaskar	not out		65	86	9	0
+FM Engineer	not out		54	93	7	0
Extras	(b 4)		4			
Total	(0 wickets, 29.5 overs)		123			

DNB: AD Gaekwad, GR Viswanath, BP Patel, ED Solkar, S Abid Ali, S Madan Lal, M Amarnath, *S Venkataraghavan, BS Bedi.

Bowling	O	M	R	W
Frasat Ali	6	1	17	0
Pringle	3	0	14	0
Zulfiqar Ali	11	3	32	0
Nana	4.5	0	36	0
Sethi	5	0	20	0

Australia v Sri Lanka, Group B
At Kennington Oval, London, 11 June 1975 (60-overs)
Result: Australia won by 52 runs. Points: Australia 4, Sri Lanka 0.
Toss: Sri Lanka. Umpires: WL Budd and AE Fagg.
Man of the Match: A Turner.

Australia innings (60 overs maximum)			R	B	4	6
RB McCosker		b de Silva	73	111	2	0
A Turner	c Mendis	b de Silva	101	113	9	1
*IM Chappell		b Kaluperuma	4	7	1	0
GS Chappell	c Opatha	b Pieris	50	50	5	1
KD Walters	c Tennekoon	b Pieris	59	66	5	0
JR Thomson	not out		9	7	0	0
+RW Marsh	not out		9	7	0	0
Extras	(b 1, lb 20, w 1, nb 1)		23			
Total	(5 wickets, 60 overs)		328			

DNB: R Edwards, MHN Walker, DK Lillee, AA Mallett.
Fall of wickets: 1-182 (Turner), 2-187 (McCosker), 3-191 (IM Chappell), 4-308 (Walters), 5-308 (GS Chappell).

Bowling	O	M	R	W
Opatha	9	0	32	0
Pieris	11	0	68	2
Warnapura	9	0	40	0
Ranasinghe	7	0	55	0
de Silva	12	3	60	2
Kaluperuma	12	0	50	1

Sri Lanka innings (target: 329 runs from 60 overs)			R	B	4	6
SRD Wettimuny	retired hurt		53	102	7	0
+ER Fernando		b Thomson	22	18	4	0
B Warnapura	st Marsh	b Mallett	31	39	5	0
LRD Mendis	retired hurt		32	45	5	0
*APB Tennekoon		b IM Chappell	48	71	6	0
MH Tissera	c Turner	b IM Chappell	52	72	7	0
AN Ranasinghe	not out		14	18	3	0
HSM Pieris	not out		0	3	0	0
Extras	(b 6, lb 8, w 8, nb 2)		24			
Total	(4 wickets, 60 overs)		276			

DNB: ARM Opatha, DS de Silva, LWS Kaluperuma.
Fall of wickets: 1-30 (Fernando), 2-84 (Warnapura), 3-246 (Tennekoon), 4-268 (Tissera).
NB: LRD Mendis retired hurt at 150/2 and SRD Wettimuny retired hurt at 164/2.

Bowling	O	M	R	W
Lillee	10	0	42	0
Thomson	12	5	84	1
Mallett	12	0	72	1
Walters	6	1	33	0
Walker	12	1	44	0
GS Chappell	4	0	25	0
IM Chappell	4	0	14	2

Pakistan v West Indies, Group B
At Edgbaston, Birmingham, 11 June 1975 (60-overs)
Result: West Indies won by 1 wicket. Points: West Indies 4, Pakistan 0.
Toss: Pakistan. Umpires: DJ Constant and JG Langridge.
Man of the Match: Sarfraz Nawaz.

Pakistan innings (60 overs maximum)			R	B	4	6
*Majid Khan	c Murray	b Lloyd	60	108	6	0
Sadiq Mohammad	c Kanhai	b Julien	7	23	1	0
Zaheer Abbas	lbw	b Richards	31	56	4	0
Mushtaq Mohammad		b Boyce	55	84	3	0
Wasim Raja		b Roberts	58	57	6	0
Javed Miandad	run out		24	32	2	0
Pervez Mir	run out		4	9	0	0
+Wasim Bari	not out		1	1	0	0
Sarfraz Nawaz	not out		0	0	0	0
Extras	(b 1, lb 15, w 4, nb 6)		26			
Total	(7 wickets, 60 overs)		266			

DNB: Asif Masood, Naseer Malik.
Fall of wickets: 1-21 (Sadiq Mohammad), 2-83 (Zaheer Abbas), 3-140 (Majid Khan), 4-202 (Mushtaq Mohammad), 5-249 (Wasim Raja), 6-263 (Pervez Mir), 7-265 (Javed Miandad).

Bowling	O	M	R	W
Roberts	12	1	47	1
Boyce	12	2	44	1
Julien	12	1	41	1
Holder	12	3	56	0
Richards	4	0	21	1
Lloyd	8	1	31	1

West Indies innings (target: 267 runs from 60 overs)			R	B	4	6
RC Fredericks	lbw	b Sarfraz Nawaz	12	11	2	0
CG Greenidge	c Wasim Bari	b Sarfraz Nawaz	4	6	1	0
AI Kallicharran	c Wasim Bari	b Sarfraz Nawaz	16	25	1	0
RB Kanhai		b Naseer Malik	24	42	3	0
*CH Lloyd	c Wasim Bari	b Javed Miandad	53	58	8	0
IVA Richards	c Zaheer Abbas	b Pervez Mir	13	23	2	0
BD Julien	c Javed Miandad	b Asif Masood	18	40	2	0
+DL Murray	not out		61	76	6	0
KD Boyce		b Naseer Malik	7	6	0	0
VA Holder	c Pervez Mir	b Sarfraz Nawaz	16	28	1	0
AME Roberts	not out		24	48	3	0
Extras	(lb 10, w 1, nb 8)		19			
Total	(9 wickets, 59.4 overs)		267			

Fall of wickets: 1-6 (Greenidge), 2-31 (Fredericks), 3-36 (Kallicharran), 4-84 (Kanhai), 5-99 (Richards), 6-145 (Julien), 7-151 (Lloyd), 8-166 (Boyce), 9-203 (Holder).

Bowling	O	M	R	W
Asif Masood	12	1	64	1
Sarfraz Nawaz	12	1	44	4
Naseer Malik	12	2	42	2
Pervez Mir	9	1	42	1
Javed Miandad	12	0	46	1
Mushtaq Mohammad	2	0	7	0
Wasim Raja	0.4	0	3	0

England v East Africa, Group A
At Edgbaston, Birmingham, 14 June 1975 (60-overs)
Result: England won by 196 runs. Points: England 4, East Africa 0.
Toss: East Africa. Umpires: WE Alley and JG Langridge.
Man of the Match: JA Snow.

England innings (60 overs maximum)			R	B	4	6
B Wood		b Mehmood Quaraishy	77	138	6	0
DL Amiss	c Nana	b Zulfiqar Ali	88	116	7	0
FC Hayes		b Zulfiqar Ali	52	50	6	2
AW Greig	lbw	b Zulfiqar Ali	9	17	0	0
+APE Knott	not out		18	19	0	0
CM Old		b Mehmood Quaraishy	18	16	3	0
*MH Denness	not out		12	6	1	0
Extras	(b 7, lb 7, w 1, nb 1)		16			
Tota	(5 wickets, 60 overs)		290			

DNB: KWR Fletcher, JA Snow, P Lever, DL Underwood.
Fall of wickets: 1-158 (Amiss), 2-192 (Wood), 3-234 (Greig), 4-244 (Hayes), 5-277 (Old).

Bowling	O	M	R	W
Frasat Ali	9	0	40	0
Pringle	12	0	41	0
Nana	12	2	46	0
Sethi	5	0	29	0
Zulfiqar Ali	12	0	63	3
Mehmood Quaraishy	10	0	55	2

East Africa innings (target: 291 runs from 60 overs)			R	B	4	6
Frasat Ali		b Snow	0	17	0	0
S Walusimbi	lbw	b Snow	7	30	0	0
Yunus Badat		b Snow	0	3	0	0
Jawahir Shah	lbw	b Snow	4	13	0	0
RK Sethi		b Lever	30	102	3	0
*Harilal Shah		b Greig	6	53	0	0
Mehmood Quaraishy	c Amiss	b Greig	19	41	2	0
Zulfiqar Ali		b Lever	7	22	0	0
+H McLeod		b Lever	0	2	0	0
PG Nana	not out		8	28	0	0
DJ Pringle		b Old	3	12	0	0
Extras	(lb 6, w 1, nb 3)		10			
Total	(all out, 52.3 overs)		94			

Fall of wickets: 1-7 (Frasat Ali), 2-7 (Yunus Badat), 3-15 (Jawahir Shah), 4-21 (Walusimbi), 5-42 (Harilal Shah), 6-72 (Mehmood Quaraishy), 7-76 (Sethi), 8-79 (McLeod), 9-88 (Zulfiqar Ali), 10-94 (Pringle).

Bowling	O	M	R	W
Snow	12	6	11	4
Lever	12	3	32	3
Underwood	10	5	11	0
Wood	7	3	10	0
Greig	10	1	18	2
Old	1.3	0	2	1

India v New Zealand, Group A
At Old Trafford, Manchester, 14 June 1975 (60-overs)
Result: New Zealand won by 4 wickets. Points: New Zealand 4, India 0.
Toss: India. Umpires: WL Budd and AE Fagg.
Man of the Match: GM Turner.

India innings (60 overs maximum)			R	B	4	6
SM Gavaskar	c RJ Hadlee	b DR Hadlee	12	14	2	0
+FM Engineer	lbw	b RJ Hadlee	24	36	3	0
AD Gaekwad	c Hastings	b RJ Hadlee	37	51	3	0
GR Viswanath	lbw	b McKechnie	2	9	0	0
BP Patel		b HJ Howarth	9	32	1	0
ED Solkar	c Wadsworth	b HJ Howarth	13	10	2	0
S Abid Ali	c HJ Howarth	b McKechnie	70	98	5	1
S Madan Lal		c & b McKechnie	20	44	4	0
M Amarnath	c Morrison	b DR Hadlee	1	3	0	0
*S Venkataraghavan	not out		26	58	3	0
BS Bedi	run out		6	10	0	0
Extras	(b 5, w 1, nb 4)		10			
Total	(all out, 60 overs)		230			

Fall of wickets: 1-17 (Gavaskar), 2-48 (Engineer), 3-59 (Viswanath), 4-81 (Gaekwad), 5-94 (Solkar), 6-101 (Patel), 7-156 (Madan Lal), 8-157 (Amarnath), 9-217 (Abid Ali), 10-230 (Bedi).

Bowling	O	M	R	W
Collinge	12	2	43	0
RJ Hadlee	12	2	48	2
DR Hadlee	12	3	32	2
McKechnie	12	1	49	3
HJ Howarth	12	0	48	2

New Zealand innings (target: 231 runs from 60 overs)			R	B	4	6
*GM Turner	not out		114	177	13	0
JFM Morrison	c Engineer	b Bedi	17	34	2	0
GP Howarth	run out		9	13	2	0
JM Parker	lbw	b Abid Ali	1	6	0	0
BF Hastings	c Solkar	b Amarnath	34	49	3	0
+KJ Wadsworth	lbw	b Madan Lal	22	38	3	0
RJ Hadlee		b Abid Ali	15	30	2	0
DR Hadlee	not out		8	7	0	0
Extras	(b 8, lb 5)		13			
Total	(6 wickets, 58.5 overs)		233			

DNB: BJ McKechnie, HJ Howarth, RO Collinge.
Fall of wickets: 1-45 (Morrison), 2-62 (GP Howarth), 3-70 (Parker), 4-135 (Hastings), 5-185 (Wadsworth), 6-224 (RJ Hadlee).

Bowling	O	M	R	W
Madan Lal	11.5	1	62	1
Amarnath	8	1	40	1
Bedi	12	6	28	1
Abid Ali	12	2	35	2
Venkataraghavan	12	0	39	0
Solkar	3	0	16	0

Australia v West Indies, Group B

At Kennington Oval, London, 14 June 1975 (60-overs)
Result: West Indies won by 7 wickets. Points: West Indies 4, Australia 0.
Toss: West Indies. Umpires: HD Bird and DJ Constant.
Man of the Match: AI Kallicharran.

Australia innings (60 overs maximum)			R	B	4	6
RB McCosker	c Fredericks	b Julien	0	3	0	0
A Turner	lbw	b Roberts	7	18	0	0
*IM Chappell	c Murray	b Boyce	25	63	0	0
GS Chappell	c Murray	b Boyce	15	33	0	0
KD Walters	run out		7	18	0	0
R Edwards		b Richards	58	74	6	0
+RW Marsh	not out		52	84	4	0
MHN Walker	lbw	b Holder	8	22	1	0
JR Thomson	c Holder	b Richards	1	3	0	0
DK Lillee		b Boyce	3	12	0	0
AA Mallett	c Murray	b Roberts	0	1	0	0
Extras	(lb 9, w 1, nb 6)		16			
Total	(all out, 53.4 overs)		192			

Fall of wickets: 1-0 (McCosker), 2-21 (Turner), 3-49 (GS Chappell), 4-56 (IM Chappell), 5-61 (Walters), 6-160 (Edwards), 7-173 (Walker), 8-174 (Thomson), 9-192 (Lillee), 10-192 (Mallett).

Bowling	O	M	R	W
Julien	12	2	31	1
Roberts	10.4	1	39	3
Boyce	11	0	38	2
Holder	10	0	31	1
Lloyd	4	1	19	0
Richards	6	0	18	2

West Indies innings (target: 193 runs from 60 overs)			R	B	4	6
RC Fredericks	c Marsh	b Mallett	58	105	5	0
CG Greenidge	lbw	b Walker	16	18	2	0
AI Kallicharran	c Mallett	b Lillee	78	83	14	1
IVA Richards	not out		15	38	2	0
RB Kanhai	not out		18	33	1	0
Extras	(b 4, lb 2, w 3, nb 1)		10			
Total	(3 wickets, 46 overs)		195			

DNB: *CH Lloyd, BD Julien, +DL Murray, KD Boyce, VA Holder, AME Roberts.
Fall of wickets: 1-29 (Greenidge), 2-153 (Kallicharran), 3-159 (Fredericks).

Bowling	O	M	R	W
Lillee	10	0	66	1
Thomson	6	1	21	0
Walker	12	2	41	1
GS Chappell	4	0	13	0
Mallett	11	2	35	1
IM Chappell	3	1	9	0

Pakistan v Sri Lanka, Group B

At Trent Bridge, Nottingham, 14 June 1975 (60-overs)
Result: Pakistan won by 192 runs. Points: Pakistan 4, Sri Lanka 0.
Toss: Sri Lanka. Umpires: A Jepson and TW Spencer.
Man of the Match: Zaheer Abbas.

Pakistan innings (60 overs maximum)			R	B	4	6
Sadiq Mohammad	c Opatha	b Warnapura	74	88	12	1
*Majid Khan	c Tennekoon	b DS de Silva	84	93	9	1
Zaheer Abbas		b Opatha	97	89	10	1
Mushtaq Mohammad	c Heyn	b Warnapura	26	48	2	0
Wasim Raja	c Opatha	b Warnapura	2	6	0	0
Javed Miandad	not out		28	35	1	0
Imran Khan		b Opatha	0	2	0	0
Pervez Mir	not out		4	7	0	0
Extras	(b 4, lb 4, w 2, nb 5)		15			
Total	(6 wickets, 60 overs)		330			

DNB: +Wasim Bari, Asif Masood, Naseer Malik.
Fall of wickets: 1-159 (Sadiq Mohammad), 2-168 (Majid Khan), 3-256 (Mushtaq Mohammad), 4-268 (Wasim Raja), 5-318 (Zaheer Abbas), 6-318 (Imran Khan).

Bowling	O	M	R	W
Opatha	12	0	67	2
Pieris	9	0	54	0
GRA de Silva	7	1	46	0
DS de Silva	12	1	61	1
Kaluperuma	9	1	35	0
Warnapura	8	0	42	3
Ranasinghe	3	0	10	0

Sri Lanka innings (target: 331 runs from 60 overs)			R	B	4	6
+ER Fernando	c & b Javed Miandad		21	42	3	0
B Warnapura		b Imran Khan	2	15	0	0
*APB Tennekoon	lbw	b Naseer Malik	30	36	4	0
MH Tissera	c Wasim Bari	b Sadiq Mohammad	12	40	2	0
PD Heyn	c Zaheer Abbas	b Javed Miandad	1	8	0	0
AN Ranasinghe		b Wasim Raja	9	23	0	0
HSM Pieris	lbw	b Pervez Mir	16	44	2	0
ARM Opatha	c Zaheer Abbas	b Sadiq Mohammad	0	10	0	0
DS de Silva		b Imran Khan	26	59	4	0
LWS Kaluperuma	not out		13	27	1	0
GRA de Silva	c Wasim Raja	b Imran Khan	0	12	0	0
Extras	(lb 1, w 3, nb 4)		8			
Tota	(all out, 50.1 overs)		138			

Fall of wickets: 1-5 (Warnapura), 2-44 (Fernando), 3-60 (Tissera), 4-61 (Heyn), 5-75 (Tennekoon), 6-79 (Ranasinghe), 7-90 (Opatha), 8-113 (Pieris), 9-135 (DS de Silva), 10-138 (GRA de Silva).

Bowling	O	M	R	W
Asif Masood	6	2	14	0
Imran Khan	7.1	3	15	3
Javed Miandad	7	2	22	2
Naseer Malik	6	1	19	1
Sadiq Mohammad	6	1	20	2
Wasim Raja	7	4	7	1
Mushtaq Mohammad	5	0	16	0
Pervez Mir	6	1	17	1

1st Semi Final
England v Australia
At Headingley, Leeds, 18 June 1975 (60-overs)
Result: Australia won by 4 wickets. Australia advances to the final.
Toss: Australia. Umpires: WE Alley and DJ Constant.
Man of the Match: GJ Gilmour.

England innings (60 overs maximum)			R	B	4	6
DL Amiss	lbw	b Gilmour	2	7	0	0
B Wood		b Gilmour	6	19	1	0
KWR Fletcher	lbw	b Gilmour	8	45	0	0
AW Greig	c Marsh	b Gilmour	7	25	1	0
FC Hayes	lbw	b Gilmour	4	6	1	0
*MH Denness		b Walker	27	60	1	0
+APE Knott	lbw	b Gilmour	0	5	0	0
CM Old	c GS Chappell	b Walker	0	3	0	0
JA Snow	c Marsh	b Lillee	2	14	0	0
GG Arnold	not out		18	30	2	0
P Lever	lbw	b Walker	5	13	0	0
Extras	(lb 5, w 7, nb 2)		14			
Total	(all out, 36.2 overs)		93			

Fall of wickets: 1-2 (Amiss), 2-11 (Wood), 3-26 (Greig), 4-33 (Hayes), 5-35 (Fletcher), 6-36 (Knott), 7-37 (Old), 8-52 (Snow), 9-73 (Denness), 10-93 (Lever).

Bowling	O	M	R	W
Lillee	9	3	26	1
Gilmour	12	6	14	6
Walker	9.2	3	22	3
Thomson	6	0	17	0

Australia innings (target: 94 runs from 60 overs)			R	B	4	6
A Turner	lbw	b Arnold	7	20	0	0
RB McCosker		b Old	15	50	0	0
*IM Chappell	lbw	b Snow	2	19	0	0
GS Chappell	lbw	b Snow	4	9	1	0
KD Walters	not out		20	43	2	0
R Edwards		b Old	0	3	0	0
+RW Marsh		b Old	5	8	0	0
GJ Gilmour	not out		28	28	5	0
Extras	(b 1, lb 6, nb 6)		13			
Total	(6 wickets, 28.4 overs)		94			

DNB: MHN Walker, DK Lillee, JR Thomson.
Fall of wickets: 1-17 (Turner), 2-24 (IM Chappell), 3-32 (GS Chappell), 4-32 (McCosker), 5-32 (Edwards), 6-39 (Marsh).

Bowling	O	M	R	W
Arnold	7.4	2	15	1
Snow	12	0	30	2
Old	7	2	29	3
Lever	2	0	7	0

2nd Semi Final
New Zealand v West Indies
At Kennington Oval, London, 18 June 1975 (60-overs)
Result: West Indies won by 5 wickets. West Indies advances to the final.
Toss: West Indies. Umpires: WL Budd and AE Fagg.
Man of the Match: AI Kallicharran.

New Zealand innings (60 overs maximum)			R	B	4	6
*GM Turner	c Kanhai	b Roberts	36	74	3	0
JFM Morrison	lbw	b Julien	5	26	0	0
GP Howarth	c Murray	b Roberts	51	93	3	0
JM Parker		b Lloyd	3	12	0	0
BF Hastings	not out		24	57	4	0
+KJ Wadsworth	c Lloyd	b Julien	11	21	1	0
BJ McKechnie	lbw	b Julien	1	9	0	0
DR Hadlee	c Holder	b Julien	0	10	0	0
BL Cairns		b Holder	10	14	1	0
HJ Howarth		b Holder	0	1	0	0
RO Collinge		b Holder	2	4	0	0
Extras	(b 1, lb 5, w 2, nb 7)		15			
Total	(all out, 52.2 overs)		158			

Fall of wickets: 1-8 (Morrison), 2-98 (Turner), 3-105 (GP Howarth), 4-106 (Parker), 5-125 (Wadsworth), 6-133 (McKechnie), 7-139 (Hadlee), 8-155 (Cairns), 9-155 (HJ Howarth), 10-158 (Collinge).

Bowling	O	M	R	W
Julien	12	5	27	4
Roberts	11	3	18	2
Holder	8.2	0	30	3
Boyce	9	0	31	0
Lloyd	12	1	37	1

West Indies innings (target: 159 runs from 60 overs)			R	B	4	6
RC Fredericks	c Hastings	b Hadlee	6	14	0	0
CG Greenidge	lbw	b Collinge	55	95	9	1
AI Kallicharran		c & b Collinge	72	92	7	1
IVA Richards	lbw	b Collinge	5	10	1	0
RB Kanhai	not out		12	18	2	0
*CH Lloyd	c Hastings	b McKechnie	3	8	0	0
BD Julien	not out		4	5	1	0
Extras	(lb 1, nb 1)		2			
Total	(5 wickets, 40.1 overs)		159			

DNB: +DL Murray, KD Boyce, VA Holder, AME Roberts.
Fall of wickets: 1-8 (Fredericks), 2-133 (Kallicharran), 3-139 (Richards), 4-142 (Greenidge), 5-151 (Lloyd).

Bowling	O	M	R	W
Collinge	12	4	28	3
Hadlee	10	0	54	0
Cairns	6.1	2	23	0
McKechnie	8	0	37	1
HJ Howarth	4	0	15	0

Final
Australia v West Indies
At Lord's, London, 21 June 1975 (60-overs)
Result: West Indies won by 17 runs.
West Indies wins the 1975 Prudential World Cup.
Toss: Australia. Umpires: HD Bird and TW Spencer.
Man of the Match: CH Lloyd.

West Indies innings (60 overs maximum)			R	B	4	6
RC Fredericks	hit wicket	b Lillee	7	13	0	0
CG Greenidge	c Marsh	b Thomson	13	61	1	0
AI Kallicharran	c Marsh	b Gilmour	12	18	2	0
RB Kanhai		b Gilmour	55	105	8	0
*CH Lloyd	c Marsh	b Gilmour	102	85	12	2
IVA Richards		b Gilmour	5	11	1	0
KD Boyce	c GS Chappell	b Thomson	34	37	3	0
BD Julien	not out		26	37	1	0
+DL Murray		c & b Gilmour	14	10	1	1
VA Holder	not out		6	2	1	0
Extras	(lb 6, nb 11)		17			
Total	(8 wickets, 60 overs)		291			

DNB: AME Roberts.
Fall of wickets: 1-12 (Fredericks), 2-27 (Kallicharran), 3-50 (Greenidge), 4-199 (Lloyd), 5-206 (Kanhai), 6-209 (Richards), 7-261 (Boyce), 8-285 (Murray).

Bowling	O	M	R	W
Lillee	12	1	55	1
Gilmour	12	2	48	5
Thomson	12	1	44	2
Walker	12	1	71	0
GS Chappell	7	0	33	0
Walters	5	0	23	0

Australia innings (target: 292 runs from 60 overs)			R	B	4	6
A Turner	run out (Richards)		40	54	4	0
RB McCosker	c Kallicharran	b Boyce	7	24	1	0
*IM Chappell	run out (Richards/Lloyd)		62	93	6	0
GS Chappell	run out (Richards)		15	23	2	0
KD Walters		b Lloyd	35	51	5	0
+RW Marsh		b Boyce	11	24	0	0
R Edwards	c Fredericks	b Boyce	28	37	2	0
GJ Gilmour	c Kanhai	b Boyce	14	11	2	0
MHN Walke	run out (Kallicharran/Holder)		7	9	1	0
JR Thomson	run out (Kallicharran/Murray)		21	21	2	0
DK Lillee	not out		16	19	1	0
Extras	(b 2, lb 9, nb 7)		18			
Total	(all out, 58.4 overs)		274			

Fall of wickets: 1-25 (McCosker), 2-81 (Turner), 3-115 (GS Chappell), 4-162 (IM Chappell), 5-170 (Walters), 6-195 (Marsh), 7-221 (Gilmour), 8-231 (Edwards), 9-233 (Walker), 10-274 (Thomson).

Bowling	O	M	R	W
Julien	12	0	58	0
Roberts	11	1	45	0
Boyce	12	0	50	4
Holder	11.4	1	65	0
Lloyd	12	1	38	1

World Cup **1979**
by Stephen Thorpe

If the inaugural World Cup had been a step into the unknown with sponsorship and branding in their infancy, the ructions prior to the second tournament in 1979 were of seismic significance, emphasising the relatively poor remuneration of elite practitioners and changing the landscape of international cricket forever.

The formation of World Series Cricket was rooted in a ratings and revenue war in Australian television, but quickly became a cause celebre for players to be paid their due worth. The repercussions are felt to this day. The media mogul and buccaneering capitalist Kerry Packer had attempted to broker an exclusive deal for his Channel 9 network to broadcast all Tests in Australia as early as June 1976, yet it was not until the following May that the *Bulletin* magazine (also Packer property) launched a barely credible story on an unsuspecting world.

Three weeks before, a leak had suggested that four pre-eminent South Africans – Graeme Pollock, Barry Richards, Mike Procter and Eddie Barlow – had signed lucrative contracts to play a series of matches, but the full magnitude of the revolution shook the game to its core. Thirty-five top players, including the cream of Australian talent, four West Indians, led by Clive Lloyd, and four Englishmen had been engaged to play unofficial "Super Tests" and one-day matches in Australia.

Negotiations had actually taken place during the Centenary Test in Melbourne in March 1977, and the World XI boasted the then England captain, 32-year-old Tony Greig, doubling up as Packer's chief henchman. Even now, to give him his due, Greig is unmoved, unequivocal in his condemnation of authority: "Packer had more influence on big-time cricket than anybody who ever held a bat. He dragged the game kicking and screaming into the 20th century and ensured its prosperity in the 21st.

Deja vu for Clive Lloyd as the West Indies captain once more lifts the Cup in triumph on the Lord's balcony in front of some of the outclassed opponents (from left): Geoff Boycott, Phil Edmonds, David Gower, Ian Botham and Bob Taylor.

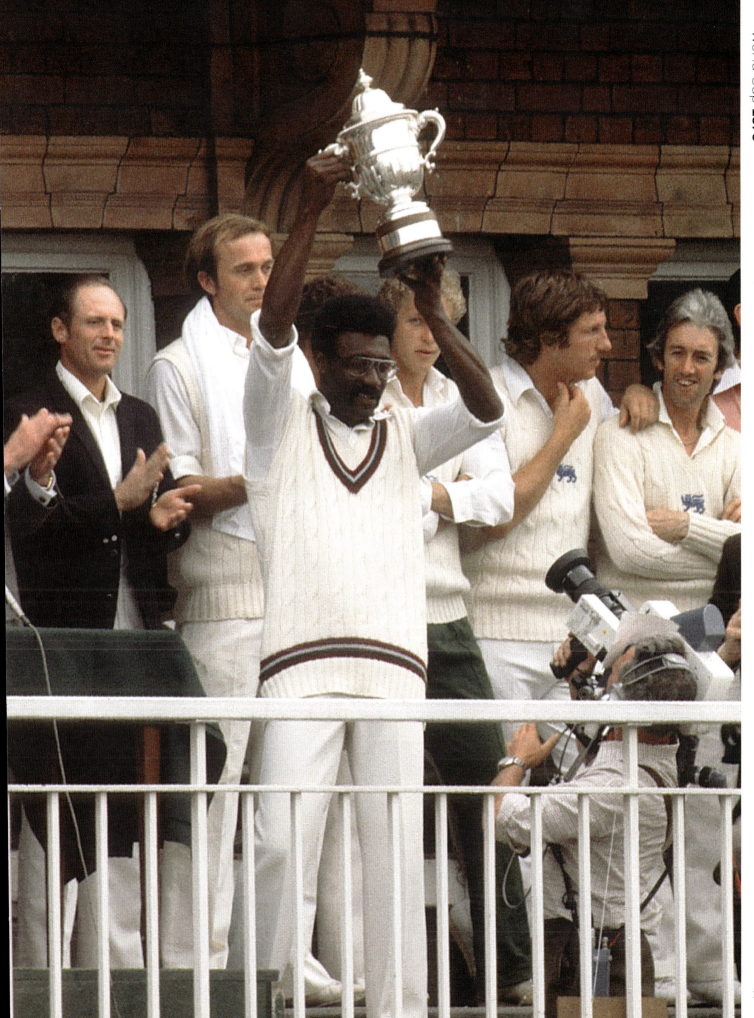

Cricketers were ill served by their masters, and the politest thing that can be said about the Establishment when he came along was that they were naïve, incompetent nincompoops."

The fallout was shattering and predictable – two years of legal and political wrangling, bans and rescisions by the International Cricket Conference (ICC) and England's Test & County Cricket Board (TCCB) after a High Court ruling citing restraint of trade, and a deeply disturbing feeling that the game would never be the same again.

Almost overnight cricket entered a new television-friendly age – one that was never destined to gain universal approval – of garish coloured clothing, helmets, floodlit matches, motorised drinks trolleys attended by glamorous girls, prizemoney and gimmicks galore. The Australian Test batsman of an earlier generation, Jack Fingleton, reckoned that "cricket as I've known and admired it has gone... it is the day, and night, of the big buck".

By the spring of 1979 the World Series circus embraced 60 players, had visited New Zealand and featured in an ill-fated Caribbean venture where crowd disturbances in Barbados and Trinidad were capped by a full-scale riot in Guyana.

The Australian Board soon capitulated, granting exclusive broadcasting rights to Channel 9 for a decade from 1981, though neither Australia nor England chose their Packer men for the imminent World Cup. World Series Cricket lost more than £2million in its first year and, though Australian TV rights were worth around £30,000 then compared to today's £20million, its true legacy is impossible to quantify.

Suffice to say that the game changed irrevocably, undeniably for the better, with players' status and monetary value increasing worldwide, and marketing and sponsorship ever more influential. The World Cup, remember, would never have started without Prudential's early involvement.

Some old values and chivalry may have disappeared along the way but, while it was never the best preamble, at least a sense of order and normality had been restored. Suddenly, after two years of trouble and strife, the 1979 competition was seen as a unifying force, a coming-together of the brotherhood of cricket. India had pitched to host it, but the vagaries of light there were deemed too problematical for the 60-overs

The eight teams line up at Lord's behind their captains. From left, Sri Lanka (Anura Tennekoon). Pakistan (Asif Iqbal), West Indies (Clive Lloyd), England (Mike Brearley), Australia (Kim Hughes), New Zealand (Mark Burgess), India (Srinivas Venkataraghavan), Canada (Brian Mauricette). For 2007, the number of teams has doubled to 16.

format and England, again, was preferred. No surprise there, with the ICC still run by the MCC at Lord's. The venerable English journalist, John Woodcock, stated the folly of this arrangement, but no one listened. "These sporting jamborees are all the better for doing the rounds," he noted, "and, although the costs of internal travel would be very much higher than in England, it would be a splendid adventure to take the great carnival to the Caribbean with the final in Trinidad." A pity his prescient musings have taken nearly 30 years to come to fruition.

In cricket's first truly global competition, South Africa's exclusion notwithstanding, preliminary matches involving 14 associate members of the ICC, plus Wales, started in May on club grounds in the English Midlands with two progressing to the main event. In 1975, Sri Lanka and East Africa were simply invited (Uganda's reviled president Idi Amin had apparently pondered the role of manager), but the members had decided their own knockout for the ICC Trophy was a far better prospect.

Nigh on 300 cricketers from 21 countries duly convened, disregarding the worst spring weather in living memory and six abandonments, before Sri Lanka, despite refusing to play Israel for some political reason, and Canada gained entry into the World Cup by qualifying for the final, eventually won by Sri Lanka at Worcester two days before the main final at Lord's. Denmark's demonstrative fast bowler Ole Mortensen sprang to prominence, and Canada's

24-year-old left-arm medium-pacer John Valentine, a French teacher from Montreal, surprised everyone, not least himself, by yorking Majid Khan and dismissing two other renowned openers in Mike Brearley and Rick Darling in the World Cup proper.

Expatriates played a significant role for several countries, and exotic cricketing outposts Singapore, Papua New Guinea and Fiji also raised their profiles, the latter more through a new-ball attack glorying in the names, on translation, of Back from Wars and Great Whale's Tooth. Sadly there was no great cutting edge, though games overall were of a decent club standard. Indeed, when the USA played Israel at somewhere called Blossomfield the supposed highlight of the American innings occurred when Lashkari was caught by Zion Moses off Reuben.

The tournament proper started on June 9, the rain briefly relenting ahead of a three-day washout at The Oval which ruined the West Indies' match against Sri Lanka. As reigning champions the West Indies were strong favourites. In the weaker group, the formidable firepower of Michael Holding, Andy Roberts, Joel Garner and Colin Croft, not forgetting Collis King, on a moisture-laden morning at Edgbaston restricted India to 190. It was never enough, and Gordon Greenidge's unbeaten hundred after an opening partnership of 138 with Desmond Haynes did the rest.

At Lord's, a sellout 25,000 crowd saw England prevail with some ease over the old enemy, Australia, depleted by the absence of the Packer players and undone by seam and swing, two wickets from Geoffrey Boycott and four run-outs. Chasing 160 and losing two early wickets, England cantered home when Graham Gooch stayed nearly three hours for 53. The Canadians had seven players of West Indian descent but lost heavily by eight wickets to Pakistan at Leeds after a decent start, eventually subsiding to Majid's off-spin, Asif Iqbal's in-duckers and an undefeated half-century from Sadiq Mohammad. New Zealand's margin over Sri Lanka at Trent Bridge was even greater, thanks to an unbroken stand of 126 between Glenn Turner and Geoff Howarth.

England then travelled north to a damp Old Trafford, sweeping aside Canada for 46 on the second day with Chris Old and Bob Willis irresistible, Mike Hendrick and Ian Botham merely unplayable. Somehow the visitors survived for 40 overs, a heavy downpour intervened and England again lost cheap wickets in victory.

Fears were expressed beforehand of an undercurrent of ill-feeling – or a possible bumper war – between the Packerites and traditionalists, but it was never a serious issue. Two years previously Pakistan's Mushtaq Mohammad had criticised the home West Indian umpiring and queried Garner's action, then in March 1979 Pakistan shared a bad-tempered short series in Australia marred by several unsavoury incidents. The tourists included eight WSC men, and the Australian Board had strained relations further in issuing a statement confirming they would play against any team selected by an ICC member. The clash at Nottingham was eagerly anticipated, a tense affair over two rain-affected days, won in the end by a distance by Pakistan's solid batting and the captain Asif's all-round acumen.

New Zealand's formula was straightforward and effective: win the toss and bowl. That is always a useful ploy at Headingley anyway, and India managed only 182 before an opening stand of 100 between the left-handers John Wright and Bruce Edgar, and 43 from Glenn Turner ensured victory. Three days later they ran the West Indies close after the usual insertion, but had done enough to reach the semi-final. England, meanwhile, won their third successive match, overcoming Pakistan by a slender margin on another seamer's paradise at Leeds. Gooch top-scored with 33 in a meagre 165, but Hendrick's inspired spell of four for three in eight balls settled it and booked their slot against the Kiwis.

Australia took scant consolation in defeating Canada and Sri Lanka recorded the only victory by an associate member, India losing by 47 runs at Manchester, which did much to hasten Sri Lanka's elevation to full status. The batting had impressed in 1975 against Australia, and the loss of skipper Anura Tennekoon to a hamstring strain in practice barely mattered.

The elements relented at last and the semi-finals were blessed with welcome sunshine, England shading New Zealand by nine runs in a cliffhanger at Old Trafford and West Indies defeating Pakistan in a high-scoring match at The Oval.

The West Indies victory in the final at Lord's owed much to the decisive fifth-wicket stand of 139 between Viv Richards, who graced the occasion with a typically commanding 138 not out, and Collis King. Richards tells a good story of greeting King at the outset and offering words of wisdom, which the Barbadian duly ignored in his whirlwind 86.

The event overall was an unmitigated success and, though attendances dropped to 132,000, this was almost entirely attributable to the adverse weather. For their part, the West Indies were coming to regard the World Cup as their personal property – but, four years on, all that was to change.

Contrasting footwork with contrasting results. Pakistan's Majid Khan gathered a boundary from his neat leg-glance off Michael Holding in the semi-final. Holding's side-kick on his follow through was wide of the mark as England's Derek Randall sprinted a single in the final.

SEMI-FINALS
England v New Zealand

At Old Trafford, June 20, 1979. England won by nine runs.
A wonderful match played in glorious sunshine before an almost capacity crowd of 22,000 ended with New Zealand covering themselves with glory but just failing to get to Lord's for the final.

All day long they fought nobly but the fortunes of the game continually fluctuated after Mark Burgess had sent in England to bat after winning the toss once more. The capable New Zealand attack, spearheaded by the fiery Richard Hadlee, tied down most of the England batsmen. Geoff Boycott, who survived a difficult chance to wicketkeeper Warren Lees off the second ball he received from the left-arm Gary Troup, fell to a smart catch at second slip in Hadlee's fifth over.

Wayne Larkins, preferred to left-arm spinner Phil Edmonds, tried to force the pace only to be taken at extra cover. Mike Brearley, content to defend, was making slow progress but Graham Gooch, in his most confident mood, set about establishing the innings.

There were further shocks for England when Brearley, having made 53 out of 96, cut Jeremy Coney to Lees and David Gower, going for a second run, was beaten by Lance Cairns' splendid long return to the bowler. There followed a bold stand between Gooch and Ian Botham, who put on 47 in 10 overs. Gooch, stepping forward, drove Bruce McKechnie high over the sightscreen for six. A low ball dismissed Botham as he attempted a mighty hook and Gooch's fine display ended when he deflected a widish ball into his stumps.

Fortunately for England, Brearley had put Derek Randall at No.7 and he played neatly, seldom attempting anything ambitious. Bob Taylor calmly put Cairns over long-on for six and England snatched 25 from the last three overs.

The left-handers, John Wright and Bruce Edgar, began New Zealand's task by putting on 47 in 16 overs before Chris Old had Edgar leg before. Boycott, trundling medium-pace from round the wicket, removed Howarth leg-before with a full toss the batsman tried to sweep towards square-leg. Wright kept New Zealand moving the right way until he succumbed to some brilliant fielding by Randall from deep square-leg. Burgess, too, was run out but New Zealand were not finished yet. Lees lifting Mike Hendrick over mid-on for six and Cairns hoisted Botham even further before Hendrick removed them both. With Bob Willis lame and Botham and Hendrick also limping, it was touch and go but, with 14 wanted from the last over, sent down by Botham, New Zealand went out of the World Cup with their flag flying.
(Wisden Cricketers' Almanack, 1980)

West Indies v Pakistan

At The Oval, June 20, 1979. West Indies won by 43 runs.
With all their leading batsmen in form, the West Indies ran up a massive score after they were sent in by Asif Iqbal. It was no day for Sarfraz Nawaz who failed with the new ball and conceded 71 runs off his 12 overs, although he did remove Collis King towards the end of the innings.

The West Indies thrived on a positive opening stand of 132 between Gordon Greenidge and Desmond Haynes. Pakistan missed one important chance when Haynes, on 32, hooked the medium-pacer Mudassar Nazar and Imran Khan, at long leg, failed at first to sight the ball which he fumbled. In the end, Asif dismissed both in the same spell and returned later to claim the next two wickets as well but not before Viv Richards and Clive Lloyd had played some glorious strokes in a partnership of 68. Some of the best Pakistan bowling was accomplished by Majid Khan with his off-breaks that yielded only 26 from the allocated 12 overs.

Michael Holding struck an early blow for the West Indies when Pakistan began their tremendous task with the bat. Bowling at great pace and hostile with the bouncer, he dismissed the left-handed Sadiq Mohammad to a keeper's catch at 10. This did not deter Majid and Zaheer Abbas who rose to the occasion in a wonderful partnership of 166 off 36 overs that put their side within striking distance. It would have been a different story had Greenidge not dropped Majid off Holding when he was 10.

Captain Lloyd, looking for a solution, brought on Richards with his spin and re-introduced Colin Croft at the Vauxhall end, instructing the big fast bowler to maintain a middle-and-leg line. The gamble worked for, although Richards' first over cost 12, Croft made the breakthrough by dismissing Zaheer, Majid and Javed Miandad in 12 balls for four runs.

Haroon Rashid was run out, Richards followed by disposing of Mudassar, Asif and Imran and, with Roberts proving too much for the tail, the West Indies gained their deserved success before a crowd of 20,000 that enjoyed the spectacle in brilliant sunshine.
(Wisden Cricketers' Almanack, 1980)

Zaheer Abbas swings to fine leg during his 93 for Pakistan in the semi-final, the highest World Cup innings against the West Indies at the time but it was in vain. Pakistan lost by 43 runs.

FINAL
West Indies v England

At Lord's, June 23, 1979. West Indies won by 92 runs.
Two innings of rare quality determined the championship. They were played by Viv Richards and Collis King at a critical time in West Indies' fortunes with the total 99 for the loss of Gordon Greenidge, Desmond Haynes, Alvin Kallicharran and Clive Lloyd

Left and above left: Having dazzled with his fielding in the 1975 final, Viv Richards dominated the 1979 final with his batting, his 138 decorated with 11 fours (one from this square-cut off Phil Edmonds) and three sixes, and his partnership of 139 with Collis King that involved the occasional tactical, mid-pitch discussion.

Above right: Captain Mike Brearley's 64 was England's top-score but occupied 130 balls in a methodical opening partnership of 129 off 38 overs with Geoff Boycott. The pull off Andy Roberts was one of his seven fours (top right) but it was a rare attacking stroke.

with wicketkeeper Deryck Murray and the four fast bowlers remaining.

As King, bareheaded, strode briskly across the lush green outfield to the crease, the match seemed in England's grasp. Greenidge was run out by Derek Randall's anticipation, speed and direct underarm hit from mid-wicket as he and Haynes tried to sneak a single, Haynes and Lloyd fell to Chris Old and Alvin Kallicharran was bowled by Mike Hendrick.

When King departed 21 overs later, to a catch on the square-leg boundary off the left-arm spinner Phil Edmonds, the outcome had been virtually decided by his partnership of 139 with Richards.

King savagely square-cut his first ball, from Ian Botham, to the ropes and so pulverised everything served up to him afterwards that he needed only 67 deliveries for his 86, three sixes and 10 fours being his most productive shots. Only one, a top-edged hook off Botham, came from anywhere but the middle of the bat.

As he and Richards took command, electrifying the thousands of their compatriots in the capacity crowd, England's usually unflustered captain Mike Brearley admitted that he "felt powerless".

Even the mighty Richards was overshadowed by the Kingley display but his was the innings of a great and mature player. A hesitant start did not trouble him nor did his team's precarious position. The pitch was true, the light clear and he was determined to make this prestigious occasion the scene of something special. When King was in his element, he made no effort to match him, playing a complementary role much as Rohan Kanhai had done to Lloyd in similar circumstances in the 1975 final.

When King entered, Richards was 49. When he left, Richards was in the 90s where he had lingered while his rampant partner scored 38. King's departure was the signal for Richards to take over the mantle of run-maker. He scored all but five of the 42 runs added from the last 10 overs and fittingly ended the innings with a nonchalant flick off his toes off Mike Hendrick's last ball that landed among the spectators at square-leg for six, a typical piece of improvisation.

England, by now regretting their decision to bolster their batting by relying on the undemanding medium-pace of Geoff Boycott, Wayne Larkins and Graham Gooch to share 12 overs, were left to score at 4.7 runs an over for victory.

It was an imposing target that called for positive methods. Instead, Brearley and Boycott batted as if laying the foundations for an innings in a timeless Test. They put together 129 runs for the first wicket but took 38 overs doing so. Brearley was dropped in the slips early on and Boycott at 38 by Lloyd at wide mid-on. It was such a dolly it looked for all the world as if the West Indies captain had put it down deliberately, which would have been an understandable tactic.

By the time the openers were finally out within six runs of each other, both to Michael Holding, there was too much to do for those better equipped to do it. Gooch played some hefty strokes in his 32 and England might have expected to at least get closer until Joel Garner returned and bowled his yorkers with lethal accuracy. The lower order crashed, mainly to the crash of shattered stumps, as the giant fast bowler took five wickets for four runs from 11 balls to formalise the result.

(Tony Cozier)

Right: Everywhere the Cup went, the crowds were sure to go. Those at The Oval for the semi-final between Pakistan and the West Indies comprised mostly West Indian expats from surrounding districts cheering their team to victory.

Far right: Collis King tears the bowling to shreds at Lord's against England in the final.

"They said at the time"

Desmond Haynes, Viv Richards' roommate in the tournament: *"On the day of the final, Viv got up and, before he went to the bathroom, before he'd even said good morning, he stretched and said, 'There's going to be a lot of people at Lord's today. It would be a good time to really turn it on'."*

Viv Richards on his partnership with Collis King: *"Every time I told him to take it easy, he hit the ball further and further. He was in that special frame of mind and, in the end, I just relaxed and let him tear the bowling to shreds. Rather than the two of us going berserk, I took time out and worked around him while his fire raged. I didn't feel that I should try to match him."*

Richards on his last-ball hit for six off Mike Hendrick: *"It was a shot that stood out for me. I had nothing to lose with over 100 on the scoreboard against my name and I had sussed that Mike would, with his long-on and long-off back, bowl a ball of fuller length to allow me to stroke for one or, if we pushed hard, two at the most. It was the correct ball, a much fuller length but slightly off line and I just stepped to the other side and flicked it. It went off the meat to perfection and sailed over the fence."*

West Indies captain Clive Lloyd, referring to the preceding split over World Series Cricket: *"It is a victory which means even more than usual for West Indies cricket – and for me personally. We've gone through a difficult period and this is the perfect way to signal an end to the problems. West Indies cricket is now back on its feet again."*

England captain Mike Brearley: *"Collis King was inspired and when he and Richards were in full flow I felt helpless. I knew there was nothing more we could do. But even with 286 to chase, we thought we had a chance."*

John Woodcock on the final in The Cricketer: *"Richards got away with bowling 10 overs of the most gentle off-breaks for 35 runs. For most of his spell, Boycott and Brearley contented themselves with hitting him to long-off for one. The situation cried out for a wholehearted assault on Richards and Boycott and Brearley failed to produce it."*

Format

As 1975.

Innovations

The minor teams emerged from a qualifying competition – the inaugural ICC Trophy, won by Sri Lanka. Australia handicapped themselves by selecting a largely unknown team (remember Graham Porter or Jeff Moss?) as their best players were still contracted to Kerry Packer's World Series Cricket. West Indies and Pakistan, fearing ructions at home if they fared badly, chose all their WSC players. By the following winter, peace had broken out and all the Packer men were back in the fold.

World Cup 1979
Scoreboards

India v West Indies, Group B
At Edgbaston, Birmingham, 9 June 1979 (60-overs)
Result: West Indies won by 9 wickets. Points: West Indies 4, India 0.
Toss: West Indies. Umpires: DGL Evans and JG Langridge.
Man of the Match: CG Greenidge.

India innings (60 overs maximum)			R	B	4	6
SM Gavaskar	c Holding	b Roberts	8	7	1	0
AD Gaekwad	c King	b Holding	11	30	2	0
DB Vengsarkar	c Kallicharran	b Holding	7	7	1	0
GR Viswanath		b Holding	75	134	7	0
BP Patel	run out		15	33	2	0
M Amarnath	c Murray	b Croft	8	15	1	0
N Kapil Dev		b King	12	12	1	0
+SC Khanna	c Haynes	b Holding	0	12	0	0
KD Ghavri	c Murray	b Garner	12	26	2	0
*S Venkataraghavan	not out		13	30	0	0
BS Bedi	c Lloyd	b Roberts	13	23	1	0
Extras	(b 6, lb 3, w 3, nb 4)		16			
Total	(all out, 53.1 overs)		190			

Fall of wickets: 1-10 (Gavaskar), 2-24 (Vengsarkar), 3-29 (Gaekwad), 4-56 (Patel), 5-77 (Amarnath), 6-112 (Kapil Dev), 7-119 (Khanna), 8-155 (Ghavri), 9-163 (Viswanath), 10-190 (Bedi).

Bowling	O	M	R	W
Roberts	9.1	0	32	2
Holding	12	2	33	4
Garner	12	1	42	1
Croft	10	1	31	1
King	10	1	36	1

West Indies innings (target: 191 runs from 60 overs)			R	B	4	6
CG Greenidge	not out		106	173	9	1
DL Haynes	lbw	b Kapil Dev	47	99	2	1
IVA Richards	not out		28	44	1	1
Extras	(lb 6, nb 7)		13			
Total	(1 wicket, 51.3 overs)		194			

DNB: AI Kallicharran, *CH Lloyd, CL King, +DL Murray, AME Roberts, J Garner, MA Holding, CEH Croft.
Fall of wickets: 1-138 (Haynes).

Bowling	O	M	R	W
Kapil Dev	10	1	46	1
Ghavri	10	2	25	0
Venkataraghavan	12	3	30	0
Bedi	12	0	45	0
Amarnath	7.3	0	35	0

New Zealand v Sri Lanka, Group B
At Trent Bridge, Nottingham, 9 June 1979 (60-overs)
Result: New Zealand won by 9 wickets. Points: New Zealand 4, Sri Lanka 0.
Toss: New Zealand. Umpires: WL Budd and KE Palmer.
Man of the Match: GP Howarth.

Sri Lanka innings (60 overs maximum)			R	B	4	6
B Warnapura		c & b McKechnie	20	58	2	0
SRD Wettimuny		b Cairns	16	20	1	0
*APB Tennekoon		b Stott	59	96	6	0
RL Dias		c & b Stott	25	46	2	0
LRD Mendis	c Turner	b Troup	14	27	2	0
DS de Silva	c Burgess	b Stott	6	24	0	0
+SA Jayasinghe	run out		1	3	0	0
SP Pasqual		b Hadlee	1	2	0	0
ARM Opatha		b McKechnie	18	27	2	0
DLS de Silva	c Wright	b McKechnie	10	35	0	0
GRA de Silva	not out		2	11	0	0
Extras	(lb 13, w 2, nb 2)		17			
Total	(all out, 56.5 overs)		189			

Fall of wickets: 1-26 (Wettimuny), 2-57 (Warnapura), 3-107 (Dias), 4-137 (Mendis), 5-149 (DS de Silva), 6-150 (Jayasinghe), 7-150 (Tennekoon), 8-154 (Pasqual), 9-178 (DLS de Silva), 10-189 (Opatha).

Bowling	O	M	R	W
Hadlee	12	3	24	1
Troup	10	0	30	1
Cairns	12	1	45	1
McKechnie	10.5	2	25	3
Stott	12	1	48	3

New Zealand innings (target: 190 runs from 60 overs)			R	B	4	6
GM Turner	not out		83	143	4	0
JG Wright	c Tennekoon	b GRA de Silva	34	69	6	0
GP Howarth	not out		63	75	8	1
Extras	(lb 7, w 2, nb 1)		10			
Total	(1 wicket, 47.4 overs)		190			

DNB: JV Coney, *MG Burgess, +WK Lees, BJ McKechnie, BL Cairns, RJ Hadlee, LW Stott, GB Troup.
Fall of wickets: 1-64 (Wright).

Bowling	O	M	R	W
Opatha	7	1	31	0
DLS de Silva	8	2	18	0
Warnapura	7	0	30	0
DS de Silva	9	0	42	0
GRA de Silva	12	1	39	1
Pasqual	4.4	0	20	0

England v Australia, Group A
At Lord's, London, 9 June 1979 (60-overs)
Result: England won by 6 wickets. Points: England 4, Australia 0.
Toss: England. Umpires: DJ Constant and BJ Meyer.
Man of the Match: GA Gooch.

Australia innings (60 overs maximum)			R	B	4	6
AMJ Hilditch		b Boycott	47	108	2	0
WM Darling	lbw	b Willis	25	61	3	0
AR Border	c Taylor	b Edmonds	34	74	4	0
*KJ Hughes	c Hendrick	b Boycott	6	13	1	0
GN Yallop	run out		10	20	1	0
GJ Cosier	run out		6	20	0	0
TJ Laughlin	run out		8	22	0	0
+KJ Wright	lbw	b Old	6	15	0	0
RM Hogg	run out		0	5	0	0
AG Hurst	not out		3	10	0	0
G Dymock	not out		4	12	0	0
Extras	(b 4, lb 5, w 1)		10			
Total	(9 wickets, 60 overs)		159			

Fall of wickets: 1-56 (Darling), 2-97 (Hilditch), 3-111 (Hughes), 4-131 (Border), 5-132 (Yallop), 6-137 (Cosier), 7-150 (Wright), 8-153 (Laughlin), 9-153 (Hogg).

Bowling	O	M	R	W
Willis	11	2	20	1
Hendrick	12	2	24	0
Old	12	2	33	1
Botham	8	0	32	0
Edmonds	11	1	25	1
Boycott	6	0	15	2

England innings (target: 160 runs from 60 overs)			R	B	4	6
*JM Brearley	c Wright	b Laughlin	44	147	2	0
G Boycott	lbw	b Hogg	1	5	0	0
DW Randall	c Wright	b Hurst	1	3	0	0
GA Gooch	lbw	b Laughlin	53	96	6	0
DI Gower	not out		22	30	2	0
IT Botham	not out		18	14	2	0
Extras	(lb 10, nb 11)		21			
Total	(4 wickets, 47.1 overs)		160			

DNB: PH Edmonds, +RW Taylor, CM Old, M Hendrick, RGD Willis.
Fall of wickets: 1-4 (Boycott), 2-5 (Randall), 3-113 (Gooch), 4-124 (Brearley).

Bowling	O	M	R	W
Hogg	9	1	25	1
Hurst	10	3	33	1
Dymock	11	2	19	0
Cosier	8	1	24	0
Laughlin	9.1	0	38	2

Canada v Pakistan, Group A

At Headingley, Leeds, 9 June 1979 (60-overs)
Result: Pakistan won by 8 wickets. Points: Pakistan 4, Canada 0.
Toss: Canada. Umpires: HD Bird and AGT Whitehead.
Man of the Match: Sadiq Mohammad.

Canada innings (60 overs maximum)			R	B	4	6
CJD Chappell		c & b Sikander Bakht	14	70	0	0
GR Sealy		c & b Asif Iqbal	45	110	5	0
FA Dennis	c Wasim Bari	b Sarfraz Nawaz	25	64	2	0
MP Stead	c Zaheer Abbas	b Asif Iqbal	10	33	1	0
CA Marshall		b Imran Khan	8	34	0	0
JCB Vaughan		c & b Asif Iqbal	0	2	0	0
*+BM Mauricette	c Zaheer Abbas	b Sarfraz Nawaz	15	38	0	1
Tariq Javed	st Wasim Bari	b Majid Khan	3	7	0	0
JM Patel		b Sarfraz Nawaz	0	5	0	0
CC Henry	not out		1	3	0	0
Extras	(lb 10, w 5, nb 3)		18			
Total	(9 wickets, 60 overs)		139			

DNB: JN Valentine.
Fall of wickets: 1-54 (Chappell), 2-85 (Sealy), 3-103 (Dennis), 4-110 (Stead), 5-110 (Vaughan), 6-129 (Marshall), 7-134 (Tariq Javed), 8-138 (Patel), 9-139 (Mauricette).

Bowling	O	M	R	W
Imran Khan	11	1	27	1
Sarfraz Nawaz	10	1	26	3
Mudassar Nazar	4	1	11	0
Sikander Bakht	12	5	18	1
Majid Khan	11	4	11	1
Asif Iqbal	12	2	28	3

Pakistan innings (target: 140 runs from 60 overs)		R	B	4	6
Majid Khan	b Valentine	1	3	0	0
Sadiq Mohammad	not out	57	122	4	0
Zaheer Abbas	run out	36	51	4	1
Haroon Rashid	not out	37	69	1	0
Extras	(b 1, lb 3, w 1, nb 4)	9			
Total	(2 wickets, 40.1 overs)	140			

DNB: Javed Miandad, *Asif Iqbal, Mudassar Nazar, Imran Khan, +Wasim Bari, Sarfraz Nawaz, Sikander Bakht.
Fall of wickets: 1-4 (Majid Khan), 2-61 (Zaheer Abbas).

Bowling	O	M	R	W
Valentine	9	3	18	1
Vaughan	5	1	21	0
Henry	5	0	26	0
Patel	11.1	0	27	0
Sealy	6	1	21	0
Stead	4	0	18	0

Sri Lanka v West Indies, Group B

At Kennington Oval, London, 13,14,15 June 1979 (60-overs)
Result: Match abandoned without a ball bowled.
Points: West Indies 2, Sri Lanka 2.
NB: 2 reserve days used. Match abandoned due to heavy rain.

India v New Zealand, Group B

At Headingley, Leeds, 13 June 1979 (60-overs)
Result: New Zealand won by 8 wickets. Points: New Zealand 4, India 0.
Toss: New Zealand. Umpires: WL Budd and AGT Whitehead.
Man of the Match: BA Edgar.

India innings (60 overs maximum)			R	B	4	6
SM Gavaskar	c Lees	b Hadlee	55	144	5	0
AD Gaekwad		b Hadlee	10	31	1	0
DB Vengsarkar	c Lees	b McKechnie	1	2	0	0
GR Viswanath	c Turner	b Cairns	9	10	0	0
BP Patel		b Troup	38	60	5	0
M Amarnath		b Troup	1	5	0	0
N Kapil Dev		c & b Cairns	25	24	3	0
KD Ghavri	c Coney	b McKechnie	20	22	2	0
+SC Khanna	c Morrison	b McKechnie	7	16	0	0
*S Venkataraghavan	c Lees	b Cairns	1	2	0	0
BS Bedi	not out		1	2	0	0
Extras	(lb 8, w 5, nb 1)		14			
Total	(all out, 55.5 overs)		182			

Fall of wickets: 1-27 (Gaekwad), 2-38 (Vengsarkar), 3-53 (Viswanath), 4-104 (Patel), 5-107 (Amarnath), 6-147 (Kapil Dev), 7-153 (Gavaskar), 8-180 (Khanna), 9-181 (Ghavri), 10-182 (Venkataraghavan).

Bowling	O	M	R	W
Hadlee	10	2	20	2
Troup	10	2	36	2
Cairns	11.5	0	36	3
McKechnie	12	1	24	3
Coney	7	0	33	0
Morrison	5	0	19	0

New Zealand innings (target: 183 runs from 60 overs)		R	B	4	6
JG Wright	c & b Amarnath	48	94	1	0
BA Edgar	not out	84	167	8	0
BL Cairns	run out	2	4	0	0
GM Turner	not out	43	76	6	0
Extras	(lb 3, nb 3)	6			
Total	(2 wickets, 57 overs)	183			

DNB: JV Coney, *MG Burgess, JFM Morrison, BJ McKechnie, +WK Lees, RJ Hadlee, GB Troup.
Fall of wickets: 1-100 (Wright), 2-103 (Cairns).

Bowling	O	M	R	W
Amarnath	12	1	39	1
Bedi	12	1	32	0
Venkataraghavan	12	0	34	0
Ghavri	10	1	34	0
Kapil Dev	11	3	38	0

Australia v Pakistan, Group A

At Trent Bridge, Nottingham, 13,14 June 1979 (60-overs)
Result: Pakistan won by 89 runs. Points: Pakistan 4, Australia 0.
Toss: Australia. Umpires: HD Bird and KE Palmer.
Man of the Match: Asif Iqbal.
Score after day 1 (reserve day used): Pak 286/7, Aus 17/0 (off 5 overs).

Pakistan innings (60 overs maximum)			R	B	4	6
Sadiq Mohammad	c Moss	b Porter	27	73	2	0
Majid Khan		b Dymock	61	100	7	1
Zaheer Abbas		c & b Cosier	16	32	1	0
Haroon Rashid	c Wright	b Cosier	16	42	2	0
Javed Miandad	c Border	b Cosier	46	46	4	0
*Asif Iqbal	c sub (DF Whatmore)	b Hurst	61	57	7	0
Wasim Raja	c Moss	b Border	18	12	2	1
Imran Khan	not out		15	9	0	0
Mudassar Nazar	not out		1	1	0	0
Extras	(b 6, lb 4, w 5, nb 10)		25			
Total	(7 wickets, 60 overs)		286			

DNB: +Wasim Bari, Sikander Bakht.
Fall of wickets: 1-99 (Majid Khan), 2-99 (Sadiq Mohammad), 3-133 (Zaheer Abbas), 4-152 (Haroon Rashid), 5-239 (Javed Miandad), 6-268 (Asif Iqbal), 7-274 (Wasim Raja).

Bowling	O	M	R	W
Porter	12	3	20	1
Dymock	12	3	28	1
Cosier	12	1	54	3
Hurst	12	0	65	1
Yallop	8	0	56	0
Border	4	0	38	1

Australia innings (target: 287 runs from 60 overs)			R	B	4	6
WM Darling	c Wasim Bari	b Imran Khan	13	25	1	0
AMJ Hilditch	c Sadiq Mohammad	b Mudassar Nazar	72	129	4	0
AR Border		b Sikander Bakht	0	5	0	0
*KJ Hughes	lbw	b Sikander Bakht	15	37	2	0
GN Yallop		b Majid Khan	37	64	2	0
JK Moss	run out		7	16	0	0
GJ Cosier		c & b Majid Khan	0	1	0	0
+KJ Wright	c Wasim Bari	b Imran Khan	23	37	0	0
GD Porter	c Sadiq Mohammad	b Majid Khan	3	9	0	0
G Dymock	lbw	b Sikander Bakht	10	18	0	0
AG Hurst	not out		3	2	0	0
Extras	(b 1, lb 5, w 8)		14			
Total	(all out, 57.1 overs)		197			

Fall of wickets: 1-22 (Darling), 2-24 (Border), 3-46 (Hughes), 4-117 (Yallop), 5-136 (Moss), 6-137 (Cosier), 7-172 (Hilditch), 8-175 (Porter), 9-193 (Dymock), 10-197 (Wright).

Bowling	O	M	R	W
Asif Iqbal	12	0	36	0
Majid Khan	12	0	53	3
Mudassar Nazar	12	0	31	1
Imran Khan	10.1	2	29	2
Sikander Bakht	11	1	34	3

England v Canada, Group A
At Old Trafford, Manchester, 13,14 June 1979 (60-overs)
Result: England won by 8 wickets. Points: England 4, Canada 0.
Toss: Canada. Umpires: JG Langridge and BJ Meyer.
Man of the Match: CM Old.
Score after day 1 (reserve day used): No play.

Canada innings (60 overs maximum)			R	B	4	6
CJD Chappell	lbw	b Botham	5	31	0	0
GR Sealy	c Botham	b Hendrick	3	9	0	0
FA Dennis	hit wicket	b Willis	21	99	2	0
Tariq Javed	lbw	b Old	4	40	0	0
JCB Vaughan		b Old	1	10	0	0
CA Marshall		b Old	2	7	0	0
*+BM Mauricette		b Willis	0	8	0	0
MP Stead		b Old	0	12	0	0
JM Patel		b Willis	1	14	0	0
RG Callender		b Willis	0	3	0	0
JN Valentine	not out		3	11	0	0
Extras	(lb 4, nb 1)		5			
Total	(all out, 40.3 overs)		45			

Fall of wickets: 1-5 (Sealy), 2-13 (Chappell), 3-25 (Tariq Javed), 4-29 (Vaughan), 5-37 (Marshall), 6-38 (Mauricette), 7-41 (Stead), 8-41 (Dennis), 9-42 (Callender), 10-45 (Patel).

Bowling	O	M	R	W
Willis	10.3	3	11	4
Hendrick	8	4	5	1
Botham	9	5	12	1
Miller	2	1	1	0
Boycott	1	0	3	0
Old	10	5	8	4

England innings (target: 46 runs from 60 overs)			R	B	4	6
*JM Brearley	lbw	b Valentine	0	10	0	0
G Boycott	not out		14	36	0	0
DW Randall		b Callender	5	11	1	0
GA Gooch	not out		21	31	2	1
Extras	(w 3, nb 3)		6			
Total	(2 wickets, 13.5 overs)		46			

DNB: DI Gower, IT Botham, G Miller, +RW Taylor, CM Old, RGD Willis, M Hendrick.
Fall of wickets: 1-3 (Brearley), 2-11 (Randall).

Bowling	O	M	R	W
Valentine	7	2	20	1
Callender	6	1	14	1
Stead	0.5	0	6	0

India v Sri Lanka, Group B
At Old Trafford, Manchester, 16,18 June 1979 (60-overs)
Result: Sri Lanka won by 47 runs. Points: Sri Lanka 4, India 0.
Toss: India. Umpires: KE Palmer and AGT Whitehead.
Man of the Match: LRD Mendis.
Score after day 1 (reserve day used): SL 238/5 (60 overs).

Sri Lanka innings (60 overs maximum)			R	B	4	6
*B Warnapura	c Gaekwad	b Amarnath	18	51	2	0
SRD Wettimuny	c Vengsarkar	b Kapil Dev	67	120	8	0
RL Dias		c & b Amarnath	50	88	2	0
LRD Mendis	run out		64	57	1	3
RS Madugalle	c Khanna	b Amarnath	4	16	0	0
SP Pasqual	not out		23	26	1	0
DS de Silva	not out		1	4	0	0
Extras	(lb 8, w 2, nb 1)		11			
Total	(5 wickets, 60 overs)		238			

DNB: +SA Jayasinghe, ARM Opatha, DLS de Silva, FRMD Gunatilleke.
Fall of wickets: 1-31 (Warnapura), 2-127 (Wettimuny), 3-147 (Dias), 4-175 (Madugalle), 5-227 (Mendis).

Bowling	O	M	R	W
Kapil Dev	12	2	53	1
Ghavri	12	0	53	0
Amarnath	12	3	40	3
Bedi	12	2	37	0
Venkataraghavan	12	0	44	0

India innings (target: 239 runs from 60 overs)			R	B	4	6
SM Gavaskar	c Dias	b Warnapura	26	54	2	0
AD Gaekwad	c sub (GRA de Silva)	b DLS de Silva	33	52	2	0
DB Vengsarkar	c DLS de Silva	b DS de Silva	36	57	3	0
GR Viswanath	run out		22	55	0	0
BP Patel		b DS de Silva	10	13	1	0
N Kapil Dev	c Warnapura	b DLS de Silva	16	19	2	0
M Amarnath		b DS de Silva	7	15	0	0
KD Ghavri	c Warnapura	b Opatha	3	8	0	0
+SC Khanna	c Dias	b Opatha	10	17	1	0
*S Venkataraghavan	not out		9	9	0	0
BS Bedi	c Jayasinghe	b Opatha	5	13	0	0
Extras	(lb 10, w 3, nb 1)		14			
Total	(all out, 54.1 overs)		191			

Fall of wickets: 1-60 (Gavaskar), 2-76 (Gaekwad), 3-119 (Viswanath), 4-132 (Patel), 5-147 (Vengsarkar), 6-160 (Kapil Dev), 7-162 (Amarnath), 8-170 (Ghavri), 9-185 (Khanna), 10-191 (Bedi).

Bowling	O	M	R	W
Opatha	10.1	0	31	3
Gunatilleke	9	1	34	0
Warnapura	12	0	47	1
DLS de Silva	12	0	36	2
DS de Silva	11	1	29	3

New Zealand v West Indies, Group B
At Trent Bridge, Nottingham, 16 June 1979 (60-overs)
Result: West Indies won by 32 runs. Points: West Indies 4, New Zealand 0.
Toss: New Zealand. Umpires: HD Bird and BJ Meyer.
Man of the Match: CH Lloyd.

West Indies innings (60 overs maximum)			R	B	4	6
CG Greenidge	c Edgar	b Coney	65	95	3	1
DL Haynes	lbw	b Hadlee	12	20		
IVA Richards	c Burgess	b Coney	9	30		
AI Kallicharran		b McKechnie	39	68	2	0
*CH Lloyd	not out		73	80	4	0
CL King	lbw	b Cairns	12	18		
+DL Murray	c Coney	b Chatfield	12	21		
AME Roberts	c Lees	b Cairns	1	3	0	0
J Garner	not out		9	25		
Extras	(b 5, lb 7)		12			
Total	(7 wickets, 60 overs)		244			

DNB: MA Holding, CEH Croft.
Fall of wickets: 1-23 (Haynes), 2-61 (Richards), 3-117 (Greenidge), 4-152 (Kallicharran), 5-175 (King), 6-202 (Murray), 7-204 (Roberts).

Bowling	O	M	R	W
Hadlee	11	2	41	1
Chatfield	11	0	45	1
Cairns	12	1	48	2
Coney	12	0	40	2
McKechnie	11	0	46	1
Morrison	3	0	12	0

New Zealand innings (target: 245 runs from 60 overs)			R	B	4	6
BA Edgar	run out		12	23		
JG Wright	c Lloyd	b Garner	15	32		
JV Coney	c Garner	b King	36	54	3	0
GM Turner	c Lloyd	b Roberts	20	44		
JFM Morrison	c Murray	b Garner	11	41		
*MG Burgess	c Richards	b Roberts	35	49	3	0
+WK Lees		b Croft	5	5	0	0
RJ Hadlee		b Roberts	42	48	4	0
BJ McKechnie	not out		13	44		
BL Cairns		b Holding	1	3	0	0
EJ Chatfield	not out		3	9	0	0
Extras	(lb 14, w 4, nb 1)		19			
Total	(9 wickets, 60 overs)		212			

Fall of wickets: 1-27 (Edgar), 2-38 (Wright), 3-90 (Turner), 4-91 (Coney), 5-138 (Morrison), 6-143 (Lees), 7-160 (Burgess), 8-199 (Hadlee), 9-202 (Cairns).

Bowling	O	M	R	W
Roberts	12	2	43	3
Holding	12	1	29	1
Croft	12	1	38	1
Garner	12	0	45	2
King	12	1	38	1

Australia v Canada, Group A
At Edgbaston, Birmingham, 16 June 1979 (60-overs)
Result: Australia won by 7 wickets. Points: Australia 4, Canada 0.
Toss: Australia. Umpires: DJ Constant and JG Langridge.
Man of the Match: AG Hurst.

Canada innings (60 overs maximum)			R	B	4	6
GR Sealy	c Porter	b Dymock	25	30	4	0
CJD Chappell	lbw	b Hurst	19	42	2	0
FA Dennis	lbw	b Hurst	1	8	0	0
Tariq Javed	c Wright	b Porter	8	30	1	0
S Baksh		b Hurst	0	6	0	0
JCB Vaughan		b Porter	29	43	4	0
*+BM Mauricette	c Hilditch	b Cosier	5	22	0	0
JM Patel		b Cosier	2	4	0	0
RG Callender	c Wright	b Hurst	0	6	0	0
CC Henry	c Hughes	b Hurst	5	11	1	0
JN Valentine	not out		0	6	0	0
Extras	(b 4, lb 5, w 1, nb 1)		11			
Total	(all out, 33.2 overs)		105			

Fall of wickets: 1-44 (Sealy), 2-50 (Dennis), 3-51 (Chappell), 4-51 (Baksh), 5-78 (Tariq Javed), 6-97 (Vaughan), 7-97 (Mauricette), 8-98 (Callender), 9-104 (Henry), 10-105 (Patel).

Bowling	O	M	R	W
Hogg	2	0	26	0
Hurst	10	3	21	5
Dymock	8	2	17	1
Porter	6	2	13	2
Cosier	7.2	2	17	2

Australia innings (target: 106 runs from 60 overs)			R	B	4	6
AMJ Hilditch	c Valentine	b Henry	24	30	3	0
WM Darling	lbw	b Valentine	13	16	2	0
AR Border		b Henry	25	53	4	0
*KJ Hughes	not out		27	40	2	0
GN Yallop	not out		13	20	0	0
Extras	(lb 1, nb 3)		4			
Total	(3 wickets, 26 overs)		106			

DNB: GJ Cosier, +KJ Wright, GD Porter, RM Hogg, G Dymock, AG Hurst.
Fall of wickets: 1-23 (Darling), 2-53 (Hilditch), 3-72 (Border).

Bowling	O	M	R	W
Valentine	3	0	28	1
Callender	3	0	12	0
Henry	10	0	27	2
Vaughan	6	0	15	0
Patel	4	0	20	0

England v Pakistan, Group A

At Headingley, Leeds, 16 June 1979 (60-overs)
Result: England won by 14 runs. Points: England 4, Pakistan 0.
Toss: Pakistan. Umpires: WL Budd and DGL Evans.
Man of the Match: M Hendrick.

England innings (60 overs maximum)			R	B	4	6
*JM Brearley	c Wasim Bari	b Imran Khan	0	2	0	0
G Boycott	lbw	b Majid Khan	18	54	2	0
DW Randall	c Wasim Bari	b Sikander Bakht	1	5	0	0
GA Gooch	c Sadiq Mohammad	b Sikander Bakht	33	90	5	0
DI Gower		b Majid Khan	27	40	3	0
IT Botham		b Majid Khan	22	48	1	1
PH Edmonds	c Wasim Raja	b Asif Iqbal	2	23	0	0
+RW Taylor	not out		20	59	1	0
CM Old		c & b Asif Iqbal	2	7	0	0
RGD Willis		b Sikander Bakht	24	37	3	0
M Hendrick	not out		1	1	0	0
Extras	(lb 3, w 7, nb 5)		15			
Total	(9 wickets, 60 overs)		165			

Fall of wickets: 1-0 (Brearley), 2-4 (Randall), 3-51 (Boycott), 4-70 (Gooch), 5-99 (Gower), 6-115 (Botham), 7-115 (Edmonds), 8-118 (Old), 9-161 (Willis).

Bowling	O	M	R	W
Imran Khan	12	3	24	1
Sikander Bakht	12	3	32	3
Mudassar Nazar	12	4	30	0
Asif Iqbal	12	3	37	2
Majid Khan	12	2	27	3

Pakistan innings (target: 166 runs from 60 overs)			R	B	4	6
Majid Khan	c Botham	b Hendrick	7	20	1	0
Sadiq Mohammad		b Hendrick	18	27	4	0
Mudassar Nazar	lbw	b Hendrick	0	2	0	0
Zaheer Abbas	c Taylor	b Botham	3	19	0	0
Haroon Rashid	c Brearley	b Hendrick	1	2	0	0
Javed Miandad	lbw	b Botham	0	4	0	0
*Asif Iqbal	c Brearley	b Willis	51	104	5	0
Wasim Raja	lbw	b Old	21	25	4	0
Imran Khan	not out		21	82	1	0
+Wasim Bari	c Taylor	b Boycott	17	33	2	0
Sikander Bakht	c Hendrick	b Boycott	2	19	0	0
Extras	(lb 8, w 1, nb 1)		10			
Total	(all out, 56 overs)		151			

Fall of wickets: 1-27 (Majid Khan), 2-27 (Mudassar Nazar), 3-28 (Sadiq Mohammad), 4-30 (Zaheer Abbas), 5-31 (Javed Miandad), 6-34 (Haroon Rashid), 7-86 (Wasim Raja), 8-115 (Asif Iqbal), 9-145 (Wasim Bari), 10-151 (Sikander Bakht).

Bowling	O	M	R	W
Willis	11	2	37	1
Hendrick	12	6	15	4
Botham	12	3	38	2
Old	12	2	28	1
Edmonds	3	0	8	0
Boycott	5	0	14	2
Gooch	1	0	1	0

1st Semi Final
England v New Zealand

At Old Trafford, Manchester, 20 June 1979 (60-overs)
Result: England won by 9 runs. England advances to the final.
Toss: New Zealand. Umpires: JG Langridge and KE Palmer.
Man of the Match: GA Gooch.

England innings (60 overs maximum)			R	B	4	6
*JM Brearley	c Lees	b Coney	53	115	3	0
G Boycott	c Howarth	b Hadlee	2	14	0	0
W Larkins	c Coney	b McKechnie	7	37	0	0
GA Gooch		b McKechnie	71	84	1	3
DI Gower	run out		1	1	0	0
IT Botham	lbw	b Cairns	21	30	2	0
DW Randall	not out		42	50	1	1
CM Old	c Lees	b Troup	0	2	0	0
+RW Taylor	run out		12	25	1	0
RGD Willis	not out		1	2	0	0
Extras	(lb 8, w 3)		11			
Total	(8 wickets, 60 overs)		221			

DNB: M Hendrick.
Fall of wickets: 1-13 (Boycott), 2-38 (Larkins), 3-96 (Brearley), 4-98 (Gower), 5-145 (Botham), 6-177 (Gooch), 7-178 (Old), 8-219 (Taylor).

Bowling	O	M	R	W
Hadlee	12	4	32	1
Troup	12	1	38	1
Cairns	12	2	47	1
Coney	12	0	47	1
McKechnie	12	1	46	2

New Zealand innings (target: 222 runs from 60 overs)			R	B	4	6
JG Wright	run out		69	137	9	0
BA Edgar	lbw	b Old	17	38	1	0
GP Howarth	lbw	b Boycott	7	12	1	0
JV Coney	lbw	b Hendrick	11	39	0	0
GM Turner	lbw	b Willis	30	51	2	0
*MG Burgess	run out		10	13	0	0
RJ Hadlee		b Botham	15	32	0	0
+WK Lees		b Hendrick	23	20	1	0
BL Cairns	c Brearley	b Hendrick	14	6	1	1
BJ McKechnie	not out		4	9	0	0
GB Troup	not out		3	3	0	0
Extras	(b 5, w 4)		9			
Total	(9 wickets, 60 overs)		212			

Fall of wickets: 1-47 (Edgar), 2-58 (Howarth), 3-104 (Coney), 4-112 (Wright), 5-132 (Burgess), 6-162 (Turner), 7-180 (Hadlee), 8-195 (Cairns), 9-208 (Lees).

Bowling	O	M	R	W
Botham	12	3	42	1
Hendrick	12	0	55	3
Old	12	1	33	1
Boycott	9	1	24	1
Gooch	3	1	8	0
Willis	12	1	41	1

2nd Semi Final
Pakistan v West Indies

At Kennington Oval, London, 20 June 1979 (60-overs)
Result: West Indies won by 43 runs. West Indies advances to the final.
Toss: Pakistan. Umpires: WL Budd and DJ Constant.
Man of the Match: CG Greenidge.

West Indies innings (60 overs maximum)			R	B	4	6
CG Greenidge	c Wasim Bari	b Asif Iqbal	73	107	5	1
DL Haynes		c & b Asif Iqbal	65	115	4	0
IVA Richards		b Asif Iqbal	42	62	1	0
*CH Lloyd	c Mudassar Nazar	b Asif Iqbal	37	38	3	0
CL King	c sub	b Sarfraz Nawaz	34	25	3	0
AI Kallicharran		b Imran Khan	11	14	0	0
AME Roberts	not out		7	4	0	0
J Garner	not out		1	1	0	0
Extras	(b 1, lb 17, w 1, nb 4)		23			
Total	6 wickets, 60 overs		293			

DNB: +DL Murray, MA Holding, CEH Croft.
Fall of wickets: 1-132 (Greenidge), 2-165 (Haynes), 3-233 (Richards), 4-236 (Lloyd), 5-285 (Kallicharran), 6-285 (King).

Bowling	O	M	R	W
Imran Khan	9	1	43	1
Sarfraz Nawaz	12	1	71	1
Sikander Bakht	6	1	24	0
Mudassar Nazar	10	0	50	0
Majid Khan	12	2	26	0
Asif Iqbal	11	0	56	4

Pakistan innings (target: 294 runs from 60 overs)

			R	B	4	6
Majid Khan	c Kallicharran	b Croft	81	124	7	0
Sadiq Mohammad	c Murray	b Holding	2	7	0	0
Zaheer Abbas	c Murray	b Croft	93	122	8	1
Haroon Rashid	run out		15	22	1	0
Javed Miandad	lbw	b Croft	0	1	0	0
*Asif Iqbal	c Holding	b Richards	17	20	1	0
Mudassar Nazar	c Kallicharran	b Richards	2	9	0	0
Imran Khan		c & b Richards	6	4	1	0
Sarfraz Nawaz	c Haynes	b Roberts	12	15	0	0
+Wasim Bari	c Murray	b Roberts	9	12	0	0
Sikander Bakht	not out		1	4	0	0
Extras	(lb 9, w 2, nb 1)		12			
Total	(all out, 56.2 overs)		250			

Fall of wickets: 1-10 (Sadiq Mohammad), 2-176 (Zaheer Abbas), 3-187 (Majid Khan), 4-187 (Javed Miandad), 5-208 (Haroon Rashid), 6-220 (Mudassar Nazar), 7-221 (Asif Iqbal), 8-228 (Imran Khan), 9-246 (Wasim Bari), 10-250 (Sarfraz Nawaz).

Bowling	O	M	R	W
Roberts	9.2	2	41	2
Holding	9	1	28	1
Croft	11	0	29	3
Garner	12	1	47	0
King	7	0	41	0
Richards	8	0	52	3

Final
England v West Indies
At Lord's, London, 23 June 1979 (60-overs)
Result: West Indies won by 92 runs. West Indies wins the 1979 Prudential World Cup.
Toss: England. Umpires: HD Bird and BJ Meyer.
Man of the Match: IVA Richards.

West Indies innings (60 overs maximum)

			R	B	4	6
CG Greenidge	run out (Randall)		9	31	0	0
DL Haynes	c Hendrick	b Old	20	27	3	0
IVA Richards	not out		138	157	11	3
AI Kallicharran		b Hendrick	4	17	0	0
*CH Lloyd		c & b Old	13	33	2	0
CL King	c Randall	b Edmonds	86	66	10	3
+DL Murray	c Gower	b Edmonds	5	9	1	0
AME Roberts	c Brearley	b Hendrick	0	7	0	0
J Garner	c Taylor	b Botham	0	5	0	0
MA Holding		b Botham	0	6	0	0
CEH Croft	not out		0	2	0	0
Extras	(b 1, lb 10)		11			
Total	(9 wickets, 60 overs)		286			

Fall of wickets: 1-22 (Greenidge), 2-36 (Haynes), 3-55 (Kallicharran), 4-99 (Lloyd), 5-238 (King), 6-252 (Murray), 7-258 (Roberts), 8-260 (Garner), 9-272 (Holding).

Bowling	O	M	R	W
Botham	12	2	44	2
Hendrick	12	2	50	2
Old	12	0	55	2
Boycott	6	0	38	0
Edmonds	12	2	40	2
Gooch	4	0	27	0
Larkins	2	0	21	0

England innings (target: 287 runs from 60 overs)

			R	B	4	6
*JM Brearley	c King	b Holding	64	130	7	0
G Boycott	c Kallicharran	b Holding	57	105	3	0
DW Randall		b Croft	15	22	0	0
GA Gooch		b Garner	32	28	4	0
DI Gower		b Garner	0	4	0	0
IT Botham	c Richards	b Croft	4	3	0	0
W Larkins		b Garner	0	1	0	0
PH Edmonds	not out		5	8	0	0
CM Old		b Garner	0	2	0	0
+RW Taylor	c Murray	b Garner	0	1	0	0
M Hendrick		b Croft	0	5	0	0
Extras	(lb 12, w 2, nb 3)		17			
Total	(all out, 51 overs)		194			

Fall of wickets: 1-129 (Brearley), 2-135 (Boycott), 3-183 (Gooch), 4-183 (Gower), 5-186 (Randall), 6-186 (Larkins), 7-192 (Botham), 8-192 (Old), 9-194 (Taylor), 10-194 (Hendrick).

Bowling	O	M	R	W
Roberts	9	2	33	0
Holding	8	1	16	2
Croft	10	1	42	3
Garner	11	0	38	5
Richards	10	0	35	0
King	3	0	13	0

World Cup **1983**
by Dicky Rutnagur

THE 1983 World Cup was momentous, not only because it featured quite the biggest upset in the competition's history to date, a win for unfancied India. The impact of such an unexpected triumph, completed with a sensational win over the mighty West Indies, was seismic for the changes it quickly evolved in the structure of world cricket and its governance, as also in India's cricket culture.

But let us set aside the political fallout for the epilogue and first review the background and exciting events of the third tournament in the World Cup series. Even allowing for the fact that there is greater scope for cricket's "glorious uncertainties" to surface in the game's shorter version than in the orthodox variety, it was hard to visualise the West Indies, who had won the Cup in 1975 and 1979 without losing a single match, failing to extend their supremacy.

England, the hosts and 1979 finalists, headed the opposite group and were seen as the West Indies' closest rivals, because Australia's fortunes were at a low ebb and Pakistan's prospects were dimmed by Imran Khan's inability to bowl due to stress fractures in his shin.

New Zealand, also drawn in England's group, were a force to reckon with, having twice before figured in the semi-finals. Sri Lanka's glory days still lay some way ahead, but they were capable of springing the odd surprise. India and Zimbabwe were regarded as the minnows. Zimbabwe had come to the top table via the qualifying competition for the Associates, but they were by no means a nonentity, for most of their players had honed their skills in the hard school of South Africa's Currie Cup, playing for Rhodesia.

India's only win in two previous World Cups was against the amateurs of East Africa in 1975 and they were quoted by the bookmakers at 66-1. But they had shown faint signs of improvement over the previous two years, and the strongest hint of it was dropped a few months earlier on their Caribbean tour when they beat the West Indies at full strength in Berbice, during a three-match series. This forward surge could

Indian heroes, Man of the Match Mohinder Amarnath and captain Kapil Dev, with the World Cup, on the Lord's balcony after their team's stunning victory over the West Indies in the final.

be attributed largely to the growing maturity as an all-rounder of Kapil Dev, who was now captain and who led the side with enterprise and inspiration.

A new format had been devised for the 1983 competition, in that the teams in each qualifying group played each other twice. The revision made it increasingly difficult for one of the lesser sides to sneak into the semi-finals, never mind snatch the Cup. In the circumstances, India's win was quite remarkable. Another factor that heightened the surprise element was that the jewel in India's batting crown, Sunil Gavaskar, was hopelessly out of form right through the campaign. In fact, there came a stage when the great opener was dropped for two consecutive matches.

The curtain rose on a first act of high drama with the underdogs holding centre stage. At Trent Bridge, Zimbabwe toppled Australia in a sensational debut. Their hero was their captain, Duncan Fletcher, who two decades later became England's celebrated Ashes-winning coach.

In another match played simultaneously at Old Trafford, but which spilled over into the reserve day because of rain, a second giant had his nose bloodied. The West Indies were beaten quite convincingly by India, who both batted and bowled with admirable calm and discipline. At the time, it was regarded as no more than an aberration, but it was to prove an early portent.

The West Indies did not encounter another serious challenge in their remaining group matches. On a blissful Oval pitch, Viv Richards brilliantly dominated the return match against India. The might of West Indies' pace attack was proving irresistible, but the substantial margins of their victories camouflaged the fact that their batting, so daunting on paper, was not firing on all cylinders.

The second semi-final place from that group remained open until the last round. India clinched it by beating Australia, at Chelmsford. Despite this win, it could have been a different story if, two days earlier, India had fallen victim to their bravado in opting to

bat first against Zimbabwe on a damp greentop at the quaint Nevill Ground in Tunbridge Wells. This reckless gamble was taken to give themselves the fullest scope to boost their scoring rate in case there was a tie on points and the issue rested on countback. The events that followed were absurdly bizarre. India's five specialist batsmen were all dispatched for a mere 17 runs. The miracle of transforming this tattered innings from pumpkin to Cinderella's gilded coach was performed by the irrepressible Kapil Dev, with noble support from all-rounders Roger Binny and Madan Lal and wicketkeeper Syed Kirmani.

After steadying the innings with circumspection, Kapil Dev cut loose with such ferocity that his epic 175 not out, off 138 balls, included 16 fours and four sixes. Zimbabwe, to their credit, were not overwhelmed by this withering onslaught and, if they came as near to India as 31 runs, and that despite a mid-innings collapse that had them floundering at 189 for eight, it was thanks to Kevin Curran, who had already left his mark on the match as a bowler. He gave them hope with a near replica of Kapil's masterpiece: 73 off 93 balls.

In the other group, England had just one hiccup – against New Zealand – on their way to the top. When New Zealand beat them at Edgbaston, their prospects burned bright but, next time out, they conceded to underperforming Sri Lanka their only win of the competition, and the Kiwis' chances ultimately rested on their final match with Pakistan, which they lost. They still finished level on points with Pakistan, but were eliminated by an inferior run rate.

During the 1970s and '80s, the West Indies could well have regarded The Oval as a home ground. The pitch was ideal and the terraces were always filled with expats from the Caribbean who supported them fervently. In that congenial environment, their semi-final with Pakistan was won effortlessly.

India's swelling self-belief and their relish of the Old Trafford pitch which had served them well in their opening victory over the West Indies stood them in good stead against England. Mohinder Amarnath did the groundwork with both ball and bat, and Yashpal Sharma and Sandeep Patil hurried them to victory with a flourish, getting the last 63 runs in nine overs.

Each of the first two finals had been adorned with a memorable century – Clive Lloyd's in 1975 and Viv Richards's in 1979. In this respect the one of 1983 was bland, but there was no dearth of thrills. Even with the distance of time it is hard to find an explanation for the most powerful and star-studded batting line-up of

Cause and effect. The notice over the poster on Lord's wall for the final leaves ticketless fans understandably crestfallen.

that era failing to achieve a modest target of 184 on a balmy afternoon at Lord's.

India were rewarded for playing excellent cricket throughout the tournament and for their never-say-die attitude. The West Indies learned the hard way the price of complacency.

After India were bowled out for 183, "victory was treated as a foregone conclusion," Michael Holding later wrote. "Each batsman seemed to go out with the attitude that if he didn't get the runs someone after him would. They played a lot of airy-fairy shots, trying to get the runs in quick time instead of just batting normally until the Cup was secured. In short, we made the cardinal mistake of underestimating the task."

The disappointment of defeat drove a distressed Lloyd to announce his resignation to his stunned team that night. It was the knee-jerk reaction of a proud captain who reconsidered his decision under the urging of the president of the West Indies Cricket Board of Control, Allan Rae, next day and remained at the helm for another two years during which the West Indies reasserted their dominance in both forms of the game. The effects of the Lord's loss on Lloyd and his players were evident when they toured India later in the year, winning all five one-day internationals and the series of six Tests 3-0.

The Test & County Cricket Board (as the ECB was then styled) never sought, or claimed, ownership of the World Cup brand-name, but it was generally accepted that England would be the competition's permanent home for at least the foreseeable future. However, India's unexpected victory in 1983 put an end to such a notion. Legend has it that a request by the president of the Board of Control for Cricket in India, NKP Salve, for some extra tickets for the final was brusquely turned down by the MCC, whereupon Mr Salve, who was also a cabinet minister in the Indian government, swore vengeance.

India's means of settling this score was to bid for the next competition, in 1987, a submission tabled as a joint Indo-Pakistani venture. Their only rivals were England, who failed only because the two Asian countries offered a 50% increase in the prizemoney England paid out in 1983.

Australia and New Zealand played hosts in 1992 (by which time South Africa had been readmitted to the fold). When it came to 1996, a gentleman's agreement was made for England to stage it again. The pact was broken with India, Pakistan and Sri Lanka jointly throwing in a late bid. Except for Zimbabwe and, of course, the three countries making the bid, all the Test-playing countries remained faithful to the original agreement, but the balance was swayed by the support of the Associate members, who were seduced by an offer of guarantee money amounting to £100,000 as compared to England's offer of

£60,000. This unsavoury episode reassured the Asian bloc that they had built up the muscle to seize power in the International Cricket Council, and not long afterwards Jagmohan Dalmiya, of India, became its president, beating Malcolm Gray, of Australia, and South Africa's Krish Makherdhuj in a three-cornered contest.

One deplorable consequence of India's 1983 victory was an overnight change in the subcontinent's cricket culture. Hitherto, one-day cricket had no appeal to speak of there, while domestic first-class matches drew substantial crowds, and Test matches usually played to full houses. But soon Test-match attendances, even in Mumbai, Chennai and Kolkata – cities with deep-rooted cricketing traditions – showed a fall, while frenzied, jingoistic crowds packed grounds for one-day games.

The Indian board, rather than strive to restore the image of Test cricket with vigorous marketing, left it shamefully abandoned and instead fondled the new golden goose. They revealed their cavalier attitude to Test cricket most brazenly when the West Indies were on tour in the winter of 1987-88. The series of five Tests had already started when the Board decided to

reduce it to four and instead added two one-day internationals to the previously arranged programme of five. The West Indian board, still administrated in those days by cricketers, objected strongly, but without avail. Never since has India staged a five-Test series.

Another unwholesome feature of the proliferation of one-day internationals in the region has been the alarming increase in illegal betting, with the accompanying evil of match-fixing, which dragged the game into the sewers at the turn of the century.

But even if foreseen at the time, such repercussions were well into the future. The immediate reality was that the remarkable result at Lord's on June 25, 1983, was as famous a victory as India had ever known and it was blissfully and interminably celebrated as such in every city, town and village back home.

The scene on the Lord's outfield as the multitude assembles to hail India's upset victory over the West Indies in the final.

SEMI-FINALS
West Indies v Pakistan

At The Oval, June 22, 1983. West Indies won by eight wickets.

While India were confounding the odds and astounding England in the other semi-final at Manchester, the West Indies were casually disposing of the other Asian semi-finalist in London and proceeding to the final for the third time.

The Pakistanis, lucky to reach so far in any case, were effectively beaten within the first hour. They had to pick their XI without their classiest batsman, Javed Miandad, who ruled himself out because of an attack of the flu. They lost the toss on a humid, misty morning and were subjected to a ball moving about in the air and off the pitch. Andy Roberts and Joel Garner were entrusted with the new ball, to be followed by Michael Holding and Malcolm Marshall, and they gave the batsmen no quarter. Pakistan took 23 overs to raise their 50 by which time two wickets were down and they were never allowed to recover, scraping together 184 for six from their 60 overs.

It was never going to be a serious threat to the West Indies and, even though the leg-spinner Abdul Qadir amply demonstrated the quality on which his

reputation was built, victory was completed with 11.2 overs unutilised, Viv Richards registering his third score over 80 and Larry Gomes his third half-century in the tournament.

Apart from a period when Qadir caused Desmond Haynes, Richards and Gomes some discomfort with his mixture of leg-breaks, googlies and top-spinners, the match was completely devoid of the brilliant strokeplay of the semi-final between the teams at the same ground in the previous tournament four years earlier, which had produced over 500 runs.

The problems confronted by the Pakistani batsmen was best illustrated by the struggle of top-scorer Mohsin Khan. He managed only one boundary, an edge to third man, in his 70 which occupied almost four hours and included 43 singles. For a time, the elegant Zaheer Abbas threatened to collar Gomes, but the occasional off-spinner bowled him in the last over before lunch.

Greenidge and Haynes went cheaply but Richards, always at ease, had a six and 11 fours in his unbeaten 80 off 96 deliveries and the left-handed Gomes, typically unobtrusive, helped him add 132 for the third wicket to seal the win.

The greatest concern for the West Indies was a muscle injury that kept captain Clive Lloyd off the field after lunch, and that was to be more significantly

aggravated three days later in the final.
(Tony Cozier, West Indies Cricket Annual, 1984)

India v England

At Old Trafford, June 22, 1983. India won by six wickets. Though England made a brisk and promising start, this was a pitch similar to those on which India are so hard to beat at home. Roger Binny, Kirti Azad and Mohinder Amarnath had only to bowl a steady length to reduce the England batsmen, as they sought to attack, to mistimings and countless uses of the bat's edge. The fact that the faster Kapil Dev was no great menace when Graeme Fowler and Chris Tavaré were adding 69 at four an over for the first wicket was an indication that England's quicker bowlers would not pose the same problems to the Indian batsmen, with their vast experience of slow pitches of low bounce.

Binny dismissed the openers, Amarnath had David Gower caught behind from a lazy stroke and found a gap between bat and pad to bowl Mike Gatting, and Azad accounted for Ian Botham with one that skidded through. The run-outs of Allan Lamb and Ian Gould made a recovery of the initiative even more unlikely. For more than an hour not a four was hit, and it needed a few rough, mostly edged, strokes by Graham Dilley and his ninth-wicket stand of 25 with Paul

Allott, along with four wides in Kapil Dev's last over, to lift England's score above 200.

India, with little need to hurry, duly found the going easier against bowling which came on to the bat more readily. The openers, Sunil Gavaskar and Kris Srikkanth, were out in successive overs, but Amarnath, who earlier took two for 27 from his 12 overs, and Yashpal Sharma added 92 with increasing belligerence. Both hit sixes, Amarnath's straight off Allott when the required rate was rising. When Man of the Match Amarnath was run out, Yashpal and Sandeep Patil hurried the match to its close, at one time making 63 off nine overs.
(Wisden Cricketers' Almanack, 1984)

Above left: In a mirror image of the square-cut of the Man of the Match in an earlier final (see page 17), Mohinder Amarnath goes on the attack in his 26 in the low-scoring final.

Above right: Hands up for jubilant India as England lose another wicket in the semi-final at Old Trafford. Allan Lamb is beaten by a direct hit on the bowler's stumps attempting a sharp single with Graham Gooch.

FINAL
India v West Indies

At Lord's, June 25, 1983. India won by 43 runs.
India triumphed in a low-scoring match of high drama that remains one of the game's most astounding upsets. Never prepared to accept the role of no-hopers to which they had been generally condemned, they dethroned the champions of the previous two tournaments and the heavy favourites by dint of steady bowling, keen fielding and an indomitable spirit.

The West Indies lost because of unbelievably inept batting, described by captain Clive Lloyd afterwards as "the performance of amateurs", that led to an all-out 140 from 52 overs. Their target was seemingly straightforward after India squandered a promising beginning with suicidal strokes to slip from 90 for two just before lunch to 183 all out with 6.2 of their 60 overs unused. Against such confident opponents, filled with batsmen of experience and proven class, the challenge was minimal. The unequal contest that had been widely predicted seemed certain.

Those who followed India's progress through the tournament knew better. They were contesting the final not by fluke but by right. They had beaten the West Indies, Australia and England on the way to

their appointment with destiny. They had reduced the West Indies to 157 for nine in the opening match before a last-wicket partnership of 71 saved some of the defending champions' blushes, had demolished Australia for 129, and limited England to 213 in the semi-final.

Above all, India believed in themselves. They had come to realise that no cause is lost until the last ball is bowled. Their limited bowling staff of medium-pacers adhered strictly to the principles of line and length, and found that they were assisted by over-confident batsmen who threw their wickets away like novices. Gordon Greenidge, in his third final, lost his off stump with bat upraised high above his shoulder, offering no shot to Balwinder Singh Sandhu, who had twice bowled with him inswingers in the Tests in the Caribbean a few months earlier and in the opening

Above: Opening salvo from India. Kris Srikkanth's savage square-cut boundary off Andy Roberts in the first over sends an immediate signal of intent to the West Indies.

Right: Madan Lal bowls, Viv Richards pulls and all eyes are on the ball. An instant later, Kapil Dev completes the running catch at mid-wicket, the defining moment in the final.

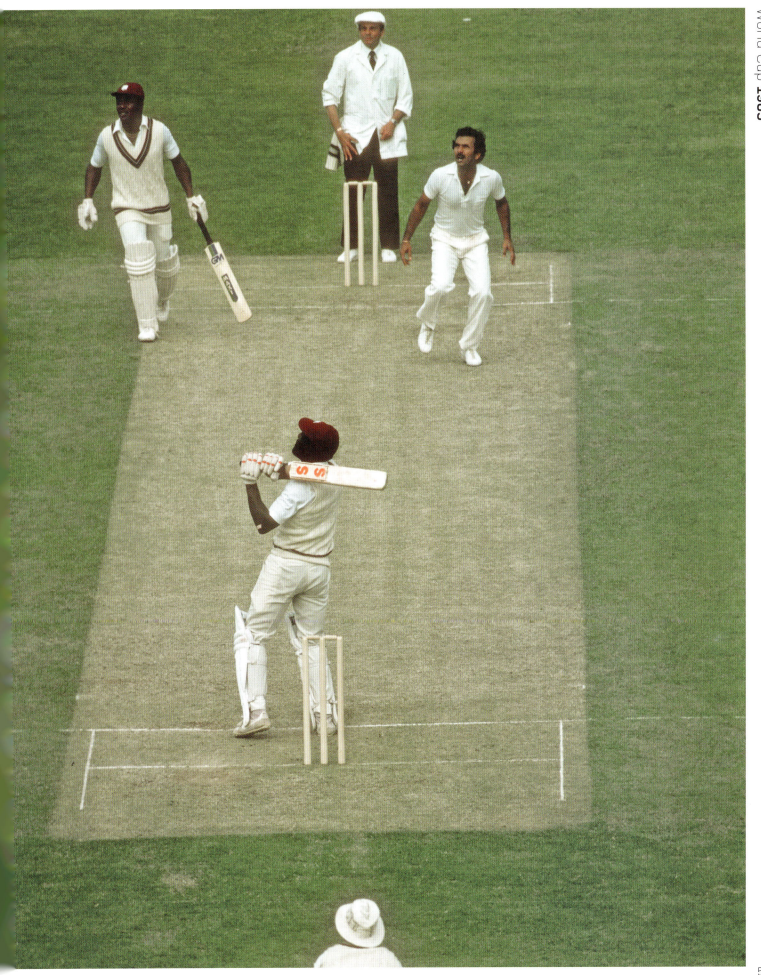

match of this tournament. Desmond Haynes drove on the up to the only fielder in the covers. Larry Gomes nibbled outside off stump several times before touching one to first slip. Jeff Dujon, after a lengthy and plucky fight, dragged a ball back into his stumps after deciding in mid-stroke to pull his bat away. Faoud Bacchus somehow managed to reach a delivery that would have been signalled wide had it not found a thin edge.

India's greatest prize was Viv Richards. Stroking the ball majestically all over the ground, the Master Blaster struck seven boundaries from 28 deliveries in scoring 33. Three of the fours were in Madan Lal's first over, but when he attempted to improve on that in the medium-pacer's second over with a hook aimed at the top tier of the grandstand, the ball got up more than anticipated, he top-edged the stroke, and Kapil Dev ran back from mid-wicket coolly and expertly to take the most vital catch of the tournament over his head.

The West Indies could not recover after that, their misery compounded when Lloyd, in taking his first run, pulled the muscle that had troubled him in the semi-final and needed to have Haynes as his runner. With his movement restricted, he soon skied a catch to mid-on off Roger Binny

At tea, the West Indies were 76 for five from 25 overs, and the large Indian element in a packed ground, hundreds of whom had flown in from India for the occasion, was already in celebratory mood. When Bacchus went in the first over after the break, the Cup had all but changed hands and only Dujon and Malcolm Marshall, who added 43, interrupted the Indian progress to their deserving triumph.

Earlier, their batsmen appeared to have relinquished any chance they had. After Sunil Gavaskar went early, Kris Srikkanth attacked with enterprising strokes, including a hooked six off Andy Roberts. When he was lbw to Marshall for 38 – as it turned out the highest score of the match – Mohinder Amarnath assumed the role of aggressor so that India were 90 for two in the 30th over before the innings imploded.

Amarnath lost his off stump to Michael Holding, Yashpal Sharma and Kapil Dev skied catches off Gomes' deceptive off-spin, as did Sandeep Patil off Joel Garner. Syed Kirmani and Sandhu added 22 for the last wicket, but 183 seemed totally inadequate.

Yet again, cricket proved itself to be a funny game.
(Tony Cozier, West Indies Cricket Annual, 1984)

Umpire Dickie Bird and India's Bishan Bedi are caught in the immediate melee of the crowd invasion at the end of the final. The West Indies last pair, Joel Garner and Michael Holding, seem oblivious to the mayhem about to engulf them – but they might have had other things on their minds.

"They said at the time"

India's captain Kapil Dev: *"Once we beat England, we said to ourselves that we had already won the tournament. Reaching the final was the greatest thing for all of us because nobody, including ourselves, imagined we would be there. I just said to the guys at the team meeting before the game that it was a bonus to have come this far and just to go out there and play as a team. We had nothing to lose and everything to gain."*

Indian all-rounder Roger Binny: *"Considering our performances in the previous two World Cups people just expected us to go and have another World Cup and come back. As a team we were looking to better that and come back with some sort of pride by winning a few more games. What really kicked us off was beating the West Indies in the first match of the tournament. That was really a morale-booster for our team."*

West Indies fast bowler Malcolm Marshall: *"I was sure we were going to win the World Cup. In fact, I was so positive about the outcome that I had even ordered a new BMW car in the misguided belief that I could pay for it out of my winnings. What utter folly! Cricket has a nasty habit of punishing those who come to believe in their infallibility and so it was at Lord's on June 25, 1983, that we paid the ultimate price for an act of complacency."*

West Indies captain Clive Lloyd: *"We only lost two games in the first three World Cup tournaments. Both were to India in 1983, in the first round and then the final. After that first loss, we should have realised the danger, but we approached a target of 184 in a complacent manner. Had it been 284 we would probably have had a better approach to it. We were the better side – there was no doubt – but they played better than us on that day. They were perhaps mentally stronger."*

Former England captain Tony Lewis: *"This was wonderful for the health of cricket as a world game of honour, skill and equal opportunity. India were supposed to have no chance of beating the West Indies in this World Cup final but they did."*

Format

Two groups of four, as in 1979; this time, though, each team played the others in its group twice, not once, to determine the four semi-finalists. As a ploy to reduce the chance of elimination by the weather, it was a good one, even if June wasn't wet and only three of the 27 games went into a reserve day anyway. For the first time, non-Test grounds were used.

Innovations

Umpires were told to apply a stricter interpretation of wides and bouncers. The result? More than twice as many wides per match as in 1979 (9.59 to 4.64). A fielding circle (actually an oval) was introduced, 30 yards away from the stumps. Four fieldsmen needed to be inside it at all times.

World Cup 1983
Scoreboards

England v New Zealand, Group A
At Kennington Oval, London, 9 June 1983 (60-overs)
Result: England won by 106 runs. Points: England 4, New Zealand 0.
Toss: England. Umpires: BJ Meyer and DO Oslear.
Man of the Match: AJ Lamb.

England innings (60 overs maximum)			R	B	4	6
G Fowler	c Coney	b Cairns	8	19	1	0
CJ Tavare	c Edgar	b Chatfield	45	91	4	0
DI Gower	c Edgar	b Coney	39	62	6	0
AJ Lamb		b Snedden	102	105	12	2
MW Gatting		b Snedden	43	47	3	0
IT Botham	c Lees	b Hadlee	22	16	0	1
+IJ Gould	not out		14	12	1	0
GR Dilley	not out		31	14	4	0
Extras	(lb 12, w 1, nb 5)		18			
Total	(6 wickets, 60 overs)		322			

DNB: VJ Marks, PJW Allott, *RGD Willis.
Fall of wickets: 1-13 (Fowler), 2-79 (Gower), 3-117 (Tavare), 4-232 (Gatting), 5-271 (Botham), 6-278 (Lamb).

Bowling	O	M	R	W
Hadlee	12	4	26	1
Cairns	12	4	57	1
Snedden	12	1	105	2
Chatfield	12	1	45	1
Coney	6	1	20	1
Crowe	6	0	51	0

New Zealand innings (target: 323 runs from 60 overs)			R	B	4	6
GM Turner	lbw	b Willis	14	28	2	0
BA Edgar	c Gould	b Willis	3	6	0	0
JG Wright	c Botham	b Dilley	10	17	1	0
*GP Howarth	c Lamb	b Marks	18	44	1	0
JV Coney	run out		23	52	2	0
MD Crowe	run out		97	118	8	0
+WK Lees		b Botham	8	23	0	0
RJ Hadlee	c Lamb	b Marks	1	9	0	0
BL Cairns	lbw	b Botham	1	2	0	0
MC Snedden	c Gould	b Gatting	21	34	1	0
EJ Chatfield	not out		9	24	1	0
Extras	(b 2, lb 4, w 4, nb 1)		11			
Total	(all out, 59 overs)		216			

Fall of wickets: 1-3 (Edgar), 2-28 (Wright), 3-31 (Turner), 4-62 (Howarth), 5-85 (Coney), 6-123 (Lees), 7-136 (Hadlee), 8-138 (Cairns), 9-190 (Snedden), 10-216 (Crowe).

Bowling	O	M	R	W
Willis	7	2	9	2
Dilley	8	0	33	1
Botham	12	0	42	2
Allott	12	1	47	0
Marks	12	1	39	2
Gatting	8	1	35	1

Pakistan v Sri Lanka, Group A
At St Helen's, Swansea, 9 June 1983 (60-overs)
Result: Pakistan won by 50 runs. Points: Pakistan 4, Sri Lanka 0.
Toss: Sri Lanka. Umpires: KE Palmer and DR Shepherd.
Man of the Match: Mohsin Khan.

Pakistan innings (60 overs maximum)			R	B	4	6
Mudassar Nazar	c de Silva	b Ratnayake	36	72	2	0
Mohsin Khan		b John	82	121	5	1
Zaheer Abbas	c Kuruppu	b de Mel	82	81	10	0
Javed Miandad	lbw	b de Mel	72	52	4	3
*Imran Khan	not out		56	33	6	2
Ijaz Faqih	run out		2	3	0	0
Tahir Naqqash	not out		0	0	0	0
Extras	(b 4, lb 4)		8			
Total	(5 wickets, 60 overs)		338			

DNB: +Wasim Bari, Rashid Khan, Shahid Mahboob, Sarfraz Nawaz.
Fall of wickets: 1-88 (Mudassar Nazar), 2-156 (Mohsin Khan), 3-229 (Zaheer Abbas), 4-325 (Javed Miandad), 5-332 (Ijaz Faqih).

Bowling	O	M	R	W
de Mel	12	2	69	2
John	12	2	58	1
Ratnayake	12	0	65	1
Ranatunga	9	0	53	0
de Silva	10	0	52	0
Samarasekera	5	0	33	0

Sri Lanka innings (target: 339 runs from 60 overs)			R	B	4	6
S Wettimuny	c Rashid Khan	b Sarfraz Nawaz	12	26	1	0
DSBP Kuruppu	run out		72	101	7	2
RL Dias		b Rashid Khan	5	21	0	0
*LRD Mendis		b Tahir Naqqash	16	17	3	0
A Ranatunga		c & b Mudassar Nazar	31	42	5	0
MAR Samarasekera	run out		0	2	0	0
DS de Silva	c Wasim Bari	b Sarfraz Nawaz	35	51	1	0
ALF de Mel	c Tahir Naqqash	b Shahid Mahboob	11	22	0	0
+RG de Alwis	not out		59	56	5	1
RJ Ratnayake	c Mudassar Nazar	b Sarfraz Nawaz	13	13	0	1
VB John	not out		12	11	2	0
Extras	(lb 8, w 10, nb 4)		22			
Total	(9 wickets, 60 overs)		288			

Fall of wickets: 1-34 (Wettimuny), 2-58 (Dias), 3-85 (Mendis), 4-142 (Ranatunga), 5-143 (Samarasekera), 6-157 (Kuruppu), 7-180 (de Mel), 8-234 (de Silva), 9-262 (Ratnayake).

Bowling	O	M	R	W
Sarfraz Nawaz	12	1	40	3
Shahid Mahboob	11	0	48	1
Tahir Naqqash	8	0	49	1
Rashid Khan	12	1	55	1
Ijaz Faqih	12	1	52	0
Mudassar Nazar	4	0	18	1
Zaheer Abbas	1	0	4	0

Australia v Zimbabwe, Group B
At Trent Bridge, Nottingham, 9 June 1983 (60-overs)
Result: Zimbabwe won by 13 runs. Points: Zimbabwe 4, Australia 0.
Toss: Australia. Umpires: DJ Constant and MJ Kitchen.
Man of the Match: DAG Fletcher.

Zimbabwe innings (60 overs maximum)			R	B	4	6
AH Omarshah	c Marsh	b Lillee	16	57	0	0
GA Paterson	c Hookes	b Lillee	27	59	2	0
JG Heron	c Marsh	b Yallop	14	40	1	0
AJ Pycroft		b Border	21	41	1	0
+DL Houghton	c Marsh	b Yallop	0	1	0	0
*DAG Fletcher	not out		69	84	5	0
KM Curran	c Hookes	b Hogg	27	46	2	0
IP Butchart	not out		34	38	2	0
Extras	(lb 18, w 7, nb 6)		31			
Total	(6 wickets, 60 overs)		239			

DNB: PWE Rawson, AJ Traicos, VR Hogg.
Fall of wickets: 1-55 (Paterson), 2-55 (Omarshah), 3-86 (Heron), 4-86 (Houghton), 5-94 (Pycroft), 6-164 (Curran).

Bowling	O	M	R	W
Lawson	11	2	33	0
Hogg	12	3	43	1
Lillee	12	1	47	2
Thomson	11	1	46	0
Yallop	9	0	28	2
Border	5	0	11	1

Australia innings (target: 240 runs from 60 overs)			R	B	4	6
GM Wood	c Houghton	b Fletcher	31	60	3	0
KC Wessels	run out		76	130	5	0
*KJ Hughes	c Omarshah	b Fletcher	0	4	0	0
DW Hookes	c Traicos	b Fletcher	20	48	1	0
GN Yallop	c Pycroft	b Fletcher	2	17	0	0
AR Border	c Pycroft	b Curran	17	33	0	0
+RW Marsh	not out		50	42	3	2
GF Lawson		b Butchart	0	4	0	0
RM Hogg	not out		19	22	1	0
Extras	(b 2, lb 7, w 2)		11			
Total	(7 wickets, 60 overs)		226			

DNB: DK Lillee, JR Thomson.
Fall of wickets: 1-61 (Wood), 2-63 (Hughes), 3-114 (Hookes), 4-133 (Yallop), 5-138 (Wessels), 6-168 (Border), 7-176 (Lawson).

Bowling	O	M	R	W
Hogg	6	2	15	0
Rawson	12	1	54	0
Butchart	10	0	39	1
Fletcher	11	1	42	4
Traicos	12	2	27	0
Curran	9	0	38	1

India v West Indies, Group B

At Old Trafford, Manchester, 9,10 June 1983 (60-overs)
Result: India won by 34 runs. Points: India 4, West Indies 0.
Toss: West Indies. Umpires: B Leadbeater and AGT Whitehead.
Man of the Match: Yashpal Sharma.
Score after day 1 (reserve day used): Ind 262/8, WI 67/2 (off 22 overs).

India innings (60 overs maximum)			R	B	4	6
SM Gavaskar	c Dujon	b Marshall	19	44		
K Srikkanth	c Dujon	b Holding	14	17		
M Amarnath	c Dujon	b Garner	21	60		
SM Patil		b Gomes	36	52		
Yashpal Sharma		b Holding	89	120	9	0
*N Kapil Dev	c Richards	b Gomes	6	13		
RMH Binny	lbw	b Marshall	27	38		
S Madan Lal	not out		21	22		
+SMH Kirmani	run out		1	2	0	0
RJ Shastri	not out		5	3	0	
Extras	(b 4, lb 10, w 1, nb 8)		23			
Total	(8 wickets, 60 overs)		262			

DNB: BS Sandhu.
Fall of wickets: 1-21 (Srikkanth), 2-46 (Gavaskar), 3-76 (Amarnath), 4-125 (Patil), 5-141 (Kapil Dev), 6-214 (Binny), 7-243 (Yashpal Sharma), 8-246 (Kirmani).

Bowling	O	M	R	W
Holding	12	3	32	2
Roberts	12	1	51	0
Marshall	12	1	48	2
Garner	12	1	49	1
Richards	2	0	13	0
Gomes	10	0	46	2

West Indies innings (target: 263 runs from 60 overs)			R	B	4	6
CG Greenidge		b Sandhu	24	55		
DL Haynes	run out		24	29		
IVA Richards	c Kirmani	b Binny	17	36		
SFAF Bacchus		b Madan Lal	14	24		
*CH Lloyd		b Binny	25	38		
+PJL Dujon	c Sandhu	b Binny	7	12		
HA Gomes	run out		8	16		
MD Marshall	st Kirmani	b Shastri	2	5	0	0
AME Roberts	not out		37	58		
MA Holding		b Shastri	8	11		
J Garner	st Kirmani	b Shastri	37	29	0	1
Extras	(b 4, lb 17, w 4)		25			
Total	(all out, 54.1 overs)		228			

Fall of wickets: 1-49 (Haynes), 2-56 (Greenidge), 3-76 (Richards), 4-96 (Bacchus), 5-107 (Dujon), 6-124 (Gomes), 7-126 (Marshall), 8-130 (Lloyd), 9-157 (Holding), 10-228 (Garner).

Bowling	O	M	R	W
Kapil Dev	10	0	34	0
Sandhu	12	1	36	1
Madan Lal	12	1	34	1
Binny	12	1	48	3
Shastri	5.1	0	26	3
Patil	3	0	25	0

England v Sri Lanka, Group A

At County Ground, Taunton, 11 June 1983 (60-overs)
Result: England won by 47 runs. Points: England 4, Sri Lanka 0.
Toss: England. Umpires: MJ Kitchen and KE Palmer.
Man of the Match: DI Gower.

England innings (60 overs maximum)			R	B	4	6
G Fowler		b John	22	59	1	0
CJ Tavare	c de Alwis	b Ranatunga	32	61	4	0
DI Gower		b de Mel	130	120	12	5
AJ Lamb		b Ratnayake	53	51	4	2
MW Gatting	run out		7	8	0	0
IT Botham	run out		0	1	0	0
+IJ Gould	c Ranatunga	b de Mel	35	40	2	0
GR Dilley		b de Mel	29	16	5	0
VJ Marks	run out		5	5	0	0
PJW Allott	not out		0	0	0	0
Extras	(lb 11, w 9)		20			
Total	(9 wickets, 60 overs)		333			

DNB: *RGD Willis.
Fall of wickets: 1-49 (Fowler), 2-78 (Tavare), 3-174 (Lamb), 4-193 (Gatting), 5-194 (Botham), 6-292 (Gould), 7-298 (Gower), 8-333 (Dilley), 9-333 (Marks).

Bowling	O	M	R	W
de Mel	12	3	62	2
John	12	0	55	1
Ratnayake	12	0	66	2
Ranatunga	12	0	65	1
de Silva	12	0	65	0

Sri Lanka innings (target: 334 runs from 60 overs)			R	B	4	6
S Wettimuny	lbw	b Marks	33	66	3	1
DSBP Kuruppu	c Gatting	b Dilley	4	3	1	0
RL Dias	c Botham	b Dilley	2	15	0	0
*LRD Mendis	c Willis	b Marks	56	64	5	1
RS Madugalle	c Tavare	b Marks	12	26	1	0
A Ranatunga	c Lamb	b Marks	34	45	4	0
DS de Silva	st Gould	b Marks	28	37	2	0
+RG de Alwis	not out		58	51	6	1
ALF de Mel	c Dilley	b Allott	27	26	2	0
RJ Ratnayake	c Lamb	b Dilley	15	18	1	0
VB John		b Dilley	0	1	0	0
Extras	(lb 12, w 2, nb 3)		17			
Total	(all out, 58 overs)		286			

Fall of wickets: 1-11 (Kuruppu), 2-17 (Dias), 3-92 (Wettimuny), 4-108 (Madugalle), 5-117 (Mendis), 6-168 (Ranatunga), 7-192 (de Silva), 8-246 (de Mel), 9-281 (Ratnayake), 10-286 (John).

Bowling	O	M	R	W
Willis	11	3	43	0
Dilley	11	0	45	4
Allott	12	1	82	1
Botham	12	0	60	0
Marks	12	3	39	5

New Zealand v Pakistan, Group A

At Edgbaston, Birmingham, 11,12 June 1983 (60-overs)
Result: New Zealand won by 52 runs. Points: New Zealand 4, Pakistan 0.
Toss: Pakistan. Umpires: HD Bird and B Leadbeater.
Man of the Match: Abdul Qadir.
Score after day 1 (reserve day used): NZ 211/8 (off 56 overs).

New Zealand innings (60 overs maximum)			R	B	4	6
GM Turner	c Wasim Bari	b Rashid Khan	27	37	5	0
BA Edgar	c Imran Khan	b Abdul Qadir	44	107	3	0
JG Wright	c Wasim Bari	b Abdul Qadir	9	14	2	0
BL Cairns		b Abdul Qadir	4	6	1	0
*GP Howarth	st Wasim Bari	b Abdul Qadir	16	35	1	0
JV Coney	c Ijaz Faqih	b Shahid Mahboob	33	65	3	0
MD Crowe	c Mohsin Khan	b Rashid Khan	34	53	2	0
RJ Hadlee	c Wasim Bari	b Sarfraz Nawaz	13	11	1	0
JG Bracewell	lbw	b Rashid Khan	3	6	0	0
+WK Lees	not out		24	21	2	0
EJ Chatfield	not out		6	8	0	0
Extras	(lb 20, w 4, nb 1)		25			
Total	(9 wickets, 60 overs)		238			

Fall of wickets: 1-57 (Turner), 2-68 (Wright), 3-80 (Cairns), 4-109 (Edgar), 5-120 (Howarth), 6-166 (Coney), 7-197 (Hadlee), 8-202 (Bracewell), 9-223 (Crowe).

Bowling	O	M	R	W
Sarfraz Nawaz	11	1	49	1
Shahid Mahboob	10	2	38	1
Rashid Khan	11	0	47	3
Mudassar Nazar	12	1	40	0
Abdul Qadir	12	4	21	4
Ijaz Faqih	1	0	6	0
Zaheer Abbas	3	0	12	0

Pakistan innings (target: 239 runs from 60 overs)			R	B	4	6
Mohsin Khan	lbw	b Hadlee	0	3	0	0
Mudassar Nazar	c Lees	b Cairns	0	2	0	0
Zaheer Abbas		b Hadlee	0	3	0	0
Javed Miandad	lbw	b Chatfield	35	61	3	0
*Imran Khan	c Chatfield	b Hadlee	9	26	1	0
Ijaz Faqih	c Edgar	b Coney	12	37	1	0
Shahid Mahboob	c Wright	b Coney	17	31	2	0
+Wasim Bari	c Edgar	b Coney	34	71	2	0
Abdul Qadir	not out		41	68	2	1
Sarfraz Nawaz	c Crowe	b Chatfield	13	14	2	0
Rashid Khan		c & b Cairns	9	21	0	0
Extras	(b 5, lb 6, w 3, nb 2)		16			
Total	(all out, 55.2 overs)		186			

Fall of wickets: 1-0 (Mohsin Khan), 2-0 (Zaheer Abbas), 3-0 (Mudassar Nazar), 4-22 (Imran Khan), 5-54 (Ijaz Faqih), 6-60 (Javed Miandad), 7-102 (Shahid Mahboob), 8-131 (Wasim Bari), 9-158 (Sarfraz Nawaz), 10-186 (Rashid Khan).

Bowling	O	M	R	W
Hadlee	9	2	20	3
Cairns	9.2	3	21	2
Chatfield	12	0	50	2
Crowe	2	0	12	0
Coney	12	3	28	3
Bracewell	11	2	39	0

Australia v West Indies, Group B

At Headingley, Leeds, 11,12 June 1983 (60-overs)
Result: West Indies won by 101 runs. Points: West Indies 4, Australia 0.
Toss: Australia. Umpires: DJ Constant and DGL Evans.
Man of the Match: WW Davis.
Score after day 1 (reserve day used): WI 160/5 (off 42 overs).

West Indies innings (60 overs maximum)			R	B	4	6
CG Greenidge	c Wood	b Hogg	4	8	1	0
DL Haynes	c Marsh	b Lawson	13	29	1	0
IVA Richards		b Lawson	7	16	1	0
HA Gomes	c Marsh	b Lillee	78	153	4	0
*CH Lloyd	lbw	b MacLeay	19	42	1	1
SFAF Bacchus	c Wessels	b Yallop	47	59	5	0
+PJL Dujon	lbw	b Lawson	12	34	0	0
AME Roberts	c Marsh	b Lillee	5	14	0	0
MA Holding	run out		20	13	2	0
WW Daniel	not out		16	12	2	0
Extras	(b 1, lb 9, w 10, nb 11)		31			
Total	(9 wickets, 60 overs)		252			

DNB: WW Davis.
Fall of wickets: 1-7 (Greenidge), 2-25 (Richards), 3-32 (Haynes), 4-78 (Lloyd), 5-154 (Bacchus), 6-192 (Dujon), 7-208 (Roberts), 8-211 (Gomes), 9-252 (Holding).

Bowling	O	M	R	W
Lawson	12	3	29	3
Hogg	12	1	49	1
MacLeay	12	1	31	1
Lillee	12	0	55	2
Yallop	5	0	26	1
Border	7	0	31	0

Australia innings (target: 253 runs from 60 overs)			R	B	4	6
GM Wood	retired hurt		2	19	0	0
KC Wessels		b Roberts	11	27	2	0
*KJ Hughes	c Lloyd	b Davis	18	16	0	2
DW Hookes	c Dujon	b Davis	45	45	5	0
GN Yallop	c Holding	b Davis	29	26	4	0
AR Border	c Lloyd	b Davis	17	22	2	0
KH MacLeay	c Haynes	b Davis	1	8	0	0
+RW Marsh	c Haynes	b Holding	8	15	1	0
GF Lawson	c Dujon	b Davis	2	8	0	0
RM Hogg	not out		0	2	0	0
DK Lillee		b Davis	0	2	0	0
Extras	(b 1, lb 4, w 5, nb 8)		18			
Total	(all out, 30.3 overs)		151			

Fall of wickets: 1-18 (Wessels), 2-55 (Hughes), 3-114 (Yallop), 4-116 (Hookes), 5-126 (MacLeay), 6-137 (Marsh), 7-141 (Lawson), 8-150 (Border), 9-151 (Lillee). NB: GM Wood retired hurt at 18/1.

Bowling	O	M	R	W
Roberts	7	0	14	1
Holding	8	2	23	1
Davis	10.3	0	51	7
Daniel	3	0	35	0
Gomes	2	0	10	0

India v Zimbabwe, Group B

At Grace Road, Leicester, 11 June 1983 (60-overs)
Result: India won by 5 wickets. Points: India 4, Zimbabwe 0.
Toss: India. Umpires: J Birkenshaw and R Palmer.
Man of the Match: S Madan Lal.

Zimbabwe innings (60 overs maximum)			R	B	4	6
AH Omarshah	c Kirmani	b Sandhu	8	32	1	0
GA Paterson	lbw	b Madan Lal	22	51	2	0
JG Heron	c Kirmani	b Madan Lal	18	30	2	0
AJ Pycroft	c Shastri	b Binny	14	21	1	0
+DL Houghton	c Kirmani	b Madan Lal	21	47	1	0
*DAG Fletcher		b Kapil Dev	13	32	0	0
KM Curran	run out		8	16	0	0
IP Butchart	not out		22	35	2	0
RD Brown	c Kirmani	b Shastri	6	27	0	0
PWE Rawson	c Kirmani	b Binny	3	6	0	0
AJ Traicos	run out		2	13	0	0
Extras	(lb 9, w 9)		18			
Total	(all out, 51.4 overs)		155			

Fall of wickets: 1-13 (Omarshah), 2-55 (Heron), 3-56 (Paterson), 4-71 (Pycroft), 5-106 (Fletcher), 6-114 (Houghton), 7-115 (Curran), 8-139 (Brown), 9-148 (Rawson), 10-155 (Traicos).

Bowling	O	M	R	W
Kapil Dev	9	3	18	1
Sandhu	9	1	29	1
Madan Lal	10.4	0	27	3
Binny	11	2	25	2
Shastri	12	1	38	1

India innings (target: 156 runs from 60 overs)			R	B	4	6
K Srikkanth	c Butchart	b Rawson	20	27	0	0
SM Gavaskar	c Heron	b Rawson	4	11	0	0
M Amarnath	c sub	b Traicos	44	79	4	0
SM Patil		b Fletcher	50	54	7	1
RJ Shastri	c Brown	b Omarshah	17	27	1	0
Yashpal Sharma	not out		18	19	2	0
*N Kapil Dev	not out		2	8	0	0
Extras	(w 2)		2			
Total	(5 wickets, 37.3 overs)		157			

DNB: RMH Binny, S Madan Lal, +SMH Kirmani, BS Sandhu.
Fall of wickets: 1-13 (Gavaskar), 2-32 (Srikkanth), 3-101 (Amarnath), 4-128 (Patil), 5-148 (Shastri).

Bowling	O	M	R	W
Rawson	5.1	1	11	2
Curran	6.5	1	33	0
Butchart	5	1	21	0
Traicos	11	1	41	1
Fletcher	6	1	32	1
Omarshah	3.3	0	17	1

England v Pakistan, Group A

At Lord's, London, 13 June 1983 (60-overs)
Result: England won by 8 wickets. Points: England 4, Pakistan 0.
Toss: Pakistan. Umpires: BJ Meyer and AGT Whitehead.
Man of the Match: Zaheer Abbas.

Pakistan innings (60 overs maximum)			R	B	4	6
Mohsin Khan	c Tavare	b Willis	3	29	0	0
Mudassar Nazar	c Gould	b Allott	26	98	2	0
Mansoor Akhtar	c Gould	b Willis	3	15	0	0
Javed Miandad	c Gould	b Botham	14	26	2	0
Zaheer Abbas	not out		83	104	7	1
*Imran Khan	run out		7	35	1	0
Wasim Raja	c Botham	b Marks	9	19	2	0
Abdul Qadir	run out		0	2	0	0
Sarfraz Nawaz		c & b Botham	11	15	2	0
+Wasim Bari	not out		18	21	1	0
Extras	(b 5, lb 8, w 3, nb 3)		19			
Total	(8 wickets, 60 overs)		193			

DNB: Rashid Khan.
Fall of wickets: 1-29 (Mohsin Khan), 2-33 (Mansoor Akhtar), 3-49 (Javed Miandad), 4-67 (Mudassar Nazar), 5-96 (Imran Khan), 6-112 (Wasim Raja), 7-118 (Abdul Qadir), 8-154 (Sarfraz Nawaz).

Bowling	O	M	R	W
Willis	12	4	24	2
Dilley	12	1	33	0
Allott	12	2	48	1
Botham	12	3	36	2
Marks	12	1	33	1

England innings (target: 194 runs from 60 overs)			R	B	4	6
G Fowler	not out		78	151	5	0
CJ Tavare	lbw	b Rashid Khan	8	21	0	0
DI Gower	c Sarfraz Nawaz	b Mansoor Akhtar	48	72	6	0
AJ Lamb	not out		48	62	5	1
Extras	(b 1, lb 12, w 2, nb 2)		17			
Total	(2 wickets, 50.4 overs)		199			

DNB: MW Gatting, IT Botham, +IJ Gould, VJ Marks, GR Dilley, PJW Allott, *RGD Willis.
Fall of wickets: 1-15 (Tavare), 2-93 (Gower).

Bowling	O	M	R	W
Rashid Khan	7	2	19	1
Sarfraz Nawaz	11	5	22	0
Wasim Raja	3	0	14	0
Mudassar Nazar	8	0	30	0
Abdul Qadir	9.4	0	53	0
Mansoor Akhtar	12	2	44	1

New Zealand v Sri Lanka, Group A
At Phoenix County Ground, Bristol, 13 June 1983 (60-overs)
Result: New Zealand won by 5 wickets. Points: New Zealand 4, Sri Lanka 0.
Toss: New Zealand. Umpires: HD Bird and DR Shepherd.
Man of the Match: RJ Hadlee.

Sri Lanka innings (60 overs maximum)			R	B	4	6
S Wettimuny	lbw	b Hadlee	7	19	1	0
DSBP Kuruppu	c Hadlee	b Chatfield	26	60	5	0
RL Dias		b Chatfield	25	43	4	0
*LRD Mendis		b Hadlee	43	70	2	0
RS Madugalle	c Snedden	b Coney	60	87	3	1
A Ranatunga	lbw	b Hadlee	0	3	0	0
DS de Silva		b Coney	13	20	0	0
+RG de Alwis	c Howarth	b Snedden	16	17	2	0
ALF de Mel		c & b Hadlee	1	6	0	0
RJ Ratnayake		b Hadlee	5	9	0	0
VB John	not out		2	5	0	0
Extras	(lb 6, w 1, nb 1)		8			
Total	(all out, 56.1 overs)		206			

Fall of wickets: 1-16 (Wettimuny), 2-56 (Kuruppu), 3-73 (Dias), 4-144 (Mendis), 5-144 (Ranatunga), 6-171 (de Silva), 7-196 (Madugalle), 8-199 (de Alwis), 9-199 (de Mel), 10-206 (Ratnayake).

Bowling	O	M	R	W
Hadlee	10.1	4	25	5
Snedden	10	1	38	1
Chatfield	12	4	24	2
Cairns	7	0	35	0
Coney	12	0	44	2
MD Crowe	5	0	32	0

New Zealand innings (target: 207 runs from 60 overs)			R	B	4	6
GM Turner	c Mendis	b de Silva	50	60	8	0
JG Wright	lbw	b de Mel	45	52	8	0
*GP Howarth	c Madugalle	b Ratnayake	76	79	14	0
MD Crowe	c de Alwis	b de Mel	0	11	0	0
JJ Crowe	lbw	b John	23	26	4	0
JV Coney	not out		2	10	0	0
+IDS Smith	not out		4	1	1	0
Extras	(lb 6, w 3)		9			
Total	(5 wickets, 39.2 overs)		209			

DNB: RJ Hadlee, BL Cairns, MC Snedden, EJ Chatfield.
Fall of wickets: 1-89 (Wright), 2-99 (Turner), 3-110 (MD Crowe), 4-176 (JJ Crowe), 5-205 (Howarth).

Bowling	O	M	R	W
de Mel	8	2	30	2
John	8.2	0	49	1
Ratnayake	12	0	60	1
de Silva	9	0	39	1
Ranatunga	2	0	22	0

Australia v India, Group B
At Trent Bridge, Nottingham, 13 June 1983 (60-overs)
Result: Australia won by 162 runs. Points: Australia 4, India 0.
Toss: Australia. Umpires: DO Oslear and R Palmer.
Man of the Match: TM Chappell.

Australia innings (60 overs maximum)			R	B	4	6
KC Wessels		b Kapil Dev	5	11	1	0
TM Chappell	c Srikkanth	b Amarnath	110	131	11	0
*KJ Hughes		b Madan Lal	52	86	3	0
DW Hookes	c Kapil Dev	b Madan Lal	1	4	0	0
GN Yallop	not out		66	73	5	0
AR Border	c Yashpal Sharma	b Binny	26	23	1	0
+RW Marsh	c Sandhu	b Kapil Dev	12	15	1	0
KH MacLeay		c & b Kapil Dev	4	5	0	0
TG Hogan		b Kapil Dev	11	9	0	1
GF Lawson	c Srikkanth	b Kapil Dev	6	3	1	0
RM Hogg	not out		2	2	0	0
Extras	(b 1, lb 14, w 8, nb 2)		25			
Total	(9 wickets, 60 overs)		320			

Fall of wickets: 1-11 (Wessels), 2-155 (Hughes), 3-159 (Hookes), 4-206 (Chappell), 5-254 (Border), 6-277 (Marsh), 7-289 (MacLeay), 8-301 (Hogan), 9-307 (Lawson).

Bowling	O	M	R	W
Kapil Dev	12	2	43	5
Sandhu	12	1	52	0
Binny	12	0	52	1
Shastri	2	0	16	0
Madan Lal	12	0	69	2
Patil	6	0	36	0
Amarnath	4	0	27	1

India innings (target: 321 runs from 60 overs)			R	B	4	6
RJ Shastri	lbw	b Lawson	11	18	1	0
K Srikkanth	c Border	b Hogan	39	63	6	0
M Amarnath	run out		2	17	0	0
DB Vengsarkar	lbw	b MacLeay	5	14	1	0
SM Patil		b MacLeay	0	7	0	0
Yashpal Sharma		c & b MacLeay	3	11	0	0
*N Kapil Dev		b Hogan	40	27	2	1
S Madan Lal	c Hogan	b MacLeay	27	39	2	0
RMH Binny	lbw	b MacLeay	0	6	0	0
+SMH Kirmani		b MacLeay	12	23	2	0
BS Sandhu	not out		9	12	0	1
Extras	(b 1, lb 4, w 3, nb 2)		10			
Total	(all out, 37.5 overs)		158			

Fall of wickets: 1-38 (Shastri), 2-43 (Amarnath), 3-57 (Vengsarkar), 4-57 (Patil), 5-64 (Yashpal Sharma), 6-66 (Srikkanth), 7-124 (Madan Lal), 8-126 (Binny), 9-136 (Kapil Dev), 10-158 (Kirmani).

Bowling	O	M	R	W
Lawson	5	1	25	1
Hogg	7	2	23	0
Hogan	12	1	48	2
MacLeay	11.5	3	39	6
Border	2	0	13	0

West Indies v Zimbabwe, Group B
At County Ground, New Road, Worcester, 13 June 1983 (60-overs)
Result: West Indies won by 8 wickets. Points: West Indies 4, Zimbabwe 0.
Toss: West Indies. Umpires: J Birkenshaw and DGL Evans.
Man of the Match: CG Greenidge.

Zimbabwe innings (60 overs maximum)			R	B	4	6
AH Omarshah		b Roberts	2	20	0	0
GA Paterson	c Dujon	b Holding	4	20	0	0
JG Heron	st Dujon	b Gomes	12	73	0	0
AJ Pycroft	run out		13	35	1	0
+DL Houghton	c Dujon	b Roberts	54	92	5	1
*DAG Fletcher	not out		71	88	7	0
KM Curran		b Roberts	7	15	1	0
IP Butchart	lbw	b Holding	0	3	0	0
GE Peckover	not out		16	21	3	0
Extras	(b 1, lb 23, w 7, nb 7)		38			
Total	(7 wickets, 60 overs)		217			

DNB: PWE Rawson, AJ Traicos.
Fall of wickets: 1-7 (Omarshah), 2-7 (Paterson), 3-35 (Pycroft), 4-65 (Heron), 5-157 (Houghton), 6-181 (Curran), 7-183 (Butchart).

Bowling	O	M	R	W
Roberts	12	4	36	3
Holding	12	2	33	2
Daniel	12	4	21	0
Davis	12	2	34	0
Gomes	8	0	42	1
Richards	4	1	13	0

West Indies innings (target: 218 runs from 60 overs)			R	B	4	6
CG Greenidge	not out		105	147	5	1
DL Haynes	c Houghton	b Rawson	2	5	0	0
IVA Richards	lbw	b Rawson	16	13	2	0
HA Gomes	not out		75	128	5	0
Extras	(b 1, lb 8, w 9, nb 2)		20			
Total	(2 wickets, 48.3 overs)		218			

DNB: SFAF Bacchus, *CH Lloyd, +PJL Dujon, AME Roberts, MA Holding, WW Daniel, WW Davis.
Fall of wickets: 1-3 (Haynes), 2-23 (Richards).

Bowling	O	M	R	W
Rawson	12	1	39	2
Curran	10.3	1	37	0
Butchart	9	1	40	0
Fletcher	4	0	22	0
Traicos	9	0	37	0
Omarshah	4	0	23	0

England v New Zealand, Group A

At Edgbaston, Birmingham, 15 June 1983 (60-overs)
Result: New Zealand won by 2 wickets. Points: New Zealand 4, England 0.
Toss: England. Umpires: J Birkenshaw and KE Palmer.
Man of the Match: JV Coney.

England innings (60 overs maximum)			R	B	4	6
G Fowler	c JJ Crowe	b Chatfield	69	112	9	0
CJ Tavare	c Cairns	b Coney	18	44	1	0
IT Botham		c & b Bracewell	12	9	1	1
DI Gower	not out		92	96	6	4
AJ Lamb	c JJ Crowe	b Cairns	8	14	1	0
MW Gatting		b Cairns	1	5	0	0
+IJ Gould	lbw	b Cairns	4	14	0	0
VJ Marks		b Hadlee	5	15	0	0
GR Dilley		b Hadlee	10	19	0	0
PJW Allott	c Smith	b Hadlee	0	1	0	0
*RGD Willis	lbw	b Chatfield	0	3	0	0
Extras	(b 4, lb 10, w 1)		15			
Total	(all out, 55.2 overs)		234			

Fall of wickets: 1-63 (Tavare), 2-77 (Botham), 3-117 (Fowler), 4-143 (Lamb), 5-154 (Gatting), 6-162 (Gould), 7-203 (Marks), 8-233 (Dilley), 9-233 (Allott), 10-234 (Willis).

Bowling	O	M	R	W
Hadlee	10	3	32	3
Cairns	11	0	44	3
Coney	12	2	27	1
Bracewell	12	0	66	1
Chatfield	10.2	0	50	2

New Zealand innings (target: 235 runs from 60 overs)			R	B	4	6
GM Turner	lbw	b Willis	2	5	0	0
BA Edgar	c Gould	b Willis	1	6	0	0
*GP Howarth	run out		60	104	5	1
JJ Crowe		b Allott	17	46	1	0
MD Crowe		b Marks	20	40	2	0
JV Coney	not out		66	97	9	0
+IDS Smith		b Botham	4	6	1	0
RJ Hadlee		b Willis	31	45	3	0
BL Cairns	lbw	b Willis	5	6	0	0
JG Bracewell	not out		4	7	1	0
Extras	(b 2, lb 22, w 1, nb 3)		28			
Total	(8 wickets, 59.5 overs)		238			

DNB: EJ Chatfield.
Fall of wickets: 1-2 (Turner), 2-3 (Edgar), 3-47 (JJ Crowe), 4-75 (MD Crowe), 5-146 (Howarth), 6-151 (Smith), 7-221 (Hadlee), 8-231 (Cairns).

Bowling	O	M	R	W
Willis	12	1	42	4
Dilley	12	1	43	0
Botham	12	1	47	1
Allott	11.5	2	44	1
Marks	12	1	34	1

India v West Indies, Group B

At Kennington Oval, London, 15 June 1983 (60-overs)
Result: West Indies won by 66 runs. Points: West Indies 4, India 0.
Toss: West Indies. Umpires: BJ Meyer and DR Shepherd.
Man of the Match: IVA Richards.

West Indies innings (60 overs maximum)			R	B	4	6
CG Greenidge	c Vengsarkar	b Kapil Dev	9	13		
DL Haynes	c Kapil Dev	b Amarnath	38	93		
IVA Richards	c Kirmani	b Sandhu	119	146	6	1
*CH Lloyd	run out		41	42		
SFAF Bacchus		b Binny	8	8		
+PJL Dujon	c Shastri	b Binny	9	13		
HA Gomes	not out		27	22		
AME Roberts	c Patil	b Binny	7	9		
MD Marshall	run out		4	7	0	
MA Holding	c sub	b Madan Lal	2	5	0	0
WW Davis	not out		0	2	0	0
Extras	(lb 13, w 5)		18			
Total	(9 wickets, 60 overs)		282			

Fall of wickets: 1-17 (Greenidge), 2-118 (Haynes), 3-198 (Lloyd), 4-213 (Bacchus), 5-239 (Dujon), 6-240 (Richards), 7-257 (Roberts), 8-270 (Marshall), 9-280 (Holding).

Bowling	O	M	R	W
Kapil Dev	12	0	46	1
Sandhu	12	2	42	1
Binny	12	0	71	3
Amarnath	12	0	58	1
Madan Lal	12	0	47	1

India innings (target: 283 runs from 60 overs)			R	B	4	6
K Srikkanth	c Dujon	b Roberts	2	9	0	0
RJ Shastri	c Dujon	b Roberts	6	15		
M Amarnath	c Lloyd	b Holding	80	139		
DB Vengsarkar	retired hurt		32	59		
SM Patil		c & b Gomes	21	31		
Yashpal Sharma	run out		9	10		
*N Kapil Dev	c Haynes	b Holding	36	46		
RMH Binny	lbw	b Holding	1	4	0	0
S Madan Lal	not out		8	15		
+SMH Kirmani		b Marshall	0	2	0	0
BS Sandhu	run out		0	2	0	0
Extras	(b 3, lb 13, nb 5)		21			
Total	(all out, 53.1 overs)		216			

Fall of wickets: 1-2 (Srikkanth), 2-21 (Shastri), 3-130 (Patil), 4-143 (Yashpal Sharma), 5-193 (Amarnath), 6-195 (Binny), 7-212 (Kapil Dev), 8-214 (Kirmani), 9-216 (Sandhu). NB: DB Vengsarkar retired hurt at 89/2.

Bowling	O	M	R	W
Roberts	9	1	29	2
Holding	9.1	0	40	3
Marshall	11	3	20	1
Davis	12	2	51	0
Gomes	12	1	55	1

Pakistan v Sri Lanka, Group A

At Headingley, Leeds, 16 June 1983 (60-overs)
Result: Pakistan won by 11 runs. Points: Pakistan 4, Sri Lanka 0.
Toss: Sri Lanka. Umpires: DO Oslear and AGT Whitehead.
Man of the Match: Abdul Qadir.

Pakistan innings (60 overs maximum)			R	B	4	6
Mohsin Khan	c Ranatunga	b de Mel	3	14	0	0
Mansoor Akhtar	c de Alwis	b de Mel	6	32	0	0
Zaheer Abbas	c Dias	b de Mel	15	28	2	0
Javed Miandad	lbw	b Ratnayake	7	14	1	0
*Imran Khan	not out		102	133	11	0
Ijaz Faqih	lbw	b Ratnayake	0	1	0	0
Shahid Mahboob	c de Silva	b de Mel	77	126	6	0
Sarfraz Nawaz	c Madugalle	b de Mel	9	10	1	0
Abdul Qadir	not out		5	7	0	0
Extras	(b 1, lb 4, w 4, nb 2)		11			
Total	(7 wickets, 60 overs)		235			

DNB: +Wasim Bari, Rashid Khan.
Fall of wickets: 1-6 (Mohsin Khan), 2-25 (Mansoor Akhtar), 3-30 (Zaheer Abbas), 4-43 (Javed Miandad), 5-43 (Ijaz Faqih), 6-187 (Shahid Mahboob), 7-204 (Sarfraz Nawaz).

Bowling	O	M	R	W
de Mel	12	1	39	5
John	12	1	48	0
Ratnayake	12	2	42	2
Ranatunga	11	0	49	0
de Silva	12	1	42	0
Wettimuny	1	0	4	0

Sri Lanka innings (target: 236 runs from 60 overs)			R	B	4	6
S Wettimuny	c Shahid Mahboob	b Rashid Khan	50	127	4	0
DSBP Kuruppu		b Rashid Khan	12	36	1	0
RL Dias	st Wasim Bari	b Abdul Qadir	47	73	7	0
*LRD Mendis	c Wasim Bari	b Abdul Qadir	33	49	5	0
RJ Ratnayake	st Wasim Bari	b Abdul Qadir	1	6	0	0
RS Madugalle	c Abdul Qadir	b Shahid Mahboob	26	20	1	1
A Ranatunga	c Zaheer Abbas	b Abdul Qadir	0	1	0	0
DS de Silva	run out		1	3	0	0
+RG de Alwis	c Javed Miandad	b Abdul Qadir	4	5	1	0
ALF de Mel	c Imran Khan	b Sarfraz Nawaz	17	19	1	0
VB John	not out		6	15	0	0
Extras	(lb 8, w 17, nb 2)		27			
Total	(all out, 58.3 overs)		224			

Fall of wickets: 1-22 (Kuruppu), 2-101 (Dias), 3-162 (Wettimuny), 4-162 (Mendis), 5-166 (Ratnayake), 6-166 (Ranatunga), 7-171 (de Silva), 8-193 (de Alwis), 9-199 (Madugalle), 10-224 (de Mel).

Bowling	O	M	R	W
Rashid Khan	12	4	31	2
Sarfraz Nawaz	11.3	2	25	1
Shahid Mahboob	10	1	62	1
Mansoor Akhtar	1	0	8	0
Ijaz Faqih	12	0	27	0
Abdul Qadir	12	1	44	5

Australia v Zimbabwe, Group B
At County Ground, Southampton, 16 June 1983 (60-overs)
Result: Australia won by 32 runs. Points: Australia 4, Zimbabwe 0.
Toss: Australia. Umpires: DGL Evans and R Palmer.
Man of the Match: DL Houghton.

Australia innings (60 overs maximum)			R	B	4	6
GM Wood	c Rawson	b Traicos	73	121	5	0
TM Chappell	c Traicos	b Rawson	22	29	4	0
*KJ Hughes		b Traicos	31	59	2	0
DW Hookes	c Brown	b Fletcher	10	21	0	0
GN Yallop	c Houghton	b Curran	20	42	3	0
AR Border		b Butchart	43	47	2	0
+RW Marsh	not out		35	28	2	1
KH MacLeay	c Rawson	b Butchart	9	9	0	1
TG Hogan	not out		5	10	0	0
Extras	(lb 16, w 2, nb 6)		24			
Total	(7 wickets, 60 overs)		272			

DNB: DK Lillee, RM Hogg.
Fall of wickets: 1-46 (Chappell), 2-124 (Hughes), 3-150 (Wood), 4-150 (Hookes), 5-219 (Yallop), 6-231 (Border), 7-249 (MacLeay).

Bowling	O	M	R	W
Hogg	9	2	34	0
Rawson	9	0	50	1
Fletcher	9	1	27	1
Butchart	10	0	52	2
Traicos	12	1	28	2
Curran	11	0	57	1

Zimbabwe innings (target: 273 runs from 60 overs)			R	B	4	6
RD Brown	c Marsh	b Hogan	38	80	4	0
GA Paterson	lbw	b Hogg	17	41	1	0
JG Heron	run out		3	11	0	0
AJ Pycroft	run out		13	24	1	0
+DL Houghton	c Hughes	b Chappell	84	108	9	1
*DAG Fletcher		b Hogan	2	11	0	0
KM Curran	lbw	b Chappell	35	53	2	0
IP Butchart	lbw	b Hogg	0	1	0	0
PWE Rawson	lbw	b Hogg	0	1	0	0
AJ Traicos		b Chappell	19	21	1	0
VR Hogg	not out		7	19	0	0
Extras	(b 1, lb 10, w 1, nb 10)		22			
Total	(all out, 59.5 overs)		240			

Fall of wickets: 1-48 (Paterson), 2-53 (Heron), 3-79 (Pycroft), 4-97 (Brown), 5-109 (Fletcher), 6-212 (Curran), 7-213 (Butchart), 8-213 (Rawson), 9-213 (Houghton), 10-240 (Traicos).

Bowling	O	M	R	W
Hogg	12	0	40	3
Lillee	9	1	23	0
Hogan	12	0	33	2
MacLeay	9	0	45	0
Border	9	1	30	0
Chappell	8.5	0	47	3

England v Pakistan, Group A
At Old Trafford, Manchester, 18 June 1983 (60-overs)
Result: England won by 7 wickets. Points: England 4, Pakistan 0.
Toss: Pakistan. Umpires: HD Bird and DO Oslear.
Man of the Match: G Fowler.

Pakistan innings (60 overs maximum)			R	B	4	6
Mohsin Khan	c Marks	b Allott	32	98	3	0
Mudassar Nazar	c Gould	b Dilley	18	23	2	0
Zaheer Abbas	c Gould	b Dilley	0	8	0	0
Javed Miandad	run out		67	100	6	0
*Imran Khan	c Willis	b Marks	13	28	2	0
Wasim Raja	c Willis	b Marks	15	24	3	0
Ijaz Faqih	not out		42	52	5	0
Sarfraz Nawaz		b Willis	17	20	1	1
Abdul Qadir	run out		6	7	0	0
+Wasim Bari	not out		2	3	0	0
Extras	(b 3, lb 14, w 2, nb 1)		20			
Total	(8 wickets, 60 overs)		232			

DNB: Rashid Khan.
Fall of wickets: 1-33 (Mudassar Nazar), 2-34 (Zaheer Abbas), 3-87 (Mohsin Khan), 4-116 (Imran Khan), 5-144 (Wasim Raja), 6-169 (Javed Miandad), 7-204 (Sarfraz Nawaz), 8-221 (Abdul Qadir).

Bowling	O	M	R	W
Willis	12	3	37	1
Dilley	12	2	46	2
Allott	12	1	33	1
Botham	12	1	51	0
Marks	12	0	45	2

England innings (target: 233 runs from 60 overs)			R	B	4	6
G Fowler	c Javed Miandad	b Mudassar Nazar	69	96	7	0
CJ Tavare	c Wasim Raja	b Zaheer Abbas	58	116	5	0
DI Gower	c Zaheer Abbas	b Mudassar Nazar	31	48	3	0
AJ Lamb	not out		38	57	4	0
MW Gatting	not out		14	27	1	0
Extras	(b 1, lb 15, w 7)		23			
Total	(3 wickets, 57.2 overs)		233			

DNB: IT Botham, +IJ Gould, VJ Marks, GR Dilley, PJW Allott, *RGD Willis.
Fall of wickets: 1-115 (Fowler), 2-165 (Tavare), 3-181 (Gower).

Bowling	O	M	R	W
Rashid Khan	11	1	58	0
Sarfraz Nawaz	10.2	2	22	0
Abdul Qadir	11	0	51	0
Ijaz Faqih	6	0	19	0
Mudassar Nazar	12	2	34	2
Zaheer Abbas	7	0	26	1

New Zealand v Sri Lanka, Group A
At County Ground, Derby, 18 June 1983 (60-overs)
Result: Sri Lanka won by 3 wickets. Points: Sri Lanka 4, New Zealand 0.
Toss: Sri Lanka. Umpires: DJ Constant and B Leadbeater.
Man of the Match: ALF de Mel.

New Zealand innings (60 overs maximum)			R	B	4	6
GM Turner	c Dias	b de Mel	6	10	1	0
JG Wright	c de Alwis	b de Mel	0	7	0	0
*GP Howarth		b Ratnayake	15	23	2	0
MD Crowe	lbw	b Ratnayake	8	32	0	0
BA Edgar	c Samarasekera	b de Silva	27	77	3	0
JV Coney	c sub	b de Silva	22	50	2	0
RJ Hadlee	c Madugalle	b de Mel	15	39	3	0
+WK Lees	c Ranatunga	b de Mel	2	16	0	0
BL Cairns	c Dias	b de Mel	6	7	1	0
MC Snedden	run out		40	55	5	0
EJ Chatfield	not out		19	48	2	0
Extras	(b 4, lb 5, w 11, nb 1)		21			
Total	(all out, 58.2 overs)		181			

Fall of wickets: 1-8 (Turner), 2-8 (Wright), 3-32 (Howarth), 4-47 (Crowe), 5-88 (Coney), 6-91 (Edgar), 7-105 (Lees), 8-115 (Cairns), 9-116 (Hadlee), 10-181 (Snedden).

Bowling	O	M	R	W
de Mel	12	4	32	5
Ratnayake	11	4	18	2
Ranatunga	10	2	50	0
de Silva	12	5	11	2
Samarasekera	11.2	2	38	0
Wettimuny	2	0	11	0

Sri Lanka innings (target: 182 runs from 60 overs)			R	B	4	6
S Wettimuny		b Cairns	4	30	0	0
DSBP Kuruppu	c & b Snedden		62	120	10	0
A Ranatunga		b Crowe	15	22	2	0
RL Dias	not out		64	101	9	0
*LRD Mendis	lbw	b Chatfield	0	2	0	0
RS Madugalle	c Lees	b Snedden	6	18	0	0
MAR Samarasekera	c Lees	b Hadlee	5	11	0	0
DS de Silva	run out		2	10	0	0
+RG de Alwis	not out		11	10	1	0
Extras	(b 1, lb 4, w 10)		15			
Total	(7 wickets, 52.5 overs)		184			

DNB: ALF de Mel, RJ Ratnayake.
Fall of wickets: 1-15 (Wettimuny), 2-49 (Ranatunga), 3-129 (Kuruppu), 4-130 (Mendis), 5-139 (Madugalle), 6-151 (Samarasekera), 7-161 (de Silva).

Bowling	O	M	R	W
Hadlee	12	3	16	1
Cairns	10	2	35	1
Snedden	10.5	1	58	2
Chatfield	12	3	23	1
Crowe	4	2	15	1
Coney	4	1	22	0

Australia v West Indies, Group B
At Lord's, London, 18 June 1983 (60-overs)
Result: West Indies won by 7 wickets. Points: West Indies 4, Australia 0.
Toss: Australia. Umpires: KE Palmer and AGT Whitehead.
Man of the Match: IVA Richards.

Australia innings (60 overs maximum)			R	B	4	6
GM Wood		b Marshall	17	24	0	0
TM Chappell	c Dujon	b Marshall	5	14	1	0
*KJ Hughes		b Gomes	69	124	8	0
DW Hookes	c Greenidge	b Davis	56	74	4	2
GN Yallop	not out		52	74	3	0
AR Border		c & b Gomes	11	24	1	0
+RW Marsh	c Haynes	b Holding	37	26	4	2
TG Hogan	not out		0	1	0	0
Extras	(b 1, lb 18, w 6, nb 1)		26			
Total	(6 wickets, 60 overs)		273			

DNB: JR Thomson, DK Lillee, RM Hogg.

Fall of wickets: 1-10 (Chappell), 2-37 (Wood), 3-138 (Hookes), 4-176 (Hughes), 5-202 (Border), 6-266 (Marsh).

Bowling	O	M	R	W
Roberts	12	0	51	0
Marshall	12	0	36	2
Davis	12	0	57	1
Holding	12	1	56	1
Gomes	12	0	47	2

West Indies innings (target: 274 runs from 60 overs)			R	B	4	6
CG Greenidge	c Hughes	b Hogg	90	140	8	0
DL Haynes		b Hogan	33	46	3	0
IVA Richards	not out		95	117	9	3
HA Gomes		b Chappell	15	26	1	0
*CH Lloyd	not out		19	22	3	0
Extras	(b 3, lb 18, w 1, nb 2)		24			
Total	(3 wickets, 57.5 overs)		276			

DNB: SFAF Bacchus, +PJL Dujon, MD Marshall, AME Roberts, MA Holding, WW Davis.
Fall of wickets: 1-79 (Haynes), 2-203 (Greenidge), 3-228 (Gomes).

Bowling	O	M	R	W
Hogg	12	0	25	1
Thomson	11	0	64	0
Hogan	12	0	60	1
Lillee	12	0	52	0
Chappell	10.5	0	51	1

India v Zimbabwe, Group B

At Nevill Ground, Tunbridge Wells, 18 June 1983 (60-overs)
Result: India won by 31 runs. Points: India 4, Zimbabwe 0.
Toss: India. Umpires: MJ Kitchen and BJ Meyer.
Man of the Match: N Kapil Dev.

India innings (60 overs maximum)			R	B	4	6
SM Gavaskar	lbw	b Rawson	0	2	0	0
K Srikkanth	c Butchart	b Curran	0	13	0	0
M Amarnath	c Houghton	b Rawson	5	20	1	0
SM Patil	c Houghton	b Curran	1	10	0	0
Yashpal Sharma	c Houghton	b Rawson	9	28	1	0
*N Kapil Dev	not out		175	138	16	6
RMH Binny	lbw	b Traicos	22	48	2	0
RJ Shastri	c Pycroft	b Fletcher	1	6	0	0
S Madan Lal	c Houghton	b Curran	17	39	1	0
+SMH Kirmani	not out		24	56	2	0
Extras	(lb 9, w 3)		12			
Total	(8 wickets, 60 overs)		266			

DNB: BS Sandhu.
Fall of wickets: 1-0 (Gavaskar), 2-6 (Srikkanth), 3-6 (Amarnath), 4-9 (Patil), 5-17 (Yashpal Sharma), 6-77 (Binny), 7-78 (Shastri), 8-140 (Madan Lal).

Bowling	O	M	R	W
Rawson	12	4	47	3
Curran	12	1	65	3
Butchart	12	2	38	0
Fletcher	12	2	59	1
Traicos	12	0	45	1

Zimbabwe innings (target: 267 runs from 60 overs)			R	B	4	6
RD Brown	run out		35	66	2	0
GA Paterson	lbw	b Binny	23	35	4	0
JG Heron	run out		3	8	0	0
AJ Pycroft	c Kirmani	b Sandhu	6	15	0	0
+DL Houghton	lbw	b Madan Lal	17	35	2	0
*DAG Fletcher	c Kapil Dev	b Amarnath	13	23	0	0
KM Curran	c Shastri	b Madan Lal	73	93	8	0
IP Butchart		b Binny	18	43	1	0
GE Peckover	c Yashpal Sharma	b Madan Lal	14	18	0	0
PWE Rawson	not out		2	6	0	0
AJ Traicos		c & b Kapil Dev	3	7	0	0
Extras	(lb 17, w 7, nb 4)		28			
Total	(all out, 57 overs)		235			

Fall of wickets: 1-44 (Paterson), 2-48 (Heron), 3-61 (Pycroft), 4-86 (Brown), 5-103 (Houghton), 6-113 (Fletcher), 7-168 (Butchart), 8-189 (Peckover), 9-230 (Curran), 10-235 (Traicos).

Bowling	O	M	R	W
Kapil Dev	11	1	32	1
Sandhu	11	2	44	1
Binny	11	2	45	2
Madan Lal	11	2	42	3
Amarnath	12	1	37	0
Shastri	1	0	7	0

England v Sri Lanka, Group A

At Headingley, Leeds, 20 June 1983 (60-overs)
Result: England won by 9 wickets. Points: England 4, Sri Lanka 0.
Toss: England. Umpires: B Leadbeater and R Palmer.
Man of the Match: RGD Willis.

Sri Lanka innings (60 overs maximum)			R	B	4	6
S Wettimuny	lbw	b Botham	22	49	3	0
DSBP Kuruppu	c Gatting	b Willis	6	36	1	0
A Ranatunga	c Lamb	b Botham	0	6	0	0
RL Dias	c Gould	b Cowans	7	24	1	0
*LRD Mendis		b Allott	10	38	0	0
RS Madugalle	c Gould	b Allott	0	16	0	0
DS de Silva	c Gower	b Marks	15	36	1	0
+RG de Alwis	c Marks	b Cowans	19	20	2	1
ALF de Mel	c Lamb	b Marks	10	23	2	0
RJ Ratnayake	not out		20	32	1	1
VB John	c Cowans	b Allott	15	27	1	0
Extras	(b 5, lb 2, w 3, nb 2)		12			
Total	(all out, 50.4 overs)		136			

Fall of wickets: 1-25 (Kuruppu), 2-30 (Ranatunga), 3-32 (Wettimuny), 4-40 (Dias), 5-43 (Madugalle), 6-54 (Mendis), 7-81 (de Silva), 8-97 (de Alwis), 9-103 (de Mel), 10-136 (John).

Bowling	O	M	R	W
Willis	9	4	9	1
Cowans	12	3	31	2
Botham	9	4	12	2
Allott	10.4	0	41	3
Gatting	4	2	13	0
Marks	6	2	18	2

England innings (target: 137 runs from 60 overs)			R	B	4	6
G Fowler	not out		81	77	11	0
CJ Tavare	c de Alwis	b de Mel	19	48	1	1
DI Gower	not out		27	24	3	0
Extras	(b 1, lb 3, w 3, nb 3)		10			
Total	(1 wicket, 24.1 overs)		137			

DNB: AJ Lamb, MW Gatting, IT Botham, +IJ Gould, VJ Marks, PJW Allott, *RGD Willis, NG Cowans.
Fall of wickets: 1-68 (Tavare).

Bowling	O	M	R	W
de Mel	10	1	33	1
Ratnayake	5	0	23	0
John	6	0	41	0
de Silva	3	0	29	0
Ranatunga	0.1	0	1	0

New Zealand v Pakistan, Group A

At Trent Bridge, Nottingham, 20 June 1983 (60-overs)
Result: Pakistan won by 11 runs. Points: Pakistan 4, New Zealand 0.
Toss: Pakistan. Umpires: DGL Evans and MJ Kitchen.
Man of the Match: Imran Khan.

Pakistan innings (60 overs maximum)			R	B	4	6
Mohsin Khan	c Cairns	b Coney	33	64	3	0
Mudassar Nazar		b Coney	15	60	0	0
Javed Miandad		b Hadlee	25	45	1	0
Zaheer Abbas	not out		103	121	6	0
*Imran Khan	not out		79	74	7	1
Extras	(b 1, lb 2, w 2, nb 1)		6			
Total	(3 wickets, 60 overs)		261			

DNB: Ijaz Faqih, Shahid Mahboob, Sarfraz Nawaz, Abdul Qadir, +Wasim Bari, Rashid Khan.
Fall of wickets: 1-48 (Mohsin Khan), 2-54 (Mudassar Nazar), 3-114 (Javed Miandad).

Bowling	O	M	R	W
Hadlee	12	1	61	1
Cairns	12	1	45	0
Chatfield	12	0	57	0
Coney	12	0	42	2
Bracewell	12	0	50	0

New Zealand innings (target: 262 runs from 60 overs)			R	B	4	6
GM Turner	c Wasim Bari	b Sarfraz Nawaz	4	16	0	0
JG Wright	c Imran Khan	b Abdul Qadir	19	57	1	0
*GP Howarth	c Javed Miandad	b Zaheer Abbas	39	51	3	0
MD Crowe		b Mudassar Nazar	43	62	4	0
BA Edgar	lbw	b Shahid Mahboob	6	22	0	0
JV Coney	run out		51	78	3	0
RJ Hadlee	c Mohsin Khan	b Mudassar Nazar	11	20	1	0
BL Cairns	c Imran Khan	b Abdul Qadir	0	3	0	0
+WK Lees	c sub (Mansoor Akhtar) b Mudassar Nazar		26	25	4	0
JG Bracewell	c Mohsin Khan	b Sarfraz Nawaz	34	24	7	0
EJ Chatfield	not out		3	6	0	0
Extras	(lb 8, w 5, nb 1)		14			
Total	(all out, 59.1 overs)		250			

Fall of wickets: 1-13 (Turner), 2-44 (Wright), 3-85 (Howarth), 4-102 (Edgar), 5-130 (Crowe), 6-150 (Hadlee), 7-152 (Cairns), 8-187 (Lees), 9-246 (Bracewell), 10-250 (Coney).

Bowling	O	M	R	W
Rashid Khan	6	1	24	0
Sarfraz Nawaz	9.1	1	50	2
Abdul Qadir	12	0	53	2
Ijaz Faqih	6	1	21	0
Shahid Mahboob	10	0	37	1
Mudassar Nazar	12	0	43	3
Zaheer Abbas	4	1	8	1

Australia v India, Group B

At County Ground, Chelmsford, 20 June 1983 (60-overs)
Result: India won by 118 runs. Points: India 4, Australia 0.
Toss: India. Umpires: J Birkenshaw and DR Shepherd.
Man of the Match: RMH Binny.

India innings (60 overs maximum)			R	B	4	6
SM Gavaskar	c Chappell	b Hogg	9	10	1	0
K Srikkanth	c Border	b Thomson	24	22	3	0
M Amarnath	c Marsh	b Thomson	13	20	2	0
Yashpal Sharma	c Hogg	b Hogg	40	40	1	0
SM Patil	c Hogan	b MacLeay	30	25	4	0
*N Kapil Dev	c Hookes	b Hogg	28	32	3	0
KBJ Azad	c Border	b Lawson	15	18	1	0
RMH Binny	run out		21	32	2	0
S Madan Lal	not out		12	15	0	0
+SMH Kirmani	lbw	b Hogg	10	20	1	0
BS Sandhu		b Thomson	8	18	1	0
Extras	(lb 13, w 9, nb 15)		37			
Total	(all out, 55.5 overs)		247			

Fall of wickets: 1-27 (Gavaskar), 2-54 (Srikkanth), 3-65 (Amarnath), 4-118 (Patil), 5-157 (Yashpal Sharma), 6-174 (Kapil Dev), 7-207 (Azad), 8-215 (Binny), 9-232 (Kirmani), 10-247 (Sandhu).

Bowling	O	M	R	W
Lawson	10	1	40	1
Hogg	12	2	40	3
Hogan	11	1	31	1
Thomson	10.5	0	51	3
MacLeay	12	2	48	1

Australia innings (target: 248 runs from 60 overs)			R	B	4	6
TM Chappell	c Madan Lal	b Sandhu	2	5	0	0
GM Wood	c Kirmani	b Binny	21	32	2	0
GN Yallop		c & b Binny	18	30	2	0
*DW Hookes		b Binny	1	2	0	0
AR Border		b Madan Lal	36	49	5	0
+RW Marsh	lbw	b Madan Lal	0	2	0	0
KH MacLeay	c Gavaskar	b Madan Lal	5	6	1	0
TG Hogan	c Srikkanth	b Binny	8	10	2	0
GF Lawson		b Sandhu	16	20	1	0
RM Hogg	not out		8	12	1	0
JR Thomson		b Madan Lal	0	5	0	0
Extras	(lb 5, w 5, nb 4)		14			
Total	(all out, 38.2 overs)		129			

Fall of wickets: 1-3 (Chappell), 2-46 (Wood), 3-48 (Hookes), 4-52 (Yallop), 5-52 (Marsh), 6-69 (MacLeay), 7-78 (Hogan), 8-115 (Lawson), 9-129 (Border), 10-129 (Thomson).

Bowling	O	M	R	W
Kapil Dev	8	2	16	0
Sandhu	10	1	26	2
Madan Lal	8.2	3	20	4
Binny	8	2	29	4
Amarnath	2	0	17	0
Azad	2	0	7	0

West Indies v Zimbabwe, Group B

At Edgbaston, Birmingham, 20 June 1983 (60-overs)
Result: West Indies won by 10 wickets. Points: West Indies 4, Zimbabwe 0.
Toss: Zimbabwe. Umpires: HD Bird and DJ Constant.
Man of the Match: SFAF Bacchus.

Zimbabwe innings (60 overs maximum)			R	B	4	6
RD Brown	c Lloyd	b Marshall	14	69	0	0
GA Paterson	c Richards	b Garner	6	28	1	0
JG Heron	c Dujon	b Garner	0	1	0	0
AJ Pycroft	c Dujon	b Marshall	4	39	0	0
+DL Houghton	c Lloyd	b Daniel	0	3	0	0
*DAG Fletcher		b Richards	23	51	2	0
KM Curran		b Daniel	62	92	4	1
IP Butchart	c Haynes	b Richards	8	27	0	0
GE Peckover		c & b Richards	3	15	0	0
PWE Rawson		b Daniel	19	40	1	0
AJ Traicos	not out		1	2	0	0
Extras	(b 4, lb 13, w 7, nb 7)		31			
Total	(all out, 60 overs)		171			

Fall of wickets: 1-17 (Paterson), 2-17 (Heron), 3-41 (Pycroft), 4-42 (Houghton), 5-42 (Brown), 6-79 (Fletcher), 7-104 (Butchart), 8-115 (Peckover), 9-170 (Curran), 10-171 (Rawson).

Bowling	O	M	R	W
Marshall	12	3	19	2
Garner	7	4	13	2
Davis	8	2	13	0
Daniel	9	2	28	3
Gomes	12	2	26	0
Richards	12	1	41	3

West Indies innings (target: 172 runs from 60 overs)		R	B	4	6
DL Haynes	not out	88	136	9	0
SFAF Bacchus	not out	80	135	8	0
Extras	(lb 1, w 3)	4			
Total	(0 wickets, 45.1 overs)	172			

DNB: AL Logie, IVA Richards, HA Gomes, *CH Lloyd, +PJL Dujon, MD Marshall, J Garner, WW Daniel, WW Davis.

Bowling	O	M	R	W
Rawson	12	3	38	0
Butchart	4	0	23	0
Traicos	12	2	24	0
Curran	9	0	44	0
Fletcher	8.1	0	39	0

1st Semi Final
England v India

At Old Trafford, Manchester, 22 June 1983 (60-overs)
Result: India won by 6 wickets. India advances to the final
Toss: England. Umpires: DGL Evans and DO Oslear.
Man of the Match: M Amarnath.

England innings (60 overs maximum)			R	B	4	6
G Fowler		b Binny	33	59	3	0
CJ Tavare	c Kirmani	b Binny	32	51	4	0
DI Gower	c Kirmani	b Amarnath	17	30	1	0
AJ Lamb	run out		29	58	1	0
MW Gatting		b Amarnath	18	46	1	0
IT Botham		b Azad	6	26	0	0
+IJ Gould	run out		13	36	0	0
VJ Marks		b Kapil Dev	8	18	0	0
GR Dilley	not out		20	26	2	0
PJW Allott	c Patil	b Kapil Dev	8	14	0	0
*RGD Willis		b Kapil Dev	0	2	0	0
Extras	(b 1, lb 17, w 7, nb 4)		29			
Total	(all out, 60 overs)		213			

Fall of wickets: 1-69 (Tavare), 2-84 (Fowler), 3-107 (Gower), 4-141 (Lamb), 5-150 (Gatting), 6-160 (Botham), 7-175 (Gould), 8-177 (Marks), 9-202 (Allott), 10-213 (Willis).

Bowling	O	M	R	W
Kapil Dev	11	1	35	3
Sandhu	8	1	36	0
Binny	12	1	43	2
Madan Lal	5	0	15	0
Azad	12	1	28	1
Amarnath	12	1	27	2

India innings (target: 214 runs from 60 overs)			R	B	4	6
SM Gavaskar	c Gould	b Allott	25	41	3	0
K Srikkanth	c Willis	b Botham	19	44	3	0
M Amarnath	run out		46	92	4	1
Yashpal Sharma	c Allott	b Willis	61	115	3	2
SM Patil	not out		51	32	8	0
*N Kapil Dev	not out		1	6	0	0
Extras	(b 5, lb 6, w 1, nb 2)		14			
Total	(4 wickets, 54.4 overs)		217			

DNB: KBJ Azad, RMH Binny, S Madan Lal, +SMH Kirmani, BS Sandhu.
Fall of wickets: 1-46 (Srikkanth), 2-50 (Gavaskar), 3-142 (Amarnath), 4-205 (Yashpal Sharma).

Bowling	O	M	R	W
Willis	10.4	2	42	1
Dilley	11	0	43	0
Allott	10	3	40	1
Botham	11	4	40	1
Marks	12	1	38	0

2nd Semi Final
Pakistan v West Indies

At Kennington Oval, London, 22 June 1983 (60-overs)
Result: West Indies won by 8 wickets. West Indies advances to the final.
Toss: West Indies. Umpires: DJ Constant and AGT Whitehead.
Man of the Match: IVA Richards.

Pakistan innings (60 overs maximum)			R	B	4	6
Mohsin Khan		b Roberts	70	176	1	0
Mudassar Nazar		c & b Garner	11	39	0	0
Ijaz Faqih	c Dujon	b Holding	5	19	0	0
Zaheer Abbas		b Gomes	30	38	1	0
*Imran Khan	c Dujon	b Marshall	17	41	0	0
Wasim Raja	lbw	b Marshall	0	3	0	0
Shahid Mahboob	c Richards	b Marshall	6	10	0	0
Sarfraz Nawaz	c Holding	b Roberts	3	12	0	0
Abdul Qadir	not out		10	21	0	0
+Wasim Bari	not out		4	7	0	0
Extras	(b 6, lb 13, w 4, nb 5)		28			
Total	(8 wickets, 60 overs)		184			

DNB: Rashid Khan.
Fall of wickets: 1-23 (Mudassar Nazar), 2-34 (Ijaz Faqih), 3-88 (Zaheer Abbas), 4-139 (Imran Khan), 5-139 (Wasim Raja), 6-159 (Shahid Mahboob), 7-164 (Sarfraz Nawaz), 8-171 (Mohsin Khan).

Bowling	O	M	R	W
Roberts	12	3	25	2
Garner	12	1	31	1
Marshall	12	2	28	3
Holding	12	1	25	1
Gomes	7	0	29	1
Richards	5	0	18	0

West Indies innings (target: 185 runs from 60 overs)			R	B	4	6
CG Greenidge	lbw	b Rashid Khan	17	3	8	
DL Haynes		b Abdul Qadir	29	58		
IVA Richards	not out		80	96	11	1
HA Gomes	not out		50	100	3	0
Extras	(b 2, lb 6, w 4)		12			
Total	(2 wickets, 48.4 overs)		188			

DNB: *CH Lloyd, SFAF Bacchus, +PJL Dujon, MD Marshall, AME Roberts, J Garner, MA Holding.
Fall of wickets: 1-34 (Greenidge), 2-56 (Haynes).

Bowling	O	M	R	W
Rashid Khan	12	2	32	1
Sarfraz Nawaz	8	0	23	0
Abdul Qadir	11	1	42	1
Shahid Mahboob	11	1	43	0
Wasim Raja	1	0	9	0
Zaheer Abbas	4.4	1	24	0
Mohsin Khan	1	0	3	0

Final
India v West Indies

At Lord's, London, 25 June 1983 (60-overs)
Result: India won by 43 runs. India wins the 1983 Prudential World Cup.
Toss: West Indies. Umpires: HD Bird and BJ Meyer.
Man of the Match: M Amarnath.

India innings (60 overs maximum)			R	B	4	6
SM Gavaskar	c Dujon	b Roberts	2	12	0	0
K Srikkanth	lbw	b Marshall	38	57	7	1
M Amarnath		b Holding	26	80	3	0
Yashpal Sharma	c sub (AL Logie)	b Gomes	11	32	1	0
SM Patil	c Gomes	b Garner	27	29	0	1
*N Kapil Dev	c Holding	b Gomes	15	8	3	0
KBJ Azad	c Garner	b Roberts	0	3	0	0
RMH Binny	c Garner	b Roberts	2	8	0	0
S Madan Lal		b Marshall	17	27	0	1
+SMH Kirmani		b Holding	14	43	0	0
BS Sandhu	not out		11	30	1	0
Extras	(b 5, lb 5, w 9, nb 1)		20			
Total	(all out, 54.4 overs)		183			

Fall of wickets: 1-2 (Gavaskar), 2-59 (Srikkanth), 3-90 (Amarnath), 4-92 (Yashpal Sharma), 5-110 (Kapil Dev), 6-111 (Azad), 7-130 (Binny), 8-153 (Patil), 9-161 (Madan Lal), 10-183 (Kirmani).

Bowling	O	M	R	W
Roberts	10	3	32	3
Garner	12	4	24	1
Marshall	11	1	24	2
Holding	9.4	2	26	2
Gomes	11	1	49	2
Richards	1	0	8	0

West Indies innings (target: 184 runs from 60 overs)			R	B	4	6
CG Greenidge		b Sandhu	1	12	0	0
DL Haynes	c Binny	b Madan Lal	13	33	2	0
IVA Richards	c Kapil Dev	b Madan Lal	33	28	7	0
*CH Lloyd	c Kapil Dev	b Binny	8	17	1	0
HA Gomes	c Gavaskar	b Madan Lal	5	16	0	0
SFAF Bacchus	c Kirmani	b Sandhu	8	25	0	0
+PJL Dujon		b Amarnath	25	73	0	1
MD Marshall	c Gavaskar	b Amarnath	18	51	0	0
AME Roberts	lbw	b Kapil Dev	4	14	0	0
J Garner	not out		5	19	0	0
MA Holding	lbw	b Amarnath	6	24	0	0
Extras	(lb 4, w 10)		14			
Total	(all out, 52 overs)		140			

Fall of wickets: 1-5 (Greenidge), 2-50 (Haynes), 3-57 (Richards), 4-66 (Gomes), 5-66 (Lloyd), 6-76 (Bacchus), 7-119 (Dujon), 8-124 (Marshall), 9-126 (Roberts), 10-140 (Holding).

Bowling	O	M	R	W
Kapil Dev	11	4	21	1
Sandhu	9	1	32	2
Madan Lal	12	2	31	3
Binny	10	1	23	1
Amarnath	7	0	12	3
Azad	3	0	7	0

World Cup **1987**

by Mike Coward

Not even the myriad seers, mystics and astrologers of the Indian sub-continent could have foretold the profound effect the 1987 World Cup was to have on global cricket.

The decision of the then International Cricket Conference (ICC) to stage the World Cup away from England for the first time began the legitimate internationalisation of the event.

No longer was it a World Cup in name only and the exclusive preserve of the English authorities which had staged highly successful tournaments under the Prudential banner in 1975, 1979 and 1983. By awarding the fourth World Cup to India and Pakistan the ICC partially broke its conservative bonds, and so created a dynamic new environment which, within ten years, led to India becoming the richest and most powerful body in world cricket.

Despite the enmities in existence since Partition in 1947, Hindu India and Muslim Pakistan linked arms to take the game of the British Empire beyond the Empire. Furthermore they chose a dove as the principal logo, and turned a deaf ear to snide and mocking laughter in the West and staged the tournament under the slogan of "Cricket for Peace".

The event, held in 14 cities in India and seven in Pakistan, was such an overwhelming success that the World Cup was placed on a rota and, by the time it reached the Caribbean in 2007, it had been hosted by Australia and New Zealand in 1992, India, Pakistan and Sri Lanka in 1996, England, Wales, Scotland, Ireland and Holland in 1999, and South Africa, Zimbabwe and Kenya in 2003.

India's unexpected triumph over the West Indies at Lord's in the final in 1983 was so stirring it prompted the then president of the Board of Control for Cricket in India, NKP Salve, loudly to question England's apparent automatic right to stage the quadrennial event. After discussions which threatened to polarise the global cricket fraternity the ICC approved the co-hosting tender on July 19, 1984. Australia did not support such radical change but, unlike England, accepted defeat graciously and pledged co-operation and support.

The fruits of a tough campaign enjoyed by Australia's captain Allan Border and his determined team after their Cup-winning final against England at Eden Gardens.

And they were as good as their word. Malcolm Gray, chairman of the then Australian Cricket Board, played a key diplomatic role when the tournament was seriously threatened by the intransigence of both Rajiv Gandhi's government and the West Indies' more radical administrators on issues centred on the old and iniquitous South Africa and its banished Cricket Union.

Given that the showcase tournament of the limited-overs game had not before been played in the conditions peculiar to the Indian subcontinent and in front of such vast and animated crowds, it was generally anticipated that the co-hosts would play off for the title at magnificent Eden Gardens in Calcutta on Sunday, November 8. As far as the masses of the region were concerned it was a fait accompli, and all that remained to be established was the identity of their opponents in the semi-finals on consecutive days in Bombay and Lahore. After all, Kapil Dev, who had held aloft the trophy in 1983, was still at the helm for India, while Pakistan, under the command of the redoubtable Imran Khan, were generally considered the favourites for the tournament.

While Viv Richards' West Indies and Mike Gatting's England attracted a good deal of enthusiasm from the outset, little attention was paid to Allan Border's Australians when the eight teams paraded before Indian Prime Minister Rajiv Gandhi at the opening ceremony at the fortress that was the Jawaharlal Nehru Stadium in New Delhi.

Indeed, the English bookmaking firm of Ladbrokes thought them to be most unfashionable and quoted them at 16-1. This was understandable given the litany of disasters from their previous home season – a 2-1 defeat in the Ashes series being compounded by failure in an inconsequential tournament to celebrate yachting's America's Cup Challenge off Fremantle near Perth, the annual World Series Cup triangular with England and the West Indies, and even in a four-nation festival at Sharjah in the desert of the United Arab Emirates.

Even in the context of the limited-overs game, historically a platform for the unexpected and improbable, the change that overcame the Australians in six weeks was extraordinary. Bereft of confidence and as low in self-esteem as in talent for the preceding 12 months, suddenly they were transformed into a highly capable and committed group with an unwavering faith in their abilities.

As the tournament unfolded over 31 days – compared with 18 in England four years earlier – it was apparent that the Australians were more comfortable with the environment and well prepared physically and, significantly, mentally. Indeed, they opened their minds and hearts to the essential India like no Australian team before them and unselfconsciously Border and coach Bob Simpson referred to a mystical "special feeling".

In the end, the essential India rewarded them beyond their wildest dreams and, after he was presented with the diamond-studded Reliance World Cup, Border spoke publicly of the "love and encouragement" his men had received from Indians everywhere. This was particularly so of the 80,000 Bengalis who cheered them to the echo in the final with England.

Forty years after independence, anti-British feeling still ran high and the Bengalis willed the Australians to conquer England, who had overcome India by 35 runs in the semi-final. And so it came to pass, by just seven runs in a match remembered as much for Gatting's ill-conceived reverse sweep to Border's first delivery as to any individual achievements.

Be that as it may, the unexpected triumph raised Australian cricket from the depths of despair and provided the impetus and spirit needed to regain the Ashes in England two years later and so embark on an era of extraordinary prosperity.

That Australia were drawn into the more manageable Group A with India, Jeff Crowe's New Zealand and John Traicos's Zimbabwe gave Border some heart. While he had no illusions about the difficulty of playing the defending champions at Madras in their opening match the Australians had established a marginal advantage against India in one-day cricket since losing the decisive qualifying match in 1983 – ten wins from 18 concluded outings in India, Australia and Sharjah. Furthermore the previous year they had survived the debilitating heat and humidity of the Chidambaram Stadium to tie a Test match with India – only the second tie in 1052 Tests since 1877.

Astonishingly, the orthodox left-arm spinner Maninder Singh was again the central figure in the drama played out before a crowd of 50,000. Leg-before to off-spinner Greg Matthews to the penultimate delivery of the tied Test a year and 17 days later, this time he was bowled by Steve Waugh with the second-last delivery of the enthralling opening game in Group A.

Any doubts about the value of taking the World Cup away from England were dispelled by the thrilling opening matches. In addition to the absorbing match in Madras which earned Steve Waugh his famous sobriquet of "Iceman", Duleep Mendis's Sri Lanka pushed Pakistan to the limit, England managed to score 35 off their last three overs to overpower the West Indies, who were significantly weakened by Malcolm Marshall's decision to take a self-imposed

Epitomising the Australian spirit, David Boon rounded off an outstanding tournament by top scoring with 75 in the final against England, his fifth fifty in six innings.

rest from the tournament and the retirements, earlier in the year, of Michael Holding and Joel Garner, while the gallant amateurs from Zimbabwe lost by just three runs to New Zealand.

England's thrilling chase proved to be especially meritorious, as 19 of the 27 matches were won by the side batting first. To this end Australia were fortunate to bat first in five of their six qualifying matches, and in the semi-final and final. To defend a total against an opponent wearied by three and a half hours' fielding in high heat was universally viewed as the logical strategy.

While many players were challenged by the vast distances that needed to be travelled in countries of such geographical dimensions – the Sri Lankans were conspicuously disadvantaged – the transition to 50 overs an innings from the 60 in previous World Cups was accomplished smoothly.

And, to the unbridled delight of the game's cognoscenti, the staging of the tournament in the region ensured that spin bowlers, rather than

metronomic seamers, had a major role to play. That said, the leading wicket-takers were pacemen – Australia's Craig McDermott with 18 and Imran Khan with 17. Imran, however, gained little comfort from his personal success as Pakistan failed in the semi-finals, just as they had in 1979 and 1983: Australia won by the 18 runs Waugh belted off Saleem Jaffer's final over.

Given that Waugh was destined to become one of the most influential figures in world cricket for the

next 17 years, it was appropriate that he came of age as an elite cricketer the very moment the tournament came of age as a world event.

Fit for a final and packed to capacity, Eden Gardens hosts the final between the game's two oldest rivals England and Australia under Calcutta's cloudless sky

SEMI-FINALS
Australia v Pakistan

At Gaddafi Stadium, Lahore, November 4, 1987.
Australia won by 18 runs.
Pakistan, losing semi-finalists in 1979 and 1983, again failed to reach the final. They were beaten by a superior all-round performance as Allan Border's Australian side, scarcely rated at the start of the tournament, came of age.

Until Imran Khan returned to take three for 17 in five overs, Australia's batsmen had contributed solidly. At the very end, Steve Waugh, previously the provider of heroic last overs with the ball, struck a vital 18 runs off Saleem Jaffer, beginning with a six over long-on. The left-arm Jaffer had earlier conceded 39 from his first five overs (the 50th was only his sixth) as Geoff Marsh and David Boon put on 73 in 18 overs. Salim Malik's direct hit from square leg ran out Marsh but Boon and Dean Jones added 82 before Pakistan broke through in the 31st and 32nd overs.

Javed Miandad, who stumped Boon, had taken the gloves when Salim Yousuf was hit on the mouth by a deflection off Jones's pad in the 19th over. Another wicket now would have put Pakistan on top, but Border and Mike Veletta kept the momentum going with a stand of 60.

Pakistan made a disastrous start, losing three wickets for 38 in 10.1 overs. Rameez Raja, sent back, was run out in the first over, Mansoor Akhtar always struggled and Malik, playing across the line, spooned the first ball of Waugh's spell to extra cover.

Miandad (104 balls, four fours) and Imran Khan (83 balls, four fours) rebuilt the innings with 112 in 26 overs, reducing the target to 118 from 15 overs. While Miandad remained it was always possible, but his dismissal, swinging at Bruce Reid in the 44th over, left the last three wickets to muster 56. Instead, Man of the Match Craig McDermott, bowling fast and

accurately, took all three to finish with the first five-wicket return of the tournament and dash the dreams of a nation.
(Wisden Cricketers' Almanack, 1988)

England v India

At Wankhede Stadium, Bombay, November 5, 1987.
England won by 35 runs.
Kapil Dev put England in on winning the toss, believing the ball would swing early in the day. In the event, it did not. The pitch, slow and providing turn, was more suited to spin bowling, thought to be India's strength but countered masterfully by Graham Gooch (136 balls, 11 fours) and Mike Gatting. Adopting a policy of sweeping and pulling the two slow left-arm bowlers, Maninder Singh and Ravi Shastri, they put on 117 in 19 overs.

When Gooch, who survived a difficult, running chance to Kris Srikkanth at 82, was fourth out, caught on the mid-wicket boundary in the 43rd over – Gatting was out in the 41st – Allan Lamb saw to it that another 51 runs were added.

India, with Dilip Vengsarkar unable to play because of a stomach upset, suffered an early setback when Phillip DeFreitas knocked over Sunil Gavaskar's off stump. It was the break England wanted and they never let India take the initiative. Srikkanth and Navjot Singh Sidhu did not manage a single boundary.

When Mohammad Azharuddin and Chandrakant Pandit took 27 from off-spinner Eddie Hemmings's first three overs, Gooch bowled three tidy overs and Neil Foster struck again to remove Pandit. Kapil Dev fell to his own impetuosity, caught on the mid-wicket boundary immediately after Gatting had stationed himself there.

For Hemmings, it was the start of a 34-ball spell in which he took four for 21, his next wicket being the important one of Azharuddin (74 balls, seven fours). With five wickets and 10 overs in hand, India were looking for five runs an over but, with Azharuddin gone, panic and recklessness set in. Shastri remained a potential threat until the last, but Lamb's marvellous running catch to put paid to Chetan Sharma's first-ball fling was testimony to England's all-round commitment.
(Scyld Berry, Wisden Cricketers' Almanack, 1988)

Above: Another setback for England in their defeat in the final. Top-scorer Bill Athey is run out as Australia tighten their grip.

Right: Spoiling the party for the expectant home crowd at Bombay's Wankhede Stadium, England's Graham Gooch on the way to his Man of the Match 115 in the semi-final.

FINAL
Australia v England

At Eden Gardens, Calcutta, November 8, 1987. Australia won by seven runs.

Batting first on winning the toss suited Australia; and, when they took the field to defend a total of 253 it was in the knowledge that no side batting second had scored 254 to win in the tournament.

At 135 for two after 31 overs, and with Australia beginning to show disarray in the field, England were almost on target but, in a moment too crass to contemplate, Mike Gatting handed back the initiative. To Allan Border's first ball, bowled on the line of his leg stump, the England captain attempted a reverse sweep. Having swept the ball on to his leg stump in the semi-final, he now contrived to hit it onto his shoulder, whence it looped into Greg Dyer's gloves. The Australians' joy was unconcealed.

England had conceded points from the start, an erratic spell from Phillip DeFreitas and Gladstone Small helping Geoff Marsh and David Boon post 52 in 10 overs. Neil Foster and the two spinners repaired the damage, with Foster's eight overs costing just 16 runs and bringing the wicket of Marsh in the 18th over.

Graham Gooch, too, was economical until coming under fire as Border and Mike Veletta added 73 in 10 overs following Boon's dismissal. Man of the Match Boon's 75 (125 balls, seven fours) was his fifth score of

50 or more in six innings. DeFreitas, brought back to bowl the last over, went for 11 to bring to 65 the runs scored from England's last six overs.

Tim Robinson, undone by pace to no one's great surprise, was out first ball to Craig McDermott's fourth. Gooch and Bill Athey put on 65 in 17 overs, Athey and Gatting 69 in 13, Athey and Lamb 35 in just over eight. Steve Waugh's throw ran out Athey as he went for a third run and, with England slipping further behind the run-rate (75 required from ten overs had drifted to 46 from five), he bowled Lamb in the 47th over. DeFreitas gave England renewed hope by hitting 4, 6 and 4 in McDermott's penultimate over, but Waugh conceded just two runs, as well as having DeFreitas caught, in the 49th. That left 17 needed from the final over, and there was no way McDermott was going to allow that.
(Scyld Berry, Wisden Cricketers' Almanack, 1988)

Left: Captains' contrasts, England's Mike Gatting reverse sweeps. He would later play a similar shot, the wrong shot to the wrong ball, the first delivered by opposite number Allan Border. It would succeed only in presenting a catch to keeper Greg Dyer off the shoulder creating, in an instant, a lifetime of criticism for Gatting.

Above: Less than an hour later Border is triumphant on the shoulders of his exultant teammates.

"They said at the time"

Australia's captain Allan Border: *"To the outside observer the odds were stacked heavily against Australia. I guess only a handful of people really believed in us – and they were the players and officials. That's precisely what got us home in the end. Belief in ourselves and each other."*

Australia's Dean Jones: *"We were the fittest Australian side ever to leave Australia. After we beat New Zealand, Bob Simpson made us get up at 6 a.m. to train on the front lawn of the hotel so the New Zealanders would see us as they boarded the coach to the airport. They sent word around that we meant business, and that bit of psychology from Simmo was vital."*

David Boon, Australia's Man of the Match in the final, on Mike Gatting's infamous reverse-sweep dismissal to Border's first ball: *"I think Gatting has been slandered enough for that dismissal. If he had got hold of that shot and it went for four then England quite possibly could have won the World Cup. But because it went the wrong way he has been criticised ever since."*

Pakistan captain Imran Khan: *"From the public's point of view it would have been great to have won the World Cup. The whole country was behind the team and that was the saddest aspect of our defeat. I have never seen the Pakistani public so disappointed as they were after our semi-final defeat. I had underestimated the depth of feeling about the World Cup: most of the people leaving the stadium had tears in their eyes."*

Format

As in 1983 but, due to the shorter daylight hours on the subcontinent, games were 50 overs per innings, not 60. There was an attempt to cheer up disappointed crowds by staging a third-place play-off between Pakistan and India, but the star players demanded too much cash.

Innovations

The first World Cup to be held away from England was also the first to feature neutral umpires.

World Cup 1987
Scoreboards

Pakistan v Sri Lanka, Group B

At Niaz Stadium, Hyderabad, Sind, 8 October 1987 (50-overs)
Result: Pakistan won by 15 runs. Points: Pakistan 4, Sri Lanka 0.
Toss: Pakistan. Umpires: VK Ramaswamy (Ind) and SJ Woodward (NZ).
Man of the Match: Javed Miandad.

Pakistan innings (50 overs maximum)			R	B	4	6
Rameez Raja	c Ratnayake	b Anurasiri	76	115	3	0
Ijaz Ahmed	c Kuruppu	b Ratnayake	16	34	2	0
Mansoor Akhtar	c Ratnayake	b Ratnayeke	12	23	0	0
Javed Miandad		b Ratnayeke	103	100	6	0
Wasim Akram	run out		14	14	0	0
Saleem Malik	not out		18	12	1	0
*Imran Khan		b Ratnayake	2	4	0	0
+Saleem Yousuf	not out		1	1	0	0
Extras	(lb 15, w 9, nb 1)		25			
Total	(6 wickets, 50 overs)		267			

DNB: Mudassar Nazar, Abdul Qadir, Tauseef Ahmed.
Fall of wickets: 1-48 (Ijaz Ahmed), 2-67 (Mansoor Akhtar), 3-180 (Rameez Raja), 4-226 (Wasim Akram), 5-259 (Javed Miandad), 6-266 (Imran Khan).

Bowling	O	M	R	W
John	10	2	37	0
Ratnayake	10	0	64	2
Ratnayeke	9	0	47	2
de Silva	10	0	44	0
Anurasiri	10	0	52	1
Gurusinha	1	0	8	0

Sri Lanka innings (target: 268 runs from 50 overs)			R	B	4	6
+DSBP Kuruppu	c Saleem Yousuf	b Imran Khan	9	24	1	0
RS Mahanama	c Javed Miandad	b Mansoor Akhtar	89	117	7	1
RL Dias		b Abdul Qadir	5	21	0	0
A Ranatunga		b Tauseef Ahmed	24	29	3	0
*LRD Mendis	run out		1	6	0	0
AP Gurusinha		b Abdul Qadir	37	39	2	1
PA de Silva		b Imran Khan	42	32	3	1
JR Ratnayeke	c Saleem Yousuf	b Wasim Akram	7	13	0	0
RJ Ratnayake	c Mudassar Nazar	b Wasim Akram	8	9	0	0
VB John	not out		1	4	0	0
SD Anurasiri	run out		0	3	0	0
Extras	(b 7, lb 14, w 7, nb 1)		29			
Total	(all out, 49.2 overs)		252			

Fall of wickets: 1-29 (Kuruppu), 2-57 (Dias), 3-100 (Ranatunga), 4-103 (Mendis), 5-182 (Mahanama), 6-190 (Gurusinha), 7-209 (Ratnayeke), 8-223 (Ratnayake), 9-251 (de Silva), 10-252 (Anurasiri).

Bowling	O	M	R	W
Imran Khan	10	2	42	2
Wasim Akram	9.2	1	41	2
Mudassar Nazar	9	0	63	0
Abdul Qadir	10	1	30	2
Tauseef Ahmed	10	0	48	1
Mansoor Akhtar	1	0	7	1

England v West Indies, Group B

At Municipal Stadium, Gujranwala, 9 October 1987 (50-overs)
Result: England won by 2 wickets. Points: England 4, West Indies 0.
Toss: England. Umpires: AR Crafter (Aus) and RB Gupta (Ind).
Man of the Match: AJ Lamb.

West Indies innings (50 overs maximum)		R	B	4	6
DL Haynes	run out	19	45	1	0
CA Best	b DeFreitas	5	15	0	0
RB Richardson	b Foster	53	80	8	0
*IVA Richards	b Foster	27	36	3	0
+PJL Dujon	run out	46	76	3	0
AL Logie	b Foster	49	41	3	0
RA Harper	b Small	24	10	3	1
CL Hooper	not out	1	2	0	0
WKM Benjamin	not out	7	2	1	0
Extras	(lb 9, nb 3)	12			
Total	(7 wickets, 50 overs)	243			

DNB: CA Walsh, BP Patterson.
Fall of wickets: 1-8 (Best), 2-53 (Haynes), 3-105 (Richards), 4-122 (Richardson), 5-205 (Dujon), 6-235 (Logie), 7-235 (Harper).

Bowling	O	M	R	W
DeFreitas	10	2	31	1
Foster	10	0	53	3
Emburey	10	1	22	0
Small	10	0	45	1
Pringle	10	0	83	0

England innings (target: 244 runs from 50 overs)			R	B	4	6
GA Gooch	c Dujon	b Hooper	47	93	3	0
BC Broad	c Dujon	b Walsh	3	12	0	0
RT Robinson	run out		12	35	1	0
*MW Gatting		b Hooper	25	23	3	0
AJ Lamb	not out		67	68	5	1
DR Pringle	c Best	b Hooper	12	23	0	0
+PR Downton	run out		3	4	0	0
JE Emburey		b Patterson	22	15	2	1
PAJ DeFreitas		b Patterson	23	21	2	0
NA Foster	not out		9	6	1	0
Extras	(lb 14, w 6, nb 3)		23			
Total	(8 wickets, 49.3 overs)		246			

DNB: GC Small.
Fall of wickets: 1-14 (Broad), 2-40 (Robinson), 3-98 (Gatting), 4-99 (Gooch), 5-123 (Pringle), 6-131 (Downton), 7-162 (Emburey), 8-209 (DeFreitas).

Bowling	O	M	R	W
Patterson	10	0	49	2
Walsh	9.3	0	65	1
Harper	10	0	44	0
Benjamin	10	2	32	0
Hooper	10	0	42	3

India v Australia, Group A

At MA Chidambaram Stadium, Chepauk, Madras, 9 October 1987 (50-overs)
Result: Australia won by 1 run. Points: Australia 4, India 0.
Toss: India. Umpires: DM Archer (WI) and HD Bird (Eng).
Man of the Match: GR Marsh.

Australia innings (50 overs maximum)			R	B	4	6
DC Boon	lbw	b Shastri	49	68	5	0
GR Marsh	c Azharuddin	b Prabhakar	110	141	7	1
DM Jones	c Sidhu	b Maninder Singh	39	35	2	2
*AR Border		b Binny	16	22	0	0
TM Moody	c Kapil Dev	b Prabhakar	8	13	1	0
SR Waugh	not out		19	17	0	0
SP O'Donnell	run out		7	10	0	0
Extras	(lb 18, w 2, nb 2)		22			
Total	(6 wickets, 50 overs)		270			

DNB: +GC Dyer, PL Taylor, CJ McDermott, BA Reid.
Fall of wickets: 1-110 (Boon), 2-174 (Jones), 3-228 (Border), 4-237 (Marsh), 5-251 (Moody), 6-270 (O'Donnell).

Bowling	O	M	R	W
Kapil Dev	10	0	41	0
Prabhakar	10	0	47	2
Binny	7	0	46	1
Maninder Singh	10	0	48	1
Shastri	10	0	50	1
Azharuddin	3	0	20	0

India innings (target: 271 runs from 50 overs)			R	B	4	6
SM Gavaskar	c Reid	b Taylor	37	32	6	1
K Srikkanth	lbw	b Waugh	70	83	7	0
NS Sidhu		b McDermott	73	79	4	5
DB Vengsarkar	c Jones	b McDermott	29	45	2	0
M Azharuddin		b McDermott	10	14	1	0
*N Kapil Dev	c Boon	b O'Donnell	6	10	0	0
RJ Shastri		c & b McDermott	12	11	1	0
+KS More	not out		12	14	2	0
RMH Binny	run out		0	3	0	0
M Prabhakar	run out		5	7	0	0
Maninder Singh		b Waugh	4	5	0	0
Extras	(b 2, lb 7, w 2)		11			
Total	(all out, 49.5 overs)		269			

Fall of wickets: 1-69 (Gavaskar), 2-131 (Srikkanth), 3-207 (Sidhu), 4-229 (Azharuddin), 5-232 (Vengsarkar), 6-246 (Shastri), 7-256 (Kapil Dev), 8-256 (Binny), 9-265 (Prabhakar), 10-269 (Maninder Singh).

Bowling	O	M	R	W
McDermott	10	0	56	4
Reid	10	2	35	0
O'Donnell	9	1	32	1
Taylor	5	0	46	1
Waugh	9.5	0	52	2
Border	6	0	39	0

New Zealand v Zimbabwe, Group A

At Lal Bahadur Shastri Stadium, Hyderabad, Deccan, 10 October 1987 (50-overs)
Result: New Zealand won by 3 runs. Points: New Zealand 4, Zimbabwe 0.
Toss: Zimbabwe. Umpires: Mahboob Shah (Pak) and PW Vidanagamage (SL).
Man of the Match: DL Houghton.

New Zealand innings (50 overs maximum)			R	B	4	6
MC Snedden	c Waller	b Rawson	64	96	3	0
JG Wright	c Houghton	b Traicos	18	40	1	0
MD Crowe		c & b Rawson	72	88	5	1
AH Jones	c Brandes	b Omarshah	0	6	0	0
*JJ Crowe	c Brown	b Curran	31	35	2	0
DN Patel	lbw	b Omarshah	0	2	0	0
JG Bracewell	not out		13	20	0	0
+IDS Smith	c Brown	b Curran	29	20	2	1
SL Boock	not out		0	0	0	0
Extras	(b 4, lb 4, w 4, nb 3)		15			
Total	(7 wickets, 50 overs)		242			

DNB: EJ Chatfield, W Watson.
Fall of wickets: 1-59 (Wright), 2-143 (Snedden), 3-145 (Jones), 4-166 (MD Crowe), 5-169 (Patel), 6-205 (JJ Crowe), 7-240 (Smith).

Bowling	O	M	R	W
Curran	10	0	51	2
Rawson	10	0	62	2
Brandes	7	2	24	0
Traicos	10	2	28	1
Butchart	4	0	27	0
Omarshah	9	0	42	2

Zimbabwe innings (target: 243 runs from 50 overs)			R	B	4	6
RD Brown	c JJ Crowe	b Chatfield	1	10	0	0
AH Omarshah	lbw	b Snedden	5	13	0	0
+DL Houghton	c MD Crowe	b Snedden	142	137	13	6
AJ Pycroft	run out		12	22	2	0
KM Curran	c Boock	b Watson	4	8	0	0
AC Waller	c Smith	b Watson	5	14	0	0
GA Paterson	c Smith	b Boock	2	11	0	0
PWE Rawson	lbw	b Boock	1	10	0	0
IP Butchart	run out		54	70	2	1
EA Brandes	run out		0	0	0	0
*AJ Traicos	not out		4	6	0	0
Extras	(lb 7, w 1, nb 1)		9			
Total	(all out, 49.4 overs)		239			

Fall of wickets: 1-8 (Brown), 2-10 (Omarshah), 3-61 (Pycroft), 4-67 (Curran), 5-86 (Waller), 6-94 (Paterson), 7-104 (Rawson), 8-221 (Houghton), 9-221 (Brandes), 10-239 (Butchart).

Bowling	O	M	R	W
Chatfield	10	2	26	1
Snedden	9	0	53	2
Watson	10	2	36	2
Bracewell	7	0	48	0
Patel	5	0	27	0
Boock	8.4	0	42	2

Pakistan v England, Group B

At Pindi Club Ground, Rawalpindi, 12,13 October 1987 (50-overs)
Result: Pakistan won by 18 runs. Points: Pakistan 4, England 0.
Toss: England. Umpires: AR Crafter (Aus) and RB Gupta (Ind).
Man of the Match: Abdul Qadir.
Score after day 1 (reserve day used): No play.

Pakistan innings (50 overs maximum)			R	B	4	6
Mansoor Akhtar	c Downton	b Foster	6	24	1	0
Rameez Raja	run out		15	40	1	0
Saleem Malik	c Downton	b DeFreitas	65	80	8	0
Javed Miandad	lbw	b DeFreitas	23	50	3	0
Ijaz Ahmed	c Robinson	b Small	59	59	4	1
*!Imran Khan		b Small	22	32	2	0
Wasim Akram		b DeFreitas	5	3	1	0
+Saleem Yousuf	not out		16	10	0	0
Abdul Qadir	not out		12	7	1	1
Extras	(lb 10, w 3, nb 3)		16			
Total	(7 wickets, 50 overs)		239			

DNB: Tauseef Ahmed, Saleem Jaffar.
Fall of wickets: 1-13 (Mansoor Akhtar), 2-51 (Rameez Raja), 3-112 (Javed Miandad), 4-123 (Saleem Malik), 5-202 (Imran Khan), 6-210 (Wasim Akram), 7-210 (Ijaz Ahmed).

Bowling	O	M	R	W
DeFreitas	10	1	42	3
Foster	10	1	35	1
Small	10	1	47	2
Pringle	10	0	54	0
Emburey	10	0	51	0

England innings (target: 240 runs from 50 overs)			R	B	4	6
GA Gooch		b Abdul Qadir	21	41	3	0
BC Broad		b Tauseef Ahmed	36	78	2	0
RT Robinson		b Abdul Qadir	33	62	1	0
*MW Gatting		b Saleem Jaffar	43	47	4	0
AJ Lamb	lbw	b Abdul Qadir	30	38	3	0
DR Pringle	run out		8	14	0	0
JE Emburey	run out		1	1	0	0
+PR Downton	c Saleem Yousuf	b Abdul Qadir	0	2	0	0
PAJ DeFreitas	not out		3	3	0	0
NA Foster	run out		6	5	0	0
GC Small	lbw	b Saleem Jaffar	0	1	0	0
Extras	(b 6, lb 26, w 8)		40			
Total	(all out, 48.4 overs)		221			

Fall of wickets: 1-52 (Gooch), 2-92 (Broad), 3-141 (Robinson), 4-186 (Gatting), 5-206 (Lamb), 6-207 (Emburey), 7-207 (Downton), 8-213 (Pringle), 9-221 (Foster), 10-221 (Small).

Bowling	O	M	R	W
Wasim Akram	9	0	32	0
Saleem Jaffar	9.4	0	42	2
Tauseef Ahmed	10	0	39	1
Abdul Qadir	10	0	31	4
Saleem Malik	7	0	29	0
Mansoor Akhtar	3	0	16	0

Australia v Zimbabwe, Group A

At MA Chidambaram Stadium, Chepauk, Madras, 13 October 1987 (50-overs)
Result: Australia won by 96 runs. Points: Australia 4, Zimbabwe 0.
Toss: Zimbabwe. Umpires: Khizer Hayat (Pak) and DR Shepherd (Eng).
Man of the Match: SR Waugh.

Australia innings (50 overs maximum)			R	B	4	6
GR Marsh	c Curran	b Omarshah	62	101	8	0
DC Boon	c Houghton	b Curran	2	15	0	0
DM Jones	run out		2	12	0	0
*AR Border	c Omarshah	b Butchart	67	88	8	0
SR Waugh	run out		45	41	3	2
SP O'Donnell	run out		3	11	0	0
+GC Dyer	c Paterson	b Butchart	27	20	1	2
PL Taylor	not out		17	13	1	0
CJ McDermott	c Brown	b Curran	1	3	0	0
TBA May	run out		1	1	0	0
Extras	(w 8)		8			
Total	(9 wickets, 50 overs)		235			

DNB: BA Reid.
Fall of wickets: 1-10 (Boon), 2-20 (Jones), 3-133 (Border), 4-143 (Marsh), 5-155 (O'Donnell), 6-202 (Waugh), 7-228 (Dyer), 8-230 (McDermott), 9-235 (May).

Bowling	O	M	R	W
Curran	8	0	29	2
Jarvis	10	0	40	0
Rawson	6	0	39	0
Butchart	10	1	59	2
Traicos	10	0	36	0
Omarshah	6	0	32	1

Zimbabwe innings (target: 236 runs from 50 overs)			R	B	4	6
RD Brown		b O'Donnell	3	30	0	0
GA Paterson	run out		16	53	1	0
+DL Houghton	c O'Donnell	b May	11	22	1	0
AJ Pycroft	run out		9	29	1	0
KM Curran		b O'Donnell	30	38	1	3
AC Waller		c & b May	19	22	1	1
AH Omarshah		b McDermott	2	9	0	0
PWE Rawson		b Reid	15	14	2	0
IP Butchart	c Jones	b O'Donnell	18	32	2	0
*AJ Traicos		c & b O'Donnell	6	5	1	0
MP Jarvis	not out		1	1	0	0
Extras	(b 2, lb 3, w 3, nb 1)		9			
Total	(all out, 42.4 overs)		139			

Fall of wickets: 1-13 (Brown), 2-27 (Paterson), 3-41 (Pycroft), 4-44 (Houghton), 5-79 (Waller), 6-97 (Omarshah), 7-97 (Curran), 8-124 (Rawson), 9-137 (Traicos), 10-139 (Butchart).

Bowling	O	M	R	W
McDermott	7	1	13	1
Reid	7	1	21	1
O'Donnell	9.4	1	39	4
Waugh	6	3	7	0
May	8	0	29	2
Taylor	5	0	25	0

Sri Lanka v West Indies, Group B
At National Stadium, Karachi, 13 October 1987 (50-overs)
Result: West Indies won by 191 runs. Points: West Indies 4, Sri Lanka 0.
Toss: Sri Lanka. Umpires: VK Ramaswamy (Ind) and SJ Woodward (NZ).
Man of the Match: IVA Richards.

West Indies innings (50 overs maximum)			R	B	4	6
DL Haynes		b Gurusinha	105	124	10	1
CA Best		b Ratnayeke	18	30	1	0
RB Richardson	c Kuruppu	b Ratnayeke	0	1	0	0
*IVA Richards	c Mahanama	b de Mel	181	125	16	7
AL Logie	not out		31	25	0	0
RA Harper	not out		5	2	0	0
Extras	(b 4, lb 8, w 4, nb 4)		20			
Total	(4 wickets, 50 overs)		360			

DNB: CL Hooper, +PJL Dujon, WKM Benjamin, CA Walsh, BP Patterson.
Fall of wickets: 1-45 (Best), 2-45 (Richardson), 3-227 (Haynes), 4-343 (Richards).

Bowling	O	M	R	W
John	10	1	48	0
Ratnayeke	8	0	68	2
Anurasiri	10	0	39	0
de Mel	10	0	97	1
de Silva	6	0	35	0
Ranatunga	2	0	18	0
Gurusinha	4	0	43	1

Sri Lanka innings (target: 361 runs from 50 overs)			R	B	4	6
RS Mahanama	c Dujon	b Walsh	12	4	3	0
+DSBP Kuruppu	lbw	b Patterson	14	14	0	0
AP Gurusinha		b Hooper	36	108	1	1
PA de Silva	c Dujon	b Hooper	9	27	0	0
A Ranatunga	not out		52	93	5	0
*LRD Mendis	not out		37	45	5	0
Extras	(b 1, lb 2, w 6)		9			
Total	(4 wickets, 50 overs)		169			

DNB: RS Madugalle, JR Ratnayeke, ALF de Mel, VB John, SD Anurasiri.
Fall of wickets: 1-24 (Mahanama), 2-31 (Kuruppu), 3-57 (de Silva), 4-112 (Gurusinha).

Bowling	O	M	R	W
Patterson	7	0	32	1
Walsh	7	2	23	1
Harper	10	2	15	0
Benjamin	4	0	11	0
Hooper	10	0	39	2
Richards	8	0	22	0
Richardson	4	0	24	0

India v New Zealand, Group A
At M.Chinnaswamy Stadium, Bangalore, 14 October 1987 (50-overs)
Result: India won by 16 runs. Points: India 4, New Zealand 0.
Toss: New Zealand. Umpires: DM Archer (WI) and HD Bird (Eng).
Man of the Match: N Kapil Dev.

India innings (50 overs maximum)			R	B	4	6
K Srikkanth	run out		9	19	1	0
SM Gavaskar	run out		2	14	0	0
NS Sidhu	c Jones	b Patel	75	71	4	4
DB Vengsarkar		c & b Watson	0	8	0	0
M Azharuddin	c Boock	b Patel	21	57	1	0
RJ Shastri		c & b Patel	22	44	0	1
*N Kapil Dev	not out		72	58	4	1
M Prabhakar		c & b Chatfield	3	5	0	0
+KS More	not out		42	26	5	0
Extras	(lb 4, w 2)		6			
Total	7 wickets, 50 overs)		252			

DNB: L Sivaramakrishnan, Maninder Singh.
Fall of wickets: 1-11 (Gavaskar), 2-16 (Srikkanth), 3-21 (Vengsarkar), 4-86 (Azharuddin), 5-114 (Sidhu), 6-165 (Shastri), 7-170 (Prabhakar).

Bowling	O	M	R	W
Chatfield	10	1	39	1
Snedden	10	1	56	0
Watson	9	0	59	1
Boock	4	0	26	0
Bracewell	7	0	32	0
Patel	10	0	36	3

New Zealand innings (target: 253 runs from 50 overs)			R	B	4	6
MC Snedden	c Shastri	b Azharuddin	33	63	2	0
KR Rutherford	c Srikkanth	b Shastri	75	95	6	2
MD Crowe	st More	b Maninder Singh	9	12	1	0
AH Jones	run out		64	86	2	0
*JJ Crowe	c Vengsarkar	b Maninder Singh	7	11	0	0
DN Patel	run out		1	3	0	0
JG Bracewell	c Maninder Singh	b Shastri	8	14	0	0
+IDS Smith		b Prabhakar	10	5	0	0
SL Boock	not out		7	8	0	0
W Watson	not out		2	3	0	0
Extras	(b 5, lb 9, w 5, nb 1)		20			
Total	(8 wickets, 50 overs)		236			

DNB: EJ Chatfield.
Fall of wickets: 1-67 (Snedden), 2-86 (MD Crowe), 3-146 (Rutherford), 4-168 (JJ Crowe), 5-170 (Patel), 6-189 (Bracewell), 7-206 (Smith), 8-225 (Jones).

Bowling	O	M	R	W
Kapil Dev	10	1	54	0
Prabhakar	8	0	38	1
Azharuddin	4	0	11	0
Sivaramakrishnan	8	0	34	0
Maninder Singh	10	0	40	2
Shastri	10	0	45	2

Pakistan v West Indies, Group B
At Gaddafi Stadium, Lahore, 16 October 1987 (50-overs)
Result: Pakistan won by 1 wicket. Points: Pakistan 4, West Indies 0.
Toss: West Indies. Umpires: AR Crafter (Aus) and SJ Woodward (NZ).
Man of the Match: Saleem Yousuf.

West Indies innings (50 overs maximum)			R	B	4	6
DL Haynes		b Saleem Jaffar	37	81	3	0
PV Simmons		c & b Tauseef Ahmed	50	57	8	0
RB Richardson	c Ijaz Ahmed	b Saleem Jaffar	11	22	1	0
*IVA Richards	c Saleem Malik	b Imran Khan	51	52	4	1
AL Logie	c Mansoor Akhtar	b Saleem Jaffar	2	4	0	0
CL Hooper	lbw	b Wasim Akram	22	37	2	0
+PJL Dujon	lbw	b Wasim Akram	5	12	0	0
RA Harper	c Mansoor Akhtar	b Imran Khan	0	1	0	0
EAE Baptiste		b Imran Khan	14	20	1	0
CA Walsh	lbw	b Imran Khan	7	6	1	0
BP Patterson	not out		0	4	0	0
Extras	(b 1, lb 14, w 2)		17			
Total	(all out, 49.3 overs)		216			

Fall of wickets: 1-91 (Haynes), 2-97 (Simmons), 3-118 (Richardson), 4-121 (Logie), 5-169 (Hooper), 6-184 (Richards), 7-184 (Harper), 8-196 (Dujon), 9-207 (Baptiste), 10-216 (Walsh).

Bowling	O	M	R	W
Imran Khan	8.3	2	37	4
Wasim Akram	10	0	45	2
Abdul Qadir	8	0	42	0
Tauseef Ahmed	10	2	35	1
Saleem Jaffar	10	0	30	3
Saleem Malik	3	0	12	0

Pakistan innings (target: 217 runs from 50 overs)			R	B	4	6
Rameez Raja	c Richards	b Harper	42	87	1	0
Mansoor Akhtar		b Patterson	10	24	2	0
Saleem Malik	c Baptiste	b Walsh	4	7	1	0
Javed Miandad		c & b Hooper	33	72	1	0
Ijaz Ahmed		b Walsh	6	14	0	0
*Imran Khan	c Logie	b Walsh	18	26	0	0
+Saleem Yousuf	c Hooper	b Walsh	56	49	7	0
Wasim Akram	c Richardson	b Patterson	7	8	0	0
Abdul Qadir	not out		16	9	0	1
Tauseef Ahmed	run out		0	1	0	0
Saleem Jaffar	not out		1	3	0	0
Extras	(b 5, lb 12, w 7)		24			
Total	(9 wickets, 50 overs)		217			

Fall of wickets: 1-23 (Mansoor Akhtar), 2-28 (Saleem Malik), 3-92 (Rameez Raja), 4-104 (Ijaz Ahmed), 5-110 (Javed Miandad), 6-183 (Imran Khan), 7-200 (Wasim Akram), 8-202 (Saleem Yousuf), 9-203 (Tauseef Ahmed).

Bowling	O	M	R	W
Patterson	10	1	51	2
Walsh	10	1	40	4
Baptiste	8	0	33	0
Harper	10	0	28	1
Hooper	10	0	38	1
Richards	2	0	10	0

England v Sri Lanka, Group B
At Arbab Niaz Stadium, Peshawar, 17 October 1987 (50-overs)
Result: England won by 108 runs (revised target). Points: England 4, Sri Lanka 0.
Toss: England. Umpires: RB Gupta (Ind) and VK Ramaswamy (Ind).
Man of the Match: AJ Lamb.

England innings (50 overs maximum)			R	B	4	6
GA Gooch		c & b Anurasiri	84	100	8	0
BC Broad	c de Silva	b Ratnayeke	28	60	1	0
*MW Gatting		b Ratnayeke	58	63	3	0
AJ Lamb	c de Silva	b Ratnayeke	76	58	3	2
JE Emburey	not out		30	19	3	0
CWJ Athey	not out		2	2	0	0
Extras	(lb 13, w 5)		18			
Total	(4 wickets, 50 overs)		296			

DNB: +PR Downton, PAJ DeFreitas, DR Pringle, EE Hemmings, GC Small.
Fall of wickets: 1-89 (Broad), 2-142 (Gooch), 3-218 (Gatting), 4-287 (Lamb).

Bowling	O	M	R	W
Ratnayeke	9	0	62	2
John	10	0	44	0
de Silva	7	0	33	0
Ratnayake	10	0	60	1
Anurasiri	8	0	44	1
Ranatunga	6	0	40	0

NB: Rain interrupted Sri Lankan innings. SL's target was reduced to 267 in 45 overs.

Sri Lanka innings (target: 267 runs from 45 overs)

			R	B	4	6
RS Mahanama	c Gooch	b Pringle	11	39	2	0
+DSBP Kuruppu	c Hemmings	b Emburey	13	26	1	0
AP Gurusinha	run out		1	12	0	0
RS Madugalle		b Hemmings	30	49	3	0
A Ranatunga	lbw	b DeFreitas	40	67	4	0
*LRD Mendis	run out		14	33	1	0
PA de Silva	c Emburey	b Hemmings	6	14	0	0
JR Ratnayeke	c Broad	b Emburey	1	5	0	0
RJ Ratnayake	not out		14	22	1	0
VB John	not out		8	7	1	0
Extras	(b 2, lb 9, w 6, nb 3)		20			
Total	(8 wickets, 45 overs)		158			

DNB: SD Anurasiri.
Fall of wickets: 1-31 (Mahanama), 2-32 (Gurusinha), 3-37 (Kuruppu), 4-99 (Madugalle), 5-105 (Ranatunga), 6-113 (de Silva), 7-119 (Ratnayeke), 8-137 (Mendis).

Bowling	O	M	R	W
DeFreitas	9	2	24	1
Small	7	0	27	0
Pringle	4	0	11	1
Emburey	10	1	26	2
Hemmings	10	1	31	2
Gooch	2	0	9	0
Athey	1	0	10	0
Broad	1	0	6	0
Lamb	1	0	3	0

India v Zimbabwe, Group A

At Wankhede Stadium, Bombay, 17 October 1987 (50-overs)
Result: India won by 8 wickets. Points: India 4, Zimbabwe 0.
Toss: Zimbabwe. Umpires: Mahboob Shah (Pak) and DR Shepherd (Eng).
Man of the Match: M Prabhakar.

Zimbabwe innings (50 overs maximum)

			R	B	4	6
GA Paterson		b Prabhakar	6	21	0	0
KJ Arnott	lbw	b Prabhakar	1	6	0	0
+DL Houghton		b Prabhakar	0	12	0	0
AJ Pycroft	st More	b Shastri	61	102	2	0
KM Curran	c More	b Prabhakar	0	1	0	0
AC Waller	st More	b Maninder Singh	16	42	1	0
IP Butchart	c Sivaramakrishnan	b Maninder Singh	10	23	1	0
AH Omarshah	c More	b Maninder Singh	0	1	0	0
MA Meman	run out		19	22	2	0
*AJ Traicos	c Gavaskar	b Sivaramakrishnan	0	1	0	0
MP Jarvis	not out		8	35	0	0
Extras	(b 2, lb 6, w 6)		14			
Total	(all out, 44.2 overs)		135			

Fall of wickets: 1-3 (Arnott), 2-12 (Houghton), 3-13 (Paterson), 4-13 (Curran), 5-47 (Waller), 6-67 (Butchart), 7-67 (Omarshah), 8-98 (Meman), 9-99 (Traicos), 10-135 (Pycroft).

Bowling	O	M	R	W
Kapil Dev	8	1	17	0
Prabhakar	8	1	19	4
Maninder Singh	10	0	21	3
Azharuddin	1	0	6	0
Sivaramakrishnan	9	0	36	1
Shastri	8.2	0	28	1

India innings (target: 136 runs from 50 overs)

			R	B	4	6
K Srikkanth	c Paterson	b Traicos	31	38	4	0
SM Gavaskar	st Houghton	b Traicos	43	52	9	0
M Prabhakar	not out		11	41	1	0
DB Vengsarkar	not out		46	37	4	3
Extras	(lb 1, w 4)		5			
Total	(2 wickets, 27.5 overs)		136			

DNB: NS Sidhu, M Azharuddin, *N Kapil Dev, RJ Shastri, +KS More, L Sivaramakrishnan, Maninder Singh.
Fall of wickets: 1-76 (Srikkanth), 2-80 (Gavaskar).

Bowling	O	M	R	W
Curran	6	0	32	0
Jarvis	4	0	22	0
Butchart	3	0	20	0
Traicos	8	0	27	2
Meman	6.5	0	34	0

Australia v New Zealand, Group A

At Nehru Stadium, Indore, 18,19 October 1987 (50-overs)
Result: Australia won by 3 runs. Points: Australia 4, New Zealand 0.
Toss: New Zealand. Umpires: DM Archer (WI) and Khizer Hayat (Pak).
Man of the Match: DC Boon.
Score after day 1 (reserve day used): No play.
NB: Match reduced to 30 overs per side after a delayed start on the reserve day.

Australia innings (30 overs maximum)

			R	B	4	6
DC Boon	c Wright	b Snedden	87	96	5	2
GR Marsh	c JJ Crowe	b Snedden	5	9	0	0
DM Jones	c Rutherford	b Patel	52	48	1	3
*AR Border	c MD Crowe	b Chatfield	34	28	3	0
SR Waugh	not out		13	8	1	1
TM Moody	not out		0	3	0	0
Extras	(b 1, lb 5, w 2)		8			
Total	(4 wickets, 30 overs)		199			

DNB: SP O'Donnell, +GC Dyer, TBA May, CJ McDermott, BA Reid.
Fall of wickets: 1-17 (Marsh), 2-134 (Jones), 3-171 (Boon), 4-196 (Border).

Bowling	O	M	R	W
Snedden	6	0	36	2
Chatfield	6	0	27	1
Watson	6	0	34	0
Patel	6	0	45	1
Bracewell	6	0	51	0

New Zealand innings (target: 200 runs from 30 overs)

			R	B	4	6
KR Rutherford		b O'Donnell	37	38	2	2
JG Wright	c Dyer	b O'Donnell	47	44	1	2
MD Crowe	c Marsh	b Waugh	58	48	5	0
AH Jones	c Marsh	b McDermott	15	23	0	0
*JJ Crowe		c & b Reid	3	10	0	0
DN Patel	run out		13	9	1	0
JG Bracewell		c & b Reid	6	4	1	0
+IDS Smith		b Waugh	1	2	0	0
MC Snedden	run out		1	1	0	0
EJ Chatfield	not out		0	0	0	0
W Watson	not out		2	3	0	0
Extras	(b 4, lb 5, w 4)		13			
Total	(9 wickets, 30 overs)		196			

Fall of wickets: 1-83 (Wright), 2-94 (Rutherford), 3-133 (Jones), 4-140 (JJ Crowe), 5-165 (Patel), 6-183 (Bracewell), 7-193 (MD Crowe), 8-193 (Smith), 9-194 (Snedden).

Bowling	O	M	R	W
McDermott	6	0	30	1
Reid	6	0	38	2
May	6	0	39	0
O'Donnell	6	0	44	2
Waugh	6	0	36	2

Pakistan v England, Group B

At National Stadium, Karachi, 20 October 1987 (50-overs)
Result: Pakistan won by 7 wickets. Points: Pakistan 4, England 0.
Toss: Pakistan. Umpires: AR Crafter (Aus) and VK Ramaswamy (Ind).
Man of the Match: Imran Khan.

England innings (50 overs maximum)

			R	B	4	6
GA Gooch	c Wasim Akram	b Imran Khan	16	27	2	0
RT Robinson		b Abdul Qadir	16	26	1	0
CWJ Athey		b Tauseef Ahmed	86	104	6	2
*MW Gatting	c Saleem Yousuf	b Abdul Qadir	60	65	3	1
AJ Lamb		b Imran Khan	9	15	0	0
JE Emburey	lbw	b Abdul Qadir	3	11	0	0
+PR Downton	c Saleem Yousuf	b Imran Khan	6	13	0	0
PAJ DeFreitas	c Saleem Yousuf	b Imran Khan	13	15	1	0
NA Foster	not out		20	20	2	0
GC Small	run out		0	1	0	0
EE Hemmings	not out		4	3	0	0
Extras	(lb 7, w 4)		11			
Total	(9 wickets, 50 overs)		244			

Fall of wickets: 1-26 (Gooch), 2-52 (Robinson), 3-187 (Athey), 4-187 (Gatting), 5-192 (Emburey), 6-203 (Lamb), 7-206 (Downton), 8-230 (DeFreitas), 9-230 (Small).

Bowling	O	M	R	W
Imran Khan	9	0	37	4
Wasim Akram	8	0	44	0
Tauseef Ahmed	10	0	46	1
Abdul Qadir	10	0	31	3
Saleem Jaffar	8	0	44	0
Saleem Malik	5	0	35	0

Pakistan innings (target: 245 runs from 50 overs)

			R	B	4	6
Rameez Raja	c Gooch	b DeFreitas	113	148	5	0
Mansoor Akhtar	run out		29	49	3	0
Saleem Malik	c Athey	b Emburey	88	92	7	0
Javed Miandad	not out		6	3	1	0
Ijaz Ahmed	not out		4	2	1	0
Extras	(lb 6, w 1)		7			
Total	(3 wickets, 49 overs)		247			

DNB: *Imran Khan, +Saleem Yousuf, Wasim Akram, Abdul Qadir, Tauseef Ahmed, Saleem Jaffar.

Fall of wickets: 1-61 (Mansoor Akhtar), 2-228 (Saleem Malik), 3-243 (Rameez Raja).

Bowling	O	M	R	W
DeFreitas	8	2	41	1
Foster	10	0	51	0
Hemmings	10	1	40	0
Emburey	10	0	34	1
Small	9	0	63	0
Gooch	2	0	12	0

Sri Lanka v West Indies, Group B

At Green Park, Kanpur, 21 October 1987 (50-overs)
Result: West Indies won by 25 runs. Points: West Indies 4, Sri Lanka 0.
Toss: Sri Lanka. Umpires: Amanullah Khan (Pak) and Mahboob Shah (Pak).
Man of the Match: PV Simmons.

West Indies innings (50 overs maximum)			R	B	4	6
DL Haynes		b Anurasiri	24	36	3	0
PV Simmons	c Madugalle	b Ratnayeke	89	126	11	0
RB Richardson	c Mahanama	b Jeganathan	4	12	0	0
*IVA Richards	c Ratnayake	b de Silva	14	25	0	0
AL Logie	not out		65	66	7	0
CL Hooper	st Kuruppu	b de Silva	6	8	1	0
+PJL Dujon	c Kuruppu	b Ratnayeke	6	14	0	0
RA Harper		b Ratnayeke	3	6	0	0
WKM Benjamin		b Ratnayeke	0	3	0	0
CA Walsh	not out		9	8	1	0
Extras	(b 2, lb 7, w 7)		16			
Total	(8 wickets, 50 overs)		236			

DNB: BP Patterson.
Fall of wickets: 1-62 (Haynes), 2-80 (Richardson), 3-115 (Richards), 4-155 (Simmons), 5-168 (Hooper), 6-199 (Dujon), 7-213 (Harper), 8-214 (Benjamin).

Bowling	O	M	R	W
Ratnayeke	10	1	41	3
John	5	1	25	0
Ratnayake	5	0	39	1
Jeganathan	10	1	33	1
Anurasiri	10	1	46	1
de Silva	10	0	43	2

Sri Lanka innings (target: 237 runs from 50 overs)			R	B	4	6
RS Mahanama		b Patterson	0	3	0	0
+DSBP Kuruppu		c & b Hooper	33	82	1	0
JR Ratnayeke	lbw	b Benjamin	15	22	1	0
RS Madugalle	c Haynes	b Harper	18	42	0	0
A Ranatunga	not out		86	100	7	2
*LRD Mendis		b Walsh	19	34	1	0
PA de Silva		b Patterson	8	9	0	0
RJ Ratnayake	c Walsh	b Patterson	5	7	0	0
S Jeganathan	run out		3	9	0	0
VB John	not out		1	3	0	0
Extras	(b 2, lb 11, nb 10)		23			
Total	(8 wickets, 50 overs)		211			

DNB: SD Anurasiri.
Fall of wickets: 1-2 (Mahanama), 2-28 (Ratnayeke), 3-66 (Madugalle), 4-86 (Kuruppu), 5-156 (Mendis), 6-184 (de Silva), 7-200 (Ratnayake), 8-209 (Jeganathan).

Bowling	O	M	R	W
Patterson	10	0	31	3
Walsh	9	2	43	1
Benjamin	10	0	43	1
Harper	10	1	29	1
Hooper	8	0	35	1
Richards	3	0	17	0

India v Australia, Group A

At Feroz Shah Kotla, Delhi, 22 October 1987 (50-overs)
Result: India won by 56 runs. Points: India 4, Australia 0.
Toss: Australia. Umpires: Khalid Aziz (Pak) and DR Shepherd (Eng).
Man of the Match: M Azharuddin.

India innings (50 overs maximum)			R	B	4	6
K Srikkanth	c Dyer	b McDermott	26	37	3	0
SM Gavaskar		b O'Donnell	61	72	7	0
NS Sidhu	c Moody	b McDermott	51	70	2	0
DB Vengsarkar	c O'Donnell	b Reid	63	60	3	2
*N Kapil Dev	c Dyer	b McDermott	3	5	0	0
M Azharuddin	not out		54	45	5	1
RJ Shastri		c & b Waugh	8	7	1	0
+KS More	not out		5	4	0	0
Extras	b 1, lb 6, w 11		18			
Total	6 wickets, 50 overs)		289			

DNB: M Prabhakar, C Sharma, Maninder Singh.
Fall of wickets: 1-50 (Srikkanth), 2-125 (Gavaskar), 3-167 (Sidhu), 4-178 (Kapil Dev), 5-243 (Vengsarkar), 6-274 (Shastri).

Bowling	O	M	R	W
O'Donnell	9	1	45	1
Reid	10	0	65	1
Waugh	10	0	59	1
McDermott	10	0	61	3
Moody	2	0	15	0
Zesers	9	1	37	0

Australia innings (target: 290 runs from 50 overs)			R	B	4	6
GR Marsh	st More	b Maninder Singh	33	56	2	0
DC Boon	c More	b Shastri	62	59	7	0
DM Jones	c Kapil Dev	b Maninder Singh	36	55	0	0
*AR Border	c Prabhakar	b Maninder Singh	12	24	0	0
SR Waugh	c Sidhu	b Kapil Dev	42	52	3	0
TM Moody	run out		2	6	0	0
SP O'Donnell		b Azharuddin	5	10	0	0
+GC Dyer	c Kapil Dev	b Prabhakar	15	12	0	1
CJ McDermott		c & b Azharuddin	4	5	0	0
AK Zesers	not out		2	11	0	0
BA Reid	c Sidhu	b Azharuddin	1	6	0	0
Extras	(lb 11, w 8)		19			
Total	(all out, 49 overs)		233			

Fall of wickets: 1-88 (Marsh), 2-104 (Boon), 3-135 (Border), 4-164 (Jones), 5-167 (Moody), 6-182 (O'Donnell), 7-214 (Dyer), 8-227 (McDermott), 9-231 (Waugh), 10-233 (Reid).

Bowling	O	M	R	W
Kapil Dev	8	1	41	1
Prabhakar	10	0	56	1
Maninder Singh	10	0	34	3
Shastri	10	0	35	1
Sharma	7.1	0	37	0
Azharuddin	3.5	0	19	3

New Zealand v Zimbabwe, Group A

At Eden Gardens, Calcutta, 23 October 1987 (50-overs)
Result: New Zealand won by 4 wickets. Points: New Zealand 4, Zimbabwe 0.
Toss: New Zealand. Umpires: Khizer Hayat (Pak) and PW Vidanagamage (SL).
Man of the Match: JJ Crowe.

Zimbabwe innings (50 overs maximum)			R	B	4	6
GA Paterson	run out		0	8	0	0
AH Omarshah	c MD Crowe	b Watson	41	90	2	0
KJ Arnott	run out		51	83	5	0
+DL Houghton	c MD Crowe	b Boock	50	57	5	0
AJ Pycroft	not out		52	46	2	1
KM Curran		b Boock	12	11	1	0
AC Waller	not out		8	5	1	0
Extras	(lb 7, w 6)		13			
Total	(5 wickets, 50 overs)		227			

DNB: IP Butchart, EA Brandes, *AJ Traicos, MP Jarvis.
Fall of wickets: 1-1 (Paterson), 2-82 (Arnott), 3-121 (Omarshah), 4-180 (Houghton), 5-216 (Curran).

Bowling	O	M	R	W
Snedden	10	2	32	0
Chatfield	10	2	47	0
Patel	10	1	53	0
Watson	10	1	45	1
Boock	10	1	43	2

New Zealand innings (target: 228 runs from 50 overs)			R	B	4	6
KR Rutherford		b Brandes	22	32	2	0
JG Wright		b Omarshah	12	32	1	0
MD Crowe	c Butchart	b Omarshah	58	58	8	0
DN Patel	c Arnott	b Brandes	1	4	0	0
*JJ Crowe	not out		88	105	8	0
AH Jones	c Jarvis	b Traicos	15	35	1	0
MC Snedden		b Jarvis	4	13	0	0
+IDS Smith	not out		17	10	1	0
Extras	(b 1, lb 5, w 4, nb 1)		11			
Total	(6 wickets, 47.4 overs)		228			

DNB: SL Boock, EJ Chatfield, W Watson.
Fall of wickets: 1-37 (Wright), 2-53 (Rutherford), 3-56 (Patel), 4-125 (MD Crowe), 5-158 (Jones), 6-182 (Snedden).

Bowling	O	M	R	W
Curran	2	0	12	0
Jarvis	7.4	0	39	1
Brandes	10	1	44	2
Omarshah	10	0	34	2
Butchart	8	0	50	0
Traicos	10	0	43	1

Pakistan v Sri Lanka, Group B

At Iqbal Stadium, Faisalabad, 25 October 1987 (50-overs)
Result: Pakistan won by 113 runs. Points: Pakistan 4, Sri Lanka 0.
Toss: Pakistan. Umpires: RB Gupta (Ind) and SJ Woodward (NZ).
Man of the Match: Saleem Malik.

Pakistan innings (50 overs maximum)			R	B	4	6
Rameez Raja		c & b Anurasiri	32	49	2	0
Mansoor Akhtar		b Jeganathan	33	61	2	0
Saleem Malik		b Ratnayeke	100	95	10	0
Javed Miandad	run out		1	8	0	0
Wasim Akram	c Ranatunga	b de Silva	39	40	2	2
Ijaz Ahmed		c & b John	30	18	5	0
*Imran Khan	run out		39	20	5	1
Manzoor Elahi	not out		4	6	0	0
+Saleem Yousuf	not out		11	6	0	1
Extras	(lb 6, w 2)		8			
Total	(7 wickets, 50 overs)		297			

DNB: Abdul Qadir, Tauseef Ahmed.
Fall of wickets: 1-64 (Rameez Raja), 2-72 (Mansoor Akhtar), 3-77 (Javed Miandad), 4-137 (Wasim Akram), 5-197 (Ijaz Ahmed), 6-264 (Imran Khan), 7-285 (Saleem Malik).

Bowling	O	M	R	W
Ratnayeke	10	0	58	0
John	8	1	53	1
de Mel	10	0	53	0
Jeganathan	9	1	45	1
Anurasiri	7	0	45	1
de Silva	6	0	37	1

Sri Lanka innings (target: 298 runs from 50 overs)			R	B	4	6
RS Mahanama	run out		8	13	1	0
+DSBP Kuruppu	c Saleem Yousuf	b Imran Khan	0	1	0	0
JR Ratnayeke	run out		22	60	2	0
RS Madugalle	c Saleem Yousuf	b Manzoor Elahi	15	38	2	0
A Ranatunga		c & b Abdul Qadir	50	66	4	0
*LRD Mendis		b Abdul Qadir	58	65	6	0
PA de Silva	not out		13	35	0	0
ALF de Mel		b Abdul Qadir	0	3	0	0
S Jeganathan	c Saleem Yousuf	b Javed Miandad	1	11	0	0
VB John	not out		1	12	0	0
Extras	(b 4, lb 4, w 6, nb 2)		16			
Total	(8 wickets, 50 overs)		184			

DNB: SD Anurasiri.
Fall of wickets: 1-4 (Kuruppu), 2-11 (Mahanama), 3-41 (Madugalle), 4-70 (Ratnayeke), 5-150 (Ranatunga), 6-173 (Mendis), 7-173 (de Mel), 8-179 (Jeganathan).

Bowling	O	M	R	W
Imran Khan	3.2	1	13	1
Wasim Akram	7	0	34	0
Manzoor Elahi	9.4	0	32	1
Tauseef Ahmed	10	1	23	0
Abdul Qadir	10	0	40	3
Saleem Malik	7	1	29	0
Javed Miandad	3	0	5	1

England v West Indies, Group B
At Sawai Mansingh Stadium, Jaipur, 26 October 1987 (50-overs)
Result: England won by 34 runs. Points: England 4, West Indies 0.
Toss: West Indies. Umpires: Mahboob Shah (Pak) and PW Vidanagamage (SL).
Man of the Match: GA Gooch.

England innings (50 overs maximum)			R	B	4	6
GA Gooch	c Harper	b Patterson	92	137	7	0
RT Robinson		b Patterson	13	19	2	0
CWJ Athey	c Patterson	b Harper	21	44	3	0
*MW Gatting	lbw	b Richards	25	24	1	0
AJ Lamb	c Richardson	b Patterson	40	52	3	0
JE Emburey	not out		24	16	4	0
PAJ DeFreitas	not out		16	9	3	0
Extras	(b 5, lb 10, w 22, nb 1)		38			
Total	(5 wickets, 50 overs)		269			

DNB: +PR Downton, NA Foster, GC Small, EE Hemmings.
Fall of wickets: 1-35 (Robinson), 2-90 (Athey), 3-154 (Gatting), 4-209 (Gooch), 5-250 (Lamb).

Bowling	O	M	R	W
Patterson	9	0	56	3
Walsh	10	0	24	0
Benjamin	10	0	63	0
Harper	10	1	52	1
Hooper	3	0	27	0
Richards	8	0	32	1

West Indies innings (target: 270 runs from 50 overs)			R	B	4	6
DL Haynes	c Athey	b DeFreitas	9	14	2	0
PV Simmons		b Emburey	25	28	5	0
RB Richardson	c Downton	b Small	93	130	8	1
*IVA Richards		b Hemmings	51	51	4	3
AL Logie	c Hemmings	b Emburey	22	21	3	0
CL Hooper	c Downton	b DeFreitas	8	11	1	0
+PJL Dujon	c Downton	b Foster	1	4	0	0
RA Harper	run out		3	4	0	0
WKM Benjamin	c Foster	b DeFreitas	8	16	0	0
CA Walsh		b Hemmings	2	3	0	0
BP Patterson	not out		4	8	0	0
Extras	(lb 7, w 1, nb 1)		9			
Total	(all out, 48.1 overs)		235			

Fall of wickets: 1-18 (Haynes), 2-65 (Simmons), 3-147 (Richards), 4-182 (Logie), 5-208 (Hooper), 6-211 (Dujon), 7-219 (Harper), 8-221 (Richardson), 9-224 (Walsh), 10-235 (Benjamin).

Bowling	O	M	R	W
DeFreitas	9.1	2	28	3
Foster	10	0	52	1
Emburey	9	0	41	2
Small	10	0	61	1
Hemmings	10	0	46	2

India v Zimbabwe, Group A
At Gujarat Stadium, Motera, Ahmedabad, 26 October 1987 (50-overs)
Result: India won by 7 wickets. Points: India 4, Zimbabwe 0.
Toss: India. Umpires: DM Archer (WI) and HD Bird (Eng).
Man of the Match: N Kapil Dev.

Zimbabwe innings (50 overs maximum)			R	B	4	6
RD Brown	c More	b Sharma	13	52	2	0
AH Omarshah	run out		0	3	0	0
KJ Arnott		b Kapil Dev	60	126	1	0
AJ Pycroft	c More	b Sharma	2	9	0	0
+DL Houghton	c Kapil Dev	b Shastri	22	35	0	0
AC Waller	c Shastri	b Maninder Singh	39	44	4	1
IP Butchart		b Kapil Dev	13	14	1	0
PWE Rawson	not out		16	17	0	0
EA Brandes	not out		3	4	0	0
Extras	(b 1, lb 12, w 9, nb 1)		23			
Total	(7 wickets, 50 overs)		191			

DNB: MP Jarvis, *AJ Traicos.
Fall of wickets: 1-4 (Omarshah), 2-36 (Brown), 3-40 (Pycroft), 4-83 (Houghton), 5-150 (Arnott), 6-155 (Waller), 7-184 (Butchart).

Bowling	O	M	R	W
Kapil Dev	10	2	44	2
Prabhakar	7	2	12	0
Sharma	10	0	41	2
Maninder Singh	10	1	32	1
Shastri	10	0	35	1
Azharuddin	3	0	14	0

India innings (target: 192 runs from 50 overs)			R	B	4	6
K Srikkanth	lbw	b Jarvis	6	9	1	0
SM Gavaskar	c Butchart	b Rawson	50	114	3	0
NS Sidhu	c Brandes	b Rawson	55	61	5	1
DB Vengsarkar	not out		33	43	1	0
*N Kapil Dev	not out		41	25	2	3
Extras	(lb 6, w 3)		9			
Total	(3 wickets, 42 overs)		194			

DNB: M Azharuddin, RJ Shastri, +KS More, M Prabhakar, C Sharma, Maninder Singh.
Fall of wickets: 1-11 (Srikkanth), 2-105 (Sidhu), 3-132 (Gavaskar).

Bowling	O	M	R	W
Brandes	6	0	28	0
Jarvis	8	1	21	1
Omarshah	8	0	40	0
Traicos	10	0	39	0
Rawson	8	0	46	2
Butchart	2	0	14	0

Australia v New Zealand, Group A
At Sector 16 Stadium, Chandigarh, 27 October 1987 (50-overs)
Result: Australia won by 17 runs. Points: Australia 4, New Zealand 0.
Toss: Australia. Umpires: Khizer Hayat (Pak) and DR Shepherd (Eng).
Man of the Match: GR Marsh.

Australia innings (50 overs maximum)			R	B	4	6
GR Marsh	not out		126	149	12	3
DC Boon	run out		14	28	1	0
DM Jones	c Smith	b Watson	56	80	1	2
*AR Border		b Snedden	1	4	0	0
MRJ Veletta	run out		0	1	0	0
SR Waugh		b Watson	1	7	0	0
+GC Dyer		b Chatfield	8	10	0	0
CJ McDermott	lbw	b Chatfield	5	7	0	0
TBA May	run out		15	10	1	0
AK Zesers	not out		8	3	1	0
Extras	(lb 10, w 7)		17			
Total	(8 wickets, 50 overs)		251			

DNB: BA Reid.
Fall of wickets: 1-25 (Boon), 2-151 (Jones), 3-158 (Border), 4-158 (Veletta), 5-175 (Waugh), 6-193 (Dyer), 7-201 (McDermott), 8-228 (May).

Bowling	O	M	R	W
Snedden	10	0	48	1
Chatfield	10	2	52	2
Boock	10	1	45	0
Bracewell	4	0	24	0
Patel	8	0	26	0
Watson	8	0	46	2

New Zealand innings (target: 252 runs from 50 overs)			R	B	4	6
MC Snedden		b Waugh	32	56	3	0
JG Wright		c & b Zesers	61	82	4	0
MD Crowe	run out		4	5	0	0
KR Rutherford	c Jones	b McDermott	44	57	4	0
*JJ Crowe		c & b Border	27	28	3	0
DN Patel	st Dyer	b Border	3	10	0	0
JG Bracewell	run out		12	20	0	0
+IDS Smith	c Boon	b Waugh	12	15	0	0
SL Boock	run out		12	8	1	0
W Watson	run out		8	8	0	1
EJ Chatfield	not out		5	6	0	0
Extras	(b 1, lb 7, w 4, nb 2)		14			
Total	(all out, 48.4 overs)		234			

Fall of wickets: 1-72 (Snedden), 2-82 (MD Crowe), 3-127 (Wright), 4-173 (JJ Crowe), 5-179 (Rutherford), 6-186 (Patel), 7-206 (Bracewell), 8-208 (Smith), 9-221 (Boock), 10-234 (Watson).

Bowling	O	M	R	W
McDermott	10	1	43	1
Reid	6	0	30	0
Waugh	9.4	0	37	2
Zesers	6	0	37	1
May	10	0	52	0
Border	7	0	27	2

Australia v Zimbabwe, Group A

At Barabati Stadium, Cuttack, 30 October 1987 (50-overs)
Result: Australia won by 70 runs. Points: Australia 4, Zimbabwe 0.
Toss: Zimbabwe. Umpires: Mahboob Shah (Pak) and PW Vidanagamage (SL).
Man of the Match: DC Boon.

Australia innings (50 overs maximum)		R	B	4	6
DC Boon	c Houghton b Butchart	93	101	9	1
GR Marsh	run out	37	65	1	0
DM Jones	not out	58	72	1	1
CJ McDermott	c Rawson b Traicos	9	10	0	1
*AR Border	st Houghton b Traicos	4	6	0	0
MRJ Veletta	run out	43	39	3	0
SR Waugh	not out	10	14	1	0
Extras	(b 3, lb 3, w 6)	12			
Total	(5 wickets, 50 overs)	266			

DNB: SP O'Donnell, +GC Dyer, TBA May, BA Reid.
Fall of wickets: 1-90 (Marsh), 2-148 (Boon), 3-159 (McDermott), 4-170 (Border), 5-248 (Veletta).

Bowling	O	M	R	W
Rawson	9	0	41	0
Jarvis	6	0	33	0
Omarshah	7	0	31	0
Brandes	10	1	58	0
Traicos	10	0	45	2
Butchart	8	0	52	1

Zimbabwe innings (target: 267 runs from 50 overs)		R	B	4	6
AH Omarshah	b Waugh	32	90	4	0
AC Waller	c Waugh b McDermott	38	83	2	0
KM Curran	c Waugh b May	29	57	2	0
AJ Pycroft	c Dyer b McDermott	38	46	2	0
+DL Houghton	lbw b May	1	11	0	0
IP Butchart	st Dyer b Border	3	5	0	0
PWE Rawson	not out	24	29	2	1
EA Brandes	not out	18	11	1	2
Extras	(lb 5, w 6, nb 2)	13			
Total	(6 wickets, 50 overs)	196			

DNB: KJ Arnott, MP Jarvis, *AJ Traicos.
Fall of wickets: 1-55 (Omarshah), 2-89 (Curran), 3-92 (Houghton), 4-97 (Butchart), 5-139 (Pycroft), 6-156 (Waller). NB: Waller retired hurt from 10/0 to 97/4.

Bowling	O	M	R	W
McDermott	10	0	43	2
Reid	9	2	30	0
Waugh	4	0	9	1
O'Donnell	7	1	21	0
May	10	1	30	2
Border	8	0	36	1
Jones	1	0	5	0
Boon	1	0	17	0

England v Sri Lanka, Group B

At Nehru Stadium, Pune, 30 October 1987 (50-overs)
Result: England won by 8 wickets. Points: England 4, Sri Lanka 0.
Toss: Sri Lanka. Umpires: DM Archer (WI) and Khizer Hayat (Pak).
Man of the Match: GA Gooch.

Sri Lanka innings (50 overs maximum)		R	B	4	6
RS Mahanama	c Emburey b DeFreitas	14	28	1	0
JR Ratnayeke	lbw b Small	7	11	1	0
+AP Gurusinha	run out	34	63	3	0
RL Dias	st Downton b Hemmings	80	105	6	3
*LRD Mendis	b DeFreitas	7	26	0	0
RS Madugalle	c sub (PW Jarvis) b Hemmings	22	38	0	1
PA de Silva	not out	23	18	2	0
ALF de Mel	c Lamb b Hemmings	0	2	0	0
S Jeganathan	not out	20	15	2	1
Extras	(lb 3, w 3, nb 5)	11			
Total	(7 wickets, 50 overs)	218			

DNB: VB John, SD Anurasiri.
Fall of wickets: 1-23 (Ratnayeke), 2-25 (Mahanama), 3-113 (Gurusinha), 4-125 (Mendis), 5-170 (Dias), 6-177 (Madugalle), 7-180 (de Mel).

Bowling	O	M	R	W
DeFreitas	10	2	46	2
Small	10	1	33	1
Foster	10	0	37	0
Emburey	10	1	42	0
Hemmings	10	0	57	3

England innings (target: 219 runs from 50 overs)		R	B	4	6
GA Gooch	c & b Jeganathan	61	79	7	0
RT Robinson	b Jeganathan	55	75	7	0
CWJ Athey	not out	40	55	0	0
*MW Gatting	not out	46	40	4	0
Extras	(b 1, lb 13, w 3)	17			
Total	(2 wickets, 41.2 overs)	219			

DNB: AJ Lamb, +PR Downton, JE Emburey, PAJ DeFreitas, NA Foster, GC Small, EE Hemmings.
Fall of wickets: 1-123 (Robinson), 2-132 (Gooch).

Bowling	O	M	R	W
Ratnayeke	8	1	37	0
John	6	2	19	0
de Mel	4.2	0	34	0
Jeganathan	10	0	45	2
Anurasiri	10	0	45	0
de Silva	3	0	25	0

Pakistan v West Indies, Group B

At National Stadium, Karachi, 30 October 1987 (50-overs)
Result: West Indies won by 28 runs. Points: West Indies 4, Pakistan 0.
Toss: West Indies. Umpires: RB Gupta (Ind) and VK Ramaswamy (Ind).
Man of the Match: RB Richardson.

West Indies innings (50 overs maximum)		R	B	4	6
DL Haynes	c Imran Khan b Mudassar Nazar	25	52	1	0
PV Simmons	b Wasim Akram	6	9	1	0
RB Richardson	c Abdul Qadir b Imran Khan	110	135	8	2
*IVA Richards	b Wasim Akram	67	75	2	2
AL Logie	c Mudassar Nazar b Imran Khan	12	17	0	0
RA Harper	b Wasim Akram	2	7	0	0
CL Hooper	not out	5	7	0	0
WKM Benjamin	c Mudassar Nazar b Imran Khan	0	1	0	0
+PJL Dujon	not out	1	1	0	0
Extras	(b 3, lb 10, w 16, nb 1)	30			
Total	(7 wickets, 50 overs)	258			

DNB: CA Walsh, BP Patterson.
Fall of wickets: 1-19 (Simmons), 2-84 (Haynes), 3-221 (Richards), 4-242 (Logie), 5-248 (Harper), 6-255 (Richardson), 7-255 (Benjamin).

Bowling	O	M	R	W
Imran Khan	9	0	57	3
Wasim Akram	10	0	45	3
Abdul Qadir	10	1	29	0
Mudassar Nazar	10	0	47	1
Saleem Jaffar	6	0	37	0
Saleem Malik	5	0	30	0

Pakistan innings (target: 259 runs from 50 overs)		R	B	4	6
Mudassar Nazar	b Harper	40	55	3	0
Rameez Raja	c Hooper b Patterson	70	111	3	0
Saleem Malik	c Richards b Walsh	23	37	0	0
Javed Miandad	b Benjamin	38	38	3	0
Ijaz Ahmed	b Benjamin	6	10	0	0
*Imran Khan	c Harper b Walsh	8	11	0	0
+Saleem Yousuf	b Patterson	7	10	0	0
Wasim Akram	lbw b Patterson	0	2	0	0
Abdul Qadir	not out	8	11	0	0
Shoaib Mohammad	b Benjamin	0	1	0	0
Saleem Jaffar	not out	8	16	0	0
Extras	(b 4, lb 6, w 10, nb 2)	22			
Total	(9 wickets, 50 overs)	230			

Fall of wickets: 1-78 (Mudassar Nazar), 2-128 (Saleem Malik), 3-147 (Rameez Raja), 4-167 (Ijaz Ahmed), 5-186 (Imran Khan), 6-202 (Saleem Yousuf), 7-202 (Wasim Akram), 8-208 (Javed Miandad), 9-208 (Shoaib Mohammad).

Bowling	O	M	R	W
Patterson	10	1	34	3
Walsh	10	1	34	2
Harper	10	0	38	1
Benjamin	10	0	69	3
Richards	10	0	45	0

India v New Zealand, Group A

At Vidarbha C.A. Ground, Nagpur, 31 October 1987 (50-overs)
Result: India won by 9 wickets. Points: India 4, New Zealand 0.
Toss: New Zealand. Umpires: HD Bird (Eng) and DR Shepherd (Eng).
Men of the Match: SM Gavaskar and C Sharma.

New Zealand innings (50 overs maximum)			R	B	4	6
JG Wright	run out		35	59	4	0
PA Horne		b Prabhakar	18	35	1	0
MD Crowe	c Pandit	b Azharuddin	21	24	2	0
KR Rutherford		b Sharma	26	54	1	0
*JJ Crowe		b Maninder Singh	24	24	3	0
DN Patel	c Kapil Dev	b Shastri	40	51	3	0
MC Snedden	run out		23	28	2	0
+IDS Smith		b Sharma	0	1	0	0
EJ Chatfield		b Sharma	0	1	0	0
W Watson	not out		12	25	1	0
Extras	(lb 14, w 7, nb 1)		22			
Total	(9 wickets, 50 overs)		221			

DNB: DK Morrison.
Fall of wickets: 1-46 (Horne), 2-84 (MD Crowe), 3-90 (Wright), 4-122 (JJ Crowe), 5-181 (Patel), 6-182 (Rutherford), 7-182 (Smith), 8-182 (Chatfield), 9-221 (Snedden).
NB: Sharma took hat-trick (Rutherford/Smith/Chatfield).

Bowling	O	M	R	W
Kapil Dev	6	0	24	0
Prabhakar	7	0	23	1
Sharma	10	2	51	3
Azharuddin	7	0	26	1
Maninder Singh	10	0	51	1
Shastri	10	1	32	1

India innings (target: 222 runs from 50 overs)			R	B	4	6
K Srikkanth	c Rutherford	b Watson	75	58	9	3
SM Gavaskar	not out		103	88	10	3
M Azharuddin	not out		41	51	5	0
Extras	(lb 1, w 2, nb 2)		5			
Total	(1 wicket, 32.1 overs)		224			

DNB: NS Sidhu, DB Vengsarkar, *N Kapil Dev, RJ Shastri, +CS Pandit, M Prabhakar, C Sharma, Maninder Singh.
Fall of wickets: 1-136 (Srikkanth).

Bowling	O	M	R	W
Morrison	10	0	69	0
Chatfield	4.1	1	39	0
Snedden	4	0	29	0
Watson	10	0	50	1
Patel	4	0	36	0

1st Semi Final
Pakistan v Australia

At Gaddafi Stadium, Lahore, 4 November 1987 (50-overs)
Result: Australia won by 18 runs. Australia advances to the final.
Toss: Australia. Umpires: HD Bird (Eng) and DR Shepherd (Eng).
Man of the Match: CJ McDermott.

Australia innings (50 overs maximum)			R	B	4	6
GR Marsh	run out		31	57	2	0
DC Boon	st +Javed Miandad	b Saleem Malik	65	91	4	0
DM Jones		b Tauseef Ahmed	38	45	3	0
*AR Border	run out		18	22	2	0
MRJ Veletta		b Imran Khan	48	50	2	0
SR Waugh	not out		32	28	4	1
SP O'Donnell	run out		0	2	0	0
+GC Dyer		b Imran Khan	0	1	0	0
CJ McDermott		b Imran Khan	1	3	0	0
TBA May	not out		0	2	0	0
Extras	(b 1, lb 19, w 13, nb 1)		34			
Total	(8 wickets, 50 overs)		267			

DNB: BA Reid.
Fall of wickets: 1-73 (Marsh), 2-155 (Boon), 3-155 (Jones), 4-215 (Border), 5-236 (Veletta), 6-236 (O'Donnell), 7-241 (Dyer), 8-249 (McDermott).

Bowling	O	M	R	W
Imran Khan	10	1	36	3
Saleem Jaffar	6	0	57	0
Wasim Akram	10	0	54	0
Abdul Qadir	10	0	39	0
Tauseef Ahmed	10	1	39	1
Saleem Malik	4	0	22	1

NB: Javed deputised as wicket-keeper after a ball deflected into Saleem Yousuf's mouth.

Pakistan innings (target: 268 runs from 50 overs)			R	B	4	6
Rameez Raja	run out		1	1	0	0
Mansoor Akhtar		b McDermott	9	19	0	0
Saleem Malik	c McDermott	b Waugh	25	31	3	0
Javed Miandad		b Reid	70	103	4	0
*Imran Khan	c Dyer	b Border	58	84	4	0
Wasim Akram		b McDermott	20	13	0	2
Ijaz Ahmed	c Jones	b Reid	8	7	1	0
+Saleem Yousuf	c Dyer	b McDermott	21	15	2	0
Abdul Qadir	not out		20	16	2	0
Saleem Jaffar	c Dyer	b McDermott	0	2	0	0
Tauseef Ahmed	c Dyer	b McDermott	1	3	0	0
Extras	(lb 6, w 10)		16			
Total	(all out, 49 overs)		249			

Fall of wickets: 1-2 (Rameez Raja), 2-37 (Mansoor Akhtar), 3-38 (Saleem Malik), 4-150 (Imran Khan), 5-177 (Wasim Akram), 6-192 (Ijaz Ahmed), 7-212 (Javed Miandad), 8-236 (Saleem Yousuf), 9-247 (Saleem Jaffar), 10-249 (Tauseef Ahmed).

Bowling	O	M	R	W
McDermott	10	0	44	5
Reid	10	2	41	2
Waugh	9	1	51	1
O'Donnell	10	1	45	0
May	6	0	36	0
Border	4	0	26	1

2nd Semi Final
India v England

At Wankhede Stadium, Bombay, 5 November 1987 (50-overs)
Result: England won by 35 runs. England advances to the final.
Toss: India. Umpires: AR Crafter (Aus) and SJ Woodward (NZ).
Man of the Match: GA Gooch.

England innings (50 overs maximum)			R	B	4	6
GA Gooch	c Srikkanth	b Maninder Singh	115	136	11	0
RT Robinson	st More	b Maninder Singh	13	36	2	0
CWJ Athey	c More	b Sharma	4	17	0	0
*MW Gatting		b Maninder Singh	56	62	5	0
AJ Lamb	not out		32	29	2	0
JE Emburey	lbw	b Kapil Dev	6	10	0	0
PAJ DeFreitas		b Kapil Dev	7	8	1	0
+PR Downton	not out		1	5	0	0
Extras	(b 1, lb 18, w 1)		20			
Total	(6 wickets, 50 overs)		254			

DNB: NA Foster, GC Small, EE Hemmings.
Fall of wickets: 1-40 (Robinson), 2-79 (Athey), 3-196 (Gatting), 4-203 (Gooch), 5-219 (Emburey), 6-231 (DeFreitas).

Bowling	O	M	R	W
Kapil Dev	10	1	38	2
Prabhakar	9	1	40	0
Maninder Singh	10	0	54	3
Sharma	9	0	41	1
Shastri	10	0	49	0
Azharuddin	2	0	13	0

India innings (target: 255 runs from 50 overs)

			R	B	4	6
K Srikkanth		b Foster	31	55	4	0
SM Gavaskar		b DeFreitas	4	7	1	0
NS Sidhu	c Athey	b Foster	22	40	0	0
M Azharuddin	lbw	b Hemmings	64	74	7	0
CS Pandit	lbw	b Foster	24	30	3	0
*N Kapil Dev	c Gatting	b Hemmings	30	22	3	0
RJ Shastri	c Downton	b Hemmings	21	32	2	0
+KS More		c & b Emburey	0	5	0	0
M Prabhakar	c Downton	b Small	4	11	0	0
C Sharma	c Lamb	b Hemmings	0	1	0	0
Maninder Singh	not out		0	0	0	0
Extras	(b 1, lb 9, w 6, nb 3)		19			
Total	(all out, 45.3 overs)		219			

Fall of wickets: 1-7 (Gavaskar), 2-58 (Srikkanth), 3-73 (Sidhu), 4-121 (Pandit), 5-168 (Kapil Dev), 6-204 (Azharuddin), 7-205 (More), 8-218 (Prabhakar), 9-219 (Sharma), 10-219 (Shastri).

Bowling	O	M	R	W
DeFreitas	7	0	37	1
Small	6	0	22	1
Emburey	10	1	35	1
Foster	10	0	47	3
Hemmings	9.3	1	52	4
Gooch	3	0	16	0

Final
Australia v England

At Eden Gardens, Calcutta, 8 November 1987 (50-overs)
Result: Australia won by 7 runs. Australia wins the 1987 Reliance World Cup.
Toss: Australia. Umpires: RB Gupta and Mahboob Shah (Pak).
Man of the Match: DC Boon.

Australia innings (50 overs maximum)

			R	B	4	6
DC Boon	c Downton	b Hemmings	75	125	7	0
GR Marsh		b Foster	24	49	3	0
DM Jones	c Athey	b Hemmings	33	57	1	1
CJ McDermott		b Gooch	14	8	2	0
*AR Border	run out (Robinson/Downton)		31	31	3	0
MRJ Veletta	not out		45	31	6	0
SR Waugh	not out		5	4	0	0
Extras	(b 1, lb 13, w 5, nb 7)		26			
Total	(5 wickets, 50 overs)		253			

DNB: SP O'Donnell, +GC Dyer, TBA May, BA Reid.
Fall of wickets: 1-75 (Marsh), 2-151 (Jones), 3-166 (McDermott), 4-168 (Boon), 5-241 (Border).

Bowling	O	M	R	W
DeFreitas	6	1	34	0
Small	6	0	33	0
Foster	10	0	38	1
Hemmings	10	1	48	2
Emburey	10	0	44	0
Gooch	8	1	42	1

England innings (target: 254 runs from 50 overs)

			R	B	4	6
GA Gooch	lbw	b O'Donnell	35	57	4	0
RT Robinson	lbw	b McDermott	0	1	0	0
CWJ Athey	run out (Waugh/Reid)		58	103	2	0
*MW Gatting	c Dyer	b Border	41	45	3	1
AJ Lamb		b Waugh	45	55	4	0
+PR Downton	c O'Donnell	b Border	9	8	1	0
JE Emburey	run out (Boon/McDermott)		10	16	0	0
PAJ DeFreitas	c Reid	b Waugh	17	10	2	1
NA Foster	not out		7	6	0	0
GC Small	not out		3	3	0	0
Extras	(b 1, lb 14, w 2, nb 4)		21			
Total	(8 wickets, 50 overs)		246			

DNB: EE Hemmings.
Fall of wickets: 1-1 (Robinson), 2-66 (Gooch), 3-135 (Gatting), 4-170 (Athey), 5-188 (Downton), 6-218 (Emburey), 7-220 (Lamb), 8-235 (DeFreitas).

Bowling	O	M	R	W
McDermott	10	1	51	1
Reid	10	0	43	0
Waugh	9	0	37	2
O'Donnell	10	1	35	1
May	4	0	27	0
Border	7	0	38	2

World Cup **1992**
by Osman Samiuddin

Appropriately enough, a decade still fresh brought a World Cup fresher, drenched in the new and the now. As noted by David Frith, the fifth World Cup was in the modern ethos of sporting events, bigger, better and shinier than its predecessors. It had more teams, more matches, more colour, more viewers, more regulations and more action. Intrinsically, it was just more.

The tournament was co-hosted by Australia and New Zealand, with nearly two-thirds of the 39 matches, including one semi-final and the final, being staged in Australia. That the man from whom the idea germinated – Bob Vance – was a Kiwi added a neat quirk as well as a co-host. Vance, a Wellington player considered by some to be among the best never to represent his country, was chairman of the New Zealand Cricket Council in June 1987 when he suggested the idea to Australian officials at an ICC meeting. They were initially hesitant, but Australia's World Cup win later in the year at Eden Gardens submerged doubts, and a formal bid followed a year on.

Australia offered romance because it was here, the home of Kerry Packer's renegade World Series Cricket, that modern one-day international cricket was born. Coloured clothing, white balls and floodlights; Packer dragged sex, albeit surreptitiously at first, into a fusty game in the late '70s. Australia and New Zealand in 1992 brought all this unabashedly out of the closet and onto a global stage.

Soon after – not immediately – all international ODIs would be as much riots of colour as action, played in pyjamas, with white balls and increasingly under lights. Packer's Channel 9 had pioneered slick television coverage of his revolutionary cricket. Satellite TV, the ideal accomplice, arrived, beaming round-the-clock coverage to the rest of the world, most significantly to a lucrative subcontinent just opening its eyes to the riches of economic liberalisation.

Everything felt new, everywhere there was

No longer a cup but a Waterford crystal trophy, the prize was just as rewarding as ever when Pakistan captain Imran Khan received it under the Melbourne Cricket Ground lights after the victory over England in the final.

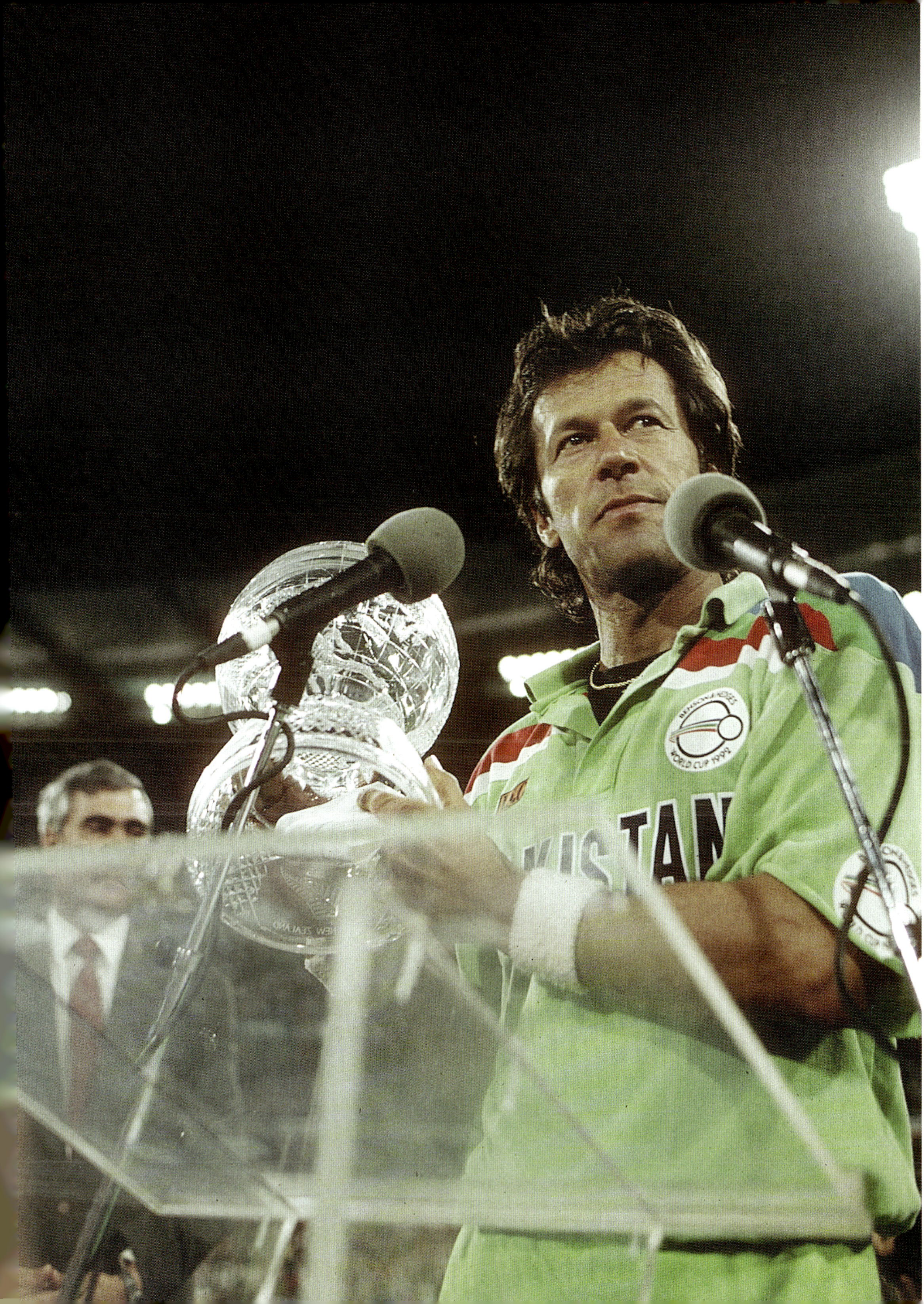

innovation. It encompassed the format, which bravely shunned customary bifurcation and instead called for all nine teams to play each other at least once in a league format. Fairer than that was difficult to imagine.

Newness gushed through South Africa's reinstatement into the cricket fold, a decision taken in Sharjah just four months before the tournament began. Their inclusion exemplified a changing global politic, mirroring the country's rehabilitation onto the world stage. Unsurprisingly a referendum was held in South Africa mid-way through the Cup on whether President F. W. de Klerk should continue reforms towards a multiracial government. Their performance held as much significance on the field as it did off it.

But most cruelly, the South Africans felt the brunt of the one novelty that wasn't so successful – the rain rule. The decision to make a reduction in the target by disregarding the lowest-scoring overs of the side batting first in case of rain was borne of an inability to schedule spare days. Ultimately, it produced only grave imbalances and a vivid sense of injustice to the side chasing in every rain-affected contest. Its absurdity was most embarrassingly exposed by the psychedelic lights of the SCG scoreboard that declared "21 to win off one ball" when South Africa were finally obliged to give up their run-chase after a succession of rain breaks in the semi-final.

More intriguing was the decision to use two white balls, one for each end. Thus emerged a tantalising double-edged sword: the extravagance of swing the balls offered invited bowlers to attack, but simultaneously demanded discipline. Lest batsmen felt neglected, a legislative tweaking was worked, allowing only two fielders outside the fielding circle during the first 15 overs, after which at least four had to remain inside. The change felt unnecessarily bureaucratic then, but its implications were deeper felt over time.

Pinch-hitting blossomed fully four years later on the docility of the subcontinent's pitches, but its genesis was here. Mark Greatbatch, the bulky left-hand New Zealand opener, understood its value, scoring over 300 runs with three fifties at a strike rate touching 90. At the time he was audacious, scything, bludgeoning uppishly, gleefully and regularly. By some distance he hit the most sixes, 14 all told. Ian Botham was another prototype, although his success was more ambivalent.

Greatbatch's shunning of convention encapsulated New Zealand's eccentricity of approach, one that took them all but to the summit. In recent memory, few

The massive new Southern Stand dwarfs all else as the shadows stretch across the packed Melbourne Cricket Ground as Pakistan bat against England in the final.

teams have defied convention as brazenly as New Zealand did here. They inaugurated the tournament by surprising the holders and favourites Australia. The shock matched that felt when they opened their bowling with Dipak Patel, an unheralded, ostensibly unthreatening off-spinner, who ended the tournament with the best economy rate.

Thereafter, they relied on an assembly line of the innocuous. Slow-medium bowlers Gavin Larsen, Willie Watson and Chris Harris stifled rates and snaffled wickets in ideal conditions, Harris finishing as the joint second-highest wicket-taker.

Martin Crowe, their wildly imaginative leader, was their only concession to conformity, through his batting. Unerringly correct and orthodox, Crowe began with a match-winning hundred and ended with a heart-breaking 91 in the semi-final loss to Pakistan. In between he was, for a month, the world's best batsman.

The change in fielding restrictions also brought forth the discipline it obviously affected the most – fielding itself. The flow of runs in the first 15 overs depended ultimately, after the skirmishes of ball and bat, upon those employed to stop them. There had been great fielders in the history of the game – Colin Bland, Gus Logie, Derek Randall and Viv Richards, among others – but few teams collectively did as much to assert fielding emphatically as a discipline equal in importance to batting and bowling as the South Africans.

At the centre was Jonty Rhodes, a pint-sized, hockey-playing, impish-batting livewire, so valuable at point that he was a match-winner. Regularly, and in considerable quantity, he saved runs. With a fully horizontal airborne run-out of Inzamam-ul-Haq in a crucial group game, he donated simultaneously one of the images of the tournament as well as a blueprint for fielding excellence for subsequent generations.

Specialists between point and cover emerged globally, an essential cog in any ODI wheel. Paul Collingwood, Herschelle Gibbs, Ricky Ponting, Mohammad Kaif and Yuvraj Singh; somewhere in all of them the spirit of Rhodes resides. Rhodes's efficiency, liberally interrupted by bouts of luminescence, captured the essence of his team. To everyone's surprise but their own, they gazumped Australia with a performance of ruthless intent. Allan Donald's macho pace led an effervescent attack, but Peter Kirsten (originally left out of the squad only to score four fifties and over 400 runs on reinstatement) and captain Kepler Wessels added critical steel to the batting. Inevitably, their inexperience often peeped through, but it never clouded a joyous and startling re-introduction to the international stage, cruelly cut short in the semi-final by a quirk of the rules.

Australia, overwhelmingly pre-tournament favourites, never recovered from the misfortune of facing supremely motivated opponents in their opening two games. Inexplicably, the pressure and an inflexible approach told. England, on the other hand, seemed perfectly equipped, becoming many people's preference after Australia. A battery of all-rounders, from explosive to workman, played with an efficacy under the ultra-efficient Graham Gooch that they, before or after, failed to replicate. But for the rain in Adelaide, which stole a point and saved Pakistan from likely exit, their organisation may well have borne triumph.

But in the spirit of Paulo Coelho's *The Alchemist*, in Pakistan's 1992 universe every element conspired eventually in their favour. Adelaide's rain, the consistent inconsistency of India and a revamped West Indies (without Viv Richards, Gordon Greenidge and Jeff Dujon), Sri Lankan and Zimbabwean virtues only of an honest endeavour occasionally translating into capacity for upset, other results; never so unequivocally was the truism that to win big tournaments everything needs to go your way proved as it was here.

Pakistan had no pinch-hitter, only the opening solidity of Rameez Raja and pugnacity of Aamer Sohail. They were a poor fielding side, and their bowling was bereft not only of discipline but its greatest threat, in Waqar Younis, who pulled out days before the tournament with stress fractures in his back. Injuries also kept Javed Miandad and captain Imran Khan – their two most experienced players – off the field at various times.

After five matches, with one win, precisely nothing was going their way. Then, the conspiring began. It was sparked by Imran asking his team to "fight like cornered tigers". In a nation conceived in blood and not unused to wars, it became a rallying call immortalised.

Pakistan, as they perennially do, had the players to render legislation, tactics and form all impotent. Their attack shunned discipline for all-out attack at Imran's insistence, thus setting a pattern that is replicated to this day. Wides and no-balls merely became currency for wickets. If Wasim Akram was the highest conceder of extras, he was also the premier wicket-taker. Patel was the tournament's most frugal spinner, but the leg-spin of Mushtaq Ahmed was its most incisive, with 16 wickets. His presence defied an international one-day tradition that Pakistan, through Abdul Qadir, had long ignored: that leg-spin had no place in limited-overs games. Aqib Javed's role, in the final and vitally against Australia, was invisibly pivotal. In pace he didn't threaten, but his demeanour was tearaway. To boot, he was mostly economical.

Reliance on the nous of Miandad and Imran was also heavy. Miandad, with 437 runs and five fifties, was at his wiliest, the World Cup the street for which

he saved his best fight. And Imran led, as always, with an aura and, after missing some early games, transformed into a cussed, essential conduit at one-down. Above all, Pakistan timed it well. England and New Zealand peaked inopportunely, but not Pakistan. Inzamam's twilight surge fulfilled Imran's prophecy that he was a batsman among the best, and also paralleled his team's late but successful swell.

While New Zealand (significantly by Pakistan) and England (in a popular upset by Zimbabwe) were beaten in their last matches leading to the semis, Pakistan reeled off three straight victories to squeeze into the last four by the point they'd grabbed from that Adelaide washout against England. Once there, their collective confidence converted them into Cup winners.

It should have been a harbinger for a golden age, but uniquely for Pakistan it wasn't. Where India's 1983 triumph opened the country's eyes to one-day cricket, where Australia's 1987 win began a renaissance, where Sri Lanka's triumph in 1996 became their graduation to the big league, Pakistan's in 1992 heralded only the unravelling of their fragile unity and a cantankerous, ramshackle descent into chaos.

The following year Imran retired, uneasily, among whiffs of unrest and acrimony. Miandad assumed the captaincy, only to be forced out by a players' revolt. In body, he stayed till the following World Cup; in mind and soul this was his last hurrah. Akram took over from Miandad, becoming the first of nine different leaders in ten years (many of them more than once). To compound the chaos, ball-tampering lurked.

After that came a period which swung intermittently between spectacular successes and debilitating failures on the field. Off it was near anarchy, with match-fixing and unprecedented factionalism.

Only Pakistan's utterly shambolic World Cup in 2003 and the wholesale cull following it, finally brought an end to this turblulent period, giving this 33-day period in early 1992 only a sense of utterly glorious serendipity.

Ian Botham's middle stump – and the TV pitch mike – are shattered by South Africa's Brian McMillan in the semi-final.

SEMI-FINALS
New Zealand v Pakistan

At Eden Park, Auckland, March 21, 1992. Pakistan won by four wickets.

Pakistan reached their first World Cup final by defeating the previously invincible New Zealanders twice in four days. This win was far less convincing than that by seven wickets at Christchurch in the qualifying that gained them their semi-final place.

It seemed unlikely when they needed 123 from 15 overs at a run rate of 8.2 an over, but the game was transformed by Man of the Match Inzamam-ul-Haq, whose aggressive hitting gave him 60 from 37 balls (one six, seven fours, 50 from 31) and a partnership of 87 in 10 overs with Javed Miandad.

When Inzamam was run out the target was 36 from five overs, which was passed with ease thanks to Wasim Akram, Moin Khan (20 not out from 11 balls) and Miandad, who chivvied his partners along for two hours and came in unbeaten on 57. Imran Khan ran out to welcome him as his opposite number, Martin Crowe, limped on for New Zealand's lap of honour. He had to sit out Pakistan's innings with a pulled hamstring, and John Wright led in the field.

Yet Crowe's day had begun happily enough. He was named Man of the Series for his batting and his captaincy to date, he won the toss and, going in at 39 for two, he re-emphasised his class with an accomplished 91 from 83 balls, including three sixes. When he arrived, New Zealand were tangled in Mushtaq Ahmed's leg-spin after Mark Greatbatch's usual explosion (sixes off Akram and Aqib Javed). Crowe accelerated smoothly, adding 107 from 113 balls with Ken Rutherford. But when Rutherford skied the ball to Moin, the batsmen crossed and Crowe's hamstring went. He continued with Greatbatch as his runner until this supposed aide ran him out. Still, Ian Smith and the tail hurried on to 262.

It was an imposing target, especially in mid-innings when Imran Khan seemed bogged down. But against Inzamam's dynamism, New Zealand's successful stratagems of the previous month had no power. Even their surprise weapon, Dipak Patel, whose opening eight overs of off-breaks garnered one for 28, yielded 22 when he returned for his last two.

(David Frith, Wisden Cricketers' Almanack, 1993)

England v South Africa

At Sydney Cricket Ground, March 22, 1992 (day/night). England won by 19 runs (rain rule).

This game's closing minutes buried South Africa's World Cup hopes, and whatever credibility the "rain rule" had retained. By putting pressure on the team batting second, the rule supposedly created exciting finishes. On this occasion, 12 minutes' heavy rain, when South Africa needed 22 from 13 balls, adjusted their target first to 22 from seven and then 21 from one. Brian McMillan could only take a single off Chris Lewis.

The losers were disconsolate, the winners embarrassed, and the crowd furious. Why, they asked, were the two overs not played out under the floodlights? The majority blamed the World Cup's organising committee and the inflexibility which prevented a second-day resumption. (The next day was set aside only for a completely new match, to be played if the second team had not faced 25 overs.)

Justice was probably done. Kepler Wessels chose to field, knowing the rules and the forecast, and his bowlers were fined for going slow and depriving England of five overs' acceleration. But it was not seen to be done, and fine performances on both sides were overshadowed by indignation.

Most of England's batsmen scored fluently, but the tour de force came from Man of the Match Graeme Hick. He survived an lbw appeal first ball and was caught off a no-ball before scoring, but went on to 83 off 90 balls, adding 71 in 14 overs with Alec Stewart and 73 with Neil Fairbrother. Dermot Reeve raced out to score 25 from 14 balls, including 17 of the 18 plundered off Allan Donald's final over.

Pursuing 5.62 an over, South Africa made 58 from their first ten. For once, they did not depend on Peter Kirsten, who was hampered by an injury. Andrew Hudson narrowly missed a fourth fifty, Adrian Kuiper hit three consecutive fours off Gladstone Small, and Jonty Rhodes proved his worth as a batsman, reducing the target to 47 from just five overs. McMillan and Dave Richardson knocked off 25 from three before the rain, and the rule, made their task impossible.

(David Frith, Wisden Cricketers' Almanack, 1993)

The equation on the Sydney Cricket Ground scoreboard does not compute but South Africa's batsmen Dave Richardson and Brian McMillan have to complete the ludicrous formality in the semi-final finally and embarrassingly discrediting the "rain rule", eliminating South Africa in their first tournament and sending England through to their third final.

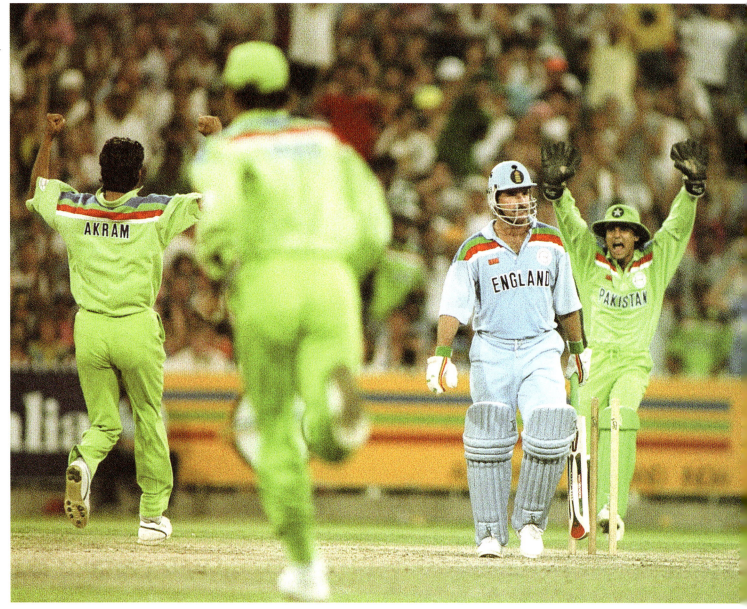

FINAL
Pakistan v England

At Melbourne Cricket Ground, March 25, 1992 (day/night). Pakistan won by 22 runs.
Imran Khan's erratically brilliant Pakistanis won their first World Cup final, while Graham Gooch and England lost their third on the broad field of the MCG with nearly 90,000 in attendance.

Afterwards Imran said it was "the most fulfilling and satisfying cricket moment of my life". He described the victory as his young team's talent over England's experience. He also stressed the role of his aggressive specialist bowlers rather than the "stereotyped" attack of Gooch's all-rounders. But he enjoyed an all-round triumph himself, with the match's highest score and the final wicket.

Imran's role went deeper, however. He had virtually hand-picked the team and, after the disappointment of losing a key player, the pace bowler Waqar Younis, to a stress fracture before leaving Pakistan, and a

disastrous start when they won only one in five matches (two of which he missed). He urged them to imitate the action of a cornered tiger before they went on to five successive wins.

They reached the giant stadium in peak form, while England looked exhausted. The players who had toured New Zealand unconquered had gradually weakened in the face of constant travel and frequent injury. As Pakistan had picked up, they had been losing, first to New Zealand and then, most embarrassingly, to Zimbabwe. "It's not the end of the world," Gooch said after the match, "but it is close to it. We got beaten fair and square."

England were worn down by the century partnership of veterans Imran and Javed Miandad which started slowly but gathered force, and the spirit of their batsmen was broken by successive balls from Man of the Match Wasim Akram which dismissed Allan Lamb and Chris Lewis, one swinging in and then straightening again, the next cutting in sharply.

Remembering the baleful potential of rain, and

knowing that no team had won a World Cup final chasing runs, Imran chose to bat. At first, England prospered. In nine overs, Derek Pringle reduced Pakistan to 24 for two. Then Imran and Miandad, the sole survivors in this World Cup of the 1975 tournament, settled down to see off the new ball.

Progress was slow. Imran was nine from 16 overs when Gooch spilled a running catch, but although Pakistan were only 70 for two half-way through and Miandad had summoned a runner, they accelerated to add 139 from 31 overs before Miandad's reverse sweep was caught at point. Inzamam-ul-Haq (35 balls) and Akram (18 balls) took up the fight. Their 52 from six overs brought the runs from the last 20 to 153, though Pringle's last over cost only two and saw them both dismissed.

England's pursuit of five an over started badly when Ian Botham was surprised to be given caught behind. The next time Moin Khan claimed a catch, Alec Stewart escaped judgment but not for long and Mushtaq Ahmed's leg-spin accounted for Graeme

Hick (baffled by the googly) and Gooch.

With England requiring 181 from 29 overs, Lamb, preferred for his experience to Robin Smith, whose fitness was in doubt, added 72 in 14 with the left-handed Neil Fairbrother. But Akram returned with devastating effect. Deprived of heavyweight partners and using a runner, Fairbrother top-edged to Moin after an hour and a half. The tail threw the bat to no avail. Imran dismissed Richard Illingworth to complete his triumph, and pledged the proceeds of his success to the cancer hospital planned in his mother's memory.

(David Frith, Wisden Cricketers' Almanack, 1993)

Two in two for the King of Swing. Pakistan's Wasim Akram bowls Allan Lamb and Chris Lewis with successive balls as England slide towards defeat in the final.

"They said at the time"

Pakistan captain Imran Khan on his advice to his team: *"I told them, you're cornered tigers. You've got nowhere to go, just go all out. Forget all these worries about no-balls and wide balls and just go out and fight."*

England captain Graham Gooch, who was in the losing team for the third time: *"I think mine's the sort of record that won't be bettered."*

England all-rounder Derek Pringle: *"Losing the final was a deflating experience. Many were inconsolable in defeat. Surprisingly though it was the senior players like Gooch, Botham and Lamb, who are unlikely to get another chance, who appeared to take the loss most graciously."*

New Zealand captain Martin Crowe: *"We haven't got a bowling attack that's going to blast sides out, that's obvious. So we've got to mix and match. We try things and we enjoy ourselves doing it that way."*

West Indies captain Richie Richardson: *"Even though we haven't been doing all that well, people back home still believe that the World Cup belongs to us and we cannot go back to the Caribbean without it. The fact is all the teams have improved a hell of a lot and they're no longer afraid of us."*

Australia captain Allan Border after the loss to South Africa: *"I wish I knew what was wrong so I could fix it."*

Imran Khan: *"I played in the other four World Cups and I can tell you this is the worst organised."*

Banner at the Sydney Cricket Ground during South Africa's opening match: *"End apartheid forever. Ban the white balls now!"*

Format

This was the Cup that thought it was a league. All played all in a qualifying round that went on for ever. It was fair, but about as exciting as the Nullarbor Plain. The good news was that South Africa joined in for the first time, following the end of apartheid.

Innovations

Four big ones – Coloured clothing, with names on the back; floodlights for most of the 36 games; the white ball, in fact two of them, one at each end (so they didn't get too grubby), which meant they swung prodigiously; and the fielding-circle rules were refined, allowing only two men outside the ring in the first 15 overs. After that, it was as before: a minimum of four inside the circle. Result: the birth of the pinch-hitter.

World Cup 1992
Scoreboards

New Zealand v Australia
At Eden Park, Auckland, 22 February 1992 (50-overs)
Result: New Zealand won by 37 runs. Points: New Zealand 2, Australia 0.
Toss: New Zealand. Umpires: Khizer Hayat (Pak) and DR Shepherd (Eng).
World Cup Referee: PD McDermott. Man of the Match: MD Crowe.

New Zealand innings (50 overs maximum)			R	B	4	6
JG Wright		b McDermott	0	1	0	0
RT Latham	c Healy	b Moody	26	44	4	0
AH Jones	lbw	b Reid	4	14	1	0
*MD Crowe	not out		100	134	11	0
KR Rutherford	run out		57	71	6	0
CZ Harris	run out		14	15	2	0
+IDS Smith	c Healy	b McDermott	14	14	1	0
CL Cairns	not out		16	11	2	0
Extras	(lb 6, w 7, nb 4)		17			
Total	(6 wickets, 50 overs)		248			

DNB: DN Patel, GR Larsen, W Watson.
Fall of wickets: 1-2 (Wright), 2-13 (Jones), 3-53 (Latham), 4-171 (Rutherford), 5-191 (Harris), 6-215 (Smith).

Bowling	O	M	R	W	
McDermott	10	1	43	2	(2w)
Reid	10	0	39	1	(4nb 2w)
Moody	9	1	37	1	
SR Waugh	10	0	60	0	(2w)
Taylor	7	0	36	0	
ME Waugh	4	0	27	0	(1w)

Australia innings (target: 249 runs from 50 overs)			R	B	4	6
DC Boon	run out		100	131	11	0
GR Marsh	c Latham	b Larsen	19	56	2	0
DM Jones	run out		21	27	3	0
*AR Border	c Cairns	b Patel	3	11	0	0
TM Moody		c & b Latham	7	11	0	0
ME Waugh	lbw	b Larsen	2	5	0	0
SR Waugh		c & b Larsen	38	34	3	1
+IA Healy	not out		7	9	0	0
CJ McDermott	run out		1	1	0	0
PL Taylor	c Rutherford	b Watson	1	2	0	0
BA Reid	c Jones	b Harris	3	4	0	0
Extras	(lb 6, w 2, nb 1)		9			
Total	(all out, 48.1 overs)		211			

Fall of wickets: 1-62 (Marsh), 2-92 (Jones), 3-104 (Border), 4-120 (Moody), 5-125 (ME Waugh), 6-199 (SR Waugh), 7-200 (Boon), 8-205 (McDermott), 9-206 (Taylor), 10-211 (Reid).

Bowling	O	M	R	W	
Cairns	4	0	30	0	(1nb 1w)
Patel	10	1	36	1	(1w)
Watson	9	1	39	1	
Larsen	10	1	30	3	
Harris	7.1	0	35	1	
Latham	8	0	35	1	

England v India
At W.A.C.A. Ground, Perth (day/night), 22 February 1992 (50-overs)
Result: England won by 9 runs. Points: England 2, India 0.
Toss: England. Umpires: DP Buultjens (SL) and PJ McConnell.
World Cup Referee: AL Mann. Man of the Match: IT Botham.

England innings (50 overs maximum)			R	B	4	6
*GA Gooch	c Tendulkar	b Shastri	51	89	1	0
IT Botham	c More	b Kapil Dev	9	21	1	0
RA Smith	c Azharuddin	b Prabhakar	91	108	8	2
GA Hick	c More	b Banerjee	5	6	1	0
NH Fairbrothe	c Srikkanth	b Srinath	24	34	1	0
+AJ Stewart		b Prabhakar	13	15	1	0
CC Lewis	c Banerjee	b Kapil Dev	10	6	1	0
DR Pringle	c Srikkanth	b Srinath	1	3	0	0
DA Reeve	not out		8	8	0	0
PAJ DeFreitas	run out		1	5	0	0
PCR Tufnell	not out		3	5	0	0
Extras	(b 1, lb 6, w 13)		20			
Total	(9 wickets, 50 overs)		236			

Fall of wickets: 1-21 (Botham), 2-131 (Gooch), 3-137 (Hick), 4-197 (Fairbrother), 5-198 (Smith), 6-214 (Lewis), 7-222 (Pringle), 8-223 (Stewart), 9-224 (DeFreitas).

Bowling	O	M	R	W	
Kapil Dev	10	0	38	2	(6w)
Prabhakar	10	3	34	2	
Srinath	9	1	47	2	(5w)
Banerjee	7	0	45	1	
Tendulkar	10	0	37	0	(1w)
Shastri	4	0	28	1	(1w)

India innings (target: 237 runs from 50 overs)			R	B	4	6
RJ Shastri	run out		57	112	2	0
K Srikkanth	c Botham	b DeFreitas	39	50	7	0
*M Azharuddin	c Stewart	b Reeve	0	1	0	0
SR Tendulkar	c Stewart	b Botham	35	44	5	0
VG Kambli	c Hick	b Botham	3	11	0	0
PK Amre	run out		22	31	0	0
N Kapil Dev	c DeFreitas	b Reeve	17	18	2	0
ST Banerjee	not out		25	16	1	1
+KS More	run out		1	4	0	0
M Prabhakar		b Reeve	0	2	0	0
J Srinath	run out		11	8	0	0
Extras	(lb 9, w 7, nb 1)		17			
Total	(all out, 49.2 overs)		227			

Fall of wickets: 1-63 (Srikkanth), 2-63 (Azharuddin), 3-126 (Tendulkar), 4-140 (Kambli), 5-149 (Shastri), 6-187 (Kapil Dev), 7-194 (Amre), 8-200 (More), 9-201 (Prabhakar), 10-227 (Srinath).

Bowling	O	M	R	W	
Pringle	10	0	53	0	(1w)
Lewis	9.2	0	36	0	(1nb 5w)
DeFreitas	10	0	39	1	
Reeve	6	0	38	3	(1w)
Botham	10	0	27	2	
Tufnell	4	0	25	0	

Sri Lanka v Zimbabwe
At Pukekura Park, New Plymouth, 23 February 1992 (50-overs)
Result: Sri Lanka won by 3 wickets. Points: Sri Lanka 2, Zimbabwe 0.
Toss: Sri Lanka. Umpires: PD Reporter (Ind) and SJ Woodward.
World Cup Referee: PW Moody. Man of the Match: A Flower.

Zimbabwe innings (50 overs maximum)			R	B	4	6
+A Flower	not out		115	152	8	1
WR James	c Tillakaratne	b Wickramasinghe	17	21	3	0
AJ Pycroft	c Ramanayake	b Gurusinha	5	22	0	0
*DL Houghton	c Tillakaratne	b Gurusinha	10	19	1	0
KJ Arnott	c Tillakaratne	b Wickramasinghe	52	56	4	1
AC Waller	not out		83	45	9	3
Extras	(b 2, lb 6, w 13, nb 9)		30			
Total	(4 wickets, 50 overs)		312			

DNB: IP Butchart, EA Brandes, KG Duers, MP Jarvis, AJ Traicos.
Fall of wickets: 1-30 (James), 2-57 (Pycroft), 3-82 (Houghton), 4-167 (Arnott).

Bowling	O	M	R	W	
Ramanayake	10	0	59	0	(1nb 3w)
Wijegunawardene	7	0	54	0	(6nb 3w)
Wickramasinghe	10	1	50	2	(2nb 1w)
Gurusinha	10	0	72	2	(6w)
Kalpage	10	0	51	0	
Jayasuriya	3	0	18	0	

Sri Lanka innings (target: 313 runs from 50 overs)			R	B	4	6
RS Mahanama	c Arnott	b Brandes	59	89	4	0
MAR Samarasekerac	Duers	b Traicos	75	61	11	1
*PA de Silva	c Houghton	b Brandes	14	24	1	0
AP Gurusinha	run out		5	6	0	0
A Ranatunga	not out		88	61	9	1
ST Jayasuriya	c Flower	b Houghton	32	23	2	2
+HP Tillakaratne		b Jarvis	18	12	1	1
RS Kalpage	c Houghton	b Brandes	11	14	1	0
CPH Ramanayake	not out		1	1	0	0
Extras	(lb 5, w 5)		10			
Total	(7 wickets, 49.2 overs)		313			

DNB: KIW Wijegunawardene, GP Wickramasinghe.
Fall of wickets: 1-128 (Samarasekera), 2-144 (Mahanama), 3-155 (Gurusinha), 4-167 (de Silva), 5-212 (Jayasuriya), 6-273 (Tillakaratne), 7-309 (Kalpage).

Bowling	O	M	R	W	
Jarvis	9.2	0	51	1	(1w)
Brandes	10	0	70	3	
Duers	10	0	72	0	
Butchart	8	0	63	0	(3w)
Traicos	10	1	33	1	(1w)
Houghton	2	0	19	1	

Pakistan v West Indies

At Melbourne Cricket Ground, 23 February 1992 (50-overs)
Result: West Indies won by 10 wickets. Points: West Indies 2, Pakistan 0.
Toss: West Indies. Umpires: SG Randell and ID Robinson (Zim).
World Cup Referee: JE Edwards. Man of the Match: BC Lara.

Pakistan innings (50 overs maximum)			R	B	4	6
Rameez Raja	not out		102	158	4	0
Aamer Sohail	c Logie	b Benjamin	23	44	3	0
Inzamam-ul-Haq	c Hooper	b Harper	27	39	0	0
*Javed Miandad	not out		57	61	5	0
Extras	(b 1, lb 3, w 5, nb 2)		11			
Total	(2 wickets, 50 overs)		220			

DNB: Saleem Malik, Ijaz Ahmed, Wasim Akram, Iqbal Sikander, Wasim Haider, +Moin Khan, Aaqib Javed.
Fall of wickets: 1-45 (Aamer Sohail), 2-97 (Inzamam-ul-Haq).

Bowling	O	M	R	W	
Marshall	10	1	53	0	(3w)
Ambrose	10	0	40	0	(2nb 1w)
Benjamin	10	0	49	1	(1w)
Hooper	10	0	41	0	
Harper	10	0	33	1	

West Indies innings (target: 221 runs from 50 overs)			R	B	4	6
DL Haynes	not out		93	144	4	0
BC Lara	retired hurt		88	101	11	0
*RB Richardson	not out		20	40	1	0
Extras	(b 2, lb 8, w 7, nb 3)		20			
Total	(0 wickets, 46.5 overs)		221			

DNB: CL Hooper, AL Logie, KLT Arthurton, RA Harper, MD Marshall, WKM Benjamin, +D Williams, CEL Ambrose.
NB: BC Lara retired hurt at 175/0.

Bowling	O	M	R	W	
Wasim Akram	10	0	37	0	(7w)
Aaqib Javed	8.5	0	42	0	(2nb)
Wasim Haider	8	0	42	0	(1nb)
Ijaz Ahmed	6	1	29	0	
Iqbal Sikander	8	1	26	0	
Aamer Sohail	6	0	35	0	

New Zealand v Sri Lanka

At Trust Bank Park, Hamilton, 25 February 1992 (50-overs)
Result: New Zealand won by 6 wickets. Points: New Zealand 2, Sri Lanka 0.
Toss: New Zealand. Umpires: PD Reporter (Ind) and DR Shepherd (Eng).
World Cup Referee: BJ Paterson. Man of the Match: KR Rutherford.

Sri Lanka innings (50 overs maximum)			R	B	4	6
RS Mahanama		c & b Harris	80	131	6	0
MAR Samarasekerac Wright		b Watson	9	20	1	0
AP Gurusinha	c Smith	b Harris	9	33	0	0
*PA de Silva	run out		31	45	2	0
A Ranatunga	c Rutherford	b Harris	20	26	2	0
ST Jayasuriya	run out		5	7	0	0
+HP Tillakaratne	c Crowe	b Watson	8	19	0	0
RS Kalpage	c Larsen	b Watson	11	17	0	0
CPH Ramanayake	run out		2	1	0	0
SD Anurasiri			3	2	0	0
GP Wickramasinghe	not out		3	4	0	0
Extras	(b 1, lb 15, w 4, nb 5)		25			
Total	(9 wickets, 50 overs)		206			

Fall of wickets: 1-18 (Samarasekera), 2-50 (Gurusinha), 3-120 (de Silva), 4-172 (Ranatunga), 5-172 (Mahanama), 6-181 (Jayasuriya), 7-195 (Tillakaratne), 8-199 (Ramanayake), 9-202 (Kalpage).

Bowling	O	M	R	W	
Morrison	8	0	36	0	(2nb 1w)
Watson	10	0	37	3	(2nb 1w)
Larsen	10	1	29	0	(1w)
Harris	10	0	43	3	(1nb 1w)
Latham	3	0	13	0	
Patel	9	0	32	0	

New Zealand innings (target: 207 runs from 50 overs)			R	B	4	6
JG Wright		c & b Kalpage	57	76	9	0
RT Latham		b Kalpage	20	41	3	0
AH Jones	c Jayasuriya	b Gurusinha	49	77	4	0
*MD Crowe	c Ramanayake	b Wickramasinghe	5	23	0	0
KR Rutherford	not out		65	71	6	1
CZ Harris	not out		5	5	0	0
Extras	(lb 3, w 3, nb 3)		9			
Total	(4 wickets, 48.2 overs)		210			

DNB: +IDS Smith, DN Patel, DK Morrison, GR Larsen, W Watson.
Fall of wickets: 1-77 (Latham), 2-91 (Wright), 3-105 (Crowe), 4-186 (Jones).

Bowling	O	M	R	W	
Ramanayake	9.2	0	46	0	(2nb 2w)
Wickramasinghe	8	1	40	1	(1w)
Anurasiri	10	1	27	0	
Kalpage	10	0	33	2	
Gurusinha	4	0	19	1	
Ranatunga	4	0	22	0	
Jayasuriya	2	0	14	0	
de Silva	1	0	6	0	(1w)

Australia v South Africa

At Sydney Cricket Ground (day/night), 26 February 1992 (50-overs)
Result: South Africa won by 9 wickets. Points: South Africa 2, Australia 0.
Toss: Australia. Umpires: BL Aldridge (NZ) and SA Bucknor (WI).
World Cup Referee: EF Wykes. Man of the Match: KC Wessels.

Australia innings (49 overs maximum)			R	B	4	6
GR Marsh	c Richardson	b Kuiper	25	72	1	0
DC Boon	run out (Snell/Cronje)		27	32	4	0
DM Jones	c Richardson	b McMillan	24	51	1	0
*AR Border		b Kuiper	0	1	0	0
TM Moody	lbw	b Donald	10	33	0	0
SR Waugh	c Cronje	b McMillan	27	51	1	0
+IA Healy	c McMillan	b Donald	16	24	2	0
PL Taylor		b Donald	4	9	0	0
CJ McDermott	run out (Rhodes/Snell)		6	12	0	0
MR Whitney	not out		9	15	1	0
BA Reid	not out		5	10	0	0
Extras	(lb 2, w 11, nb 4)		17			
Total	(9 wickets, 49 overs, 215 mins)		170			

Fall of wickets: 1-42 (Boon), 2-76 (Marsh), 3-76 (Border), 4-97 (Jones), 5-108 (Moody), 6-143 (Healy), 7-146 (Waugh), 8-156 (Taylor), 9-161 (McDermott).
NB: IA Healy used a runner (DM Jones) after pulling a hamstring at 118/5.

Bowling	O	M	R	W	
Donald	10	0	34	3	(5w)
Pringle	10	0	52	0	(1w, 2nb)
Snell	9	1	15	0	
McMillan	10	0	35	2	(3w, 2nb)
Kuiper	5	0	15	2	(1w)
Cronje	5	1	17	0	(1w)

South Africa innings (target: 171 runs from 49 overs)			R	B	4	6
*KC Wessels	not out		81	148	9	0
AC Hudson		b Taylor	28	52	3	0
PN Kirsten	not out		49	88	1	0
Extras	(lb 5, w 6, nb 2)		13			
Total	(1 wicket, 46.5 overs, 173 mins)		171			

DNB: WJ Cronje, AP Kuiper, JN Rhodes, BM McMillan, +DJ Richardson, RP Snell, MW Pringle, AA Donald.
Fall of wickets: 1-74 (Hudson).
NB: DC Boon kept wicket throughout the South African innings.

Bowling	O	M	R	W	
McDermott	10	1	23	0	(2nb)
Reid	8.5	0	41	0	(4w)
Whitney	6	0	26	0	
Waugh	4	1	16	0	(1w)
Taylor	10	1	32	1	(1w)
Border	4	0	13	0	
Moody	4	0	15	0	

Pakistan v Zimbabwe

At Bellerive Oval, Hobart, 27 February 1992 (50-overs)
Result: Pakistan won by 53 runs. Points: Pakistan 2, Zimbabwe 0.
Toss: Zimbabwe. Umpires: DP Buultjens (SL) and SG Randell.
World Cup Referee: DW Rogers. Man of the Match: Aamer Sohail.

Pakistan innings (50 overs maximum)			R	B	4	6
Rameez Raja	c Flower	b Jarvis	9	16	1	0
Aamer Sohail	c Pycroft	b Butchart	114	136	12	0
Inzamam-ul-Haq	c Brandes	b Butchart	14	43	0	0
Javed Miandad	lbw	b Butchart	89	94	5	0
Saleem Malik	not out		14	12	0	0
Wasim Akram	not out		1	1	0	0
Extras	(lb 9, nb 4)		13			
Total	(4 wickets, 50 overs)		254			

DNB: *Imran Khan, Mushtaq Ahmed, Iqbal Sikander, +Moin Khan, Aaqib Javed.
Fall of wickets: 1-29 (Rameez Raja), 2-63 (Inzamam-ul-Haq), 3-208 (Aamer Sohail), 4-253 (Javed Miandad).

Bowling	O	M	R	W	
Brandes	10	1	49	0	(4nb)
Jarvis	10	1	52	1	
Omarshah	10	1	24	0	
Butchart	10	0	57	3	
Traicos	10	0	63	0	

Zimbabwe innings (target: 255 runs from 50 overs)			R	B	4	6
KJ Arnott	c Wasim Akram	b Iqbal Sikander	7	61	0	0
+A Flower	c Inzamam-ul-Haq	b Wasim Akram	6	21	0	0
AJ Pycroft		b Wasim Akram	0	4	0	0
*DL Houghton	c Rameez Raja	b Aamer Sohail	44	82	3	0
AH Omarshah		b Aamer Sohail	33	58	2	0
AC Waller		b Wasim Akram	44	36	3	1
IP Butchart	c Javed Miandad	b Aaqib Javed	33	27	4	0
EA Brandes	not out		2	3	0	0
AJ Traicos	not out		8	7	0	0
Extras	(b 3, lb 15, w 6)		24			
Total	(7 wickets, 50 overs)		201			

DNB: WR James, MP Jarvis.
Fall of wickets: 1-14 (Flower), 2-14 (Pycroft), 3-33 (Arnott), 4-103 (Omarshah), 5-108 (Houghton), 6-187 (Butchart), 7-190 (Waller).

Bowling	O	M	R	W	
Wasim Akram	10	2	21	3	(3w)
Aaqib Javed	10	1	49	1	(1w)
Iqbal Sikander	10	1	35	1	(1w)
Mushtaq Ahmed	10	1	34	0	
Aamer Sohail	6	1	26	2	
Saleem Malik	4	0	18	0	(1w)

England v West Indies

At Melbourne Cricket Ground (day/night), 27 February 1992 (50-overs)
Result: England won by 6 wickets. Points: England 2, West Indies 0.
Toss: England. Umpires: KE Liebenberg (SA) and SJ Woodward (NZ).
World Cup Referee: JW Mann. Man of the Match: CC Lewis.

West Indies innings (50 overs maximum)			R	B	4	6
DL Haynes	c Fairbrother	b DeFreitas	38	68	5	0
BC Lara	c Stewart	b Lewis	0	2	0	0
*RB Richardson	c Botham	b Lewis	5	17	1	0
CL Hooper	c Reeve	b Botham	5	20	0	0
KLT Arthurton	c Fairbrother	b DeFreitas	54	101	2	2
AL Logie	run out		20	27	0	1
RA Harper	c Hick	b Reeve	3	14	0	0
MD Marshall	run out		3	8	0	0
+D Williams	c Pringle	b DeFreitas	6	19	0	0
CEL Ambrose	c DeFreitas	b Lewis	4	6	0	0
WKM Benjamin	not out		11	15	1	0
Extras	(lb 4, w 3, nb 1)		8			
Total	(all out, 49.2 overs)		157			

Fall of wickets: 1-0 (Lara), 2-22 (Richardson), 3-36 (Hooper), 4-55 (Haynes), 5-91 (Logie), 6-102 (Harper), 7-116 (Marshall), 8-131 (Williams), 9-145 (Arthurton), 10-157 (Ambrose).

Bowling	O	M	R	W	
Pringle	7	3	16	0	
Lewis	8.2	1	30	3	(1nb)
DeFreitas	9	2	34	3	(2w)
Botham	10	0	30	1	
Reeve	10	1	23	1	(1w)
Tufnell	5	0	20	0	

England innings (target: 158 runs from 50 overs)			R	B	4	6
*GA Gooch	st Williams	b Hooper	65	101	7	0
IT Botham	c Williams	b Benjamin	8	28	0	0
RA Smith	c Logie	b Benjamin	8	28	1	0
GA Hick		c & b Harper	54	55	3	1
NH Fairbrother	not out		13	28	1	0
+AJ Stewart	not out		0	1	0	0
Extras	(lb 7, w 4, nb 1)		12			
Total	(4 wickets, 39.5 overs)		160			

DNB: DA Reeve, CC Lewis, DR Pringle, PAJ DeFreitas, PCR Tufnell.
Fall of wickets: 1-50 (Botham), 2-71 (Smith), 3-126 (Gooch), 4-156 (Hick).

Bowling	O	M	R	W	
Ambrose	8	1	26	0	
Marshall	8	0	37	0	(2w)
Benjamin	9.5	2	22	2	(1nb 2w)
Hooper	10	1	38	1	
Harper	4	0	30	1	

India v Sri Lanka

At Harrup Park, Mackay, 28 February 1992 (50-overs)
Result: No result. Points: India 1, Sri Lanka 1.
Toss: Sri Lanka. Umpires: ID Robinson (Zim) and DR Shepherd (Eng).
World Cup Referee: A Pettigrew.

India innings (20 overs maximum)		R	B	4	6
K Srikkanth	not out	1	2	0	0
N Kapil Dev	not out	0	0	0	0
Extras		0			
Total	(0 wickets, 0.2 overs)	1			

DNB: *M Azharuddin, SR Tendulkar, VG Kambli, PK Amre, A Jadeja, SLV Raju, M Prabhakar, +KS More, J Srinath.

Bowling	O	M	R	W
Ramanayake	0.2	0	1	0

Sri Lanka team:
RS Mahanama, UC Hathurusingha, AP Gurusinha, *PA de Silva, A Ranatunga, ST Jayasuriya, +HP Tillakaratne, RS Kalpage, CPH Ramanayake, KIW Wijegunawardene, GP Wickramasinghe.
NB: The match was initially reduced to 20 overs a side due to rain. A helicopter was used to dry the pitch but as play began rain fell again, washing out the game.

New Zealand v South Africa

At Eden Park, Auckland, 29 February 1992 (50-overs)
Result: New Zealand won by 7 wickets. Points: New Zealand 2, South Africa 0.
Toss: South Africa. Umpires: Khizer Hayat (Pak) and PD Reporter (Ind).
World Cup Referee: PD McDermott. Man of the Match: MJ Greatbatch.

South Africa innings (50 overs maximum)			R	B	4	6
*KC Wessels	c Smith	b Watson	3	18	0	0
AC Hudson		b Patel	1	16	0	0
PN Kirsten	c Cairns	b Watson	90	129	10	0
WJ Cronje	c Smith	b Harris	7	22	0	0
+DJ Richardson	c Larsen	b Cairns	28	53	1	0
AP Kuiper	run out		2	2	0	0
JN Rhodes	c Crowe	b Cairns	6	13	0	0
BM McMillan	not out		33	40	1	0
RP Snell	not out		11	8	1	0
Extras	(lb 8, nb 1)		9			
Total	(7 wickets, 50 overs)		190			

DNB: AA Donald, T Bosch.
Fall of wickets: 1-8 (Hudson), 2-10 (Wessels), 3-29 (Cronje), 4-108 (Richardson), 5-111 (Kuiper), 6-121 (Rhodes), 7-162 (Kirsten).

Bowling	O	M	R	W	
Watson	10	2	30	2	
Patel	10	1	28	1	
Larsen	10	1	29	0	
Harris	10	2	33	1	
Latham	2	0	19	0	
Cairns	8	0	43	2	(1nb)

New Zealand innings (target: 191 runs from 50 overs)			R	B	4	6
MJ Greatbatch		b Kirsten	68	60	9	2
RT Latham	c Wessels	b Snell	60	69	7	0
AH Jones	not out		34	63	4	0
+IDS Smith	c Kirsten	b Donald	19	8	4	0
*MD Crowe	not out		3	9	0	0
Extras	(b 1, w 5, nb 1)		7			
Total	(3 wickets, 34.3 overs)		191			

DNB: KR Rutherford, CZ Harris, CL Cairns, DN Patel, GR Larsen, W Watson.
Fall of wickets: 1-114 (Greatbatch), 2-155 (Latham), 3-179 (Smith).

Bowling	O	M	R	W	
Donald	10	0	38	1	(1nb 1w)
McMillan	5	1	23	0	(3w)
Snell	7	0	56	1	
Bosch	2.3	0	19	0	
Cronje	2	0	14	0	(1w)
Kuiper	1	0	18	0	
Kirsten	7	1	22	1	

West Indies v Zimbabwe

At Brisbane Cricket Ground, Woolloongabba, Brisbane, 29 February 1992 (50-overs)
Result: West Indies won by 75 runs. Points: West Indies 2, Zimbabwe 0.
Toss: Zimbabwe. Umpires: KE Liebenberg (SA) and SJ Woodward (NZ).
World Cup Referee: MW Johnson. Man of the Match: BC Lara.

West Indies innings (50 overs maximum)			R	B	4	6
PV Simmons		b Brandes	21	45	1	0
BC Lara	c Houghton	b Omarshah	72	71	12	0
*RB Richardson	c Brandes	b Jarvis	56	76	2	2
CL Hooper	c Pycroft	b Traicos	63	67	5	1
KLT Arthurton		b Duers	26	18	2	2
AL Logie	run out		5	6	0	0
MD Marshall	c Houghton	b Brandes	2	10	0	0
+D Williams	not out		8	6	1	0
WKM Benjamin		b Brandes	1	4	0	0
Extras	(b 1, lb 6, w 2, nb 1)		10			
Total	(8 wickets, 50 overs)		264			

DNB: AC Cummins, BP Patterson.
Fall of wickets: 1-78 (Simmons), 2-103 (Lara), 3-220 (Hooper), 4-221 (Richardson), 5-239 (Logie), 6-254 (Marshall), 7-255 (Arthurton), 8-264 (Benjamin).

Bowling	O	M	R	W	
Brandes	10	1	45	3	(1nb 2w)
Jarvis	10	1	71	1	
Duers	10	0	52	1	
Omarshah	10	2	39	1	
Traicos	10	0	50	1	

Zimbabwe innings (target: 265 runs from 50 overs)			R	B	4	6
KJ Arnott	retired hurt		16	36	1	0
+A Flower		b Patterson	6	20	0	0
AJ Pycroft	c Williams	b Benjamin	10	24	0	0
*DL Houghton	c Patterson	b Hooper	55	88	3	0
AC Waller	c Simmons	b Benjamin	9	9	0	0
ADR Campbell	c Richardson	b Hooper	1	18	0	0
AH Omarshah	not out		60	87	4	0
EA Brandes		c & b Benjamin	6	9	0	0
AJ Traicos	run out		8	19	0	0
MP Jarvis	not out		5	4	1	0
Extras	(lb 9, w 5, nb 8)		22			
Total	(7 wickets, 50 overs)		189			

DNB: KG Duers.
Fall of wickets: 1-21 (Flower), 2-43 (Pycroft), 3-48 (Waller), 4-63 (Campbell), 5-132 (Houghton), 6-161 (Brandes), 7-181 (Traicos). NB: KJ Arnott retired hurt at 43/2.

Bowling	O	M	R	W	
Patterson	10	0	25	1	(1w)
Marshall	6	0	23	0	(2nb)
Benjamin	10	2	27	3	(3nb 3w)
Cummins	10	0	33	0	(3nb 1w)
Hooper	10	0	47	2	
Arthurton	4	0	25	0	

Australia v India

At Brisbane Cricket Ground, Woolloongabba, Brisbane, 1 March 1992 (50-overs)
Result: Australia won by 1 run (revised target). Points: Australia 2, India 0.
Toss: Australia. Umpires: BL Aldridge (NZ) and ID Robinson (Zim).
World Cup Referee: MW Johnson. Man of the Match: DM Jones.

Australia innings (50 overs maximum)			R	B	4	6
MA Taylor	c More	b Kapil Dev	13	18	0	0
GR Marsh		b Kapil Dev	8	28	1	0
+DC Boon	c Shastri	b Raju	43	60	4	0
DM Jones		c & b Prabhakar	90	108	6	2
SR Waugh		b Srinath	29	48	1	0
TM Moody		b Prabhakar	25	23	3	0
*AR Border	c Jadeja	b Kapil Dev	10	10	0	0
CJ McDermott	c Jadeja	b Prabhakar	2	5	0	0
PL Taylor	run out		1	1	0	0
MG Hughes	not out		0	4	0	0
Extras	(lb 7, w 5, nb 4)		16			
Total	(9 wickets, 50 overs)		237			

DNB: MR Whitney.
Fall of wickets: 1-18 (MA Taylor), 2-31 (Marsh), 3-102 (Boon), 4-156 (Waugh), 5-198 (Moody), 6-230 (Jones), 7-235 (McDermott), 8-236 (Border), 9-237 (PL Taylor).

Bowling	O	M	R	W	
Kapil Dev	10	2	41	3	(1nb 1w)
Prabhakar	10	0	41	3	(1nb 2w)
Srinath	8	0	48	1	(2nb 1w)
Tendulkar	5	0	29	0	(1w)
Raju	10	0	37	1	
Jadeja	7	0	34	0	

India innings (target: 236 runs from 47 overs)			R	B	4	6
RJ Shastri	c Waugh	b Moody	25	67	1	0
K Srikkanth		b McDermott	0	10	0	0
*M Azharuddin	run out		93	103	10	0
SR Tendulkar	c Waugh	b Moody	11	19	1	0
N Kapil Dev	lbw	b Waugh	21	21	3	0
SV Manjrekar	run out		47	42	3	1
A Jadeja		b Hughes	1	4	0	0
+KS More		b Moody	14	8	2	0
J Srinath	not out		8	8	0	0
M Prabhakar	run out		1	1	0	0
SLV Raju	run out		0	0	0	0
Extras	(lb 8, w 5)		13			
Total	(all out, 47 overs)		234			

Fall of wickets: 1-6 (Srikkanth), 2-53 (Shastri), 3-86 (Tendulkar), 4-128 (Kapil Dev), 5-194 (Azharuddin), 6-199 (Jadeja), 7-216 (Manjrekar), 8-231 (More), 9-232 (Prabhakar), 10-234 (Raju).

Bowling	O	M	R	W
McDermott	9	1	35	1
Whitney	10	2	36	0
Hughes	9	1	49	1
Moody	9	0	56	3
Waugh	10	0	50	1

NB: India were 45/1 off 16.2 overs when rain interrupted play. Target recalculated to 236 off 47 overs.

England v Pakistan

At Adelaide Oval, 1 March 1992 (50-overs)
Result: No result. Points: England 1, Pakistan 1.
Toss: England. Umpires: SA Bucknor (WI) and PJ McConnell.
World Cup Referee: B Gibbs. Man of the Match: No award.

Pakistan innings (50 overs maximum)			R	B	4	6
Rameez Raja	c Reeve	b DeFreitas	1	10	0	0
Aamer Sohail		c & b Pringle	9	39	0	0
Inzamam-ul-Haq	c Stewart	b DeFreitas	0	10	0	0
*Javed Miandad		b Pringle	3	22	0	0
Saleem Malik	c Reeve	b Botham	17	20	3	0
Ijaz Ahmed	c Stewart	b Small	0	15	0	0
Wasim Akram		b Botham	1	13	0	0
+Moin Khan	c Hick	b Small	2	14	0	0
Wasim Haider	c Stewart	b Reeve	13	46	1	0
Mushtaq Ahmed	c Reeve	b Pringle	17	42	1	0
Aaqib Javed	not out		1	21	0	0
Extras	(lb 1, w 8, nb 1)		10			
Total	(all out, 40.2 overs)		74			

Fall of wickets: 1-5 (Rameez Raja), 2-5 (Inzamam-ul-Haq), 3-14 (Javed Miandad), 4-20 (Aamer Sohail), 5-32 (Ijaz Ahmed), 6-35 (Wasim Akram), 7-42 (Saleem Malik), 8-47 (Moin Khan), 9-62 (Wasim Haider), 10-74 (Mushtaq Ahmed).

Bowling	O	M	R	W	
Pringle	8.2	5	8	3	(1nb)
DeFreitas	7	1	22	2	(7w)
Small	10	1	29	2	(1w)
Botham	10	4	12	2	
Reeve	5	3	2	1	

England innings (target: 64 runs from 16 overs)			R	B	4	6
*GA Gooch	c Moin Khan	b Wasim Akram	3	14	0	0
IT Botham	not out		6	22	0	0
RA Smith	not out		5	13	1	0
Extras	(b 1, lb 3, w 5, nb 1)		10			
Total	(1 wicket, 8 overs)		24			

DNB: GA Hick, NH Fairbrother, +AJ Stewart, CC Lewis, DA Reeve, DR Pringle, PAJ DeFreitas, GC Small.
Fall of wickets: 1-14 (Gooch).

Bowling	O	M	R	W	
Wasim Akram	3	0	7	1	(1nb 3w)
Aaqib Javed	3	1	7	0	(2w)
Wasim Haider	1	0	1	0	
Ijaz Ahmed	1	0	5	0	

South Africa v Sri Lanka

At Basin Reserve, Wellington, 2 March 1992 (50-overs)
Result: Sri Lanka won by 3 wickets. Points: Sri Lanka 2, South Africa 0.
Toss: Sri Lanka. Umpires: Khizer Hayat (Pak) and SJ Woodward.
World Cup Referee: AR Isaac. Man of the Match: A Ranatunga.

South Africa innings (50 overs maximum)			R	B	4	6
*KC Wessels		c & b Ranatunga	40	94	0	0
AP Kuiper		b Anurasiri	18	44	3	0
PN Kirsten	c Hathurusingha	b Kalpage	47	81	5	1
JN Rhodes	c Jayasuriya	b Wickramasinghe	28	21	2	0
MW Rushmere	c Jayasuriya	b Ranatunga	4	9	0	0
WJ Cronje	st Tillakaratne	b Anurasiri	3	6	0	0
RP Snell		b Anurasiri	9	5	2	0
BM McMillan	not out		18	22	1	0
+DJ Richardson	run out		0	0	0	0
O Henry	c Kalpage	b Ramanayake	11	13	1	0
AA Donald	run out		3	6	0	0
Extras	(lb 9, w 4, nb 1)		14			
Total	(all out, 50 overs)		195			

Fall of wickets: 1-27 (Kuiper), 2-114 (Kirsten), 3-114 (Wessels), 4-128 (Rushmere), 5-149 (Cronje), 6-153 (Rhodes), 7-165 (Snell), 8-165 (Richardson), 9-186 (Henry), 10-195 (Donald).

Bowling	O	M	R	W
Ramanayake	9	2	19	1
Wickramasinghe	7	0	32	1
Anurasiri	10	1	41	3
Kalpage	10	0	38	1
Gurusinha	8	0	30	0
Ranatunga	6	0	26	2

Sri Lanka innings (target: 196 runs from 50 overs)			R	B	4	6
RS Mahanama	c Richardson	b McMillan	68	121	6	0
UC Hathurusingha	c Wessels	b Donald	5	9	1	0
AP Gurusinha	lbw	b Donald	0	4	0	0
*PA de Silva		b Donald	7	16	1	0
+HP Tillakaratne	c Rushmere	b Henry	17	63	0	0
A Ranatunga	not out		64	73	6	0
ST Jayasuriya	st Richardson	b Kirsten	3	7	0	0
RS Kalpage	run out		5	11	0	0
CPH Ramanayake	not out		4	2	1	0
Extras	(b 1, lb 7, w 13, nb 4)		25			
Total	(7 wickets, 49.5 overs)		198			

DNB: SD Anurasiri, GP Wickramasinghe.
Fall of wickets: 1-11 (Hathurusingha), 2-12 (Gurusinha), 3-35 (de Silva), 4-87 (Tillakaratne), 5-154 (Mahanama), 6-168 (Jayasuriya), 7-189 (Kalpage).

Bowling	O	M	R	W	
McMillan	10	2	34	1	(3nb)
Donald	9.5	0	42	3	(9w)
Snell	10	1	33	0	(2w)
Henry	10	0	31	1	(1nb 2w)
Kuiper	5	0	25	0	
Kirsten	5	0	25	1	

New Zealand v Zimbabwe

At McLean Park, Napier, 3 March 1992 (50-overs)
Result: New Zealand won by 48 runs (revised target).
Points: New Zealand 2, Zimbabwe 0.
Toss: Zimbabwe. Umpires: DP Buultjens (SL) and KE Liebenberg (SA).
World Cup Referee: PW Moody. Man of the Match: MD Crowe.

New Zealand innings (20.5 overs maximum)			R	B	4	6
MJ Greatbatch		b Duers	15	16	2	0
RT Latham		b Brandes	2	6	0	0
AH Jones	c Waller	b Butchart	57	58	9	0
*MD Crowe	not out		74	44	8	2
CL Cairns	not out		1	2	0	0
Extras	(b 6, lb 7)		13			
Total	(3 wickets, 20.5 overs)		162			

DNB: KR Rutherford, CZ Harris, +IDS Smith, DN Patel, DK Morrison, GR Larsen.
Fall of wickets: 1-9 (Latham), 2-25 (Greatbatch), 3-154 (Jones).

Bowling	O	M	R	W
Brandes	5	1	28	1
Duers	6	0	17	1
Omarshah	4	0	34	0
Butchart	4	0	53	1
Burmester	1.5	0	17	0

Zimbabwe innings (target: 154 runs from 18 overs)			R	B	4	6
+A Flower		b Larsen	30	27	5	0
AC Waller		b Morrison	11	11	1	1
*DL Houghton		b Larsen	10	14	2	0
IP Butchart	c Cairns	b Larsen	3	7	0	0
EA Brandes		b Harris	6	8	0	0
AJ Pycroft	not out		13	20	0	0
ADR Campbell	c Crowe	b Harris	8	9	1	0
AH Omarshah		b Harris	7	8	1	0
MG Burmester	not out		4	8	0	0
Extras	(lb 9, w 3, nb 1)		13			
Total	(7 wickets, 18 overs)		105			

DNB: AJ Traicos, KG Duers.
Fall of wickets: 1-21 (Waller), 2-41 (Houghton), 3-63 (Flower), 4-63 (Butchart), 5-75 (Brandes), 6-86 (Campbell), 7-97 (Omarshah).

Bowling	O	M	R	W
Morrison	4	0	14	1 (1nb 2w)
Cairns	2	0	27	0
Larsen	4	0	16	3
Harris	4	0	15	3 (1w)
Latham	3	0	18	0
Crowe	1	0	6	0

NB: Rain stopped play during the NZ innings three times and, according to the rules, Zimbabwe were set a target of 154 to within 18 overs.

India v Pakistan
At Sydney Cricket Ground (day/night), 4 March 1992 (50-overs)
Result: India won by 43 runs. Points: India 2, Pakistan 0.
Toss: India. Umpires: PJ McConnell and DR Shepherd (Eng).
World Cup Referee: EF Wykes. Man of the Match: SR Tendulkar.

India innings (49 overs maximum)			R	B	4	6
A Jadeja	c Zahid Fazal	b Wasim Haider	46	81	2	0
K Srikkanth	c Moin Khan	b Aaqib Javed	5	40	0	0
*M Azharuddin	c Moin Khan	b Mushtaq Ahmed	32	51	4	0
VG Kambli	c Inzamam-ul-Haq	b Mushtaq Ahmed	24	42	0	0
SR Tendulkar	not out		54	62	3	0
SV Manjrekar		b Mushtaq Ahmed	0	1	0	0
N Kapil Dev	c Imran Khan	b Aaqib Javed	35	26	2	1
+KS More	run out		4	4	0	0
M Prabhakar	not out		2	1	0	0
Extras	(lb 3, w 9, nb 2)		14			
Total	(7 wickets, 49 overs)		216			

DNB: J Srinath, SLV Raju.
Fall of wickets: 1-25 (Srikkanth), 2-86 (Azharuddin), 3-101 (Jadeja), 4-147 (Kambli), 5-148 (Manjrekar), 6-208 (Kapil Dev), 7-213 (More).

Bowling	O	M	R	W
Wasim Akram	10	0	45	0
Aaqib Javed	8	2	28	2
Imran Khan	8	0	25	0
Wasim Haider	10	1	36	1
Mushtaq Ahmed	10	0	59	3
Aamer Sohail	3	0	20	0

Pakistan innings (target: 217 runs from 49 overs)			R	B	4	6
Aamer Sohail	c Srikkanth	b Tendulkar	62	103	6	0
Inzamam-ul-Haq	lbw	b Kapil Dev	2	7	0	0
Zahid Fazal	c More	b Prabhakar	2	10	0	0
Javed Miandad		b Srinath	40	113	2	0
Saleem Malik	c More	b Prabhakar	12	9	2	0
*Imran Khan	run out		0	5	0	0
Wasim Akram	st More	b Raju	4	8	0	0
Wasim Haider		b Srinath	13	25	0	0
+Moin Khan	c Manjrekar	b Kapil Dev	12	12	1	0
Mushtaq Ahmed	run out		3	4	0	0
Aaqib Javed	not out		1	12	0	0
Extras	(lb 6, w 15, nb 1)		22			
Total	(all out, 48.1 overs)		173			

Fall of wickets: 1-8 (Inzamam-ul-Haq), 2-17 (Zahid Fazal), 3-105 (Aamer Sohail), 4-127 (Saleem Malik), 5-130 (Imran Khan), 6-141 (Wasim Akram), 7-141 (Javed Miandad), 8-161 (Moin Khan), 9-166 (Mushtaq Ahmed), 10-173 (Wasim Haider).

Bowling	O	M	R	W
Kapil Dev	10	0	30	2
Prabhakar	10	1	22	2
Srinath	8.1	0	37	2
Tendulkar	10	0	37	1
Raju	10	1	41	1

South Africa v West Indies
At Lancaster Park, Christchurch, 5 March 1992 (50-overs)
Result: South Africa won by 64 runs. Points: South Africa 2, West Indies 0.
Toss: West Indies. Umpires: BL Aldridge and SG Randell (Aus).
World Cup Referee: CL Bull. Man of the Match: MW Pringle.

South Africa innings (50 overs maximum)			R	B	4	6
AC Hudson	c Lara	b Cummins	22	60	3	0
*KC Wessels	c Haynes	b Marshall	1	9	0	0
PN Kirsten	c Williams	b Marshall	56	91	2	0
MW Rushmere	st Williams	b Hooper	10	24	0	0
AP Kuiper		b Ambrose	23	29	0	1
JN Rhodes	c Williams	b Cummins	22	27	0	0
BM McMillan	c Lara	b Benjamin	20	29	2	0
+DJ Richardson	not out		20	26	1	0
RP Snell	c Haynes	b Ambrose	3	6	0	0
MW Pringle	not out		5	6	0	0
Extras	(lb 8, w 3, nb 7)		18			
Total	(8 wickets, 50 overs)		200			

DNB: AA Donald.
Fall of wickets: 1-8 (Wessels), 2-52 (Hudson), 3-73 (Rushmere), 4-118 (Kuiper), 5-127 (Kirsten), 6-159 (Rhodes), 7-181 (McMillan), 8-187 (Snell).

Bowling	O	M	R	W
Ambrose	10	1	34	2 (3nb)
Marshall	10	1	26	2
Hooper	10	0	45	1 (2w)
Cummins	10	0	40	2 (4nb)
Benjamin	10	0	47	1 (1w)

West Indies innings (target: 201 runs from 50 overs)			R	B	4	6
DL Haynes	c Richardson	b Kuiper	30	83	3	0
BC Lara	c Rhodes	b Pringle	9	13	2	0
*RB Richardson	lbw	b Pringle	1	3	0	0
CL Hooper	c Wessels	b Pringle	0	4	0	0
KLT Arthurton	c Wessels	b Pringle	0	4	0	0
AL Logie	c Pringle	b Kuiper	61	69	9	1
MD Marshall	c Rhodes	b Snell	6	10	1	0
+D Williams	c Richardson	b Snell	0	3	0	0
CEL Ambrose	run out		12	15	2	0
AC Cummins	c McMillan	b Donald	6	24	0	0
WKM Benjamin	not out		1	4	0	0
Extras	(lb 9, w 1)		10			
Total	(all out, 38.4 overs)		136			

Fall of wickets: 1-10 (Lara), 2-19 (Richardson), 3-19 (Hooper), 4-19 (Arthurton), 5-70 (Marshall), 6-70 (Williams), 7-116 (Haynes), 8-117 (Logie), 9-132 (Ambrose), 10-136 (Cummins). NB: DL Haynes retired hurt on 13* from 50/4 to 70/6.

Bowling	O	M	R	W
Donald	6.4	2	13	1 (1w)
Pringle	8	4	11	4
Snell	7	2	16	2
McMillan	8	2	36	0
Kuiper	9	0	51	2

Australia v England
At Sydney Cricket Ground (day/night), 5 March 1992 (50-overs)
Result: England won by 8 wickets. Points: England 2, Australia 0.
Toss: Australia. Umpires: SA Bucknor (WI) and Khizer Hayat (Pak).
World Cup Referee: EF Wykes. Man of the Match: IT Botham.

Australia innings (50 overs maximum)			R	B	4	6
TM Moody		b Tufnell	51	88	3	0
MA Taylor	lbw	b Pringle	0	11	0	0
DC Boon	run out		18	27	2	0
DM Jones	c Lewis	b DeFreitas	22	49	2	0
SR Waugh	run out		27	43	2	0
*AR Border		b Botham	16	22	1	0
+IA Healy	c Fairbrother	b Botham	9	7	0	1
PL Taylor	lbw	b Botham	0	2	0	0
CJ McDermott	c DeFreitas	b Botham	0	2	0	0
MR Whitney	not out		8	27	1	0
BA Reid		b Reeve	1	21	0	0
Extras	(b 2, lb 8, w 5, nb 4)		19			
Total	(all out, 49 overs)		171			

Fall of wickets: 1-5 (MA Taylor), 2-35 (Boon), 3-106 (Jones), 4-114 (Moody), 5-145 (Border), 6-155 (Healy), 7-155 (PL Taylor), 8-155 (McDermott), 9-164 (Waugh), 10-171 (Reid).

Bowling	O	M	R	W
Pringle	9	1	24	1 (3nb 1w)
Lewis	10	2	28	0 (2w)
DeFreitas	10	3	23	1 (1w)
Botham	10	1	31	4 (1w)
Tufnell	9	0	52	1 (1nb)
Reeve	1	0	3	1

England innings (target: 172 runs from 50 overs)			R	B	4	6
*GA Gooch		b Waugh	58	112	7	0
IT Botham	c Healy	b Whitney	53	77	6	0
RA Smith	not out		30	58	5	0
GA Hick	not out		7	5	1	0
Extras	(lb 13, w 8, nb 4)		25			
Total	(2 wickets, 40.5 overs)		173			

DNB: NH Fairbrother, +AJ Stewart, CC Lewis, DA Reeve, DR Pringle, PAJ DeFreitas, PCR Tufnell.
Fall of wickets: 1-107 (Botham), 2-153 (Gooch).

Bowling	O	M	R	W
McDermott	10	1	29	0 (1nb 3w)
Reid	7.5	0	49	0 (5nb 2w)
Whitney	10	2	28	1 (1w)
Waugh	6	0	29	1 (2w)
PL Taylor	3	0	7	0
Moody	4	0	18	0

India v Zimbabwe
At Trust Bank Park, Hamilton, 7 March 1992 (50-overs)
Result: India won by 55 runs (revised target). Points: India 2, Zimbabwe 0.
Toss: India. Umpires: DP Buultjens (SL) and SG Randell (Aus).
World Cup Referee: BJ Paterson. Man of the Match: SR Tendulkar.

India innings (32 overs maximum)			R	B	4	6
K Srikkanth		b Burmester	32	32	5	0
N Kapil Dev	lbw	b Brandes	10	14	0	1
*M Azharuddin	c Flower	b Burmester	12	15	2	0
SR Tendulkar	c Campbell	b Burmester	81	77	8	1
SV Manjrekar	c Duers	b Traicos	34	34	2	0
VG Kambli		b Traicos	1	2	0	0
A Jadeja	c Omarshah	b Traicos	6	6	0	0
+KS More	not out		15	8	0	1
J Srinath	not out		6	4	1	0
Extras	(lb 3, w 3)		6			
Total	(7 wickets, 32 overs)		203			

DNB: M Prabhakar, SLV Raju.
Fall of wickets: 1-23 (Kapil Dev), 2-43 (Azharuddin), 3-69 (Srikkanth), 4-168 (Manjrekar), 5-170 (Kambli), 6-182 (Jadeja), 7-184 (Tendulkar).

Bowling	O	M	R	W	
Brandes	7	0	43	1	
Duers	7	0	48	0	
Burmester	6	0	36	3	(3w)
Omarshah	6	1	38	0	
Traicos	6	0	35	3	

Zimbabwe innings (target: 159 runs from 19 overs)			R	B	4	6
AH Omarshah		b Tendulkar	31	51	3	0
+A Flower	not out		43	56	3	0
AC Waller	not out		13	7	2	0
Extras	(b 1, lb 11, w 5)		17			
Total	(1 wicket, 19.1 overs)		104			

DNB: AJ Pycroft, *DL Houghton, ADR Campbell, IP Butchart, EA Brandes, MG Burmester, AJ Traicos, KG Duers.
Fall of wickets: 1-79 (Omarshah).

Bowling	O	M	R	W	
Kapil Dev	4	0	6	0	(2w)
Prabhakar	3	0	14	0	(1w)
Srinath	4	0	20	0	(1w)
Tendulkar	6	0	35	1	(1w)
Raju	2.1	0	17	0	

NB: After rain forced the early close of the Zimbabwe innings, their target was recalculated to 159 runs in the 19 overs. After 19 overs, Zimbabwe were 103.

Australia v Sri Lanka
At Adelaide Oval, 7 March 1992 (50-overs)
Result: Australia won by 7 wickets. Points: Australia 2, Sri Lanka 0.
Toss: Australia. Umpires: PD Reporter (Ind) and ID Robinson (Zim).
World Cup Referee: B Gibbs. Man of the Match: TM Moody.

Sri Lanka innings (50 overs maximum)			R	B	4	6
RS Mahanama	run out		7	10	1	0
MAR Samarasekera	c Healy	b Taylor	34	63	3	0
AP Gurusinha	lbw	b Whitney	5	23	1	0
*PA de Silva	c Moody	b McDermott	62	83	2	0
A Ranatunga	c Jones	b Taylor	23	52	0	0
ST Jayasuriya	lbw	b Border	15	29	1	0
+HP Tillakaratne	run out		5	13	0	0
RS Kalpage	run out		14	15	1	0
CPH Ramanayake	run out		5	10	0	0
SD Anurasiri	not out		4	4	0	0
Extras	(b 3, lb 6, w 5, nb 1)		15			
Total	(9 wickets, 50 overs)		189			

DNB: GP Wickramasinghe.
Fall of wickets: 1-8 (Mahanama), 2-28 (Gurusinha), 3-72 (Samarasekera), 4-123 (Ranatunga), 5-151 (Jayasuriya), 6-163 (de Silva), 7-166 (Tillakaratne), 8-182 (Ramanayake), 9-189 (Kalpage).

Bowling	O	M	R	W	
McDermott	10	0	28	1	(1w)
SR Waugh	7	0	34	0	(1nb 4w)
Whitney	10	3	26	1	
Moody	3	0	18	0	
Taylor	10	0	34	2	
Border	10	0	40	1	

Australia innings (target: 190 runs from 50 overs)			R	B	4	6
TM Moody	c Mahanama	b Wickramasinghe	57	86	4	0
GR Marsh	c Anurasiri	b Kalpage	60	113	3	1
ME Waugh	c Mahanama	b Wickramasinghe	26	37	1	0
DC Boon	not out		27	26	0	2
DM Jones	not out		12	8	0	1
Extras	(lb 2, w 3, nb 3)		8			
Total	(3 wickets, 44 overs)		190			

DNB: SR Waugh, *AR Border, +IA Healy, PL Taylor, CJ McDermott, MR Whitney.
Fall of wickets: 1-120 (Moody), 2-130 (Marsh), 3-165 (ME Waugh).

Bowling	O	M	R	W	
Wickramasinghe	10	3	29	2	(1nb 1w)
Ramanayake	9	1	44	0	(2nb 2w)
Anurasiri	10	0	43	0	
Gurusinha	6	0	20	0	
Kalpage	8	0	41	1	
Ranatunga	1	0	11	0	

New Zealand v West Indies
At Eden Park, Auckland, 8 March 1992 (50-overs)
Result: New Zealand won by 5 wickets. Points: New Zealand 2, West Indies 0.
Toss: New Zealand. Umpires: KE Liebenberg (SA) and PJ McConnell (Aus).
World Cup Referee: PD McDermott. Man of the Match: MD Crowe.

West Indies innings (50 overs maximum)			R	B	4	6
DL Haynes	c & b Harris		22	61	0	1
BC Lara	c Rutherford	b Larsen	52	81	0	0
*RB Richardson	c Smith	b Watson	29	54	1	0
CL Hooper	c Greatbatch	b Patel	2	9	0	0
KLT Arthurton		b Morrison	40	54	3	0
AL Logie		b Harris	3	4	0	0
MD Marshall		b Larsen	5	14	0	0
+D Williams	not out		32	24	5	0
WKM Benjamin	not out		2	1	0	0
Extras	(lb 8, w 7, nb 1)		16			
Total	(7 wickets, 50 overs)		203			

DNB: CEL Ambrose, AC Cummins.
Fall of wickets: 1-65 (Haynes), 2-95 (Lara), 3-100 (Hooper), 4-136 (Richardson), 5-142 (Logie), 6-156 (Marshall), 7-201 (Arthurton).

Bowling	O	M	R	W	
Morrison	9	1	33	1	(1nb 2w)
Patel	10	2	19	1	(1w)
Watson	10	2	56	1	
Larsen	10	0	41	2	
Harris	10	2	32	2	
Latham	1	0	14	0	(4w)

New Zealand innings (target: 204 runs from 50 overs)			R	B	4	6
MJ Greatbatch	c Haynes	b Benjamin	63	77	7	3
RT Latham	c Williams	b Cummins	14	27	1	0
AH Jones	c Williams	b Benjamin	10	35	0	0
*MD Crowe	not out		81	81	12	0
KR Rutherford	c Williams	b Ambrose	8	32	1	0
CZ Harris	c Williams	b Cummins	7	23	0	0
DN Patel	not out		10	18	0	0
Extras	(lb 7, w 5, nb 1)		13			
Total	(5 wickets, 48.3 overs)		206			

DNB: +IDS Smith, DK Morrison, GR Larsen, W Watson.
Fall of wickets: 1-67 (Latham), 2-97 (Jones), 3-100 (Greatbatch), 4-135 (Rutherford), 5-174 (Harris).

Bowling	O	M	R	W	
Ambrose	10	1	41	1	(3w)
Marshall	9	1	35	0	(1nb 1w)
Cummins	10	0	53	2	(1w)
Benjamin	9.3	3	34	2	
Hooper	10	0	36	0	

Pakistan v South Africa
At Brisbane Cricket Ground, Woolloongabba, Brisbane, 8 March 1992 (50-overs)
Result: South Africa won by 20 runs (revised target).
Points: South Africa 2, Pakistan 0.
Toss: Pakistan. Umpires: BL Aldridge (NZ) and SA Bucknor (WI).
World Cup Referee: MW Johnson. Man of the Match: AC Hudson.

South Africa innings (50 overs maximum)			R	B	4	6
AC Hudson	c Ijaz Ahmed	b Imran Khan	54	81	8	0
*KC Wessels	c Moin Khan	b Aaqib Javed	7	26	0	0
MW Rushmere	c Aamer Sohail	b Mushtaq Ahmed	35	70	2	0
AP Kuiper	c Moin Khan	b Imran Khan	5	12	0	0
JN Rhodes	lbw	b Iqbal Sikander	5	17	0	0
WJ Cronje	not out		47	53	4	0
BM McMillan		b Wasim Akram	33	44	1	0
+DJ Richardson		b Wasim Akram	5	10	0	0
RP Snell	not out		1	1	0	0
Extras	(lb 8, w 9, nb 2)		19			
Total	(7 wickets, 50 overs)		211			

DNB: MW Pringle, AA Donald.
Fall of wickets: 1-31 (Wessels), 2-98 (Hudson), 3-110 (Kuiper), 4-111 (Rushmere), 5-127 (Rhodes), 6-198 (McMillan), 7-207 (Richardson).

Bowling	O	M	R	W	
Wasim Akram	10	0	42	2	(2nb 7w)
Aaqib Javed	7	1	36	1	(2w)
Imran Khan	10	0	34	2	
Iqbal Sikander	8	0	30	1	
Ijaz Ahmed	7	0	26	0	
Mushtaq Ahmed	8	1	35	1	

Pakistan innings (target: 194 runs from 36 overs)			R	B	4	6
Aamer Sohail		b Snell	23	53	2	0
Zahid Fazal	c Richardson	b McMillan	11	46	1	0
Inzamam-ul-Haq	run out		48	45.5		
*Imran Khan	c Richardson	b McMillan	34	53	5	0
Saleem Malik	c Donald	b Kuiper	12	11	0	0
Wasim Akram	c Snell	b Kuiper	9	8	1	0
Ijaz Ahmed	c Rhodes	b Kuiper	6	3	1	0
+Moin Khan	not out		5	5	0	0
Mushtaq Ahmed	run out		4	4	0	0
Iqbal Sikander	not out		1	3	0	0
Extras	(lb 2, w 17, nb 1)		20			
Total	(8 wickets, 36 overs)		173			

DNB: Aaqib Javed.
Fall of wickets: 1-50 (Aamer Sohail), 2-50 (Zahid Fazal), 3-135 (Inzamam-ul-Haq), 4-136 (Imran Khan), 5-156 (Saleem Malik), 6-157 (Wasim Akram), 7-163 (Ijaz Ahmed), 8-171 (Mushtaq Ahmed).

Bowling	O	M	R	W	
Donald	7	1	31	0	(7w)
Pringle	7	0	31	0	(1nb 3w)
Snell	8	2	26	1	(1w)
McMillan	7	0	34	2	(4w)
Kuiper	6	0	40	3	(2w)
Cronje	1	0	9	0	

NB: With Pakistan 74/2 in the 22nd over, rain halted the play and the target was revised to 194 in 36 overs.

England v Sri Lanka

At Eastern Oval, Ballarat, 9 March 1992 (50-overs)
Result: England won by 106 runs. Points: England 2, Sri Lanka 0.
Toss: England. Umpires: Khizer Hayat (Pak) and PD Reporter (Ind).
World Cup Referee: RJ Merriman. Man of the Match: CC Lewis.

England innings (50 overs maximum)			R	B	4	6
*GA Gooch		b Labrooy	8	28	1	0
IT Botham		b Anurasiri	47	63	5	2
RA Smith	run out		19	39	2	0
GA Hick		b Ramanayake	41	62	3	0
NH Fairbrother	c Ramanayake	b Gurusinha	63	70	3	2
+AJ Stewart	c Jayasuriya	b Gurusinha	59	36	7	1
CC Lewis	not out		20	6	1	2
DR Pringle	not out		0	0	0	0
Extras	(b 1, lb 9, w 9, nb 4)		23			
Total	(6 wickets, 50 overs)		280			

DNB: DA Reeve, PAJ DeFreitas, RK Illingworth.
Fall of wickets: 1-44 (Gooch), 2-80 (Smith), 3-105 (Botham), 4-164 (Hick), 5-244 (Fairbrother), 6-268 (Stewart).

Bowling	O	M	R	W	
Wickramasinghe	9	0	54	0	(3w)
Ramanayake	10	1	42	1	(4nb 3w)
Labrooy	10	1	68	1	(2w)
Anurasiri	10	1	27	1	
Gurusinha	10	0	67	2	(1w)
Jayasuriya	1	0	12	0	

Sri Lanka innings (target: 281 runs from 50 overs)			R	B	4	6
RS Mahanama	c Botham	b Lewis	9	19	1	0
MAR Samarasekera	c Illingworth	b Lewis	23	29	4	0
AP Gurusinha		c & b Lewis	7	9	0	0
*PA de Silva	c Fairbrother	b Lewis	7	10	1	0
A Ranatunga	c Stewart	b Botham	36	51	6	0
+HP Tillakaratne	run out		4	30	0	0
ST Jayasuriya	c DeFreitas	b Illingworth	19	16	2	0
GF Labrooy	c Smith	b Illingworth	19	34	1	0
CPH Ramanayake		c & b Reeve	12	38	1	0
SD Anurasiri	lbw	b Reeve	11	19	0	0
GP Wickramasinghe	not out		6	16	0	0
Extras	(lb 7, w 8, nb 6)		21			
Total	(all out, 44 overs)		174			

Fall of wickets: 1-33 (Mahanama), 2-46 (Samarasekera), 3-56 (de Silva), 4-60 (Gurusinha), 5-91 (Tillakaratne), 6-119 (Ranatunga), 7-123 (Jayasuriya), 8-156 (Ramanayake), 9-158 (Labrooy), 10-174 (Anurasiri).

Bowling	O	M	R	W	
Pringle	7	1	27	0	(3nb 1w)
Lewis	8	0	30	4	(2nb 2w)
DeFreitas	5	1	31	0	(1nb 3w)
Botham	10	0	33	1	(1w)
Illingworth	10	0	32	2	
Reeve	4	0	14	2	(1w)

India v West Indies

At Basin Reserve, Wellington, 10 March 1992 (50-overs)
Result: West Indies won by 5 wickets (revised target).
Points: West Indies 2, India 0.
Toss: India. Umpires: SG Randell (Aus) and SJ Woodward.
World Cup Referee: AR Isaac. Man of the Match: AC Cummins.

India innings (50 overs maximum)			R	B	4	6
A Jadeja	c Benjamin	b Simmons	27	61	2	0
K Srikkanth	c Logie	b Hooper	40	70	2	0
*M Azharuddin	c Ambrose	b Cummins	61	84	4	0
SR Tendulkar	c Williams	b Ambrose	4	11	0	0
SV Manjrekar	run out		27	40	0	0
N Kapil Dev	c Haynes	b Cummins	3	4	0	0
PK Amre	c Hooper	b Ambrose	4	8	0	0
+KS More	c Hooper	b Cummins	5	5	1	0
M Prabhakar	c Richardson	b Cummins	8	10	1	0
J Srinath	not out		5	5	0	0
SLV Raju	run out		1	1	0	0
Extras	(lb 6, w 5, nb 1)		12			
Total	(all out, 49.4 overs)		197			

Fall of wickets: 1-56 (Jadeja), 2-102 (Srikkanth), 3-115 (Tendulkar), 4-166 (Azharuddin), 5-171 (Kapil Dev), 6-173 (Manjrekar), 7-180 (More), 8-186 (Amre), 9-193 (Prabhakar), 10-197 (Raju).

Bowling	O	M	R	W	
Ambrose	10	1	24	2	
Benjamin	9.4	0	35	0	(4w)
Cummins	10	0	33	4	
Simmons	9	0	48	1	(1nb 1w)
Hooper	10	0	46	1	
Arthurton	1	0	5	0	

West Indies innings (target: 195 runs from 46 overs)			R	B	4	6
DL Haynes	c Manjrekar	b Kapil Dev	16	16	3	0
BC Lara	c Manjrekar	b Srinath	41	37	6	1
PV Simmons	c Tendulkar	b Prabhakar	22	20	2	1
*RB Richardson	c Srikkanth	b Srinath	3	8	0	0
KLT Arthurton	not out		58	99	3	0
AL Logie	c More	b Raju	7	10	1	0
CL Hooper	not out		34	57	3	0
Extras	(lb 8, w 2, nb 4)		14			
Total	(5 wickets, 40.2 overs)		195			

DNB: +D Williams, WKM Benjamin, CEL Ambrose, AC Cummins.
Fall of wickets: 1-57 (Haynes), 2-81 (Lara), 3-88 (Simmons), 4-98 (Richardson), 5-112 (Logie).

Bowling	O	M	R	W	
Kapil Dev	8	0	45	1	
Prabhakar	9	0	55	1	(1nb 1w)
Raju	10	2	32	1	(1w)
Srinath	9	2	23	2	(3nb)
Tendulkar	3	0	20	0	
Srikkanth	1	0	7	0	
Jadeja	0.2	0	5	0	

South Africa v Zimbabwe

At Manuka Oval, Canberra, 10 March 1992 (50-overs)
Result: South Africa won by 7 wickets. Points: South Africa 2, Zimbabwe 0.
Toss: South Africa. Umpires: SA Bucknor (WI) and DR Shepherd (Eng).
World Cup Referee: R Webb. Man of the Match: PN Kirsten.

Zimbabwe innings (50 overs maximum)			R	B	4	6
WR James	lbw	b Pringle	5	12	0	0
+A Flower	c Richardson	b Cronje	19	44	0	0
AJ Pycroft	c Wessels	b McMillan	19	47	0	0
*DL Houghton	c Cronje	b Kirsten	15	53	0	0
AC Waller	c Cronje	b Kirsten	15	28	1	0
AH Omarshah	c Wessels	b Kirsten	3	4	0	0
EA Brandes	c Richardson	b McMillan	20	28	1	1
MG Burmester	c Kuiper	b Cronje	1	10	0	0
AJ Traicos	not out		16	40	1	0
MP Jarvis		c & b McMillan	17	21	1	1
KG Duers		b Donald	5	10	0	0
Extras	(lb 11, w 13, nb 4)		28			
Total	(all out, 48.3 overs)		163			

Fall of wickets: 1-7 (James), 2-51 (Pycroft), 3-72 (Waller), 4-80 (Houghton), 5-80 (Omarshah), 6-115 (Flower), 7-117 (Burmester), 8-123 (Brandes), 9-151 (Jarvis), 10-163 (Duers).

Bowling	O	M	R	W	
Donald	9.3	1	25	1	(2nb 1w)
Pringle	9	0	25	1	(3nb 6w)
Snell	10	3	24	0	
McMillan	10	1	30	3	(6w)
Cronje	5	0	17	2	
Kirsten	5	0	31	3	

South Africa innings (target: 164 runs from 50 overs)			R	B	4	6
*KC Wessels		b Omarshah	70	137	6	0
AC Hudson		b Jarvis	13	22	1	0
PN Kirsten	not out		62	103	3	0
AP Kuiper	c Burmester	b Brandes	7	9	0	0
JN Rhodes	not out		3	3	0	0
Extras	(lb 4, w 2, nb 3)		9			
Total	(3 wickets, 45.1 overs)		164			

DNB: WJ Cronje, BM McMillan, +DJ Richardson, RP Snell, MW Pringle, AA Donald.
Fall of wickets: 1-27 (Hudson), 2-139 (Wessels), 3-152 (Kuiper).

Bowling	O	M	R	W	
Brandes	9.1	0	40	1	(1nb 1w)
Jarvis	9	2	23	1	(2nb)
Burmester	5	0	20	0	(1w)
Omarshah	8	2	32	1	
Duers	8	1	19	0	
Traicos	6	0	26	0	

Australia v Pakistan

At W.A.C.A. Ground, Perth (day/night), 11 March 1992 (50-overs)
Result: Pakistan won by 48 runs. Points: Pakistan 2, Australia 0.
Toss: Pakistan. Umpires: KE Liebenberg (SA) and PD Reporter (Ind).
World Cup Referee: AL Mann. Man of the Match: Aamer Sohail.

Pakistan innings (50 overs maximum)			R	B	4	6
Aamer Sohail	c Healy	b Moody	76	106	8	0
Rameez Raja	c Border	b Whitney	34	61	4	0
Saleem Malik		b Moody	0	6	0	0
Javed Miandad	c Healy	b SR Waugh	46	75	3	0
*Imran Khan	c Moody	b SR Waugh	13	22	0	1
Inzamam-ul-Haq	run out		16	16	0	0
Ijaz Ahmed	run out		0	2	0	0
Wasim Akram	c ME Waugh	b SR Waugh	0	1	0	0
+Moin Khan	c Healy	b McDermott	5	8	0	0
Mushtaq Ahmed	not out		3	5	0	0
Extras	(lb 9, w 16, nb 2)		27			
Total	(9 wickets, 50 overs)		220			

DNB: Aaqib Javed.
Fall of wickets: 1-78 (Rameez Raja), 2-80 (Saleem Malik), 3-157 (Aamer Sohail), 4-193 (Javed Miandad), 5-194 (Imran Khan), 6-205 (Ijaz Ahmed), 7-205 (Wasim Akram), 8-214 (Inzamam-ul-Haq), 9-220 (Moin Khan).

Bowling	O	M	R	W	
McDermott	10	0	33	1	(3w)
Reid	9	0	37	0	(2nb 4w)
SR Waugh	10	0	36	3	(2w)
Whitney	10	1	50	1	(2w)
Moody	10	0	42	2	(1w)
ME Waugh	1	0	13	0	(1nb)

Australia innings (target: 221 runs from 50 overs)

			R	B	4	6
TM Moody	c Saleem Malik	b Aaqib Javed	4	18	0	0
GR Marsh	c Moin Khan	b Imran Khan	39	91	1	0
DC Boon	c Mushtaq Ahmed	b Aaqib Javed	5	15	1	0
DM Jones	c Aaqib Javed	b Mushtaq Ahmed	47	79	2	0
ME Waugh	c Ijaz Ahmed	b Mushtaq Ahmed	30	42	2	0
*AR Border	c Ijaz Ahmed	b Mushtaq Ahmed	1	4	0	0
SR Waugh	c Moin Khan	b Imran Khan	5	6	1	0
+IA Healy	c Ijaz Ahmed	b Aaqib Javed	8	15	0	0
CJ McDermott	lbw	b Wasim Akram	0	2	0	0
MR Whitney		b Wasim Akram	0	0	0	0
BA Reid	not out		0	0	0	0
Extras	(lb 7, w 14, nb 7)		28			
Total	(all out, 45.2 overs)		172			

Fall of wickets: 1-13 (Moody), 2-31 (Boon), 3-116 (Jones), 4-122 (Marsh), 5-123 (Border), 6-130 (SR Waugh), 7-156 (Healy), 8-162 (McDermott), 9-167 (ME Waugh), 10-172 (Whitney).

Bowling	O	M	R	W	
Wasim Akram	7.2	0	28	2	(5nb 4w)
Aaqib Javed	8	1	21	3	(1nb 5w)
Imran Khan	10	1	32	0	
Ijaz Ahmed	10	0	43	0	(3nb 4w)
Mushtaq Ahmed	10	0	41	3	

New Zealand v India

At Carisbrook, Dunedin, 12 March 1992 (50-overs)
Result: New Zealand won by 4 wickets. Points: New Zealand 2, India 0.
Toss: New Zealand. Umpires: PJ McConnell (Aus) and ID Robinson (Zim).
World Cup Referee: WJ Henderson. Man of the Match: MJ Greatbatch.

India innings (50 overs maximum)

			R	B	4	6
A Jadeja	retired hurt		13	32	1	0
K Srikkanth	c Latham	b Patel	0	3	0	0
*M Azharuddin	c Greatbatch	b Patel	55	98	3	1
SR Tendulkar	c Smith	b Harris	84	107	6	0
SV Manjrekar		c & b Harris	18	25	0	0
N Kapil Dev	c Larsen	b Harris	33	16	5	0
ST Banerjee	c Greatbatch	b Watson	11	9	1	0
+KS More	not out		2	8	0	0
J Srinath	not out		4	3	0	0
Extras	(b 1, lb 4, w 4, nb 1)		10			
Total	(6 wickets, 50 overs)		230			

DNB: M Prabhakar, SLV Raju.
Fall of wickets: 1-4 (Srikkanth), 2-149 (Azharuddin), 3-166 (Tendulkar), 4-201 (Manjrekar), 5-222 (Kapil Dev), 6-223 (Banerjee). NB: A Jadeja retired hurt at 22/1.

Bowling	O	M	R	W	
Cairns	8	1	40	0	(1nb)
Patel	10	0	29	2	
Watson	10	1	34	1	
Larsen	9	0	43	0	
Harris	9	0	55	3	(2w)
Latham	4	0	24	0	(2w)

New Zealand innings (target: 231 runs from 50 overs)

			R	B	4	6
MJ Greatbatch	c Banerjee	b Raju	73	77	5	4
RT Latham		b Prabhakar	8	22	1	0
AH Jones	not out		67	107	8	0
*MD Crowe	run out		26	28	3	1
+IDS Smith	c sub (PK Amre)	b Prabhakar	9	8	1	0
KR Rutherford	lbw	b Raju	21	22	3	1
CZ Harris		b Prabhakar	4	17	0	0
CL Cairns	not out		4	5	1	0
Extras	(b 4, lb 3, w 4, nb 8)		19			
Total	(6 wickets, 47.1 overs)		231			

DNB: DN Patel, GR Larsen, W Watson.
Fall of wickets: 1-36 (Latham), 2-118 (Greatbatch), 3-162 (Crowe), 4-172 (Smith), 5-206 (Rutherford), 6-225 (Harris).

Bowling	O	M	R	W	
Kapil Dev	10	0	55	0	(1nb 1w)
Prabhakar	10	0	46	3	(2w)
Banerjee	6	1	40	0	(1nb)
Srinath	9	0	35	0	(3nb 2w)
Raju	10	0	38	2	
Tendulkar	1	0	2	0	
Srikkanth	1.1	0	8	0	(1nb)

England v South Africa

At Melbourne Cricket Ground (day/night), 12 March 1992 (50-overs)
Result: England won by 3 wickets (revised target).
Points: England 2, South Africa 0.
Toss: England. Umpires: BL Aldridge (NZ) and DP Buultjens (SL).
World Cup Referee: JE Edwards. Man of the Match: AJ Stewart.

South Africa innings (50 overs maximum)

			R	B	4	6
*KC Wessels	c Smith	b Hick	85	126	6	0
AC Hudson		c & b Hick	79	115	7	0
PN Kirsten	c Smith	b DeFreitas	11	12	0	1
JN Rhodes	run out		18	23	0	0
AP Kuiper	not out		15	12	1	0
WJ Cronje	not out		13	15	0	0
Extras	(b 4, lb 4, w 4, nb 3)		15			
Total	(4 wickets, 50 overs)		236			

DNB: BM McMillan, +DJ Richardson, RP Snell, MW Pringle, AA Donald.
Fall of wickets: 1-151 (Hudson), 2-170 (Kirsten), 3-201 (Wessels), 4-205 (Rhodes).

Bowling	O	M	R	W	
Pringle	9	2	34	0	(3nb 2w)
DeFreitas	10	1	41	1	(1w)
Botham	8	0	37	0	
Small	2	0	14	0	(1w)
Illingworth	10	0	43	0	
Reeve	2.4	0	15	0	
Hick	8.2	0	44	2	

England innings (target: 226 runs from 41 overs)

			R	B	4	6
*+AJ Stewart	run out		77	88	7	0
IT Botham		b McMillan	22	30	1	0
RA Smith	c Richardson	b McMillan	0	2	0	0
GA Hick	c Richardson	b Snell	1	4	0	0
NH Fairbrother	not out		75	83	6	0
DA Reeve	c McMillan	b Snell	10	15	0	0
CC Lewis	run out		33	22	4	0
DR Pringle	c Kuiper	b Snell	1	3	0	0
PAJ DeFreitas	not out		1	1	0	0
Extras	(lb 3, w 1, nb 2)		6			
Total	(7 wickets, 40.5 overs)		226			

DNB: RK Illingworth, GC Small.
Fall of wickets: 1-63 (Botham), 2-63 (Smith), 3-64 (Hick), 4-132 (Stewart), 5-166 (Reeve), 6-216 (Lewis), 7-225 (Pringle).

Bowling	O	M	R	W	
Donald	9	1	43	0	(1nb)
Pringle	8	0	44	0	(1nb 1w)
Snell	7.5	0	42	3	
McMillan	8	1	39	2	
Kuiper	4	0	32	0	
Cronje	3	0	14	0	
Kirsten	1	0	9	0	

NB: Rain disrupted play in England's innings when they were 62/0 at the end of 12 overs. The target was revised to 226 in 41 overs.

Sri Lanka v West Indies

At Berri Oval, 13 March 1992 (50-overs)
Result: West Indies won by 91 runs. Points: West Indies 2, Sri Lanka 0.
Toss: Sri Lanka. Umpires: DR Shepherd (Eng) and SJ Woodward (NZ).
World Cup Referee: BE Martin. Man of the Match: PV Simmons.

West Indies innings (50 overs maximum)

			R	B	4	6
DL Haynes	c Tillakaratne	b Ranatunga	38	47	3	1
BC Lara		c & b Ramanayake	1	6	0	0
PV Simmons	c Wickramasinghe	b Hathurusingha	110	125	8	2
*RB Richardson	run out		8	23	0	0
KLT Arthurton	c Tillakaratne	b Hathurusingha	40	54	1	0
AL Logie		b Anurasiri	0	2	0	0
CL Hooper	c Gurusinha	b Hathurusingha	12	12	1	0
+D Williams	c Tillakaratne	b Hathurusingha	2	3	0	0
CEL Ambrose	not out		15	14	0	1
WKM Benjamin	not out		24	20	1	0
Extras	(lb 9, w 3, nb 6)		18			
Total	(8 wickets, 50 overs)		268			

DNB: AC Cummins.
Fall of wickets: 1-6 (Lara), 2-72 (Haynes), 3-103 (Richardson), 4-197 (Simmons), 5-199 (Logie), 6-219 (Hooper), 7-223 (Williams), 8-228 (Arthurton).

Bowling	O	M	R	W	
Wickramasinghe	7	0	30	0	(1nb 2w)
Ramanayake	7	1	17	1	(1nb 1w)
Anurasiri	10	0	46	1	
Gurusinha	1	0	10	0	
Ranatunga	7	0	35	1	
Kalpage	10	0	64	0	
Hathurusingha	8	0	57	4	(4nb)

Sri Lanka innings (target: 269 runs from 50 overs)

			R	B	4	6
RS Mahanama	c Arthurton	b Cummins	11	50	0	0
MAR Samarasekera	lbw	b Hooper	40	41	4	1
UC Hathurusingha	run out		16	25	0	0
*PA de Silva		c & b Hooper	11	19	0	0
A Ranatunga	c Benjamin	b Arthurton	24	40	0	1
AP Gurusinha	c Richardson	b Ambrose	10	30	0	0
+HP Tillakaratne		b Ambrose	3	9	0	0
RS Kalpage	not out		13	40	0	0
CPH Ramanayake		b Arthurton	1	13	0	0
SD Anurasiri		b Benjamin	3	11	0	0
GP Wickramasinghe	not out		21	21	1	0
Extras	(lb 8, w 14, nb 2)		24			
Total	(9 wickets, 50 overs)		177			

Fall of wickets: 1-56 (Samarasekera), 2-80 (Hathurusingha), 3-86 (Mahanama), 4-99 (de Silva), 5-130 (Gurusinha), 6-135 (Tillakaratne), 7-137 (Ranatunga), 8-139 (Ramanayake), 9-149 (Anurasiri).

Bowling	O	M	R	W	
Ambrose	10	2	24	2	(6w)
Benjamin	10	0	34	1	(5w)
Cummins	9	0	49	1	(1nb 3w)
Hooper	10	1	19	2	
Arthurton	10	0	40	2	(1nb)
Simmons	1	0	3	0	

Australia v Zimbabwe

At Bellerive Oval, Hobart, 14 March 1992 (50-overs)
Result: Australia won by 128 runs. Points: Australia 2, Zimbabwe 0.
Toss: Australia. Umpires: BL Aldridge (NZ) and SA Bucknor (WI).
World Cup Referee: BAH Palfreyman. Man of the Match: SR Waugh.

Australia innings (46 overs maximum)			R	B	4	6
TM Moody	run out		6	8	0	0
DC Boon		b Omarshah	48	84	4	0
DM Jones		b Burmester	54	71	4	0
*AR Border	st Flower	b Traicos	22	29	2	0
ME Waugh	not out		66	39	5	2
SR Waugh		b Brandes	55	43	4	0
+IA Healy	lbw	b Duers	0	2	0	0
PL Taylor	not out		1	1	0	0
Extras	(b 2, lb 8, w 2, nb 1)		13			
Total	(6 wickets, 46 overs)		265			

DNB: CJ McDermott, MR Whitney, BA Reid.
Fall of wickets: 1-8 (Moody), 2-102 (Boon), 3-134 (Border), 4-144 (Jones), 5-257 (SR Waugh), 6-258 (Healy).

Bowling	O	M	R	W	
Brandes	9	0	59	1	(1nb)
Duers	9	1	48	1	(1w)
Burmester	9	0	65	1	(1w)
Omarshah	9	0	53	1	
Traicos	10	0	30	1	

Zimbabwe innings (target: 266 runs from 46 overs)			R	B	4	6
AH Omarshah	run out		23	47	2	0
+A Flower	c Border	b SR Waugh	20	49	1	0
ADR Campbell	c ME Waugh	b Whitney	4	20	1	0
AJ Pycroft	c ME Waugh	b SR Waugh	0	1	0	0
*DL Houghton		b McDermott	2	10	0	0
AC Waller	c Taylor	b Moody	18	39	2	0
KJ Arnott		b Whitney	8	15	0	0
EA Brandes	c McDermott	b Taylor	23	28	3	0
MG Burmester	c Border	b Reid	12	24	0	0
AJ Traicos	c Border	b Taylor	3	9	0	0
KG Duers	not out		2	10	0	0
Extras	(lb 12, w 8, nb 2)		22			
Total	(all out, 41.4 overs)		137			

Fall of wickets: 1-47 (Omarshah), 2-51 (Flower), 3-51 (Pycroft), 4-57 (Campbell), 5-69 (Houghton), 6-88 (Waller), 7-97 (Arnott), 8-117 (Burmester), 9-132 (Traicos), 10-137 (Brandes).

Bowling	O	M	R	W	
McDermott	8	0	26	1	(1nb 3w)
Reid	9	2	17	1	(1nb)
SR Waugh	7	0	28	2	(4w)
Whitney	10	3	15	2	
Moody	4	0	25	1	(1w)
Taylor	3.4	0	14	2	

New Zealand v England

At Basin Reserve, Wellington, 15 March 1992 (50-overs)
Result: New Zealand won by 7 wickets. Points: New Zealand 2, England 0.
Toss: New Zealand. Umpires: SG Randell (Aus) and ID Robinson (Zim).
World Cup Referee: BJ Paterson. Man of the Match: AH Jones.

England innings (50 overs maximum)			R	B	4	6
*+AJ Stewart	c Harris	b Patel	41	59	7	0
IT Botham		b Patel	8	25	1	0
GA Hick	c Greatbatch	b Harris	56	70	6	1
RA Smith	c Patel	b Jones	38	72	3	0
AJ Lamb	c Cairns	b Watson	12	29	0	0
CC Lewis		c & b Watson	0	1	0	0
DA Reeve	not out		21	27	1	0
DR Pringle	c sub (RT Latham)	b Jones	10	16	0	0
PAJ DeFreitas	c Cairns	b Harris	0	1	0	0
RK Illingworth	not out		2	2	0	0
Extras	(b 1, lb 7, w 4)		12			
Total	(8 wickets, 50 overs)		200			

DNB: GC Small.
Fall of wickets: 1-25 (Botham), 2-95 (Stewart), 3-135 (Hick), 4-162 (Smith), 5-162 (Lewis), 6-169 (Lamb), 7-189 (Pringle), 8-195 (DeFreitas).

Bowling	O	M	R	W	
Patel	10	1	26	2	
Harris	8	0	39	2	(1w)
Watson	10	0	40	2	(1w)
Cairns	3	0	21	0	(1w)
Larsen	10	3	24	0	(1w)
Jones	9	0	42	2	

New Zealand innings (target: 201 runs from 50 overs)			R	B	4	6
MJ Greatbatch	c DeFreitas	b Botham	35	37	4	1
JG Wright		b DeFreitas	1	5	0	0
AH Jones	run out		78	113	13	0
*MD Crowe	not out		73	81	4	0
KR Rutherford	not out		3	12	0	0
Extras	(b 1, lb 8, w 1, nb 1)		11			
Total	(3 wickets, 40.5 overs)		201			

DNB: CZ Harris, CL Cairns, +IDS Smith, DN Patel, GR Larsen, W Watson.
Fall of wickets: 1-5 (Wright), 2-64 (Greatbatch), 3-172 (Jones).

Bowling	O	M	R	W	
Pringle	6.2	1	34	0	(1nb 1w)
DeFreitas	8.3	1	45	1	
Botham	4	0	19	1	
Illingworth	9	1	46	0	
Hick	6	0	26	0	
Reeve	3	0	9	0	
Small	4	0	13	0	

India v South Africa

At Adelaide Oval, 15 March 1992 (50-overs)
Result: South Africa won by 6 wickets. Points: South Africa 2, India 0.
Toss: South Africa. Umpires: DP Buultjens (SL) and Khizer Hayat (Pak).
World Cup Referee: B Gibbs. Man of the Match: PN Kirsten.

India innings (30 overs maximum)			R	B	4	6
K Srikkanth	c Kirsten	b Donald	0	5	0	0
SV Manjrekar		b Kuiper	28	53	0	0
*M Azharuddin	c Kuiper	b Pringle	79	77	6	0
SR Tendulkar	c Wessels	b Kuiper	14	14	1	0
N Kapil Dev		b Donald	42	29	3	1
VG Kambli	run out		1	3	0	0
PK Amre	not out		1	1	0	0
J Srinath	not out		0	0	0	0
Extras	(lb 7, w 6, nb 2)		15			
Total	(6 wickets, 30 overs)		180			

DNB: +KS More, M Prabhakar, SLV Raju.
Fall of wickets: 1-1 (Srikkanth), 2-79 (Manjrekar), 3-103 (Tendulkar), 4-174 (Kapil Dev), 5-177 (Kambli), 6-179 (Azharuddin).

Bowling	O	M	R	W	
Donald	6	0	34	2	(3w)
Pringle	6	0	37	1	(2nb 2w)
Snell	6	1	46	0	
McMillan	6	0	28	0	
Kuiper	6	0	28	2	(1w)

South Africa innings (target: 181 runs from 30 overs)			R	B	4	6
AC Hudson		b Srinath	53	73	4	0
PN Kirsten		b Kapil Dev	84	86	7	0
AP Kuiper	run out		7	6	0	0
JN Rhodes	c Raju	b Prabhakar	7	3	0	1
*KC Wessels	not out		9	6	1	0
WJ Cronje	not out		8	6	1	0
Extras	(lb 10, nb 3)		13			
Total	(4 wickets, 29.1 overs)		181			

DNB: BM McMillan, +DJ Richardson, RP Snell, MW Pringle, AA Donald.
Fall of wickets: 1-128 (Hudson), 2-149 (Kuiper), 3-157 (Kirsten), 4-163 (Rhodes).

Bowling	O	M	R	W	
Kapil Dev	6	0	36	1	
Prabhakar	5.1	1	33	1	
Tendulkar	6	0	20	0	
Srinath	6	0	39	1	(3nb)
Raju	6	0	43	0	

NB: Rain reduced the match to 30 overs per side.

Pakistan v Sri Lanka

At W.A.C.A. Ground, Perth, 15 March 1992 (50-overs)
Result: Pakistan won by 4 wickets. Points: Pakistan 2, Sri Lanka 0.
Toss: Sri Lanka. Umpires: KE Liebenberg (SA) and PJ McConnell.
World Cup Referee: JW Mann. Man of the Match: Javed Miandad.

Sri Lanka innings (50 overs maximum)			R	B	4	6
RS Mahanama		b Wasim Akram	12	36	1	0
MAR Samarasekera	st Moin Khan	b Mushtaq Ahmed	38	59	1	0
UC Hathurusingha		b Mushtaq Ahmed	5	29	0	0
*PA de Silva	c Aamer Sohail	b Ijaz Ahmed	43	56	2	0
AP Gurusinha	c Saleem Malik	b Imran Khan	37	54	2	0
A Ranatunga	c sub (Zahid Fazal)	b Aamer Sohail	7	19	0	0
+HP Tillakaratne	not out		25	34	3	0
RS Kalpage	not out		13	14	0	0
Extras	(lb 15, w 11, nb 6)		32			
Total	(6 wickets, 50 overs)		212			

DNB: CPH Ramanayake, KIW Wijegunawardene, GP Wickramasinghe.
Fall of wickets: 1-29 (Mahanama), 2-48 (Hathurusingha), 3-99 (Samarasekera), 4-132 (de Silva), 5-158 (Ranatunga), 6-187 (Gurusinha).

Bowling	O	M	R	W	
Wasim Akram	10	0	37	1	(4nb 2w)
Aaqib Javed	10	0	39	0	(2nb 3w)
Imran Khan	8	1	36	1	
Mushtaq Ahmed	10	0	43	2	(2w)
Ijaz Ahmed	8	0	28	1	(3w)
Aamer Sohail	4	0	14	1	(1w)

Pakistan innings (target: 213 runs from 50 overs)			R	B	4	6
Aamer Sohail	c Mahanama	b Ramanayake	1	10	0	0
Rameez Raja	c Gurusinha	b Wickramasinghe	32	56	3	0
*Imran Khan	c de Silva	b Hathurusingha	22	69	2	0
Javed Miandad	c Wickramasinghe	b Gurusinha	57	84	3	0
Saleem Malik	c Kalpage	b Ramanayake	51	66	2	0
Inzamam-ul-Haq	run out		11	11	0	0
Ijaz Ahmed	not out		8	6	1	0
Wasim Akram	not out		5	5	1	0
Extras	(lb 12, w 9, nb 8)		29			
Total	(6 wickets, 49.1 overs)		216			

DNB: +Moin Khan, Mushtaq Ahmed, Aaqib Javed.

Fall of wickets: 1-7 (Aamer Sohail), 2-68 (Rameez Raja), 3-84 (Imran Khan), 4-185 (Javed Miandad), 5-201 (Saleem Malik), 6-205 (Inzamam-ul-Haq).

Bowling	O	M	R	W	
Wijegunawardene	10	1	34	0	(7nb)
Ramanayake	10	1	37	2	(4w)
Wickramasinghe	9.1	0	41	1	(1w)
Gurusinha	9	0	38	1	(1w)
Hathurusingha	9	0	40	1	(1nb 2w)
Kalpage	2	0	14	0	(1w)

New Zealand v Pakistan
At Lancaster Park, Christchurch, 18 March 1992 (50-overs)
Result: Pakistan won by 7 wickets. Points: Pakistan 2, New Zealand 0.
Toss: Pakistan. Umpires: SA Bucknor (WI) and SG Randell (Aus).
World Cup Referee: CL Bull. Man of the Match: Mushtaq Ahmed.

New Zealand innings (50 overs maximum)			R	B	4	6
MJ Greatbatch	c Saleem Malik	b Mushtaq Ahmed	42	67	5	1
RT Latham	c Inzamam-ul-Haq	b Aaqib Javed	6	9	1	0
AH Jones	lbw	b Wasim Akram	2	3	0	0
*MD Crowe	c Aamer Sohail	b Wasim Akram	3	20	0	0
KR Rutherford	run out		8	35	0	0
CZ Harris	st Moin Khan	b Mushtaq Ahmed	1	6	0	0
DN Patel	c Mushtaq Ahmed	b Aamer Sohail	7	13	0	0
+IDS Smith		b Imran Khan	1	4	0	0
GR Larsen		b Wasim Akram	37	80	3	0
DK Morrison	c Inzamam-ul-Haq	b Wasim Akram	12	45	1	0
W Watson	not out		5	13	0	0
Extras	(b 3, lb 23, w 12, nb 4)		42			
Total	(all out, 48.2 overs)		166			

Fall of wickets: 1-23 (Latham), 2-26 (Jones), 3-39 (Crowe), 4-85 (Rutherford), 5-88 (Harris), 6-93 (Greatbatch), 7-96 (Smith), 8-106 (Patel), 9-150 (Morrison), 10-166 (Larsen).

Bowling	O	M	R	W
Wasim Akram	9.2	0	32	4
Aaqib Javed	10	1	34	1
Mushtaq Ahmed	10	0	18	2
Imran Khan	8	0	22	1
Aamer Sohail	10	1	29	1
Ijaz Ahmed	1	0	5	0

Pakistan innings (target: 167 runs from 50 overs)			R	B	4	6
Aamer Sohail	c Patel	b Morrison	0	1	0	0
Rameez Raja	not out		119	155	16	0
Inzamam-ul-Haq		b Morrison	5	8	1	0
Javed Miandad	lbw	b Morrison	30	85	1	0
Saleem Malik	not out		9	23	1	0
Extras	(lb 1, w 1, nb 2)		4			
Total	(3 wickets, 44.4 overs)		167			

DNB: *Imran Khan, Wasim Akram, Ijaz Ahmed, +Moin Khan, Mushtaq Ahmed, Aaqib Javed.
Fall of wickets: 1-0 (Aamer Sohail), 2-9 (Inzamam-ul-Haq), 3-124 (Javed Miandad).

Bowling	O	M	R	W
Morrison	10	0	42	3
Patel	10	2	25	0
Watson	10	3	26	0
Harris	4	0	18	0
Larsen	3	0	16	0
Jones	3	0	10	0
Latham	2	0	13	0
Rutherford	1.4	0	11	0
Greatbatch	1	0	5	0

England v Zimbabwe
At Lavington Sports Oval, Albury, 18 March 1992 (50-overs)
Result: Zimbabwe won by 9 runs. Points: Zimbabwe 2, England 0.
Toss: England. Umpires: BL Aldridge (NZ) and Khizer Hayat (Pak).
World Cup Referee: B Stanton. Man of the Match: EA Brandes.

Zimbabwe innings (50 overs maximum)			R	B	4	6
WR James	c & b Illingworth		13	46	1	0
+A Flower		b DeFreitas	7	16	1	0
AJ Pycroft	c Gooch	b Botham	3	13	0	0
KJ Arnott	lbw	b Botham	11	33	0	0
*DL Houghton	c Fairbrother	b Small	29	74	2	0
AC Waller		b Tufnell	8	16	1	0
AH Omarshah	c Lamb	b Tufnell	3	16	0	0
IP Butchart	c Fairbrother	b Botham	24	36	2	0
EA Brandes	st Stewart	b Illingworth	14	24	1	0
AJ Traicos	not out		0	6	0	0
MP Jarvis	lbw	b Illingworth	6	6	0	0
Extras	(lb 8, w 8)		16			
Total	(all out, 46.1 overs)		134			

Fall of wickets: 1-12 (Flower), 2-19 (Pycroft), 3-30 (James), 4-52 (Arnott), 5-65 (Waller), 6-77 (Omarshah), 7-96 (Houghton), 8-127 (Butchart), 9-127 (Brandes), 10-134 (Jarvis).

Bowling	O	M	R	W
DeFreitas	8	1	14	1
Small	9	1	20	1
Botham	10	2	23	3
Illingworth	9.1	0	33	3
Tufnell	10	2	36	2

England innings (target: 135 runs from 50 overs)			R	B	4	6
*GA Gooch	lbw	b Brandes	0	1	0	0
IT Botham	c Flower	b Omarshah	18	34	4	0
AJ Lamb	c James	b Brandes	17	26	2	0
RA Smith		b Brandes	2	13	0	0
GA Hick		b Brandes	0	6	0	0
NH Fairbrother	c Flower	b Butchart	20	77	0	0
+AJ Stewart	c Waller	b Omarshah	29	96	3	0
PAJ DeFreitas	c Flower	b Butchart	4	17	0	0
RK Illingworth	run out		11	20	0	0
GC Small	c Pycroft	b Jarvis	5	18	0	0
PCR Tufnell	not out		0	0	0	0
Extras	(b 4, lb 3, w 11, nb 1)		19			
Total	(all out, 49.1 overs)		125			

Fall of wickets: 1-0 (Gooch), 2-32 (Lamb), 3-42 (Botham), 4-42 (Smith), 5-43 (Hick), 6-95 (Stewart), 7-101 (DeFreitas), 8-108 (Fairbrother), 9-124 (Illingworth), 10-125 (Small).

Bowling	O	M	R	W
Brandes	10	4	21	4
Jarvis	9.1	0	32	1
Omarshah	10	3	17	2
Traicos	10	4	16	0
Butchart	10	1	32	2

Australia v West Indies
At Melbourne Cricket Ground (day/night), 18 March 1992 (50-overs)
Result: Australia won by 57 runs. Points: Australia 2, West Indies 0.
Toss: Australia. Umpires: PD Reporter (Ind) and DR Shepherd (Eng).
World Cup Referee: JW Mann. Man of the Match: DC Boon.

Australia innings (50 overs maximum)			R	B	4	6
TM Moody	c Benjamin	b Simmons	42	70	3	0
DC Boon	c Williams	b Cummins	100	147	8	0
DM Jones	c Williams	b Cummins	6	14	0	0
*AR Border	lbw	b Simmons	8	10	1	0
ME Waugh	st Williams	b Hooper	21	31	0	0
SR Waugh		b Cummins	6	14	0	0
+IA Healy	not out		11	11	0	0
PL Taylor	not out		10	6	1	0
Extras	(lb 3, w 3, nb 6)		12			
Total	(6 wickets, 50 overs)		216			

DNB: CJ McDermott, MR Whitney, BA Reid.
Fall of wickets: 1-107 (Moody), 2-128 (Jones), 3-141 (Border), 4-185 (ME Waugh), 5-189 (Boon), 6-200 (SR Waugh).

Bowling	O	M	R	W
Ambrose	10	0	46	0
Benjamin	10	1	49	0
Cummins	10	1	38	3
Hooper	10	0	40	1
Simmons	10	1	40	2

West Indies innings (target: 217 runs from 50 overs)			R	B	4	6
DL Haynes	c Jones	b McDermott	14	24	2	0
BC Lara	run out		70	97	3	0
PV Simmons	lbw	b McDermott	0	1	0	0
*RB Richardson	c Healy	b Whitney	10	44	0	0
KLT Arthurton	c McDermott	b Whitney	15	21	1	0
AL Logie	c Healy	b Whitney	5	15	0	0
CL Hooper	c ME Waugh	b Whitney	4	11	0	0
+D Williams	c Border	b Reid	4	15	0	0
WKM Benjamin	lbw	b SR Waugh	15	15	2	0
CEL Ambrose	run out		2	7	0	0
AC Cummins	not out		5	10	0	0
Extras	(b 3, lb 5, w 3, nb 4)		15			
Total	(all out, 42.4 overs)		159			

Fall of wickets: 1-27 (Haynes), 2-27 (Simmons), 3-59 (Richardson), 4-83 (Arthurton), 5-99 (Logie), 6-117 (Hooper), 7-128 (Williams), 8-137 (Lara), 9-150 (Ambrose), 10-159 (Benjamin).

Bowling	O	M	R	W
McDermott	6	1	29	2
Reid	10	1	26	1
Whitney	10	1	34	4
SR Waugh	6.4	0	24	1
Taylor	4	0	24	0
Moody	6	1	14	0

1st Semi Final
New Zealand v Pakistan

At Eden Park, Auckland, 21 March 1992 (50-overs)
Result: Pakistan won by 4 wickets. Pakistan advances to the final.
Toss: New Zealand. Umpires: SA Bucknor (WI) and DR Shepherd (Eng).
Match Referee: PJP Burge (Aus). Man of the Match: Inzamam-ul-Haq.

New Zealand innings (50 overs maximum)			R	B	4	6
MJ Greatbatch		b Aaqib Javed	17	22	0	2
JG Wright	c Rameez Raja	b Mushtaq Ahmed	13	44	1	0
AH Jones	lbw	b Mushtaq Ahmed	21	53	2	0
*MD Crowe	run out		91	83	7	3
KR Rutherford	c Moin Khan	b Wasim Akram	50	68	5	1
CZ Harris	st Moin Khan	b Iqbal Sikander	13	12	1	0
+IDS Smith	not out		18	10	3	0
DN Patel	lbw	b Wasim Akram	8	6	1	0
GR Larsen	not out		8	6	1	0
Extras	(lb 11, w 8, nb 4)		23			
Total	(7 wickets, 50 overs)		262			

DNB: DK Morrison, W Watson.
Fall of wickets: 1-35 (Greatbatch), 2-39 (Wright), 3-87 (Jones), 4-194 (Rutherford), 5-214 (Harris), 6-221 (Crowe), 7-244 (Patel).

Bowling	O	M	R	W	
Wasim Akram	10	1	40	2	(4nb 2w)
Aaqib Javed	10	2	45	1	(2w)
Mushtaq Ahmed	10	0	40	2	
Imran Khan	10	0	59	0	(3w)
Iqbal Sikander	9	0	56	1	(1w)
Aamer Sohail	1	0	11	0	

Pakistan innings (target: 263 runs from 50 overs)			R	B	4	6
Aamer Sohail	c Jones	b Patel	14	20	1	0
Rameez Raja	c Morrison	b Watson	44	55	6	0
*Imran Khan	c Larsen	b Harris	44	93	1	2
Javed Miandad	not out		57	69	4	0
Saleem Malik	c sub	b Larsen	1	2	0	0
Inzamam-ul-Haq	run out		60	37	7	1
Wasim Akram		b Watson	9	8	1	0
+Moin Khan	not out		20	11	2	1
Extras	(b 4, lb 10, w 1)		15			
Total	(6 wickets, 49 overs)		264			

DNB: Mushtaq Ahmed, Iqbal Sikander, Aaqib Javed.
Fall of wickets: 1-30 (Aamer Sohail), 2-84 (Rameez Raja), 3-134 (Imran Khan), 4-140 (Saleem Malik), 5-227 (Inzamam-ul-Haq), 6-238 (Wasim Akram).

Bowling	O	M	R	W	
Patel	10	1	50	1	
Morrison	9	0	55	0	(1w)
Watson	10	2	39	2	(1nb)
Larsen	10	1	34	1	
Harris	10	0	72	1	

2nd Semi Final
England v South Africa

At Sydney Cricket Ground (day/night), 22 March 1992 (50-overs)
Result: England won by 19 runs (revised target). England advances to the final.
Toss: South Africa. Umpires: BL Aldridge (NZ) and SG Randell.
Match Referee: FJ Cameron (NZ). Man of the Match: GA Hick.

England innings (45 overs maximum)			R	B	4	6
*GA Gooch	c Richardson	b Donald	2	9	0	0
IT Botham		b Pringle	21	23	3	0
+AJ Stewart	c Richardson	b McMillan	33	54	4	0
GA Hick	c Rhodes	b Snell	83	90	9	0
NH Fairbrother		b Pringle	28	50	1	0
AJ Lamb	c Richardson	b Donald	19	22	1	0
CC Lewis	not out		18	16	2	0
DA Reeve	not out		25	14	4	0
Extras	(b 1, lb 7, w 9, nb 6)		23			
Total	(6 wickets, 45 overs)		252			

DNB: PAJ DeFreitas, GC Small, RK Illingworth.
Fall of wickets: 1-20 (Gooch), 2-39 (Botham), 3-110 (Stewart), 4-183 (Fairbrother), 5-187 (Hick), 6-221 (Lamb).

Bowling	O	M	R	W	
Donald	10	0	69	2	(2nb 5w)
Pringle	9	2	36	2	(4nb 1w)
Snell	8	0	52	1	(2w)
McMillan	9	0	47	1	
Kuiper	5	0	26	0	
Cronje	4	0	14	0	

South Africa innings (target: 252 runs from 43 overs)			R	B	4	6
*KC Wessels	c Lewis	b Botham	17	21	1	0
AC Hudson	lbw	b Illingworth	46	52	6	0
PN Kirsten		b DeFreitas	11	26	0	0
AP Kuiper		b Illingworth	36	44	5	0
WJ Cronje	c Hick	b Small	24	45	1	0
JN Rhodes	c Lewis	b Small	43	38	3	0
BM McMillan	not out		21	21	0	0
+DJ Richardson	not out		13	10	1	0
Extras	(lb 17, w 4)		21			
Total	(6 wickets, 43 overs)		232			

DNB: RP Snell, MW Pringle, AA Donald.

Fall of wickets: 1-26 (Wessels), 2-61 (Kirsten), 3-90 (Hudson), 4-131 (Kuiper), 5-176 (Cronje), 6-206 (Rhodes).

Bowling	O	M	R	W	
Botham	10	0	52	1	(3w)
Lewis	5	0	38	0	
DeFreitas	8	1	28	1	(1w)
Illingworth	10	1	46	2	
Small	10	1	51	2	

NB: The England innings was shortened when the overs weren't completed by the time for the innings to end. Rain interrupted the South African innings after 42.5 overs, 2 overs were lost, the target remained unchanged, 22 were needed from the one ball that remained.

Final
England v Pakistan

At Melbourne Cricket Ground (day/night), 25 March 1992 (50-overs)
Result: Pakistan won by 22 runs. Pakistan wins the 1992 Benson & Hedges World Cup.
Toss: Pakistan. Umpires: BL Aldridge (NZ) and SA Bucknor (WI).
Match Referee: PJP Burge. Man of the Match: Wasim Akram.
Man of the series: MD Crowe (NZ).

Pakistan innings (50 overs maximum)			R	B	4	6
Aamer Sohail	c Stewart	b Pringle	4	19	0	0
Rameez Raja	lbw	b Pringle	8	26	1	0
*Imran Khan	c Illingworth	b Botham	72	110	5	1
Javed Miandad	c Botham	b Illingworth	58	98	4	0
Inzamam-ul-Haq		b Pringle	42	35	4	0
Wasim Akram	run out		33	19	4	0
Saleem Malik	not out		0	1	0	0
Extras	(lb 19, w 6, nb 7)		32			
Total	(6 wickets, 50 overs)		249			

DNB: Ijaz Ahmed, +Moin Khan, Mushtaq Ahmed, Aaqib Javed.
Fall of wickets: 1-20 (Aamer Sohail), 2-24 (Rameez Raja), 3-163 (Javed Miandad), 4-197 (Imran Khan), 5-249 (Inzamam-ul-Haq), 6-249 (Wasim Akram).

Bowling	O	M	R	W	
Pringle	10	2	22	3	(5nb 3w)
Lewis	10	2	52	0	(2nb 1w)
Botham	7	0	42	1	
DeFreitas	10	1	42	0	(1w)
Illingworth	10	0	50	1	
Reeve	3	0	22	0	(1w)

England innings (target: 250 runs from 50 overs)			R	B	4	6
*GA Gooch	c Aaqib Javed	b Mushtaq Ahmed	29	66	1	0
IT Botham	c Moin Khan	b Wasim Akram	0	6	0	0
+AJ Stewart	c Moin Khan	b Aaqib Javed	7	16	1	0
GA Hick	lbw	b Mushtaq Ahmed	17	36	1	0
NH Fairbrother	c Moin Khan	b Aaqib Javed	62	70	3	0
AJ Lamb		b Wasim Akram	31	41	2	0
CC Lewis		b Wasim Akram	0	6	0	0
DA Reeve	c Rameez Raja	b Mushtaq Ahmed	15	32	0	0
DR Pringle	not out		18	16	1	0
PAJ DeFreitas	run out		10	8	0	0
RK Illingworth	c Rameez Raja	b Imran Khan	14	11	2	0
Extras	(lb 5, w 13, nb 6)		24			
Total	(all out, 49.2 overs)		227			

Fall of wickets: 1-6 (Botham), 2-21 (Stewart), 3-59 (Hick), 4-69 (Gooch), 5-141 (Lamb), 6-141 (Lewis), 7-180 (Fairbrother), 8-183 (Reeve), 9-208 (DeFreitas), 10-227 (Illingworth).

Bowling	O	M	R	W	
Wasim Akram	10	0	49	3	(4nb 6w)
Aaqib Javed	10	2	27	2	(1nb 3w)
Mushtaq Ahmed	10	1	41	3	(1w)
Ijaz Ahmed	3	0	13	0	(2w)
Imran Khan	6.2	0	43	1	(1nb)
Aamer Sohail	10	0	49	0	(1w)

World Cup **1996**
by Alan Lee

There were some good, uplifting aspects to the sixth cricket World Cup, not least the style and smiles of its unsuspected winners, Sri Lanka, but overall this was not a tournament to linger fondly in the memory.

Wounded by events beyond its control even before its opening, the competition proceeded to frustrate and bewilder through an interminable and largely irrelevant saga of group matches in India, Pakistan and Sri Lanka before hastening frantically through its knockout games in little more than a week.

The event was poorly conceived in its format and its logistics and suffered throughout from the threat – and ultimately the reality – of crowd disorder. The abandonment of the semi-final at Eden Gardens, Calcutta, following bottle-throwing and fire-lighting on the terraces, was a shameful reflection on standards of sportsmanship in an area until recently renowned for its appreciation of all things good in the game of cricket.

Perhaps, however, we should not be too harsh on the individuals responsible for the riot in Calcutta. They were merely responding to the seductions created for them by the promoters of the Wills World Cup, an event that plainly, disastrously, put money-making above all the fundamentals of organising a global sporting competition. As the glamorising of the Indian and Pakistani cricketers reached new and absurd heights, so too did the unshakeable belief of the masses in their invincibility. Defeat, of the kind that came to India that night in Calcutta, was popularly unimaginable, with consequences for which many must share the blame.

It was all markedly at odds with the 1987 World Cup, also co-hosted by India and Pakistan and widely judged to be an organisational triumph. Players and observers alike enjoyed that competition far more than the 1996 event. Yet the paradox is that, when the accounts were complete, they showed a negligible profit.

Within a decade, the profile of the game had altered substantially. So too, it transpired, had the methods and ambitions of those charged with running the tournament. Suddenly, it was deemed more important

---

Somehow managing to squeeze onto an overpopulated presentation platform, Arjuna Ranatunga lifts the Cup for Sri Lanka. Pakistan Prime Minister Benazir Bhutto leads the applause, a strategically placed operative manages to ensure the sponsor isn't forgotten.

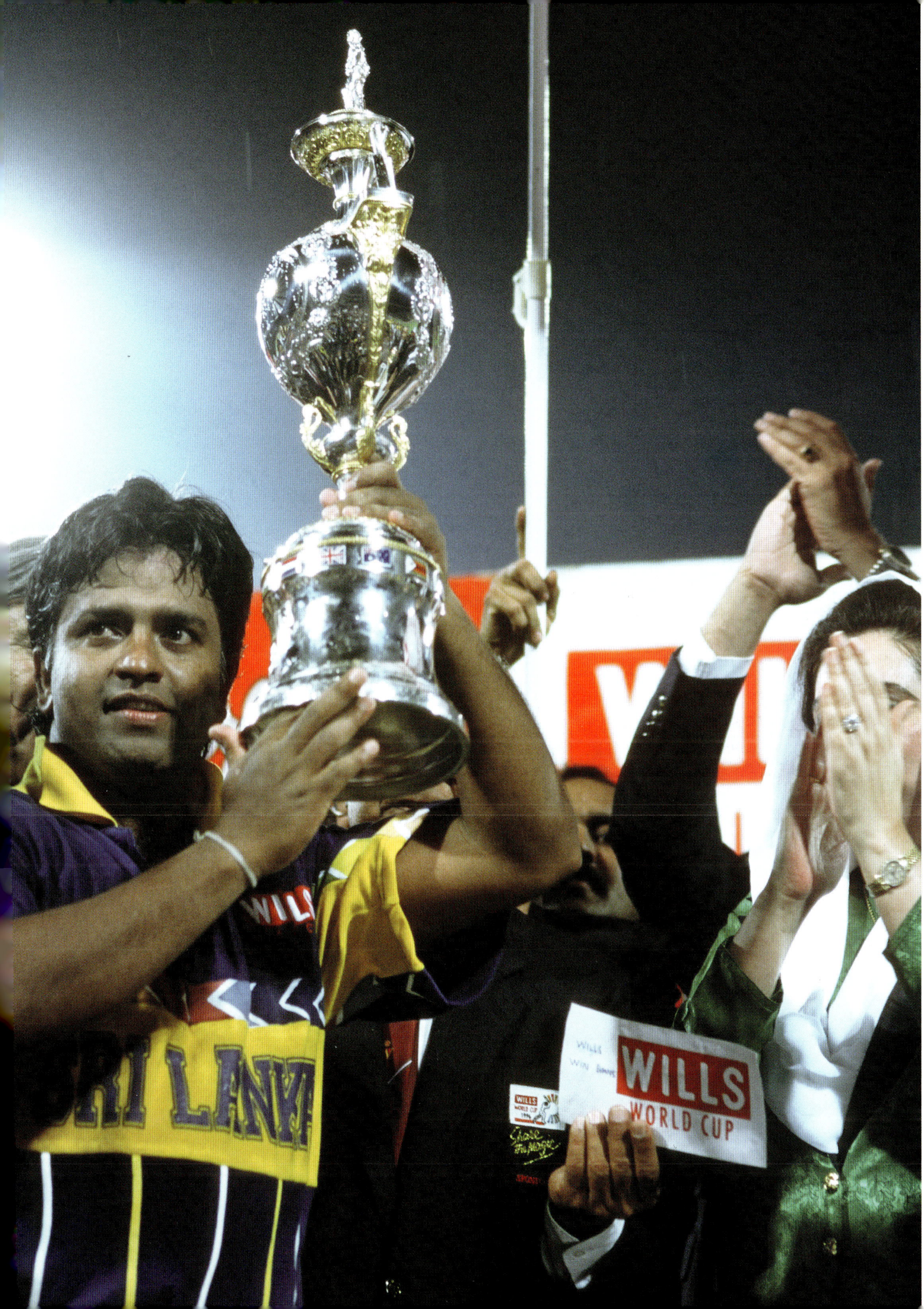
WILLS
WORLD CUP

to register a company as supplier of official chewing gum – and take its money – than to pay proper attention to the welfare of the competing teams.

Of course, it is possible to become too nannyish about professional sportsmen, who by and large lead a pretty pampered existence, but the wearisome travel schedules, illogical playing itineraries and inadequate practice facilities inflicted on most of the visiting teams would have caused a serious rebellion had this been a football championship.

In fact, such elementary flaws should have been dealt with at source, long before they became a millstone around the event. The reason they were not – the handing-over by the International Cricket Council of all responsibility for the tournament to the World Cup committee, Pilcom – reflects poorly on all those responsible. What function does ICC perform if it is not to be a vigilant monitor of events like this? Cricket must never permit such complacency again.

ICC must also take the blame for the format. The expansion of the field to 12, from nine in 1992, was quite right. By embracing three of ICC's Associate members, the non-Test countries, the World Cup was fulfilling its missionary aim (though whether the Associates, wooed by financial guarantees, had too much say in the venue is another serious matter for ICC to consider).

The problem arose when the extra teams were accommodated by a complete change from the successful 1992 system, a round-robin producing four semi-finalists. Instead, the teams were divided into two groups of six, from which not four but eight sides would proceed to the knockout rounds. The effect of this, obvious in advance, was to reduce virtually a month of cricket to the status of little more than practice games: duly, almost inevitably, the three Associate nations and the junior Test-playing team, Zimbabwe, were eliminated.

A genuinely competitive group programme could have been installed, by discarding the idea of quarter-finals and going straight to a last four. Presumably, the attraction of four big crowds, four big television games, was too great, but this was a decision taken on flawed grounds. The people were not all fooled; the group games in Pakistan, particularly, drew very small crowds.

The logistical chaos of the competition stemmed largely from the decision, laudable in theory but utterly unrealistic, to spread the tournament to virtually every corner of the vast country of India. The 17 games scheduled for the country were all staged in different cities, and insufficient attention had been paid to the practicalities of moving teams (let alone TV crews and

Cricket's latest marketing gimmick makes its mark as India belt a boundary against Pakistan at Bangalore.

media people) between games.

Travel in India is problematical at best; a few specific alterations were made to airline schedules to oblige the competition organisers but nowhere near enough to surmount the problem, the size of which became clear during the first, eventful weekend. The teams were all due to gather in Calcutta for a variety of briefing meetings before the much-vaunted opening ceremony, a celebration of technology for which the organisers had outlaid considerable capital.

As it transpired, the weekend was dominated by the issue of two teams, Australia and the West Indies, adamantly refusing to play their scheduled group games in Colombo. The bomb blast in the city a fortnight earlier, was the clinching factor, but Australia's players were already uncomfortable about visiting Sri Lanka, with whom they had just played an acrimonious Test series. In truth, they were reluctant to participate in the Cup at all, the backwash of their bribery allegations against Salim Malik having brought

threats of an unpleasant nature from a number of fanatics around Pakistan.

The West Indies had far less reason for prudence on the Colombo issue, but the condemnatory tone of the organisers against the two defectors gave the episode an unwarranted tone, intensified by a press conference that touched heights of incoherent rancour. It was even suggested that Australia and the West Indies were indulging in a vendetta against the Third World, until it was gently pointed out, by ICC's chairman, Sir Clyde Walcott, himself West Indian, that the Caribbean forms part of the Third World.

Positions being entrenched, the matches were forfeited, though it was a commentary on the cosiness of the format that Australia and the West Indies could make such a sacrifice without seriously endangering their progress to the business end of the tournament. Sri Lanka were both winners and losers – winners because they received four points, and a comfortable passage to the last eight, without playing, but losers because their lovely island was deprived of its two biggest matches at a time when the public was most in need of rousing diversions. For them, however, the grandest of compensations awaited.

The opening ceremony was attended by more than 100,000 people, most of whom must have left wondering what on earth they had been watching. The laser show malfunctioned, the compère was embarrassing, and the grand launch was a complete flop – so much so that there were subsequent calls at Calcuttan government level for the arrest of the Pilcom convenor, Jagmohan Dalmiya, on a charge of wasting public money.

At 4 a.m. the following morning, four teams gathered blearily in the lobby of Calcutta's Oberoi hotel. They were all slated for the 6 a.m. flight to Delhi (India's internal flights tended to run before dawn and after dusk), whereafter they were required to wait many hours before connecting to flights for their various first-game destinations. Had no one thought of organising a charter flight at a civilised hour? Apparently not.

Given this, the choice of the unlovely city of Ahmedabad, and the teams of England and New Zealand, for the opening game of the tournament, should perhaps not seem curious. It was, however, a deflating start, and not just for England, whose obsolete one-day tactics and lack of specific preparation for the only limited-overs event that matters were exposed from the beginning.

England were destined to win only two games in the competition, both against non-league opposition, and one of those, against Holland, by an unflatteringly narrow margin. England once dictated the terms in one-day cricket; unnoticed by them, other countries have caught up and left them behind, developing new and innovative ways of overcoming the essentially negative restrictions of the limited-overs game.

The use of pinch-hitters was one such method, much discussed and granted more significance than it merited, but it was certainly the case that the successful teams no longer looked to accrue the majority of their runs in the closing overs of their innings. Instead of settling for 60 or 70 runs from the initial 15 overs, when fielding restrictions applied, teams were now looking to pass the 100 mark.

On the blissful batting pitches encountered, it was seldom impossible. Sri Lanka, through their fearless openers, Sanath Jayasuriya – later named the Most Valued Player of the Tournament – and Romesh Kaluwitharana, were the trend-setters and, as the outcome proved, nobody did it better. Jayasuriya's assault on England's bowling in the quarter-final at Faisalabad was authentic, aggressive batting without insult to the coaching manual.

There were some memorable images from the over-long group stages. Mark Taylor's sportsmanship, in refusing to claim a slip catch at a pivotal stage against the West Indies, was one. The imperious batting of Mark Waugh and Sachin Tendulkar provided more. But the majority involved the minnow nations.

The best of them was the catch by Kenya's portly, bespectacled and none-too-nimble wicket-keeper, Tariq Iqbal, to dismiss Brian Lara. That it led to a Kenyan victory by 73 runs was part of the romance. Here was the greatest upset the World Cup has known and, perhaps, a salutary lesson to a West Indies team that had become surly and unattractive. Kenya played their cricket as the West Indians once loved to do, without inhibition.

Defeat paradoxically restored pride to the West Indies. They not only rallied to reach the last eight – roused by 93 not out from their beleaguered captain, Richie Richardson, against Australia – but, there, beat the team that had hitherto looked the slickest in the event, South Africa.

The two main host nations predictably reached the quarter-finals, but it was not in the preferred script that they should meet each other so soon. Bangalore had the dubious honour of staging the game, and this beautiful, bustling city has never known such an event. The fact that India won it, before an intensely partisan crowd, perhaps averted the kind of disgraceful scenes witnessed four days later in Calcutta, where Sri Lanka utterly outplayed the Indians.

In the other semi-final, Australia recovered from an apparently hopeless position to beat the West Indies, whose collective nerve crumbled.

Thus was created a meeting, in the final, between two teams who were prevented by politics and expediency from playing each other earlier. Sri Lanka's victory was to the great approval and acclaim of much of the cricket world. It was also a result that, to some degree, rescued this World Cup from an abiding image of bungling mediocrity.

The tournament achieved one aim in increasing the profile of cricket, through TV coverage on an impressive but largely uncritical scale, and undoubtedly it satisfied the organisers in the amount of money accrued. But the impression was that the cricket was secondary to the commercialism.

Even in a game newly awakened to its financial opportunities, that could not be right.

(Wisden Cricketers' Almanack, 1997)

No joy for Shane Warne who has to go wicketless in the final, denied despite his typically vociferous appeal against Arjuna Ranatunga and the support of wicketkeeper Ian Healy.

SEMI-FINALS
India v Sri Lanka

At Eden Gardens, Calcutta, March 13, 1996 (day/night). Sri Lanka won by default after a crowd riot.

Sri Lanka played brilliantly after a disastrous first over to achieve an unbeatable advantage. But the headlines were devoted to the riot which ended the match. Enraged by an Indian collapse of seven wickets for 22, some home supporters threw bottles on to the outfield and set fire to the seating.

Referee Clive Lloyd took the teams off for 15 minutes, attempted a restart and then awarded Sri Lanka the game by default. Nobody questioned the result. India needed a near-impossible 132 from 15.5 overs, with only two wickets standing. But the Indian board smarted at the word "default", and asked for Sri Lanka to be declared winners on run-rate.

The authorities – and many home fans – were intensely embarrassed by the trouble. Even as the match was abandoned, one Indian raised a banner reading: "Congratulation [sic] Sri Lanka – we are sorry." Some took out apologetic advertisements in the Sri Lankan press. But, like the Pakistani fans four days before, others raged against their unsuccessful players, and a guard was placed on captain Mohammad Azharuddin's house.

Azharuddin took much criticism for fielding first. He knew Sri Lanka preferred to chase, as they did to beat India in Delhi in the earlier round, but critics argued that he should play to his team's strengths, not his opponents' weaknesses.

There were few objections, however, when Romesh Kaluwitharana and Sanath Jayasuriya, Sri Lanka's celebrated pinch-hitters, hit straight to third man in the first four balls of the match. Asanka Gurusinha soon followed, but Aravinda de Silva determinedly stuck to the strategy of scoring as heavily as possible early on: he hit 22 off Venkatesh Prasad's first two overs. Though he was bowled in the 15th over, de Silva had scored 66, with 14 fours, off 47 balls, and Sri Lanka already had 85. Arjuna Ranatunga and Roshan Mahanama (who eventually succumbed to cramp) kept up a steady five an over.

A target of 252 was not necessarily beyond India's batting heroes. Sachin Tendulkar, their tidiest bowler earlier, and Sanjay Manjrekar advanced confidently to

Left above: Eden Gardens' combustible crowd vents its anger at India's collapse in the semi-final.

Left: Referee Clive Lloyd, an earlier World Cup hero (in tie, in conversation with umpire Cyril Mitchley), abandons the match and declares jubilant Sri Lanka winners by default.

98 for one, but when Tendulkar was stumped and, seven balls later, Azharuddin gave Kumar Dharmasena a return catch, the 100,000 crowd was stunned into silence. That did not last, as the collapse fuelled their fury and no play was possible after the loss of Aashish Kapoor to de Silva's running catch in the deep.

The presentation ceremony went ahead as if nothing untoward had occurred and, against the smoking background, Tony Greig conducted post-match interviews so normal they were bizarre. A day later, Jayasuriya was named Most Valued Player of the Tournament, an award clinched by his three for 12 in seven overs in addition to two catches and a run-out. *(Wisden Cricketers' Almanack, 1997)*

Australia v West Indies

At Mohali, March 14, 1996 (day/night). Australia won by five runs.
The West Indies pulled off an extraordinary defeat, losing eight wickets in the final 50 minutes. After 41 overs, they were 165 for two, needing 43 from the last nine. Brian Lara had gone for a run-a-ball 45, but Shivnarine Chanderpaul was heading for a century and Richie Richardson for a glorious conclusion to his captaincy. But once Chanderpaul, hampered by cramp, fell, the innings swerved out of control.

Big hitters Roger Harper and Ottis Gibson were promoted in the order but their wickets, in quick succession, placed more pressure on the recognised batsmen, Jimmy Adams and the out-of-form Keith Arthurton, who soon followed.

Australia were on top for the first time in the game, and a devastating three-over spell from Shane Warne culled three for six. Richardson was still there to face the final over, from Damien Fleming. When he struck the first ball for four, the West Indies needed six from five balls, with two wickets left, and victory was within his grasp.

The final fatal misjudgment was to set off for a single for, even if Curtly Ambrose had got home, it was Richardson who needed the strike. In fact, Ambrose was given out on a TV replay. Last man Courtney Walsh heaved at his first ball and was bowled.

Mark Taylor had controlled the closing stages perfectly, but said afterwards that the West Indies had

won 95% of the match. The game had seemed dead after 40 minutes when Australia, electing to bat on one of the grassier pitches of the tournament, were 15 for four. Ambrose and Ian Bishop had fired out both Waughs, Ricky Ponting, who scored 102 in their previous meeting, and Taylor himself for a combined four runs, and a rout threatened. But Stuart Law and Michael Bevan batted with determination and growing confidence to add 138 in 32 overs, and the later order pushed the total past 200. Though Warne dismissed Courtney Browne with his first ball, the West Indies seemed to have the task well in hand until panic overtook them.

(*Wisden Cricketers' Almanack, 1997*)

FINAL
Australia v Sri Lanka

At Gaddafi Stadium, Lahore, March 17 (day/night). Sri Lanka won by seven wickets.
Contrary to most expectations, Sri Lanka controlled their first World Cup final after the initial stages. Their batting was vastly more proficient against spin, their catching was flawless where the Australians held

one chance out of five, their ground fielding was sure while the Australians frequently fumbled, and their spinner obtained enough turn on what was otherwise a batsman's pitch to stifle the Australians after their confident start.

Only in pace bowling were the Sri Lankans the lesser side on the day, and their two opening bowlers did not feature again after the first 13 overs cost 72 runs.

The first day/night international in Pakistan was played in cool conditions and there was no sun, even in daytime. Storms the previous night were followed by rain just as Prime Minister Benazir Bhutto presented the Wills World Cup to Arjuna Ranatunga, one of the longest survivors among contemporary

Above left: Cup in sight for Arjuna Ranatunga as Sri Lanka's captain steers more runs to third man in his match-winning partnership with Aravinda de Silva.

Above right: Quick but futile work by Sri Lanka's wicket-keeper Romesh Kaluwitharana was not quite fast enough to remove Australia's finisher, Michael Bevan.

international cricketers.

In spite of the dampness, the Australians would have batted first in any event, but Ranatunga chose to field first in the hope of some early wickets for the seamers and because his batsmen had shown exceptional maturity of temperament in their earlier run-chases. If his plan did not work out exactly – the hitherto impressive Chaminda Vaas pitching too short – his seamers did succeed in removing Australia's best player of spin, Mark Waugh, who clipped a half-volley to square leg.

The significance of his dismissal was not apparent while Mark Taylor and Ricky Ponting took the score to 137 by the 27th over. Then Taylor was caught sweeping at de Silva, who began his various contributions with a spell of five overs for two wickets and 19 runs. Four overs later, Ponting missed his cut at an off-break which left Australia without a settled batsman to take on four spinners as they tightened their grip. The balance shifted and Australia's incoming batsmen

were unable to work the ball through the gaps in the infield often enough, let alone score boundaries. After 20 overs, their score was 110 for one, after 40 overs 178 for five. From the 24th over to their 49th, they did not reach the boundary except for a pulled six by Stuart Law. Whereas Taylor hit eight fours and a six, his team-mates mustered just five fours between them as Ranatunga shrewdly kept his three off-spinners and Sanath Jayasuriya going until the end.

Given the excellence of Sri Lanka's batting, the Australians had to take early wickets and catch everything. By the sixth over they did have two wickets, Jayasuriya run out by the narrowest of margins on a TV replay and Romesh Kaluwitharana mis-pulling to square leg. That, however, was the extent of Australia's catching. Law dropped Asanka Gurusinha when 53 off a straightforward pull to deep mid-wicket, and three half-chances were not taken.

Considerable dew made the ball slippery, especially for the spinners, Shane Warne and Mark Waugh, and

the Australians seemed to have little left in their tank for their third high-intensity match in seven days.

Gurusinha flat-batted Warne for four to long-on and for six over long-off from consecutive balls, and provided steadily accelerating support for de Silva, who began with a model on-drive for three first ball and whipped Damien Fleming's straight slower ball in front of square to give Sri Lanka's innings a momentum it never lost. In mid-innings, he was content to push the spinners around and hit only the bad ball hard, and he made sure of his wicket after Gurusinha was out to a wild swing and while Ranatunga was playing himself in.

Just as the required rate was climbing towards a run a ball, Mark Waugh conceded 12 runs from an over, so Sri Lanka needed just 51 off their last ten overs, which became a mere ten from five. de Silva went on to score the third hundred in a World Cup final (after Clive Lloyd and Viv Richards), and finished with 107 from 127 balls, including 13 fours, a remarkable strike-rate

given his certainty of application. It was the first time in six attempts that the side batting second had won the World Cup final.

While a light-hearted crowd favoured Sri Lanka throughout, no malice was directed towards the Australians, worried though they had been about the repercussions from the Salim Malik affair. A well-lit and well-staged match was enjoyed by considerably more than the official capacity of 23,826 spectators.
(Scyld Berry, Wisden Cricketers' Almanack, 1997)

Man of the Match Aravinda de Silva punches more runs on his way to his unbeaten 107, carrying Sri Lanka to the championship, in partnership with captain Arjuna Ranatunga and prompting an embrace of ecstasy and relief as the deed is done.

"They said at the time"

Sri Lanka captain Arjuna Ranatunga: *"We are four years ahead of ourselves in winning the World Cup. Now comes the task of finding a couple of fast bowlers who can lead us to the top in Test cricket by the year 2000."*

Sri Lankan President Chandrika Kumaratunga: *"We have shown that even a small country can achieve great heights. We have proved we are world-class in cricket. My personal greetings as well as those of the nation go out to Arjuna and his team-mates."*

Australia captain Mark Taylor: *"Sri Lanka have improved a hell of a lot in the past few years in one-day cricket and they now have a game-plan – positive batting and defensive bowling. They deserve to be World Cup champions. We didn't play very well against the West Indies [in the semi-final] but we got out of jail in the last ten overs. Today we didn't get out of jail."*

Pakistan captain Wasim Akram after his team's quarter-final loss to India: *"I don't mind criticism. But stoning my house, abusing my family and threatening my life are some things which don't reflect the sporting attitude of the game's enthusiasts."*

Australia coach Bob Simpson: *"If anything, losing that World Cup final has made me more determined to go on. I know the boys are hurting. It's one that got away for me too and I don't like that."*

Christopher Martin-Jenkins in the London Daily Telegraph: *"Sri Lanka were not only unbeaten, but never looked like being bettered by anyone. The way that they expanded everyone's horizons, by exploiting the 15-over rule with such wonderful boldness and by batting of rare quality, was wholly admirable and justly rewarded."*

The Nation newspaper, Barbados, after the West Indies' loss to Kenya, pre-empting captain Richardson's resignation a few days later: *"Richie Richardson is the man who must ultimately pay the price and his resignation must now be properly offered to the Board in a timely manner."*

Format

Two qualifying groups of six: each team played the other five in its group to determine the quarter-finalists. In other words, it took 30 matches to eliminate Zimbabwe and the three minnows, then seven more to reduce the remaining Test nations to one winner.

Innovations

15-over fielding restrictions had made their debut in 1992, but 1996 was the year the pinch-hitters really seized their opportunity. Sri Lanka, Australia and India exploited the wide open spaces with aggressive early batting. England didn't. The third umpire also made his first appearance in front of the TV monitor.

World Cup 1996
Scoreboards

England v New Zealand, Group B
At Gujarat Stadium, Motera, Ahmedabad, 14 February 1996 (50-overs)
Result: New Zealand won by 11 runs. Points: New Zealand 2, England 0.
Toss: England. Umpires: BC Cooray (SL) and SG Randell (Aus).
TV Umpire: S Toohey (Neth). Match Referee: MAK Pataudi.
Man of the Match: NJ Astle.

New Zealand innings (50 overs maximum)			R	B	4	6
CM Spearman		c & b Cork	5	16	0	0
NJ Astle	c Hick	b Martin	101	132	8	2
SP Fleming	c Thorpe	b Hick	28	47	3	0
RG Twose	c Thorpe	b Hick	17	26	1	0
CL Cairns	c Cork	b Illingworth	36	30	4	1
CZ Harris	run out		10	16	1	0
SA Thomson	not out		17	23	1	0
*+LK Germon	not out		13	12	0	0
Extras	(b 4, lb 2, w 4, nb 2)		12			
Total	(6 wickets, 50 overs)		239			

DNB: GR Larsen, DJ Nash, DK Morrison.
Fall of wickets: 1-12 (Spearman), 2-108 (Fleming), 3-141 (Twose), 4-196 (Cairns), 5-204 (Astle), 6-212 (Harris).

Bowling	O	M	R	W	
Cork	10	1	36	1	(1nb, 1w)
Martin	6	0	37	1	
Gough	10	0	63	0	
Illingworth	10	1	31	1	
Hick	9	0	45	2	(3w)
White	5	0	21	0	(1nb)

England innings (target: 240 runs from 50 overs)		R	B	4	6
*MA Atherton	b Nash	1	3	0	0
AJ Stewart	c & b Harris	34	71	3	0
GA Hick	run out	85	102	9	0
GP Thorpe	b Larsen	9	21	0	0
NH Fairbrother	b Morrison	36	46	1	0
+RC Russell	c Morrison	b Larsen	2	9	0	0
C White	c Cairns	b Thomson	13	12	0	1
DG Cork	c Germon	b Nash	19	11	2	1
D Gough	not out	15	17	0	0
PJ Martin	c Cairns	b Nash	3	7	0	0
RK Illingworth	not out	3	4	0	0
Extras	(b 1, lb 4, w 1, nb 2)	8			
Total	(9 wickets, 50 overs)	228			

Fall of wickets: 1-1 (Atherton), 2-100 (Stewart), 3-123 (Thorpe), 4-144 (Hick), 5-151 (Russell), 6-180 (White), 7-185 (Fairbrother), 8-210 (Cork), 9-222 (Martin).

Bowling	O	M	R	W	
Morrison	8	0	38	1	(1nb, 1w)
Nash	7	1	26	3	(1w)
Cairns	4	0	24	0	
Larsen	10	1	33	2	
Thomson	10	0	51	1	
Harris	9	0	45	1	
Astle	2	0	6	0	

South Africa v United Arab Emirates, Group B
At Rawalpindi Cricket Stadium, 16 February 1996 (50-overs)
Result: South Africa won by 169 runs. Points: South Africa 2, United Arab Emirates 0.
Toss: United Arab Emirates. Umpires: SA Bucknor (WI) and VK Ramaswamy (Ind).
TV Umpire: A Sarkar (Ken). Match Referee: RS Madugalle (SL).
Man of the Match: G Kirsten.

South Africa innings (50 overs maximum)		R	B	4	6
AC Hudson	b Samarasekera	27	33	5	0
G Kirsten	not out	188	159	13	4
*WJ Cronje	st Imtiaz Abbasi	b Zarawani	57	62	1	1
DJ Cullinan	not out	41	50	2	0
Extras	(b 1, lb 1, w 3, nb 3)	8			
Total	(2 wickets, 50 overs)	321			

DNB: JH Kallis, JN Rhodes, BM McMillan, SM Pollock, +SJ Palframan, CR Matthews, AA Donald.
Fall of wickets: 1-60 (Hudson), 2-176 (Cronje).

Bowling	O	M	R	W	
Samarasekera	9	2	39	1	(2w, 2nb)
Shehzad Altaf	3	0	22	0	(1w)
Arshad Laeeq	6	0	52	0	
Dukanwala	10	0	64	0	
Azhar Saeed	7	0	41	0	
Zarawani	10	0	69	1	
Mazhar Hussain	5	0	32	0	(1nb)

United Arab Emirates innings (target: 322 runs from 50 overs)		R	B	4	6
Azhar Saeed	c McMillan	b Pollock	11	24	2	0
G Mylvaganam	c Palframan	b Donald	23	36	3	0
Mazhar Hussain		b Donald	14	42	0	0
V Mehra	run out (McMillan)		2	12	0	0
Mohammad Aslam		b McMillan	9	5	1	0
Arshad Laeeq	not out		43	79	4	0
JA Samarasekera	c Hudson	b Donald	4	12	0	0
*Sultan Zarawani	c Cronje	b McMillan	0	7	0	0
+Imtiaz Abbasi	c Palframan	b McMillan	1	7	0	0
SF Dukanwala	not out		40	78	4	0
Extras	(w 3, nb 2)		5			
Total	(8 wickets, 50 overs)		152			

DNB: Shehzad Altaf.
Fall of wickets: 1-24 (Azhar Saeed), 2-42 (Mylvaganam), 3-46 (Mehra), 4-60 (Mohammad Aslam), 5-62 (Mazhar Hussain), 6-68 (Samarasekera), 7-70 (Zarawani), 8-72 (Imtiaz Abbasi).

Bowling	O	M	R	W
Pollock	9	2	28	1
Matthews	10	0	39	0
Donald	10	0	21	3
Cronje	4	0	17	0
McMillan	8	1	11	3
Kallis	6	0	27	0
Kirsten	3	1	9	0

NB: Match was delayed from 15 February due to rain and a flooded ground.

West Indies v Zimbabwe, Group A
At Lal Bahadur Shastri Stadium, Hyderabad, Deccan (day/night), 16 February 1996 (50-overs)
Result: West Indies won by 6 wickets. Points: West Indies 2, Zimbabwe 0.
Toss: Zimbabwe. Umpires: RS Dunne (NZ) and S Venkataraghavan.
TV Umpire: Mian Mohammad Aslam (Pak). Match Referee: R Subba Row (Eng).
Man of the Match: CEL Ambrose.

Zimbabwe innings (50 overs maximum)			R	B	4	6
*+A Flower	c Browne	b Ambrose	3	4	0	0
GW Flower		c & b Gibson	31	54	6	0
GJ Whittall	run out		14	62	0	0
ADR Campbell	run out (Lara)		0	8	0	0
AC Waller	st Browne	b Harper	21	44	2	0
CN Evans	c Browne	b Ambrose	21	31	2	0
SG Davies	run out (Bishop)		9	35	0	0
HH Streak	lbw	b Walsh	7	18	0	0
PA Strang	not out		22	28	2	0
EA Brandes	c Chanderpaul	b Ambrose	7	13	1	0
ACI Lock	not out		1	5	0	0
Extras	(lb 10, w 4, nb 1)		15			
Total	(9 wickets, 50 overs)		151			

Fall of wickets: 1-11 (A Flower), 2-53 (GW Flower), 3-56 (Campbell), 4-59 (Whittall), 5-91 (Evans), 6-103 (Waller), 7-115 (Davies), 8-125 (Streak), 9-142 (Brandes).

Bowling	O	M	R	W	
Ambrose	10	2	28	3	(4w)
Walsh	10	3	27	1	
Gibson	9	1	27	1	
Bishop	10	3	18	0	(1nb)
Harper	10	1	30	1	
Arthurton	1	0	11	0	

West Indies innings (target: 152 runs from 50 overs)			R	B	4	6
SL Campbell		b Strang	47	88	5	0
*RB Richardson	c Campbell	b Strang	32	47	3	0
BC Lara	not out		43	31	5	2
S Chanderpaul		b Strang	8	4	2	0
KLT Arthurton	c Campbell	b Strang	1	3	0	0
RA Harper	not out		5	6	1	0
Extras	(b 5, lb 3, w 10, nb 1)		19			
Total	(4 wickets, 29.3 overs)		155			

DNB: +CO Browne, OD Gibson, IR Bishop, CEL Ambrose, CA Walsh.
Fall of wickets: 1-78 (Richardson), 2-115 (Campbell), 3-123 (Chanderpaul), 4-136 (Arthurton).

Bowling	O	M	R	W	
Streak	7	0	34	0	(5w, 1nb)
Lock	6	0	23	0	(4w)
Brandes	7	0	42	0	(1w)
Whittall	2	0	8	0	
Strang	7.3	1	40	4	

Netherlands v New Zealand, Group B
At I.P.C.L. Sports Complex Ground, Baroda, 17 February 1996 (50-overs)
Result: New Zealand won by 119 runs. Points: New Zealand 2, Netherlands 0.
Toss: New Zealand. Umpires: Khizer Hayat (Pak) and ID Robinson (Zim).
TV Umpire: Shakeel Khan (Pak). Match Referee: MAK Pataudi.
Man of the Match: CM Spearman.

New Zealand innings (50 overs maximum)

			R	B	4	6
CM Spearman	c Zuiderent	b Lubbers	68	59	8	0
NJ Astle	run out		0	5	0	0
SP Fleming	c Zuiderent	b Lubbers	66	79	4	0
RG Twose	st Schewe	b Lubbers	25	32	1	0
CL Cairns		b Cantrell	52	37	4	2
AC Parore	c Clarke	b Aponso	55	55	0	3
CZ Harris	c Schewe	b Bakker	8	12	0	0
*+LK Germon	not out		14	11	1	0
DN Patel	c Schewe	b Bakker	11	10	1	0
DK Morrison	not out		0	0	0	0
Extras	(lb 7, w 1)		8			
Total	(8 wickets, 50 overs)		307			

DNB: RJ Kennedy.
Fall of wickets: 1-1 (Astle), 2-117 (Spearman), 3-155 (Fleming), 4-165 (Twose), 5-253 (Cairns), 6-279 (Parore), 7-292 (Harris), 8-306 (Patel).

Bowling	O	M	R	W	
Lefebvre	10	0	48	0	
Bakker	10	0	51	2	
de Leede	7	0	58	0	(1w)
Aponso	10	0	60	1	
Lubbers	9	0	48	3	
Cantrell	4	0	35	1	

Netherlands innings (target: 308 runs from 50 overs)

			R	B	4	6
NE Clarke		b Kennedy	14	21	2	0
PE Cantrell	c Astle	b Harris	45	86	5	0
GJAF Aponso	c Astle	b Harris	11	31	2	0
*SW Lubbers	run out		5	19	0	0
RP Lefebvre		b Kennedy	45	64	3	0
TBM de Leede	lbw	b Harris	1	4	0	0
KJJ van Noortwijk	not out		36	54	3	0
+MMC Schewe	st Germon	b Fleming	12	16	1	0
B Zuiderent	not out		1	6	0	0
Extras	(b 3, lb 5, w 8, nb 2)		18			
Total	(7 wickets, 50 overs)		188			

DNB: EL Gouka, PJ Bakker.
Fall of wickets: 1-18 (Clarke), 2-52 (Aponso), 3-66 (Lubbers), 4-100 (Cantrell), 5-102 (de Leede), 6-147 (Lefebvre), 7-181 (Schewe).

Bowling	O	M	R	W	
Morrison	4	1	11	0	
Kennedy	10	2	36	2	(1nb, 4w)
Cairns	7	1	24	0	(1nb)
Harris	10	1	24	3	
Patel	10	0	43	0	
Astle	5	0	20	0	
Fleming	2	0	8	1	
Twose	2	0	14	0	(4w)

Sri Lanka v Australia, Group A

At R.Premadasa Stadium, Khettarama, Colombo, 17 February 1996 (50-overs)
Result: Sri Lanka won by a walkover. Points: Sri Lanka 2, Australia 0.
Toss: None. Umpires: Mahboob Shah (Pak) and CJ Mitchley (SA).
TV Umpire: Farid Malik (UAE). Match Referee: Nasim-ul-Ghani (Pak).
Man of the Match: No award
NB: Australia were not in attendance - forfeited the match due to safety concerns.

India v Kenya, Group A

At Barabati Stadium, Cuttack, 18 February 1996 (50-overs)
Result: India won by 7 wickets. Points: India 2, Kenya 0.
Toss: India. Umpires: KT Francis (SL) and DR Shepherd (Eng).
TV Umpire: S Toohey (Neth). Match Referee: CH Lloyd (WI).
Man of the Match: SR Tendulkar.

Kenya innings (50 overs maximum)

			R	B	4	6
DN Chudasama	c Mongia	b Prasad	29	51	5	0
+KO Otieno	c Mongia	b Raju	27	58	3	0
SO Tikolo	c Kumble	b Raju	65	83	4	1
*MO Odumbe	st Mongia	b Kumble	26	57	0	0
HS Modi	c Jadeja	b Kumble	2	3	0	0
TM Odoyo	c Prabhakar	b Kumble	8	18	0	0
EO Odumbe	not out		15	21	0	0
AY Karim	not out		6	11	0	0
Extras	(b 2, lb 11, w 7, nb 1)		21			
Total	(6 wickets, 50 overs)		199			

DNB: LO Tikolo, MA Suji, RW Ali.
Fall of wickets: 1-41 (Chudasama), 2-65 (Otieno), 3-161 (MO Odumbe), 4-161 (SO Tikolo), 5-165 (Modi), 6-184 (Odoyo).

Bowling	O	M	R	W	
Prabhakar	5	1	19	0	
Srinath	10	0	38	0	(5w)
Prasad	10	0	41	1	(2w)
Kumble	10	0	28	3	
Raju	10	2	34	2	
Tendulkar	5	0	26	0	

India innings (target: 200 runs from 50 overs)

			R	B	4	6
A Jadeja	c Ali	b Karim	53	85	4	1
SR Tendulkar	not out		127	138	15	1
NS Sidhu	c Suji	b SO Tikolo	1	11	0	0
VG Kambli	c LO Tikolo	b MO Odumbe	2	11	0	0
+NR Mongia	not out		8	7	1	0
Extras	(lb 5, w 6, nb 1)		12			
Total	(3 wickets, 41.5 overs)		203			

DNB: *M Azharuddin, M Prabhakar, J Srinath, A Kumble, BKV Prasad, SLV Raju.
Fall of wickets: 1-163 (Jadeja), 2-167 (Sidhu), 3-182 (Kambli).

Bowling	O	M	R	W	
Ali	5	0	25	0	
EO Odumbe	3	0	18	0	(3w)
Suji	5	0	20	0	
Odoyo	3	0	22	0	(1nb)
Karim	10	1	27	1	
LO Tikolo	3	0	21	0	(3w)
MO Odumbe	9.5	1	39	1	
SO Tikolo	3	0	26	1	

England v United Arab Emirates, Group B

At Arbab Niaz Stadium, Peshawar, 18 February 1996 (50-overs)
Result: England won by 8 wickets. Points: England 2, United Arab Emirates 0.
Toss: United Arab Emirates. Umpires: BC Cooray (SL) and VK Ramaswamy (Ind).
TV Umpire: RC Sharma (Ind). Match Referee: JR Reid (NZ).
Man of the Match: NMK Smith.

United Arab Emirates innings (50 overs maximum)

			R	B	4	6
Azhar Saeed	lbw	b DeFreitas	9	36	1	0
G Mylvaganam	c Fairbrother	b DeFreitas	0	6	0	0
Mazhar Hussain		b Smith	33	59	6	0
V Mehra	c Russell	b Smith	1	34	0	0
Mohammad Aslam		b Gough	23	47	1	0
Arshad Laeeq		b Smith	0	6	0	0
Saleem Raza		b Cork	10	31	0	0
JA Samarasekera	run out		29	39	3	0
*Sultan Zarawani		b Cork	2	8	0	0
SF Dukanwala	lbw	b Illingworth	15	21	1	0
+Imtiaz Abbasi	not out		1	5	0	0
Extras	(b 4, lb 4, w 4, nb 1)		13			
Total	(all out, 48.3 overs)		136			

Fall of wickets: 1-3 (Mylvaganam), 2-32 (Azhar Saeed), 3-48 (Mehra), 4-49 (Mazhar Hussain), 5-49 (Arshad Laeeq), 6-80 (Mohammad Aslam), 7-88 (Saleem Raza), 8-100 (Zarawani), 9-135 (Dukanwala), 10-136 (Samarasekera).

Bowling	O	M	R	W	
Cork	10	1	33	2	(2w)
DeFreitas	9.3	3	16	2	(2w, 1nb)
Gough	8	3	23	1	
White	1.3	1	2	0	
Smith	9.3	2	29	3	
Illingworth	10	2	25	1	

England innings (target: 137 runs from 50 overs)

			R	B	4	6
AJ Stewart	c Mylvaganam	b Arshad Laeeq	23	52	3	0
NMK Smith	retired ill		27	31	4	0
GP Thorpe	not out		44	66	5	0
*MA Atherton		b Azhar Saeed	20	40	1	0
NH Fairbrother	not out		12	29	1	0
Extras	(b 4, lb 2, w 2, nb 6)		14			
Total	(2 wickets, 35 overs)		140			

DNB: +RC Russell, C White, DG Cork, PAJ DeFreitas, D Gough, RK Illingworth.
Fall of wickets: 1-52 (Stewart), 2-109 (Atherton). NB: NMK Smith retired ill at 59/1.

Bowling	O	M	R	W	
Samarasekera	7	1	35	0	(1w, 3nb)
Arshad Laeeq	7	0	25	1	(5nb)
Saleem Raza	5	1	20	0	
Azhar Saeed	10	1	26	1	
Zarawani	6	0	28	0	

New Zealand v South Africa, Group B

At Iqbal Stadium, Faisalabad, 20 February 1996 (50-overs)
Result: South Africa won by 5 wickets. Points: South Africa 2, New Zealand 0.
Toss: New Zealand. Umpires: SG Randell (Aus) and S Venkataraghavan (Ind).
TV Umpire: SK Bansal (Ind). Match Referee: RS Madugalle (SL).
Man of the Match: WJ Cronje.

New Zealand innings (50 overs maximum)

			R	B	4	6
CM Spearman	c Palframan	b Matthews	14	14	3	0
NJ Astle	run out		1	4	0	0
SP Fleming		b McMillan	33	79	2	0
RG Twose	c McMillan	b Pollock	13	17	2	0
CL Cairns		b Donald	9	20	2	0
AC Parore	run out		27	48	0	0
CZ Harris	run out		8	21	0	0
SA Thomson	c Cronje	b Donald	29	54	4	0
*+LK Germon	not out		31	33	2	0
GR Larsen	c Cullinan	b Donald	1	7	0	0
DK Morrison	not out		5	6	0	0
Extras	(lb 4, nb 2)		6			
Total	(9 wickets, 50 overs)		177			

Fall of wickets: 1-7 (Astle), 2-17 (Spearman), 3-36 (Twose), 4-54 (Cairns), 5-85 (Fleming), 6-103 (Harris), 7-116 (Parore), 8-158 (Thomson), 9-165 (Larsen).

Bowling	O	M	R	W	
Pollock	10	1	45	1	
Matthews	10	2	30	1	(1nb)
Donald	10	0	34	3	
Cronje	3	0	13	0	
Symcox	10	1	25	0	
McMillan	7	1	26	1	(1nb)

South Africa innings (target: 178 runs from 50 overs)			R	B	4	6
G Kirsten	lbw	b Harris	35	46	5	0
+SJ Palframan		b Morrison	16	26	3	0
*WJ Cronje	c Fleming	b Astle	78	64	11	3
DJ Cullinan	c Thomson	b Astle	27	42	2	0
JH Kallis	not out		11	25	1	0
JN Rhodes		c & b Larsen	9	13	1	0
BM McMillan	not out		2	10	0	0
Extras			0			
Total	(5 wickets, 37.3 overs)		178			

DNB: SM Pollock, PL Symcox, CR Matthews, AA Donald.
Fall of wickets: 1-41 (Palframan), 2-87 (Kirsten), 3-146 (Cronje), 4-159 (Cullinan), 5-170 (Rhodes).

Bowling	O	M	R	W
Morrison	8	0	44	1
Cairns	6	0	24	0
Larsen	8	1	41	1
Harris	4	0	25	1
Thomson	8.3	0	34	0
Astle	3	1	10	2

Sri Lanka v Zimbabwe, Group A
At Sinhalese Sports Club Ground, Colombo, 21 February 1996 (50-overs)
Result: Sri Lanka won by 6 wickets. Points: Sri Lanka 2, Zimbabwe 0.
Toss: Zimbabwe. Umpires: RS Dunne (NZ) and Mahboob Shah (Pak).
TV Umpire: Farid Malik (UAE). Match Referee: Nasim-ul-Ghani (Pak).
Man of the Match: PA de Silva.

Zimbabwe innings (50 overs maximum)			R	B	4	6
*+A Flower	run out (Vaas)		8	18	1	0
GW Flower	run out (Jayasuriya)		15	32	0	0
GJ Whittall	c Jayasuriya	b Muralitharan	35	64	5	0
ADR Campbell	c Muralitharan	b Vaas	75	102	8	0
AC Waller		b Jayasuriya	19	36	1	0
CN Evans	not out		39	34	5	0
HH Streak	c de Silva	b Vaas	15	13	0	0
PA Strang	not out		0	1	0	0
Extras	(b 1, lb 16, w 4, nb 1)		22			
Total	(6 wickets, 50 overs)		228			

DNB: ACI Lock, EA Brandes, SG Peall.
Fall of wickets: 1-19 (A Flower), 2-51 (GW Flower), 3-92 (Whittall), 4-160 (Waller), 5-194 (Campbell), 6-227 (Streak).

Bowling	O	M	R	W
Vaas	10	0	30	2
Wickramasinghe	8	0	36	0
Ranatunga	2	0	14	0
Dharmasena	10	1	50	0
Muralitharan	10	0	37	1
Jayasuriya	10	0	44	1

Sri Lanka innings (target: 229 runs from 50 overs)			R	B	4	6
ST Jayasuriya		b Streak	6	11	1	0
+RS Kaluwitharana	c Peall	b Streak	0	1	0	0
AP Gurusinha	run out		87	100	5	6
PA de Silva	lbw	b Streak	91	86	10	2
*A Ranatunga	not out		13	11	1	0
HP Tillakaratne	not out		7	16	1	0
Extras	(lb 5, w 17, nb 3)		25			
Total	(4 wickets, 37 overs)		229			

DNB: RS Mahanama, WPUJC Vaas, HDPK Dharmasena, GP Wickramasinghe, M Muralitharan.
Fall of wickets: 1-5 (Kaluwitharana), 2-23 (Jayasuriya), 3-195 (Gurusinha), 4-209 (de Silva).

Bowling	O	M	R	W
Streak	10	0	60	3 (12w, 2nb)
Lock	4	0	17	0 (4w)
Brandes	8	0	35	0 (1w, 1nb)
Peall	3	0	23	0
Strang	5	0	43	0
Whittall	2	0	20	0
GW Flower	5	1	26	0

India v West Indies, Group A
At Captain Roop Singh Stadium, Gwalior (day/night), 21 February 1996 (50-overs)
Result: India won by 5 wickets. Points: India 2, West Indies 0.
Toss: West Indies. Umpires: Khizer Hayat (Pak) and ID Robinson (Zim).
TV Umpire: S Toohey (Neth). Match Referee: R Subba Row (Eng).
Man of the Match: SR Tendulkar.

West Indies innings (50 overs maximum)			R	B	4	6
SL Campbell		b Srinath	5	14	1	0
*RB Richardson	c Kambli	b Prabhakar	47	70	4	0
BC Lara	c Mongia	b Srinath	2	5	0	0
S Chanderpaul	c Azharuddin	b Kapoor	38	66	6	0
RIC Holder		b Kumble	0	3	0	0
RA Harper		b Kumble	23	40	1	1
+CO Browne		b Prabhakar	18	45	0	0
OD Gibson		b Kumble	6	5	1	0
IR Bishop	run out		9	28	0	0
CEL Ambrose	c Kumble	b Prabhakar	8	15	1	0
CA Walsh	not out		9	11	2	0
Extras	(lb 2, w 5, nb 1)		8			
Total	(all out, 50 overs)		173			

Fall of wickets: 1-16 (Campbell), 2-24 (Lara), 3-91 (Richardson), 4-99 (Holder), 5-99 (Chanderpaul), 6-141 (Harper), 7-141 (Browne), 8-149 (Gibson), 9-162 (Ambrose), 10-173 (Bishop).

Bowling	O	M	R	W
Prabhakar	10	0	39	3 (1nb)
Srinath	10	0	22	2
Kumble	10	0	35	3 (5w)
Prasad	10	0	34	0
Kapoor	10	2	41	1

India innings (target: 174 runs from 50 overs)			R	B	4	6
A Jadeja		b Ambrose	1	3	0	0
SR Tendulkar	run out		70	91	8	0
NS Sidhu		b Ambrose	1	5	0	0
*M Azharuddin	c Walsh	b Harper	32	59	4	0
VG Kambli	not out		33	48	4	1
M Prabhakar		c & b Harper	1	12	0	0
+NR Mongia	not out		24	33	3	0
Extras	(lb 3, w 1, nb 8)		12			
Total	(5 wickets, 39.4 overs)		174			

DNB: AR Kapoor, A Kumble, J Srinath, BKV Prasad.
Fall of wickets: 1-2 (Jadeja), 2-15 (Sidhu), 3-94 (Azharuddin), 4-125 (Tendulkar), 5-127 (Prabhakar).

Bowling	O	M	R	W
Ambrose	8	1	41	2 (2nb, 1w)
Walsh	9	3	18	0 (2nb)
Bishop	5	0	28	0 (3nb)
Gibson	8.4	0	50	0 (1nb)
Harper	9	1	34	2

England v Netherlands, Group B
At Arbab Niaz Stadium, Peshawar, 22 February 1996 (50-overs)
Result: England won by 49 runs. Points: England 2, Netherlands 0.
Toss: England. Umpires: SA Bucknor (WI) and KT Francis (SL).
TV Umpire: A Sarkar (Ken). Match Referee: JR Reid (NZ).
Man of the Match: GA Hick.

England innings (50 overs maximum)			R	B	4	6
AJ Stewart		b Bakker	5	13	0	0
NMK Smith	c Clarke	b Jansen	31	33	5	0
GA Hick	not out		104	133	6	2
GP Thorpe	lbw	b Lefebvre	89	82	7	1
*MA Atherton		b Lubbers	10	10	0	0
NH Fairbrother	not out		24	29	1	0
Extras	(lb 12, w 4)		16			
Total	(4 wickets, 50 overs)		279			

DNB: +RC Russell, DG Cork, PAJ DeFreitas, D Gough, PJ Martin.
Fall of wickets: 1-11 (Stewart), 2-42 (Smith), 3-185 (Thorpe), 4-212 (Atherton).

Bowling	O	M	R	W
Lefebvre	10	1	40	1
Bakker	8	0	46	1 (4w)
Jansen	7	0	40	1
Aponso	8	0	55	0
Lubbers	10	0	51	1
de Leede	2	0	9	0
Cantrell	5	0	26	0

Netherlands innings (target: 280 runs from 50 overs)			R	B	4	6
NE Clarke	lbw	b Cork	0	8	0	0
PE Cantrell	lbw	b DeFreitas	28	44	4	0
TBM de Leede	lbw	b DeFreitas	41	42	7	0
*SW Lubbers	c Russell	b DeFreitas	9	8	1	0
KJJ van Noortwijk	c Gough	b Martin	64	82	3	2
B Zuiderent	c Thorpe	b Martin	54	93	2	0
RP Lefebvre	not out		11	14	0	0
+MMC Schewe	not out		11	12	1	0
Extras	(lb 4, w 6, nb 2)		12			
Total	(6 wickets, 50 overs)		230			

DNB: GJAF Aponso, F Jansen, PJ Bakker.
Fall of wickets: 1-1 (Clarke), 2-46 (Cantrell), 3-70 (Lubbers), 4-81 (de Leede), 5-195 (van Noortwijk), 6-210 (Zuiderent).

Bowling	O	M	R	W
Cork	8	0	52	1 (4w, 2nb)
DeFreitas	10	3	31	3
Smith	8	0	27	0
Gough	3	0	23	0
Martin	10	1	42	2 (1w)
Hick	5	0	23	0
Thorpe	6	0	28	0 (1w)

Australia v Kenya, Group A
At Indira Priyadarshini Stadium, Visakhapatnam, 23 February 1996 (50-overs)
Result: Australia won by 97 runs. Points: Australia 2, Kenya 0.
Toss: Kenya. Umpires: CJ Mitchley (SA) and DR Shepherd (Eng).
TV Umpire: Shakeel Khan (Pak). Match Referee: CH Lloyd (WI).
Man of the Match: ME Waugh.

Australia innings (50 overs maximum)			R	B	4	6
*MA Taylor	c Modi	b Suji	6	20	0	0
ME Waugh	c Suji	b Ali	130	128	14	1
RT Ponting	c Otieno	b Ali	6	12	1	0
SR Waugh		c & b Suji	82	88	5	1
SG Law	run out (MO Odumbe)		35	30	3	0
MG Bevan		b Ali	12	12	0	0
+IA Healy	c EO Odumbe	b Karim	17	11	2	0
PR Reiffel	not out		3	2	0	0
SK Warne	not out		0	2	0	0
Extras	(b 1, w 10, nb 2)		13			
Total	(7 wickets, 50 overs)		304			

DNB: CJ McDermott, GD McGrath.
Fall of wickets: 1-10 (Taylor), 2-26 (Ponting), 3-233 (ME Waugh), 4-237 (SR Waugh), 5-261 (Bevan), 6-301 (Law), 7-301 (Healy).

Bowling	O	M	R	W	
Suji	10	1	55	2	(1w, 1nb)
Ali	10	0	45	3	(4w)
Odoyo	8	0	58	0	(1w, 1nb)
EO Odumbe	4	0	21	0	(2w)
Karim	10	1	54	1	
MO Odumbe	4	0	35	0	(1w)
LO Tikolo	3	0	21	0	
SO Tikolo	1	0	14	0	(1w)

Kenya innings (target: 305 runs from 50 overs)			R	B	4	6
+KO Otieno		b McGrath	85	137	8	1
DN Chudasama	c Healy	b McDermott	5	7	1	0
SO Tikolo	c Ponting	b Reiffel	6	8	1	0
*MO Odumbe	c Reiffel	b Bevan	50	53	7	0
HS Modi		b Bevan	10	20	1	0
EO Odumbe	c Bevan	b Reiffel	14	33	0	0
LO Tikolo	not out		11	35	0	0
TM Odoyo	st Healy	b Warne	10	6	2	0
MA Suji	not out		1	4	0	0
Extras	(lb 7, w 6, nb 2)		15			
Total	(7 wickets, 50 overs)		207			

DNB: AY Karim, RW Ali.
Fall of wickets: 1-12 (Chudasama), 2-30 (SO Tikolo), 3-132 (MO Odumbe), 4-167 (Modi), 5-188 (EO Odumbe), 6-195 (Otieno), 7-206 (Odoyo).

Bowling	O	M	R	W	
McDermott	3	0	12	1	(1w)
Reiffel	7	1	18	2	(1w, 1nb)
McGrath	10	0	44	1	(1w)
SR Waugh	7	0	43	0	(1nb)
Warne	10	0	25	1	
Bevan	8	0	35	2	(2w)
ME Waugh	5	0	23	0	(1w)

Pakistan v United Arab Emirates, Group B

At Jinnah Stadium, Gujranwala, 24 February 1996 (50-overs)
Result: Pakistan won by 9 wickets. Points: Pakistan 2, United Arab Emirates 0.
Toss: Pakistan. Umpires: BC Cooray (SL) and S Venkataraghavan (Ind).
TV Umpire: SK Bansal (Ind). Match Referee: RS Madugalle (SL)
Man of the Match: Mushtaq Ahmed.

United Arab Emirates innings (33 overs maximum)			R	B	4	6
G Mylvaganam		b Mushtaq Ahmed	13	50	1	0
Saleem Raza	c Javed Miandad	b Aaqib Javed	22	20	2	1
Azhar Saeed	run out		1	13	0	0
Mazhar Hussain	c Waqar Younis	b Mushtaq Ahmed	7	21	0	0
Mohammad Aslam		b Mushtaq Ahmed	5	9	1	0
Mohammad Ishaq		b Wasim Akram	12	20	1	0
Arshad Laeeq	c Ijaz Ahmed	b Aaqib Javed	9	19	2	0
JA Samarasekera		b Waqar Younis	10	22	0	0
SF Dukanwala	not out		21	19	1	1
*Sultan Zarawani		b Wasim Akram	1	3	0	0
+Imtiaz Abbasi	not out		0	4	0	0
Extras	(lb 1, w 5, nb 2)		8			
Total	(9 wickets, 33 overs)		109			

Fall of wickets: 1-27 (Saleem Raza), 2-40 (Azhar Saeed), 3-47 (Mylvaganam), 4-53 (Mohammad Aslam), 5-54 (Mazhar Hussain), 6-70 (Arshad Laeeq), 7-80 (Mohammad Ishaq), 8-108 (Samarasekera), 9-109 (Zarawani).

Bowling	O	M	R	W	
Wasim Akram	7	1	25	2	(2nb, 1w)
Waqar Younis	7	1	33	1	(1w)
Aaqib Javed	6	0	18	2	(2w)
Mushtaq Ahmed	7	0	16	3	(1w)
Aamer Sohail	6	1	16	0	

Pakistan innings (target: 110 runs from 33 overs)			R	B	4	6
Aamer Sohail		b Samarasekera	5	5	1	0
Saeed Anwar	not out		40	50	4	0
Ijaz Ahmed	not out		50	57	4	1
Extras	(lb 1, w 12, nb 4)		17			
Total	(1 wicket, 18 overs)		112			

DNB: Inzamam-ul-Haq, Javed Miandad, Saleem Malik, *Wasim Akram, +Rashid Latif, Mushtaq Ahmed, Aaqib Javed, Waqar Younis.
Fall of wickets: 1-7 (Aamer Sohail).

Bowling	O	M	R	W	
Samarasekera	3	0	17	1	(2nb, 6w)
Arshad Laeeq	4	0	24	0	(2nb, 3w)
Dukanwala	3	1	14	0	
Saleem Raza	3	0	17	0	
Zarawani	3	0	23	0	(3w)
Azhar Saeed	2	0	16	0	

NB: Match delayed due to rain - shortened to 33 overs a side.

England v South Africa, Group B

At Rawalpindi Cricket Stadium, 25 February 1996 (50-overs)
Result: South Africa won by 78 runs. Points: South Africa 2, England 0.
Toss: South Africa. Umpires: SG Randell (Aus) and ID Robinson (Zim).
TV Umpire: K Parthasarathy (Ind). Match Referee: JR Reid (NZ).
Man of the Match: JN Rhodes.

South Africa innings (50 overs maximum)			R	B	4	6
G Kirsten	run out		38	60	4	0
+SJ Palframan	c Russell	b Martin	28	36	3	0
*WJ Cronje	c Russell	b Gough	15	31	1	0
DJ Cullinan		b DeFreitas	34	42	2	0
JH Kallis	c Russell	b Cork	26	42	2	0
JN Rhodes		b Martin	37	32	3	0
BM McMillan		b Smith	11	17	0	0
SM Pollock	c Fairbrother	b Cork	12	13	0	0
PL Symcox	c Thorpe	b Martin	1	4	0	0
CR Matthews	not out		9	13	0	0
PS de Villiers	c Smith	b Gough	12	11	1	0
Extras	(lb 1, w 5, nb 1)		7			
Total	(all out, 50 overs)		230			

Fall of wickets: 1-56 (Palframan), 2-85 (Kirsten), 3-88 (Cronje), 4-137 (Cullinan), 5-163 (Kallis), 6-195 (Rhodes), 7-199 (McMillan), 8-202 (Symcox), 9-213 (Pollock), 10-230 (de Villiers).

Bowling	O	M	R	W	
Cork	10	0	36	2	(1w)
DeFreitas	10	0	55	1	(1nb, 1w)
Gough	10	0	48	2	
Martin	10	0	33	3	(3w)
Smith	8	0	40	1	
Thorpe	2	0	17	0	

England innings (target: 231 runs from 50 overs)			R	B	4	6
*MA Atherton	c Palframan	b Pollock	0	4	0	0
NMK Smith		b de Villiers	11	24	1	0
GA Hick	c McMillan	b de Villiers	14	27	1	0
GP Thorpe	c Palframan	b Symcox	46	69	3	0
AJ Stewart	run out		7	29	0	0
NH Fairbrother	c Palframan	b Symcox	3	10	0	0
+RC Russell	c Rhodes	b Pollock	12	32	0	0
DG Cork		b Matthews	17	33	1	0
PAJ DeFreitas	run out		22	24	1	1
D Gough		b Matthews	11	12	0	0
PJ Martin	not out		1	3	0	0
Extras	(lb 7, w 1)		8			
Total	(all out, 44.3 overs)		152			

Fall of wickets: 1-0 (Atherton), 2-22 (Hick), 3-33 (Smith), 4-52 (Stewart), 5-62 (Fairbrother), 6-97 (Thorpe), 7-97 (Russell), 8-139 (DeFreitas), 9-141 (Cork), 10-152 (Gough).

Bowling	O	M	R	W	
Pollock	8	1	16	2	
de Villiers	7	1	27	2	(1w)
Matthews	9.3	0	30	2	
McMillan	6	0	17	0	
Symcox	10	0	38	2	
Cronje	4	0	17	0	

Sri Lanka v West Indies, Group A

At R.Premadasa Stadium, Khettarama, Colombo, 25 February 1996 (50-overs)
Result: Sri Lanka won by a walkover. Points: Sri Lanka 2, West Indies 0.
Toss: No toss. Umpires: Mahboob Shah (Pak) and VK Ramaswamy (Ind).
TV Umpire: Mian Mohammad Aslam (Pak). Match Referee: Nasim-ul-Ghani (Pak).
Man of the Match: No award.
NB: West Indies were not in attendance - forfeited the match due to safety concerns.

Kenya v Zimbabwe, Group A

At Moin-ul-Haq Stadium, Patna, 26 February 1996 (50-overs)
Result: No result. Match to be replayed on 27 February 1996. Points: No points.
Toss: Zimbabwe. Umpires: Khizer Hayat (Pak) and CJ Mitchley (SA).
TV Umpire: Farid Malik (UAE). Match Referee: MAK Pataudi.
Man of the Match: No award.

Zimbabwe innings (50 overs maximum)			R	B	4	6
GW Flower	not out		25	40		
AC Waller	c EO Odumbe	b Ali	3	14	0	0
GJ Whittall	c MO Odumbe	b EO Odumbe	12	33		
ADR Campbell	lbw	b EO Odumbe	0	1	0	0
*+A Flower	not out		0	0	0	0
Extras	(lb 2, w 3)		5			
Total	(3 wickets, 15.5 overs)		45			

DNB: CN Evans, HH Streak, PA Strang, BC Strang, SG Peall, ACI Lock.
Fall of wickets: 1-8 (Waller), 2-44 (Whittall), 3-45 (Campbell).

Bowling	O	M	R	W
Suji	5	1	11	0
Ali	5	0	14	1
Odoyo	3	0	10	0
EO Odumbe	2.5	0	8	2

Kenya team:
DN Chudasama, +IT Iqbal, KO Otieno, SO Tikolo, *MO Odumbe, HS Modi, EO Odumbe, TM Odoyo, AY Karim, MA Suji, RW Ali.
NB: Match abandoned due to rain.

Kenya v Zimbabwe, Group A

At Moin-ul-Haq Stadium, Patna, 27 February 1996 (50-overs)
Result: Zimbabwe won by 5 wickets. Points: Zimbabwe 2, Kenya 0.
Toss: Zimbabwe. Umpires: Khizer Hayat (Pak) and CJ Mitchley (SA).
TV Umpire: Farid Malik (UAE). Match Referee: MAK Pataudi.
Man of the Match: PA Strang.

Kenya innings (50 overs maximum)			R	B	4	6
DN Chudasama	run out		34	66	5	0
+IT Iqbal		b Lock	1	20	0	0
KO Otieno		b Peall	19	51	0	0
SO Tikolo	st A Flower	b BC Strang	0	6	0	0
*MO Odumbe	c BC Strang	b PA Strang	30	64	1	0
HS Modi		b BC Strang	3	10	0	0
EO Odumbe	c Campbell	b PA Strang	20	55	0	0
TM Odoyo	c GW Flower	b PA Strang	0	2	0	0
AY Karim	lbw	b PA Strang	0	1	0	0
MA Suji	c GW Flower	b PA Strang	15	23	1	0
RW Ali	not out		0	0	0	0
Extras	(lb 3, w 8, nb 1)		12			
Total	(all out, 49.4 overs)		134			

Fall of wickets: 1-7 (Iqbal), 2-60 (Otieno), 3-61 (Tikolo), 4-63 (Chudasama), 5-67 (Modi), 6-109 (EO Odumbe), 7-109 (Odoyo), 8-109 (Karim), 9-134 (Suji), 10-134 (MO Odumbe).

Bowling	O	M	R	W
Streak	7	2	23	0	(4w)
Lock	8	2	19	1
Whittall	5	0	21	0	(3w, 1nb)
Peall	10	1	23	1	(1w)
BC Strang	10	0	24	2
PA Strang	9.4	1	21	5

Zimbabwe innings (target: 135 runs from 50 overs)			R	B	4	6
AC Waller	c Tikolo	b MO Odumbe	30	32	3	0
GW Flower		b Ali	45	112	4	0
ADR Campbell	c Tikolo	b MO Odumbe	6	26	1	0
GJ Whittall	c EO Odumbe	b Ali	6	36	0	0
*+A Flower	lbw	b Ali	5	8	1	0
CN Evans	not out		8	18	1	0
HH Streak	not out		15	27	1	0
Extras	(b 3, lb 4, w 12, nb 3)		22			
Total	(5 wickets, 42.2 overs)		137			

DNB: PA Strang, SG Peall, BC Strang, ACI Lock.
Fall of wickets: 1-59 (Waller), 2-79 (Campbell), 3-104 (GW Flower), 4-108 (Whittall), 5-113 (A Flower).

Bowling	O	M	R	W
Suji	9.2	0	37	0
Ali	8	1	22	3
EO Odumbe	2	0	14	0
Odoyo	2	0	7	0
Karim	10	1	21	0
MO Odumbe	10	2	24	2
Tikolo	1	0	5	0

Pakistan v Netherlands, Group B

At Gaddafi Stadium, Lahore, 26 February 1996 (50-overs)
Result: Pakistan won by 8 wickets. Points: Pakistan 2, Netherlands 0.
Toss: Netherlands. Umpires: SA Bucknor (WI) and KT Francis (SL).
TV Umpire: RC Sharma (Ind). Match Referee: R Subba Row (Eng).
Man of the Match: Waqar Younis.

Netherlands innings (50 overs maximum)			R	B	4	6
NE Clarke	c Rashid Latif	b Aaqib Javed	4	26	0	0
PE Cantrell	c Ijaz Ahmed	b Waqar Younis	17	32	1	0
TBM de Leede	c Rashid Latif	b Waqar Younis	0	19	0	0
KJJ van Noortwijk	c Mushtaq Ahmed	b Aaqib Javed	33	89	2	1
GJAF Aponso		b Waqar Younis	58	105	3	1
*RP Lefebvre		b Waqar Younis	10	26	0	0
B Zuiderent	run out		6	6	1	0
EL Gouka	not out		0	1	0	0
Extras	(lb 7, w 4, nb 6)		17			
Total	(7 wickets, 50 overs)		145			

DNB: +MMC Schewe, F Jansen, PJ Bakker.
Fall of wickets: 1-16 (Clarke), 2-28 (Cantrell), 3-29 (de Leede), 4-102 (van Noortwijk), 5-130 (Aponso), 6-143 (Lefebvre), 7-145 (Zuiderent).

Bowling	O	M	R	W
Wasim Akram	10	1	30	0	(3nb, 1w)
Waqar Younis	10	0	26	4	(2nb, 1w)
Aaqib Javed	9	2	25	2	(1nb, 1w)
Mushtaq Ahmed	10	2	27	0
Aamer Sohail	9	0	21	0	(1w)
Saleem Malik	2	0	9	0

Pakistan innings (target: 146 runs from 50 overs)			R	B	4	6
Aamer Sohail	c Jansen	b Lefebvre	9	24	1	0
Saeed Anwar	not out		83	92	9	3
Ijaz Ahmed	c Lefebvre	b Cantrell	39	55	2	1
Inzamam-ul-Haq	not out		18	13	0	1
Extras	(lb 1, w 1)		2			
Total	(2 wickets, 30.4 overs)		151			

DNB: Javed Miandad, Saleem Malik, *Wasim Akram, +Rashid Latif, Mushtaq Ahmed, Aaqib Javed, Waqar Younis.
Fall of wickets: 1-10 (Aamer Sohail), 2-104 (Ijaz Ahmed).

Bowling	O	M	R	W
Lefebvre	7	1	20	1
Bakker	7	1	13	0
Jansen	2	0	22	0	(1w)
de Leede	4	0	20	0
Aponso	5	0	38	0
Cantrell	4	0	18	1
Gouka	1.4	0	19	0

New Zealand v United Arab Emirates, Group B

At Iqbal Stadium, Faisalabad, 27 February 1996 (50-overs)
Result: New Zealand won by 109 runs. Points: New Zealand 2, United Arab Emirates 0.
Toss: United Arab Emirates. Umpires: BC Cooray (SL) and S Venkataraghavan (Ind).
TV Umpire: Ikram Rabbani. Match Referee: RS Madugalle (SL).
Man of the Match: RG Twose.

New Zealand innings (47 overs maximum)			R	B	4	6
CM Spearman		b Saleem Raza	78	77	10	0
NJ Astle		b Samarasekera	2	2	0	0
SP Fleming		c & b Dukanwala	16	11	4	0
RG Twose	c Mazhar Hussain	b Azhar Saeed	92	112	8	0
CL Cairns	c Imtiaz Abbasi	b Zarawani	6	20	0	0
AC Parore	c Azhar Saeed	b Zarawani	15	18	0	0
SA Thomson	not out		31	35	2	0
*+LK Germon		b Azhar Saeed	3	6	0	0
DJ Nash	lbw	b Azhar Saeed	8	12	0	0
DK Morrison	not out		10	2	1	1
Extras	(b 2, lb 12, nb 1)		15			
Total	(8 wickets, 47 overs)		276			

DNB: RJ Kennedy.
Fall of wickets: 1-11 (Astle), 2-42 (Fleming), 3-162 (Spearman), 4-173 (Cairns), 5-210 (Parore), 6-228 (Twose), 7-239 (Germon), 8-266 (Nash).

Bowling	O	M	R	W
Samarasekera	6	0	30	1
Arshad Laeeq	2	0	16	0
Saleem Raza	9	0	48	1
Dukanwala	10	0	46	1	(1nb)
Mazhar Hussain	3	0	28	0
Azhar Saeed	7	0	45	3
Zarawani	10	0	49	2

United Arab Emirates innings (target: 277 runs from 47 overs)			R	B	4	6
Azhar Saeed	c Fleming	b Nash	5	20	0	0
Saleem Raza	c Kennedy	b Morrison	21	17	1	1
Mazhar Hussain	c Cairns	b Thomson	29	53	5	0
V Mehra	c Cairns	b Thomson	12	21	1	0
Mohammad Ishaqc Fleming		b Kennedy	8	9	0	0
Mohammad Aslamc Twose		b Thomson	1	12	0	0
SF Dukanwala		c & b Cairns	8	21	0	0
Arshad Laeeq	run out		14	36	3	0
JA Samarasekera	not out		47	59	5	0
*Sultan Zarawani	c Thomson	b Nash	13	18	1	0
+Imtiaz Abbasi	not out		2	6	0	0
Extras	(lb 2, w 3, nb 2)		7			
Total	(9 wickets, 47 overs)		167			

Fall of wickets: 1-23 (Azhar Saeed), 2-29 (Saleem Raza), 3-65 (Mehra), 4-70 (Mazhar Hussain), 5-81 (Mohammad Ishaq), 6-88 (Mohammad Aslam), 7-92 (Dukanwala), 8-124 (Arshad Laeeq), 9-162 (Zarawani).

Bowling	O	M	R	W
Morrison	7	0	37	1	(2nb)
Nash	9	1	34	2	(2w)
Cairns	10	2	31	1
Kennedy	6	0	20	1	(1w)
Thomson	10	2	20	3
Astle	5	0	30	2

NB: Match reduced to 47 overs a side due to heavy fog at the start of the match.

India v Australia, Group A

At Wankhede Stadium, Mumbai (day/night), 27 February 1996 (50-overs)
Result: Australia won by 16 runs. Points: Australia 2, India 0.
Toss: Australia. Umpires: RS Dunne (NZ) and DR Shepherd (Eng).
TV Umpire: TM Samarasinghe (SL). Match Referee: CH Lloyd (WI).
Man of the Match: ME Waugh.

Australia innings (50 overs maximum)			R	B	4	6
ME Waugh	run out (Prasad)		126	135	8	3
*MA Taylor	c Srinath	b Raju	59	73	8	1
RT Ponting	c Manjrekar	b Raju	12	21	0	0
SR Waugh	run out (Raju)		7	15	0	0
SG Law		c & b Kumble	21	31	1	0
MG Bevan	run out (Jadeja)		6	5	0	0
S Lee	run out (Mongia)		9	10	0	0
+IA Healy	c Kumble	b Prasad	6	10	0	0
SK Warne	c Azharuddin	b Prasad	0	1	0	0
DW Fleming	run out (Mongia/Prasad)		0	1	0	0
GD McGrath	not out		0	0	0	0
Extras	(lb 8, w 2, nb 2)		12			
Total	(all out, 50 overs)		258			

Fall of wickets: 1-103 (Taylor), 2-140 (Ponting), 3-157 (SR Waugh), 4-232 (ME Waugh), 5-237 (Law), 6-244 (Bevan), 7-258 (Lee), 8-258 (Warne), 9-258 (Healy), 10-258 (Fleming).

Bowling	O	M	R	W	
Prabhakar	10	0	55	0	
Srinath	10	1	51	0	
Prasad	10	0	49	2	(2nb, 2w)
Kumble	10	1	47	1	
Raju	10	0	48	2	

India innings (target: 259 runs from 50 overs)			R	B	4	6
A Jadeja	lbw	b Fleming	1	17	0	0
SR Tendulkar	st Healy	b ME Waugh	90	84	14	1
VG Kambli		b Fleming	0	2	0	0
*M Azharuddin		b Fleming	10	17	1	0
SV Manjrekar	c Healy	b SR Waugh	62	91	7	0
M Prabhakar	run out (Ponting)		3	6	0	0
+NR Mongia	c Taylor	b Warne	27	32	3	0
A Kumble		b Fleming	17	22	3	0
J Srinath	c Lee	b Fleming	7	12	1	0
BKV Prasad	c Bevan	b SR Waugh	0	2	0	0
SLV Raju	not out		3	4	0	0
Extras	(b 5, lb 8, w 8, nb 1)		22			
Total	(all out, 48 overs)		242			

Fall of wickets: 1-7 (Jadeja), 2-7 (Kambli), 3-70 (Azharuddin), 4-143 (Tendulkar), 5-147 (Prabhakar), 6-201 (Mongia), 7-205 (Manjrekar), 8-224 (Srinath), 9-231 (Prasad), 10-242 (Kumble).

Bowling	O	M	R	W	
McGrath	8	3	48	0	(1nb)
Fleming	9	0	36	5	(2w)
Warne	10	1	28	1	(2w)
Lee	3	0	23	0	(2w)
ME Waugh	10	0	44	1	(1w)
Bevan	5	0	28	0	
SR Waugh	3	0	22	2	(1w)

Kenya v West Indies, Group A

At Nehru Stadium, Poona, 29 February 1996 (50-overs)
Result: Kenya won by 73 runs. Points: Kenya 2, West Indies 0.
Toss: West Indies. Umpires: Khizer Hayat (Pak) and VK Ramaswamy.
TV Umpire: SK Bansal. Match Referee: MAK Pataudi.
Man of the Match: MO Odumbe.

Kenya innings (50 overs maximum)			R	B	4	6
DN Chudasama	c Lara	b Walsh	8	7	2	0
+IT Iqbal	c Cuffy	b Walsh	16	32	2	0
KO Otieno	c Adams	b Walsh	2	5	0	0
SO Tikolo	c Adams	b Harper	29	50	3	1
*MO Odumbe	hit wicket	b Bishop	6	30	0	0
HS Modi	c Adams	b Ambrose	26	74	1	0
MA Suji	c Lara	b Harper	0	4	0	0
TM Odoyo	st Adams	b Harper	24	59	3	0
EO Odumbe		b Cuffy	1	4	0	0
AY Karim	c Adams	b Ambrose	11	27	1	0
RW Ali	not out		6	19	0	0
Extras	(lb 10, w 14, nb 13)		37			
Total	(all out, 49.3 overs)		166			

Fall of wickets: 1-15 (Chudasama), 2-19 (Otieno), 3-45 (Iqbal), 4-72 (MO Odumbe), 5-77 (Tikolo), 6-81 (Suji), 7-125 (Odoyo), 8-126 (EO Odumbe), 9-155 (Modi), 10-166 (Karim).

Bowling	O	M	R	W	
Ambrose	8.3	1	21	2	(5w)
Walsh	9	0	46	3	(6nb, 3w)
Bishop	10	2	30	1	(2nb, 1w)
Cuffy	8	0	31	1	(7nb, 5w)
Harper	10	4	15	3	
Arthurton	4	0	13	0	

West Indies innings (target: 167 runs from 50 overs)			R	B	4	6
SL Campbell		b Suji	4	12	1	0
*RB Richardson		b Ali	5	11	1	0
BC Lara	c Iqbal	b Ali	8	11	1	0
S Chanderpaul	c Tikolo	b MO Odumbe	19	48	3	0
KLT Arthurton	run out		0	6	0	0
+JC Adams	c Modi	b MO Odumbe	9	37	1	0
RA Harper	c Iqbal	b MO Odumbe	17	18	3	0
IR Bishop	not out		6	42	0	0
CEL Ambrose	run out		3	13	0	0
CA Walsh	c Chudasama	b Karim	4	8	1	0
CE Cuffy		b Ali	1	8	0	0
Extras	(b 5, lb 6, w 4, nb 2)		17			
Total	(all out, 35.2 overs)		93			

Fall of wickets: 1-18 (Richardson), 2-22 (Campbell), 3-33 (Lara), 4-35 (Arthurton), 5-55 (Chanderpaul), 6-65 (Adams), 7-78 (Harper), 8-81 (Ambrose), 9-89 (Walsh), 10-93 (Cuffy).

Bowling	O	M	R	W	
Suji	7	2	16	1	
Ali	7.2	2	17	3	
Karim	8	1	19	1	
MO Odumbe	10	3	15	3	
Odoyo	3	0	15	0	

Pakistan v South Africa, Group B

At National Stadium, Karachi, 29 February 1996 (50-overs)
Result: South Africa won by 5 wickets. Points: South Africa 2, Pakistan 0.
Toss: Pakistan. Umpires: SA Bucknor (WI) and KT Francis (SL).
TV Umpire: K Parthasarathy (Ind). Match Referee: R Subba Row (Eng).
Man of the Match: WJ Cronje.

Pakistan innings (50 overs maximum)			R	B	4	6
Aamer Sohail	c Cronje	b Pollock	111	139	8	0
Saeed Anwar	c McMillan	b Cronje	25	30	3	0
Ijaz Ahmed	lbw	b Cronje	0	2	0	0
Inzamam-ul-Haq	run out		23	39	3	0
Saleem Malik	c Palframan	b Adams	40	66	3	0
*Wasim Akram	not out		32	25	3	0
+Rashid Latif	lbw	b Matthews	0	1	0	0
Rameez Raja	not out		2	2	0	0
Extras	(b 1, lb 2, w 4, nb 2)		9			
Total	(6 wickets, 50 overs)		242			

DNB: Mushtaq Ahmed, Saqlain Mushtaq, Waqar Younis.
Fall of wickets: 1-52 (Saeed Anwar), 2-52 (Ijaz Ahmed), 3-112 (Inzamam-ul-Haq), 4-189 (Saleem Malik), 5-233 (Aamer Sohail), 6-235 (Rashid Latif).

Bowling	O	M	R	W	
Pollock	9	0	49	1	(1nb)
Matthews	10	0	47	1	(1w)
Cronje	5	0	20	2	
Donald	8	0	50	0	(1nb, 1w)
Adams	10	0	42	1	(2w)
McMillan	8	0	31	0	

South Africa innings (target: 243 runs from 50 overs)			R	B	4	6
AC Hudson		b Waqar Younis	33	26	6	0
G Kirsten		b Saqlain Mushtaq	44	57	5	0
BM McMillan	lbw	b Waqar Younis	1	4	0	0
DJ Cullinan		b Waqar Younis	65	76	6	0
JH Kallis		c & b Saqlain Mushtaq	9	14	0	0
*WJ Cronje	not out		45	73	2	0
SM Pollock	not out		20	28	1	0
Extras	(b 8, lb 4, w 6, nb 8)		26			
Total	(5 wickets, 44.2 overs)		243			

DNB: +SJ Palframan, CR Matthews, AA Donald, PR Adams.
Fall of wickets: 1-51 (Hudson), 2-53 (McMillan), 3-111 (Kirsten), 4-125 (Kallis), 5-203 (Cullinan).

Bowling	O	M	R	W	
Wasim Akram	9.2	0	49	0	(4nb)
Waqar Younis	8	0	50	3	(2nb, 3w)
Mushtaq Ahmed	10	0	54	0	
Aamer Sohail	6	0	35	0	(2nb, 2w)
Saqlain Mushtaq	10	1	38	2	(1w)
Saleem Malik	1	0	5	0	

Australia v Zimbabwe, Group A

At Vidarbha C.A. Ground, Nagpur, 1 March 1996 (50-overs)
Result: Australia won by 8 wickets. Points: Australia 2, Zimbabwe 0.
Toss: Zimbabwe. Umpires: RS Dunne (NZ) and DR Shepherd (Eng).
TV Umpire: TM Samarasinghe (SL). Match Referee: CH Lloyd (WI).
Man of the Match: SK Warne.

Zimbabwe innings (50 overs maximum)			R	B	4	6
AC Waller	run out		67	101	10	0
GW Flower		b McGrath	4	16	0	0
GJ Whittall		c & b SR Waugh	6	22	1	0
ADR Campbell	c ME Waugh	b SR Waugh	5	10	1	0
*+A Flower	st Healy	b Warne	7	15	1	0
CN Evans	c Healy	b Warne	18	24	2	1
HH Streak	c SR Waugh	b Fleming	13	41	0	0
PA Strang	not out		16	29	1	0
BC Strang		b Fleming	0	2	0	0
SG Peall	c Healy	b Warne	0	4	0	0
ACI Lock		b Warne	5	11	1	0
Extras	(lb 8, w 3, nb 2)		13			
Total	(all out, 45.3 overs)		154			

Fall of wickets: 1-21 (GW Flower), 2-41 (Whittall), 3-55 (Campbell), 4-68 (A Flower), 5-106 (Evans), 6-126 (Waller), 7-140 (Streak), 8-140 (BC Strang), 9-145 (Peall), 10-154 (Lock).

Bowling	O	M	R	W	
McGrath	8	2	12	1	
Fleming	9	1	30	2	(1nb)
Lee	4	2	8	0	(1nb)
SR Waugh	7	2	22	2	
Warne	9.3	1	34	4	(3w)
ME Waugh	5	0	30	0	
Law	3	0	10	0	

Australia innings (target: 155 runs from 50 overs)			R	B	4	6
*MA Taylor	c BC Strang	b PA Strang	34	50	5	0
ME Waugh	not out		76	109	10	0
RT Ponting		c & b PA Strang	33	51	4	0
SR Waugh	not out		5	7	1	0
Extras	(b 6, lb 2, w 1, nb 1)		10			
Total	(2 wickets, 36 overs)		158			

DNB: SG Law, MG Bevan, S Lee, +IA Healy, SK Warne, DW Fleming, GD McGrath.
Fall of wickets: 1-92 (Taylor), 2-150 (Ponting).

Bowling	O	M	R	W	
Streak	10	3	29	0	(1nb, 1w)
Lock	4	0	25	0	
BC Strang	3	0	20	0	
Whittall	2	0	11	0	
PA Strang	10	2	33	2	
Peall	4	0	20	0	
GW Flower	3	0	12	0	

Netherlands v United Arab Emirates, Group B

At Gaddafi Stadium, Lahore, 1 March 1996 (50-overs)
Result: United Arab Emirates won by 7 wickets.
Points: United Arab Emirates 2, Netherlands 0.
Toss: United Arab Emirates. Umpires: Mahboob Shah and SG Randell (Aus).
TV Umpire: RC Sharma (Ind). Match Referee: Nasim-ul-Ghani.
Men of the Match: SF Dukanwala and Saleem Raza.

Netherlands innings (50 overs maximum)			R	B	4	6
NE Clarke	c Mehra	b Shehzad Altaf	0	11	0	0
PE Cantrell	c Imtiaz Abbasi	b Azhar Saeed	47	106	1	0
GJAF Aponso		c & b Dukanwala	45	80	6	0
TBM de Leede		c & b Azhar Saeed	36	47	3	0
KJJ van Noortwijk	c Zarawani	b Dukanwala	26	19	3	0
*SW Lubbers	c Saeed-al-Saffar	b Zarawani	8	8	1	0
RP Lefebvre	c Mohammad Ishaqb	Dukanwala	12	8	0	1
B Zuiderent	st Imtiaz Abbasi	b Dukanwala	3	5	0	0
+MMC Schewe		b Dukanwala	6	6	0	0
RF van Oosterom	not out		2	4	0	0
PJ Bakker	not out		1	4	0	0
Extras	(b 4, lb 15, w 11)		30			
Total	(9 wickets, 50 overs)		216			

Fall of wickets: 1-3 (Clarke), 2-77 (Aponso), 3-148 (de Leede), 4-153 (Cantrell), 5-168 (Lubbers), 6-200 (van Noortwijk), 7-200 (Lefebvre), 8-209 (Zuiderent), 9-210 (Schewe).

Bowling	O	M	R	W	
Shehzad Altaf	10	3	15	1	
Samarasekera	9	1	36	0	
Saeed-al-Saffar	3	0	25	0	
Dukanwala	10	0	29	5	
Zarawani	8	0	40	1	
Saleem Raza	5	0	23	0	
Azhar Saeed	5	0	29	2	

United Arab Emirates innings (target: 217 runs from 50 overs)			R	B	4	6
Azhar Saeed	run out		32	82	2	0
Saleem Raza	c Zuiderent	b Lubbers	84	68	7	6
Mazhar Hussain	c Clarke	b Lefebvre	16	14	3	0
V Mehra	not out		29	45	2	0
Mohammad Ishaq	not out		51	55	8	0
Extras	(lb 7, w 1)		8			
Total	(3 wickets, 44.2 overs)		220			

DNB: JA Samarasekera, SF Dukanwala, *Sultan Zarawani, Saeed-al-Saffar, +Imtiaz Abbasi, Shehzad Altaf.
Fall of wickets: 1-117 (Saleem Raza), 2-135 (Mazhar Hussain), 3-138 (Azhar Saeed).

Bowling	O	M	R	W	
Bakker	8	0	41	0	
Lefebvre	8	0	24	1	(1w)
Lubbers	9	0	38	1	
Cantrell	8	0	30	0	
Aponso	7.2	0	47	0	
de Leede	4	0	33	0	

India v Sri Lanka, Group A

At Feroz Shah Kotla, Delhi, 2 March 1996 (50-overs)
Result: Sri Lanka won by 6 wickets. Points: Sri Lanka 2, India 0.
Toss: Sri Lanka. Umpires: CJ Mitchley (SA) and ID Robinson (Zim).
TV Umpire: Ikram Rabbani (Pak). Match Referee: JR Reid (NZ).
Man of the Match: ST Jayasuriya.

India innings (50 overs maximum)			R	B	4	6
M Prabhakar	c Gurusinha	b Pushpakumara	7	36	1	0
SR Tendulkar	run out		137	137	8	5
SV Manjrekar	c Kaluwitharana	b Dharmasena	32	46	2	1
*M Azharuddin	not out		72	80	4	0
VG Kambli	not out		1	1	0	0
Extras	(b 4, lb 7, w 11)		22			
Total	(3 wickets, 50 overs)		271			

DNB: A Jadeja, +NR Mongia, J Srinath, A Kumble, SA Ankola, BKV Prasad.
Fall of wickets: 1-27 (Prabhakar), 2-93 (Manjrekar), 3-268 (Tendulkar).

Bowling	O	M	R	W	
Vaas	9	3	37	0	(2w)
Pushpakumara	8	0	53	1	(7w)
Muralitharan	10	1	42	0	(1w)
Dharmasena	9	0	53	1	(1w)
Jayasuriya	10	0	52	0	
Ranatunga	4	0	23	0	

Sri Lanka innings (target: 272 runs from 50 overs)			R	B	4	6
ST Jayasuriya	c Prabhakar	b Kumble	79	76	9	2
+RS Kaluwitharana	c Kumble	b Prasad	26	16	6	0
AP Gurusinha	run out		25	27	2	1
PA de Silva	st Mongia	b Kumble	8	14	1	0
*A Ranatunga	not out		46	63	2	0
HP Tillakaratne	not out		70	98	6	0
Extras	(b 4, lb 9, w 3, nb 2)		18			
Total	(4 wickets, 48.4 overs)		272			

DNB: RS Mahanama, HDPK Dharmasena, WPUJC Vaas, KR Pushpakumara, M Muralitharan.
Fall of wickets: 1-53 (Kaluwitharana), 2-129 (Gurusinha), 3-137 (Jayasuriya), 4-141 (de Silva).

Bowling	O	M	R	W	
Prabhakar	4	0	47	0	
Srinath	9.4	0	51	0	
Prasad	10	1	53	1	(1w, 2nb)
Ankola	5	0	28	0	
Kumble	10	1	39	2	
Tendulkar	10	0	41	0	(2w)

Pakistan v England, Group B

At National Stadium, Karachi, 3 March 1996 (50-overs)
Result: Pakistan won by 7 wickets. Points: Pakistan 2, England 0.
Toss: England. Umpires: BC Cooray (SL) and S Venkataraghavan (Ind).
TV Umpire: K Parthasarathy (Ind). Match Referee: RS Madugalle (SL).
Man of the Match: Aamer Sohail.

England innings (50 overs maximum)			R	B	4	6
RA Smith	c Waqar Younis	b Saleem Malik	75	92	8	1
*MA Atherton		b Aamer Sohail	66	91	6	0
GA Hick	st Rashid Latif	b Aamer Sohail	1	2	0	0
GP Thorpe	not out		52	64	3	0
NH Fairbrother	c Wasim Akram	b Mushtaq Ahmed	13	21	1	0
+RC Russell		c & b Mushtaq Ahmed	4	7	0	0
DA Reeve		b Mushtaq Ahmed	3	5	0	0
DG Cork	lbw	b Waqar Younis	0	2	0	0
D Gough		b Wasim Akram	14	15	1	0
PJ Martin	run out		2	4	0	0
RK Illingworth	not out		1	1	0	0
Extras	(lb 11, w 4, nb 3)		18			
Total	(9 wickets, 50 overs)		249			

Fall of wickets: 1-147 (Smith), 2-151 (Hick), 3-156 (Atherton), 4-194 (Fairbrother), 5-204 (Russell), 6-212 (Reeve), 7-217 (Cork), 8-241 (Gough), 9-247 (Martin).

Bowling	O	M	R	W	
Wasim Akram	7	1	31	2	(3w)
Waqar Younis	10	1	45	1	
Aaqib Javed	7	0	34	0	(3nb)
Mushtaq Ahmed	10	0	53	3	
Aamer Sohail	10	0	48	2	(1nb, 1w)
Saleem Malik	6	1	27	1	

Pakistan innings (target: 250 runs from 50 overs)			R	B	4	6
Aamer Sohail	c Thorpe	b Illingworth	42	56	6	0
Saeed Anwar	c Russell	b Cork	71	72	8	0
Ijaz Ahmed	c Russell	b Cork	70	83	6	0
Inzamam-ul-Haq	not out		53	54	6	0
Javed Miandad	not out		11	21	1	0
Extras	(lb 1, w 2)		3			
Total	(3 wickets, 47.4 overs)		250			

DNB: Saleem Malik, *Wasim Akram, +Rashid Latif, Mushtaq Ahmed, Waqar Younis, Aaqib Javed.
Fall of wickets: 1-81 (Aamer Sohail), 2-139 (Saeed Anwar), 3-214 (Ijaz Ahmed).

Bowling	O	M	R	W	
Cork	10	0	59	2	(2w)
Martin	9	0	45	0	
Gough	10	0	45	0	
Illingworth	10	0	46	1	
Reeve	6.4	0	37	0	
Hick	2	0	17	0	

Australia v West Indies, Group A

At Sawai Mansingh Stadium, Jaipur, 4 March 1996 (50-overs)
Result: West Indies won by 4 wickets. Points: West Indies 2, Australia 0.
Toss: Australia. Umpires: Mahboob Shah (Pak) and DR Shepherd (Eng).
TV Umpire: Shakeel Khan (Pak). Match Referee: R Subba Row (Eng).
Man of the Match: RB Richardson.

Australia innings (50 overs maximum)			R	B	4	6
ME Waugh	st Browne	b Harper	30	62	1	0
*MA Taylor	c Browne	b Walsh	9	38	0	0
RT Ponting	run out		102	112	5	1
SR Waugh		b Walsh	57	64	3	1
MG Bevan	run out		2	3	0	0
SG Law	not out		12	12	0	0
+IA Healy	run out		3	4	0	0
PR Reiffel	not out		4	6	0	0
Extras	(lb 3, w 6, nb 1)		10			
Total	(6 wickets, 50 overs)		229			

DNB: SK Warne, DW Fleming, GD McGrath.
Fall of wickets: 1-22 (Taylor), 2-84 (ME Waugh), 3-194 (SR Waugh), 4-200 (Bevan), 5-216 (Ponting), 6-224 (Healy).

Bowling	O	M	R	W
Ambrose	10	4	25	0 (1w)
Walsh	9	2	35	2
Bishop	9	0	52	0 (1nb, 4w)
Harper	10	0	46	1
Arthurton	9	0	53	0
Adams	3	0	15	0 (1w)

West Indies innings (target: 230 runs from 50 overs)			R	B	4	6
SL Campbel	c Healy	b Fleming	1	5	0	0
+CO Browne	run out		10	18	2	0
BC Lara	c McGrath	b ME Waugh	60	70	7	0
*RB Richardson	not out		93	133	10	1
S Chanderpaul		b ME Waugh	10	17	0	0
RA Harper	lbw	b Reiffel	22	27	2	0
KLT Arthurton	lbw	b ME Waugh	0	3	0	0
JC Adams	not out		17	22	3	0
Extras	(lb 12, w 5, nb 2)		19			
Total	(6 wickets, 48.5 overs)		232			

DNB: IR Bishop, CEL Ambrose, CA Walsh.
Fall of wickets: 1-1 (Campbell), 2-26 (Browne), 3-113 (Lara), 4-146 (Chanderpaul), 5-194 (Harper), 6-196 (Arthurton).

Bowling	O	M	R	W
Reiffel	10	2	45	1 (2nb, 1w)
Fleming	7.5	1	44	1 (1w)
McGrath	9	0	46	0 (1w)
Warne	10	1	30	0 (1w)
ME Waugh	10	1	38	3 (1w)
Bevan	2	0	17	0

Netherlands v South Africa, Group B
At Rawalpindi Cricket Stadium, 5 March 1996 (50-overs)
Result: South Africa won by 160 runs. Points: South Africa 2, Netherlands 0.
Toss: South Africa. Umpires: Khizer Hayat and SG Randell (Aus).
TV Umpire: Mian Mohammad Aslam. Match Referee: Nasim-ul-Ghani.
Man of the Match: AC Hudson.

South Africa innings (50 overs maximum)			R	B	4	6
G Kirsten	c Zuiderent	b Aponso	83	98	6	0
AC Hudson	c van Oosterom	b Gouka	161	132	13	4
*WJ Cronje	c Lubbers	b Cantrell	41	39	3	0
DJ Cullinan	not out		19	17	1	0
JH Kallis	not out		17	16	0	0
Extras	(lb 5, w 2)		7			
Total	(3 wickets, 50 overs)		328			

DNB: BM McMillan, SM Pollock, +SJ Palframan, PL Symcox, CR Matthews, AA Donald.
Fall of wickets: 1-186 (Kirsten), 2-274 (Hudson), 3-301 (Cronje).

Bowling	O	M	R	W
Bakker	10	1	64	0 (1w)
Lubbers	8	0	50	0
de Leede	10	0	59	0 (1w)
Aponso	10	0	57	1
Cantrell	10	0	61	1
Gouka	2	0	32	1 (1nb)

Netherlands innings (target: 329 runs from 50 overs)			R	B	4	6
NE Clarke	c Pollock	b Donald	32	46	6	1
PE Cantrell		c & b Matthews	23	39	3	0
TBM de Leede		b Donald	12	26	1	0
KJJ van Noortwijk	c Palframan	b Symcox	9	24	1	0
GJAF Aponso	c Kirsten	b Symcox	6	31	0	0
B Zuiderent	run out		27	50	2	0
+MMC Schewe		b Matthews	20	34	1	0
EL Gouka	c Kallis	b Pollock	19	35	2	0
RF van Oosterom	not out		5	15	0	0
*SW Lubbers	not out		2	2	0	0
Extras	(lb 7, w 5, nb 1)		13			
Total	(8 wickets, 50 overs)		168			

DNB: PJ Bakker.
Fall of wickets: 1-56 (Cantrell), 2-70 (Clarke), 3-81 (de Leede), 4-86 (van Noortwijk), 5-97 (Aponso), 6-126 (Zuiderent), 7-158 (Gouka), 8-163 (Schewe).

Bowling	O	M	R	W
Pollock	8	0	35	1 (5w)
Matthews	10	0	38	2
Donald	6	0	21	2 (1w)
Cronje	3	1	3	0
Symcox	10	1	22	2
McMillan	4	2	5	0
Kallis	7	1	30	0
Cullinan	2	0	7	0

Sri Lanka v Kenya, Group A
At Asgiriya Stadium, Kandy, 6 March 1996 (50-overs)
Result: Sri Lanka won by 144 runs. Points: Sri Lanka 2, Kenya 0.
Toss: Kenya. Umpires: RS Dunne (NZ) and VK Ramaswamy (Ind).
TV Umpire: Ikram Rabbani (Pak). Match Referee: MAK Pataudi (Ind).
Man of the Match: PA de Silva.

Sri Lanka innings (50 overs maximum)			R	B	4	6
ST Jayasuriya	c LO Tikolo	b EO Odumbe	44	27	5	3
+RS Kaluwitharana		b EO Odumbe	33	18	4	2
AP Gurusinha	c Onyango	b Karim	84	103	7	3
PA de Silva	c Modi	b Suji	145	115	14	5
*A Ranatunga	not out		75	40	13	1
HP Tillakaratne	run out		0	1	0	0
RS Mahanama	not out		0	0	0	0
Extras	(b 1, lb 5, w 11)		17			
Total	(5 wickets, 50 overs)		398			

DNB: WPUJC Vaas, HDPK Dharmasena, KR Pushpakumara, M Muralitharan.
Fall of wickets: 1-83 (Jayasuriya), 2-88 (Kaluwitharana), 3-271 (Gurusinha), 4-377 (de Silva), 5-383 (Tillakaratne).

Bowling	O	M	R	W
Suji	9	0	85	1
Ali	6	0	67	0
Onyango	4	0	31	0
EO Odumbe	5	0	34	2
Karim	10	0	50	1
LO Tikolo	2	0	13	0
MO Odumbe	9	0	74	0
SO Tikolo	5	0	38	0

Kenya innings (target: 399 runs from 50 overs)			R	B	4	6
DN Chudasama		b Muralitharan	27	23	5	0
+KO Otieno		b Vaas	14	28	1	1
SO Tikolo		b Dharmasena	96	95	8	4
*MO Odumbe	st Kaluwitharana	b Muralitharan	0	2	0	0
HS Modi	run out (Muralitharan)		41	82	2	0
LO Tikolo	not out		25	40	2	1
EO Odumbe	c Muralitharan	b Ranatunga	4	17	0	0
LN Onyango	c sub (MS Atapattu)	b Ranatunga	23	18	2	1
MA Suji	not out		2	4	0	0
Extras	(b 1, lb 9, w 7, nb 5)		22			
Total	(7 wickets, 50 overs)		254			

DNB: AY Karim, RW Ali.
Fall of wickets: 1-47 (Otieno), 2-51 (Chudasama), 3-51 (MO Odumbe), 4-188 (SO Tikolo), 5-196 (Modi), 6-215 (EO Odumbe), 7-246 (Onyango).

Bowling	O	M	R	W
Vaas	10	0	44	1
Muralitharan	10	1	40	2
Pushpakumara	7	0	46	0
Ranatunga	5	0	31	2
Dharmasena	10	0	45	1
Jayasuriya	7	0	34	0
Tillakaratne	1	0	4	0

India v Zimbabwe, Group A
At Green Park, Kanpur, 6 March 1996 (50-overs)
Result: India won by 40 runs. Points: India 2, Zimbabwe 0.
Toss: Zimbabwe. Umpires: SA Bucknor (WI) and CJ Mitchley (SA).
TV Umpire: TM Samarasinghe (SL). Match Referee: JR Reid (NZ).
Man of the Match: A Jadeja.

India innings (50 overs maximum)			R	B	4	6
SR Tendulkar		b Streak	3	12	0	0
NS Sidhu	c Streak	b PA Strang	80	116	5	0
SV Manjrekar	c Campbell	b Lock	21	8	0	0
*M Azharuddin	c Campbell	b BC Strang	2	10	0	0
VG Kambli	c GW Flower	b Lock	106	110	11	0
A Jadeja	not out		44	27	3	2
+NR Mongia	not out		6	9	0	0
Extras	(lb 1, w 3)		4			
Total	(5 wickets, 50 overs)		247			

DNB: A Kumble, J Srinath, BKV Prasad, SLV Raju.
Fall of wickets: 1-5 (Tendulkar), 2-25 (Manjrekar), 3-32 (Azharuddin), 4-174 (Sidhu), 5-219 (Kambli).

Bowling	O	M	R	W
Streak	10	3	29	1 (1nb)
Lock	10	1	57	2 (2w)
BC Strang	5	1	22	1
PA Strang	10	0	55	1
Peall	6	0	35	0 (1w)
Whittall	3	0	19	0
GW Flower	3	0	16	0
Campbell	3	0	13	0

Zimbabwe innings (target: 248 runs from 50 overs)			R	B	4	6
AC Waller	c Tendulkar	b Kumble	22	36	1	0
GW Flower	c Azharuddin	b Raju	30	42	1	0
GJ Whittall	run out		10	29	0	0
ADR Campbell		c & b Jadeja	28	55	4	0
*+A Flower		b Raju	28	40	1	0
CN Evans	c Srinath	b Jadeja	6	5	1	0
HH Streak	lbw	b Raju	30	39	3	0
PA Strang		b Srinath	14	21	1	0
BC Strang	lbw	b Srinath	3	13	0	0
SG Peall	c Raju	b Kumble	9	14	2	0
ACI Lock	not out		2	4	0	0
Extras	(b 4, lb 9, w 11, nb 1)		25			
Total	(all out, 49.4 overs)		207			

Fall of wickets: 1-59 (GW Flower), 2-59 (Waller), 3-96 (Campbell), 4-99 (Whittall), 5-106 (Evans), 6-168 (Streak), 7-173 (A Flower), 8-193 (PA Strang), 9-195 (BC Strang), 10-207 (Peall).

Bowling	O	M	R	W
Srinath	10	1	36	2 (1w)
Prasad	7	0	40	0 (4w)
Kumble	9.4	0	33	2 (1w)
Raju	10	2	30	3
Tendulkar	6	0	23	0
Jadeja	7	0	32	2 (1w)

Pakistan v New Zealand, Group B

At Gaddafi Stadium, Lahore, 6 March 1996 (50-overs)
Result: Pakistan won by 46 runs. Points: Pakistan 2, New Zealand 0.
Toss: New Zealand. Umpires: KT Francis (SL) and ID Robinson (Zim).
TV Umpire: RC Sharma (Ind). Match Referee: CH Lloyd (WI).
Man of the Match: Saleem Malik.

Pakistan innings (50 overs maximum)			R	B	4	6
Aamer Sohail	c Thomson	b Kennedy	50	62	10	0
Saeed Anwar	run out (Thomson)		62	67	0	0
Ijaz Ahmed	c Spearman	b Cairns	26	46	0	0
Inzamam-ul-Haq	run out		39	41	4	1
Javed Miandad	run out (sub [CZ Harris])		5	19	0	0
Saleem Malik	not out		55	47	5	0
*Wasim Akram	not out		28	26	2	0
Extras	(lb 5, w 5, nb 6)		16			
Total	(5 wickets, 50 overs)		281			

DNB: +Rashid Latif, Waqar Younis, Mushtaq Ahmed, Aaqib Javed.
Fall of wickets: 1-70 (Aamer Sohail), 2-139 (Saeed Anwar), 3-155 (Ijaz Ahmed), 4-173 (Javed Miandad), 5-201 (Inzamam-ul-Haq).

Bowling	O	M	R	W	
Morrison	2	0	17	0	
Nash	10	1	49	0	
Cairns	10	1	53	1	
Kennedy	5	0	32	1	
Astle	9	0	50	0	
Thomson	6	0	35	0	
Twose	8	0	40	0	

New Zealand innings (target: 282 runs from 50 overs)			R	B	4	6
CM Spearman	c Rashid Latif	b Aaqib Javed	14	13	2	0
NJ Astle	c Rashid Latif	b Waqar Younis	6	17	1	0
*+LK Germon	c sub (Ata-ur-Rehman) b Mushtaq Ahmed		41	67	1	0
SP Fleming	st Rashid Latif	b Saleem Malik	42	43	7	0
RG Twose	c Saleem Malik	b Mushtaq Ahmed	24	38	0	0
CL Cairns	c Rashid Latif	b Aamer Sohail	32	34	1	2
AC Parore	c Mushtaq Ahmed	b Saleem Malik	36	34	3	0
SA Thomson	c Rashid Latif	b Waqar Younis	13	25	0	0
DJ Nash	not out		5	12	0	0
RJ Kennedy		b Aaqib Javed	2	3	0	0
DK Morrison	absent hurt		-			
Extras	(b 4, lb 9, w 6, nb 1)		20			
Total	(all out, 47.3 overs)		235			

Fall of wickets: 1-23 (Astle), 2-23 (Spearman), 3-83 (Fleming), 4-132 (Germon), 5-138 (Twose), 6-182 (Cairns), 7-221 (Parore), 8-228 (Thomson), 9-235 (Kennedy).

Bowling	O	M	R	W	
Waqar Younis	9	2	32	2	(1w)
Aaqib Javed	7.3	0	45	2	(2w)
Mushtaq Ahmed	10	0	32	2	
Saleem Malik	7	0	41	2	(1w)
Ijaz Ahmed	4	0	21	0	(1nb)
Aamer Sohail	10	0	51	1	

England v Sri Lanka

At Iqbal Stadium, Faisalabad, 9 March 1996 (50-overs)
Result: Sri Lanka won by 5 wickets. Sri Lanka advances to the semi finals.
Toss: England. Umpires: Mahboob Shah and ID Robinson (Zim).
TV Umpire: VK Ramaswamy (Ind). Match Referee: Nasim-ul-Ghani.
Man of the Match: ST Jayasuriya.

England innings (50 overs maximum)			R	B	4	6
RA Smith	run out		25	41	3	0
*MA Atherton	c Kaluwitharana	b Vaas	22	27	2	0
GA Hick	c Ranatunga	b Muralitharan	8	21	0	0
GP Thorpe		b Dharmasena	14	31	1	0
PAJ DeFreitas	lbw	b Jayasuriya	67	64	5	2
AJ Stewart		b Muralitharan	17	38	0	0
+RC Russell		b Dharmasena	9	17	0	0
DA Reeve		b Jayasuriya	35	34	2	0
D Gough	not out		26	26	5	0
PJ Martin	not out		0	1	0	0
Extras	(lb 8, w 4)		12			
Total	(8 wickets, 50 overs)		235			

DNB: RK Illingworth.
Fall of wickets: 1-31 (Atherton), 2-58 (Hick), 3-66 (Smith), 4-94 (Thorpe), 5-145 (Stewart), 6-171 (Russell), 7-173 (DeFreitas), 8-235 (Reeve).

Bowling	O	M	R	W	
Wickramasinghe	7	0	43	0	(1w)
Vaas	8	1	29	1	(1w)
Muralitharan	10	1	37	2	(1w)
Dharmasena	10	0	30	2	
Jayasuriya	9	0	46	2	
de Silva	6	0	42	0	(1w)

Sri Lanka innings (target: 236 runs from 50 overs)			R	B	4	6
ST Jayasuriya	st Russell	b Reeve	82	44	13	3
+RS Kaluwitharana		b Illingworth	8	3	2	0
AP Gurusinha	run out		45	63	5	0
PA de Silva	c Smith	b Hick	31	30	5	0
*A Ranatunga	lbw	b Gough	25	17	5	0
HP Tillakaratne	not out		19	50	1	0
RS Mahanama	not out		22	38	2	0
Extras	(lb 1, w 2, nb 1)		4			
Total	(5 wickets, 40.4 overs)		236			

DNB: HDPK Dharmasena, WPUJC Vaas, M Muralitharan, GP Wickramasinghe.
Fall of wickets: 1-12 (Kaluwitharana), 2-113 (Jayasuriya), 3-165 (de Silva), 4-194 (Ranatunga), 5-198 (Gurusinha).

Bowling	O	M	R	W	
Martin	9	1	41	0	(2w)
Illingworth	10	1	72	1	
Gough	10	1	36	1	
DeFreitas	3.4	0	38	0	
Reeve	4	1	14	1	(1nb)
Hick	4	0	34	1	

India v Pakistan

At M.Chinnaswamy Stadium, Bangalore (day/night), 9 March 1996 (50-overs)
Result: India won by 39 runs. India advances to the semi finals.
Toss: India. Umpires: SA Bucknor (WI) and DR Shepherd (Eng).
TV Umpire: RS Dunne (NZ). Match Referee: R Subba Row (Eng).
Man of the Match: NS Sidhu.

India innings (50 overs maximum)			R	B	4	6
NS Sidhu		b Mushtaq Ahmed	93	115	11	0
SR Tendulkar		b Ata-ur-Rehman	31	59	3	0
SV Manjrekar	c Javed Miandad	b Aamer Sohail	20	43	0	0
*M Azharuddin	c Rashid Latif	b Waqar Younis	27	22	1	1
VG Kambli		b Mushtaq Ahmed	24	26	1	0
A Jadeja	c Aamer Sohail	b Waqar Younis	45	25	4	2
+NR Mongia	run out		3	3	0	0
A Kumble	c Javed Miandad	b Aaqib Javed	10	6	2	0
J Srinath	not out		12	4	2	0
BKV Prasad	not out		0	0	0	0
Extras	(lb 3, w 15, nb 4)		22			
Total	(8 wickets, 50 overs)		287			

DNB: SLV Raju.
Fall of wickets: 1-90 (Tendulkar), 2-138 (Manjrekar), 3-168 (Sidhu), 4-200 (Azharuddin), 5-226 (Kambli), 6-236 (Mongia), 7-260 (Kumble), 8-279 (Jadeja).

Bowling	O	M	R	W	
Waqar Younis	10	1	67	2	(1w)
Aaqib Javed	10	0	67	1	(1nb, 4w)
Ata-ur-Rehman	10	0	40	1	(3nb, 1w)
Mushtaq Ahmed	10	0	56	2	(3w)
Aamer Sohail	5	0	29	1	(4w)
Saleem Malik	5	0	25	0	(2w)

Pakistan innings (target: 288 runs from 49 overs)			R	B	4	6
*Aamer Sohail		b Prasad	55	46	9	1
Saeed Anwar	c Kumble	b Srinath	48	32	5	2
Ijaz Ahmed	c Srinath	b Prasad	12	23	1	0
Inzamam-ul-Haq	c Mongia	b Prasad	12	20	1	0
Saleem Malik	lbw	b Kumble	38	50	4	0
Javed Miandad	run out		38	64	2	0
+Rashid Latif	st Mongia	b Raju	26	25	1	2
Mushtaq Ahmed		c & b Kumble	0	0	0	0
Waqar Younis	not out		4	21	0	0
Ata-ur-Rehman	lbw	b Kumble	0	1	0	0
Aaqib Javed	not out		6	10	0	0
Extras	(b 1, lb 3, w 5)		9			
Total	(9 wickets, 49 overs)		248			

Fall of wickets: 1-84 (Saeed Anwar), 2-113 (Aamer Sohail), 3-122 (Ijaz Ahmed), 4-132 (Inzamam-ul-Haq), 5-184 (Saleem Malik), 6-231 (Rashid Latif), 7-232 (Mushtaq Ahmed), 8-239 (Javed Miandad), 9-239 (Ata-ur-Rehman).

Bowling	O	M	R	W	
Srinath	9	0	61	1	(1w)
Prasad	10	0	45	3	(2w)
Kumble	10	0	48	3	
Raju	10	0	46	1	(1w)
Tendulkar	5	0	25	0	
Jadeja	5	0	19	0	(1w)

South Africa v West Indies

At National Stadium, Karachi, 11 March 1996 (50-overs)
Result: West Indies won by 19 runs. West Indies advances to the semi finals.
Toss: West Indies. Umpires: KT Francis (SL) and SG Randell (Aus).
TV Umpire: BC Cooray (SL). Match Referee: RS Madugalle (SL).
Man of the Match: BC Lara.

West Indies innings (50 overs maximum)			R	B	4	6
S Chanderpaul	c Cullinan	b McMillan	56	93	4	0
+CO Browne	c Cullinan	b Matthews	26	18	3	0
BC Lara	c Pollock	b Symcox	111	94	16	0
*RB Richardson	c Kirsten	b Symcox	10	27	0	0
RA Harper	lbw	b McMillan	9	15	1	0
RIC Holder	run out (Adams)		5	9	0	0
KLT Arthurton	c Hudson	b Adams	1	5	0	0
JC Adams	not out		13	17	1	0
IR Bishop		b Adams	17	22	1	1
CEL Ambrose	not out		0	1	0	0
Extras	(b 2, lb 11, w 2, nb 1)		16			
Total	(8 wickets, 50 overs)		264			

DNB: CA Walsh.
Fall of wickets: 1-42 (Browne), 2-180 (Chanderpaul), 3-210 (Richardson), 4-214 (Lara), 5-227 (Harper), 6-230 (Arthurton), 7-230 (Holder), 8-254 (Bishop).

Bowling	O	M	R	W	
Pollock	9	0	46	0	(1w)
Matthews	10	0	42	1	
Cronje	3	0	17	0	
McMillan	10	1	37	2	(1nb)
Symcox	10	0	64	2	
Adams	8	0	45	2	(1w)

South Africa innings (target: 265 runs from 50 overs)			R	B	4	6
AC Hudson	c Walsh	b Adams	54	80	8	0
G Kirsten	hit wicket	b Ambrose	3	14	0	0
DJ Cullinan	c Bishop	b Adams	69	78	3	3
*WJ Cronje	c Arthurton	b Adams	40	47	2	2
JN Rhodes	c Adams	b Harper	13	24	0	0
BM McMillan	lbw	b Harper	6	7	0	0
SM Pollock	c Adams	b Harper	6	7	0	0
+SJ Palframan		c & b Harper	1	2	0	0
PL Symcox	c Harper	b Arthurton	24	20	1	2
CR Matthews	not out		8	12	0	0
PR Adams		b Walsh	10	14	0	0
Extras	(b 1, lb 4, w 2, nb 4)		11			
Total	(all out, 49.3 overs)		245			

Fall of wickets: 1-21 (Kirsten), 2-118 (Hudson), 3-140 (Cullinan), 4-186 (Cronje), 5-196 (Rhodes), 6-196 (McMillan), 7-198 (Palframan), 8-227 (Pollock), 9-228 (Symcox), 10-245 (Adams).

Bowling	O	M	R	W	
Ambrose	10	0	29	1	
Walsh	8.3	0	51	1	(1w, 2nb)
Bishop	5	0	31	0	(3nb)
Harper	10	0	47	4	(1nb)
Adams	10	0	53	3	
Arthurton	6	0	29	1	

Australia v New Zealand

At MA Chidambaram Stadium, Chepauk, Madras (day/night), 11 March 1996 (50-overs)
Result: Australia won by 6 wickets. Australia advances to the semi finals.
Toss: New Zealand. Umpires: CJ Mitchley (SA) and S Venkataraghavan.
TV Umpire: Khizer Hayat (Pak). Match Referee: MAK Pataudi.
Man of the Match: ME Waugh.

New Zealand innings (50 overs maximum)			R	B	4	6
CM Spearman	c Healy	b Reiffel	12	12	3	0
NJ Astle	c Healy	b Fleming	1	6	0	0
*+LK Germon	c Fleming	b McGrath	89	96	9	1
SP Fleming	c SR Waugh	b McGrath	8	18	0	0
CZ Harris	c Reiffel	b Warne	130	124	13	4
RG Twose		b Bevan	4	12	0	0
CL Cairns	c Reiffel	b ME Waugh	4	9	0	0
AC Parore	lbw	b Warne	11	13	0	0
SA Thomson	run out		11	10	1	0
DN Patel	not out		3	4	0	0
Extras	(lb 6, w 3, nb 4)		13			
Total	(9 wickets, 50 overs)		286			

DNB: DJ Nash.
Fall of wickets: 1-15 (Astle), 2-16 (Spearman), 3-44 (Fleming), 4-212 (Germon), 5-227 (Twose), 6-240 (Cairns), 7-259 (Parore), 8-282 (Harris), 9-286 (Thomson).

Bowling	O	M	R	W	
Reiffel	4	0	38	1	(3nb, 1w)
Fleming	5	1	20	1	
McGrath	9	2	50	2	(1nb)
ME Waugh	8	0	43	1	
Warne	10	0	52	2	(1w)
Bevan	10	0	52	1	(1nb, 1w)
SR Waugh	4	0	25	0	

Australia innings (target: 287 runs from 50 overs)			R	B	4	6
*MA Taylor	c Germon	b Patel	10	24	1	0
ME Waugh	c Parore	b Nash	110	112	6	2
RT Ponting	c sub (RJ Kennedy)	b Thomson	31	43	4	0
SK Warne	lbw	b Astle	24	14	1	2
SR Waugh	not out		59	68	5	0
SG Law	not out		42	30	3	1
Extras	(b 1, lb 6, w 3, nb 3)		13			
Total	(4 wickets, 47.5 overs)		289			

DNB: MG Bevan, +IA Healy, PR Reiffel, DW Fleming, GD McGrath.
Fall of wickets: 1-19 (Taylor), 2-84 (Ponting), 3-127 (Warne), 4-213 (ME Waugh).

Bowling	O	M	R	W	
Nash	9	1	44	1	(1w)
Patel	8	0	45	1	
Cairns	6.5	0	51	0	(1nb)
Harris	10	0	41	0	(2nb, 1w)
Thomson	8	0	57	1	(1w)
Astle	3	0	21	1	
Twose	3	0	23	0	

1st Semi-Final
India v Sri Lanka

At Eden Gardens, Calcutta (day/night), 13 March 1996 (50-overs)
Result: Sri Lanka won by default. Sri Lanka advances to the final.
Toss: India. Umpires: RS Dunne (NZ) and CJ Mitchley (SA).
TV Umpire: Mahboob Shah (Pak). Match Referee: CH Lloyd (WI).
Man of the Match: PA de Silva.

Sri Lanka innings (50 overs maximum)			R	B	4	6
ST Jayasuriya	c Prasad	b Srinath	1	3	0	0
+RS Kaluwitharana	c Manjrekar	b Srinath	0	1	0	0
AP Gurusinha	c Kumble	b Srinath	1	16	0	0
PA de Silva		b Kumble	66	47	14	0
RS Mahanama	retired hurt		58	101	6	0
*A Ranatunga	lbw	b Tendulkar	35	42	4	0
HP Tillakaratne	c Tendulkar	b Prasad	32	43	1	0
HDPK Dharmasena		b Tendulkar	9	20	0	0
WPUJC Vaas	run out (Azharuddin)		23	16	3	0
GP Wickramasinghe	not out		4	9	0	0
M Muralitharan	not out		5	4	0	0
Extras	(b 1, lb 10, w 4, nb 2)		17			
Total	(8 wickets, 50 overs)		251			

Fall of wickets: 1-1 (Kaluwitharana), 2-1 (Jayasuriya), 3-35 (Gurusinha), 4-85 (de Silva), 5-168 (Ranatunga), 6-206 (Dharmasena), 7-236 (Tillakaratne), 8-244 (Vaas). NB: RS Mahanama retired hurt (leg injury) at 182/5 off 37.2 overs.

Bowling	O	M	R	W	
Srinath	7	1	34	3	
Kumble	10	0	51	1	(1w)
Prasad	8	0	50	1	(2nb, 2w)
Kapoor	10	0	40	0	
Jadeja	5	0	31	0	
Tendulkar	10	1	34	2	(1w)

India innings (target: 252 runs from 50 overs)			R	B	4	6
SR Tendulkar	st Kaluwitharana	b Jayasuriya	65	88	9	0
NS Sidhu	c Jayasuriya	b Vaas	3	8	0	0
SV Manjrekar		b Jayasuriya	25	48	1	0
*M Azharuddin		c & b Dharmasena	0	6	0	0
VG Kambli	not out		10	29	0	0
J Srinath	run out		6	6	1	0
A Jadeja		b Jayasuriya	0	11	0	0
+NR Mongia	c Jayasuriya	b de Silva	1	8	0	0
AR Kapoor	c de Silva	b Muralitharan	0	1	0	0
A Kumble	not out		0	0	0	0
Extras	(lb 5, w 5)		10			
Total	(8 wickets, 34.1 overs)		120			

DNB: BKV Prasad.
Fall of wickets: 1-8 (Sidhu), 2-98 (Tendulkar), 3-99 (Azharuddin), 4-101 (Manjrekar), 5-110 (Srinath), 6-115 (Jadeja), 7-120 (Mongia), 8-120 (Kapoor).

Bowling	O	M	R	W	
Wickramasinghe	5	0	24	0	(2w)
Vaas	6	1	23	1	
Muralitharan	7.1	0	29	1	(1w)
Dharmasena	7	0	24	1	
Jayasuriya	7	1	12	3	(1w)
de Silva	2	0	3	1	(1w)

NB: At the fall of the 8th Indian wicket, sections of the crowd vented their disgust with the state of the match by setting fire to some areas of the stands and throwing fruit and waterbottles onto the field. The match was briefly stopped and when play was about to resume, the crowd again threw bottles at the deep fielders. The match referee stopped the game and the game was awarded to Sri Lanka by default.

2nd Semi-Final
Australia v West Indies

At Punjab C.A. Stadium, Mohali, Chandigarh (day/night), 14 March 1996 (50-overs)
Result: Australia won by 5 runs. Australia advances to the final.
Toss: Australia. Umpires: BC Cooray (SL) and S Venkataraghavan.
TV Umpire: Khizer Hayat (Pak). Match Referee: JR Reid (NZ).
Man of the Match: SK Warne.

Australia innings (50 overs maximum)			R	B	4	6
ME Waugh	lbw	b Ambrose	0	2	0	0
*MA Taylor		b Bishop	1	11	0	0
RT Ponting	lbw	b Ambrose	0	15	0	0
SR Waugh		b Bishop	3	18	0	0
SG Law	run out		72	105	5	0
MG Bevan	c Richardson	b Harper	69	110	4	1
+IA Healy	run out		31	28	2	0
PR Reiffel	run out		7	11	0	0
SK Warne	not out		6	6	0	0
Extras	(lb 11, w 5, nb 2)		18			
Total	(8 wickets, 50 overs)		207			

DNB: DW Fleming, GD McGrath.
Fall of wickets: 1-0 (ME Waugh), 2-7 (Taylor), 3-8 (Ponting), 4-15 (SR Waugh), 5-153 (Law), 6-171 (Bevan), 7-186 (Reiffel), 8-207 (Healy).

Bowling	O	M	R	W	
Ambrose	10	1	26	2	(3w)
Bishop	10	1	35	2	(3nb, 1w)
Walsh	10	1	33	0	(1nb)
Gibson	2	0	13	0	(1nb)
Harper	9	0	47	1	
Adams	9	0	42	0	(1w)

West Indies innings (target: 208 runs from 50 overs)			R	B	4	6
S Chanderpaul	c Fleming	b McGrath	80	126	7	0
+CO Browne		c & b Warne	10	18	0	0
BC Lara		b SR Waugh	45	45	4	0
*RB Richardson	not out		49	83	4	0
RA Harper	lbw	b McGrath	2	5	0	0
OD Gibson	c Healy	b Warne	1	2	0	0
JC Adams	lbw	b Warne	2	11	0	0
KLT Arthurton	c Healy	b Fleming	0	4	0	0
IR Bishop	lbw	b Warne	3	3	0	0
CEL Ambrose	run out		2	2	0	0
CA Walsh		b Fleming	0	1	0	0
Extras	(lb 4, w 2, nb 2)		8			
Total	(all out, 49.3 overs)		202			

Fall of wickets: 1-25 (Browne), 2-93 (Lara), 3-165 (Chanderpaul), 4-173 (Harper), 5-178 (Gibson), 6-183 (Adams), 7-187 (Arthurton), 8-194 (Bishop), 9-202 (Ambrose), 10-202 (Walsh).

Bowling	O	M	R	W	
McGrath	10	2	30	2	(1nb)
Fleming	8.3	0	48	2	(1w)
Warne	9	0	36	4	(1w)
ME Waugh	4	0	16	0	
SR Waugh	7	0	30	1	
Reiffel	5	0	13	0	(2nb)
Bevan	4	1	12	0	
Law	2	0	13	0	

Final
Australia v Sri Lanka
At Gaddafi Stadium, Lahore (day/night), 17 March 1996 (50-overs)
Result: Sri Lanka won by 7 wickets. Sri Lanka wins the 1996 Wills World Cup.
Toss: Sri Lanka. Umpires: SA Bucknor (WI) and DR Shepherd (Eng).
TV Umpire: CJ Mitchley (SA). Match Referee: CH Lloyd (WI).
Man of the Match: PA de Silva. Man of the Series: ST Jayasuriya.

Australia innings (50 overs maximum)			R	B	4	6
*MA Taylor	c Jayasuriya	b de Silva	74	83	8	1
ME Waugh	c Jayasuriya	b Vaas	12	15	1	0
RT Ponting		b de Silva	45	73	2	0
SR Waugh	c de Silva	b Dharmasena	13	25	0	0
SK Warne	st Kaluwitharana	b Muralitharan	2	5	0	0
SG Law	c de Silva	b Jayasuriya	22	30	0	1
MG Bevan	not out		36	49	2	0
+IA Healy		b de Silva	2	3	0	0
PR Reiffel	not out		13	18	0	0
Extras	(lb 10, w 11, nb 1)		22			
Total	(7 wickets, 50 overs)		241			

DNB: DW Fleming, GD McGrath.
Fall of wickets: 1-36 (ME Waugh), 2-137 (Taylor), 3-152 (Ponting), 4-156 (Warne), 5-170 (SR Waugh), 6-202 (Law), 7-205 (Healy).

Bowling	O	M	R	W	
Wickramasinghe	7	0	38	0	(2w)
Vaas	6	1	30	1	
Muralitharan	10	0	31	1	(1w)
Dharmasena	10	0	47	1	(1nb)
Jayasuriya	8	0	43	1	(5w)
de Silva	9	0	42	3	(3w)

Sri Lanka innings (target: 242 runs from 50 overs)			R	B	4	6
ST Jayasuriya	run out		9	7	1	0
+RS Kaluwitharana	c Bevan	b Fleming	6	13	0	0
AP Gurusinha		b Reiffel	65	99	6	1
PA de Silva	not out		107	124	13	0
*A Ranatunga	not out		47	37	4	1
Extras	(b 1, lb 4, w 5, nb 1)		11			
Total	(3 wickets, 46.2 overs)		245			

DNB: HP Tillakaratne, RS Mahanama, HDPK Dharmasena, WPUJC Vaas, GP Wickramasinghe, M Muralitharan.
Fall of wickets: 1-12 (Jayasuriya), 2-23 (Kaluwitharana), 3-148 (Gurusinha).

Bowling	O	M	R	W	
McGrath	8.2	1	28	0	
Fleming	6	0	43	1	(4w)
Warne	10	0	58	0	(1nb, 1w)
Reiffel	10	0	49	1	
ME Waugh	6	0	35	0	
SR Waugh	3	0	15	0	(1nb)
Bevan	3	0	12	0	

World Cup **1999**

by Matthew Engel

With about five playable hours of daylight remaining on the longest Sunday of the year, Darren Lehmann struck the ball towards the Lord's Grand Stand for the boundary that gave the seventh World Cup to Australia.

This concluded a final so one-sided that it descended from anticlimax into bathos. A match that had started at 11.15 a.m., half an hour late, was all over by 4.35 p.m. because Pakistan, the most exciting side in the tournament, had gone to pieces when it mattered most.

The first World Cup final, at the same ground 24 years earlier almost to the day, had lasted nearly ten hours. This one was over shortly after it started. Thus the best Test team in the world became the world one-day champions, uniting the two forms of cricket into one undisputed title for the first time since the West Indies lost their invincibility in the last Lord's final 16 years before.

When Australia had gone to Old Trafford three Sundays earlier for their final group match, they were in severe danger of the earliest possible exit. Two Sundays after that, during the last Super Six match at Headingley, Australian journalists and officials had been making calls to check on airline-seat availability, which would have been firmed up had Herschelle Gibbs not celebrated too soon and literally thrown away a catch offered by Steve Waugh at 56 of his eventual 120 not out.

In the semi-final four days later, as Damien Fleming prepared to bowl to Lance Klusener – the player of the tournament – with South Africa needing one to win, Australia were effectively goners. But that game, arguably the greatest in the history of one-day cricket, produced a final twist that no one could have foreseen or invented. Klusener and Allan Donald had a horrendous running mix-up, the match was tied, and Australia went through on net run-rate.

Australia's improbable lurch into the final was in complete contrast to their opponents' confident strut.

Euphoric – and relieved – Australians rejoice after their one-sided victory over Pakistan in the final. But for a dropped catch in one and a frenzied run-out in the other, they would have been eliminated in their previous two matches. Significantly, Ricky Ponting is the man in the middle (surrounded by Adam Gilchrist, Damien Martyn, Damien Fleming, captain Steve Waugh and Shane Warne). Four years later, he would raise the Cup as captain.

The Pakistanis lost three successive games which did not matter, but returned to form in time to earn their place at Lord's by blowing Zimbabwe and New Zealand away by huge margins. But it has been noticed before that the way to win World Cups – and not just in cricket – is to fiddle quietly through the early matches and peak at the end.

The overall quality of the Australian team meant that no one could begrudge their right to the trophy. But Pakistan and South Africa would have been worthy winners too. The class of these three teams (one might add India's batting as well) gave the tournament enough lustre to make the whole thing seem like a triumph.

Yet the success came against a background of travail almost as great as Australia's. England's main objective in staging the World Cup was to reinvigorate the nation's love of the game, which had been flagging after so many years of failure by the national team. For the organisers, the worst-case scenario was that England would go out quickly.

By the time they had completed no-nonsense wins over Sri Lanka, Kenya and Zimbabwe, that fear had receded to vanishing point. Some newspapers claimed that England were already through to the Super Six stage. For them to fail, Zimbabwe had to beat South Africa, which in advance seemed improbable bordering on impossible, and then

England had to lose to India very badly. It all happened.

Only 16 days into the tournament, with a further 21 to go, England were gone. It was an outcome wholly in keeping with many of the farcical organisational aspects of the whole competition. The hosts were reduced to just that: handing round the cucumber sandwiches at their own tea party.

The fact that the tournament maintained public interest, even in England, in spite of this disaster, represented its greatest achievement. The fact that it got into such a pickle in the first place was its biggest failure.

The system used in Australasia in 1992, when all played all in a round robin with the top four going into the semi-finals, was widely admired and enjoyed. But this became impossible once it was decided to admit the top three non-Test countries (Bangladesh, Kenya and Scotland) making 12 teams in all. They were split into two groups, and the top three in each group went into the Super Six, with the subsequent top four going into the semi-finals. Notionally, ties on points from the qualifying groups were to be resolved by the result between the teams involved. Unfortunately, there were three-way ties in both, and New Zealand and Zimbabwe, fourth and fifth in the Super Six, had shared the one washed-out game of the entire tournament. The next determinant was net

run-rate, familiar for many years from one-day cricket's triangulars and quadrangulars. This vile technicality decided the whole tournament, since the tied semi-final was resolved by the teams' positions in the Super Six, and net run-rate had put Australia ahead of South Africa.

Net run-rate was responsible for the failure of both England and the West Indies to reach the last six. Bad luck? To an extent. But if the West Indies had won more quickly against Bangladesh they would have qualified. And it is hard to see why England, who did after all make the rules as hosts, were so slow to realise the dangers.

The tournament's many shortcomings were worsened by the slogan chosen – a "Carnival of Cricket". The trouble is that one man's carnival is another man's nightmare. It is difficult to find much accommodation between those who want to sit down and concentrate on the game, and those who want to shout, chant, cheer and sing. For English cricket, this is an intractable problem.

The old English custom of running on the field at the end of a match – or sometimes earlier – returned with gusto. Australia were spooked by this early on and demanded greater protection. There was much mockery of the Trent Bridge authorities at the New Zealand-India match for their undue strictness. Yet India's previous match, at Old Trafford, had taken

place amid fears of full-scale warfare as they were playing Pakistan at a time when the always-simmering conflict between the countries over Kashmir had boiled over into bloodshed. This match, heavily policed, passed off calmly. It was the next Old Trafford match – the semi-final between Pakistan and New Zealand – where a pitch invasion nearly led to disaster.

Given the briefness of the home team's involvement, it was the supporters of the other countries, and the Indians and Pakistanis in particular, who gave the World Cup its vibrancy. The bearded Pakistani cheerleader, Abdul Jalil, was by the end of the competition more recognisable than Steve Waugh. It began to be noticed that Asians in England were the one community who had absolutely not fallen out of love with cricket and that their loyalties were an expression of their individuality, and a perfectly legitimate one.

There was criticism of the decision to spread the 42 matches among 21 grounds. All the county headquarters staged at least one match. Clearly, many of these matches could have attracted bigger crowds

Lord's, overlooked by the new, space-age media centre at the Nursery End, in all its summer splendour for the opening match between England and Sri Lanka.

on bigger grounds: Pakistan v Bangladesh at Northampton could have been sold at least three times over, but English cricket had only six available stadia which could hold much more than 10,000 people.

The greatest success was the cricket. From the start, it took on a completely different flavour from the 1996 tournament. There was a huge meteorological risk attached to starting as early as May 14 but, miraculously, only one of the 42 matches was left unfinished, only one other spilled over to the second day, and the dreaded Duckworth/Lewis system – much talked about, little understood – was never invoked.

It was generally believed that the team batting second had an advantage, because at 10.45 a.m. there was still early-morning damp. In 27 of the games, the captain winning the toss inserted. In fact, the team batting first won 19 times and lost 21 times – there was one tie and one no-result – which proves nothing. Captains changed tack in June, when the sun came out: 24 of the insertions had occurred in the 30 group games.

The lacquered white ball was thought to be harder than the red one by batsmen who were hit by it. It often seemed to swing more, especially late in the innings. This was one reason for the astonishing number of wides, 979, called by umpires who were stern – too stern, and often inconsistent – about anything wide of off stump as well as leg.

What was certain was that the pattern established in 1996 was turned upside down. The bowlers, reduced to mere helots by conditions in India and Pakistan, suddenly re-established themselves as equals of the batsmen, or even their masters. Little was heard or seen of pinch-hitters, and lashing the ball over the infield. Indeed, the end of the 15th over, when captains were allowed to place a more defensive field, often passed unnoticed.

The three makeweight teams – Bangladesh, Kenya and Scotland – emphasised that the gap between the worst of the nine Test sides and the best of the rest

---

Far right: Player of the tournament, Lance Klusener, clubs another boundary in the opening round against England. His 10 sixes and 26 fours yielded him a strike rate of 140.5.

Top: Fans were forced to find alternative seating for the Australia-Pakistan match at Headingly.

Middle/bottom: South Africa's wicketkeeper Mark Boucher dismantles the stumps against Pakistan; England's Andy Flintoff dismantles camera and advertising boundary board at Edgbaston.

was enormous. The one great shock occurred on the final day of preliminary competition when Bangladesh, already eliminated, beat Pakistan, already qualified, in an extraordinary match at Northampton. Legal English bookmakers had rated Pakistan 33-1 on to win. Illegal Indian ones had apparently refused to take any bets on Pakistan's preliminary matches because of the team's association with general hocus-pocus. Inevitably, this result led to rumours that it was fixed, because there was nothing at all in the run-up to suggest it was even feasible.

After six teams had been eliminated in the first round (Bangladesh, England, Kenya, Scotland, Sri Lanka, West Indies), a new incipient table was formed for the Super Six, incorporating the relevant results from the first phase. Zimbabwe almost had enough momentum to be carried into the semi-finals. They were saved by rain against New Zealand, who finally managed to secure some justice by beating India and squeezing Zimbabwe out on net run-rate.

So Zimbabwe and India went out, leaving the semi-finals to what people were beginning to regard as The Big Three – plus New Zealand, who had quietly been doing just enough to keep in the contest. Once they came up against a class team in prime form, however, they were exposed. Pakistan had lost three successive

matches, but had judged their defeats so well that they still qualified at the top of the Super Six. And in the first semi-final they were devastating.

Something had to give at Edgbaston. But it was hard to imagine who or what. South Africa essentially stuck to their methods: athletic fielding, fierce if spin-free bowling, and all-round batting efficiency. Indeed, the most feared batsman of all had been marching in at No. 8 or 9. Klusener, one of the most successful bowlers in the Cup, had turned tail-end hitting into something close to an exact science.

Australia, in contrast, adjusted. Originally, they denied Glenn McGrath the new ball and tried to fiddle through without a real fifth bowler. By the end of the first phase, they had reconsidered, bringing in Tom Moody to improve the balance. McGrath moved into top form. And, slowly, much more slowly, so did Shane Warne. In the semi-final, he found a pitch that gave him bounce and turn, and he responded by performing with much of his old exuberance.

In a sense, nothing did give; the match was tied. But Australia went into the final with momentum and, on the day, found a Pakistan team that suddenly could not summon up their best form when they needed it. (*Abridged version from Wisden Cricketers' Almanack, 2000*)

SEMI-FINALS
Pakistan v New Zealand

AT Old Trafford, June 16, 1999. Pakistan won by nine wickets.

IT was more Karachi than Manchester or, more to the point, Auckland or Wellington as Pakistan turned a virtual home match into a resounding triumph. They were inspired principally by the electrifying speed and control of Shoaib Akhtar, whose three wickets and mere menacing presence were responsible for restricting New Zealand to a modest 241 for seven. The limitations of New Zealand's bowling in the ideal conditions were then exposed by Saeed Anwar and Wajahatullah Wasti, who effectively settled the result with a new World Cup first-wicket record of 194.

Wasti made 84 off 123 balls with ten fours and a six with confident, straight-batted correctness before he wasted the chance of a hundred by lifting an outfield catch. The left-handed Anwar, in his 172nd one-day international, remained unbeaten with his 17th hundred in such matches, his second in succession, 113 from 148 balls with ten fours.

Yet Shoaib was chosen as Man of the Match. Although 55 off his ten overs made him the most expensive Pakistani bowler, the decision was not a surprise for no one made more of an impact.

The sun shone from a clear sky throughout the hottest day of the tournament. The pitch was as hard and as dry as those that abound in the sub-continent and the stands, packed to their 20,000 capacity, were a canvas of green and white and a cacophony of horns and whistles from the majority Pakistani support. Midway through the game and at the end, rockets and

---

At left and middle above: Two of the victims that made Australia's Shane Warne and New Zealand's Geoff Allott the leading wicket-takers with 20 each. Warne snares South Africa captain Hansie Cronje in the tied semi-final (left), Allott claims Mark Waugh lbw in Australia's first-round defeat.

Middle below: Bangladesh wicketkeeper Khaled Mashud gets ready to complete the first of three run-outs in Pakistan's stunning demise in the first round. Saeed Anwar is the stranded victim.

Right: India's support took all shapes and forms. Whether the gaily bedecked, and clearly bewildered, mascot had an influence on the first-round victory over England at Edgbaston was not clear.

143

fire-crackers shot into the air, a common occurrence on Pakistan's grounds but certainly not England's.

For New Zealand, with hardly a flag-waving supporter in sight, home had been the chilly, overcast weather and slow, seaming pitches that prevailed in the first round. Here, their batsmen were hard-pressed to resist Shoaib's thunderbolts and the penetration of his colleagues. In contrast, their own nagging medium-pacers could get nothing out of the pitch after Geoff Allott did not snare his usual early wicket or two.

Shoaib, consistently clocked at between 90 and 95mph, unsettled the New Zealanders from the start after Stephen Fleming chose to bat on winning the toss. In his opening spell, he knocked out Nathan Astle's leg stump, while Wasim Akram removed Craig McMillan and Abdul Razzaq yorked Matthew Horne to leave New Zealand 58 for three in the 16th over.

The left-handers Fleming and Roger Twose slowly but surely negotiated them out of the crisis with a stand of 94 from 18.4 overs before Akram summoned Shoaib for another explosive spell. It took him less then two overs to propel a yorker, fired in from round the wicket, that plucked out the mesmerised Fleming's leg stump.

It also took a special piece of cricket to shift Twose, Ijaz Ahmed leaping far to his right at point to claim a low catch. Chris Cairns and Chris Harris were threatening a late surge when Shoaib came back for his last spell and produced a change of pace from 90 to 75mph that dumbfounded and bowled the left-handed Harris.

Anwar and Wasti soon made it obvious that New Zealand's total was inadequate, and that Pakistan would be in the World Cup final for the second time. *(Tony Cozier, Caribbean Cricket Quarterly, 1999)*

Australia v South Africa

At Edgbaston, June 17, 1999. Tied.
This was not only the match of the tournament. It must have been the best one-day international of the 1,483 then played. The essence of the one-day game is a close finish, and this was by far the most significant to finish in the closest way of all, with both teams all out for the same score.

It was a compressed epic all the way through, and it ended in a savage twist. The tie meant that South Africa, for the third World Cup in a row, failed to reach the final despite making much of the early running. The crucial fact was that Australia finished higher in the Super Six table, and that was determined by the obscurity of net run-rate. Many spectators were left baffled.

Lance Klusener's brawn had powered South Africa to the brink of the final but, when he got there, his

brain short-circuited. Only he could have smashed and grabbed 31 runs off 14 balls, cutting a daunting target down to a doddle – one needed off four balls, Klusener himself on strike, and a decent, experienced tail-ender at the other end in Allan Donald.

The bowler, Damien Fleming, had only one thing going for him. He had bowled the final over that beat the West Indies in the 1996 World Cup semi-final. Having allowed Klusener to pummel consecutive fours to level the scores, he tightened up. Steve Waugh, knowing a tie would be enough, set a field that gave new meaning to the phrase "a ring saving one". Klusener thumped the ball straight and Donald, backing up too far, would have been run out if Darren Lehmann had hit the stumps.

The scare should have been a warning. But Klusener repeated his straight biff and charged. Donald grounded his bat, dropped it and finally set off while the Australians were demonstrating the benefits of a recent visit to a bowling alley. Mark Waugh, at mid-on, flicked the ball to Fleming, who rolled it to wicket-keeper Adam Gilchrist who broke the wicket, and South African hearts.

The rest of the match was studded with outstanding performances. When Australia batted, Shaun Pollock, finally finding the edge, was magnificently incisive. Donald twice took two wickets in an over. Steve Waugh and Michael Bevan then performed a repair job which showed first self-control, then controlled aggression. Jacques Kallis, carrying a stomach injury, bowled fast and tight and held the batting together with a cool 53.

Above all, there was Shane Warne. The ball that bowled Herschelle Gibbs was a miraculous replay of his most famous delivery, to Mike Gatting six years earlier. His first spell of eight overs went for only 12 runs. He pocketed three more wickets and the Man of the Match award.

The match was the last as South Africa's coach for Bob Woolmer, whose blend of science and imagination had produced a 73% success rate in one-day internationals. He deserved better than to go out on a technicality.

(Tim de Lisle, Wisden Cricketers' Almanack, 2000)

Left: Pakistan v New Zealand at Old Trafford, Pakistan celebrate the dismissal of McMillan caught by Moin Khan off the bowling of Wasim Akram.

Right: South Africa's heart-breaking exit and Australia's place in the final are about to be sealed. Adam Gilchrist prepares to run out Alan Donald, batless and hopeless, to complete the semi-final tie at Edgbaston.

FINAL
Australia v Pakistan

At Lord's, June 20, 1999. Australia won by eight wickets.
AUSTRALIA won the seventh World Cup with such
single-minded ruthlessness that even an eight-wicket
victory failed to do them justice. Pakistan, the most
exciting team in the tournament, were totally
outplayed and outwitted at the crucial moment. There
were barely four and a half hours of cricket, most of it
one-sided. For all but the most fervent Australian, it
was not a pretty sight.

It was a sight, though, spared many Pakistanis by a
controversial ticketing policy. This favoured not the
fans of the competing teams but those who has
ostensibly proved their loyalty to the game – and the

depth of their pocket – by buying a package of tickets
long before. So Lord's was awash with disinterested
observers while from outside came the klaxon, whistle
and bugle of fanatical Pakistan support.

On a pitch that Steve Waugh believed was good for
260 or so, Wasim Akram chose to bat. Saeed Anwar
cut the third ball of the match for four, and added two
more boundaries in the fourth over as Damien
Fleming struggled for consistency. For Pakistan, this
was as good as it got. Next over, Wajahatullah Wasti
followed a ball from Glenn McGrath that bounced
and left him. Mark Waugh, at second slip, flew to his
right and clung on with both hands. It set the tone for
the match.

After Anwar had played on, Abdul Razzaq and Ijaz
Ahmed briefly looked more at home. Razzaq

benefited from Australia's one false move – McGrath dropped a comfortable catch at long-off – but was later smartly caught by Steve Waugh, lunging forward at extra cover. With Pakistan faltering at 69 for three after 21 overs, Waugh brought on Warne. It was, literally, the turning point of the match.

Warne produced an astounding delivery to dismiss Ijaz, who had hung around doggedly for 22. The ball pitched on or just outside leg and hit off. It was not quite the famous Gatting ball, nor the one that dismissed Herschelle Gibbs in the semi-final, but it sent shock-waves through the lower order.

Pakistan tried to get out of trouble with all guns blazing, but for every ball that ricocheted off the boards, another landed in Australian hands. Luck was against them, too. A ball from Paul Reiffel clipped Inzamam-ul-Haq's pad on its way to Adam Gilchrist. The Australians went up in appeal, umpire David Shepherd's finger went up in judgment. An incredulous batsman plodded off at funeral pace.

When Akram holed out, Warne had claimed four wickets for the second game running, taking his tally to 20, a World Cup record shared with Geoff Allott of New Zealand. McGrath brought the innings to a swift end when Ricky Ponting held a superlative catch at third slip in the 39th over. The target was just 133.

Akram later claimed that he could have defended 180, but the way Gilchrist began, 300 would have been within reach. Shoaib Akhtar was desperately unlucky when his first ball was edged by Gilchrist and fell agonisingly short of long leg. Thereafter, boundaries came thick and fast and off the middle of the bat. Gilchrist's 50 took 33 balls. When he fell to the first ball of the 11th over, the broadcasters felt the end was close enough to remove the stump cameras.

In fact, it took another ten overs, in which time Mark Waugh passed 1,000 World Cup runs. Australia needed a mere 121 balls to win, and the game was over at 4.32 p.m. – despite a heavy shower which had delayed the start by half an hour and a half-hearted pitch invasion moments after an announcement in Urdu had requested restraint. This, the 200th World Cup match, spanned less than 60 overs. The people who reportedly paid touts £5,000 for a pair of £100 tickets might have felt short-changed. Or maybe not; they were Australians.

(Hugh Chevallier, Wisden Cricketers' Almanack, 2000)

Left: Man of the Match and leading tournament wicket-taker Shane Warne strikes again in the final, comprehensively bowling Ijaz Ahmed.

Above: Job complete in quick time, cock-a-hoop Australians head for the pavilion and early celebrations after the final.

"They said at the time"

Australian captain Steve Waugh: *"At one stage, we were virtually down and out... but we hung on to every moment we could. I would put a lot of it down to inner strength. We couldn't believe we got out alive from the South African semi-final. Perhaps there was someone looking over us."*

Waugh's purported comment to Herschelle Gibbs after his missed catch when he was 56 in the Super Six match: *"Hersch, you've just dropped the World Cup."*

Australian leg-spinner Shane Warne, Man of the Match in both the semi-final and final: *"I have been doing a lot of thinking about my future. I am now going home to spend some time with my family and have a good think about where I go from here."*

Pakistan captain Wasim Akram: *"Australia showed they are the best side in the world. I don't think we have let our supporters down. After the game, I thanked all the players for their efforts in getting us to the final."*

Pakistan wicket-keeper Moin Khan on the public's reaction to defeat in the final: *"I don't think this is the way to treat us. It's time the people realise that cricket is a sport and in sport one team has to end up on the losing side. No team in the world is invincible."*

South Africa captain Hansie Cronje after the semi-final tie that eliminated his team: *"You experience a lot of highs and lows in your career. It doesn't get more exciting than this and it's unfortunate to be on the wrong side of it. At the moment it feels like a cruel game."*

South Africa coach Bob Woolmer: *"There's no doubt in my mind that the two best sides played in our semi-final. That was really the 'final'."*

Writer John Etheridge's comment in The Sun newspaper after the loss to India in the first round that eliminated England: *"Let's get things fully in proportion – this was only the most catastrophic day ever for English cricket."*

Format

Twelve seeded teams divided into two groups, each playing the other. The top three in each progressed to the 'Super Six', taking forward the points gained against the other three qualifiers from their group and playing the three qualifiers from the other group. The top four moved into the semis. In event of ties, the ultimate factor was 'net run-rate', a system that eliminated England and the West Indies after the first round and put Australia into the final after their semi-final tie against South Africa

Innovations

Almost....An official World Cup anthem, 'All Over the World', sung by Dave Stewart, was commissioned but not released until after England had been knocked out in the first round. South Africa coach Bob Woolmer's attempt to communicate tactics with his captain Hansie Cronje through an earpiece was banned by the ICC after the first match.

World Cup 1999
Scoreboards

England v Sri Lanka, Group A

At Lord's, London, 14 May 1999 (50-overs)
Result: England won by 8 wickets. Points: England 2, Sri Lanka 0.
Toss: England. Umpires: RE Koertzen (SA) and S Venkataraghavan (Ind).
TV Umpire: DL Orchard (SA). Match Referee: CW Smith (WI).
Man of the Match: AJ Stewart.

Sri Lanka innings (50 overs maximum)			R	B	4	6
ST Jayasuriya	c Hick	b Mullally	29	52	4	0
RS Mahanama	c Hick	b Mullally	16	30	2	0
MS Atapattu	c Thorpe	b Austin	3	9	0	0
HP Tillakaratne	c Stewart	b Ealham	0	12	0	0
PA de Silva	c Thorpe	b Mullally	0	6	0	0
*A Ranatunga	c Hussain	b Ealham	32	42	1	1
+RS Kaluwitharana	c Stewart	b Mullally	57	66	7	0
WPUJC Vaas	not out		12	27	0	0
KEA Upashantha	c Thorpe	b Hollioake	11	25	1	0
GP Wickramasinghe	c Stewart	b Austin	11	18	1	0
M Muralitharan		b Gough	12	8	2	0
Extras	(lb 9, w 9, nb 3)		21			
Total	(all out, 48.4 overs)		204			

Fall of wickets: 1-42 (Mahanama, 10.6 ov), 2-50 (Atapattu, 13.2 ov), 3-63 (Jayasuriya, 16.5 ov), 4-63 (Tillakaratne, 17.1 ov), 5-65 (de Silva, 18.5 ov), 6-149 (Ranatunga, 33.6 ov), 7-155 (Kaluwitharana, 36.5 ov), 8-174 (Upashantha, 43.5 ov), 9-190 (Wickramasinghe, 47.2 ov), 10-204 (Muralitharan, 48.4 ov).

Bowling	O	M	R	W	
Gough	8.4	0	50	1	(2nb, 1w)
Austin	9	1	25	2	(5w)
Mullally	10	1	37	4	(1nb, 1w)
Ealham	10	0	31	2	
Flintoff	2	0	12	0	
Hick	3	0	19	0	(1w)
Hollioake	6	0	21	1	

England innings (target: 205 runs from 50 overs)			R	B	4	6
N Hussain	st Kaluwitharana	b Muralitharan	14	33	1	0
*+AJ Stewart	c Kaluwitharana	b Vaas	88	146	6	0
GA Hick	not out		73	88	2	2
GP Thorpe	not out		13	15	1	0
Extras	(lb 6, w 12, nb 1)		19			
Total	(2 wickets, 46.5 overs)		207			

DNB: NH Fairbrother, A Flintoff, AJ Hollioake, MA Ealham, ID Austin, D Gough, AD Mullally.
Fall of wickets: 1-50 (Hussain, 14.5 ov), 2-175 (Stewart, 41.3 ov).

Bowling	O	M	R	W	
Vaas	10	2	27	1	
Wickramasinghe	10	0	41	0	
Upashantha	8	0	38	0	(1nb, 8w)
Muralitharan	10	0	33	1	(2w)
Jayasuriya	7.5	0	55	0	(2w)
de Silva	1	0	7	0	

India v South Africa, Group A

At New County Ground, Hove, 15 May 1999 (50-overs)
Result: South Africa won by 4 wickets. Points: South Africa 2, India 0.
Toss: India. Umpires: SA Bucknor (WI) and DR Shepherd.
TV Umpire: ID Robinson (Zim). Match Referee: Talat Ali (Pak).
Man of the Match: JH Kallis.

India innings (50 overs maximum)			R	B	4	6
SC Ganguly	run out (Rhodes/Kallis)		97	142	11	1
SR Tendulkar	c Boucher	b Klusener	28	46	5	0
R Dravid		b Klusener	54	75	5	0
*M Azharuddin	c Boje	b Klusener	24	24	2	0
A Jadeja	c Kirsten	b Donald	16	14	2	0
RR Singh	not out		4	3	0	0
+NR Mongia	not out		5	2	1	0
Extras	(b 6, lb 2, w 11, nb 6)		25			
Total	(5 wickets, 50 overs)		253			

DNB: AB Agarkar, J Srinath, A Kumble, BKV Prasad.
Fall of wickets: 1-67 (Tendulkar, 15.3 ov), 2-197 (Dravid, 41.4 ov), 3-204 (Ganguly, 43.4 ov), 4-235 (Jadeja, 48.2 ov), 5-247 (Azharuddin, 49.3 ov).

Bowling	O	M	R	W	
Pollock	10	0	47	0	(4nb)
Kallis	10	1	43	0	(2w)
Donald	10	0	34	1	(2w)
Klusener	10	0	66	3	(2nb, 2w)
Boje	5	0	31	0	(1w)
Cronje	5	0	24	0	

South Africa innings (target: 254 runs from 50 overs)			R	B	4	6
G Kirsten		b Srinath	3	22	0	0
HH Gibbs	lbw	b Srinath	7	8	1	0
+MV Boucher		b Kumble	34	36	4	1
JH Kallis	run out (Prasad/Srinath)		96	128	7	0
DJ Cullinan	c Singh	b Ganguly	19	35	3	0
*WJ Cronje	c Jadeja	b Agarkar	27	30	3	0
JN Rhodes	not out		39	31	5	0
L Klusener	not out		12	4	3	0
Extras	(lb 4, w 3, nb 10)		17			
Total	(6 wickets, 47.2 overs)		254			

DNB: SM Pollock, N Boje, AA Donald.
Fall of wickets: 1-13 (Gibbs, 2.4 ov), 2-22 (Kirsten, 6.5 ov), 3-68 (Boucher, 13.6 ov), 4-116 (Cullinan, 25.4 ov), 5-180 (Cronje, 38.4 ov), 6-227 (Kallis, 45.4 ov).

Bowling	O	M	R	W	
Srinath	10	0	69	2	(4nb, 1w)
Prasad	8.2	0	32	0	(1w)
Kumble	10	0	44	1	(1w)
Agarkar	9	0	57	1	(5nb)
Singh	2	0	10	0	
Ganguly	4	0	16	1	(1nb)
Tendulkar	4	0	22	0	

Kenya v Zimbabwe, Group A

At County Ground, Taunton, 15 May 1999 (50-overs)
Result: Zimbabwe won by 5 wickets. Points: Zimbabwe 2, Kenya 0.
Toss: Zimbabwe. Umpires: DB Cowie (NZ) and Javed Akhtar (Pak).
TV Umpire: KT Francis (SL). Match Referee: JR Reid (NZ).
Man of the Match: NC Johnson.

Kenya innings (50 overs maximum)			R	B	4	6
+KO Otieno	c GW Flower	b Johnson	16	35	2	0
RD Shah	c Strang	b AR Whittall	37	43	5	0
SO Tikolo	c A Flower	b Johnson	9	17	1	0
MO Odumbe	lbw	b Strang	20	57	0	0
HS Modi		b Johnson	7	19	1	0
AV Vadher	c AR Whittall	b Strang	54	90	5	1
TM Odoyo		b Johnson	28	20	2	2
*AY Karim	not out		19	19	2	1
AO Suji	not out		3	4	0	0
Extras	(b 2, lb 5, w 25, nb 4)		36			
Total	(7 wickets, 50 overs)		229			

DNB: MA Suji, JK Kamande.
Fall of wickets: 1-62 (Otieno, 12.5 ov), 2-64 (Shah, 13.1 ov), 3-74 (Tikolo, 16.2 ov), 4-87 (Modi, 20.4 ov), 5-171 (Odumbe, 42.2 ov), 6-181 (Vadher, 44.1 ov), 7-219 (Odoyo, 48.4 ov).

Bowling	O	M	R	W	
Streak	9	1	50	0	(8w)
Mbangwa	8	0	37	0	(1nb, 3w)
Johnson	10	0	42	4	(3nb, 2w)
AR Whittall	9	0	51	1	(2w)
GJ Whittall	6	0	20	0	(5w)
Strang	8	0	22	2	

Zimbabwe innings (target: 230 runs from 50 overs)			R	B	4	6
NC Johnson	c Modi	b Odoyo	59	70	7	2
GW Flower	c Shah	b Karim	20	33	1	0
PA Strang	c AO Suji	b Odoyo	29	21	3	2
MW Goodwin	c Karim	b Odumbe	17	22	2	0
+A Flower	c Tikolo	b Odumbe	34	46	3	0
*ADR Campbell	not out		33	50	5	0
GJ Whittall	not out		11	11	1	1
Extras	(lb 5, w 16, nb 7)		28			
Total	(5 wickets, 41 overs)		231			

DNB: SV Carlisle, HH Streak, AR Whittall, M Mbangwa.
Fall of wickets: 1-81 (GW Flower, 13.4 ov), 2-119 (Strang, 18.2 ov), 3-123 (Johnson, 20.3 ov), 4-147 (Goodwin, 25.2 ov), 5-213 (A Flower, 38.2 ov).

Bowling	O	M	R	W	
MA Suji	7	0	47	0	(1nb, 4w)
AO Suji	6	1	32	0	(1w)
Odoyo	9	0	40	2	(5nb)
Kamande	9	0	38	0	(1nb, 3w)
Karim	3	0	30	1	
Odumbe	7	1	39	2	(3w)

Australia v Scotland, Group B

At County Ground, New Road, Worcester, 16 May 1999 (50-overs)
Result: Australia won by 6 wickets. Points: Australia 2, Scotland 0.
Toss: Australia. Umpires: RS Dunne (NZ) and P Willey.
TV Umpire: G Sharp. Match Referee: RS Madugalle (SL).
Man of the Match: ME Waugh.

Scotland innings (50 overs maximum)			R	B	4	6
BMW Patterson	c Gilchrist	b Fleming	10	36	2	0
IL Philip	c SR Waugh	b McGrath	17	66	0	0
MJD Allingham	st Gilchrist	b Warne	3	28	0	0
MJ Smith	c Bevan	b Lee	13	32	1	0
*G Salmond	c Gilchrist	b SR Waugh	31	54	2	0
GM Hamilton		b Warne	34	42	3	0
JE Brinkley	c Dale	b Warne	23	32	3	0
+AG Davies	not out		8	11	0	0
JAR Blain	not out		3	7	0	0
Extras	(lb 9, w 22, nb 8)		39			
Total	(7 wickets, 50 overs)		181			

DNB: Asim Butt, NR Dyer.
Fall of wickets: 1-19 (Patterson, 10.5 ov), 2-37 (Allingham, 17.6 ov), 3-52 (Philip, 22.5 ov), 4-87 (Smith, 32.1 ov), 5-105 (Salmond, 37.1 ov), 6-167 (Brinkley, 46.4 ov), 7-169 (Hamilton, 46.6 ov).

Bowling	O	M	R	W	
Fleming	9	2	19	1	
Dale	10	2	35	0	(3nb, 7w)
McGrath	9	0	32	1	(5nb, 6w)
Warne	10	0	39	3	(2w)
Lee	6	1	25	1	(3w)
SR Waugh	6	0	22	1	(4w)

Australia innings (target: 182 runs from 50 overs)			R	B	4	6
+AC Gilchrist	c Philip	b Asim Butt	6	16	1	0
ME Waugh		c & b Dyer	67	114	5	0
RT Ponting	c Allingham	b Blain	33	62	3	0
DS Lehmann		b Dyer	0	2	0	0
*SR Waugh	not out		49	69	7	0
MG Bevan	not out		11	14	1	0
Extras	(lb 3, w 4, nb 9)		16			
Total	(4 wickets, 44.5 overs)		182			

DNB: S Lee, SK Warne, DW Fleming, AC Dale, GD McGrath.
Fall of wickets: 1-17 (Gilchrist, 5.2 ov), 2-101 (Ponting, 26.6 ov), 3-101 (Lehmann, 27.2 ov), 4-141 (ME Waugh, 35.5 ov).

Bowling	O	M	R	W	
Blain	8	0	35	1	(5nb, 1w)
Asim Butt	10	3	21	1	(1nb, 1w)
Brinkley	8	0	43	0	
Hamilton	8.5	0	37	0	(2nb, 2w)
Dyer	10	1	43	2	

Pakistan v West Indies, Group B

At County Ground, Bristol, 16 May 1999 (50-overs)
Result: Pakistan won by 27 runs. Points: Pakistan 2, West Indies 0.
Toss: Pakistan. Umpires: DB Hair (Aus) and DL Orchard (SA).
TV Umpire: KE Palmer. Match Referee: R Subba Row.
Man of the Match: Azhar Mahmood.

Pakistan innings (50 overs maximum)			R	B	4	6
Saeed Anwar	c Lara	b Walsh	10	31	2	0
Shahid Afridi	c Jacobs	b Walsh	11	19	1	0
Abdul Razzaq		b Dillon	7	34	1	0
Ijaz Ahmed	lbw	b Dillon	36	70	4	0
Inzamam-ul-Haq	c Jacobs	b Dillon	0	1	0	0
Yousuf Youhana		c & b Simmons	34	53	2	0
Azhar Mahmood	c sub (NO Perry)	b Ambrose	37	51	1	2
*Wasim Akram		b Walsh	43	29	4	2
+Moin Khan	not out		11	10	0	0
Saqlain Mushtaq	not out		2	3	0	0
Extras	(b 1, lb 12, w 23, nb 2)		38			
Total	(8 wickets, 50 overs)		229			

DNB: Shoaib Akhtar.
Fall of wickets: 1-22 (Shahid Afridi, 7.6 ov), 2-23 (Saeed Anwar, 9.2 ov), 3-42 (Abdul Razzaq, 18.3 ov), 4-42 (Inzamam-ul-Haq, 18.4 ov), 5-102 (Ijaz Ahmed, 30.1 ov), 6-135 (Yousuf Youhana, 38.3 ov), 7-209 (Azhar Mahmood, 47.3 ov), 8-217 (Wasim Akram, 48.5 ov).

Bowling	O	M	R	W	
Ambrose	10	1	36	1	(1nb)
Walsh	10	3	28	3	(1nb)
Dillon	10	1	29	3	(10w)
Simmons	10	0	40	1	(4w)
Arthurton	1	0	10	0	
Adams	8	0	57	0	(3w)
Powell	1	0	16	0	(1w)

West Indies innings (target: 230 runs from 50 overs)			R	B	4	6
SL Campbell		b Shoaib Akhtar	9	14	0	1
+RD Jacobs	c Inzamam-ul-Haq	b Abdul Razzaq	25	53	3	1
JC Adams	c Inzamam-ul-Haq	b Azhar Mahmood	23	45	4	0
*BC Lara	c sub (Mushtaq Ahmed)	b Abdul Razzaq	11	9	2	0
S Chanderpaul	c Yousuf Youhana	b Shoaib Akhtar	77	96	6	0
RL Powell	c Yousuf Youhana	b Saqlain Mushtaq	4	18	0	0
PV Simmons	c Moin Khan	b Azhar Mahmood	5	16	0	0
CEL Ambrose	c Moin Khan	b Abdul Razzaq	1	9	0	0
KLT Arthurton	c Saeed Anwar	b Azhar Mahmood	6	14	0	0
M Dillon	run out (Shoaib Akhtar)		6	23	0	0
CA Walsh	not out		0	1	0	0
Extras	(b 1, lb 8, w 20, nb 6)		35			
Total	(all out, 48.5 overs)		202			

Fall of wickets: 1-14 (Campbell, 3.2 ov), 2-72 (Adams, 16.1 ov), 3-84 (Lara, 18.2 ov), 4-101 (Jacobs, 22.2 ov), 5-121 (Powell, 29.4 ov), 6-141 (Simmons, 35.2 ov), 7-142 (Ambrose, 36.6 ov), 8-161 (Arthurton, 41.1 ov), 9-195 (Dillon, 48.1 ov), 10-202 (Chanderpaul, 48.5 ov).

Bowling	O	M	R	W	
Wasim Akram	10	3	37	0	(3nb, 6w)
Shoaib Akhtar	9.5	1	54	2	(3w)
Saqlain Mushtaq	9	0	22	1	(1w)
Azhar Mahmood	10	0	48	3	(5w)
Abdul Razzaq	10	3	32	3	(3nb, 4w)

Bangladesh v New Zealand, Group B

At County Ground, Chelmsford, 17 May 1999 (50-overs)
Result: New Zealand won by 6 wickets. Points: New Zealand 2, Bangladesh 0.
Toss: New Zealand. Umpires: ID Robinson (Zim) and S Venkataraghavan (Ind).
TV Umpire: DR Shepherd. Match Referee: PJP Burge (Aus).
Man of the Match: GR Larsen.

Bangladesh innings (50 overs maximum)			R	B	4	6
Shahriar Hossain	lbw	b Allott	0	3	0	0
Mehrab Hossain	lbw	b Allott	2	4	0	0
Akram Khan		c & b Larsen	16	33	2	0
*Aminul Islam		b Cairns	15	41	0	0
+Khaled Mashud		b Larsen	4	15	0	0
Naimur Rahman	lbw	b Larsen	18	51	0	0
Khaled Mahmud	c Twose	b Cairns	3	7	0	0
Mohammad Rafique	lbw	b Cairns	0	1	0	0
Enamul Haque		b Harris	19	41	3	0
Hasibul Hossain	c Horne	b Allott	16	28	1	1
Manjural Islam	not out		6	6	0	0
Extras	(lb 4, w 5, nb 8)		17			
Total	(all out, 37.4 overs)		116			

Fall of wickets: 1-0 (Shahriar Hossain, 0.3 ov), 2-7 (Mehrab Hossain, 2.3 ov), 3-38 (Aminul Islam, 12.4 ov), 4-38 (Akram Khan, 13.3 ov), 5-46 (Khaled Mashud, 17.2 ov), 6-49 (Khaled Mahmud, 18.6 ov), 7-51 (Mohammad Rafique, 20.1 ov), 8-85 (Naimur Rahman, 29.5 ov), 9-96 (Enamul Haque, 33.5 ov), 10-116 (Hasibul Hossain, 37.4 ov).

Bowling	O	M	R	W	
Allott	8.4	0	30	3	(1nb, 3w)
Nash	10	1	30	0	(1nb)
Cairns	7	1	19	3	(1nb, 1w)
Larsen	10	0	19	3	(1nb, 1w)
Harris	2	0	14	1	

New Zealand innings (target: 117 runs from 50 overs)			R	B	4	6
MJ Horne	lbw	b Naimur Rahman	35	86	4	0
NJ Astle	c Aminul Islam	b Manjural Islam	4	5	1	0
CD McMillan	c Naimur Rahman	b Hasibul Hossain	20	26	4	0
*SP Fleming	c Khaled Mashud	b Mohammad Rafique	16	33	2	0
RG Twose	not out		30	36	3	1
CL Cairns	not out		7	12	0	0
Extras	(lb 1, w 4)		5			
Total	(4 wickets, 33 overs)		117			

DNB: +AC Parore, CZ Harris, DJ Nash, GR Larsen, GI Allott.
Fall of wickets: 1-5 (Astle, 1.5 ov), 2-33 (McMillan, 10.4 ov), 3-78 (Fleming, 23.2 ov), 4-105 (Horne, 29.5 ov).

Bowling	O	M	R	W	
Hasibul Hossain	10	2	33	1	(2w)
Manjural Islam	8	3	23	1	(2w)
Khaled Mahmud	7	2	12	0	
Enamul Haque	3	0	21	0	
Mohammad Rafique	3	0	22	1	
Naimur Rahman	2	0	5	1	

England v Kenya, Group A

At St Lawrence Ground, Canterbury, 18 May 1999 (50-overs)
Result: England won by 9 wickets. Points: England 2, Kenya 0.
Toss: England. Umpires: KT Francis (SL) and RE Koertzen (SA).
TV Umpire: DB Cowie (NZ). Match Referee: Talat Ali (Pak).
Man of the Match: SO Tikolo.

Kenya innings (50 overs maximum)			R	B	4	6
+KO Otieno	c Thorpe	b Austin	0	8	0	0
RD Shah	c Stewart	b Gough	46	80	4	0
SO Tikolo	c Gough	b Ealham	71	107	8	0
MO Odumbe		b Gough	6	13	0	0
HS Modi	run out (Fairbrother)		5	11	1	0
AV Vadher		b Croft	6	19	1	0
TM Odoyo	not out		34	32	3	1
*AY Karim		b Ealham	9	17	1	0
AO Suji		b Gough	4	5	0	0
M Sheikh		b Gough	7	6	1	0
MA Suji	run out (Thorpe)		0	3	0	0
Extras	(b 1, lb 5, w 6, nb 3)		15			
Total	(all out, 49.4 overs)		203			

Fall of wickets: 1-7 (Otieno, 3.5 ov), 2-107 (Shah, 26.3 ov), 3-115 (Odumbe, 28.6 ov), 4-130 (Modi, 33.1 ov), 5-142 (Vadher, 37.5 ov), 6-150 (Tikolo, 40.1 ov), 7-181 (Karim, 45.4 ov), 8-186 (AO Suji, 46.4 ov), 9-202 (Sheikh, 48.5 ov), 10-203 (MA Suji, 49.4 ov).

Bowling	O	M	R	W	
Gough	10	1	34	4	(1nb, 2w)
Austin	9.4	0	41	1	(2w)
Mullally	10	0	41	0	(2nb, 2w)
Ealham	10	0	49	2	
Croft	10	1	32	1	

England innings (target: 204 runs from 50 overs)			R	B	4	6
N Hussain	not out		88	127	11	1
*+AJ Stewart		b Odoyo	23	26	4	0
GA Hick	not out		61	89	9	0
Extras	(b 5, lb 6, w 13, nb 8)		32			
Total	(1 wicket, 39 overs)		204			

DNB: GP Thorpe, NH Fairbrother, A Flintoff, MA Ealham, RDB Croft, ID Austin, D Gough, AD Mullally.
Fall of wickets: 1-45 (Stewart, 9.4 ov).

Bowling	O	M	R	W	
MA Suji	9	0	46	0	(4nb, 4w)
AO Suji	3	0	6	0	(2w)
Odoyo	10	0	65	1	(4nb, 2w)
Karim	8	0	39	0	(4w)
Odumbe	6	1	23	0	(1w)
Sheikh	3	0	14	0	

India v Zimbabwe, Group A

At Grace Road, Leicester, 19 May 1999 (50-overs)
Result: Zimbabwe won by 3 runs. Points: Zimbabwe 2, India 0.
Toss: India. Umpires: DL Orchard (SA) and P Willey.
TV Umpire: DB Hair (Aus). Match Referee: CW Smith (WI).
Man of the Match: GW Flower.

Zimbabwe innings (50 overs maximum)			R	B	4	6
NC Johnson	c Mongia	b Srinath	7	10	1	0
GW Flower	c Mongia	b Jadeja	45	89	4	0
PA Strang		b Agarkar	18	26	1	0
MW Goodwin	c Singh	b Ganguly	17	40	3	0
+A Flower	not out		68	85	2	0
*ADR Campbell	st Mongia	b Kumble	24	29	3	0
GJ Whittal		b Kumble	4	8	0	0
SV Carlisle		b Srinath	1	2	0	0
HH Streak	c Mongia	b Prasad	14	18	2	0
EA Brandes	c Mongia	b Prasad	2	5	0	0
HK Olonga	not out		1	4	0	0
Extras	(lb 14, w 21, nb 16)		51			
Total	(9 wickets, 50 overs)		252			

Fall of wickets: 1-12 (Johnson, 2.4 ov), 2-45 (Strang, 9.5 ov), 3-87 (Goodwin, 21.2 ov), 4-144 (GW Flower, 31.1 ov), 5-204 (Campbell, 40.3 ov), 6-211 (Whittall, 42.4 ov), 7-214 (Carlisle, 43.2 ov), 8-244 (Streak, 47.6 ov), 9-250 (Brandes, 49.2 ov).

Bowling	O	M	R	W	
Srinath	10	1	35	2	(5nb, 1w)
Prasad	10	1	37	2	(1nb, 4w)
Agarkar	9	0	70	1	(5nb, 4w)
Ganguly	5	0	22	1	(3nb, 1w)
Singh	2	0	11	0	
Kumble	10	0	41	2	(1nb, 2w)
Jadeja	4	0	22	1	(3w)

India innings (target: 253 runs from 46 overs)			R	B	4	6
SC Ganguly	c Brandes	b Johnson	9	8	2	0
S Ramesh	c Goodwin	b GW Flower	55	77	3	1
R Dravid	c GW Flower	b Streak	13	14	2	0
*M Azharuddin	c Campbell	b Streak	7	11	1	0
A Jadeja	lbw	b Streak	43	76	3	0
RR Singh	c Campbell	b Olonga	35	47	1	0
AB Agarkar	run out (Goodwin)		1	5	0	0
+NR Mongia		b Whittall	28	24	2	1
J Srinath		b Olonga	18	12	0	2
A Kumble	not out		1	1	0	0
BKV Prasad	lbw	b Olonga	0	1	0	0
Extras	(b 1, lb 4, w 24, nb 10)		39			
Total	(all out, 45 overs)		249			

Fall of wickets: 1-13 (Ganguly, 1.5 ov), 2-44 (Dravid, 6.4 ov), 3-56 (Azharuddin, 8.6 ov), 4-155 (Ramesh, 27.5 ov), 5-174 (Jadeja, 32.2 ov), 6-175 (Agarkar, 33.2 ov), 7-219 (Mongia, 40.5 ov), 8-246 (Singh, 44.2 ov), 9-249 (Srinath, 44.5 ov), 10-249 (Prasad, 44.6 ov).

Bowling	O	M	R	W	
Brandes	3	0	27	0	(3w)
Johnson	7	0	51	1	(5nb, 1w)
Streak	9	0	36	3	(1nb, 7w)
Olonga	4	0	22	3	(6w)
Whittall	4	0	26	1	(2w)
Strang	8	0	49	0	
GW Flower	10	0	33	1	(1w)

South Africa v Sri Lanka, Group A

At County Ground, Northampton, 19 May 1999 (50-overs)
Result: South Africa won by 89 runs. Points: South Africa 2, Sri Lanka 0.
Toss: Sri Lanka. Umpires: SA Bucknor (WI) and RS Dunne (NZ).
TV Umpire: KE Palmer. Match Referee: JR Reid (NZ).
Man of the Match: L Klusener.

South Africa innings (50 overs maximum)			R	B	4	6
G Kirsten		b Vaas	14	14	3	0
HH Gibbs	c Kaluwitharana	b Vaas	5	15	1	0
+MV Boucher		b Wickramasinghe	1	10	0	0
JH Kallis	c Mahanama	b Wickramasinghe	12	26	0	0
DJ Cullinan	c Vaas	b Muralitharan	49	82	4	0
*WJ Cronje	run out (Jayawardene/Kaluwitharana)		8	21	0	0
JN Rhodes	c Jayasuriya	b Muralitharan	17	25	2	0
SM Pollock		c & b Muralitharan	2	9	0	0
L Klusener	not out		52	45	5	2
S Elworthy	c Kaluwitharana	b Vaas	23	40	3	0
AA Donald	not out		3	16	0	0
Extras	(lb 2, w 7, nb 4)		13			
Total	(9 wickets, 50 overs)		199			

Fall of wickets: 1-22 (Kirsten, 3.3 ov), 2-24 (Gibbs, 5.5 ov), 3-24 (Boucher, 6.3 ov), 4-53 (Kallis, 14.5 ov), 5-69 (Cronje, 20.4 ov), 6-103 (Rhodes, 28.2 ov), 7-115 (Pollock, 32.2 ov), 8-122 (Cullinan, 34.2 ov), 9-166 (Elworthy, 45.3 ov).

Bowling	O	M	R	W	
Wickramasinghe	10	1	45	2	(1nb, 4w)
Vaas	10	0	46	3	(3nb)
Jayawardene	10	0	46	0	(1w)
Muralitharan	10	1	25	3	(1w)
Chandana	7	0	26	0	(1w)
Jayasuriya	3	1	9	0	

Sri Lanka innings (target: 200 runs from 50 overs)			R	B	4	6
ST Jayasuriya		b Kallis	5	14	0	0
+RS Kaluwitharana	c Cullinan	b Kallis	5	10	1	0
MS Atapattu	c Boucher	b Kallis	1	10	0	0
PA de Silva	lbw	b Pollock	1	8	0	0
RS Mahanama	lbw	b Pollock	36	71	3	0
*A Ranatunga	c Boucher	b Donald	7	19	1	0
DPMD Jayawardene	c Kallis	b Elworthy	22	32	4	0
UDU Chandana	c Cullinan	b Klusener	9	22	1	0
WPUJC Vaas	c Pollock	b Klusener	1	10	0	0
GP Wickramasinghe		b Klusener	6	17	0	0
M Muralitharan	not out		0	0	0	0
Extras	(lb 5, w 10, nb 2)		17			
Total	(all out, 35.2 overs)		110			

Fall of wickets: 1-12 (Kaluwitharana, 3.3 ov), 2-13 (Jayasuriya, 3.6 ov), 3-14 (Atapattu, 5.5 ov), 4-14 (de Silva, 6.6 ov), 5-31 (Ranatunga, 13.2 ov), 6-66 (Jayawardene, 22.1 ov), 7-87 (Chandana, 27.6 ov), 8-98 (Vaas, 31.1 ov), 9-110 (Mahanama, 34.6 ov), 10-110 (Wickramasinghe, 35.2 ov).

Bowling	O	M	R	W	
Pollock	8	3	10	2	(2nb)
Kallis	8	0	26	3	(6w)
Elworthy	8	1	23	1	
Donald	6	1	25	1	(3w)
Klusener	5.2	1	21	3	

Australia v New Zealand, Group B

At Sophia Gardens, Cardiff, 20 May 1999 (50-overs)
Result: New Zealand won by 5 wickets. Points: New Zealand 2, Australia 0.
Toss: Australia. Umpires: Javed Akhtar (Pak) and DR Shepherd.
TV Umpire: RE Koertzen (SA). Match Referee: R Subba Row.
Man of the Match: RG Twose.

Australia innings (50 overs maximum)			R	B	4	6
ME Waugh	lbw	b Allott	2	5	0	0
+AC Gilchrist	c Astle	b Allott	14	28	1	0
RT Ponting	c Harris	b Astle	47	88	4	0
DS Lehmann	c Astle	b Harris	76	94	8	0
*SR Waugh	c Astle	b Harris	7	18	0	0
MG Bevan		b Allott	21	32	1	0
S Lee	run out (Nash)		2	8	0	0
SK Warne		b Allott	15	14	2	0
DW Fleming	not out		8	11	0	0
AC Dale	not out		3	5	0	0
Extras	(lb 10, w 5, nb 3)		18			
Total	(8 wickets, 50 overs)		213			

DNB: GD McGrath.
Fall of wickets: 1-7 (ME Waugh, 2.1 ov), 2-32 (Gilchrist, 8.1 ov), 3-126 (Ponting, 30.6 ov), 4-149 (SR Waugh, 35.5 ov), 5-172 (Lehmann, 41.4 ov), 6-175 (Lee, 43.4 ov), 7-192 (Bevan, 46.2 ov), 8-204 (Warne, 48.3 ov).

Bowling	O	M	R	W	
Allott	10	0	37	4	(2nb, 2w)
Nash	8	1	30	0	
Cairns	7	0	44	0	(1nb, 2w)
Larsen	10	2	26	0	(1w)
Harris	10	0	50	2	
Astle	5	0	16	1	

New Zealand innings (target: 214 runs from 50 overs)			R	B	4	6
MJ Horne	c Gilchrist	b Dale	5	8	1	0
NJ Astle	c Ponting	b Fleming	4	8	0	0
CD McMillan	c Fleming	b Warne	29	55	3	0
*SP Fleming		b McGrath	9	20	1	0
RG Twose	not out		80	99	10	0
CL Cairns	c Dale	b Fleming	60	77	5	3
+AC Parore	not out		10	9	1	1
Extras	(lb 2, w 11, nb 4)		17			
Total	(5 wickets, 45.2 overs)		214			

DNB: CZ Harris, DJ Nash, GR Larsen, GI Allott.
Fall of wickets: 1-5 (Horne, 1.2 ov), 2-21 (Astle, 6.1 ov), 3-47 (Fleming, 14.4 ov), 4-49 (McMillan, 15.3 ov), 5-197 (Cairns, 43.1 ov).

Bowling	O	M	R	W	
Fleming	8.2	1	43	2	(3w)
Dale	5	1	18	1	(1w)
McGrath	9	0	43	1	(4nb)
Lee	6	0	24	0	(1w)
Warne	10	1	44	0	(4w)
SR Waugh	4	0	25	0	(1w)
Bevan	3	0	15	0	(1w)

Pakistan v Scotland, Group B
At Riverside Ground, Chester-le-Street, 20 May 1999 (50-overs)
Result: Pakistan won by 94 runs. Points: Pakistan 2, Scotland 0.
Toss: Scotland. Umpires: DB Cowie (NZ) and ID Robinson (Zim).
TV Umpire: JH Hampshire. Match Referee: PJP Burge (Aus).
Man of the Match: Yousuf Youhana.

Pakistan innings (50 overs maximum)			R	B	4	6
Saeed Anwar	c Davies	b Asim Butt	6	22	0	0
Shahid Afridi	run out (Stanger)		7	9	1	0
Abdul Razzaq	lbw	b Brinkley	12	53	0	0
Inzamam-ul-Haq	st Davies	b Dyer	12	50	0	0
Saleem Malik	lbw	b Hamilton	0	3	0	0
Yousuf Youhana	not out		81	119	6	0
+Moin Khan	c Brinkley	b Hamilton	47	41	5	0
*Wasim Akram	not out		37	19	2	2
Extras	(b 5, lb 6, w 33, nb 15)		59			
Total	(6 wickets, 50 overs)		261			

DNB: Saqlain Mushtaq, Shoaib Akhtar, Azhar Mahmood.
Fall of wickets: 1-21 (Shahid Afridi, 3.6 ov), 2-35 (Saeed Anwar, 7.5 ov), 3-55 (Abdul Razzaq, 15.6 ov), 4-58 (Saleem Malik, 16.6 ov), 5-92 (Inzamam-ul-Haq, 26.4 ov), 6-195 (Moin Khan, 44.4 ov).

Bowling	O	M	R	W	
Blain	7	0	49	0	(6nb, 6w)
Asim Butt	9	1	55	1	(3nb, 8w)
Hamilton	10	1	36	2	(3nb, 8w)
Brinkley	10	0	29	1	(6w)
Dyer	9	0	48	1	
Stanger	5	0	33	0	(3nb, 1w)

NB: Scotland were fined 1 over for a slow over rate.

Scotland innings (target: 262 runs from 49 overs)			R	B	4	6
BMW Patterson		b Wasim Akram	0	5	0	0
IL Philip	lbw	b Shoaib Akhtar	0	6	0	0
MJ Smith		b Shoaib Akhtar	3	3	0	0
IM Stanger		b Wasim Akram	3	24	0	0
*G Salmond	c Moin Khan	b Shoaib Akhtar	5	7	0	0
GM Hamilton		b Wasim Akram	76	111	3	3
JE Brinkley	c Moin Khan	b Saqlain Mushtaq	22	43	3	0
+AG Davies	c sub (Wajahatullah Wasti) b Abdul Razzaq		19	28	1	0
JAR Blain	lbw	b Abdul Razzaq	0	5	0	0
Asim Butt	c Moin Khan	b Abdul Razzaq	1	5	0	0
NR Dyer	not out		1	4	0	0
Extras	(b 1, lb 11, w 17, nb 8)		37			
Total	(all out, 38.5 overs)		167			

Fall of wickets: 1-1 (Patterson, 0.5 ov), 2-5 (Smith, 1.2 ov), 3-9 (Philip, 3.5 ov), 4-16 (Salmond, 7.1 ov), 5-19 (Stanger, 8.4 ov), 6-78 (Brinkley, 24.6 ov), 7-139 (Davies, 33.6 ov), 8-149 (Blain, 35.5 ov), 9-160 (Asim Butt, 37.1 ov), 10-167 (Hamilton, 38.5 ov).

Bowling	O	M	R	W	
Wasim Akram	7.5	0	23	3	(6w)
Shoaib Akhtar	6	2	11	3	(1nb, 2w)
Azhar Mahmood	7	2	21	0	(3w)
Abdul Razzaq	10	0	38	3	(5nb, 1w)
Saqlain Mushtaq	6	0	46	1	(2w)
Shahid Afridi	2	0	16	0	(2nb)

Bangladesh v West Indies, Group B
At Castle Avenue, Dublin, 21 May 1999 (50-overs)
Result: West Indies won by 7 wickets. Points: West Indies 2, Bangladesh 0.
Toss: Bangladesh. Umpires: KT Francis (SL) and DB Hair (Aus).
TV Umpire: G Sharp (Eng). Match Referee: RS Madugalle (SL).
Man of the Match: CA Walsh.

Bangladesh innings (50 overs maximum)			R	B	4	6
Shahriar Hossain	c Campbell	b Walsh	2	5	0	0
Mehrab Hossain	c Chanderpaul	b Simmons	64	129	4	1
Akram Khan	c Lara	b Dillon	4	19	0	0
*Aminul Islam	c Jacobs	b King	2	24	0	0
Minhajul Abedin	c Jacobs	b King	5	20	0	0
Naimur Rahman	lbw	b Walsh	45	72	4	0
Khaled Mahmud	c Bryan	b Walsh	13	15	0	0
+Khaled Mashud		b King	4	6	0	0
Enamul Haque	c Lara	b Walsh	4	7	0	0
Hasibul Hossain		b Bryan	1	3	0	0
Manjural Islam	not out		0	2	0	0
Extras	(lb 8, w 25, nb 5)		38			
Total	(all out, 49.2 overs)		182			

Fall of wickets: 1-8 (Shahriar Hossain, 2.1 ov), 2-29 (Akram Khan, 9.6 ov), 3-39 (Aminul Islam, 16.3 ov), 4-55 (Minhajul Abedin, 22.2 ov), 5-140 (Mehrab Hossain, 42.3 ov), 6-159 (Naimur Rahman, 44.3 ov), 7-167 (Khaled Mashud, 45.6 ov), 8-180 (Khaled Mahmud, 48.1 ov), 9-182 (Enamul Haque, 48.4 ov), 10-182 (Hasibul Hossain, 49.2 ov).

Bowling	O	M	R	W	
Walsh	10	0	25	4	(4nb, 1w)
Dillon	10	0	43	1	(6w)
Bryan	9.2	0	30	1	(11w)
King	10	1	30	3	(3w)
Simmons	10	0	46	1	(1nb, 4w)

West Indies innings (target: 183 runs from 50 overs)			R	B	4	6
SL Campbell	c Manjural Islam	b Khaled Mahmud	36	70	4	0
+RD Jacobs	run out (Shahriar Hossain/Khaled Mashud)		51	82	4	1
JC Adams	not out		53	82	6	0
*BC Lara	c Hasibul Hossain	b Minhajul Abedin	25	25	4	0
S Chanderpaul	not out		11	19	2	0
Extras	(lb 2, w 5)		7			
Total	(3 wickets, 46.3 overs)		183			

DNB: SC Williams, PV Simmons, HR Bryan, M Dillon, RD King, CA Walsh.
Fall of wickets: 1-67 (Campbell, 20.3 ov), 2-115 (Jacobs, 32.2 ov), 3-150 (Lara, 38.6 ov).

Bowling	O	M	R	W	
Hasibul Hossain	7	1	28	0	(3w)
Manjural Islam	7	1	15	0	
Khaled Mahmud	8	0	36	1	
Enamul Haque	8	1	31	0	(1w)
Naimur Rahman	9.3	0	43	0	(1w)
Minhajul Abedin	7	0	28	1	

England v South Africa, Group A
At Kennington Oval, London, 22 May 1999 (50-overs)
Result: South Africa won by 122 runs. Points: South Africa 2, England 0.
Toss: England. Umpires: RS Dunne (NZ) and S Venkataraghavan (Ind).
TV Umpire: Javed Akhtar (Pak). Match Referee: CW Smith (WI).
Man of the Match: L Klusener.

South Africa innings (50 overs maximum)			R	B	4	6
G Kirsten	c Stewart	b Ealham	45	62	3	0
HH Gibbs	c Hick	b Ealham	60	94	6	1
JH Kallis		b Mullally	0	5	0	0
DJ Cullinan	c Fraser	b Mullally	10	20	2	0
*WJ Cronje	c Stewart	b Flintoff	16	28	2	0
JN Rhodes	c sub (NV Knight)	b Gough	18	24	1	0
L Klusener	not out		48	40	3	1
SM Pollock		b Gough	0	1	0	0
+MV Boucher	not out		16	27	0	0
Extras	(lb 7, w 5)		12			
Total	(7 wickets, 50 overs)		225			

DNB: S Elworthy, AA Donald.
Fall of wickets: 1-111 (Gibbs, 24.6 ov), 2-112 (Kirsten, 26.2 ov), 3-112 (Kallis, 27.2 ov), 4-127 (Cullinan, 31.6 ov), 5-146 (Cronje, 36.5 ov), 6-168 (Rhodes, 40.3 ov), 7-168 (Pollock, 40.4 ov).

Bowling	O	M	R	W	
Gough	10	1	33	2	
Fraser	10	0	54	0	(1w)
Mullally	10	1	28	2	(2w)
Croft	2	0	13	0	(1w)
Ealham	10	2	48	2	
Flintoff	8	0	42	1	(1w)

England innings (target: 226 runs from 50 overs)			R	B	4	6
N Hussain	c Boucher	b Kallis	2	14	0	0
*+AJ Stewart	lbw	b Kallis	0	1	0	0
GA Hick	c Gibbs	b Elworthy	21	50	2	0
GP Thorpe	lbw	b Donald	14	29	1	0
NH Fairbrother	lbw	b Donald	21	44	1	0
A Flintoff	c Rhodes	b Donald	0	9	0	0
MA Ealham	c Cullinan	b Donald	5	17	1	0
RDB Croft	c Rhodes	b Klusener	12	25	2	0
D Gough	c Cronje	b Elworthy	10	34	1	0
ARC Fraser	c Kirsten	b Pollock	3	18	0	0
AD Mullally	not out		1	6	0	0
Extras	(lb 4, w 9, nb 1)		14			
Total	(all out, 41 overs)		103			

Fall of wickets: 1-2 (Stewart, 0.6 ov), 2-6 (Hussain, 2.6 ov), 3-39 (Thorpe, 13.5 ov), 4-44 (Hick, 16.1 ov), 5-45 (Flintoff, 17.5 ov), 6-60 (Ealham, 23.3 ov), 7-78 (Croft, 29.3 ov), 8-97 (Gough, 36.2 ov), 9-99 (Fairbrother, 37.5 ov), 10-103 (Fraser, 40.6 ov).

Bowling	O	M	R	W	
Kallis	8	0	29	2	(6w)
Pollock	9	3	13	1	(1nb)
Elworthy	10	3	24	2	(1w)
Donald	8	1	17	4	(2w)
Klusener	6	0	16	1	

Sri Lanka v Zimbabwe, Group A

At County Ground, New Road, Worcester, 22 May 1999 (50-overs)
Result: Sri Lanka won by 4 wickets. Points: Sri Lanka 2, Zimbabwe 0.
Toss: Sri Lanka. Umpires: SA Bucknor (WI) and DR Shepherd.
TV Umpire: MJ Kitchen. Match Referee: Talat Ali (Pak).
Man of the Match: MS Atapattu.

Zimbabwe innings (50 overs maximum)			R	B	4	6
NC Johnson	c Wickramasinghe	b Upashantha	8	17	1	0
GW Flower	c Kaluwitharana	b Wickramasinghe	42	69	6	0
PA Strang		b Wickramasinghe	5	8	1	0
MW Goodwin	run out (Jayasuriya/Muralitharan)		21	29	2	0
+A Flower	c Kaluwitharana	b Jayasuriya	41	60	3	0
*ADR Campbell	c Kaluwitharana	b Wickramasinghe	6	8	1	0
GJ Whittall	c Ranatunga	b Muralitharan	4	11	1	0
SV Carlisle	run out (Vaas/Jayasuriya)		27	36	1	1
HH Streak	c Atapattu	b Muralitharan	10	23	0	0
EA Brandes	not out		19	29	1	1
HK Olonga	not out		5	10	1	0
Extras	(lb 3, w 6)		9			
Total	(9 wickets, 50 overs)		197			

Fall of wickets: 1-21 (Johnson, 7.3 ov), 2-34 (Strang, 10.5 ov), 3-78 (Goodwin, 19.2 ov), 4-81 (GW Flower, 20.4 ov), 5-89 (Campbell, 22.4 ov), 6-94 (Whittall, 25.5 ov), 7-162 (Carlisle, 39.3 ov), 8-162 (A Flower, 39.4 ov), 9-176 (Streak, 46.6 ov).

Bowling	O	M	R	W	
Vaas	10	1	47	0	(1w)
Upashantha	10	1	43	1	(4w)
Wickramasinghe	10	1	30	3	
Jayawardene	1	0	8	0	
Muralitharan	10	2	29	2	(1w)
Jayasuriya	7	0	28	1	
de Silva	2	0	9	0	

Sri Lanka innings (target: 198 runs from 50 overs)			R	B	4	6
ST Jayasuriya	c Goodwin	b Johnson	6	17	0	0
RS Mahanama		b Whittall	31	64	3	0
MS Atapattu	c Campbell	b Streak	54	90	4	0
PA de Silva	c sub (AR Whittall)	b Whittall	6	15	0	0
*A Ranatunga		c & b Whittall	3	12	0	0
DPMD Jayawardene	lbw	b Streak	31	36	4	0
+RS Kaluwitharana	not out		18	30	2	0
WPUJC Vaas	not out		17	17	2	0
Extras	(lb 6, w 21, nb 5)		32			
Total	(6 wickets, 46 overs)		198			

DNB: KEA Upashantha, GP Wickramasinghe, M Muralitharan.
Fall of wickets: 1-13 (Jayasuriya, 5.4 ov), 2-75 (Mahanama, 19.1 ov), 3-93 (de Silva, 25.2 ov), 4-108 (Ranatunga, 29.2 ov), 5-150 (Atapattu, 36.3 ov), 6-157 (Jayawardene, 38.5 ov).

Bowling	O	M	R	W	
Brandes	8	0	28	0	(2w)
Johnson	7	1	29	1	(5w)
Streak	8	1	30	2	(6w)
Whittall	10	1	35	3	(1nb, 2w)
Olonga	9	0	50	0	(4nb, 3w)
GW Flower	2	0	10	0	
Strang	2	0	10	0	

India v Kenya, Group A

At County Ground, Bristol, 23 May 1999 (50-overs)
Result: India won by 94 runs. Points: India 2, Kenya 0.
Toss: Kenya. Umpires: DB Cowie (NZ) and ID Robinson (Zim).
TV Umpire: JW Holder. Match Referee: PJP Burge (Aus).
Man of the Match: SR Tendulkar.

India innings (50 overs maximum)			R	B	4	6
S Ramesh	run out (Tikolo)		44	66	7	0
SC Ganguly	lbw	b Suji	13	26	3	0
R Dravid	not out		104	109	10	0
SR Tendulkar	not out		140	101	16	3
Extras	(lb 5, w 21, nb 2)		28			
Total	(2 wickets, 50 overs)		329			

DNB: *M Azharuddin, A Jadeja, +NR Mongia, N Chopra, AB Agarkar, J Srinath, DS Mohanty.
Fall of wickets: 1-50 (Ganguly, 10.4 ov), 2-92 (Ramesh, 20.5 ov).

Bowling	O	M	R	W	
Suji	10	2	26	1	(3w)
Angara	7	0	66	0	(1nb, 6w)
Odoyo	9	0	59	0	(1nb, 2w)
Tikolo	9	1	62	0	(2w)
Karim	7	0	52	0	(5w)
Odumbe	8	0	59	0	

Kenya innings (target: 330 runs from 50 overs)			R	B	4	6
+KO Otieno	c Agarkar	b Chopra	56	82	5	0
RD Shah	c sub (RR Singh)	b Mohanty	9	29	1	0
SK Gupta	lbw	b Mohanty	0	1	0	0
SO Tikolo	lbw	b Mohanty	58	75	6	1
MO Odumbe	c sub (RR Singh)	b Mohanty	14	28	1	0
TM Odoyo		b Agarkar	39	55	2	2
*AY Karim		b Srinath	8	15	1	0
AV Vadher	not out		6	13	1	0
MA Suji	not out		1	4	0	0
Extras	(lb 10, w 31, nb 3)		44			
Total	(7 wickets, 50 overs)		235			

DNB: HS Modi, JO Angara.
Fall of wickets: 1-29 (Shah, 11.1 ov), 2-29 (Gupta, 11.2 ov), 3-147 (Otieno, 27.6 ov), 4-165 (Tikolo, 32.3 ov), 5-193 (Odumbe, 40.2 ov), 6-209 (Karim, 44.4 ov), 7-233 (Odoyo, 49.1 ov).

Bowling	O	M	R	W	
Srinath	10	3	31	1	(4w)
Agarkar	10	0	35	1	(1nb, 7w)
Mohanty	10	0	56	4	(1nb)
Ganguly	9	0	47	0	(1nb, 3w)
Chopra	10	2	33	1	(2w)
Tendulkar	1	0	23	0	(2w)

Australia v Pakistan, Group B

At Headingley, Leeds, 23 May 1999 (50-overs)
Result: Pakistan won by 10 runs. Points: Pakistan 2, Australia 0.
Toss: Australia. Umpires: RE Koertzen (SA) and P Willey.
TV Umpire: R Julian. Match Referee: R Subba Row.
Man of the Match: Inzamam-ul-Haq.

Pakistan innings (50 overs maximum)			R	B	4	6
Wajahatullah Wasti	c SR Waugh	b McGrath	9	31	1	0
Saeed Anwar	c Gilchrist	b Reiffel	25	23	5	0
Abdul Razzaq	c Fleming	b Warne	60	99	3	1
Ijaz Ahmed	lbw	b Fleming	0	6	0	0
Inzamam-ul-Haq	run out (Fleming)		81	104	6	1
Yousuf Youhana	run out (Warne/Lehmann)		29	16	4	1
*Wasim Akram	c Gilchrist	b Fleming	13	12	1	0
+Moin Khan	not out		31	12	2	3
Azhar Mahmood	run out (Martyn/McGrath)		1	1	0	0
Saqlain Mushtaq	not out		0	0	0	0
Extras	(b 1, lb 5, w 15, nb 5)		26			
Total	(8 wickets, 50 overs)		275			

DNB: Shoaib Akhtar.
Fall of wickets: 1-32 (Saeed Anwar, 7.4 ov), 2-44 (Wajahatullah, 11.1 ov), 3-46 (Ijaz Ahmed, 12.3 ov), 4-164 (Abdul Razzaq, 39.3 ov), 5-216 (Yousuf Youhana, 44.4 ov), 6-230 (Inzamam-ul-Haq, 46.2 ov), 7-262 (Wasim Akram, 48.6 ov), 8-265 (Azhar Mahmood, 49.3 ov).

Bowling	O	M	R	W	
Fleming	10	3	37	2	(1nb, 4w)
Reiffel	10	1	49	1	(1nb, 4w)
McGrath	10	1	54	1	(1nb, 4w)
Warne	10	0	50	1	(1w)
SR Waugh	6	0	37	0	(1w)
Martyn	2	0	25	0	(1nb)
Lehmann	2	0	17	0	

Australia innings (target: 276 runs from 50 overs)			R	B	4	6
+AC Gilchrist		b Wasim Akram	0	3	0	0
ME Waugh	c Moin Khan	b Abdul Razzaq	41	49	6	0
RT Ponting	c Saeed Anwar	b Saqlain Mushtaq	47	60	7	0
DS Lehmann	c Moin Khan	b Saqlain Mushtaq	5	9	1	0
*SR Waugh		b Shoaib Akhtar	49	65	2	1
MG Bevan	c Ijaz Ahmed	b Wasim Akram	61	80	3	1
DR Martyn		b Wasim Akram	18	25	0	0
SK Warne	run out (Ijaz Ahmed)		1	6	0	0
PR Reiffel	c Wasim Akram	b Saqlain Mushtaq	1	4	0	0
DW Fleming	not out		4	3	0	0
GD McGrath		b Wasim Akram	0	2	0	0
Extras	(b 7, lb 10, w 14, nb 7)		38			
Total	(all out, 49.5 overs)		265			

Fall of wickets: 1-0 (Gilchrist, 0.3 ov), 2-91 (ME Waugh, 16.6 ov), 3-100 (Ponting, 19.2 ov), 4-101 (Lehmann, 19.4 ov), 5-214 (Bevan, 41.3 ov), 6-238 (SR Waugh, 44.5 ov), 7-248 (Warne, 46.2 ov), 8-251 (Reiffel, 47.2 ov), 9-265 (Martyn, 49.3 ov), 10-265 (McGrath, 49.5 ov).

Bowling	O	M	R	W	
Wasim Akram	9.5	1	40	4	(5nb, 1w)
Shoaib Akhtar	10	0	46	1	(3w)
Azhar Mahmood	10	0	61	0	(3w)
Saqlain Mushtaq	10	1	51	3	(2nb)
Abdul Razzaq	10	0	50	1	(5w)

Scotland v Bangladesh, Group B

At Raeburn Place, Edinburgh, 24 May 1999 (50-overs)
Result: Bangladesh won by 22 runs. Points: Bangladesh 2, Scotland 0.
Toss: Scotland. Umpires: KT Francis (SL) and DL Orchard (SA).
TV Umpire: B Dudleston (Eng). Match Referee: JR Reid (NZ).
Man of the Match: Minhajul Abedin.

Bangladesh innings (50 overs maximum)			R	B	4	6
+Khaled Mashud	c Philip	b Blain	0	9	0	0
Mehrab Hossain	c Dyer	b Asim Butt	3	20	0	0
Faruk Ahmed		b Blain	7	24	1	0
*Aminul Islam	lbw	b Blain	0	1	0	0
Akram Khan	c Philip	b Asim Butt	0	14	0	0
Minhajul Abedin	not out		68	116	6	0
Naimur Rahman	c Stanger	b Brinkley	36	58	5	0
Khaled Mahmud	c Salmond	b Dyer	0	4	0	0
Enamul Haque	c Philip	b Dyer	19	40	1	0
Hasibul Hossain		c & b Blain	6	18	0	0
Manjural Islam	not out		2	7	0	0
Extras	(lb 5, w 28, nb 11)		44			
Total	(9 wickets, 50 overs)		185			

Fall of wickets: 1-6 (Khaled Mashud, 2.3 ov), 2-12 (Mehrab Hossain, 5.3 ov), 3-13 (Aminul Islam, 6.1 ov), 4-24 (Akram Khan, 9.4 ov), 5-26 (Faruk Ahmed, 10.3 ov), 6-95 (Naimur Rahman, 29.4 ov), 7-96 (Khaled Mahmud, 30.6 ov), 8-133 (Enamul Haque, 40.5 ov), 9-164 (Hasibul Hossain, 46.6 ov).

Bowling	O	M	R	W	
Blain	10	1	37	4	(8nb, 7w)
Asim Butt	9	1	24	2	(1nb, 7w)
Hamilton	10	3	25	0	(2nb, 5w)
Brinkley	10	0	45	1	(4w)
Stanger	4	0	23	0	(1w)
Dyer	7	1	26	2	(2w)

NB; Scotland were fined 1 over for a slow over rate.

Scotland innings (target: 186 runs from 49 overs)			R	B	4	6
BMW Patterson	lbw	b Hasibul Hossain	0	2	0	0
IL Philip	lbw	b Manjural Islam	3	17	0	0
MJ Smith	c Khaled Mashud	b Hasibul Hossain	1	13	0	0
IM Stanger	lbw	b Minhajul Abedin	10	35	0	0
*G Salmond	c Faruk Ahmed	b Manjural Islam	19	31	3	0
GM Hamilton	run out (Manjural Islam)		63	71	4	1
JE Brinkley	c Hasibul Hossain	b Khaled Mahmud	5	31	0	0
+AG Davies	c Manjural Islam	b Khaled Mahmud	32	65	3	0
JAR Blain	run out (Naimur Rahman)		9	16	0	0
Asim Butt	c Aminul Islam	b Enamul Haque	1	3	0	0
NR Dyer	not out		0	0	0	0
Extras	(lb 1, w 13, nb 6)		20			
Total	(all out, 46.2 overs)		163			

Fall of wickets: 1-0 (Patterson, 0.2 ov), 2-8 (Smith, 4.5 ov), 3-8 (Philip, 5.2 ov), 4-37 (Salmond, 13.6 ov), 5-49 (Stanger, 17.3 ov), 6-83 (Brinkley, 26.3 ov), 7-138 (Hamilton, 41.3 ov), 8-158 (Davies, 45.2 ov), 9-163 (Blain, 46.1 ov), 10-163 (Asim Butt, 46.2 ov).

Bowling	O	M	R	W	
Hasibul Hossain	8	1	26	2	(4nb, 4w)
Manjural Islam	9	0	33	2	(3w)
Khaled Mahmud	9	2	27	2	(2nb, 1w)
Minhajul Abedin	3	0	12	1	(1w)
Naimur Rahman	10	0	41	0	(2w)
Enamul Haque	7.2	0	23	1	

New Zealand v West Indies, Group B

At County Ground, Southampton, 24 May 1999 (50-overs)
Result: West Indies won by 7 wickets. Points: West Indies 2, New Zealand 0.
Toss: West Indies. Umpires: Javed Akhtar (Pak) and S Venkataraghavan (Ind).
TV Umpire: JH Hampshire. Match Referee: RS Madugalle (SL).
Man of the Match: RD Jacobs.

New Zealand innings (50 overs maximum)			R	B	4	6
MJ Horne	c Lara	b Walsh	2	21	0	0
NJ Astle	c Jacobs	b Ambrose	2	6	0	0
CD McMillan	c Jacobs	b Simmons	32	78	1	0
*SP Fleming	c Jacobs	b King	0	17	0	0
RG Twose	c Williams	b King	0	12	0	0
CL Cairns	c Lara	b Dillon	23	40	2	0
+AC Parore	c Jacobs	b Dillon	23	41	4	0
CZ Harris	c Campbell	b Dillon	30	50	2	0
DJ Nash	c Williams	b Dillon	1	10	0	0
GR Larsen	c Jacobs	b Simmons	14	18	2	0
GI Allott	not out		0	2	0	0
Extras	(lb 6, w 17, nb 6)		29			
Total	(all out, 48.1 overs)		156			

Fall of wickets: 1-2 (Astle, 1.6 ov), 2-13 (Horne, 4.5 ov), 3-22 (Fleming, 10.3 ov), 4-31 (Twose, 16.4 ov), 5-59 (McMillan, 25.1 ov), 6-75 (Cairns, 30.5 ov), 7-125 (Parore, 40.3 ov), 8-130 (Nash, 42.5 ov), 9-155 (Larsen, 47.4 ov), 10-156 (Harris, 48.1 ov).

Bowling	O	M	R	W	
Walsh	10	1	23	1	(4nb, 2w)
Ambrose	10	0	19	1	(2w)
King	10	1	29	2	(1nb, 5w)
Simmons	9	2	33	2	(1nb, 4w)
Dillon	9.1	0	46	4	(3w)

West Indies innings (target: 157 runs from 50 overs)			R	B	4	6
SL Campbell	lbw	b Nash	8	32	0	0
+RD Jacobs	not out		80	131	8	1
JC Adams	c Parore	b Allott	3	29	0	0
*BC Lara	c Nash	b Harris	36	54	3	1
SC Williams	not out		14	28	1	0
Extras	(lb 4, w 5, nb 8)		17			
Total	(3 wickets, 44.2 overs)		158			

DNB: S Chanderpaul, PV Simmons, CEL Ambrose, M Dillon, RD King, CA Walsh.
Fall of wickets: 1-29 (Campbell, 9.6 ov), 2-49 (Adams, 20.5 ov), 3-121 (Lara, 35.4 ov).

Bowling	O	M	R	W	
Allott	10	2	39	1	(2nb, 1w)
Nash	10	2	25	1	(3nb, 3w)
Cairns	9.2	1	42	0	(3nb, 1w)
Larsen	7	1	29	0	
Harris	8	2	19	1	

England v Zimbabwe, Group A

At Trent Bridge, Nottingham, 25 May 1999 (50-overs)
Result: England won by 7 wickets. Points: England 2, Zimbabwe 0.
Toss: England. Umpires: SA Bucknor (WI) and DB Hair (Aus).
TV Umpire: RE Koertzen (SA). Match Referee: Talat Ali (Pak).
Man of the Match: AD Mullally.

Zimbabwe innings (50 overs maximum)			R	B	4	6
NC Johnson		b Gough	6	12	0	0
GW Flower	c Thorpe	b Ealham	35	90	4	0
PA Strang	c Hick	b Mullally	0	17	0	0
MW Goodwin	c Thorpe	b Mullally	4	18	0	0
+A Flower	run out (Hussain)		10	24	0	0
*ADR Campbell	c Stewart	b Fraser	24	35	2	0
GJ Whittall	lbw	b Ealham	28	51	3	0
SV Carlisle	c Fraser	b Gough	14	38	1	0
HH Streak	not out		11	13	1	0
HK Olonga	not out		1	3	0	0
Extras	(lb 16, w 17, nb 1)		34			
Total	(8 wickets, 50 overs)		167			

DNB: M Mbangwa.
Fall of wickets: 1-21 (Johnson, 6.1 ov), 2-29 (Strang, 11.5 ov), 3-47 (Goodwin, 17.3 ov), 4-79 (A Flower, 26.2 ov), 5-86 (GW Flower, 28.1 ov), 6-124 (Campbell, 38.1 ov), 7-141 (Whittall, 44.3 ov), 8-159 (Carlisle, 48.5 ov).

Bowling	O	M	R	W	
Gough	10	2	24	2	(3w)
Fraser	10	0	27	1	(1nb, 2w)
Mullally	10	4	16	2	(4w)
Ealham	10	1	35	2	(1w)
Flintoff	3	0	14	0	(5w)
Hollioake	7	0	35	0	(2w)

England innings (target: 168 runs from 50 overs)			R	B	4	6
N Hussain	not out		57	93	7	0
*+AJ Stewart	c Goodwin	b Johnson	12	31	1	0
GA Hick	c A Flower	b Mbangwa	4	11	0	0
GP Thorpe	c Campbell	b Mbangwa	62	80	7	0
NH Fairbrother	not out		7	23	0	0
Extras	(lb 3, w 16, nb 7)		26			
Total	(3 wickets, 38.3 overs)		168			

DNB: A Flintoff, AJ Hollioake, MA Ealham, D Gough, ARC Fraser, AD Mullally.
Fall of wickets: 1-21 (Stewart, 8.3 ov), 2-36 (Hick, 11.2 ov), 3-159 (Thorpe, 33.3 ov).

Bowling	O	M	R	W	
Johnson	7	2	20	1	(3nb)
Streak	8	0	37	0	(8w)
Mbangwa	7	1	28	2	(2w)
Whittall	4	0	23	0	(2w)
Olonga	3	0	27	0	(4nb, 4w)
Strang	9.3	1	30	0	

Kenya v South Africa, Group A

At VRA Ground, Amstelveen, 26 May 1999 (50-overs)
Result: South Africa won by 7 wickets. Points: South Africa 2, Kenya 0.
Toss: South Africa. Umpires: DB Cowie (NZ) and P Willey (Eng).
TV Umpire: DJ Constant (Eng). Match Referee: R Subba Row (Eng).
Man of the Match: L Klusener.

Kenya innings (50 overs maximum)			R	B	4	6
+KO Otieno	lbw	b Elworthy	26	42	3	0
RD Shah	c Boucher	b Donald	50	64	7	0
SK Gupta		b Elworthy	1	7	0	0
SO Tikolo	c Cronje	b Klusener	10	35	0	0
MO Odumbe		b Donald	7	15	1	0
AV Vadher		c & b Klusener	2	24	0	0
TM Odoyo	lbw	b Klusener	0	1	0	0
*AY Karim	lbw	b Cronje	22	40	2	0
M Sheikh		b Klusener	8	26	0	0
MA Suji	not out		6	10	1	0
JO Angara		b Klusener	6	5	1	0
Extras	(lb 5, w 7, nb 2)		14			
Total	(all out, 44.3 overs)		152			

Fall of wickets: 1-66 (Otieno, 15.2 ov), 2-80 (Gupta, 17.6 ov), 3-82 (Shah, 18.3 ov), 4-91 (Odumbe, 22.5 ov), 5-104 (Tikolo, 30.3 ov), 6-104 (Odoyo, 30.4 ov), 7-107 (Vadher, 32.1 ov), 8-138 (Karim, 41.4 ov), 9-140 (Sheikh, 42.2 ov), 10-152 (Angara, 44.3 ov).

Bowling	O	M	R	W	
Pollock	8	1	22	0	(1nb, 1w)
Kallis	8	0	37	0	(1w)
Donald	8	1	42	2	(1nb, 3w)
Elworthy	10	2	20	2	(1w)
Klusener	8.3	3	21	5	
Cronje	2	0	5	1	(1w)

South Africa innings (target: 153 runs from 50 overs)			R	B	4	6
G Kirsten		b Odumbe	27	71	3	0
HH Gibbs	lbw	b Odoyo	38	38	4	1
+MV Boucher	c Sheikh	b Angara	3	6	0	0
JH Kallis	not out		44	81	4	1
DJ Cullinan	not out		35	51	3	2
Extras	(b 4, w 1, nb 1)		6			
Total	(3 wickets, 41 overs)		153			

DNB: JN Rhodes, L Klusener, SM Pollock, *WJ Cronje, S Elworthy, AA Donald.
Fall of wickets: 1-55 (Gibbs, 10.6 ov), 2-58 (Boucher, 13.3 ov), 3-86 (Kirsten, 22.5 ov).

Bowling	O	M	R	W	
Suji	6	0	18	0	(1nb)
Karim	7	0	43	0	(1w)
Angara	8	1	34	1	
Odoyo	9	3	18	1	
Sheikh	4	0	21	0	
Odumbe	7	1	15	1	

India v Sri Lanka, Group A

At County Ground, Taunton, 26 May 1999 (50-overs)
Result: India won by 157 runs. Points: India 2, Sri Lanka 0.
Toss: Sri Lanka. Umpires: RS Dunne (NZ) and DR Shepherd.
TV Umpire: R Julian. Match Referee: CW Smith (WI).
Man of the Match: SC Ganguly.

India innings (50 overs maximum)			R	B	4	6
S Ramesh		b Vaas	5	4	1	0
SC Ganguly	c sub (UDU Chandana)	b Wickramasinghe	183	158	17	7
+R Dravid	run out (Muralitharan)		145	129	17	1
SR Tendulkar		b Jayasuriya	2	3	0	0
A Jadeja		c & b Wickramasinghe	5	4	0	0
RR Singh	c de Silva	b Wickramasinghe	0	1	0	0
*M Azharuddin	not out		12	7	0	1
J Srinath	not out		0	0	0	0
Extras	(lb 3, w 12, nb 6)		21			
Total	(6 wickets, 50 overs)		373			

DNB: A Kumble, BKV Prasad, DS Mohanty.
Fall of wickets: 1-6 (Ramesh, 0.5 ov), 2-324 (Dravid, 45.4 ov), 3-344 (Tendulkar, 46.5 ov), 4-349 (Jadeja, 47.3 ov), 5-349 (Singh, 47.4 ov), 6-372 (Ganguly, 49.5 ov).

Bowling	O	M	R	W	
Vaas	10	0	84	1	(3nb, 1w)
Upashantha	10	0	80	0	(3nb, 3w)
Wickramasinghe	10	0	65	3	(1w)
Muralitharan	10	0	60	0	(2w)
Jayawardene	3	0	21	0	
Jayasuriya	3	0	37	1	(2w)
de Silva	4	0	23	0	(1w)

Sri Lanka innings (target: 374 runs from 50 overs)			R	B	4	6
ST Jayasuriya	run out (Srinath)		3	7	0	0
+RS Kaluwitharana	lbw	b Srinath	7	15	1	0
MS Atapattu	lbw	b Mohanty	29	29	5	0
PA de Silva	lbw	b Singh	56	74	7	0
DPMD Jayawardene	lbw	b Kumble	4	5	1	0
*A Ranatunga		b Singh	42	57	7	0
RS Mahanama	run out (Tendulkar)		32	45	3	0
WPUJC Vaas	c Ramesh	b Singh	1	4	0	0
KEA Upashantha		b Singh	5	17	0	0
GP Wickramasinghe	not out		2	6	0	0
M Muralitharan	c Tendulkar	b Singh	4	3	1	0
Extras	(b 4, lb 12, w 8, nb 7)		31			
Total	(all out, 42.3 overs)		216			

Fall of wickets: 1-5 (Jayasuriya, 2.1 ov), 2-23 (Kaluwitharana, 4.3 ov), 3-74 (Atapattu, 14.2 ov), 4-79 (Jayawardene, 15.3 ov), 5-147 (de Silva, 28.1 ov), 6-181 (Ranatunga, 34.3 ov), 7-187 (Vaas, 36.4 ov), 8-203 (Upashantha, 40.6 ov), 9-204 (Mahanama, 41.3 ov), 10-216 (Muralitharan, 42.3 ov).

Bowling	O	M	R	W	
Srinath	7	0	33	1	(1nb, 2w)
Prasad	8	0	41	0	
Mohanty	5	0	31	1	
Kumble	8	0	27	1	(2w)
Ganguly	5	0	37	0	(2nb, 1w)
Singh	9.3	0	31	5	(4nb, 2w)

Australia v Bangladesh, Group B

At Riverside Ground, Chester-le-Street, 27 May 1999 (50-overs)
Result: Australia won by 7 wickets. Points: Australia 2, Bangladesh 0.
Toss: Australia. Umpires: SA Bucknor (WI) and DL Orchard (SA).
TV Umpire: MJ Kitchen. Match Referee: JR Reid (NZ).
Man of the Match: TM Moody.

Bangladesh innings (50 overs maximum)			R	B	4	6
Khaled Mahmud	lbw	b McGrath	6	19	0	0
Mehrab Hossain	c Ponting	b Moody	42	75	7	0
Faruk Ahmed	c Ponting	b McGrath	9	16	1	0
Naimur Rahman	c Ponting	b Moody	2	5	0	0
*Aminul Islam		b Fleming	13	30	1	0
Minhajul Abedin	not out		53	99	6	0
Akram Khan	lbw	b Warne	0	7	0	0
+Khaled Mashud	lbw	b Moody	17	42	1	0
Enamul Haque	not out		17	14	2	0
Extras	(b 2, w 10, nb 7)		19			
Total	(7 wickets, 50 overs)		178			

DNB: Hasibul Hossain, Manjural Islam.
Fall of wickets: 1-10 (Khaled Mahmud, 4.2 ov), 2-39 (Faruk Ahmed, 10.6 ov), 3-47 (Naimur Rahman, 13.2 ov), 4-72 (Mehrab Hossain, 21.2 ov), 5-91 (Aminul Islam, 26.3 ov), 6-99 (Akram Khan, 31.2 ov), 7-143 (Khaled Mashud, 44.3 ov).

Bowling	O	M	R	W	
McGrath	10	0	44	2	(4nb, 2w)
Fleming	10	0	45	1	(4w)
Moody	10	4	25	3	(1w)
Julian	10	1	44	0	(3nb, 1w)
Warne	10	2	18	1	(2w)

Australia innings (target: 179 runs from 50 overs)			R	B	4	6
ME Waugh	st Khaled Mashud	b Enamul Haque	33	35	3	0
+AC Gilchrist	st Khaled Mashud	b Minhajul Abedin	63	39	12	0
BP Julian		b Enamul Haque	9	6	2	0
TM Moody	not out		56	29	6	2
RT Ponting	not out		18	10	1	1
Extras	(w 2)		2			
Total	(3 wickets, 19.5 overs)		181			

DNB: MG Bevan, DS Lehmann, *SR Waugh, SK Warne, DW Fleming, GD McGrath.
Fall of wickets: 1-98 (Gilchrist, 11.5 ov), 2-98 (ME Waugh, 12.3 ov), 3-111 (Julian, 14.1 ov).

Bowling	O	M	R	W	
Hasibul Hossain	4	0	24	0	
Manjural Islam	3	0	23	0	
Khaled Mahmud	2.5	0	39	0	
Naimur Rahman	2	0	17	0	
Enamul Haque	5	0	40	2	
Minhajul Abedin	3	0	38	1	(2w)

Scotland v West Indies, Group B

At Grace Road, Leicester, 27 May 1999 (50-overs)
Result: West Indies won by 8 wickets. Points: West Indies 2, Scotland 0.
Toss: Scotland. Umpires: Javed Akhtar (Pak) and ID Robinson (Zim).
TV Umpire: S Venkataraghavan (Ind). Match Referee: PJP Burge (Aus).
Man of the Match: CA Walsh.

Scotland innings (50 overs maximum)			R	B	4	6
MJ Smith	c Jacobs	b Simmons	1	23	0	0
MJD Allingham	c Jacobs	b Ambrose	6	43	0	0
IM Stanger	c Jacobs	b Walsh	7	27	0	0
*G Salmond	c Jacobs	b Ambrose	1	4	0	0
GM Hamilton	not out		24	43	3	0
JG Williamson	c Williams	b Bryan	1	11	0	0
JE Brinkley	c Simmons	b Walsh	2	6	0	0
+AG Davies	lbw	b Walsh	0	2	0	0
JAR Blain	lbw	b Bryan	3	21	0	0
Asim Butt	c Williams	b King	11	10	0	1
NR Dyer	c Williams	b King	0	2	0	0
Extras	(w 9, nb 3)		12			
Total	(all out, 31.3 overs)		68			

Fall of wickets: 1-6 (Smith, 5.6 ov), 2-18 (Allingham, 14.2 ov), 3-20 (Stanger, 15.5 ov), 4-20 (Salmond, 16.2 ov), 5-25 (Williamson, 20.3 ov), 6-29 (Brinkley, 21.4 ov), 7-29 (Davies, 21.6 ov), 8-47 (Blain, 28.2 ov), 9-67 (Asim Butt, 31.2 ov), 10-68 (Dyer, 31.3 ov).

Bowling	O	M	R	W	
Ambrose	10	4	8	2	(1nb, 1w)
Simmons	7	1	15	1	(4w)
Walsh	7	1	7	3	(1nb, 1w)
Bryan	6	0	29	2	(3w)
King	1.3	0	9	2	(1nb)

West Indies innings (target: 69 runs from 50 overs)			R	B	4	6
PV Simmons	c Stanger	b Blain	7	15	1	0
S Chanderpaul	not out		30	30	6	0
SC Williams	lbw	b Blain	0	1	0	0
*BC Lara	not out		25	17	3	1
Extras	(lb 2, w 4, nb 2)		8			
Total	(2 wickets, 10.1 overs)		70			

DNB: JC Adams, +RD Jacobs, SL Campbell, RD King, CEL Ambrose, HR Bryan, CA Walsh.
Fall of wickets: 1-21 (Simmons, 4.5 ov), 2-22 (Williams, 6.1 ov).

Bowling	O	M	R	W
Blain	5.1	0	36	2 (1nb, 2w)
Asim Butt	4	1	15	0 (1nb, 1w)
Hamilton	1	0	17	0 (1w)

New Zealand v Pakistan, Group B

At County Ground, Derby, 28 May 1999 (50-overs)
Result: Pakistan won by 62 runs. Points: Pakistan 2, New Zealand 0.
Toss: New Zealand. Umpires: KT Francis (SL) and RE Koertzen (SA).
TV Umpire: P Willey. Match Referee: RS Madugalle (SL).
Man of the Match: Inzamam-ul-Haq.

Pakistan innings (50 overs maximum)			R	B	4	6
Saeed Anwar		b Allott	28	25	4	0
Shahid Afridi	c Parore	b Allott	17	22	2	1
Abdul Razzaq	run out (Astle)		33	82	4	0
Ijaz Ahmed	run out (Harris)		51	68	0	0
Inzamam-ul-Haq	not out		73	61	7	0
Saleem Malik		b Allott	8	9	1	0
+Moin Khan	c McMillan	b Astle	19	17	3	0
*Wasim Akram	lbw	b Cairns	1	7	0	0
Azhar Mahmood	c Twose	b Allott	14	12	2	0
Saqlain Mushtaq	not out		0	0	0	0
Extras	(b 4, lb 10, w 8, nb 3)		25			
Total	(8 wickets, 50 overs)		269			

DNB: Shoaib Akhtar.
Fall of wickets: 1-40 (Shahid Afridi, 5.3 ov), 2-51 (Saeed Anwar, 9.5 ov), 3-127 (Abdul Razzaq, 28.3 ov), 4-163 (Ijaz Ahmed, 36.2 ov), 5-180 (Saleem Malik, 38.5 ov), 6-221 (Moin Khan, 43.4 ov), 7-226 (Wasim Akram, 45.2 ov), 8-255 (Azhar Mahmood, 48.6 ov).

Bowling	O	M	R	W
Nash	10	1	36	0 (1nb)
Allott	10	0	64	4 (2nb, 5w)
Larsen	10	0	35	0
Cairns	7	0	46	1 (1w)
Harris	8	0	47	1 (1w)
Astle	5	0	27	1 (1w)

New Zealand innings (target: 270 runs from 50 overs)			R	B	4	6
MJ Horne	c Moin Khan	b Shoaib Akhtar	1	20	0	0
NJ Astle	c Moin Khan	b Shoaib Akhtar	0	6	0	0
CD McMillan	c Saleem Malik	b Wasim Akram	20	25	3	0
*SP Fleming	c Wasim Akram	b Azhar Mahmood	69	100	4	0
RG Twose	c Inzamam-ul-Haq	b Saqlain Mushtaq	13	25	0	1
CL Cairns	lbw	b Azhar Mahmood	0	4	0	0
+AC Parore	lbw	b Azhar Mahmood	0	1	0	0
CZ Harris	c Abdul Razzaq	b Saqlain Mushtaq	42	96	0	0
DJ Nash	not out		21	32	0	0
GR Larsen	not out		3	4	0	0
Extras	(lb 15, w 13, nb 10)		38			
Total	(8 wickets, 50 overs)		207			

DNB: GI Allott.
Fall of wickets: 1-2 (Astle, 1.5 ov), 2-12 (Horne, 5.1 ov), 3-35 (McMillan, 10.4 ov), 4-70 (Twose, 18.4 ov), 5-71 (Cairns, 19.4 ov), 6-71 (Parore, 19.5 ov), 7-154 (Fleming, 38.5 ov), 8-200 (Harris, 48.6 ov).

Bowling	O	M	R	W
Wasim Akram	9	0	27	1 (5nb, 2w)
Shoaib Akhtar	7	1	31	2 (4nb, 1w)
Azhar Mahmood	10	0	38	3 (2w)
Saqlain Mushtaq	10	1	34	2 (1nb, 1w)
Shahid Afridi	6	1	26	0 (2nb, 1w)
Abdul Razzaq	8	0	36	0 (2w)

England v India, Group A

At Edgbaston, Birmingham, 29,30 May 1999 (50-overs)
Result: India won by 63 runs. Points: India 2, England 0.
Toss: England. Umpires: DB Hair (Aus) and Javed Akhtar (Pak).
TV Umpire: DB Cowie (NZ). Match Referee: PJP Burge (Aus).
Man of the Match: SC Ganguly.
Score after day 1 (reserve day used): India 232/8, England 73/3 (off 20.3 overs).

India innings (50 overs maximum)			R	B	4	6
SC Ganguly	run out (Ealham)		40	59	6	0
S Ramesh	c Hick	b Mullally	20	41	2	0
R Dravid	c Ealham	b Flintoff	53	82	6	0
SR Tendulkar	c Hick	b Ealham	22	40	2	0
*M Azharuddin	c Hussain	b Ealham	26	35	3	0
A Jadeja	c Fraser	b Gough	39	30	5	0
+NR Mongia		b Mullally	2	5	0	0
J Srinath		b Gough	1	2	0	0
A Kumble	not out		6	8	0	0
BKV Prasad	not out		2	3	0	0
Extras	(lb 7, w 10, nb 4)		21			
Total	(8 wickets, 50 overs)		232			

DNB: DS Mohanty.
Fall of wickets: 1-49 (Ramesh, 12.5 ov), 2-93 (Ganguly, 21.2 ov), 3-139 (Tendulkar, 33.3 ov), 4-174 (Dravid, 39.5 ov), 5-188 (Azharuddin, 43.5 ov), 6-209 (Mongia, 46.4 ov), 7-210 (Srinath, 47.1 ov), 8-228 (Jadeja, 49.1 ov).

Bowling	O	M	R	W
Gough	10	0	51	2 (2nb, 3w)
Fraser	10	2	30	0 (2w)
Mullally	10	0	54	2 (1nb, 4w)
Ealham	10	2	28	2 (1nb, 1w)
Flintoff	5	0	28	1
Hollioake	5	0	34	0

England innings (target: 233 runs from 50 overs)			R	B	4	6
N Hussain		b Ganguly	33	63	3	0
*+AJ Stewart	c Azharuddin	b Mohanty	2	9	0	0
GA Hick		b Mohanty	0	1	0	0
GP Thorpe	lbw	b Srinath	36	57	7	0
NH Fairbrother	c Mongia	b Ganguly	29	62	2	0
A Flintoff	lbw	b Kumble	15	21	1	1
AJ Hollioake	lbw	b Kumble	6	13	0	0
MA Ealham	c Azharuddin	b Ganguly	0	3	0	0
D Gough	c Kumble	b Prasad	19	25	1	0
ARC Fraser	not out		15	17	3	0
AD Mullally		b Srinath	0	2	0	0
Extras	(b 4, lb 4, w 5, nb 1)		14			
Total	(all out, 45.2 overs)		169			

Fall of wickets: 1-12 (Stewart, 3.1 ov), 2-13 (Hick, 3.2 ov), 3-72 (Hussain, 19.1 ov), 4-81 (Thorpe, 23.4 ov), 5-118 (Flintoff, 31.3 ov), 6-130 (Hollioake, 35.5 ov), 7-131 (Ealham, 36.5 ov), 8-132 (Fairbrother, 38.4 ov), 9-161 (Gough, 44.1 ov), 10-169 (Mullally, 45.2 ov).

Bowling	O	M	R	W
Srinath	8.2	3	25	2
Mohanty	10	0	54	2 (1nb, 5w)
Prasad	9	1	25	1
Ganguly	8	0	27	3
Kumble	10	1	30	2

South Africa v Zimbabwe, Group A

At County Ground, Chelmsford, 29 May 1999 (50-overs)
Result: Zimbabwe won by 48 runs. Points: Zimbabwe 2, South Africa 0.
Toss: Zimbabwe. Umpires: DR Shepherd and S Venkataraghavan (Ind).
TV Umpire: JW Holder. Match Referee: R Subba Row.
Man of the Match: NC Johnson.

Zimbabwe innings (50 overs maximum)			R	B	4	6
NC Johnson	c Pollock	b Donald	76	117	10	0
GW Flower	c Cullinan	b Elworthy	19	43	3	0
MW Goodwin	c Kirsten	b Klusener	34	45	5	0
+A Flower	run out (Pollock/Boucher)		29	35	3	1
*ADR Campbell	lbw	b Donald	0	1	0	0
GJ Whittall	c Cullinan	b Donald	20	31	0	1
SV Carlisle	not out		18	19	1	0
HH Streak	not out		9	13	1	0
Extras	(b 1, lb 15, w 8, nb 4)		28			
Total	(6 wickets, 50 overs)		233			

DNB: AR Whittall, AG Huckle, HK Olonga.
Fall of wickets: 1-65 (GW Flower, 13.4 ov), 2-131 (Goodwin, 30.4 ov), 3-170 (Johnson, 38.1 ov), 4-175 (Campbell, 38.4 ov), 5-186 (A Flower, 41.3 ov), 6-214 (GJ Whittall, 46.4 ov).

Bowling	O	M	R	W
Pollock	10	1	39	0 (2nb)
Kallis	6	0	36	0 (1nb, 2w)
Donald	10	1	41	3 (1w)
Elworthy	6	0	32	1 (1w)
Klusener	9	0	36	1 (1nb, 1w)
Cronje	9	0	33	0 (2w)

South Africa innings (target: 234 runs from 50 overs)			R	B	4	6
G Kirsten	c AR Whittall	b Johnson	0	1	0	0
HH Gibbs	run out (Huckle/A Flower)		9	21	0	0
+MV Boucher	lbw	b Streak	8	23	1	0
JH Kallis	c A Flower	b Johnson	0	4	0	0
DJ Cullinan		c & b AR Whittall	29	67	3	0
*WJ Cronje		b Johnson	4	6	1	0
JN Rhodes	lbw	b Streak	5	5	1	0
SM Pollock	c Olonga	b AR Whittall	52	81	4	0
L Klusener	not out		52	58	3	2
S Elworthy	c AR Whittall	b Streak	1	6	0	0
AA Donald	c Streak	b Olonga	7	18	0	0
Extras	(b 2, lb 1, w 8, nb 7)		18			
Total	(all out, 47.2 overs)		185			

Fall of wickets: 1-0 (Kirsten, 0.1 ov), 2-24 (Gibbs, 6.4 ov), 3-25 (Boucher, 7.3 ov), 4-25 (Kallis, 8.2 ov), 5-34 (Cronje, 10.1 ov), 6-40 (Rhodes, 11.4 ov), 7-106 (Cullinan, 29.2 ov), 8-149 (Pollock, 41.2 ov), 9-150 (Elworthy, 42.2 ov), 10-185 (Donald, 47.2 ov).

Bowling	O	M	R	W
Johnson	8	1	27	3 (3nb, 3w)
Streak	9	1	35	3 (1nb, 4w)
GJ Whittall	4	0	20	0 (1w)
Olonga	4.2	0	17	1 (2nb)
Huckle	10	1	35	0
AR Whittall	10	0	41	2
GW Flower	2	0	7	0

Kenya v Sri Lanka, Group A

At County Ground, Southampton, 30 May 1999 (50-overs)
Result: Sri Lanka won by 45 runs. Points: Sri Lanka 2, Kenya 0.
Toss: Kenya. Umpires: DL Orchard (SA) and P Willey.
TV Umpire: B Dudleston. Match Referee: Talat Ali (Pak).
Man of the Match: MO Odumbe.

Sri Lanka innings (50 overs maximum)			R	B	4	6
ST Jayasuriya	lbw	b Odoyo	39	50	5	1
RS Mahanama		b Odoyo	21	45	2	0
MS Atapattu	c Otieno	b Angara	52	67	3	0
PA de Silva	c Suji	b Odoyo	10	19	2	0
*A Ranatunga	run out (Angara)		50	61	4	0
UDU Chandana	c Otieno	b Kamande	0	1	0	0
DPMD Jayawardene	c Shah	b Suji	45	33	7	0
+RS Kaluwitharana	c Chudasama	b Angara	3	5	0	0
WPUJC Vaas	not out		29	22	1	2
GP Wickramasinghe	not out		0	0	0	0
Extras	(lb 7, w 16, nb 3)		26			
Total	(8 wickets, 50 overs)		275			

DNB: M Muralitharan.
Fall of wickets: 1-72 (Jayasuriya, 14.6 ov), 2-74 (Mahanama, 16.2 ov), 3-87 (de Silva, 20.3 ov), 4-191 (Ranatunga, 39.3 ov), 5-191 (Chandana, 39.4 ov), 6-199 (Atapattu, 40.5 ov), 7-209 (Kaluwitharana, 42.2 ov), 8-273 (Jayawardene, 49.5 ov).

Bowling	O	M	R	W	
Suji	9	1	58	1	(2nb, 2w)
Angara	10	0	50	2	(1nb, 1w)
Odoyo	10	2	56	3	(2w)
Karim	10	0	35	0	(1w)
Kamande	9	0	51	1	(3w)
Odumbe	2	0	18	0	(1w)

Kenya innings (target: 276 runs from 50 overs)			R	B	4	6
+KO Otieno	lbw	b Vaas	0	2	0	0
RD Shah	c Muralitharan	b Jayawardene	12	40	1	0
DN Chudasama		b Vaas	3	24	0	0
SO Tikolo	lbw	b Wickramasinghe	19	17	4	0
*AY Karim	lbw	b Jayawardene	4	16	1	0
MO Odumbe		b Jayasuriya	82	95	7	0
AV Vadher	not out		73	98	6	0
TM Odoyo	not out		16	9	2	1
Extras	(b 4, lb 8, w 8, nb 1)		21			
Total	(6 wickets, 50 overs)		230			

DNB: MA Suji, JO Angara, JK Kamande.
Fall of wickets: 1-0 (Otieno, 0.2 ov), 2-10 (Chudasama, 6.6 ov), 3-33 (Tikolo, 11.6 ov), 4-36 (Shah, 14.1 ov), 5-52 (Karim, 18.3 ov), 6-213 (Odumbe, 47.4 ov).

Bowling	O	M	R	W	
Vaas	7	1	26	1	
Wickramasinghe	9	1	27	1	(1w)
Jayawardene	10	0	56	2	(2w)
Muralitharan	3	0	11	0	
Chandana	1	0	13	0	
Jayasuriya	10	1	39	1	(1nb, 3w)
de Silva	10	0	46	0	

Australia v West Indies, Group B

At Old Trafford, Manchester, 30 May 1999 (50-overs)
Result: Australia won by 6 wickets. Points: Australia 2, West Indies 0.
Toss: Australia. Umpires: RS Dunne (NZ) and KT Francis (SL).
TV Umpire: DJ Constant. Match Referee: JR Reid (NZ).
Man of the Match: GD McGrath.

West Indies innings (50 overs maximum)			R	B	4	6
SL Campbell	c ME Waugh	b McGrath	2	14	0	0
+RD Jacobs	not out		49	142	3	0
JC Adams	lbw	b McGrath	0	1	0	0
*BC Lara		b McGrath	9	15	1	0
S Chanderpaul		b Warne	16	38	0	0
SC Williams	c ME Waugh	b Moody	3	6	0	0
PV Simmons		b Fleming	1	8	0	0
CEL Ambrose	lbw	b Warne	1	7	0	0
M Dillon	lbw	b McGrath	0	9	0	0
RD King	lbw	b Warne	1	30	0	0
CA Walsh		b McGrath	6	11	1	0
Extras	(lb 3, w 18, nb 1)		22			
Total	(all out, 46.4 overs)		110			

Fall of wickets: 1-7 (Campbell, 4.2 ov), 2-7 (Adams, 4.3 ov), 3-20 (Lara, 8.2 ov), 4-64 (Chanderpaul, 22.3 ov), 5-67 (Williams, 23.4 ov), 6-69 (Simmons, 25.2 ov), 7-70 (Ambrose, 26.4 ov), 8-71 (Dillon, 29.5 ov), 9-88 (King, 40.5 ov), 10-110 (Walsh, 46.4 ov).

Bowling	O	M	R	W	
McGrath	8.4	3	14	5	
Fleming	7	1	12	1	(2w)
Moody	7	0	16	1	(1w)
Julian	7	1	36	0	(1nb, 4w)
Warne	10	4	11	3	(1w)
Bevan	7	0	18	0	(5w)

Australia innings (target: 111 runs from 50 overs)			R	B	4	6
+AC Gilchrist		b Ambrose	21	36	1	0
ME Waugh	c Jacobs	b Ambrose	3	5	0	0
RT Ponting	c Chanderpaul	b King	20	56	1	0
DS Lehmann	c Adams	b Ambrose	9	13	1	0
*SR Waugh	not out		19	73	2	0
MG Bevan	not out		20	69	2	0
Extras	(lb 4, w 7, nb 8)		19			
Total	(4 wickets, 40.4 overs)		111			

DNB: TM Moody, BP Julian, SK Warne, DW Fleming, GD McGrath.
Fall of wickets: 1-10 (ME Waugh, 2.1 ov), 2-43 (Gilchrist, 10.1 ov), 3-53 (Lehmann, 16.2 ov), 4-62 (Ponting, 19.3 ov).

Bowling	O	M	R	W	
Ambrose	10	0	31	3	(1w)
Walsh	10	3	25	0	(7nb, 1w)
Dillon	7.4	1	22	0	(1nb, 2w)
King	10	2	27	1	(1w)
Simmons	3	2	2	0	(2w)

Bangladesh v Pakistan, Group B

At County Ground, Northampton, 31 May 1999 (50-overs)
Result: Bangladesh won by 62 runs. Points: Bangladesh 2, Pakistan 0.
Toss: Pakistan. Umpires: DB Cowie (NZ) and DB Hair (Aus).
TV Umpire: DR Shepherd. Match Referee: RS Madugalle (SL).
Man of the Match: Khaled Mahmud.

Bangladesh innings (50 overs maximum)			R	B	4	6
Shahriar Hossain	lbw	b Saqlain Mushtaq	39	60	5	0
Mehrab Hossain	st Moin Khan	b Saqlain Mushtaq	9	42	0	0
Akram Khan	c Wasim Akram	b Waqar Younis	42	66	6	0
*Aminul Islam		b Shahid Afridi	15	26	2	0
Naimur Rahman		b Waqar Younis	13	20	2	0
Minhajul Abedin		c & b Saqlain Mushtaq	14	14	2	0
Khaled Mahmud	st Moin Khan	b Saqlain Mushtaq	27	34	3	0
+Khaled Mashud	not out		15	21	1	0
Mohammad Rafique	c Shoaib Akhtar	b Saqlain Mushtaq	6	19	0	0
Niamur Rashid	lbw	b Wasim Akram	1	2	0	0
Shafiuddin Ahmed	not out		2	3	0	0
Extras	(lb 5, w 28, nb 7)		40			
Total	(9 wickets, 50 overs)		223			

Fall of wickets: 1-69 (Mehrab Hossain, 15.3 ov), 2-70 (Shahriar Hossain, 17.4 ov), 3-120 (Aminul Islam, 29.1 ov), 4-148 (Akram Khan, 34.3 ov), 5-148 (Naimur Rahman, 34.5 ov), 6-187 (Minhajul Abedin, 41.1 ov), 7-195 (Khaled Mahmud, 43.1 ov), 8-208 (Mohammad Rafique, 47.1 ov), 9-212 (Niamur Rashid, 48.1 ov).

Bowling	O	M	R	W	
Waqar Younis	9	1	36	2	(1w)
Shoaib Akhtar	8	0	30	0	(2nb, 1w)
Wasim Akram	10	0	35	1	(4nb, 8w)
Azhar Mahmood	8	0	56	0	(3w)
Saqlain Mushtaq	10	1	35	5	(6w)
Shahid Afridi	5	0	26	1	(1nb, 1w)

NB: Pakistan were fined 1 over for a slow over rate.

Pakistan innings (target: 224 runs from 49 overs)			R	B	4	6
Saeed Anwar	run out (Khaled Mashud)		9	20	0	0
Shahid Afridi	c Mehrab Hossain	b Khaled Mahmud	2	4	0	0
Ijaz Ahmed		b Shafiuddin Ahmed	0	5	0	0
Inzamam-ul-Haq	lbw	b Khaled Mahmud	7	16	1	0
Saleem Malik	lbw	b Khaled Mahmud	5	17	0	0
Azhar Mahmood	run out (Khaled Mashud)		29	61	3	0
*Wasim Akram	c Shahriar Hossain	b Minhajul Abedin	29	52	2	1
+Moin Khan	c Mehrab Hossain	b Naimur Rahman	18	17	1	0
Saqlain Mushtaq	run out (Khaled Mashud)		21	51	2	0
Waqar Younis		b Mohammad Rafique	11	20	2	0
Shoaib Akhtar	not out		1	5	0	0
Extras	(b 1, lb 6, w 21, nb 1)		29			
Total	(all out, 44.3 overs)		161			

Fall of wickets: 1-5 (Shahid Afridi, 0.5 ov), 2-7 (Ijaz Ahmed, 1.6 ov), 3-26 (Saeed Anwar, 7.1 ov), 4-29 (Inzamam-ul-Haq, 8.1 ov), 5-42 (Saleem Malik, 12.3 ov), 6-97 (Azhar Mahmood, 27.5 ov), 7-102 (Wasim Akram, 29.1 ov), 8-124 (Moin Khan, 34.6 ov), 9-160 (Waqar Younis, 43.3 ov), 10-161 (Saqlain Mushtaq, 44.3 ov).

Bowling	O	M	R	W	
Khaled Mahmud	10	2	31	3	(1nb, 7w)
Shafiuddin Ahmed	8	0	26	1	(6w)
Niamur Rashid	5	1	20	0	
Mohammad Rafique	8	0	28	1	(1w)
Minhajul Abedin	7	2	29	1	(1w)
Naimur Rahman	6.3	2	20	1	(1w)

Scotland v New Zealand, Group B

At Raeburn Place, Edinburgh, 31 May 1999 (50-overs)
Result: New Zealand won by 6 wickets. Points: New Zealand 2, Scotland 0.
Toss: New Zealand. Umpires: RE Koertzen (SA) and ID Robinson (Zim).
TV Umpire: SA Bucknor (WI). Match Referee: CW Smith (WI).
Man of the Match: GI Allott.

Scotland innings (50 overs maximum)			R	B	4	6
MJ Smith	c Cairns	b Nash	1	14	0	0
MJD Allingham	c Fleming	b Allott	2	25	0	0
*G Salmond	lbw	b Allott	1	13	0	0
GM Hamilton	c Allott	b Astle	20	49	2	0
IM Stanger	c Astle	b Cairns	27	58	1	0
JE Brinkley	c Parore	b Allott	0	6	0	0
JG Williamson		c & b Harris	10	24	0	0
+AG Davies	c sub (DL Vettori)	b Harris	24	48	3	0
JAR Blain	lbw	b Harris	0	1	0	0
Asim Butt	c Twose	b Harris	10	10	0	1
NR Dyer	not out		2	8	0	0
Extras	(b 1, lb 7, w 13, nb 3)		24			
Total	(all out, 42.1 overs)		121			

Fall of wickets: 1-2 (Smith, 3.4 ov), 2-11 (Salmond, 6.6 ov), 3-12 (Allingham, 10.1 ov), 4-66 (Hamilton, 24.4 ov), 5-68 (Brinkley, 26.4 ov), 6-68 (Stanger, 27.2 ov), 7-100 (Williamson, 35.1 ov), 8-100 (Blain, 35.2 ov), 9-110 (Asim Butt, 37.2 ov), 10-121 (Davies, 42.1 ov).

Bowling	O	M	R	W	
Allott	10	3	15	3	(1w)
Nash	10	3	16	1	(1nb)
Bulfin	6	0	31	0	(1nb, 2w)
Cairns	8	0	26	1	(1nb, 3w)
Astle	5	1	18	1	(2w)
Harris	3.1	0	7	4	(1w)

New Zealand innings (target: 122 runs from 50 overs)			R	B	4	6
MN Hart		b Blain	0	2	0	0
NJ Astle	c Davies	b Blain	11	10	1	0
CD McMillan		c & b Hamilton	19	27	2	0
RG Twose	not out		54	49	5	1
*SP Fleming		b Blain	7	7	1	0
CL Cairns	not out		20	16	1	1
Extras	(b 1, lb 2, w 5, nb 4)		12			
Total	(4 wickets, 17.5 overs)		123			

DNB: +AC Parore, CZ Harris, CE Bulfin, DJ Nash, GI Allott.
Fall of wickets: 1-0 (Hart, 0.2 ov), 2-19 (Astle, 2.3 ov), 3-81 (McMillan, 11.5 ov), 4-92 (Fleming, 12.6 ov).

Bowling	O	M	R	W	
Blain	7	0	53	3	(3nb, 2w)
Asim Butt	5	0	33	0	(1nb, 2w)
Hamilton	5.5	0	34	1	

SUPER SIX
Australia v India
At Kennington Oval, London, 4 June 1999 (50-overs)
Result: Australia won by 77 runs. Points: Australia 2, India 0.
Toss: India. Umpires: SA Bucknor (WI) and P Willey.
TV Umpire: ID Robinson (Zim). Match Referee: RS Madugalle (SL).
Man of the Match: GD McGrath.

Australia innings (50 overs maximum)			R	B	4	6
ME Waugh	c Prasad	b Singh	83	99	8	1
+AC Gilchrist	c Mohanty	b Ganguly	31	52	1	0
RT Ponting		b Singh	23	36	1	1
DS Lehmann	run out (Jadeja)		26	33	2	0
*SR Waugh	c Kumble	b Mohanty	36	40	3	0
MG Bevan	c Mongia	b Prasad	22	27	1	1
TM Moody	not out		26	20	3	0
SK Warne	not out		0	0	0	0
Extras	(lb 14, w 10, nb 11)		35			
Total	(6 wickets, 50 overs)		282			

DNB: PR Reiffel, DW Fleming, GD McGrath.
Fall of wickets: 1-97 (Gilchrist, 20.1 ov), 2-157 (ME Waugh, 30.1 ov), 3-158 (Ponting, 30.4 ov), 4-218 (SR Waugh, 41.5 ov), 5-231 (Lehmann, 43.6 ov), 6-275 (Bevan, 49.3 ov).

Bowling	O	M	R	W	
Srinath	10	2	34	0	(2nb, 4w)
Mohanty	7	0	47	1	(1nb, 1w)
Prasad	10	0	60	1	(1nb, 1w)
Kumble	10	0	49	0	
Ganguly	5	0	31	1	(1nb, 1w)
Singh	7	0	43	2	(2nb, 3w)
Tendulkar	1	0	4	0	

India innings (target: 283 runs from 50 overs)			R	B	4	6
SC Ganguly		b Fleming	8	12	0	0
SR Tendulkar	c Gilchrist	b McGrath	0	4	0	0
R Dravid	c Gilchrist	b McGrath	2	6	0	0
A Jadeja	not out		100	138	7	2
*M Azharuddin	c SR Waugh	b McGrath	3	9	0	0
RR Singh	c Reiffel	b Moody	75	94	5	3
+NR Mongia	run out (Bevan)		2	9	0	0
J Srinath	c Gilchrist	b SR Waugh	0	2	0	0
A Kumble	c Gilchrist	b SR Waugh	3	6	0	0
BKV Prasad	lbw	b Fleming	2	9	0	0
DS Mohanty	run out (Warne/Gilchrist)		0	3	0	0
Extras	(lb 3, w 4, nb 3)		10			
Total	(all out, 48.2 overs)		205			

Fall of wickets: 1-1 (Tendulkar, 0.6 ov), 2-10 (Dravid, 2.5 ov), 3-12 (Ganguly, 3.4 ov), 4-17 (Azharuddin, 6.2 ov), 5-158 (Singh, 37.3 ov), 6-181 (Mongia, 42.2 ov), 7-186 (Srinath, 42.6 ov), 8-192 (Kumble, 44.4 ov), 9-204 (Prasad, 47.4 ov), 10-205 (Mohanty, 48.2 ov).

Bowling	O	M	R	W	
McGrath	10	1	34	3	(2nb, 1w)
Fleming	9	1	33	2	(1w)
Reiffel	10	1	30	0	
Moody	10	0	41	1	(1w)
ME Waugh	1	0	7	0	
Warne	6.2	0	49	0	(1w)
SR Waugh	2	0	8	2	

SUPER SIX
Pakistan v South Africa
At Trent Bridge, Nottingham, 5 June 1999 (50-overs)
Result: South Africa won by 3 wickets. Points: South Africa 2, Pakistan 0.
Toss: Pakistan. Umpires: DB Hair (Aus) and DR Shepherd.
TV Umpire: DB Cowie (NZ). Match Referee: JR Reid (NZ).
Man of the Match: L Klusener.

Pakistan innings (50 overs maximum)			R	B	4	6
Saeed Anwar	c Boucher	b Elworthy	23	37	2	0
Wajahatullah Wasti	c Boucher	b Donald	17	56	2	0
Abdul Razzaq	c Kirsten	b Elworthy	30	60	2	0
Ijaz Ahmed	c Cullinan	b Klusener	23	36	1	1
Inzamam-ul-Haq	run out (Rhodes)		4	15	0	0
Yousuf Youhana	run out (Klusener)		17	27	1	0
+Moin Khan	run out (Cronje/Boucher)		63	56	6	2
Azhar Mahmood	not out		15	10	1	0
*Wasim Akram			5	3	1	0
Extras	(b 4, lb 8, w 11)		23			
Total	(7 wickets, 50 overs)		220			

DNB: Saqlain Mushtaq, Shoaib Akhtar.
Fall of wickets: 1-41 (Saeed Anwar, 13.2 ov), 2-58 (Wajahatullah, 18.4 ov), 3-102 (Abdul Razzaq, 29.5 ov), 4-111 (Ijaz Ahmed, 32.3 ov), 5-118 (Inzamam-ul-Haq, 35.1 ov), 6-150 (Yousuf Youhana, 42.6 ov), 7-206 (Moin Khan, 48.5 ov).

Bowling	O	M	R	W	
Pollock	10	1	42	0	
Kallis	10	0	47	0	(7w)
Donald	10	2	49	1	(2w)
Elworthy	10	2	23	2	(1w)
Klusener	9	0	41	1	
Cronje	1	0	6	0	(1w)

South Africa innings (target: 221 runs from 50 overs)			R	B	4	6
G Kirsten	lbw	b Wasim Akram	19	38	3	0
HH Gibbs	c Ijaz Ahmed	b Shoaib Akhtar	0	3	0	0
*WJ Cronje	c Saqlain Mushtaq	b Shoaib Akhtar	4	15	1	0
DJ Cullinan	c Saeed Anwar	b Azhar Mahmood	18	42	2	0
JH Kallis	c Moin Khan	b Saqlain Mushtaq	54	98	3	0
JN Rhodes	lbw	b Azhar Mahmood	0	6	0	0
SM Pollock	c Inzamam-ul-Haq	b Azhar Mahmood	30	45	3	0
L Klusener	not out		46	41	3	3
+MV Boucher	not out		12	15	0	1
Extras	(lb 11, w 14, nb 13)		38			
Total	(7 wickets, 49 overs)		221			

DNB: S Elworthy, AA Donald.
Fall of wickets: 1-7 (Gibbs, 1.3 ov), 2-19 (Cronje, 5.4 ov), 3-39 (Kirsten, 10.6 ov), 4-55 (Cullinan, 17.4 ov), 5-58 (Rhodes, 19.6 ov), 6-135 (Pollock, 36.1 ov), 7-176 (Kallis, 44.2 ov).

Bowling	O	M	R	W	
Wasim Akram	10	0	44	1	(5nb, 2w)
Shoaib Akhtar	9	1	51	2	(3nb, 1w)
Azhar Mahmood	10	1	24	3	(3w)
Abdul Razzaq	10	1	40	0	(1nb, 3w)
Saqlain Mushtaq	10	0	51	1	(3w)

SUPER SIX
New Zealand v Zimbabwe
At Headingley, Leeds, 6,7 June 1999 (50-overs)
Result: No result. Points: New Zealand 1, Zimbabwe 1.
Toss: Zimbabwe. Umpires: DL Orchard (SA) and S Venkataraghavan (Ind).
TV Umpire: RE Koertzen (SA). Match Referee: PJP Burge (Aus).
Man of the Match: No award.
Score after day 1 (reserve day used - no play possible): Zimbabwe 175, New Zealand 70/3 (off 15 overs).

Zimbabwe innings (50 overs maximum)			R	B	4	6
NC Johnson		b Allott	25	32	5	0
GW Flower	run out (Horne)		1	9	0	0
MW Goodwin	c Parore	b Harris	57	90	6	0
+A Flower	c McMillan	b Allott	0	2	0	0
*ADR Campbell	c Nash	b Larsen	40	101	2	0
GJ Whittall	c Astle	b Allott	21	34	1	0
SV Carlisle	c McMillan	b Astle	2	11	0	0
HH Streak		c Cairns	4	13	0	0
AR Whittall	c Astle	b Cairns	3	6	0	0
AG Huckle	c Twose	b Cairns	1	0	0	0
HK Olonga	not out		1	1	0	0
Extras	(b 4, lb 11, w 3, nb 3)		21			
Total	(all out, 49.3 overs)		175			

Fall of wickets: 1-10 (GW Flower, 2.5 ov), 2-35 (Johnson, 8.5 ov), 3-45 (A Flower, 10.1 ov), 4-136 (Goodwin, 36.3 ov), 5-148 (Campbell, 41.4 ov), 6-154 (Carlisle, 44.5 ov), 7-163 (Streak, 47.2 ov), 8-174 (GJ Whittall, 48.6 ov), 9-174 (Huckle, 49.1 ov), 10-175 (AR Whittall, 49.3 ov).

Bowling	O	M	R	W	
Allott	10	1	24	3	(1nb)
Nash	10	2	48	0	(1nb)
Larsen	10	0	27	1	
Cairns	6.3	2	24	3	(1nb, 3w)
Harris	4	0	12	1	
Astle	9	0	25	1	

New Zealand innings (target: 176 runs from 50 overs)			R	B	4	6
MJ Horne	lbw	b GJ Whittall	35	35	6	0
NJ Astle	c Streak	b Olonga	20	28	4	0
CD McMillan	lbw	b Streak	1	9	0	0
*SP Fleming	not out		9	17	1	0
RG Twose	not out		0	5	0	0
Extras	(lb 1, nb 4)		5			
Total	(3 wickets, 15 overs)		70			

DNB: CL Cairns, +AC Parore, CZ Harris, GR Larsen, DJ Nash, GI Allott.
Fall of wickets: 1-58 (Horne, 8.6 ov), 2-59 (Astle, 9.6 ov), 3-65 (McMillan, 12.3 ov).

Bowling	O	M	R	W	
Johnson	3	0	21	0	(1nb)
Streak	5	0	25	1	
GJ Whittall	3	0	9	1	
Olonga	4	1	14	1	(3nb)

SUPER SIX
India v Pakistan
At Old Trafford, Manchester, 8 June 1999 (50-overs)
Result: India won by 47 runs. Points: India 2, Pakistan 0.
Toss: India. Umpires: SA Bucknor (WI) and DR Shepherd.
TV Umpire: DB Hair (Aus). Match Referee: R Subba Row.
Man of the Match: BKV Prasad.

India innings (50 overs maximum)			R	B	4	6
SR Tendulkar	c Saqlain Mushtaq	b Azhar Mahmood	45	65	5	0
S Ramesh		b Abdul Razzaq	20	31	2	0
R Dravid	c Shahid Afridi	b Wasim Akram	61	89	4	0
A Jadeja	c Inzamam-ul-Haq	b Azhar Mahmood	6	14	0	0
*M Azharuddin	c Ijaz Ahmed	b Wasim Akram	59	77	3	1
RR Singh	c Wasim Akram	b Shoaib Akhtar	16	21	0	1
+NR Mongia	not out		6	4	0	0
Extras	(b 1, lb 3, w 8, nb 2)		14			
Total	(6 wickets, 50 overs)		227			

DNB: J Srinath, A Kumble, BKV Prasad, DS Mohanty.
Fall of wickets: 1-37 (Ramesh, 11.2 ov), 2-95 (Tendulkar, 20.5 ov), 3-107 (Jadeja, 24.3 ov), 4-158 (Dravid, 39.5 ov), 5-218 (Azharuddin, 48.5 ov), 6-227 (Singh, 49.6 ov).

Bowling	O	M	R	W	
Wasim Akram	10	0	27	2	(1nb)
Shoaib Akhtar	10	0	54	1	(2w)
Abdul Razzaq	10	0	40	1	(4w)
Azhar Mahmood	10	0	35	2	
Saqlain Mushtaq	10	0	67	0	(2w)

Pakistan innings (target: 228 runs from 50 overs)			R	B	4	6
Saeed Anwar	c Azharuddin	b Prasad	36	44	6	0
Shahid Afridi	c Kumble	b Srinath	6	5	1	0
Ijaz Ahmed	c Azharuddin	b Srinath	11	24	1	0
Saleem Malik	lbw	b Prasad	6	19	1	0
Inzamam-ul-Haq	lbw	b Prasad	41	93	1	0
Azhar Mahmood	c Mongia	b Kumble	10	17	1	0
+Moin Khan	c Tendulkar	b Prasad	34	37	2	1
Abdul Razzaq		b Srinath	11	12	0	1
*Wasim Akram	c Kumble	b Prasad	12	16	1	0
Saqlain Mushtaq	lbw	b Kumble	0	4	0	0
Shoaib Akhtar	not out		0	3	0	0
Extras	(lb 11, w 2)		13			
Total	(all out, 45.3 overs)		180			

Fall of wickets: 1-19 (Shahid Afridi, 2.3 ov), 2-44 (Ijaz Ahmed, 9.4 ov), 3-52 (Saleem Malik, 13.5 ov), 4-65 (Saeed Anwar, 17.4 ov), 5-78 (Azhar Mahmood, 24.2 ov), 6-124 (Moin Khan, 34.2 ov), 7-146 (Abdul Razzaq, 39.1 ov), 8-175 (Inzamam-ul-Haq, 43.4 ov), 9-176 (Saqlain Mushtaq, 44.3 ov), 10-180 (Wasim Akram, 45.3 ov).

Bowling	O	M	R	W	
Srinath	8	1	37	3	
Mohanty	10	2	31	0	(2w)
Prasad	9.3	2	27	5	
Kumble	10	0	43	2	
Singh	8	1	31	0	

SUPER SIX
Australia v Zimbabwe
At Lord's, London, 9 June 1999 (50-overs)
Result: Australia won by 44 runs. Points: Australia 2, Zimbabwe 0.
Toss: Zimbabwe. Umpires: DB Cowie (NZ) and RE Koertzen (SA).
TV Umpire: DL Orchard (SA). Match Referee: Talat Ali (Pak).
Man of the Match: NC Johnson.

Australia innings (50 overs maximum)			R	B	4	6
+AC Gilchrist	lbw	b Johnson	10	28	1	0
ME Waugh	c Goodwin	b Johnson	104	120	13	0
RT Ponting		b Olonga	36	35	4	0
DS Lehmann	retired hurt		6	8	0	0
*SR Waugh		b GJ Whittall	62	61	5	2
MG Bevan	not out		37	35	2	0
TM Moody	not out		20	22	0	1
Extras	(lb 6, w 13, nb 9)		28			
Total	(4 wickets, 50 overs)		303			

DNB: SK Warne, DW Fleming, PR Reiffel, GD McGrath.
Fall of wickets: 1-18 (Gilchrist, 6.2 ov), 2-74 (Ponting, 14.1 ov), 3-226 (SR Waugh, 38.5 ov), 4-248 (ME Waugh, 42.5 ov). NB: DS Lehmann retired hurt at 97/2.

Bowling	O	M	R	W	
Johnson	8	0	43	2	(1nb, 3w)
Streak	10	0	50	0	(2nb, 1w)
Olonga	7	0	62	1	(5nb, 1w)
GJ Whittall	4	0	24	1	(2w)
Strang	10	1	47	0	(1w)
AR Whittall	8	1	51	0	(1nb, 1w)
GW Flower	3	0	20	0	

Zimbabwe innings (target: 304 runs from 50 overs)			R	B	4	6
NC Johnson	not out		132	144	14	2
GW Flower	lbw	b McGrath	21	32	1	0
MW Goodwin	c Moody	b Bevan	47	56	7	0
+A Flower	c Gilchrist	b Reiffel	0	1	0	0
*ADR Campbell	c Fleming	b Reiffel	17	22	2	0
GJ Whittall	c ME Waugh	b Reiffel	0	3	0	0
DP Viljoen	st Gilchrist	b Warne	5	13	0	0
HH Streak	not out		18	29	0	0
Extras	(lb 6, w 13)		19			
Total	(6 wickets, 50 overs)		259			

DNB: PA Strang, AR Whittall, HK Olonga.
Fall of wickets: 1-39 (GW Flower, 10.1 ov), 2-153 (Goodwin, 28.2 ov), 3-154 (A Flower, 29.1 ov), 4-188 (Campbell, 35.2 ov), 5-189 (GJ Whittall, 35.5 ov), 6-200 (Viljoen, 38.5 ov).

Bowling	O	M	R	W	
McGrath	10	1	33	1	(2w)
Fleming	10	0	46	0	(3w)
Warne	9	0	55	1	(1w)
Reiffel	10	0	55	3	(4w)
Moody	6	0	38	0	
Bevan	5	1	26	1	(2w)

SUPER SIX
New Zealand v South Africa
At Edgbaston, Birmingham, 10 June 1999 (50-overs)
Result: South Africa won by 74 runs. Points: South Africa 2, New Zealand 0.
Toss: South Africa. Umpires: ID Robinson (Zim) and S Venkataraghavan (Ind).
TV Umpire: P Willey. Match Referee: CW Smith (WI).
Man of the Match: JH Kallis.

South Africa innings (50 overs maximum)			R	B	4	6
G Kirsten	c Nash	b Astle	82	121	6	1
HH Gibbs		b Allott	91	118	6	1
L Klusener		b Larsen	4	5	1	0
JH Kallis	not out		53	36	1	3
DJ Cullinan		c & b Cairns	0	2	0	0
*WJ Cronje	run out (Nash)		39	22	2	2
JN Rhodes	not out		0	0	0	0
Extras	(lb 11, w 3, nb 4)		18			
Total	(5 wickets, 50 overs)		287			

DNB: SM Pollock, +MV Boucher, S Elworthy, AA Donald.
Fall of wickets: 1-176 (Kirsten, 36.3 ov), 2-187 (Klusener, 37.5 ov), 3-228 (Gibbs, 43.6 ov), 4-229 (Cullinan, 44.3 ov), 5-283 (Cronje, 49.4 ov).

Bowling	O	M	R	W	
Allott	10	0	42	1	(1nb, 1w)
Nash	8	0	44	0	(1w)
Cairns	7	0	55	1	(3nb)
Larsen	9	0	47	1	
Harris	10	0	59	0	
Astle	6	0	29	1	(1w)

New Zealand innings (target: 288 runs from 50 overs)			R	B	4	6
MJ Horne	c Pollock	b Kallis	12	20	3	0
NJ Astle	c Cullinan	b Kallis	9	32	1	0
CD McMillan	c Gibbs	b Cronje	23	54	1	0
*SP Fleming	c Pollock	b Cronje	42	64	6	0
RG Twose	c Cronje	b Klusener	35	40	3	1
CL Cairns		b Klusener	17	16	1	1
+AC Parore	run out (Kirsten/Boucher)		3	5	0	0
CZ Harris	not out		27	38	1	0
DJ Nash		b Pollock	9	22	1	0
GR Larsen	not out		13	13	1	0
Extras	(lb 9, w 11, nb 3)		23			
Total	(8 wickets, 50 overs)		213			

DNB: GI Allott.
Fall of wickets: 1-20 (Horne, 5.3 ov), 2-34 (Astle, 11.3 ov), 3-93 (McMillan, 25.6 ov), 4-107 (Fleming, 29.4 ov), 5-144 (Cairns, 34.3 ov), 6-148 (Parore, 35.4 ov), 7-171 (Twose, 40.4 ov), 8-194 (Nash, 46.3 ov).

Bowling	O	M	R	W	
Pollock	10	1	29	1	
Kallis	6	2	15	2	(4w)
Elworthy	8	0	35	0	(1nb, 2w)
Donald	10	0	42	0	(1nb, 1w)
Klusener	9	0	46	2	(1nb, 3w)
Cronje	7	0	37	2	(1w)

SUPER SIX
Pakistan v Zimbabwe
At Kennington Oval, London, 11 June 1999 (50-overs)
Result: Pakistan won by 148 runs. Points: Pakistan 2, Zimbabwe 0.
Toss: Pakistan. Umpires: SA Bucknor (WI) and DL Orchard (SA).
TV Umpire: DB Cowie (NZ). Match Referee: PJP Burge (Aus).
Man of the Match: Saeed Anwar.

Pakistan innings (50 overs maximum)			R	B	4	6
Saeed Anwar	c A Flower	b Olonga	103	144	11	0
Wajahatullah Wasti	c Huckle	b Whittall	40	42	5	1
Ijaz Ahmed	run out (Goodwin/A Flower)		5	5	0	0
Inzamam-ul-Haq	st A Flower	b Strang	21	36	0	0
*Wasim Akram	lbw	b Huckle	0	2	0	0
+Moin Khan	run out (GW Flower)		13	17	0	0
Shahid Afridi	c Johnson	b Olonga	37	29	1	2
Azhar Mahmood	c A Flower	b Streak	2	3	0	0
Abdul Razzaq		b Streak	0	1	0	0
Saqlain Mushtaq	not out		17	22	0	0
Shoaib Akhtar	not out		1	1	0	0
Extras	(b 6, lb 3, w 20, nb 3)		32			
Total	(9 wickets, 50 overs)		271			

Fall of wickets: 1-95 (Wajahatullah, 18.5 ov), 2-116 (Ijaz Ahmed, 21.2 ov), 3-183 (Inzamam-ul-Haq, 35.6 ov), 4-194 (Saeed Anwar, 37.6 ov), 5-195 (Wasim Akram, 38.4 ov), 6-228 (Moin Khan, 43.3 ov), 7-231 (Azhar Mahmood, 44.1 ov), 8-231 (Abdul Razzaq, 44.2 ov), 9-260 (Shahid Afridi, 48.3 ov).

Bowling	O	M	R	W	
Streak	10	0	63	2	(1nb, 5w)
Mbangwa	8	0	28	0	(3w)
Whittall	8	1	39	1	(3w)
Olonga	5	0	38	2	(1nb, 5w)
Huckle	10	0	43	1	(1w)
GW Flower	2	0	13	0	(2w)
Strang	7	0	38	1	(1w)

NB: Zimbabwe were fined 1 over for a slow over rate.

Zimbabwe innings (target: 272 runs from 49 overs)			R	B	4	6
NC Johnson	lbw	b Azhar Mahmood	54	94	5	0
GW Flower		b Shoaib Akhtar	2	9	0	0
MW Goodwin	c Shahid Afridi	b Abdul Razzaq	4	15	0	0
+A Flower		b Abdul Razzaq	4	12	0	0
*ADR Campbell	c Wasim Akram	b Abdul Razzaq	3	7	0	0
GJ Whittall	c Shahid Afridi	b Azhar Mahmood	16	31	2	0
HH Streak	not out		16	31	1	0
PA Strang	c Azhar Mahmood	b Shoaib Akhtar	5	15	0	0
HK Olonga	st Moin Khan	b Saqlain Mushtaq	5	31	0	0
AG Huckle	st Moin Khan	b Saqlain Mushtaq	0	1	0	0
M Mbangwa	lbw	b Saqlain Mushtaq	0	1	0	0
Extras	(lb 3, w 7, nb 4)		14			
Total	(all out, 40.3 overs)		123			

Fall of wickets: 1-12 (GW Flower, 5.5 ov), 2-28 (Goodwin, 9.3 ov), 3-46 (A Flower, 13.4 ov), 4-50 (Campbell, 15.2 ov), 5-83 (Whittall, 26.1 ov), 6-95 (Johnson, 28.2 ov), 7-110 (Strang, 33.2 ov), 8-123 (Olonga, 40.1 ov), 9-123 (Huckle, 40.2 ov), 10-123 (Mbangwa, 40.3 ov).

Bowling	O	M	R	W	
Wasim Akram	6	1	23	0	(1nb)
Shoaib Akhtar	7	1	22	2	(3nb, 1w)
Abdul Razzaq	9	1	25	3	(1w)
Saqlain Mushtaq	6.3	1	16	3	
Shahid Afridi	4	0	20	0	(1w)
Azhar Mahmood	8	1	14	2	

NB: Saqlain took hat-trick (Olonga, Huckle, Mbangwa).

SUPER SIX
India v New Zealand
At Trent Bridge, Nottingham, 12 June 1999 (50-overs)
Result: New Zealand won by 5 wickets. Points: New Zealand 2, India 0.
Toss: India. Umpires: DB Hair (Aus) and DR Shepherd.
TV Umpire: RE Koertzen (SA). Match Referee: Talat Ali (Pak).
Man of the Match: RG Twose.

India innings (50 overs maximum)			R	B	4	6
SR Tendulkar		b Nash	16	22	2	0
SC Ganguly		b Allott	29	62	0	0
R Dravid	c Fleming	b Cairns	29	35	5	0
A Jadeja	c Parore	b Cairns	76	103	6	2
*M Azharuddin	c Parore	b Larsen	30	43	2	0
RR Singh	run out (Fleming/Cairns)		27	29	1	1
J Srinath	not out		6	7	0	0
+NR Mongia	not out		3	6	0	0
Extras	(b 4, lb 8, w 13, nb 10)		35			
Total	(6 wickets, 50 overs)		251			

DNB: A Kumble, BKV Prasad, DS Mohanty.
Fall of wickets: 1-26 (Tendulkar, 5.1 ov), 2-71 (Dravid, 14.6 ov), 3-97 (Ganguly, 22.6 ov), 4-187 (Azharuddin, 40.4 ov), 5-241 (Jadeja, 47.3 ov), 6-243 (Singh, 47.6 ov).

Bowling	O	M	R	W	
Allott	10	1	33	1	(2w)
Nash	10	1	57	1	(3nb, 5w)
Cairns	10	0	44	2	(2nb)
Larsen	10	0	40	1	(1nb, 1w)
Astle	7	0	49	0	
Harris	3	0	16	0	

New Zealand innings (target: 252 runs from 50 overs)			R	B	4	6
MJ Horne	run out (sub [N Chopra])		74	116	10	0
NJ Astle	c Dravid	b Mohanty	26	27	4	0
CD McMillan	c Dravid	b Srinath	6	7	1	0
*SP Fleming	c Mongia	b Mohanty	15	23	3	0
RG Twose	not out		60	77	5	0
CL Cairns	c Kumble	b Singh	11	30	0	0
+AC Parore	not out		26	14	5	0
Extras	(b 4, lb 11, w 16, nb 4)		35			
Total	(5 wickets, 48.2 overs)		253			

DNB: CZ Harris, DJ Nash, GR Larsen, GI Allott.
Fall of wickets: 1-45 (Astle, 9.3 ov), 2-60 (McMillan, 13.1 ov), 3-90 (Fleming, 21.5 ov), 4-173 (Horne, 34.4 ov), 5-218 (Cairns, 45.1 ov).

Bowling	O	M	R	W	
Srinath	10	1	49	1	(2nb, 1w)
Mohanty	10	0	41	2	(1w)
Prasad	10	0	44	0	(2w)
Singh	4	0	27	1	
Ganguly	2	0	15	0	(2nb)
Kumble	9.2	0	48	0	(2w)
Tendulkar	3	0	14	0	(2w)

SUPER SIX
Australia v South Africa
At Headingley, Leeds, 13 June 1999 (50-overs)
Result: Australia won by 5 wickets. Points: Australia 2, South Africa 0.
Toss: South Africa. Umpires: S Venkataraghavan (Ind) and P Willey.
TV Umpire: ID Robinson (Zim). Match Referee: JR Reid (NZ).
Man of the Match: SR Waugh.

South Africa innings (50 overs maximum)			R	B	4	6
G Kirsten	c Ponting	b Reiffel	21	46	3	0
HH Gibbs		b McGrath	101	134	10	1
DJ Cullinan		b Warne	50	62	4	1
*WJ Cronje	lbw	b Warne	0	3	0	0
JN Rhodes	c ME Waugh	b Fleming	39	36	2	2
L Klusener	c Warne	b Fleming	36	21	4	1
SM Pollock		b Fleming	3	4	0	0
+MV Boucher	not out		0	0	0	0
Extras	(lb 7, w 8, nb 6)		21			
Total	(7 wickets, 50 overs)		271			

DNB: N Boje, S Elworthy, AA Donald.
Fall of wickets: 1-45 (Kirsten, 12.4 ov), 2-140 (Cullinan, 32.3 ov), 3-141 (Cronje, 32.5 ov), 4-219 (Gibbs, 44.2 ov), 5-250 (Rhodes, 47.5 ov), 6-271 (Klusener, 49.5 ov), 7-271 (Pollock, 49.6 ov).

Bowling	O	M	R	W	
McGrath	10	0	49	1	(4nb, 1w)
Fleming	10	0	57	3	(3w)
Reiffel	9	0	47	1	(1w)
Moody	8	1	56	0	(1w)
Warne	10	1	33	2	(2nb, 1w)
Bevan	3	0	22	0	(1w)

Australia innings (target: 272 runs from 50 overs)			R	B	4	6
ME Waugh	run out (Boje/Boucher)		5	9	0	0
+AC Gilchrist		b Elworthy	5	7	1	0
RT Ponting	c Donald	b Klusener	69	110	5	2
DR Martyn	c Boje	b Elworthy	11	20	1	0
*SR Waugh	not out		120	110	10	2
MG Bevan	c Cullinan	b Cronje	27	33	2	0
TM Moody	not out		15	16	2	0
Extras	(lb 6, w 7, nb 7)		20			
Total	(5 wickets, 49.4 overs)		272			

DNB: SK Warne, PR Reiffel, DW Fleming, GD McGrath.
Fall of wickets: 1-6 (Gilchrist, 1.4 ov), 2-20 (ME Waugh, 5.2 ov), 3-48 (Martyn, 11.3 ov), 4-174 (Ponting, 34.1 ov), 5-247 (Bevan, 45.4 ov).

Bowling	O	M	R	W	
Pollock	9.4	0	45	0	(3nb, 1w)
Elworthy	10	1	46	2	(2nb)
Donald	10	0	43	0	(1nb, 2w)
Klusener	10	0	53	1	(1w)
Cronje	7	0	50	1	(1w)
Boje	3	0	29	0	(1nb, 2w)

Semi-Final
New Zealand v Pakistan

At Old Trafford, Manchester, 16 June 1999 (50-overs)
Result: Pakistan won by 9 wickets. Pakistan advances to the final.
Toss: New Zealand. Umpires: DB Hair (Aus) and P Willey.
TV Umpire: DL Orchard (SA). Match Referee: CW Smith (WI).
Man of the Match: Shoaib Akhtar.

New Zealand innings (50 overs maximum)			R	B	4	6
MJ Horne		b Abdul Razzaq	35	48	5	0
NJ Astle		b Shoaib Akhtar	3	18	0	0
CD McMillan	c Moin Khan	b Wasim Akram	3	19	0	0
*SP Fleming		b Shoaib Akhtar	41	57	5	0
RG Twose	c Ijaz Ahmed	b Abdul Razzaq	46	83	3	0
CL Cairns	not out		44	48	3	0
CZ Harris		b Shoaib Akhtar	16	21	0	0
+AC Parore		b Wasim Akram	0	4	0	0
DJ Nash	not out		6	10	1	0
Extras	(b 4, lb 14, w 17, nb 12)		47			
Total	(7 wickets, 50 overs)		241			

DNB: GR Larsen, GI Allott.
Fall of wickets: 1-20 (Astle, 5.3 ov), 2-38 (McMillan, 10.3 ov), 3-58 (Horne, 15.1 ov), 4-152 (Fleming, 33.5 ov), 5-176 (Twose, 39.3 ov), 6-209 (Harris, 45.4 ov), 7-211 (Parore, 46.4 ov).

Bowling	O	M	R	W	
Wasim Akram	10	0	45	2	(4nb, 7w)
Shoaib Akhtar	10	0	55	3	(2nb, 1w)
Abdul Razzaq	8	0	28	2	(1w)
Saqlain Mushtaq	8	0	36	0	(1w)
Azhar Mahmood	9	0	32	0	(3w)
Shahid Afridi	5	0	27	0	(2nb, 2w)

Pakistan innings (target: 242 runs from 50 overs)			R	B	4	6
Saeed Anwar	not out		113	148	9	0
Wajahatullah Wasti	c Fleming	b Cairns	84	123	10	1
Ijaz Ahmed	not out		28	21	4	1
Extras	(lb 3, w 7, nb 7)		17			
Total	(1 wicket, 47.3 overs)		242			

DNB: Inzamam-ul-Haq, Abdul Razzaq, Shahid Afridi, +Moin Khan, *Wasim Akram, Azhar Mahmood, Saqlain Mushtaq, Shoaib Akhtar.
Fall of wickets: 1-194 (Wajahatullah, 40.3 ov).

Bowling	O	M	R	W	
Allott	9	0	41	0	(1nb, 1w)
Nash	5	0	34	0	(2nb, 2w)
Larsen	10	0	40	0	(1nb)
Cairns	8	0	33	1	(3nb)
Harris	6	0	31	0	
Astle	7.3	0	41	0	(1w)
McMillan	2	0	19	0	(1w)

Semi-Final
Australia v South Africa

At Edgbaston, Birmingham, 17 June 1999 (50-overs)
Result: Match tied. Australia advances to the final.
NB: Australia qualify for the final after finishing higher on the Super Six table.
Toss: South Africa. Umpires: DR Shepherd and S Venkataraghavan (Ind).
TV Umpire: SA Bucknor (WI). Match Referee: R Subba Row.
Man of the Match: SK Warne.

Australia innings (50 overs maximum)			R	B	4	6
+AC Gilchrist	c Donald	b Kallis	20	39	1	1
ME Waugh	c Boucher	b Pollock	0	4	0	0
RT Ponting	c Kirsten	b Donald	37	48	3	1
DS Lehmann	c Boucher	b Donald	1	4	0	0
*SR Waugh	c Boucher	b Pollock	56	76	6	1
MG Bevan	c Boucher	b Pollock	65	101	6	0
TM Moody	lbw	b Pollock	0	3	0	0
SK Warne	c Cronje	b Pollock	18	24	1	0
PR Reiffel		b Donald	0	1	0	0
DW Fleming		b Donald	0	2	0	0
GD McGrath	not out		0	1	0	0
Extras	(b 1, lb 6, w 3, nb 6)		16			
Total	(all out, 49.2 overs)		213			

Fall of wickets: 1-3 (ME Waugh, 0.5 ov), 2-54 (Ponting, 13.1 ov), 3-58 (Lehmann, 13.6 ov), 4-68 (Gilchrist, 16.6 ov), 5-158 (SR Waugh, 39.3 ov), 6-158 (Moody, 39.6 ov), 7-207 (Warne, 47.6 ov), 8-207 (Reiffel, 48.1 ov), 9-207 (Fleming, 48.3 ov), 10-213 (Bevan, 49.2 ov).

Bowling	O	M	R	W	
Pollock	9.2	1	36	5	
Elworthy	10	0	59	0	(2nb, 1w)
Kallis	10	2	27	1	(1nb, 1w)
Donald	10	1	32	4	(1w)
Klusener	9	1	50	0	(3nb)
Cronje	1	0	2	0	

South Africa innings (target: 214 runs from 50 overs)			R	B	4	6
G Kirsten		b Warne	18	42	1	0
HH Gibbs		b Warne	30	36	6	0
DJ Cullinan	run out (Bevan)		6	30	0	0
*WJ Cronje	c ME Waugh	b Warne	0	2	0	0
JH Kallis	c SR Waugh	b Warne	53	92	3	0
JN Rhodes	c Bevan	b Reiffel	43	55	2	1
SM Pollock		b Fleming	20	14	1	1
L Klusener	not out		31	16	4	1
+MV Boucher		b McGrath	5	10	0	0
S Elworthy	run out (Reiffel/McGrath)		1	1	0	0
AA Donald	run out (ME Waugh/Fleming/Gilchrist)		0	0	0	0
Extras	(lb 1, w 5)		6			
Total	(all out, 49.4 overs)		213			

Fall of wickets: 1-48 (Gibbs, 12.2 ov), 2-53 (Kirsten, 14.1 ov), 3-53 (Cronje, 14.3 ov), 4-61 (Cullinan, 21.2 ov), 5-145 (Rhodes, 40.3 ov), 6-175 (Kallis, 44.5 ov), 7-183 (Pollock, 45.5 ov), 8-196 (Boucher, 48.2 ov), 9-198 (Elworthy, 48.4 ov), 10-213 (Donald, 49.4 ov).

Bowling	O	M	R	W	
McGrath	10	0	51	1	(1w)
Fleming	8.4	1	40	1	(3w)
Reiffel	8	0	28	1	
Warne	10	4	29	4	(1w)
ME Waugh	8	0	37	0	
Moody	5	0	27	0	

Final
Australia v Pakistan

At Lord's, London, 20 June 1999 (50-overs)
Result: Australia won by 8 wickets. Australia wins the 1999 ICC World Cup.
Toss: Pakistan. Umpires: SA Shepherd and DR Shepherd.
TV Umpire: S Venkataraghavan (Ind). Match Referee: RS Madugalle (SL).
Man of the Match: SK Warne. Player of the Tournament: L Klusener (SA).

Pakistan innings (50 overs maximum)			R	B	4	6
Saeed Anwar		b Fleming	15	17	3	0
Wajahatullah Wasti	c ME Waugh	b McGrath	1	14	0	0
Abdul Razzaq	c SR Waugh	b Moody	17	51	2	0
Ijaz Ahmed		b Warne	22	46	2	0
Inzamam-ul-Haq	c Gilchrist	b Reiffel	15	33	0	0
+Moin Khan	c Gilchrist	b Warne	6	12	0	0
Shahid Afridi	lbw	b Warne	13	16	2	0
Azhar Mahmood		c & b Moody	8	17	1	0
*Wasim Akram	c SR Waugh	b Warne	8	20	0	1
Saqlain Mushtaq	c Ponting	b McGrath	0	4	0	0
Shoaib Akhtar	not out		2	6	0	0
Extras	(lb 10, w 13, nb 2)		25			
Total	(all out, 39 overs)		132			

Fall of wickets: 1-21 (Wajahatullah, 4.4 ov), 2-21 (Saeed Anwar, 5.1 ov), 3-68 (Abdul Razzaq, 19.4 ov), 4-77 (Ijaz Ahmed, 23.4 ov), 5-91 (Moin Khan, 27.1 ov), 6-104 (Inzamam-ul-Haq, 30.1 ov), 7-113 (Shahid Afridi, 31.6 ov), 8-129 (Azhar Mahmood, 36.6 ov), 9-129 (Wasim Akram, 37.2 ov), 10-132 (Saqlain Mushtaq, 38.6 ov).

Bowling	O	M	R	W	
McGrath	9	3	13	2	
Fleming	6	0	30	1	(2nb, 4w)
Reiffel	10	1	29	1	(2w)
Moody	5	0	17	2	(1w)
Warne	9	1	33	4	(2w)

Australia innings (target: 133 runs from 50 overs)			R	B	4	6
ME Waugh	not out		37	52	4	0
+AC Gilchrist	c Inzamam-ul-Haq	b Saqlain Mushtaq	54	36	8	1
RT Ponting	c Moin Khan	b Wasim Akram	24	27	3	0
DS Lehmann	not out		13	9	2	0
Extras	(lb 1, w 1, nb 3)		5			
Total	(2 wickets, 20.1 overs)		133			

DNB: *SR Waugh, MG Bevan, TM Moody, SK Warne, PR Reiffel, DW Fleming, GD McGrath.
Fall of wickets: 1-75 (Gilchrist, 10.1 ov), 2-112 (Ponting, 17.4 ov).

Bowling	O	M	R	W	
Wasim Akram	8	1	41	1	(2nb, 1w)
Shoaib Akhtar	4	0	37	0	(1nb)
Abdul Razzaq	2	0	13	0	
Azhar Mahmood	2	0	20	0	
Saqlain Mushtaq	4.1	0	21	1	

World Cup **2003**
by Peter Roebuck

Africa's eagerly awaited first World Cup was marred by a succession of controversies that distracted attention and energy from the competition proper.

Political confrontations, protests, court cases, scandals and various other sideshows took centre stage and the tournament was fatally compromised.

Despite impressive organisation and the hard work undertaken by thousands of cheerful volunteers determined to show their country in the best possible light, the Cup stumbled along from crisis to crisis and will be remembered fondly only by spectators lucky enough to witness the best matches, humble teams that achieved fleeting glory and the victors, a dominant side that saved its best till last.

The troubles began long before the first ball was bowled. Boycotts were the heart of the problem. Surprisingly, Geoffrey of that ilk was blameless.

England had discovered that Zimbabwe, their former colony, was ruled by a tyrant, a point that had eluded them when tens of thousands of Ndebele were massacred in the 1980s. Meanwhile the New Zealanders had been warned by some especially nervous security people not to risk playing a match in Nairobi. Soon points were being given away like presents at a wedding.

England's withdrawal was the most vainglorious. It was also astonishingly clumsy.

Finding themselves obliged by the happenstance of the draw to play a first-round match in Harare, fearful of an encounter with the patron of Zimbabwean cricket, the hated President of the country, but anxious not to lose any money or points, English officials commenced wriggling and wrangling like one of Charles Dickens' fillibustering lawyers.

Protesting principle but confined by guidelines accepted by every competing country, English officials tried to convince other nations that Zimbabwe was not a safe place to visit. Belatedly abandoning this

Familiar faces in a familiar pose. Just as they were four years earlier at Lord's, Adam Gilchrist, captain Ricky Ponting and Damien Martyn are in the forefront of celebrating Australians after victory over India in the final.

absurd position, they pointed, less contentiously, towards the nastiness of the incumbent regime. Critics replied that other governments were even worse, and yet escaped sporting censure.

In the event England conceded the match. This refusal to meet their obligations to promoters, hosts and other competitors undermined the tournament. India and Australia played their matches in Zimbabwe. England caught an early aeroplane home. British Airways flights continued to land at Harare Airport, and British companies continued to buy and sell locally.

New Zealand's refusal to play in Kenya likewise upset the balance of the tournament. Stephen Fleming's players had previously been traumatised by the carnage they had witnessed in Colombo and Karachi after terrorists set off bombs outside their hotels. Although they had merely been in the wrong place at the wrong time, the Kiwi cricketers were understandably reluctant to push their luck. Accordingly they treated warnings about their safety extremely seriously. After an agonised debate and a vote, and with the greatest reluctance, they decided to pull out.

Had Kenya lost the rest of their matches this withdrawal might not have mattered. Instead they played a crafty and composed game and beat a poorly prepared and complacent Sri Lankan outfit before

their jubiliant, if disbelieving, home crowd in Nairobi, thereby advancing to the Super Six round by finishing second in their group. Significantly, they carried forward the points earned from their victory over Sri Lanka and gifted by New Zealand.

Kenya's win provoked celebrations in a soccer-mad country. Unfortunately the victory did not have any lasting effect. Before long Kenyan cricket was making headlines for all the wrong reasons.

Kenya's feat in overcoming the Sri Lankans was not the only highlight of the early rounds. Nor was it the only time a minnow inconvenienced a whale.

Hitherto known for its fondness for bears, maple syrup and ice hockey, Canada had reached the World Cup finals and wanted to make a mark. Their champion was a long-haired and much-travelled character going by the name of John Davison, an off-spinner previously regarded as Australian to his Ugg boots but now able to carry the Canadian flag owing to the discovery that his birth coincided with his parents' brief sojourn in Vancouver.

Over the years, Davison had plied his trade mildly and enthusiastically. He had taken a few wickets for two States but was generally regarded as not quite up to scratch. No one had thought much about his batting.

Given the chance to open the innings, and taking the opportunity presented by field restrictions with

the relish detected in students in the happy hour, Davison was soon driving, cutting, pulling and slashing like a latterday Jessop. Indeed he had much the same effect on bowlers as did Sanath Jayasuriya during the 1996 World Cup. West Indies felt the full force of his blade and responded by examining his back-foot game, an experiment that did not work. Davison was, if only unofficially, the player of the tournament.

Needless to say Shane Warne provided the scandal. A month before the Cup was due to begin, he dislocated a shoulder diving to intercept a straight drive. Much to his dismay, he was not expected to recover in time to take part in the greatest cricketing show of them all.

To widespread surprise he reappeared ahead of schedule and as slim as a shorn sheep. His dedication was praised alongside his heroic disdain of pizza and toasted cheese sandwiches. Then a routine drugs test revealed a banned substance that could serve two purposes, assisting dieting and disguising the use of steroids. A press conference was called on the morning of Australia's first match. Warne was going home.

At last the cricket began and some memorable matches took place. No sooner had Warne announced his premature departure than Andrew Symonds gave notice of Australia's intentions with a blistering assault upon an ageing Pakistani attack. Waqar Younis responded with two beamers, thereby touching the lowest point of his career.

Elsewhere Brian Lara had launched the Cup and his team's campaign with a thrilling century, an innings of elan that swept his side to victory. Although both of the age's batting champions, Lara and Sachin Tendulkar, contributed one mighty performance, the tournament continued to splutter along. Appropriately the Cup was won not by an individual but by an efficient team containing numerous match-winners.

Amongst the other serious contenders, India had begun badly, a mishap that persuaded supporters to throw stones at players' houses and cars. Tendulkar and Rahul Dravid appealed for calm and said the players were trying their hardest and that defeats were

Left: Their team might have crashed out in the first round but three of South African Airways' new jetliners marked the half-way break in the final with a spectacular, low flyover of the Wanderers Stadium.

Centre/right: Two new, omnipresent features of the tournament. The green jackets were charged with applying the ICC's strict security code, those in purple were the smiling volunteers who made everything more tolerable.

part and parcel of the game. In the nick of time Tendulkar turned his team's fortunes around with a carefully constructed innings in Pietermaritzburg.

As the tournament went along so the charlatans started to falter.

West Indies discovered that, with all his brilliance, Lara could not carry an entire world on his shoulders. Pakistan huffed and puffed till they encountered Tendulkar at Centurion Park whereupon they were put to the proverbial sword by an innings as thrilling as any seen in this form of the game. England lost its last chance when it allowed the Australians back into their match at Port Elizabeth. Ricky Ponting and chums did not need a second invitation. Michael Bevan and Andrew Bichel scored the vital runs. Nasser Hussain went home as a captain unfulfilled

Nor did South Africa reach the second round. Needing to beat Sri Lanka in Durban, and finding an opponent prepared to stay out in steady rain to give them a chance, Shaun Pollock's side still managed to make a hash of it.

With one more run needed in two balls as the rain became torrential, supporters watched in bewilderment as Mark Boucher patted both deliveries back to the bowler and then hurried from the field as pleased as a child clutching an ice-cream cone. Pollock and his advisors had misread the Duckworth/Lewis form. South Africa were one run shy of victory.

The faces of Pollock and company as realisation dawned and the rain tumbled down told the tale. General Custer might as well have been directing operations.

In the event, Sri Lanka and Australia qualified to meet in one semi-final whilst India played Kenya in the second. Kenya achieved such dizzying heights through a solitary Super Six win, over a Zimbabwe team so undermined by the political intrigue of the country that two of its most prominent players, one white (Andy Flower), one black (Henry Olonga) announced their retirements, having earlier mourned "the death of democracy in our beloved Zimbabwe" by wearing black armbands.

Australia's comfortable victory over the lacklustre Lankans was notable chiefly for Adam Gilchrist's decision to walk after a gloved sweep had been taken by his counterpart. Had a dodo chosen this moment to fly past it could not have provoked more surprise than the sight of an Australian batsman leaving the

Who got it right – the captain with all his computers and advisers or his counterpart with a little slip of paper giving the correct scores needed by the end of every over? The pictures give the answer. South Africa's Shaun Pollock realises that the Proteas had miscalculated and are one run short, while Sri Lanka's Sanath Jayasuriya, who knew that South Africa had not won, bubbles with joy as his side goes through to the next stage of the Cup.

Fit for the final: Australia bat, India field before a packed, sunlit Wanderers Stadium.

Below: the headlines in the South African press reflect the agony of the home team's first-round exit and the glory of the champions' repeat triumph.

OUT FOR THE COUNT

Miscalculation ends Pollock's quest for World Cup

Australia, the true kings of cricket

Clinical and professional display puts Ricky Ponting's men on top where, in truth, they belong

ICC hits India and others for painful six

THE settling of financial scores starts now, with the International Cricket Council's (ICC's) announcement yesterday of penalties incurred by various teams, for a variety of reasons, at this 2003 World Cup, writes Mark Smit.

The biggest penalty is being levied against India, whose players refused to sign World Cup contracts, containing clauses that would result in curbs on players' private endorsement deals, in a long-running wrangle before the showpiece event started.

India stand to lose between $8m and $9m, pending compensation claims from the Global Cricket Corporation of the IDI, which is the ICC's commercial arm.

England will have to forfeit $3.5m for their decision not to play against Zimbabwe in Harare; and there will, in terms of a very acrimonious announcement made after the World Cup had started, be no compensation to the England and Wales Cricket Board.

SCOREBOARD

Photo by Gordon Brooks

Photo by Gordon Brooks

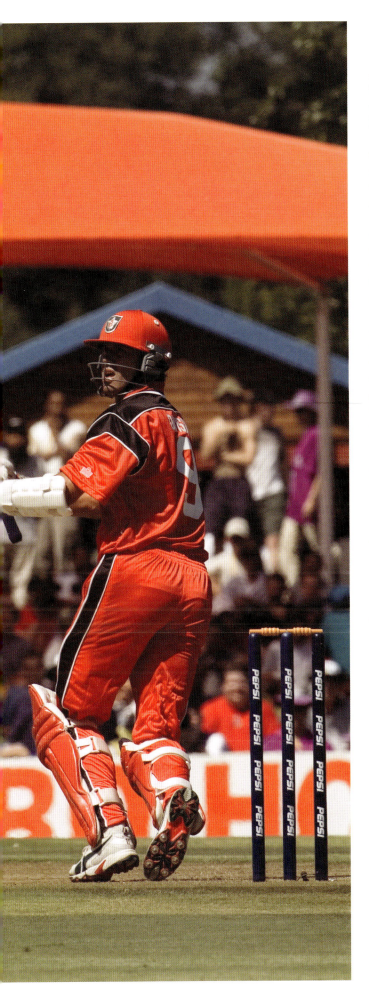

crease before the umpire had delivered his verdict. This phenomenon became the main talking point of the tournament, never mind that Lara and Tendulkar had been walking their entire careers.

Afterwards Ponting regarded his deputy's conduct with all the enthusiasm of a parent contemplating a son's new hairstyle. Nothing else lingers from the match. One fact was indisputable. Despite everything, Australia romped into the final.

India also timed their run well. Tendulkar had led the way with some composed and sporadically majestic work. Almost by default Sourav Ganguly's men reached the final to be played at the Wanderers before a vast audience and in the presence of Thabo Mbeki, the South African President.

Afterwards, the exact moment the final was decided was widely debated. In some opinions Ganguly's timid decision to bowl first on a slightly cloudy morning was an effective concession of defeat. Others maintained that Zaheer Khan's wayward and profligate opening over sealed his team's fate. Optimists thought India had a chance till Tendulkar was dismissed in the first over of the chase.

At any rate, India were slaughtered. Matthew Hayden tore the opening attack apart, Ricky Ponting built a superb and sustained century and Damien Martyn cut loose brilliantly in the second half of the innings. Every bowler was left nursing sore figures.

India were doomed. Tendulkar pulled one boundary and lost his wicket pursuing another. Virender Schwag batted gamely but it was all an exercise in futility. Australia romped home.

If the African World Cup was ill-starred it had at least found a worthy winner. Still, it was a missed opportunity. A memorable tournament was needed to help to capture the imagination of a continent devoted to soccer, enthusiastic about athletics and unconvinced about this game of bat and ball.

If only the West Indies were strong, Warne available, every match played and a thrilling climax reached with South Africa in the thick of the action. Instead exciting matches were few and far between, and apart from the winners, only the weaker nations rose to the occasion.

Far left: Brian Lara launched the tournament with a thrilling hundred that stunned South Africa in the opening match at Cape Town.

Left: John Davison, Canadian by birth and team, Australian by upbringing, stunned the world with his power-hitting, never more so than with his 111 off 76 balls with six sixes and eight fours against the West Indies at Centurion.

SEMI-FINALS
Australia v Sri Lanka

At St George's Park, Port Elizabeth, March 18, 2003. Australia won by 48 runs (Duckworth/Lewis method).
When Michael Bevan was caught behind first ball to put Sanath Jayasuriya on a hat-trick, a wave of belief wafted around St George's Park that this might just be the day when the world champions were finally brought to their knees.

The great finisher had been finished. Samson had lost his hair. Now, surely, with Australia 144 for five in the 37th over, Sri Lanka had the favourites where they wanted them. But they had missed their chance with Andrew Symonds. Kumar Sangakkara's woeful tournament continued when he fumbled the ball behind the stumps with Symonds, who had 33 at the time, stretching forward out of his ground. The new Symonds of this World Cup (a "more thinking cricketer", said Ricky Ponting) made them pay. He calmly worked the ball around before gearing up for a final onslaught with his fellow Queenslander and other chance-grabber, Andy Bichel. The pair put on 37 in the last 7.1 overs of the innings.

Sri Lanka still thought they could get 212 to win. The pitch was quicker than previous ones at the venue, but it was still pretty slow. The thing about pace is that is does not matter how slow the pitch, the ball is still the same speed through the air.

When Brett Lee shattered Marvan Atapattu's stumps with a full-length ball of 99.49 mph, the pitch could have been made of plasticine, it would have made no difference.

Sri Lanka's relatively comfortable start was demolished in one ball. The violence of Lee's celebration, which looked as if he was finishing off a hunted animal, showed just how pumped up he was. His other two scalps came from well-angled balls across the left-handers, Avishka Gunawardene and Hashan Tillekeratne. With a little help from Glenn McGrath, Sri Lanka were 43 for four off 11 overs, dead and almost buried.

The final – and rather sad – nail was the dismissal of Aravinda de Silva in his last international match. He was their last hope and what a story if he could have turned it around, He was run out by a piece of athletic brilliance from Bichel, aka King Midas. He swooped in his follow-through, picked up a push into the off side, turned and threw down the stumps at the keeper's end with de Silva a yard short. The replay was called for but de Silva was already half-way back to the pavilion and his retirement.

When the expected deluge came, no one, just this once, moaned about Duckworth-Lewis – and there was only going to be one winner.
(*John Stern, Wisden Cricket Monthly*)

India v Kenya

At Kingsmead, Durban, March 20, 2003 (day/night). India won by 91 runs.
The steel instilled into the Indian team and distilled by Sourav Ganguly, drop by steady drop, ensured there were no Disneyworld endings for Kenya. Captaining India for the 99th time in an ODI, Ganguly re-emphasised his batting mastery against modest attacks to guide his team to an imposing, if not unanswerable, total. He then sat back as his pace trio did the needful.

India equalled their record for consecutive successes, set in 1985, with win No. 8. They began carefully enough, but Ganguly was in no mood to accept dictation. After five runs had been squeezed from leg-spinner Collins Obuya's opening two overs, he darted out to launch a six off the first ball of the third, then repeated the message four balls later. The chastened Obuya lasted just six overs.

Sachin Tendulkar seemed destined for a hundred until he pulled Steve Tikolo to deep mid-wicket, but Ganguly matched Mark Waugh's 1996 feat of three centuries in a World Cup tournament, getting there with his fifth six, the product of a golfer's swing and that unmistakeable superiority complex. Arms aloft, he drank in the acclaim.

His opposite number, Tikolo, also top-scored in the Kenyan reply before his men took a weary lap of honour, smiles intact, their place in the pantheon assured.
(*Wisden Cricketers' Almanack, 2004*)

Left: Andrew Symonds hits out during his commanding, unbeaten 91 for Australia in the semi-final against Sri Lanka, his second decisive innings of the tournament.

Middle: India's semi-final hero up in lights as the scoreboard records captain Sourav Ganguly's hundred in the semi-final against Kenya at Durban, his third to match Mark Waugh's 1996 record.

Above: Player of the Tournament Sachin Tendulkar falls short of another hundred, swinging Steve Tikolo to deep mid-wicket in the semi-final.

FINAL
Australia v India

At The Wanderers, Johannesburg, March 23, 2003. Australia won by 125 runs.

Of the host of adjectives applicable to Australia's demolition of India, "unsurprising" fits the bill as accurately as any. Awesome, ruthless, clinical, impeccable, breathtaking and others of that ilk had been exhausted over their previous record of 16 consecutive victories, ten of them in this tournament. Yet another brilliant performance that created a multitude of records should not have been unexpected.

Apart from two late missed catches, when the result was long since known, their cricket was flawless as they captured the game's most prestigious and, with its US$2 million first prize, richest trophy, becoming the first team to claim three World Cups, following their successes in 1987 in India and 1999 in England.

Fittingly, their one-day captain of 15 months, Ricky Ponting, was the inspiration for the victory with his commanding, chanceless, unbeaten 140 off 121 balls. It was the highest of the four hundreds scored in the eight finals, surpassing Viv Richards's 138 for the West Indies against England in 1979. His eight massive, cleanly hit sixes were not only the most by any batsman in a final but in any World Cup match. He waited until he reached 50 before smashing his first, after which he went into overdrive, compiling his last 90 runs from just 48 balls.

Yet another World Cup record was Ponting's unbeaten third-wicket partnership of 234 in 30.1 overs with Damien Martyn, who disregarded the pain of a chipped bone in his right index finger which had kept him out of the semi-final to stroke 88 from 64 balls.

It set up the mammoth total of 359 for two, both Australia's highest in all one-day internationals at the time and the highest in a World Cup final, 68 more than the West Indies' 291 for eight, off 60 overs, in the first showpiece.

The target completely broke the spirit of the Indians, who had entered the final after eight consecutive victories. Such was the public optimism of repeating

Left above: High flyer Andy Bichel, consistently Australia's man for all occasions, dispatches Rahul Dravid in the final.

Left: India's lone star in the final Virender Sehwag drives during his futile 82.

Right: The fans make the difference. For Damien Martyn that sinking feeling after dropping Yuvraj Singh is exaggerated by the derision of a sea of Indian supporters. Minutes later Brett Lee's sensational catch triggers the opposite response from his energised countrymen.

their upset over the West Indies at Lord's in 1983 that thousands of their fans poured into Johannesburg from all points in India and the diaspora by scheduled and chartered flights, bringing with them their flags, banners and dreams.

When Sachin Tendulkar, their revered champion, lobbed a return catch to Glenn McGrath off a top-edged hook from the fifth ball of their response, the groan from the disheartened supporters was as audible as the roar of the three South African Airways jets on their special interval flypast a few minutes earlier. Tendulkar had already been confirmed as Player of the Tournament for his record tally of 669 runs. With him at the crease, all was possible; now nothing was.

Virender Sehwag substituted impressively for Tendulkar, on whom he has cloned his method, scoring 82 from 81 balls with thumping cuts and pulls that brought him three sixes and ten fours. But the target was out of reach and the Australians, as ever tigerish in the field and disciplined with their bowling, allowed no one else more than Rahul Dravid's 47.

There was brief hope that a passing thunderstorm would save India's humiliation and force a replayed match over the two reserve days, but the break lasted only 25 minutes and there was no necessity to resort to the much-maligned Duckworth/Lewis method.

An immediate clue to India's uncertainty was Sourav Ganguly's decision to bowl on winning the toss and, more dramatically, the left-armer Zaheer Khan's opening spell. Heavy overnight rain was a consideration in Ganguly's judgment, for it might have freshened the pitch for the opening salvo. As it turned out, it was an unblemished surface of even pace and bounce. Whatever early help there was, Zaheer, Javagal Srinath and Ashish Nehra wasted it.

Zaheer had been superb throughout the tournament but, as taut as a tassa drum, his first three overs cost 28 and set the tone for a typically boisterous opening partnership of 105 from 14 overs between Adam Gilchrist and Matthew Hayden before Harbhajan Singh removed both within 20 runs of each other. That was where Indian joy ended and Australian mastery resumed. Ponting and Martyn initially took care to ensure there was no repetition of the middle-order failures of their three previous matches. Towards the end, the two were doing as they pleased, blazing 103 off the last 10 overs, 74 off the last five.

The result was effectively known as the African dancers started their half-time entertainment. When Tendulkar fell, it was certain.

(Tony Cozier)

For the second successive time, Australians celebrate World Cup success after India's heavy defeat in the final – a result set up by captain Ricky Ponting's unbeaten 140, the highest score in a World Cup final, studded with eight sixes, of which this was one.

"They said at the time"

Australia's captain Ricky Ponting: *"We were outstanding. We remained unbeaten in the whole tournament, but what matters much more is the high standards we set for ourselves. We've been tested throughout this World Cup with injuries and the Warne issue. Andrew Bichel and Andy Symonds have had sensational World Cups. Well done to them."*

India's captain Sourav Ganguly on the final: *"Hats off to Australia, they played like great champions. It was a good wicket to bowl on in the morning, but unfortunately our bowlers did not put the ball in the right place. It was one bad day for the seamers but I am proud of the way they bowled through the tournament. I am proud of the whole team. India had a fantastic World Cup even though we may not have won it. We could not take the cup home because Australia were the better team, but we can go home with our heads held high."*

India's Sachin Tendulkar: *"It's an honour to be named the best player of the World Cup, but I would have been happier if India had won the title. It was just one of those off days when nothing went right for us. We had a bad start and the pressure kept building."*

Australia's Damien Martyn: *"This is one of the best moments in my career. I was a spare batsman in 1999 and the last four years have seen a lot of hard work since then. Leading up to the game there were doubts about my injury and there was nervous tension."*

Australia's Michael Bevan: *"It's great to be part of the Australian side like it is at the moment. It's awesome. Everyone's challenging each other to become better. You definitely feel the presence, or the aura, of being part of a side like this."*

Former India left-arm spinner Bishan Singh Bedi: *"The Indians were just not geared up for the big stage – right from Tendulkar downwards."*

Formats

Two teams were added bringing the total to 14, the number of matches to 54 and the number of playing days to 43, all Cup records. Otherwise the same as 1999 – seedings, qualifying round leading to Super Six, semis and final.

Innovations

Olympic-style security, rigorous anti-ambush marketing, a workforce of volunteers. Cricket's World Cup entered the 21st century. Reserve days for rain-affected first-round matches were eliminated for logistical reasons (almost certainly costing the West Indies a place in the Super Six after their match with Bangladesh was abandoned).

World Cup 2003
Scoreboards

South Africa v West Indies, Pool B
At Newlands, Cape Town (day/night), 9 February 2003 (50-overs)
Result: West Indies won by 3 runs. Points: West Indies 4, South Africa 0.
Toss: West Indies. Umpires: DJ Harper (Aus) and S Venkataraghavan (Ind).
TV Umpire: P Willey (Eng). Match Referee: RS Madugalle (SL).
Man of the Match: BC Lara.

West Indies innings (50 overs maximum)			R	B	4	6
CH Gayle		b Pollock	2	21	0	0
WW Hinds	c Boucher	b Pollock	0	16	0	0
BC Lara	c Pollock	b Ntini	116	134	12	2
S Chanderpaul	c Boucher	b Klusener	34	60	3	0
*CL Hooper	c Kallis	b Ntini	40	40	3	0
RL Powell	not out		40	18	5	1
RR Sarwan	not out		32	15	2	2
Extras	(lb 6, w 4, nb 4)		14			
Total	(5 wickets, 50 overs, 222 mins)		278			

DNB: +RD Jacobs, VC Drakes, M Dillon, PT Collins.
Fall of wickets: 1-4 (Hinds, 4.6 ov), 2-7 (Gayle, 6.4 ov), 3-109 (Chanderpaul, 30.3 ov), 4-198 (Hooper, 43.2 ov), 5-215 (Lara, 45.2 ov).

Bowling	O	M	R	W	
Pollock	10	2	52	2	(1nb)
Ntini	10	1	37	2	(2w)
Donald	9	0	54	0	(1nb, 1w)
Kallis	10	2	52	0	
Klusener	8	0	53	1	(2nb)
Boje	3	0	24	0	(1w)

South Africa innings (target: 279 runs from 49 overs)			R	B	4	6
HH Gibbs	c Jacobs	b Dillon	24	28	4	0
G Kirsten		c & b Dillon	69	92	6	1
HH Dippenaar	st Jacobs	b Hooper	20	25	2	1
JH Kallis	c Jacobs	b Collins	13	18	2	0
JN Rhodes		b Hooper	2	6	0	0
+MV Boucher		b Gayle	49	49	4	1
*SM Pollock	c Hooper	b Gayle	4	4	0	0
L Klusener	c Hooper	b Drakes	57	48	1	5
N Boje	not out		25	25	2	0
M Ntini	c Sarwan	b Drakes	0	2	0	0
AA Donald	not out		0	0	0	0
Extras	(lb 4, w 5, nb 3)		12			
Total	(9 wickets, 49 overs, 220 mins)		275			

Fall of wickets: 1-46 (Gibbs, 8.4 ov), 2-79 (Dippenaar, 16.2 ov), 3-104 (Kallis, 21.3 ov), 4-117 (Rhodes, 24.1 ov), 5-155 (Kirsten, 31.5 ov), 6-160 (Pollock, 32.4 ov), 7-204 (Boucher, 40.5 ov), 8-271 (Klusener, 48.3 ov), 9-271 (Ntini, 48.5 ov).

Bowling	O	M	R	W	
Dillon	10	0	47	2	(1w)
Collins	9	0	54	1	(1nb, 1w)
Drakes	8	1	33	2	(1nb)
Hooper	10	0	63	2	(1nb)
Gayle	10	1	60	2	(2w)
Powell	2	0	14	0	(1w)

Zimbabwe v Namibia, Pool A
At Harare Sports Club, 10 February 2003 (50-overs)
Result: Zimbabwe won by 86 runs (D/L method). Points: Zimbabwe 4, Namibia 0.
Toss: Namibia. Umpires: DL Orchard (SA) and SJA Taufel (Aus).
TV Umpire: DB Hair (Aus). Match Referee: Wasim Raja (Pak).
Man of the Match: CB Wishart.

Zimbabwe innings (50 overs maximum)			R	B	4	6
CB Wishart	not out		172	151	18	3
MA Vermeulen		c & b Louw	39	66	7	0
A Flower	c Karg	b AJ Burger	39	29	3	1
GW Flower	not out		78	55	4	2
Extras	(lb 7, w 4, nb 1)		12			
Total	(2 wickets, 50 overs, 191 mins)		340			

DNB: DD Ebrahim, GJ Whittall, +T Taibu, *HH Streak, BA Murphy, DT Hondo, HK Olonga.
Fall of wickets: 1-107 (Vermeulen, 21.4 ov), 2-174 (A Flower, 30.3 ov).

Bowling	O	M	R	W	
Snyman	10	0	49	0	(1nb, 1w)
LJ Burger	10	1	70	0	
BL Kotze	10	1	75	0	(2w)
Louw	10	0	60	1	(1w)
DB Kotze	7	0	56	0	
AJ Burger	3	0	23	1	

Namibia innings (target: 191 runs from 25.1 overs)			R	B	4	6
R Walters	c Taibu	b Streak	0	1	0	0
SJ Swanepoel	c Streak	b Whittall	23	47	2	0
AJ Burger	c A Flower	b Streak	26	18	3	1
D Keulder	c Ebrahim	b Whittall	27	46	3	0
BG Murgatroyd	c Wishart	b GW Flower	10	26	1	0
LJ Burger	not out		4	10	0	0
*DB Kotze	not out		5	3	0	0
Extras	(lb 1, w 8)		9			
Total	(5 wickets, 25.1 overs, 98 mins)		104			

DNB: +M Karg, G Snyman, JL Louw, BL Kotze.
Fall of wickets: 1-0 (Walters, 0.1 ov), 2-40 (AJ Burger, 6.6 ov), 3-80 (Swanepoel, 16.4 ov), 4-94 (Keulder, 22.4 ov), 5-98 (Murgatroyd, 23.6 ov).

Bowling	O	M	R	W	
Streak	5	0	35	2	(2w)
Hondo	6	1	20	0	(1w)
Olonga	3	1	8	0	
Murphy	1	0	7	0	
GW Flower	5.1	1	13	1	
Whittall	5	0	20	2	(1w)

New Zealand v Sri Lanka, Pool B
At Goodyear Park, Bloemfontein, 10 February 2003 (50-overs)
Result: Sri Lanka won by 47 runs. Points: Sri Lanka 4, New Zealand 0.
Toss: New Zealand. Umpires: SA Bucknor (WI) and NA Mallender (Eng).
TV Umpire: RB Tiffin (Zim). Match Referee: MJ Procter.
Man of the Match: ST Jayasuriya.

Sri Lanka innings (50 overs maximum)			R	B	4	6
MS Atapattu	c Styris	b Bond	6	17	0	0
*ST Jayasuriya	lbw	b Astle	120	125	14	0
HP Tillakaratne	not out		81	106	5	0
DPMD Jayawardene	lbw	b Adams	1	3	0	0
PA de Silva	c Styris	b Astle	12	11	2	0
+KC Sangakkara	c Adams	b Astle	13	18	0	0
RP Arnold		b Bond	12	14	0	0
WPUJC Vaas		b Adams	5	4	0	0
M Muralitharan	not out		4	6	0	0
Extras	(b 3, lb 6, w 4, nb 5)		18			
Total	(7 wickets, 50 overs, 215 mins)		272			

DNB: CRD Fernando, PW Gunaratne.
Fall of wickets: 1-23 (Atapattu, 5.1 ov), 2-193 (Jayasuriya, 34.5 ov), 3-196 (Jayawardene, 35.5 ov), 4-213 (de Silva, 38.5 ov), 5-240 (Sangakkara, 44.2 ov), 6-256 (Arnold, 47.3 ov), 7-263 (Vaas, 48.4 ov).

Bowling	O	M	R	W	
Tuffey	5	0	36	0	(1nb)
Bond	10	1	44	2	(2nb, 3w)
Oram	10	0	37	0	(1nb)
Adams	9	0	58	2	
Harris	4	0	26	0	
Styris	5	0	28	0	(1w)
Astle	7	0	34	3	

New Zealand innings (target: 273 runs from 50 overs)			R	B	4	6
*SP Fleming	c Sangakkara	b Gunaratne	1	4	0	0
NJ Astle	run out (Vaas)		0	5	0	0
CD McMillan	c Sangakkara	b Gunaratne	3	12	0	0
SB Styris	c Vaas	b Arnold	141	125	3	6
CL Cairns		c & b de Silva	32	56	2	0
+L Vincent	c Muralitharan	b Jayasuriya	1	4	0	0
CZ Harris		b Muralitharan	13	35	0	0
JDP Oram	st Sangakkara	b Muralitharan	12	20	0	0
AR Adams	c sub (J Mubarak)	b Arnold	1	4	0	0
DR Tuffey	c Sangakkara	b Arnold	4	3	0	0
SE Bond	not out		2	5	0	0
Extras	(lb 10, w 5)		15			
Total	(all out, 45.3 overs, 186 mins)		225			

Fall of wickets: 1-1 (Astle, 0.6 ov), 2-2 (Fleming, 1.5 ov), 3-15 (McMillan, 5.3 ov), 4-93 (Cairns, 22.4 ov), 5-94 (Vincent, 23.2 ov), 6-150 (Harris, 34.4 ov), 7-179 (Oram, 40.4 ov), 8-182 (Adams, 41.4 ov), 9-200 (Tuffey, 43.3 ov), 10-225 (Styris, 45.3 ov).

Bowling	O	M	R	W	
Vaas	7	0	22	0	
Gunaratne	5	0	24	2	(1w)
Fernando	3	1	19	0	
Muralitharan	9	1	42	2	
Jayasuriya	8	0	32	1	(2w)
de Silva	5	0	29	1	(1w)
Arnold	8.3	0	47	3	(1w)

Australia v Pakistan, Pool A
At New Wanderers Stadium, Johannesburg, 11 February 2003 (50-overs)
Result: Australia won by 82 runs. Points: Australia 4, Pakistan 0.
Toss: Pakistan. Umpires: EAR de Silva (SL) and DR Shepherd (Eng).
TV Umpire: BF Bowden (NZ). Match Referee: CH Lloyd (WI).
Man of the Match: A Symonds.

Australia innings (50 overs maximum)			R	B	4	6
+AC Gilchrist	c Waqar Younis	b Wasim Akram	1	3	0	0
ML Hayden		b Wasim Akram	27	41	3	0
*RT Ponting	c Taufeeq Umar	b Shoaib Akhtar	53	67	7	0
DR Martyn		b Wasim Akram	0	1	0	0
JP Maher	c Rashid Latif	b Waqar Younis	9	19	1	0
A Symonds	not out		143	125	18	2
GB Hogg	run out (Younis Khan/Rashid Latif)		14	22	0	0
IJ Harvey	c Waqar Younis	b Shoaib Akhtar	24	19	3	0
B Lee	c Inzamam-ul-Haq	b Waqar Younis	2	6	0	0
JN Gillespie	not out		6	4	1	0
Extras	(b 1, lb 9, w 12, nb 9)		31			
Total	(8 wickets, 50 overs, 219 mins)		310			

DNB: GD McGrath.
Fall of wickets: 1-10 (Gilchrist, 2.2 ov), 2-52 (Hayden, 10.2 ov), 3-52 (Martyn, 10.3 ov), 4-86 (Maher, 15.5 ov), 5-146 (Ponting, 29.3 ov), 6-216 (Hogg, 38.5 ov), 7-270 (Harvey, 46.3 ov), 8-292 (Lee, 48.3 ov).

Bowling	O	M	R	W	
Wasim Akram	10	0	64	3	(2nb, 5w)
Shoaib Akhtar	10	0	45	2	(3w)
Waqar Younis	8.3	1	50	2	(2nb, 3w)
Abdul Razzaq	6	0	42	0	(2nb)
Shahid Afridi	9.3	0	63	0	(1w)
Younis Khan	6	0	36	0	(1nb)

Pakistan innings (target: 311 runs from 49 overs)			R	B	4	6
Taufeeq Umar	c Hogg	b Lee	21	43	4	0
Shahid Afridi	c Gilchrist	b Gillespie	1	8	0	0
Saleem Elahi	c Lee	b Harvey	30	40	3	0
Inzamam-ul-Haq	c Gilchrist	b McGrath	6	13	1	0
Yousuf Youhana	c Symonds	b Harvey	27	37	4	0
Younis Khan	c Ponting	b Hogg	19	28	0	0
Abdul Razzaq		c & b Hogg	25	33	2	0
+Rashid Latif		b Hogg	33	23	1	3
Wasim Akram	c Ponting	b Harvey	33	11	4	1
*Waqar Younis	c McGrath	b Harvey	6	11	0	0
Shoaib Akhtar	not out		0	5	0	0
Extras	(b 3, lb 9, w 10, nb 5)		27			
Total	(all out, 44.3 overs, 205 mins)		228			

Fall of wickets: 1-9 (Shahid Afridi, 3.6 ov), 2-38 (Taufeeq Umar, 11.2 ov), 3-49 (Inzamam-ul-Haq, 14.2 ov), 4-81 (Saleem Elahi, 19.1 ov), 5-103 (Yousuf Youhana, 25.1 ov), 6-125 (Younis Khan, 30.1 ov), 7-147 (Abdul Razzaq, 34.1 ov), 8-201 (Rashid Latif, 38.6 ov), 9-223 (Wasim Akram, 42.6 ov), 10-228 (Waqar Younis, 44.3 ov).

Bowling	O	M	R	W	
McGrath	10	2	39	1	(1w)
Gillespie	8	1	28	1	(3w)
Lee	7	0	37	1	(5nb)
Harvey	9.3	0	58	4	(3w)
Hogg	10	0	54	3	(3w)

Bangladesh v Canada, Pool B
At Kingsmead, Durban (day/night), 11 February 2003 (50-overs)
Result: Canada won by 60 runs. Points: Canada 4, Bangladesh 0.
Toss: Canada. Umpires: Aleem Dar (Pak) and BG Jerling.
TV Umpire: AV Jayaprakash (Ind). Match Referee: GR Viswanath (Ind).
Man of the Match: A Codrington.

Canada innings (50 overs maximum)			R	B	4	6
I Maraj	c Sanwar Hossain	b Tapash Baisya	24	43	3	0
JM Davison		b Mashrafe Mortaza	8	14	2	0
DR Chumney	run out (Al Sahariar)		28	25	3	1
IS Billcliff	run out (Hannan Sarkar)		42	63	6	0
*JV Harris	c Khaled Mashud	b Sanwar Hossain	4	23	0	0
NA de Groo	c Alok Kapali	b Sanwar Hossain	0	4	0	0
AF Sattaur	lbw	b Alok Kapali	13	40	0	1
+A Bagai		b Mashrafe Mortaza	7	24	0	0
S Thuraisingam	lbw	b Mohammad Rafique	6	14	1	0
A Codrington	c Tapash Baisya	b Manjural Islam	16	31	1	0
D Joseph	not out		9	17	1	0
Extras	(lb 7, w 14, nb 2)		23			
Total	(all out, 49.1 overs, 201 mins)		180			

Fall of wickets: 1-18 (Davison, 4.5 ov), 2-47 (Maraj, 11.5 ov), 3-70 (Chumney, 14.3 ov), 4-92 (Harris, 21.6 ov), 5-104 (de Groot, 23.5 ov), 6-130 (Sattaur, 34.3 ov), 7-134 (Billcliff, 36.2 ov), 8-146 (Bagai, 39.5 ov), 9-159 (Thuraisingam, 43.3 ov), 10-180 (Codrington, 49.1 ov).

Bowling	O	M	R	W	
Manjural Islam	8.1	1	30	1	(1w)
Mashrafe Mortaza	8	0	38	2	(2nb, 5w)
Tapash Baisya	3	0	26	1	(1w)
Mohammad Rafique	10	2	34	1	(5w)
Sanwar Hossain	10	0	26	2	(1w)
Alok Kapali	10	0	19	1	(1w)

Bangladesh innings (target: 181 runs from 50 overs)			R	B	4	6
Hannan Sarkar	c Bagai	b Codrington	25	35	4	0
Al Sahariar	c sub (AM Samad)	b Joseph	9	18	2	0
Habibul Bashar	c Bagai	b Thuraisingam	0	8	0	0
Ehsanul Haque	c Bagai	b Joseph	13	17	2	0
Sanwar Hossain	lbw	b Davison	25	24	2	0
Alok Kapali	lbw	b Codrington	19	25	2	0
*+Khaled Mashud	c sub (AM Samad)	b Davison	1	8	0	0
Mohammad Rafique	c Davison	b Codrington	12	19	2	0
Tapash Baisya	c Sattaur	b Codrington	0	8	0	0
Mashrafe Mortaza	c Sattaur	b Codrington	0	2	0	0
Manjural Islam	not out		0	4	0	0
Extras	(lb 2, w 14)		16			
Total	(all out, 28 overs, 139 mins)		120			

Fall of wickets: 1-33 (Al Sahariar, 6.2 ov), 2-44 (Habibul Bashar, 9.3 ov), 3-46 (Hannan Sarkar, 10.4 ov), 4-76 (Ehsanul Haque, 15.2 ov), 5-106 (Sanwar Hossain, 20.5 ov), 6-108 (Alok Kapali, 21.6 ov), 7-108 (Khaled Mashud, 22.3 ov), 8-119 (Tapash Baisya, 25.2 ov), 9-119 (Mashrafe Mortaza, 25.4 ov), 10-120 (Mohammad Rafique, 27.6 ov).

Bowling	O	M	R	W	
Joseph	8	1	42	2	(8w)
Thuraisingam	6	0	34	1	(5w)
Codrington	9	3	27	5	(1w)
Davison	5	1	15	2	

South Africa v Kenya, Pool B
At North West Cricket Stadium, Potchefstroom, 12 February 2003 (50-overs)
Result: South Africa won by 10 wickets. Points: South Africa 4, Kenya 0.
Toss: Kenya. Umpires: KC Barbour (Zim) and TH Wijewardene (SL).
TV Umpire: NA Mallender (Eng). Match Referee: RS Madugalle (SL).
Man of the Match: L Klusener.

Kenya innings (50 overs maximum)			R	B	4	6
+KO Otieno	run out (Gibbs)		1	7	0	0
RD Shah	run out (Klusener/Boje)		60	87	7	0
BJ Patel	c Boucher	b Pollock	1	4	0	0
*SO Tikolo	c Kirsten	b Pollock	3	16	0	0
HS Modi	c Pollock	b Boje	9	24	0	0
MO Odumbe	c Gibbs	b Klusener	16	33	0	0
TM Odoyo	c Boucher	b Ntini	22	41	2	1
CO Obuya	lbw	b Klusener	0	1	0	0
MA Suji	c Pollock	b Klusener	0	5	0	0
PJ Ongondo	c Kirsten	b Klusener	13	13	1	1
AY Karim	not out		0	1	0	0
Extras	(b 1, lb 3, w 7, nb 4)		15			
Total	(all out, 38 overs, 165 mins)		140			

Fall of wickets: 1-4 (Otieno, 1.6 ov), 2-7 (Patel, 2.5 ov), 3-26 (Tikolo, 8.4 ov), 4-62 (Modi, 17.5 ov), 5-92 (Shah, 25.2 ov), 6-105 (Odumbe, 30.4 ov), 7-105 (Obuya, 30.5 ov), 8-120 (Suji, 32.4 ov), 9-139 (Ongondo, 36.2 ov), 10-140 (Odoyo, 37.6 ov).

Bowling	O	M	R	W	
Pollock	6	2	15	2	(2nb, 1w)
Ntini	7	1	14	1	(1w)
Kallis	3	0	23	0	
Langeveldt	5	0	24	0	(1nb)
Boje	9	1	44	1	
Klusener	8	2	16	4	(1nb, 1w)

South Africa innings (target: 141 runs from 50 overs)			R	B	4	6
HH Gibbs	not out		87	66	12	4
G Kirsten	not out		52	63	9	0
Extras	(w 2, nb 1)		3			
Total	(0 wickets, 21.2 overs, 84 mins)		142			

DNB: N Boje, HH Dippenaar, +MV Boucher, JH Kallis, *SM Pollock, L Klusener, CK Langeveldt, M Ntini, JN Rhodes.

Bowling	O	M	R	W	
Suji	4	0	21	0	(1w)
Odoyo	6	0	34	0	(1w)
Karim	2	0	17	0	
Obuya	5	1	32	0	(1nb)
Odumbe	2	0	21	0	
Ongondo	2.2	0	17	0	

India v Netherlands, Pool A
At Boland Bank Park, Paarl, 12 February 2003 (50-overs)
Result: India won by 68 runs. Points: India 4, Netherlands 0.
Toss: India. Umpires: DJ Harper (Aus) and P Willey (Eng).
TV Umpire: Nadeem Ghauri (Pak). Match Referee: DT Lindsay.
ODI Debut: J Smits (NL). Man of the Match: TBM de Leede.

India innings (50 overs maximum)			R	B	4	6
*SC Ganguly	c Smits	b Lefebvre	8	32	0	0
SR Tendulkar	c Smits	b de Leede	52	72	7	0
V Sehwag	c Zuiderent	b Kloppenburg	6	9	1	0
+R Dravid		b de Leede	17	38	0	0
Yuvraj Singh		c & b Adeel Raja	37	56	3	0
M Kaif	c Lefebvre	b Adeel Raja	9	21	0	0
D Mongia	run out (Kloppenburg/de Leede)		42	49	2	0
Harbhajan Singh		b de Leede	13	8	0	1
A Kumble	run out (Scholte/de Leede)		9	7	0	0
Z Khan	lbw	b de Leede	0	2	0	0
J Srinath	not out		0	0	0	0
Extras	(lb 2, w 8, nb 1)		11			
Total	(all out, 48.5 overs, 206 mins)		204			

Fall of wickets: 1-30 (Ganguly, 11.5 ov), 2-56 (Sehwag, 14.6 ov), 3-81 (Tendulkar, 23.3 ov), 4-91 (Dravid, 25.6 ov), 5-114 (Kaif, 31.5 ov), 6-169 (Yuvraj Singh, 43.5 ov), 7-186 (Harbhajan Singh, 46.2 ov), 8-203 (Kumble, 48.2 ov), 9-204 (Mongia, 48.4 ov), 10-204 (Khan, 48.5 ov).

Bowling	O	M	R	W	
Schiferli	10	2	49	0	
Lefebvre	9	1	27	1	(2w)
de Leede	9.5	0	35	4	(2w)
Kloppenburg	10	0	40	1	(1nb, 3w)
Adeel Raja	9	0	47	2	
van Troost	1	0	4	0	

Netherlands innings (target: 205 runs from 50 overs)		R	B	4	6
JF Kloppenburg	c Sehwag b Srinath	0	4	0	0
DLS van Bunge	b Srinath	62	116	5	0
HJC Mol	c Dravid b Srinath	2	30	0	0
B Zuiderent	c Sehwag b Khan	0	6	0	0
TBM de Leede	c Dravid b Harbhajan Singh	0	9	0	0
LP van Troost	c Dravid b Kumble	1	10	0	0
RH Scholte	lbw b Kumble	1	5	0	0
*RP Lefebvre	lbw b Kumble	3	14	0	0
E Schiferli	c Mongia b Kumble	13	21	2	0
+J Smits	c Sehwag b Srinath	26	66	0	0
Adeel Raja	not out	0	10	0	0
Extras	(b 2, lb 6, w 18, nb 2)	28			
Total	(all out, 48.1 overs, 204 mins)	136			

Fall of wickets: 1-0 (Kloppenburg, 0.4 ov), 2-29 (Mol, 8.2 ov), 3-31 (Zuiderent, 9.4 ov), 4-38 (de Leede, 12.6 ov), 5-42 (van Troost, 15.5 ov), 6-44 (Scholte, 17.1 ov), 7-54 (Lefebvre, 21.3 ov), 8-82 (Schiferli, 27.5 ov), 9-131 (van Bunge, 44.4 ov), 10-136 (Smits, 48.1 ov).

Bowling	O	M	R	W	
Srinath	9.1	1	30	4	(1nb, 1w)
Khan	8	1	17	1	(9w)
Harbhajan Singh	10	1	20	1	
Kumble	10	1	32	4	(1nb, 1w)
Ganguly	4	0	14	0	(2w)
Tendulkar	4	0	9	0	
Sehwag	3	0	6	0	

Zimbabwe v England, Pool A

At Harare Sports Club, 13 February 2003 (50-overs)
Result: Zimbabwe won by a walkover. Points: Zimbabwe 4, England 0.
Toss: None. Umpires: SA Bucknor (WI) and DL Orchard (SA).
TV Umpire: SJA Taufel (Aus). Match Referee: Wasim Raja (Pak).
Man of the Match: No Award.
NB: England were not in attendance - forfeited the match due to safety concerns.

New Zealand v West Indies, Pool B

At St. George's Park, Port Elizabeth, 13 February 2003 (50-overs)
Result: New Zealand won by 20 runs. Points: New Zealand 4, West Indies 0.
Toss: West Indies. Umpires: DB Hair (Aus) and RE Koertzen.
TV Umpire: S Venkataraghavan (Ind). Match Referee: MJ Procter.
Man of the Match: AR Adams.

New Zealand innings (50 overs maximum)		R	B	4	6
*SP Fleming	c & b Dillon	25	25	4	1
DL Vettori	b Drakes	13	25	2	0
NJ Astle	c Jacobs b Hinds	46	70	6	0
SB Styris	c Powell b Drakes	5	15	1	0
CL Cairns	c Dillon b Hinds	37	44	2	1
L Vincent	c Hooper b Hinds	9	11	1	0
CZ Harris	b Gayle	19	35	1	0
+BB McCullum	not out	36	53	1	0
AR Adams	not out	35	24	1	2
Extras	(lb 10, w 4, nb 2)	16			
Total	(7 wickets, 50 overs, 202 mins)	241			

DNB: JDP Oram, SE Bond.
Fall of wickets: 1-42 (Fleming, 6.6 ov), 2-58 (Vettori, 11.6 ov), 3-66 (Styris, 15.6 ov), 4-130 (Astle, 28.2 ov), 5-141 (Cairns, 30.6 ov), 6-147 (Vincent, 32.2 ov), 7-188 (Harris, 43.1 ov).

Bowling	O	M	R	W	
Dillon	10	1	30	1	(1w)
McLean	6	0	38	0	(1w)
Drakes	10	1	49	2	(2nb)
Hinds	10	0	35	3	
Hooper	9	0	42	0	
Gayle	5	0	37	1	(2w)

West Indies innings (target: 242 runs from 50 overs)		R	B	4	6
CH Gayle	c Fleming b Adams	22	29	5	0
WW Hinds	c Styris b Adams	14	31	2	0
BC Lara	run out (Vincent/Cairns)	2	4	0	0
S Chanderpaul	lbw b Oram	2	7	0	0
*CL Hooper	c Bond b Adams	3	11	0	0
RR Sarwan	b Vettori	75	99	7	0
RL Powell	b Oram	14	14	1	1
+RD Jacobs	c Oram b Styris	50	73	3	1
VC Drakes	not out	16	18	1	0
NAM McLean	run out (Adams)	5	7	0	0
M Dillon	b Adams	8	6	0	0
Extras	(b 1, lb 3, w 5, nb 1)	10			
Total	(all out, 49.4 overs, 209 mins)	221			

Fall of wickets: 1-34 (Gayle, 9.2 ov), 2-36 (Lara, 9.6 ov), 3-42 (Hinds, 11.2 ov), 4-46 (Hooper, 13.3 ov), 5-46 (Chanderpaul, 14.1 ov), 6-80 (Powell, 20.1 ov), 7-178 (Sarwan, 43.3 ov), 8-191 (Jacobs, 44.6 ov), 9-200 (McLean, 47.1 ov), 10-221 (Dillon, 49.4 ov).

Bowling	O	M	R	W	
Bond	10	2	43	0	(2w)
Adams	9.4	1	44	4	(1w)
Oram	10	2	26	2	
Cairns	1	0	21	0	(1nb, 1w)
Vettori	10	0	38	1	
Astle	4	0	14	0	
Styris	5	0	31	1	(1w)

Bangladesh v Sri Lanka, Pool B

At City Oval, Pietermaritzburg, 14 February 2003 (50-overs)
Result: Sri Lanka won by 10 wickets. Points: Sri Lanka 4, Bangladesh 0.
Toss: Sri Lanka. Umpires: BF Bowden (NZ) and RB Tiffin (Zim).
TV Umpire: Aleem Dar (Pak). Match Referee: GR Viswanath (Ind).
Man of the Match: WPUJC Vaas.

Bangladesh innings (50 overs maximum)		R	B	4	6
Hannan Sarkar	b Vaas	0	1	0	0
Al Sahariar	c de Silva b Vaas	10	13	1	0
Mohammad Ashraful	c & b Vaas	0	1	0	0
Ehsanul Haque	c Jayawardene b Vaas	0	1	0	0
Sanwar Hossain	lbw b Vaas	4	2	1	0
Alok Kapali	c Jayasuriya b Fernando	32	38	2	1
*+Khaled Mashud	lbw b Muralitharan	20	67	2	0
Mohammad Rafique	c Sangakkara b Muralitharan	6	16	0	0
Tapash Baisya	c Arnold b Muralitharan	5	19	0	0
Mashrafe Mortaza	c Muralitharan b Vaas	28	23	4	1
Manjural Islam	not out	3	9	0	0
Extras	(b 1, lb 4, w 8, nb 3)	16			
Total	(all out, 31.1 overs, 145 mins)	124			

Fall of wickets: 1-0 (Hannan Sarkar, 0.1 ov), 2-0 (Mohammad Ashraful, 0.2 ov), 3-0 (Ehsanul Haque, 0.3 ov), 4-5 (Sanwar Hossain, 0.5 ov), 5-25 (Al Sahariar, 4.4 ov), 6-70 (Alok Kapali, 13.6 ov), 7-82 (Mohammad Rafique, 20.1 ov), 8-88 (Khaled Mashud, 24.5 ov), 9-98 (Tapash Baisya, 26.2 ov), 10-124 (Mashrafe Mortaza, 31.1 ov).

Bowling	O	M	R	W	
Vaas	9.1	2	25	6	(2w)
Nissanka	5	0	22	0	(2nb, 2w)
Fernando	7	0	47	1	(4w, 1nb)
Muralitharan	10	4	25	3	

NB: Vaas took a hat-trick with the first 3 balls of the match (Hannan Sarkar, Mohammad Ashraful, Ehsanul Haque).

Sri Lanka innings (target: 125 runs from 50 overs)		R	B	4	6
MS Atapattu	not out	69	71	11	0
*ST Jayasuriya	not out	55	57	7	1
Extras	(w 1, nb 1)	2			
Total	(0 wickets, 21.1 overs, 81 mins)	126			

DNB: HP Tillakaratne, DPMD Jayawardene, PA de Silva, +KC Sangakkara, RP Arnold, WPUJC Vaas, M Muralitharan, CRD Fernando, RAP Nissanka.

Bowling	O	M	R	W	
Manjural Islam	6	1	22	0	
Mashrafe Mortaza	5	0	38	0	(1w)
Tapash Baisya	3	0	21	0	(1nb)
Mohammad Rafique	4.1	1	22	0	
Sanwar Hossain	2	0	14	0	
Alok Kapali	1	0	9	0	

Australia v India, Pool A

At SuperSport Park, Centurion, 15 February 2003 (50-overs)
Result: Australia won by 9 wickets. Points: Australia 4, India 0.
Toss: India. Umpires: EAR de Silva (SL) and DR Shepherd (Eng).
TV Umpire: BG Jerling. Match Referee: CH Lloyd (WI).
Man of the Match: JN Gillespie.

India innings (50 overs maximum)		R	B	4	6
*SC Ganguly	c Gilchrist b Lee	9	21	1	0
SR Tendulkar	lbw b Gillespie	36	59	3	0
V Sehwag	c Gilchrist b Lee	4	4	1	0
+R Dravid	b Gillespie	1	23	0	0
Yuvraj Singh	lbw b McGrath	0	8	0	0
M Kaif	c Symonds b Gillespie	1	16	0	0
D Mongia	c Symonds b Lee	13	39	1	0
A Kumble	not out	16	38	1	0
Harbhajan Singh	lbw b Hogg	28	32	4	1
Z Khan	lbw b Lehmann	1	9	0	0
J Srinath	run out (Lehmann)	0	2	0	0
Extras	(lb 5, w 10, nb 1)	16			
Total	(all out, 41.4 overs, 176 mins)	125			

Fall of wickets: 1-22 (Ganguly, 5.4 ov), 2-41 (Sehwag, 7.2 ov), 3-44 (Dravid, 13.1 ov), 4-45 (Yuvraj Singh, 14.6 ov), 5-50 (Kaif, 17.6 ov), 6-78 (Tendulkar, 27.3 ov), 7-80 (Mongia, 28.3 ov), 8-120 (Harbhajan Singh, 37.2 ov), 9-125 (Khan, 40.4 ov), 10-125 (Srinath, 41.4 ov).

Bowling	O	M	R	W	
McGrath	8	3	23	1	
Lee	9	1	36	3	(1nb, 3w)
Gillespie	10	2	13	3	(1w)
Symonds	6	0	25	0	(4w)
Hogg	4.4	0	16	1	
Lehmann	4	0	7	1	

Australia innings (target: 126 runs from 50 overs)

			R	B	4	6
+AC Gilchrist	st Dravid	b Kumble	48	61	6	0
ML Hayden	not out		45	49	1	2
*RT Ponting	not out		24	24	4	0
Extras	(lb 3, w 8)		11			
Total	(1 wicket, 22.2 overs, 91 mins)		128			

DNB: DR Martyn, DS Lehmann, MG Bevan, A Symonds, GB Hogg, B Lee, GD McGrath, JN Gillespie.
Fall of wickets: 1-100 (Gilchrist, 17.3 ov).

Bowling	O	M	R	W
Srinath	4	0	26	0 (1w)
Khan	4	0	26	0 (1w)
Harbhajan Singh	7.2	0	49	0 (1w)
Kumble	7	0	24	1 (1w)

Canada v Kenya, Pool B

At Newlands, Cape Town (day/night), 15 February 2003 (50-overs)
Result: Kenya won by 4 wickets. Points: Kenya 4, Canada 0.
Toss: Canada. Umpires: AV Jayaprakash (Ind) and Nadeem Ghauri (Pak).
TV Umpire: KC Barbour (Zim). Match Referee: RS Madugalle (SL).
Man of the Match: TM Odoyo.

Canada innings (50 overs maximum)

			R	B	4	6
I Maraj		b Odoyo	5	17	1	0
JM Davison	c CO Obuya	b Ongondo	31	32	2	2
DR Chumney	c Shahb CO Obuya		10	20	2	0
IS Billcliff		b AO Suji	71	100	8	2
*JV Harris	c AO Suji	b CO Obuya	31	74	2	1
AF Sattaur		b Odumbe	7	10	0	0
NA de Groot	lbw	b Odumbe	0	4	0	0
+A Bagai	c DO Obuya	b Odoyo	12	15	1	0
S Thuraisingam	c DO Obuya	b Odoyo	13	10	1	1
A Codrington		b Odoyo	5	7	0	0
D Joseph	not out		4	6	0	0
Extras	(lb 2, w 5, nb 1)		8			
Total	(all out, 49 overs, 198 mins)		197			

Fall of wickets: 1-18 (Maraj, 5.2 ov), 2-47 (Davison, 10.4 ov), 3-48 (Chumney, 11.2 ov), 4-134 (Harris, 38.2 ov), 5-158 (Billcliff, 41.3 ov), 6-159 (de Groot, 42.2 ov), 7-162 (Sattaur, 42.6 ov), 8-186 (Thuraisingam, 46.2 ov), 9-186 (Bagai, 46.5 ov), 10-197 (Codrington, 48.6 ov).

Bowling	O	M	R	W
MA Suji	7	1	23	0
Odoyo	10	1	28	4 (2w)
Ongondo	6	1	12	1 (1nb, 1w)
CO Obuya	10	1	46	2 (1w)
Odumbe	9	0	41	2
AO Suji	7	0	45	1 (1w)

Kenya innings (target: 198 runs from 50 overs)

			R	B	4	6
KO Otieno		b Thuraisingam	4	17	1	0
RD Shah	c Maraj	b Thuraisingam	61	95	9	0
*SO Tikolo	lbw	b Davison	42	49	6	0
HS Modi	c Harris	b Davison	6	48	0	0
MO Odumbe	lbw	b Davison	26	19	2	1
TM Odoyo	not out		27	42	2	0
PJ Ongondo		b Codrington	16	16	2	0
+DO Obuya	not out		4	5	0	0
Extras	(lb 3, w 9)		12			
Total	(6 wickets, 48.3 overs, 215 mins)		198			

DNB: CO Obuya, MA Suji, AO Suji.
Fall of wickets: 1-15 (Otieno, 5.1 ov), 2-99 (Tikolo, 22.1 ov), 3-116 (Shah, 30.3 ov), 4-148 (Odumbe, 36.5 ov), 5-154 (Modi, 38.4 ov), 6-192 (Ongondo, 47.2 ov).

Bowling	O	M	R	W
Joseph	10	1	39	0 (3w)
Thuraisingam	10	1	53	2 (2w)
Codrington	10	1	44	1 (1w)
Davison	10	3	15	3 (3w)
de Groot	4	0	22	0
Maraj	4.3	0	22	0

England v Netherlands, Pool A

At Buffalo Park, East London, 16 February 2003 (50-overs)
Result: England won by 6 wickets. Points: England 4, Netherlands 0.
Toss: England. Umpires: DB Hair (Aus) and RE Koertzen.
TV Umpire: TH Wijewardene (SL). Match Referee: MJ Procter.
Man of the Match: JM Anderson.

Netherlands innings (50 overs maximum)

			R	B	4	6
LP van Troost	lbw	b Anderson	8	31	1	0
DLS van Bunge	c White	b Anderson	4	19	1	0
NA Statham	lbw	b Flintoff	7	35	0	0
B Zuiderent	c Hussain	b Anderson	2	16	0	0
KJJ van Noortwijk	c Stewart	b Anderson	0	2	0	0
TBM de Leede	not out		58	96	6	0
JF Kloppenburg	c Knight	b Blackwell	10	30	1	0
E Schiferli	st Stewart	b Blackwell	12	16	2	0
*RP Lefebvre		b White	6	14	1	0
Adeel Raja	lbw	b White	2	5	0	0
+J Smits	not out		17	38	2	0
Extras	(lb 10, w 4, nb 2)		16			
Total	(9 wickets, 50 overs, 205 mins)		142			

Fall of wickets: 1-15 (van Bunge, 5.5 ov), 2-22 (van Troost, 9.5 ov), 3-31 (Zuiderent, 15.3 ov), 4-31 (van Noortwijk, 15.5 ov), 5-31 (Statham, 16.6 ov), 6-67 (Kloppenburg, 27.3 ov), 7-90 (Schiferli, 31.6 ov), 8-108 (Lefebvre, 36.4 ov), 9-112 (Adeel Raja, 38.1 ov).

Bowling	O	M	R	W
Caddick	10	4	19	0 (2nb, 1w)
Anderson	10	1	25	4 (1w)
Flintoff	10	2	29	1 (1w)
White	10	3	22	2
Blackwell	10	0	37	2 (1w)

England innings (target: 143 runs from 50 overs)

			R	B	4	6
ME Trescothick		b Schiferli	12	14	2	0
NV Knight	c Zuiderent	b van Bunge	51	58	8	0
MP Vaughan	c de Leede	b van Bunge	51	47	8	0
A Flintoff	c Lefebvre	b van Bunge	0	2	0	0
ID Blackwell	not out		22	11	5	0
PD Collingwood	not out		5	8	1	0
Extras	(w 3)		3			
Total	(4 wickets, 23.2 overs, 95 mins)		144			

DNB: *N Hussain, C White, +AJ Stewart, AR Caddick, JM Anderson.
Fall of wickets: 1-18 (Trescothick, 4.1 ov), 2-107 (Vaughan, 18.3 ov), 3-107 (Flintoff, 18.5 ov), 4-126 (Knight, 20.5 ov).

Bowling	O	M	R	W
Schiferli	5	0	33	1 (2w)
Lefebvre	5	0	18	0 (1w)
de Leede	4	0	29	0
Adeel Raja	5	0	34	0
van Bunge	3	0	16	3
Kloppenburg	1.2	0	14	0

Namibia v Pakistan, Pool A

At De Beers Diamond Oval, Kimberley, 16 February 2003 (50-overs)
Result: Pakistan won by 171 runs. Points: Pakistan 4, Namibia 0.
Toss: Pakistan. Umpires: NA Mallender (Eng) and DL Orchard.
TV Umpire: SJA Taufel (Aus). Match Referee: DT Lindsay.
Man of the Match: Wasim Akram.

Pakistan innings (50 overs maximum)

			R	B	4	6
Saeed Anwar	c LJ Burger	b BL Kotze	23	35	3	0
Saleem Elahi	c DB Kotze	b AJ Burger	63	100	5	0
Younis Khan	c van Schoor	b LJ Burger	28	39	2	0
Inzamam-ul-Haq		b DB Kotze	4	15	0	0
Yousuf Youhana	c LJ Burger	b BL Kotze	43	55	3	0
+Rashid Latif		b Snyman	36	30	4	0
Wasim Akram	not out		20	14	3	0
Abdul Razzaq	c van Schoor	b Snyman	4	2	1	0
*Waqar Younis	run out (Snyman)		8	7	1	0
Saqlain Mushtaq	run out (BL Kotze/van Schoor)		1	1	0	0
Shoaib Akhtar	not out		3	3	0	0
Extras	(lb 11, w 10, nb 1)		22			
Total	(9 wickets, 50 overs, 205 mins)		255			

Fall of wickets: 1-47 (Saeed Anwar, 12.2 ov), 2-105 (Younis Khan, 23.4 ov), 3-118 (Inzamam-ul-Haq, 28.4 ov), 4-150 (Saleem Elahi, 35.1 ov), 5-208 (Yousuf Youhana, 44.1 ov), 6-223 (Rashid Latif, 46.3 ov), 7-227 (Abdul Razzaq, 46.5 ov), 8-247 (Waqar Younis, 48.5 ov), 9-248 (Saqlain Mushtaq, 48.6 ov).

Bowling	O	M	R	W
Snyman	8	0	51	2 (1nb, 4w)
van Vuuren	10	1	47	0 (1w)
BL Kotze	10	1	51	2 (3w)
LJ Burger	10	0	45	1 (2w)
DB Kotze	8	0	32	1
AJ Burger	4	0	18	1

Namibia innings (target: 256 runs from 50 overs)

			R	B	4	6
R Walters	c Rashid Latif	b Wasim Akram	0	4	0	0
SJ Swanepoel	c Inzamam-ul-Haq	b Shoaib Akhtar	1	2	0	0
AJ Burger	c Younis Khan	b Shoaib Akhtar	14	18	1	0
D Keulder		b Shoaib Akhtar	0	2	0	0
BG Murgatroyd	lbw	b Wasim Akram	4	4	1	0
LJ Burger	lbw	b Wasim Akram	0	1	0	0
*DB Kotze	lbw	b Shoaib Akhtar	8	25	0	0
G Snyman	lbw	b Shoaib Akhtar	0	1	0	0
+M van Schoor	lbw	b Wasim Akram	2	4	0	0
BL Kotze	not out		24	29	3	0
RJ van Vuuren	c Waqar Younis	b Saqlain Mushtaq	14	19	2	0
Extras	(lb 9, w 4, nb 4)		17			
Total	(all out, 17.4 overs, 101 mins)		84			

Fall of wickets: 1-1 (Walters, 0.4 ov), 2-3 (Swanepoel, 1.1 ov), 3-3 (Keulder, 1.3 ov), 4-17 (Murgatroyd, 2.5 ov), 5-17 (LJ Burger, 2.6 ov), 6-32 (AJ Burger, 7.2 ov), 7-32 (Snyman, 7.3 ov), 8-35 (van Schoor, 8.2 ov), 9-42 (DB Kotze, 10.6 ov), 10-84 (van Vuuren, 17.4 ov).

Bowling	O	M	R	W
Wasim Akram	9	1	28	5 (2nb, 2w)
Shoaib Akhtar	8	1	46	4 (2nb, 2w)
Saqlain Mushtaq	0.4	0	1	1

South Africa v New Zealand, Pool B

At New Wanderers Stadium, Johannesburg, 16 February 2003 (50-overs)
Result: New Zealand won by 9 wickets (D/L method). Points: New Zealand 4, South Africa 0. Toss: South Africa. Umpires: SA Bucknor (WI) and P Willey (Eng).
TV Umpire: DJ Harper (Aus). Match Referee: Wasim Raja (Pak).
Man of the Match: SP Fleming.

South Africa innings (50 overs maximum)			R	B	4	6
GC Smith	c McCullum	b Bond	23	28	5	0
HH Gibbs	c McMillan	b Oram	143	141	19	3
N Boje		b Styris	29	37	4	0
JH Kallis	c Vincent	b Vettori	33	48	1	1
+MV Boucher	c Cairns	b Oram	10	14	1	0
L Klusener	not out		33	21	4	1
*SM Pollock	c Oram	b Adams	10	10	0	0
G Kirsten	not out		5	4	0	0
Extras	(lb 6, w 11, nb 3)		20			
Total	(6 wickets, 50 overs, 218 mins)		306			

DNB: HH Dippenaar, M Ntini, AA Donald.
Fall of wickets: 1-60 (Smith, 9.5 ov), 2-126 (Boje, 23.2 ov), 3-193 (Kallis, 38.1 ov), 4-243 (Boucher, 43.2 ov), 5-260 (Gibbs, 45.2 ov), 6-287 (Pollock, 48.2 ov).

Bowling	O	M	R	W	
Bond	10	0	73	1	(2nb, 3w)
Adams	9	0	57	1	(4w)
Oram	8	0	52	2	(1nb, 3w)
Styris	10	0	44	1	(1w)
Vettori	10	0	58	1	
Astle	3	0	16	0	

New Zealand innings (target: 226 runs from 39 overs)			R	B	4	6
CD McMillan	c Boucher	b Donald	25	32	1	1
*SP Fleming	not out		134	132	21	0
NJ Astle	not out		54	57	4	0
Extras	(lb 8, w 8)		16			
Total	(1 wicket, 36.5 overs, 158 mins)		229			

DNB: SB Styris, CL Cairns, L Vincent, +BB McCullum, JDP Oram, AR Adams, DL Vettori, SE Bond.
Fall of wickets: 1-89 (McMillan, 14.1 ov).

Bowling	O	M	R	W	
Pollock	8	0	36	0	
Ntini	8	1	33	0	(3w)
Donald	5.5	0	52	1	(3w)
Kallis	8	0	47	0	(1w)
Boje	2	0	16	0	(1w)
Klusener	5	0	37	0	

Play delayed three times due to rain: 1st: NZ 76/0 off 12 overs; 2nd: 97/1 off 15 overs; 3rd: NZ 182/1 off 30.2 overs.

Bangladesh v West Indies, Pool B

At Willowmoore Park, Benoni, 18 February 2003 (50-overs)
Result: No result. Points: Bangladesh 2, West Indies 2.
Toss: Bangladesh. Umpires: BG Jerling and RB Tiffin (Zim).
TV Umpire: BF Bowden (NZ). Match Referee: GR Viswanath (Ind).
Man of the Match: No Award.

West Indies innings (50 overs maximum)			R	B	4	6
WW Hinds	c Al Sahariar	b Khaled Mahmud	18	39	3	0
CH Gayle	c Sanwar Hossain	b Manjural Islam	0	5	0	0
BC Lara	c Al Sahariar	b Ehsanul Haque	46	76	5	0
S Chanderpaul	lbw	b Ehsanul Haque	29	53	3	0
*CL Hooper		c & b Alok Kapali	45	58	0	1
RR Sarwan		c & b Khaled Mahmud	13	28	1	0
RL Powell	c Sanwar Hossain	b Manjural Islam	50	31	3	4
+RD Jacobs	not out		6	8	0	0
VC Drakes	run out (Mohammad Rafique/Khaled Mashud)		0	3	0	0
M Dillon	c Mohammad Ashraful b Manjural Islam		10	6	1	1
CD Collymore	not out		0	0	0	0
Extras	(b 1, lb 6, w 13, nb 7)		27			
Total	(9 wickets, 50 overs, 203 mins)		244			

Fall of wickets: 1-19 (Gayle, 4.1 ov), 2-40 (Hinds, 9.3 ov), 3-108 (Chanderpaul, 25.4 ov), 4-130 (Lara, 31.3 ov), 5-158 (Sarwan, 39.3 ov), 6-217 (Hooper, 46.3 ov), 7-231 (Powell, 47.6 ov), 8-231 (Drakes, 48.3 ov), 9-242 (Dillon, 49.4 ov).

Bowling	O	M	R	W	
Manjural Islam	10	0	62	3	(4w)
Talha Jubair	8	0	46	0	(6nb, 5w)
Khaled Mahmud	10	1	48	2	(1nb)
Ehsanul Haque	10	0	34	2	(1w)
Mohammad Rafique	10	0	44	0	
Alok Kapali	2	1	3	1	

Bangladesh innings (target: 245 runs from 50 overs)			R	B	4	6
Al Sahariar	c Gayle	b Drakes	5	14	0	0
Ehsanul Haque		b Dillon	12	24	2	0
Mohammad Ashraful	not out		8	4	1	0
Sanwar Hossain	not out		2	7	0	0
Extras	(lb 2, w 3)		5			
Total	(2 wickets, 8.1 overs, 41 mins)		32			

DNB: Tushar Imran, Alok Kapali, *+Khaled Mashud, Mohammad Rafique, Khaled Mahmud, Talha Jubair, Manjural Islam.
Fall of wickets: 1-19 (Al Sahariar, 5.6 ov), 2-19 (Ehsanul Haque, 6.2 ov).

Bowling	O	M	R	W	
Dillon	4.1	0	13	1	(3w)
Drakes	4	1	17	1	

Zimbabwe v India, Pool A

At Harare Sports Club, 19 February 2003 (50-overs)
Result: India won by 83 runs. Points: India 4, Zimbabwe 0.
Toss: Zimbabwe. Umpires: EAR de Silva (SL) and RE Koertzen (SA).
TV Umpire: DB Hair (Aus). Match Referee: CH Lloyd (WI).
Man of the Match: SR Tendulkar.

India innings (50 overs maximum)			R	B	4	6
V Sehwag	c Taibu	b Whittall	36	38	6	0
SR Tendulkar		b GW Flower	81	91	10	0
D Mongia	c Hondo	b GW Flower	12	37	0	0
*SC Ganguly	c Streak	b Blignaut	24	36	0	1
+R Dravid	not out		43	55	2	0
Yuvraj Singh	c Taibu	b Murphy	1	5	0	0
M Kaif	lbw	b Hondo	25	24	1	1
Harbhajan Singh	c Murphy	b Streak	3	5	0	0
Z Khan	not out		13	8	2	0
Extras	(b 4, lb 4, w 9)		17			
Total	(7 wickets, 50 overs)		255			

DNB: A Nehra, J Srinath.
Fall of wickets: 1-99 (Sehwag, 16.4 ov), 2-142 (Mongia, 27.3 ov), 3-142 (Tendulkar, 27.5 ov), 4-182 (Ganguly, 37.6 ov), 5-184 (Yuvraj Singh, 38.6 ov), 6-227 (Kaif, 46.3 ov), 7-234 (Harbhajan Singh, 47.6 ov).

Bowling	O	M	R	W	
Streak	9	0	46	1	(1w)
Blignaut	10	0	54	1	(5w)
Hondo	9	1	56	1	
Whittall	6	0	37	1	
GW Flower	6	0	14	2	(1w)
Murphy	10	0	40	1	(2w)

Zimbabwe innings (target: 256 runs from 50 overs)			R	B	4	6
CB Wishart		b Srinath	12	19	2	0
MA Vermeulen	c Dravid	b Srinath	0	5	0	0
A Flower		b Harbhajan Singh	22	54	1	0
GW Flower	c Harbhajan Singh	b Ganguly	23	39	1	0
DD Ebrahim	c sub (AB Agarkar) b Ganguly		19	27	1	0
AM Blignaut	c Mongia	b Ganguly	2	5	0	0
+T Taibu	not out		29	44	0	0
GJ Whittall	c Khan	b Sehwag	28	26	3	0
*HH Streak	c Kaif	b Harbhajan Singh	20	33	1	0
BA Murphy		b Khan	2	9	0	0
DT Hondo		b Khan	2	9	0	0
Extras	(b 4, lb 2, w 5, nb 2)		13			
Total	(all out, 44.4 overs)		172			

Fall of wickets: 1-1 (Vermeulen, 0.6 ov), 2-23 (Wishart, 8.1 ov), 3-48 (A Flower, 16.3 ov), 4-83 (GW Flower, 23.4 ov), 5-83 (Ebrahim, 23.5 ov), 6-87 (Blignaut, 25.3 ov), 7-124 (Whittall, 31.6 ov), 8-160 (Streak, 39.5 ov), 9-165 (Murphy, 42.1 ov), 10-172 (Hondo, 44.4 ov).

Bowling	O	M	R	W	
Srinath	8	1	14	2	
Khan	7.4	0	23	2	(1nb, 3w)
Nehra	7	0	35	0	(1nb)
Harbhajan Singh	10	0	42	2	(2w)
Ganguly	5	1	22	3	
Sehwag	3	0	14	1	
Mongia	4	0	16	0	

Canada v Sri Lanka, Pool B

At Boland Bank Park, Paarl, 19 February 2003 (50-overs)
Result: Sri Lanka won by 9 wickets. Points: Sri Lanka 4, Canada 0.
Toss: Sri Lanka. Umpires: NA Mallender (Eng) and DR Shepherd (Eng).
TV Umpire: KC Barbour (Zim). Match Referee: Wasim Raja (Pak).
Man of the Match: RAP Nissanka.

Canada innings (50 overs maximum)			R	B	4	6
DR Chumney	c Sangakkara	b Vaas	9	25	2	0
JM Davison	c Sangakkara	b Nissanka	0	4	0	0
AF Sattaur	lbw	b Vaas	0	10	0	0
IS Billcliff	lbw	b Vaas	1	9	0	0
NA de Groot	lbw	b Nissanka	0	2	0	0
*JV Harris	hit wicket	b Nissanka	9	13	2	0
I Maraj	lbw	b Nissanka	0	1	0	0
+A Bagai	c Jayawardene	b Fernando	6	25	0	0
S Thuraisingam	lbw	b Fernando	6	15	1	0
A Codrington		b Muralitharan	0	9	0	0
BB Seebaran	not out		0	0	0	0
Extras	(lb 2, w 2, nb 1)		5			
Total	(all out, 18.4 overs, 87 mins)		36			

Fall of wickets: 1-0 (Davison, 1.4 ov), 2-6 (Sattaur, 4.5 ov), 3-11 (Chumney, 6.6 ov), 4-12 (Billcliff, 8.1 ov), 5-12 (de Groot, 9.1 ov), 6-12 (Maraj, 9.2 ov), 7-21 (Harris, 11.2 ov), 8-31 (Thuraisingam, 15.1 ov), 9-36 (Bagai, 17.6 ov), 10-36 (Codrington, 18.4 ov).

Bowling	O	M	R	W	
Vaas	7	4	15	3	
Nissanka	7	1	12	4	(1nb, 1w)
Muralitharan	2.4	0	3	1	
Fernando	2	0	4	2	(1w)

Sri Lanka innings (target: 37 runs from 50 overs)			R	B	4	6
MS Atapattu	not out		24	14	4	0
*ST Jayasuriya	lbw	b Thuraisingam	9	10	1	0
+KC Sangakkara	not out		4	4	1	0
Extras			0			
Total	(1 wicket, 4.4 overs, 18 mins)		37			

DNB: PA de Silva, DPMD Jayawardene, HP Tillakaratne, RP Arnold, WPUJC Vaas, M Muralitharan, CRD Fernando, RAP Nissanka.
Fall of wickets: 1-23 (Jayasuriya, 2.6 ov).

Bowling	O	M	R	W
Thuraisingam	2.4	0	22	1
Davison	2	0	15	0

England v Namibia, Pool A

At St. George's Park, Port Elizabeth, 19 February 2003 (50-overs)
Result: England won by 55 runs. Points: England 4, Namibia 0.
Toss: Namibia. Umpires: SJA Taufel (Aus) and S Venkataraghavan (Ind).
TV Umpire: Nadeem Ghauri (Pak). Match Referee: MJ Procter.
Man of the Match: AJ Burger.

England innings (50 overs maximum)			R	B	4	6
ME Trescothick	c LJ Burger	b AJ Burger	58	66	8	1
NV Knight	c LJ Burger	b van Vuuren	6	12	1	0
MP Vaughan	c LJ Burger	b van Vuuren	14	18	2	0
*+AJ Stewart	c BL Kotze	b DB Kotze	60	77	6	1
PD Collingwood	c Keulder	b Snyman	38	49	3	0
A Flintoff	c Keulder	b Snyman	21	24	0	2
ID Blackwell	c van Schoor	b Snyman	16	19	1	0
C White	c SF Burger	b van Vuuren	35	29	2	0
RC Irani	c DB Kotze	b van Vuuren	12	7	2	0
AR Caddick		b van Vuuren	4	2	1	0
JM Anderson	not out		0	0	0	0
Extras	(lb 1, w 4, nb 3)		8			
Total	(all out, 50 overs, 201 mins)		272			

Fall of wickets: 1-26 (Knight, 5.2 ov), 2-43 (Vaughan, 9.2 ov), 3-121 (Trescothick, 24.3 ov), 4-159 (Stewart, 31.4 ov), 5-202 (Collingwood, 40.1 ov), 6-205 (Flintoff, 40.6 ov), 7-242 (Blackwell, 46.3 ov), 8-264 (White, 49.2 ov), 9-268 (Irani, 49.4 ov), 10-272 (Caddick, 49.6 ov).

Bowling	O	M	R	W	
Snyman	10	0	69	3	(2nb, 2w)
van Vuuren	10	2	43	5	
LJ Burger	9	0	45	0	(1nb)
BL Kotze	3	0	24	0	
DB Kotze	10	0	35	1	
AJ Burger	2	0	23	1	(2w)
SF Burger	6	0	32	0	

Namibia innings (target: 273 runs from 50 overs)			R	B	4	6
SJ Swanepoel	c Vaughan	b Anderson	8	16	1	0
AJ Burger	c Collingwood	b White	85	86	10	1
LJ Burger		c & b Flintoff	5	25	1	0
D Keulder	run out (Trescothick/Stewart)		46	66	6	0
BG Murgatroyd		b Irani	24	44	1	1
G Snyman		b White	0	1	0	0
*DB Kotze		b Flintoff	7	14	0	0
SF Burger	c Collingwood	b Irani	5	14	0	0
+M van Schoor	not out		11	23	1	0
BL Kotze	lbw	b Irani	0	1	0	0
RJ van Vuuren	not out		12	12	0	1
Extras	(lb 5, w 6, nb 3)		14			
Total	(9 wickets, 50 overs, 206 mins)		217			

Fall of wickets: 1-12 (Swanepoel, 3.2 ov), 2-42 (LJ Burger, 11.4 ov), 3-139 (AJ Burger, 29.1 ov), 4-174 (Keulder, 37.2 ov), 5-174 (Snyman, 37.3 ov), 6-188 (Murgatroyd, 40.5 ov), 7-190 (DB Kotze, 41.6 ov), 8-200 (SF Burger, 44.3 ov), 9-200 (BL Kotze, 44.4 ov).

Bowling	O	M	R	W	
Caddick	8	2	28	0	(2w)
Anderson	8	0	44	1	(3w)
Flintoff	10	0	33	2	(1w)
White	10	0	46	2	(2nb)
Vaughan	6	0	31	0	(1nb)
Irani	8	0	30	3	

Australia v Netherlands, Pool A

At North West Cricket Stadium, Potchefstroom, 20 February 2003 (50-overs)
Result: Australia won by 75 runs (D/L Method). Points: Australia 4, Netherlands 0.
Toss: Netherlands. Umpires: DL Orchard and P Willey (Eng).
TV Umpire: Aleem Dar (Pak). Match Referee: RS Madugalle (SL).
Man of the Match: DR Martyn.

Australia innings (36 overs maximum)			R	B	4	6
+JP Maher	c van Bunge	b de Leede	26	41	4	0
ML Hayden	c Schiferli	b de Leede	33	60	4	0
DR Martyn	not out		67	76	6	0
DS Lehmann	not out		29	39	2	0
Extras	(b 4, lb 3, w 8)		15			
Total	(2 wickets, 36 overs, 139 mins)		170			

DNB: *RT Ponting, MG Bevan, A Symonds, IJ Harvey, AJ Bichel, JN Gillespie, GD McGrath.
Fall of wickets: 1-52 (Maher, 12.6 ov), 2-103 (Hayden, 22.4 ov).

Bowling	O	M	R	W	
Schiferli	7	0	42	0	(1w)
Lefebvre	8	2	19	0	(2w)
de Leede	7	0	34	2	(4w)
Kloppenburg	7	0	32	0	(1w)
Esmeijer	5	0	16	0	
van Bunge	2	0	20	0	

Netherlands innings (target: 198 runs from 36 overs)			R	B	4	6
LP van Troost	c Bichel	b Lehmann	23	33	3	0
DLS van Bunge	c Martyn	b Gillespie	1	3	0	0
B Zuiderent	c Maher	b Gillespie	5	17	0	0
KJJ van Noortwijk	lbw	b Lehmann	13	22	2	0
TBM de Leede	c Maher	b Bichel	24	38	1	1
RH Scholte	lbw	b Bichel	8	25	0	0
E Schiferli		b Harvey	9	8	0	1
JF Kloppenburg		b Bichel	9	11	2	0
*RP Lefebvre	not out		14	20	1	0
+J Smits	c Maher	b Harvey	0	2	0	0
JJ Esmeijer	c Ponting	b Harvey	0	4	0	0
Extras	(lb 4, w 11, nb 1)		16			
Total	(all out, 30.2 overs, 103 mins)		122			

Fall of wickets: 1-8 (van Bunge, 1.1 ov), 2-18 (Zuiderent, 5.4 ov), 3-42 (van Troost, 10.4 ov), 4-59 (van Noortwijk, 14.2 ov), 5-85 (de Leede, 21.5 ov), 6-90 (Scholte, 23.5 ov), 7-96 (Schiferli, 24.3 ov), 8-112 (Kloppenburg, 27.6 ov), 9-118 (Smits, 28.4 ov), 10-122 (Esmeijer, 30.2 ov).

Bowling	O	M	R	W	
McGrath	3	1	10	0	(1w)
Gillespie	3	0	7	2	(3w)
Lehmann	8	0	27	2	(1w)
Symonds	7	0	36	0	(4w)
Bichel	5	0	13	3	(1w)
Harvey	4.2	0	25	3	(1nb, 1w)

Kenya v New Zealand, Pool B

At Gymkhana Club Ground, Nairobi, 21 February 2003 (50-overs)
Result: Kenya won by a walkover. Points: Kenya 4, New Zealand 0.
Toss: None. Umpires: DJ Harper (Aus) and RB Tiffin (Zim).
TV Umpire: AV Jayaprakash (Ind). Match Referee: GR Viswanath (Ind).
Man of the Match: No Award.
NB: New Zealand were not in attendance - forfeited the match due to safety concerns.

South Africa v Bangladesh, Pool B

At Goodyear Park, Bloemfontein, 22 February 2003 (50-overs)
Result: South Africa won by 10 wickets. Points: South Africa 4, Bangladesh 0.
Toss: South Africa. Umpires: BF Bowden (NZ) and S Venkataraghavan (Ind).
TV Umpire: TH Wijewardene (SL). Match Referee: CH Lloyd (WI).
Man of the Match: M Ntini.

Bangladesh innings (50 overs maximum)			R	B	4	6
Al Sahariar	c Peterson	b Pollock	0	12	0	0
Ehsanul Haque	c Zondeki	b Pollock	3	30	0	0
Mohammad Ashraful	c Boucher	b Ntini	6	10	1	0
Sanwar Hossain	c Kallis	b Hall	11	14	1	0
Alok Kapali	c Dippenaar	b Zondeki	2	15	0	0
Tushar Imran	c Dippenaar	b Hall	9	24	0	0
*+Khaled Mashud	c Boucher	b Ntini	29	67	3	0
Khaled Mahmud	c Klusener	b Ntini	23	35	1	1
Mohammad Rafique	run out (Kallis/Peterson)		1	2	0	0
Manjural Islam	c Dippenaar	b Ntini	0	2	0	0
Talha Jubair	not out		4	8	1	0
Extras	(lb 4, w 8, nb 8)		20			
Total	(all out, 35.1 overs, 164 mins)		108			

Fall of wickets: 1-3 (Al Sahariar, 2.4 ov), 2-14 (Mohammad Ashraful, 7.1 ov), 3-21 (Ehsanul Haque, 8.5 ov), 4-33 (Sanwar Hossain, 12.2 ov), 5-33 (Alok Kapali, 13.2 ov), 6-56 (Tushar Imran, 20.2 ov), 7-91 (Khaled Mashud, 31.5 ov), 8-93 (Mohammad Rafique, 32.5 ov), 9-99 (Manjural Islam, 33.2 ov), 10-108 (Khaled Mahmud, 35.1 ov).

Bowling	O	M	R	W	
Pollock	6	2	8	2	(3nb)
Ntini	7.1	1	24	4	(2nb)
Zondeki	5	1	17	1	(4w)
Hall	6	2	15	2	(2nb, 3w)
Kallis	5	0	19	0	(1nb, 1w)
Peterson	6	0	21	0	

South Africa innings (target: 109 runs from 50 overs)		R	B	4	6
HH Gibbs	not out	49	40	8	1
G Kirsten	not out	52	32	9	1
Extras	(lb 1, w 7)	8			
Total	(0 wickets, 12 overs, 48 mins)	109			

DNB: JH Kallis, HH Dippenaar, AJ Hall, L Klusener, +MV Boucher, *SM Pollock, RJ Peterson, M Ntini, M Zondeki.

Bowling	O	M	R	W	
Manjural Islam	4	0	26	0	
Talha Jubair	2	0	24	0	(6w)
Khaled Mahmud	2	0	20	0	(1w)
Mohammad Rafique	2	0	20	0	
Alok Kapali	2	0	18	0	

England v Pakistan, Pool A

At Newlands, Cape Town (day/night), 22 February 2003 (50-overs)
Result: England won by 112 runs. Points: England 4, Pakistan 0.
Toss: England. Umpires: BG Jerling and RE Koertzen.
TV Umpire: SA Bucknor (WI). Match Referee: MJ Procter.
Man of the Match: JM Anderson.

England innings (50 overs maximum)			R	B	4	6
ME Trescothick	c Rashid Latif	b Wasim Akram	1	11	0	0
NV Knight	c Abdul Razzaq	b Waqar Younis	15	28	0	1
MP Vaughan	c Younis Khan	b Shoaib Akhtar	52	64	7	0
*N Hussain	c Rashid Latif	b Waqar Younis	8	9	1	0
+AJ Stewart		b Shahid Afridi	30	34	4	0
PD Collingwood	not out		66	73	4	0
A Flintoff	st Rashid Latif	b Saqlain Mushtaq	26	38	3	0
C White	c Younis Khan	b Shahid Afridi	15	22	2	0
AF Giles	c Shahid Afridi	b Saqlain Mushtaq	17	23	0	1
AR Caddick	not out		3	3	0	0
Extras	(lb 1, w 7, nb 5)		13			
Total	(8 wickets, 50 overs, 218 mins)		246			

DNB: JM Anderson..
Fall of wickets: 1-7 (Trescothick, 2.6 ov), 2-45 (Knight, 9.4 ov), 3-59 (Hussain, 13.3 ov), 4-110 (Vaughan, 23.2 ov), 5-118 (Stewart, 24.5 ov), 6-160 (Flintoff, 34.5 ov), 7-194 (White, 40.3 ov), 8-223 (Giles, 46.3 ov).

Bowling	O	M	R	W	
Wasim Akram	10	1	37	1	(3nb, 3w)
Shoaib Akhtar	9	1	63	1	(1nb, 3w)
Waqar Younis	7	0	37	2	
Saqlain Mushtaq	10	0	44	2	
Shahid Afridi	8	0	36	2	
Abdul Razzaq	6	0	28	0	(1nb, 1w)

Pakistan innings (target: 247 runs from 50 overs)			R	B	4	6
Saeed Anwar	lbw	b Anderson	29	60	3	0
Shahid Afridi	c Stewart	b Caddick	6	6	0	1
Inzamam-ul-Haq	c Knight	b Anderson	0	1	0	0
Yousuf Youhana		b Anderson	0	1	0	0
Younis Khan	c Stewart	b Flintoff	5	27	0	0
Abdul Razzaq		b White	11	21	1	0
+Rashid Latif	c Stewart	b Anderson	0	4	0	0
Wasim Akram	c Giles	b White	7	14	1	0
Saqlain Mushtaq	not out		12	33	2	0
*Waqar Younis	c Knight	b White	2	3	0	0
Shoaib Akhtar		b Flintoff	43	16	5	3
Extras	(b 4, lb 4, w 11)		19			
Total	(all out, 31 overs, 143 mins)		134			

Fall of wickets: 1-13 (Shahid Afridi, 2.6 ov), 2-17 (Inzamam-ul-Haq, 3.5 ov), 3-17 (Yousuf Youhana, 3.6 ov), 4-52 (Younis Khan, 14.5 ov), 5-59 (Saeed Anwar, 17.1 ov), 6-59 (Rashid Latif, 17.5 ov), 7-71 (Abdul Razzaq, 21.1 ov), 8-78 (Wasim Akram, 25.2 ov), 9-80 (Waqar Younis, 25.5 ov), 10-134 (Shoaib Akhtar, 30.6 ov).

Bowling	O	M	R	W	
Caddick	7	0	27	1	(4w)
Anderson	10	2	29	4	(3w)
Flintoff	9	2	37	2	(4w)
White	5	0	33	3	

Canada v West Indies, Pool B

At SuperSport Park, Centurion, 23 February 2003 (50-overs)
Result: West Indies won by 7 wickets. Points: West Indies 4, Canada 0.
Toss: West Indies. Umpires: EAR de Silva (SL) and DB Hair (Aus).
TV Umpire: Nadeem Ghauri (Pak). Match Referee: RS Madugalle (SL).
Man of the Match: JM Davison.

Canada innings (50 overs maximum)			R	B	4	6
I Maraj	c Hooper	b Collins	16	34	2	0
JM Davison	c Drakes	b Hinds	111	76	8	6
DR Chumney	c Gayle	b Hinds	19	25	1	1
IS Billcliff	c Jacobs	b Drakes	16	33	2	0
N Ifill	c Jacobs	b Drakes	9	28	1	0
*JV Harris	c Hooper	b Drakes	6	23	0	0
NA de Groot	run out (Hinds/Jacobs)		11	32	1	0
+A Bagai	run out (Powell)		2	9	0	0
A Codrington	c Jacobs	b Drakes	0	1	0	0
BB Seebaran	lbw	b Drakes	0	1	0	0
D Joseph	not out		0	1	0	0
Extras	(lb 3, w 3, nb 6)		12			
Total	(all out, 42.5 overs, 172 mins)		202			

Fall of wickets: 1-96 (Maraj, 11.6 ov), 2-155 (Chumney, 20.6 ov), 3-156 (Davison, 22.1 ov), 4-174 (Ifill, 28.4 ov), 5-185 (Billcliff, 34.1 ov), 6-190 (Harris, 38.3 ov), 7-197 (Bagai, 42.1 ov), 8-202 (Codrington, 42.3 ov), 9-202 (Seebaran, 42.4 ov), 10-202 (de Groot, 42.5 ov).

Bowling	O	M	R	W	
Dillon	5	0	41	0	(1w)
Collins	7	1	35	1	(3nb, 1w)
Drakes	9.5	1	44	5	(3nb)
Hooper	8	1	31	0	(1w)
Gayle	9	1	29	0	
Hinds	4	1	19	2	

West Indies innings (target: 203 runs from 50 overs)			R	B	4	6
CH Gayle	c Bagai	b Joseph	8	13	1	0
WW Hinds	st Bagai	b Davison	64	31	10	3
BC Lara		b de Groot	73	40	8	5
RR Sarwan	not out		42	32	9	0
*CL Hooper	not out		5	8	0	0
Extras	(lb 5, w 8, nb 1)		14			
Total	(3 wickets, 20.3 overs, 91 mins)		206			

DNB: S Chanderpaul, RL Powell, +RD Jacobs, VC Drakes, M Dillon, PT Collins.
Fall of wickets: 1-32 (Gayle, 4.2 ov), 2-134 (Hinds, 11.3 ov), 3-177 (Lara, 16.5 ov).

Bowling	O	M	R	W	
Joseph	4	0	47	1	(2w)
Codrington	4	0	25	0	(1w)
Ifill	4	0	46	0	(1nb, 4w)
Seebaran	1	0	26	0	
Davison	5	0	36	1	(1w)
de Groot	2.3	0	21	1	

India v Namibia, Pool A

At City Oval, Pietermaritzburg, 23 February 2003 (50-overs)
Result: India won by 181 runs. Points: India 4, Namibia 0.
Toss: Namibia. Umpires: Aleem Dar (Pak) and DR Shepherd (Eng).
TV Umpire: KC Barbour (Zim). Match Referee: Wasim Raja (Pak).
Man of the Match: SR Tendulkar.

India innings (50 overs maximum)			R	B	4	6
V Sehwag	c Keulder	b van Vuuren	24	24	4	0
SR Tendulkar		b van Vuuren	152	151	18	0
*SC Ganguly	not out		112	119	6	4
Yuvraj Singh	not out		7	7	1	0
Extras	(lb 2, w 13, nb 1)		16			
Total	(2 wickets, 50 overs, 207 mins)		311			

DNB: +R Dravid, D Mongia, M Kaif, Harbhajan Singh, Z Khan, A Nehra, J Srinath.
Fall of wickets: 1-46 (Sehwag, 7.5 ov), 2-290 (Tendulkar, 47.4 ov).

Bowling	O	M	R	W	
Snyman	10	0	57	0	(1nb, 3w)
van Vuuren	10	1	53	2	(1w)
LJ Burger	6	0	49	0	(1w)
van Rooi	6	0	36	0	(1w)
BL Kotze	10	0	64	0	
DB Kotze	8	0	50	0	(3w)

Namibia innings (target: 312 runs from 50 overs)			R	B	4	6
SJ Swanepoel	lbw	b Khan	9	21	1	0
AJ Burger		b Mongia	29	30	4	1
LJ Burger	lbw	b Khan	0	12	0	0
D Keulder	c Mongia	b Harbhajan Singh	4	19	0	0
BG Murgatroyd	lbw	b Harbhajan Singh	0	6	0	0
*DB Kotze	c & b Mongia		27	50	1	1
+M van Schoor	c Dravid	b Yuvraj Singh	24	61	1	0
BO van Rooi	c Mongia	b Yuvraj Singh	17	31	2	0
BL Kotze	c Dravid	b Yuvraj Singh	3	18	0	0
G Snyman	c Srinath	b Yuvraj Singh	5	6	1	0
RJ van Vuuren	not out		0	4	0	0
Extras	(lb 1, w 8, nb 3)		12			
Total	(all out, 42.3 overs, 163 mins)		130			

Fall of wickets: 1-19 (Swanepoel, 5.2 ov), 2-21 (LJ Burger, 7.4 ov), 3-43 (Keulder, 12.5 ov), 4-47 (AJ Burger, 13.3 ov), 5-47 (Murgatroyd, 14.6 ov), 6-98 (DB Kotze, 31.6 ov), 7-99 (van Schoor, 33.2 ov), 8-124 (van Rooi, 40.3 ov), 9-124 (BL Kotze, 40.6 ov), 10-130 (Snyman, 42.3 ov).

Bowling	O	M	R	W	
Srinath	6	0	25	0	(1w)
Nehra	0.1	0	0	0	
Khan	7.5	0	24	2	(2nb, 1w)
Harbhajan Singh	10	1	34	2	(1w)
Mongia	10	1	24	2	(1w)
Sehwag	4	0	16	0	(1nb)
Yuvraj Singh	4.3	2	6	4	

Kenya v Sri Lanka, Pool B

At Gymkhana Club Ground, Nairobi, 24 February 2003 (50-overs)
Result: Kenya won by 53 runs. Points: Kenya 4, Sri Lanka 0.
Toss: Sri Lanka. Umpires: DJ Harper (Aus) and RB Tiffin (Zim).
TV Umpire: AV Jayaprakash (Ind). Match Referee: DT Lindsay (SA).
Man of the Match: CO Obuya.

Kenya innings (50 overs maximum)			R	B	4	6
+KO Otieno	c Muralitharan	b de Silva	60	88	8	2
RD Shah	lbw	b Vaas	0	1	0	0
BJ Patel	c Sangakkara	b Vaas	12	21	2	0
*SO Tikolo	lbw	b Muralitharan	10	22	2	0
HS Modi		b Muralitharan	26	56	2	0
MO Odumbe	c Arnold	b Muralitharan	26	44	1	0
TM Odoyo	c Sangakkara	b Vaas	6	15	1	0
CO Obuya	not out		13	21	1	0
AO Suji		b Muralitharan	6	14	0	0
PJ Ongondo		b Jayasuriya	20	18	1	0
MA Suji	not out		3	2	0	0
Extras	(b 5, lb 11, w 10, nb 2)		28			
Total	(9 wickets, 50 overs, 207 mins)		210			

Fall of wickets: 1-1 (Shah, 0.2 ov), 2-46 (Patel, 6.6 ov), 3-75 (Tikolo, 15.3 ov), 4-112 (Otieno, 27.3 ov), 5-152 (Modi, 37.3 ov), 6-163 (Odoyo, 40.3 ov), 7-163 (Odumbe, 41.2 ov), 8-173 (AO Suji, 45.1 ov), 9-205 (Ongondo, 49.3 ov).

Bowling	O	M	R	W
Vaas	10	1	41	3 (2nb, 2w)
Nissanka	7	2	29	0 (4w)
Fernando	7	0	33	0
Muralitharan	10	1	28	4 (1w)
Jayasuriya	9	1	30	1 (1w)
de Silva	5	1	23	1
Arnold	2	0	10	0 (1w)

Sri Lanka innings (target: 211 runs from 50 overs)			R	B	4	6
MS Atapattu		b Odoyo	23	38	4	0
*ST Jayasuriya	c Patel	b MA Suji	3	7	0	0
HP Tillakaratne	c AO Suji	b Obuya	23	47	3	0
PA de Silva	c Otieno	b Obuya	41	53	4	1
DPMD Jayawardene		c & b Obuya	5	13	0	0
+KC Sangakkara	c Otieno	b Obuya	5	13	0	0
RP Arnold	not out		25	37	1	0
WPUJC Vaas		c & b Obuya	4	10	0	0
RAP Nissanka	c Odoyo	b Tikolo	2	23	0	0
M Muralitharan	c AO Suji	b Tikolo	10	21	1	0
CRD Fernando		b Odumbe	7	8	1	0
Extras	(b 2, w 6, nb 1)		9			
Total	(all out, 45 overs, 185 mins)		157			

Fall of wickets: 1-13 (Jayasuriya, 4.2 ov), 2-39 (Atapattu, 11.5 ov), 3-71 (Tillakaratne, 17.3 ov), 4-87 (Jayawardene, 23.3 ov), 5-105 (Sangakkara, 27.4 ov), 6-112 (de Silva, 29.3 ov), 7-119 (Vaas, 31.6 ov), 8-131 (Nissanka, 37.5 ov), 9-149 (Muralitharan, 43.1 ov), 10-157 (Fernando, 44.6 ov).

Bowling	O	M	R	W
MA Suji	8	1	24	1
Odoyo	7	0	33	1 (1w)
Obuya	10	0	24	5 (1nb, 1w)
Ongondo	5	0	22	0 (1w)
Odumbe	10	0	39	1 (2w)
Tikolo	5	1	13	2

Zimbabwe v Australia, Pool A
At Queens Sports Club, Bulawayo, 24 February 2003 (50-overs)
Result: Australia won by 7 wickets. Points: Australia 4, Zimbabwe 0.
Toss: Zimbabwe. Umpires: BF Bowden (NZ) and DL Orchard (SA).
TV Umpire: BG Jerling (SA). Match Referee: GR Viswanath (Ind).
Man of the Match: AM Blignaut.

Zimbabwe innings (50 overs maximum)			R	B	4	6
CB Wishart		b Gillespie	10	24	1	0
GJ Whittall	c Hogg	b Gillespie	1	6	0	0
A Flower		b Hogg	62	91	8	0
GW Flower	run out (Gilchrist)		37	58	4	0
DD Ebrahim		b Hogg	15	30	2	0
+T Taibu		b McGrath	23	44	1	0
DA Marillier	c Ponting	b Hogg	0	1	0	0
AM Blignaut		c & b Lee	54	28	8	2
*HH Streak	not out		28	19	2	1
BA Murphy		b McGrath	1	2	0	0
DT Hondo	not out		1	1	0	0
Extras	(b 4, lb 3, w 3, nb 4)		14			
Total	(9 wickets, 50 overs, 214 mins)		246			

Fall of wickets: 1-13 (Whittall, 3.1 ov), 2-28 (Wishart, 7.2 ov), 3-112 (GW Flower, 28.1 ov), 4-121 (A Flower, 30.1 ov), 5-142 (Ebrahim, 36.5 ov), 6-142 (Marillier, 36.6 ov), 7-208 (Blignaut, 44.3 ov), 8-242 (Taibu, 49.1 ov), 9-244 (Murphy, 49.4 ov).

Bowling	O	M	R	W
McGrath	9	2	24	2 (1w)
Gillespie	9	1	50	2 (1w)
Symonds	10	1	35	0
Lee	10	0	63	1 (3nb, 1w)
Hogg	8	0	46	3 (1nb)
Martyn	4	0	21	0

Australia innings (target: 247 runs from 50 overs)			R	B	4	6
+AC Gilchrist	c sub (SM Ervine)	b Marillier	61	64	8	0
ML Hayden	c GW Flower	b Hondo	34	39	5	0
*RT Ponting		c & b Murphy	38	63	2	0
DR Martyn	not out		50	70	2	0
DS Lehmann	not out		56	48	6	0
Extras	(lb 1, w 8)		9			
Total	(3 wickets, 47.3 overs, 199 mins)		248			

DNB: A Symonds, MG Bevan, GB Hogg, B Lee, JN Gillespie, GD McGrath.
Fall of wickets: 1-89 (Hayden, 14.1 ov), 2-113 (Gilchrist, 21.4 ov), 3-156 (Ponting, 32.4 ov).

Bowling	O	M	R	W
Streak	6	0	38	0 (1w)
Blignaut	10	0	54	0 (4w)
Hondo	9	0	49	1
Whittall	3.3	0	26	0
Marillier	10	1	32	1 (3w)
Murphy	9	0	48	1

Netherlands v Pakistan, Pool A
At Boland Bank Park, Paarl, 25 February 2003 (50-overs)
Result: Pakistan won by 97 runs. Points: Pakistan 4, Netherlands 0.
Toss: Netherlands. Umpires: SA Bucknor (WI) and S Venkataraghavan (Ind).
TV Umpire: TH Wijewardene (SL). Match Referee: CH Lloyd (WI).
Man of the Match: Yousuf Youhana.

Pakistan innings (50 overs maximum)			R	B	4	6
Taufeeq Umar	run out (Esmeijer)		48	71	6	0
Saeed Anwar	c Esmeijer	b de Leede	25	37	3	0
Abdul Razzaq	c Smits	b van Bunge	47	63	4	0
Inzamam-ul-Haq	lbw	b de Leede	0	2	0	0
Yousuf Youhana		b Lefebvre	58	59	4	0
Saleem Elahi	c Zuiderent	b van Bunge	5	7	0	0
+Rashid Latif	c van Bunge	b Schiferli	24	25	2	0
Wasim Akram	run out (Lefebvre/Schiferli)		1	4	0	0
Shoaib Akhtar	not out		26	27	0	1
*Waqar Younis		c & b Mol	1	2	0	0
Saqlain Mushtaq	not out		3	3	0	0
Extras	(b 1, lb 8, w 6)		15			
Total	(9 wickets, 50 overs, 200 mins)		253			

Fall of wickets: 1-61 (Saeed Anwar, 13.5 ov), 2-106 (Taufeeq Umar, 22.2 ov), 3-108 (Inzamam-ul-Haq, 23.5 ov), 4-143 (Abdul Razzaq, 31.5 ov), 5-153 (Saleem Elahi, 33.4 ov), 6-192 (Rashid Latif, 40.3 ov), 7-196 (Wasim Akram, 42.1 ov), 8-238 (Yousuf Youhana, 47.4 ov), 9-245 (Waqar Younis, 48.5 ov).

Bowling	O	M	R	W
Schiferli	10	1	48	1
Lefebvre	10	1	39	1 (1w)
de Leede	10	0	53	2 (4w)
van Troost	2	0	18	0
Esmeijer	10	0	35	0
van Bunge	4	0	27	2
Mol	4	0	24	1 (1w)

Netherlands innings (target: 254 runs from 50 overs)			R	B	4	6
NA Statham		b Wasim Akram	0	9	0	0
E Schiferli	c Abdul Razzaq	b Shoaib Akhtar	9	24	1	0
B Zuiderent	lbw	b Waqar Younis	8	17	1	0
KJJ van Noortwijk	c Rashid Latif	b Wasim Akram	7	7	1	0
TBM de Leede	c Shoaib Akhtar	b Saqlain Mushtaq	15	35	0	1
DLS van Bunge	c Rashid Latif	b Abdul Razzaq	31	60	3	1
LP van Troost	c Rashid Latif	b Shoaib Akhtar	22	30	3	0
HJC Mol		b Shoaib Akhtar	13	24	1	0
JJ Esmeijer	lbw	b Saeed Anwar	0	2	0	0
*RP Lefebvre	not out		4	14	0	0
+J Smits	lbw	b Wasim Akram	7	21	1	0
Extras	(b 6, lb 11, w 17, nb 6)		40			
Total	(all out, 39.3 overs, 192 mins)		156			

Fall of wickets: 1-6 (Statham, 2.1 ov), 2-31 (Schiferli, 7.3 ov), 3-35 (Zuiderent, 8.3 ov), 4-43 (van Noortwijk, 9.6 ov), 5-78 (de Leede, 21.1 ov), 6-108 (van Bunge, 26.4 ov), 7-135 (Mol, 32.5 ov), 8-136 (Esmeijer, 33.2 ov), 9-138 (van Troost, 34.1 ov), 10-156 (Smits, 39.3 ov).

Bowling	O	M	R	W
Wasim Akram	8.3	2	24	3 (4nb, 5w)
Shoaib Akhtar	7	0	26	3 (6w)
Waqar Younis	6	1	19	1 (1w)
Saqlain Mushtaq	8	2	32	1
Abdul Razzaq	6	0	23	1 (2nb, 1w)
Saeed Anwar	4	0	15	1

Bangladesh v New Zealand, Pool B
At De Beers Diamond Oval, Kimberley, 26 February 2003 (50-overs)
Result: New Zealand won by 7 wickets. Points: New Zealand 4, Bangladesh 0.
Toss: Bangladesh. Umpires: DB Hair (Aus) and DR Shepherd (Eng).
TV Umpire: BG Jerling. Match Referee: MJ Procter.
Man of the Match: CD McMillan.

Bangladesh innings (50 overs maximum)			R	B	4	6
Hannan Sarkar	c McCullum	b Bond	9	24	2	0
Mohammad Ashraful		c & b Bond	56	82	6	1
Sanwar Hossain		b Oram	5	11	0	0
Habibul Bashar	c McCullum	b Oram	0	1	0	0
Alok Kapali	c Bond	b Adams	9	22	0	0
Akram Khan	c Fleming	b Bond	13	38	0	0
*+Khaled Mashud	not out		35	54	1	0
Khaled Mahmud	c McCullum	b Oram	12	29	1	0
Mohammad Rafique	not out		41	42	3	2
Extras	(b 1, lb 4, w 10, nb 3)		18			
Total	(7 wickets, 50 overs, 212 mins)		198			

DNB: Manjural Islam, Tapash Baisya.
Fall of wickets: 1-19 (Hannan Sarkar, 6.4 ov), 2-37 (Sanwar Hossain, 10.1 ov), 3-37 (Habibul Bashar, 10.2 ov), 4-71 (Alok Kapali, 19.1 ov), 5-105 (Akram Khan, 28.1 ov), 6-107 (Mohammad Ashraful, 30.2 ov), 7-128 (Khaled Mahmud, 38.3 ov).

Bowling	O	M	R	W
Bond	10	1	33	3 (5w)
Mills	6	0	32	0 (2nb)
Adams	10	0	50	1 (2w)
Oram	10	1	32	3 (2w)
Cairns	3	0	17	0 (1nb, 1w)
Vettori	10	0	19	0
Styris	1	0	10	0

New Zealand innings (target: 199 runs from 50 overs)		R	B	4	6
CD McMillan	b Khaled Mahmud	75	83	9	2
*SP Fleming	c & b Khaled Mahmud	32	40	4	1
AR Adams	c Mohammad Ashraful b Khaled Mahmud	18	22	2	1
SB Styris	not out	37	36	2	1
CL Cairns	not out	33	21	3	1
Extras	(w 3, nb 1)	4			
Total	(3 wickets, 33.3 overs, 130 mins)	199			

DNB: MS Sinclair, +BB McCullum, JDP Oram, KD Mills, DL Vettori, SE Bond.
Fall of wickets: 1-71 (Fleming, 14.1 ov), 2-99 (Adams, 20.1 ov), 3-138 (McMillan, 26.4 ov).

Bowling	O	M	R	W	
Manjural Islam	7	1	37	0	
Tapash Baisya	8	0	56	0	(1w)
Khaled Mahmud	10	0	46	3	(1nb, 1w)
Alok Kapali	6	0	38	0	(1w)
Sanwar Hossain	2	0	19	0	
Mohammad Ashraful	0.3	0	3	0	

England v India, Pool A

At Kingsmead, Durban (day/night), 26 February 2003 (50-overs)
Result: India won by 82 runs. Points: India 4, England 0.
Toss: India. Umpires: RE Koertzen and SJA Taufel (Aus).
TV Umpire: EAR de Silva (SL). Match Referee: RS Madugalle (SL).
Man of the Match: A Nehra.

India innings (50 overs maximum)		R	B	4	6
V Sehwag	c & b Flintoff	23	29	4	0
SR Tendulkar	c Collingwood b Flintoff	50	52	8	1
*SC Ganguly	c Trescothick b White	19	38	2	0
D Mongia	lbw b Collingwood	32	66	3	0
+R Dravid	c Collingwood b Caddick	62	72	3	1
Yuvraj Singh	c Hussain b Anderson	42	38	4	1
M Kaif	c Flintoff b Caddick	5	6	0	0
Harbhajan Singh	not out	0	1	0	0
Z Khan	run out (Stewart)	0	0	0	0
J Srinath	c Trescothick b Caddick	0	1	0	0
Extras	(b 1, lb 4, w 9, nb 3)	17			
Total	(9 wickets, 50 overs, 223 mins)	250			

DNB: A Nehra.
Fall of wickets: 1-60 (Sehwag, 9.5 ov), 2-91 (Tendulkar, 15.2 ov), 3-107 (Ganguly, 22.1 ov), 4-155 (Mongia, 36.2 ov), 5-217 (Yuvraj Singh, 46.2 ov), 6-250 (Kaif, 49.3 ov), 7-250 (Dravid, 49.4 ov), 8-250 (Khan, 49.5 ov), 9-250 (Srinath, 49.6 ov).

Bowling	O	M	R	W	
Caddick	10	0	69	3	(2nb, 2w)
Anderson	10	0	61	1	(5w)
Flintoff	10	2	15	2	(1w)
White	10	0	57	1	(1nb)
Irani	6	0	28	0	
Collingwood	4	0	15	1	

England innings (target: 251 runs from 50 overs)		R	B	4	6
ME Trescothick	c Tendulkar b Khan	8	23	1	0
NV Knight	run out (Kaif)	1	3	0	0
MP Vaughan	c Dravid b Nehra	20	47	2	0
*N Hussain	c Dravid b Nehra	15	30	2	0
+AJ Stewart	lbw b Nehra	0	1	0	0
PD Collingwood	c Sehwag b Nehra	18	38	2	0
A Flintoff	c Sehwag b Srinath	64	73	5	3
C White	c Dravid b Nehra	13	9	1	0
RC Irani	c Sehwag b Nehra	0	2	0	0
AR Caddick	not out	13	41	1	0
JM Anderson	lbw b Khan	2	8	0	0
Extras	(lb 5, w 7, nb 2)	14			
Total	(all out, 45.3 overs, 211 mins)	168			

Fall of wickets: 1-6 (Knight, 1.1 ov), 2-18 (Trescothick, 6.4 ov), 3-52 (Hussain, 16.2 ov), 4-52 (Stewart, 16.3 ov), 5-62 (Vaughan, 18.6 ov), 6-93 (Collingwood, 26.1 ov), 7-107 (White, 30.1 ov), 8-107 (Irani, 30.3 ov), 9-162 (Flintoff, 42.5 ov), 10-168 (Anderson, 45.3 ov).

Bowling	O	M	R	W	
Khan	9.3	1	29	2	(3w)
Srinath	10	0	37	1	(1w)
Nehra	10	2	23	6	
Ganguly	6	0	34	0	(2nb)
Harbhajan Singh	10	0	40	0	(2w)

Australia v Namibia, Pool A

At North West Cricket Stadium, Potchefstroom, 27 February 2003 (50-overs)
Result: Australia won by 256 runs. Points: Australia 4, Namibia 0.
Toss: Australia. Umpires: BF Bowden (NZ) and RB Tiffin (Zim).
TV Umpire: NA Mallender (Eng). Match Referee: GR Viswanath (Ind).
Man of the Match: GD McGrath.

Australia innings (50 overs maximum)		R	B	4	6
+AC Gilchrist	b van Rooi	13	22	2	0
ML Hayden	b LJ Burger	88	73	9	3
MG Bevan	c & b LJ Burger	17	42	1	0
A Symonds	run out (Swanepoel/van Schoor)	59	63	2	2
*RT Ponting	c DB Kotze b LJ Burger	2	9	0	0
DR Martyn	b BL Kotze	35	50	2	0
DS Lehmann	not out	50	31	5	3
GB Hogg	not out	19	14	3	0
Extras	(lb 8, w 6, nb 4)	18			
Total	(6 wickets, 50 overs, 195 mins)	301			

DNB: B Lee, AJ Bichel, GD McGrath.
Fall of wickets: 1-26 (Gilchrist, 5.6 ov), 2-104 (Bevan, 19.6 ov), 3-140 (Hayden, 23.5 ov), 4-146 (Ponting, 25.5 ov), 5-230 (Symonds, 42.2 ov), 6-231 (Martyn, 42.5 ov).

Bowling	O	M	R	W	
van Vuuren	10	0	92	0	(2nb, 1w)
van Rooi	6	0	24	1	(4w)
BL Kotze	10	0	62	1	(2nb, 1w)
LJ Burger	10	1	39	3	
DB Kotze	10	0	54	0	
AJ Burger	4	0	22	0	

Namibia innings (target: 302 runs from 50 overs)		R	B	4	6
AJ Burger	c Ponting b McGrath	4	4	1	0
SJ Swanepoel	c Ponting b Lee	2	8	0	0
M Karg	c Gilchrist b McGrath	4	14	0	0
D Keulder	c Gilchrist b McGrath	3	20	0	0
BG Murgatroyd	lbw b McGrath	0	3	0	0
*DB Kotze	c Gilchrist b McGrath	10	14	1	0
LJ Burger	c Gilchrist b McGrath	1	11	0	0
+M van Schoor	c Gilchrist b Bichel	6	10	1	0
BL Kotze	b McGrath	0	3	0	0
BO van Rooi	not out	0	1	0	0
RJ van Vuuren	c Gilchrist b Bichel	0	1	0	0
Extras	(lb 4, w 6, nb 5)	15			
Total	(all out, 14 overs, 75 mins)	45			

Fall of wickets: 1-5 (AJ Burger, 0.4 ov), 2-14 (Swanepoel, 3.2 ov), 3-16 (Karg, 4.6 ov), 4-17 (Murgatroyd, 6.3 ov), 5-28 (Keulder, 8.4 ov), 6-34 (LJ Burger, 10.5 ov), 7-45 (DB Kotze, 12.2 ov), 8-45 (BL Kotze, 12.5 ov), 9-45 (van Schoor, 13.5 ov), 10-45 (van Vuuren, 13.6 ov).

Bowling	O	M	R	W	
McGrath	7	4	15	7	(2w)
Lee	6	1	26	1	(5nb)
Bichel	1	1	0	2	

South Africa v Canada, Pool B

At Buffalo Park, East London, 27 February 2003 (50-overs)
Result: South Africa won by 118 runs. Points: South Africa 4, Canada 0.
Toss: Canada. Umpires: KC Barbour (Zim) and DJ Harper (Aus).
TV Umpire: Aleem Dar (Pak). Match Referee: Wasim Raja (Pak)
Man of the Match: HH Dippenaar.

South Africa innings (50 overs maximum)		R	B	4	6
GC Smith	b Davison	63	79	6	0
HH Gibbs	c Bagai b Patel	8	18	2	0
G Kirsten	c Bagai b Joseph	0	5	0	0
JH Kallis	c Ifill b Patel	1	4	0	0
HH Dippenaar	c Seebaran b de Groot	80	118	7	0
+MV Boucher	b de Groot	21	36	1	0
*SM Pollock	c Bagai b Joseph	32	23	0	2
AJ Hall	not out	22	11	2	1
M Ntini	b Patel	14	6	1	1
M Zondeki	not out	1	1	0	0
Extras	(lb 3, w 8, nb 1)	12			
Total	(8 wickets, 50 overs, 207 mins)	254			

DNB: AA Donald.
Fall of wickets: 1-19 (Gibbs, 5.2 ov), 2-22 (Kirsten, 6.2 ov), 3-23 (Kallis, 7.2 ov), 4-132 (Smith, 29.1 ov), 5-174 (Boucher, 39.2 ov), 6-197 (Dippenaar, 45.2 ov), 7-227 (Pollock, 48.1 ov), 8-249 (Ntini, 49.4 ov).

Bowling	O	M	R	W	
Joseph	9	1	42	2	(3w)
Patel	7	0	41	3	(3w)
Ifill	7	0	35	0	(1nb, 1w)
Davison	10	1	45	1	(1w)
Seebaran	10	0	43	0	
de Groot	7	0	45	2	

Canada innings (target: 255 runs from 50 overs)		R	B	4	6
I Maraj	not out	53	155	6	0
JM Davison	c Zondeki b Ntini	1	2	0	0
DR Chumney	c Smith b Pollock	2	16	0	0
IS Billcliff	b Zondeki	9	24	0	0
NA de Groot	c Boucher b Hall	16	36	2	0
*JV Harris	c Boucher b Ntini	15	32	2	0
+A Bagai	not out	28	37	4	0
Extras	(lb 6, w 4, nb 2)	12			
Total	(5 wickets, 50 overs, 214 mins)	136			

DNB: N Ifill, D Joseph, BB Seebaran, A Patel.
Fall of wickets: 1-2 (Davison, 1.4 ov), 2-8 (Chumney, 6.3 ov), 3-28 (Billcliff, 15.1 ov), 4-58 (de Groot, 27.1 ov), 5-84 (Harris, 37.3 ov).

Bowling	O	M	R	W	
Pollock	8	5	13	2	
Ntini	10	2	19	2	
Donald	10	2	27	0	(1w)
Zondeki	9	1	24	1	
Hall	7	1	26	1	(2nb, 2w)
Kallis	5	1	11	0	(1w)
Smith	1	0	10	0	

Zimbabwe v Netherlands, Pool A

At Queens Sports Club, Bulawayo, 28 February 2003 (50-overs)
Result: Zimbabwe won by 99 runs. Points: Zimbabwe 4, Netherlands 0.
Toss: Netherlands. Umpires: SA Bucknor (WI) and TH Wijewardene (SL).
TV Umpire: Nadeem Ghauri (Pak). Match Referee: CH Lloyd (WI).
Man of the Match: HH Streak.

Zimbabwe innings (50 overs maximum)			R	B	4	6
CB Wishart	c Smits	b Lefebvre	21	21	4	0
MA Vermeulen		b Kloppenburg	27	62	4	0
A Flower	c Esmeijer	b Schiferli	71	72	7	0
GJ Whittall	c Zuiderent	b Kloppenburg	30	37	2	1
DD Ebrahim		b de Leede	32	41	1	0
AM Blignaut	c Kloppenburg	b Schiferli	58	38	7	0
*HH Streak	c Esmeijer	b de Leede	44	22	6	1
DA Marillier	lbw	b Lefebvre	1	2	0	0
+T Taibu	not out		7	5	0	0
Extras	(lb 3, w 7)		10			
Total	(8 wickets, 50 overs, 210 mins)		301			

DNB: BA Murphy, DT Hondo.
Fall of wickets: 1-24 (Wishart, 5.6 ov), 2-82 (Vermeulen, 19.1 ov), 3-135 (Whittall, 29.3 ov), 4-165 (Flower, 34.2 ov), 5-245 (Blignaut, 44.3 ov), 6-274 (Ebrahim, 47.3 ov), 7-281 (Marillier, 48.2 ov), 8-301 (Streak, 49.6 ov).

Bowling	O	M	R	W	
Schiferli	10	2	43	2	(1w)
Lefebvre	8	0	38	2	(3w)
de Leede	7	0	69	2	
Kloppenburg	10	0	40	2	
Esmeijer	9	0	60	0	(1w)
van Bunge	3	0	22	0	(1w)
Mol	3	0	26	0	(1w)

Netherlands innings (target: 302 runs from 50 overs)			R	B	4	6
JF Kloppenburg	c Streak	b Hondo	18	56	2	0
E Schiferli		b Streak	22	27	3	0
B Zuiderent	run out (Ebrahim/Taibu)		15	31	0	1
DLS van Bunge	lbw	b Whittall	37	47	5	0
TBM de Leede	lbw	b Murphy	1	2	0	0
LP van Troost	c Hondo	b Murphy	26	25	2	1
RH Scholte	c Blignaut	b Murphy	7	26	0	0
HJC Mol	c sub (HK Olonga)	b Marillier	23	40	2	0
*RP Lefebvre		b Marillier	30	23	4	1
+J Smits	not out		8	11	0	0
JJ Esmeijer	not out		3	13	0	0
Extras	(b 1, lb 7, w 3, nb 1)		12			
Total	(9 wickets, 50 overs, 213 mins)		202			

Fall of wickets: 1-41 (Schiferli, 11.1 ov), 2-49 (Kloppenburg, 16.2 ov), 3-80 (Zuiderent, 23.1 ov), 4-85 (de Leede, 24.1 ov), 5-127 (van Troost, 30.3 ov), 6-128 (van Bunge, 31.5 ov), 7-148 (Scholte, 38.1 ov), 8-190 (Lefebvre, 44.6 ov), 9-191 (Mol, 46.4 ov).

Bowling	O	M	R	W	
Blignaut	10	1	30	0	(1w)
Streak	10	1	36	1	
Hondo	6	1	16	1	
Murphy	10	3	44	3	(1nb)
Marillier	9	0	49	2	(1w)
Whittall	5	1	19	1	(1w)

Sri Lanka v West Indies, Pool B

At Newlands, Cape Town (day/night), 28 February 2003 (50-overs)
Result: Sri Lanka won by 6 runs. Points: Sri Lanka 4, West Indies 0.
Toss: Sri Lanka. Umpires: DL Orchard and S Venkataraghavan (Ind).
TV Umpire: BG Jerling. Match Referee: DT Lindsay.
Man of the Match: WPUJC Vaas.

Sri Lanka innings (50 overs maximum)			R	B	4	6
MS Atapattu	run out (Collins)		3	8	0	0
*ST Jayasuriya	c Chanderpaul	b Gayle	66	99	4	0
HP Tillakaratne	c Hinds		36	68	4	0
PA de Silva	run out (Chanderpaul)		13	13	2	0
DPMD Jayawardene	c Powell	b Hooper	9	16	1	0
RP Arnold	not out		34	44	1	0
+KC Sangakkara	c Lara	b Drakes	24	30	2	0
WPUJC Vaas	not out		28	25	3	0
Extras	(lb 5, w 8, nb 2)		15			
Total	(6 wickets, 50 overs, 210 mins)		228			

DNB: M Muralitharan, CRD Fernando, PW Gunaratne.
Fall of wickets: 1-11 (Atapattu, 3.1 ov), 2-96 (Tillakaratne, 23.6 ov), 3-113 (de Silva, 26.6 ov), 4-131 (Jayawardene, 32.2 ov), 5-139 (Jayasuriya, 35.1 ov), 6-178 (Sangakkara, 42.6 ov).

Bowling	O	M	R	W	
Dillon	10	0	30	0	(2w)
Collins	10	0	62	0	(2nb, 2w)
Drakes	10	1	32	1	(1w)
Hooper	6	0	30	1	(1w)
Hinds	4	0	27	1	
Gayle	10	0	42	1	(2w)

West Indies innings (target: 229 runs from 50 overs)			R	B	4	6
CH Gayle	lbw	b Vaas	55	76	8	0
WW Hinds	c Jayasuriya	b Vaas	2	8	0	0
BC Lara	c Sangakkara	b Vaas	1	22	0	0
RR Sarwan	not out		47	44	4	2
*CL Hooper	lbw	b Fernando	0	1	0	0
S Chanderpaul	c Atapattu	b de Silva	65	90	6	0
+RD Jacobs	c Sangakkara	b Vaas	0	3	0	0
RL Powell		b Muralitharan	1	3	0	0
VC Drakes	c Vaas	b Jayasuriya	25	48	1	0
M Dillon	run out (Gunaratne)		4	7	0	0
PT Collins	not out		1	1	0	0
Extras	(lb 6, w 12, nb 3)		21			
Total	(9 wickets, 50 overs, 223 mins)		222			

Fall of wickets: 1-10 (Hinds, 2.4 ov), 2-27 (Lara, 8.3 ov), 3-62 (Hooper, 14.2 ov), 4-121 (Gayle, 28.2 ov), 5-121 (Jacobs, 28.5 ov), 6-122 (Powell, 29.2 ov), 7-169 (Chanderpaul, 42.1 ov), 8-186 (Drakes, 46.1 ov), 9-219 (Dillon, 49.3 ov). NB: RR Sarwan retired hurt (10*) from 62/2 to 169/7.

Bowling	O	M	R	W	
Vaas	10	3	22	4	(1w)
Gunaratne	6	1	41	0	(4w)
de Silva	10	0	48	1	
Fernando	6	0	33	1	(2nb, 3w)
Muralitharan	10	1	26	1	(1nb, 2w)
Jayasuriya	8	0	46	1	(1w)

Bangladesh v Kenya, Pool B

At New Wanderers Stadium, Johannesburg, 1 March 2003 (50-overs)
Result: Kenya won by 32 runs. Points: Kenya 4, Bangladesh 0.
Toss: Kenya. Umpires: EAR de Silva (SL) and NA Mallender (Eng).
TV Umpire: SJA Taufel (Aus). Match Referee: RS Madugalle (SL).
Man of the Match: MO Odumbe.

Kenya innings (50 overs maximum)			R	B	4	6
+KO Otieno	c Khaled Mashud	b Manjural Islam	0	3	0	0
RD Shah	c Akram Khan	b Mohammad Rafique	37	54	6	0
BJ Patel	c Manjural Islam	b Khaled Mahmud	32	60	6	0
*SO Tikolo		b Sanwar Hossain	27	45	2	0
HS Modi		c & b Sanwar Hossain	12	38	1	0
MO Odumbe	not out		52	46	4	0
TM Odoyo	lbw	b Sanwar Hossain	19	29	1	0
CO Obuya		b Tapash Baisya	22	21	1	1
PJ Ongondo	not out		2	4	0	0
Extras	(b 1, lb 2, w 11)		14			
Total	(7 wickets, 50 overs, 197 mins)		217			

DNB: MA Suji, AO Suji.
Fall of wickets: 1-1 (Otieno, 0.3 ov), 2-68 (Patel, 17.6 ov), 3-80 (Shah, 20.4 ov), 4-116 (Tikolo, 32.3 ov), 5-124 (Modi, 34.4 ov), 6-164 (Odoyo, 42.5 ov), 7-197 (Obuya, 47.5 ov).

Bowling	O	M	R	W	
Manjural Islam	7	0	30	1	(5w)
Tapash Baisya	8	1	22	1	(1w)
Khaled Mahmud	10	1	39	1	(4w)
Mohammad Rafique	7	0	35	1	
Sanwar Hossain	10	0	49	3	(1w)
Alok Kapali	2	0	9	0	
Mohammad Ashraful	6	0	30	0	

Bangladesh innings (target: 218 runs from 50 overs)			R	B	4	6
Al Shahariar	c Otieno	b MA Suji	14	12	2	1
Mohammad Ashraful	lbw	b MA Suji	1	9	0	0
Tushar Imran	c sub (JO Angara)	b Odumbe	48	81	3	1
*+Khaled Mashud	c Shah	b Obuya	14	41	1	0
Alok Kapali	c Otieno	b Odumbe	18	26	1	1
Akram Khan	c sub (JO Angara)	b Tikolo	44	60	3	0
Sanwar Hossain	c MA Suji	b Odumbe	16	28	1	0
Khaled Mahmud	st Otieno	b Odumbe	3	7	0	0
Mohammad Rafique	c Modi	b Tikolo	5	14	0	0
Tapash Baisya	not out		2	4	0	0
Manjural Islam	st Otieno	b Tikolo	2	5	0	0
Extras	(b 2, lb 3, w 10, nb 3)		18			
Total	(all out, 47.2 overs, 207 mins)		185			

Fall of wickets: 1-16 (Al Shahariar, 2.6 ov), 2-17 (Mohammad Ashraful, 4.1 ov), 3-53 (Khaled Mashud, 16.3 ov), 4-99 (Alok Kapali, 26.3 ov), 5-111 (Tushar Imran, 28.5 ov), 6-151 (Sanwar Hossain, 38.1 ov), 7-158 (Khaled Mahmud, 40.5 ov), 8-180 (Mohammad Rafique, 45.4 ov), 9-180 (Akram Khan, 45.5 ov), 10-185 (Manjural Islam, 47.2 ov).

Bowling	O	M	R	W	
MA Suji	8	1	27	2	(1w)
Odoyo	4	0	9	0	(4w)
Ongondo	7	0	29	0	(1nb, 1w)
Obuya	9	0	40	1	(1nb)
AO Suji	4	0	23	0	(1nb, 1w)
Odumbe	10	0	38	4	(1w)
Tikolo	5.2	0	14	3	(2w)

India v Pakistan, Pool A

At SuperSport Park, Centurion, 1 March 2003 (50-overs)
Result: India won by 6 wickets. Points: India 4, Pakistan 0.
Toss: Pakistan. Umpires: RE Koertzen and DR Shepherd (Eng).
TV Umpire: BF Bowden (NZ). Match Referee: MJ Procter.
Man of the Match: SR Tendulkar.

Pakistan innings (50 overs maximum)			R	B	4	6
Saeed Anwar		b Nehra	101	126	7	0
Taufeeq Umar		b Khan	22	32	4	0
Abdul Razzaq	c Dravid	b Nehra	12	29	2	0
Inzamam-ul-Haq	run out (Sehwag/Kumble)		6	3	1	0
Yousuf Youhana	c Khan	b Srinath	25	42	0	0
Younis Khan	c Mongia	b Khan	32	36	2	0
Shahid Afridi	c Kumble	b Mongia	9	7	2	0
+Rashid Latif	not out		29	25	2	0
Wasim Akram	not out		10	6	2	0
Extras	(b 2, lb 7, w 11, nb 7)		27			
Total	(7 wickets, 50 overs, 215 mins)		273			

DNB: *Waqar Younis, Shoaib Akhtar.
Fall of wickets: 1-58 (Taufeeq Umar, 10.5 ov), 2-90 (Abdul Razzaq, 20.6 ov), 3-98 (Inzamam-ul-Haq, 21.6 ov), 4-171 (Yousuf Youhana, 36.1 ov), 5-195 (Saeed Anwar, 40.1 ov), 6-208 (Shahid Afridi, 41.3 ov), 7-256 (Younis Khan, 48.1 ov).

Bowling	O	M	R	W	
Khan	10	0	46	2	(5nb, 5w)
Srinath	10	0	41	1	(1nb, 1w)
Nehra	10	0	74	2	(2w)
Kumble	10	0	51	0	(1w)
Ganguly	3	0	14	0	
Sehwag	4	0	19	0	(1w)
Mongia	3	0	19	1	

India innings (target: 274 runs from 50 overs)			R	B	4	6
SR Tendulkar	c Younis Khan	b Shoaib Akhtar	98	75	12	1
V Sehwag	c Shahid Afridi	b Waqar Younis	21	14	3	1
*SC Ganguly	lbw	b Waqar Younis	0	1	0	0
M Kaif		b Shahid Afridi	35	60	5	0
+R Dravid	not out		44	76	2	0
Yuvraj Singh	not out		50	53	6	0
Extras	(b 1, lb 3, w 19, nb 5)		28			
Total	(4 wickets, 45.4 overs, 238 mins)		276			

DNB: D Mongia, A Kumble, Z Khan, J Srinath, A Nehra.
Fall of wickets: 1-53 (Sehwag, 5.4 ov), 2-53 (Ganguly, 5.5 ov), 3-155 (Kaif, 21.4 ov), 4-177 (Tendulkar, 27.4 ov).

Bowling	O	M	R	W	
Wasim Akram	10	0	48	0	(3nb, 1w)
Shoaib Akhtar	10	0	72	1	(7w)
Waqar Younis	8.4	0	71	2	(2w)
Shahid Afridi	9	0	45	1	
Abdul Razzaq	8	0	36	0	(2nb, 1w)

Australia v England, Pool A

At St. George's Park, Port Elizabeth, 2 March 2003 (50-overs)
Result: Australia won by 2 wickets. Points: Australia 4, England 0.
Toss: England. Umpires: Aleem Dar (Pak) and RB Tiffin (Zim).
TV Umpire: DL Orchard. Match Referee: Wasim Raja (Pak).
Man of the Match: AJ Bichel.

England innings (50 overs maximum)			R	B	4	6
ME Trescothick	c Martyn	b McGrath	37	36	6	1
NV Knight	c Martyn	b Bichel	30	33	4	0
MP Vaughan	c Gilchrist		2	5	0	0
*N Hussain		b Bichel	1	3	0	0
+AJ Stewart		b Bichel	46	92	1	0
PD Collingwood	c Gilchrist	b Bichel	10	16	0	1
A Flintoff	c Gilchrist	b Bichel	45	80	3	1
C White	not out		16	21	1	0
AF Giles	c Bevan	b Bichel	2	7	0	0
AR Caddick	not out		5	11	0	0
Extras	(lb 3, w 3, nb 4)		10			
Total	(8 wickets, 50 overs, 204 mins)		204			

DNB: JM Anderson.
Fall of wickets: 1-66 (Knight, 9.5 ov), 2-72 (Vaughan, 11.1 ov), 3-74 (Hussain, 11.6 ov), 4-74 (Trescothick, 12.2 ov), 5-87 (Collingwood, 17.5 ov), 6-177 (Flintoff, 42.3 ov), 7-180 (Stewart, 44.2 ov), 8-187 (Giles, 46.1 ov).

Bowling	O	M	R	W	
McGrath	9	2	41	1	(1w)
Lee	9	0	58	0	(4nb, 1w)
Bichel	10	0	20	7	
Hogg	10	1	28	0	(1w)
Lehmann	10	0	34	0	
Symonds	2	0	20	0	

Australia innings (target: 205 runs from 50 overs)			R	B	4	6
+AC Gilchrist	c Vaughan	b Caddick	22	18	5	0
ML Hayden	c Giles	b Caddick	1	4	0	0
*RT Ponting	c Giles	b Caddick	18	21	2	1
DR Martyn	lbw	b Caddick	0	3	0	0
DS Lehmann	c Stewart	b White	37	62	3	0
MG Bevan	not out		74	126	6	1
A Symonds		c & b Giles	0	5	0	0
GB Hogg	c Stewart	b Giles	1	3	0	0
B Lee	run out (White)		6	23	0	0
AJ Bichel	not out		34	36	3	1
Extras	(b 4, lb 4, w 4, nb 3)		15			
Total	(8 wickets, 49.4 overs, 218 mins)		208			

DNB: GD McGrath.
Fall of wickets: 1-15 (Hayden, 2.2 ov), 2-33 (Gilchrist, 4.2 ov), 3-33 (Martyn, 4.5 ov), 4-48 (Ponting, 8.4 ov), 5-111 (Lehmann, 28.2 ov), 6-112 (Symonds, 29.5 ov), 7-114 (Hogg, 31.5 ov), 8-135 (Lee, 37.4 ov).

Bowling	O	M	R	W	
Caddick	9	2	35	4	(3nb, 1w)
Anderson	9	0	66	0	(1w)
Flintoff	9.4	1	26	0	(1w)
White	10	2	21	1	
Giles	10	0	42	2	(1w)
Vaughan	2	0	10	0	

Canada v New Zealand, Pool B

At Willowmoore Park, Benoni, 3 March 2003 (50-overs)
Result: New Zealand won by 5 wickets. Points: New Zealand 4, Canada 0.
Toss: New Zealand. Umpires: AV Jayaprakash (Ind) and BG Jerling.
TV Umpire: TH Wijewardene (SL). Match Referee: DT Lindsay.
Man of the Match: JM Davison.

Canada innings (50 overs maximum)			R	B	4	6
I Maraj	lbw	b Bond	0	14	0	0
JM Davison	c Cairns	b Harris	75	62	9	4
N Ifill	c McCullum	b Oram	7	15	1	0
IS Billcliff	c Fleming	b Styris	8	24	0	0
NA de Groot	lbw	b Oram	17	49	3	0
*JV Harris	c McCullum	b Bond	26	39	3	0
+A Bagai		b Oram	1	2	0	0
AM Samad	lbw	b Bond	12	20	2	0
A Codrington		b Oram	7	17	1	0
A Patel		b Styris	25	29	3	0
BB Seebaran	not out		4	12	0	0
Extras	(lb 1, w 12, nb 1)		14			
Total	(all out, 47 overs, 197 mins)		196			

Fall of wickets: 1-21 (Maraj, 4.2 ov), 2-43 (Ifill, 7.6 ov), 3-80 (Billcliff, 14.5 ov), 4-98 (Davison, 22.4 ov), 5-123 (de Groot, 29.6 ov), 6-129 (Bagai, 31.1 ov), 7-152 (Samad, 36.3 ov), 8-153 (Harris, 38.1 ov), 9-173 (Codrington, 42.3 ov), 10-196 (Patel, 46.6 ov).

Bowling	O	M	R	W	
Bond	10	3	29	3	(3w)
Adams	6	0	38	0	
Oram	10	1	52	4	(7w)
Vettori	10	0	34	0	(1nb, 1w)
Styris	4	0	23	2	(1w)
Harris	7	1	19	1	

New Zealand innings (target: 197 runs from 50 overs)			R	B	4	6
CD McMillan	c Bagai	b Davison	14	13	3	0
*SP Fleming	run out (Maraj)		5	2	1	0
NJ Astle	st Bagai	b Davison	11	8	2	0
CL Cairns	c Maraj	b Davison	31	28	2	1
AR Adams	c sub (S Thuraisingam) b Seebaran		36	20	3	3
SB Styris	not out		54	38	4	2
CZ Harris	not out		38	29	4	0
Extras	(lb 3, w 5)		8			
Total	(5 wickets, 23 overs, 94 mins)		197			

DNB: JDP Oram, DL Vettori, +BB McCullum, SE Bond.
Fall of wickets: 1-19 (Fleming, 1.4 ov), 2-31 (Astle, 3.4 ov), 3-32 (McMillan, 3.6 ov), 4-97 (Adams, 10.4 ov), 5-114 (Cairns, 13.2 ov).

Bowling	O	M	R	W	
Patel	3	0	32	0	(3w)
Davison	10	0	61	3	(1w)
Codrington	2	0	33	0	(1w)
Seebaran	7	0	61	1	
Ifill	1	0	7	0	

Namibia v Netherlands, Pool A

At Goodyear Park, Bloemfontein, 3 March 2003 (50-overs)
Result: Netherlands won by 64 runs. Points: Netherlands 4, Namibia 0.
Toss: Netherlands. Umpires: DJ Harper (Aus) and Nadeem Ghauri (Pak).
TV Umpire: DB Hair (Aus). Match Referee: GR Viswanath (Ind).
Man of the Match: JF Kloppenburg.

Netherlands innings (50 overs maximum)			R	B	4	6
JF Kloppenburg	c van Schoor	b Snyman	121	142	6	4
E Schiferli		b van Vuuren	10	15	2	0
KJJ van Noortwijk	not out		134	129	11	3
B Zuiderent		b LJ Burger	5	7	0	0
TBM de Leede		b LJ Burger	0	1	0	0
*LP van Troost	not out		16	10	0	0
Extras	(b 4, lb 2, w 18, nb 4)		28			
Total	(4 wickets, 50 overs)		314			

DNB: DLS van Bunge, HJC Mol, JJ Esmeijer, +J Smits, Adeel Raja.
Fall of wickets: 1-25 (Schiferli, 5.4 ov), 2-253 (Kloppenburg, 43.6 ov), 3-270 (Zuiderent, 46.2 ov), 4-270 (de Leede, 46.3 ov).

Bowling	O	M	R	W	
Snyman	10	0	55	1	(4nb, 7w)
van Vuuren	10	1	63	1	(2w)
van Rooi	8	0	59	0	(5w)
LJ Burger	10	1	49	2	(2w)
AJ Burger	3	0	18	0	
Kotze	4	0	29	0	
SF Burger	5	0	35	0	(2w)

Namibia innings (target: 315 runs from 50 overs)			R	B	4	6
AJ Burger	c sub (RG Nijman)	b Kloppenburg	41	42	6	0
M Karg	c sub (RG Nijman)	b de Leede	41	51	4	1
D Keulder		b Kloppenburg	52	67	2	0
BG Murgatroyd	c Zuiderent	b Mol	52	62	4	0
*DB Kotze	lbw	b Adeel Raja	25	29	1	0
LJ Burger		b Kloppenburg	1	3	0	0
G Snyman	c de Leede	b Kloppenburg	0	1	0	0
SF Burger	st Smits	b Adeel Raja	6	6	1	0
+M van Schoor		b Adeel Raja	15	13	0	1
BO van Rooi	not out		9	6	1	0
RJ van Vuuren	c Mol	b Adeel Raja	0	2	0	0
Extras	(lb 5, w 2, nb 1)		8			
Total	(all out, 46.5 overs, 192 mins)		250			

Fall of wickets: 1-76 (AJ Burger, 13.4 ov), 2-87 (Karg, 16.4 ov), 3-179 (Keulder, 34.5 ov), 4-209 (Murgatroyd, 39.2 ov), 5-213 (LJ Burger, 40.2 ov), 6-213 (Snyman, 40.3 ov), 7-224 (SF Burger, 42.5 ov), 8-237 (Kotze, 44.3 ov), 9-250 (van Schoor, 46.3 ov), 10-250 (van Vuuren, 46.5 ov).

Bowling	O	M	R	W	
Schiferli	7	0	46	0	(1w)
Esmeijer	7	0	43	0	(1nb, 1w)
de Leede	8	0	33	1	
Kloppenburg	10	0	42	4	
Adeel Raja	8.5	0	42	4	
Mol	6	0	39	1	

South Africa v Sri Lanka, Pool B
At Kingsmead, Durban (day/night), 3 March 2003 (50-overs)
Result: Match tied (D/L method). Points: South Africa 2, Sri Lanka 2.
Toss: Sri Lanka. Umpires: SA Bucknor (WI) and S Venkataraghavan (Ind).
TV Umpire: P Willey (Eng). Match Referee: CH Lloyd (WI).
Man of the Match: MS Atapattu.

Sri Lanka innings (50 overs maximum)			R	B	4	6
MS Atapattu	c sub (RJ Peterson)	b Hall	124	129	18	0
*ST Jayasuriya	run out (Kirsten)		16	30	1	0
HP Tillakaratne	c Boucher	b Kallis	14	28	2	0
DPMD Jayawardene	c Boucher	b Hall	1	11	0	0
PA de Silva	c Smith	b Ntini	73	78	6	2
RP Arnold		b Pollock	8	11	0	0
+KC Sangakkara	c Pollock	b Kallis	6	8	0	0
WPUJC Vaas	run out (Boucher)		3	4	0	0
M Muralitharan		b Kallis	4	3	1	0
CRD Fernando	not out		1	3	0	0
Extras	(lb 2, w 11, nb 5)		18			
Total	(9 wickets, 50 overs, 210 mins)		268			

DNB: PW Gunaratne.
Fall of wickets: 1-37 (Jayasuriya, 8.6 ov), 2-77 (Tillakaratne, 17.4 ov), 3-90 (Jayawardene, 22.1 ov), 4-242 (Atapattu, 44.5 ov), 5-243 (de Silva, 45.1 ov), 6-258 (Sangakkara, 47.5 ov), 7-261 (Arnold, 48.4 ov), 8-266 (Muralitharan, 49.2 ov), 9-268 (Vaas, 49.6 ov).

Bowling	O	M	R	W	
Pollock	10	1	48	1	(1nb, 2w)
Ntini	10	0	49	1	(2nb, 3w)
Zondeki	6	0	35	0	(3w)
Kallis	10	0	41	3	(1w)
Hall	10	0	62	2	(1nb, 1w)
Klusener	4	0	31	0	(1nb, 1w)

South Africa innings (target: 230 runs from 45 overs)			R	B	4	6
GC Smith	c Gunaratne	b de Silva	35	34	5	0
HH Gibbs		b Muralitharan	73	88	7	2
G Kirsten		b de Silva	8	21	0	0
JH Kallis		b Jayasuriya	16	19	1	0
HH Dippenaar	lbw	b Jayasuriya	8	15	0	0
+MV Boucher	not out		45	50	2	1
*SM Pollock	run out (Sangakkara/Muralitharan)		25	37	1	0
L Klusener	not out		1	8	0	0
Extras	(lb 4, w 12, nb 2)		18			
Total	(6 wickets, 45 overs, 189 mins)		229			

DNB: M Ntini, M Zondeki, AJ Hall.
Fall of wickets: 1-65 (Smith, 11.1 ov), 2-91 (Kirsten, 17.2 ov), 3-124 (Kallis, 23.1 ov), 4-149 (Gibbs, 28.6 ov), 5-149 (Dippenaar, 29.1 ov), 6-212 (Pollock, 42.3 ov).

Bowling	O	M	R	W	
Vaas	7	1	33	0	(1nb)
Gunaratne	6	0	26	0	
Fernando	1	0	14	0	(1nb)
de Silva	8	0	36	2	(1w)
Arnold	4	0	16	0	(1w)
Muralitharan	9	0	51	1	(1w)
Jayasuriya	10	0	49	2	(3w)

Zimbabwe v Pakistan, Pool A
At Queens Sports Club, Bulawayo, 4 March 2003 (50-overs)
Result: No result. Points: Zimbabwe 2, Pakistan 2.
Toss: Pakistan. Umpires: BF Bowden (NZ) and EAR de Silva (SL).
TV Umpire: RE Koertzen (SA). Match Referee: RS Madugalle (SL).
Man of the Match: No Award.

Pakistan innings (38 overs maximum)			R	B	4	6
Saeed Anwar	not out		40	45	3	1
Saleem Elahi	lbw	b Hondo	4	3	1	0
Yousuf Youhana	c Taibu	b Streak	17	27	1	0
Inzamam-ul-Haq	c Whittall	b Ervine	3	8	0	0
Younis Khan	not out		0	0	0	0
Extras	(b 1, lb 6, w 2)		9			
Total	(3 wickets, 14 overs, 64 mins)		73			

DNB: Azhar Mahmood, +Rashid Latif, Mohammad Sami, Wasim Akram, *Waqar Younis, Shoaib Akhtar.
Fall of wickets: 1-4 (Saleem Elahi, 1.3 ov), 2-55 (Yousuf Youhana, 10.5 ov), 3-72 (Inzamam-ul-Haq, 13.3 ov).

Bowling	O	M	R	W	
Streak	7	1	25	1	(2w)
Hondo	4	0	22	1	
Ervine	3	0	19	1	

Zimbabwe team: DD Ebrahim, CB Wishart, A Flower, GW Flower, GJ Whittall, +T Taibu, AM Blignaut, *HH Streak, DA Marillier, SM Ervine, DT Hondo.

Kenya v West Indies, Pool B
At De Beers Diamond Oval, Kimberley, 4 March 2003 (50-overs)
Result: West Indies won by 142 runs. Points: West Indies 4, Kenya 0.
Toss: West Indies. Umpires: DR Shepherd (Eng) and SJA Taufel (Aus).
TV Umpire: KC Barbour (Zim). Match Referee: MJ Procter.
Man of the Match: VC Drakes.

West Indies innings (50 overs maximum)			R	B	4	6
CH Gayle	c DO Obuya	b Angara	119	151	8	2
S Chanderpaul	c Angara	b CO Obuya	66	72	7	2
BC Lara	c DO Obuya	b Tikolo	10	30	0	0
MN Samuels	c Patel	b Odumbe	14	17	0	1
RL Powell	c Otieno	b Odumbe	8	6	1	0
*CL Hooper	st Otieno	b Angara	6	6	0	0
WW Hinds		b Suji	10	9	1	0
+RD Jacobs	not out		9	8	0	0
VC Drakes	not out		1	1	0	0
Extras	(w 3)		3			
Total	(7 wickets, 50 overs, 191 mins)		246			

DNB: M Dillon, JJC Lawson.
Fall of wickets: 1-122 (Chanderpaul, 28.1 ov), 2-158 (Lara, 37.1 ov), 3-182 (Samuels, 41.3 ov), 4-196 (Powell, 43.6 ov), 5-222 (Gayle, 46.4 ov), 6-224 (Hooper, 46.6 ov), 7-245 (Hinds, 49.5 ov).

Bowling	O	M	R	W	
Suji	10	1	38	1	
Angara	7	0	53	2	(2w)
Ongondo	5	0	17	0	
Odumbe	10	0	62	2	
CO Obuya	10	0	48	1	
Tikolo	8	0	28	1	

Kenya innings (target: 247 runs from 50 overs)			R	B	4	6
+KO Otieno	c Dillon	b Drakes	3	16	0	0
RD Shah	c Gayle	b Dillon	12	22	1	0
BJ Patel	c Lara	b Drakes	11	30	1	0
*SO Tikolo	lbw	b Drakes	12	27	2	0
HS Modi	c Jacobs	b Drakes	0	2	0	0
MO Odumbe	hit wicket	b Lawson	0	2	0	0
DO Obuya	c Powell	b Drakes	4	6	1	0
CO Obuya	c Powell	b Lawson	13	35	1	0
PJ Ongondo		b Powell	24	43	1	0
MA Suji	c Chanderpaul	b Hinds	13	32	0	0
JO Angara	not out		0	2	0	0
Extras	(lb 3, w 8, nb 1)		12			
Total	(all out, 35.5 overs, 164 mins)		104			

Fall of wickets: 1-8 (Otieno, 3.6 ov), 2-26 (Shah, 8.4 ov), 3-34 (Patel, 13.5 ov), 4-34 (Modi, 13.6 ov), 5-43 (Tikolo, 15.6 ov), 6-43 (Odumbe, 16.1 ov), 7-54 (DO Obuya, 19.1 ov), 8-62 (CO Obuya, 24.5 ov), 9-102 (Ongondo, 34.4 ov), 10-104 (Suji, 35.5 ov).

Bowling	O	M	R	W	
Dillon	10	1	31	1	(3w)
Drakes	10	2	33	5	(1nb)
Lawson	8	0	16	2	(4w)
Powell	4	2	8	1	
Chanderpaul	2	0	6	0	
Hinds	1.5	0	7	1	(1w)

SUPER SIX
Australia v Sri Lanka

At SuperSport Park, Centurion, 7 March 2003 (50-overs)
Result: Australia won by 96 runs. Points: Australia 4, Sri Lanka 0.
Toss: Australia. Umpires: BF Bowden (NZ) and DR Shepherd (Eng).
TV Umpire: BG Jerling. Match Referee: MJ Procter.
Man of the Match: RT Ponting.

Australia innings (50 overs maximum)			R	B	4	6
+AC Gilchrist	run out (Vaas)		99	88	14	2
ML Hayden	c Tillakaratne	b Muralitharan	22	34	3	0
*RT Ponting	c Sangakkara	b Fernando	114	109	8	4
DR Martyn		b Fernando	52	58	1	0
DS Lehmann	c de Silva	b Fernando	10	10	1	0
IJ Harvey	not out		5	3	1	0
MG Bevan	not out		1	1	0	0
Extras	(lb 4, w 5, nb 7)		16			
Total	(5 wickets, 50 overs, 205 mins)		319			

DNB: GB Hogg, B Lee, AJ Bichel, GD McGrath.
Fall of wickets: 1-75 (Hayden, 12.2 ov), 2-181 (Gilchrist, 29.5 ov), 3-293 (Ponting, 45.4 ov), 4-313 (Martyn, 49.1 ov), 5-314 (Lehmann, 49.3 ov).

Bowling	O	M	R	W	
Vaas	8	0	59	0	(2nb, 1w)
Gunaratne	6	0	46	0	
de Silva	5	0	36	0	
Muralitharan	10	0	47	1	(1nb, 1w)
Arnold	2	0	21	0	(1w)
Fernando	9	0	47	3	(1w)
Jayasuriya	10	0	59	0	(1w)

Sri Lanka innings (target: 320 runs from 50 overs)			R	B	4	6
MS Atapattu		c & b Lee	16	24	3	0
*ST Jayasuriya	retired hurt		1	5	0	0
HP Tillakaratne		b McGrath	21	41	3	0
DPMD Jayawardene	c Gilchrist	b Lee	0	3	0	0
PA de Silva		c & b Hogg	92	94	9	4
RP Arnold	lbw	b Lee	1	6	0	0
+KC Sangakkara	run out (Hogg)		20	38	2	0
WPUJC Vaas	lbw	b Hogg	21	45	2	0
M Muralitharan	c Lee	b Lehmann	4	5	0	0
CRD Fernando	lbw	b McGrath	9	13	2	0
PW Gunaratne	not out		15	15	3	0
Extras	(b 6, lb 8, w 6, nb 3)		23			
Total	(all out, 47.4 overs, 205 mins)		223			

Fall of wickets: 1-42 (Atapattu, 9.5 ov), 2-46 (Jayawardene, 11.2 ov), 3-47 (Tillakaratne, 12.3 ov), 4-48 (Arnold, 13.3 ov), 5-100 (Sangakkara, 26.1 ov), 6-144 (Vaas, 36.4 ov), 7-149 (Muralitharan, 37.4 ov), 8-203 (de Silva, 44.1 ov), 9-223 (Fernando, 47.4 ov). NB: ST Jayasuriya retired hurt at 6/0.

Bowling	O	M	R	W	
McGrath	9.4	1	25	2	(3w)
Lee	10	1	52	3	(3nb, 2w)
Harvey	7	0	29	0	
Bichel	7	1	32	0	(1w)
Hogg	9	1	45	2	
Lehmann	5	0	26	1	

SUPER SIX
India v Kenya

At Newlands, Cape Town (day/night), 7 March 2003 (50-overs)
Result: India won by 6 wickets. Points: India 4, Kenya 0.
Toss: Kenya. Umpires: DJ Harper (Aus) and P Willey (Eng).
TV Umpire: SJA Taufel (Aus). Match Referee: Wasim Raja (Pak).
Man of the Match: SC Ganguly.

Kenya innings (50 overs maximum)			R	B	4	6
+KO Otieno		b Harbhajan Singh	79	134	6	2
RD Shah	run out (Khan)		34	52	3	0
*SO Tikolo	c Khan	b Harbhajan Singh	3	11	0	0
TM Odoyo	lbw	b Mongia	32	55	2	0
MO Odumbe	not out		34	24	2	0
CO Obuya	c Mongia	b Srinath	8	11	0	0
PJ Ongondo	c Tendulkar	b Srinath	8	7	1	0
MA Suji	not out		11	6	1	0
Extras	(b 4, lb 8, w 4)		16			
Total	(6 wickets, 50 overs, 210 mins)		225			

DNB: AO Suji, BJ Patel, HS Modi.
Fall of wickets: 1-75 (Shah, 20.6 ov), 2-81 (Tikolo, 23.2 ov), 3-157 (Otieno, 39.6 ov), 4-165 (Odoyo, 42.4 ov), 5-191 (Obuya, 46.1 ov), 6-206 (Ongondo, 48.1 ov).

Bowling	O	M	R	W	
Khan	10	1	53	0	(2w)
Srinath	10	0	43	2	(1w)
Nehra	10	2	30	0	(1w)
Harbhajan Singh	10	0	41	2	
Mongia	8	0	37	1	
Yuvraj Singh	2	0	9	0	

India innings (target: 226 runs from 50 overs)			R	B	4	6
V Sehwag	c Tikolo	b Odoyo	3	8	0	0
SR Tendulkar	c AO Suji	b MA Suji	5	12	1	0
*SC Ganguly	not out		107	120	11	2
M Kaif	lbw	b Odoyo	5	13	1	0
+R Dravid		c & b Obuya	32	73	3	0
Yuvraj Singh	not out		58	64	7	0
Extras	(lb 5, w 8, nb 3)		16			
Total	(4 wickets, 47.5 overs, 205 mins)		226			

DNB: D Mongia, Harbhajan Singh, Z Khan, A Nehra, J Srinath.
Fall of wickets: 1-5 (Sehwag, 1.5 ov), 2-11 (Tendulkar, 4.3 ov), 3-24 (Kaif, 9.2 ov), 4-108 (Dravid, 29.3 ov).

Bowling	O	M	R	W	
MA Suji	10	3	27	1	
Odoyo	7	0	27	2	(1nb)
Ongondo	5	0	31	0	(1w)
AO Suji	7	0	25	0	(1nb)
Obuya	9.5	2	50	1	(1nb, 3w)
Odumbe	3	0	25	0	
Tikolo	6	0	36	0	

SUPER SIX
New Zealand v Zimbabwe

At Goodyear Park, Bloemfontein, 8 March 2003 (50-overs)
Result: New Zealand won by 6 wickets. Points: New Zealand 4, Zimbabwe 0.
Toss: Zimbabwe. Umpires: DB Hair (Aus) and RE Koertzen.
TV Umpire: EAR de Silva (SL). Match Referee: GR Viswanath (Ind).
Man of the Match: NJ Astle.

Zimbabwe innings (50 overs maximum)			R	B	4	6
CB Wishart	c Styris	b Cairns	30	50	4	0
DD Ebrahim		b Adams	0	1	0	0
A Flower	run out (Astle)		37	61	5	0
GW Flower	c Cairns	b Oram	1	6	0	0
GJ Whittall	c McCullum	b Cairns	0	2	0	0
+T Taibu	lbw	b Harris	53	79	3	1
AM Blignaut	run out (McCullum/Vettori)		4	5	0	0
*HH Streak	not out		72	84	6	2
SM Ervine	not out		31	14	4	1
Extras	(lb 9, w 13, nb 2)		24			
Total	(7 wickets, 50 overs, 204 mins)		252			

DNB: BA Murphy, DT Hondo.
Fall of wickets: 1-5 (Ebrahim, 1.1 ov), 2-59 (Wishart, 14.3 ov), 3-63 (GW Flower, 15.5 ov), 4-65 (Whittall, 16.6 ov), 5-98 (A Flower, 21.6 ov), 6-106 (Blignaut, 23.6 ov), 7-174 (Taibu, 43.5 ov).

Bowling	O	M	R	W	
Bond	10	1	37	0	(2w)
Adams	5	0	54	1	(1nb, 5w)
Oram	10	4	28	1	(1w)
Cairns	4	0	16	2	(1w)
Vettori	10	0	52	0	
Harris	10	0	45	1	(1nb)
Astle	1	0	11	0	

New Zealand innings (target: 253 runs from 50 overs)			R	B	4	6
CD McMillan	c Taibu	b Hondo	8	16	1	0
*SP Fleming	lbw	b Blignaut	46	42	10	0
NJ Astle	not out		102	122	11	0
SB Styris	c sub (TJ Friend)	b Blignaut	13	22	1	0
CL Cairns		b Ervine	54	73	3	2
CZ Harris	not out		14	10	3	0
Extras	(lb 5, w 10, nb 1)		16			
Total	(4 wickets, 47.2 overs, 213 mins)		253			

DNB: +BB McCullum, JDP Oram, AR Adams, DL Vettori, SE Bond.
Fall of wickets: 1-27 (McMillan, 5.6 ov), 2-72 (Fleming, 13.3 ov), 3-97 (Styris, 19.2 ov), 4-218 (Cairns, 43.6 ov).

Bowling	O	M	R	W	
Streak	10	0	59	0	(1w)
Hondo	8.2	0	52	1	(2w)
Blignaut	10	0	41	2	(3w)
GW Flower	10	0	33	0	(1nb, 1w)
Whittall	3	0	19	0	
Ervine	6	0	44	1	(1w)

SUPER SIX
India v Sri Lanka

At New Wanderers Stadium, Johannesburg, 10 March 2003 (50-overs)
Result: India won by 183 runs. Points: India 4, Sri Lanka 0.
Toss: Sri Lanka. Umpires: DR Shepherd (Eng) and SJA Taufel (Aus).
TV Umpire: DJ Harper (Aus). Match Referee: CH Lloyd (WI).
Man of the Match: J Srinath.

India innings (50 overs maximum)			R	B	4	6
SR Tendulkar	c Sangakkara	b de Silva	97	120	7	1
V Sehwag	c de Silva	b Muralitharan	66	76	5	3
*SC Ganguly		b Vaas	48	53	2	2
M Kaif		b Muralitharan	19	24	1	0
Yuvraj Singh		b Vaas	5	6	0	0
+R Dravid	not out		18	12	2	0
D Mongia	c de Silva	b Muralitharan	9	7	0	1
Harbhajan Singh	not out		7	5	1	0
Extras	(b 4, lb 9, w 7, nb 3)		23			
Total	(6 wickets, 50 overs, 210 mins)		292			

DNB: Z Khan, A Nehra, J Srinath.
Fall of wickets: 1-153 (Sehwag, 26.2 ov), 2-214 (Tendulkar, 38.5 ov), 3-243 (Ganguly, 43.4 ov), 4-251 (Yuvraj Singh, 45.2 ov), 5-265 (Kaif, 46.5 ov), 6-277 (Mongia, 48.3 ov).

Bowling	O	M	R	W	
Vaas	10	2	34	2	(1nb)
Nissanka	6	0	49	0	(5w)
Fernando	10	1	61	0	(1nb, 1w)
Muralitharan	10	0	46	3	
Jayasuriya	3	0	27	0	
de Silva	6	0	32	1	(1w)
Arnold	5	0	30	0	(1nb)

Sri Lanka innings (target: 293 runs from 50 overs)			R	B	4	6
MS Atapattu	c Kaif	b Srinath	0	7	0	0
*ST Jayasuriya	c Kaif	b Srinath	12	19	1	0
J Mubarak	c Dravid	b Srinath	0	2	0	0
DPMD Jayawardene	lbw	b Khan	0	4	0	0
PA de Silva	lbw	b Srinath	0	3	0	0
+KC Sangakkara	c Yuvraj Singh	b Nehra	30	33	4	0
RP Arnold	lbw	b Khan	8	28	1	0
WPUJC Vaas	c Tendulkar	b Nehra	9	15	1	0
RAP Nissanka	c Kaif	b Nehra	0	4	0	0
CRD Fernando	not out		13	10	2	0
M Muralitharan	c Kaif	b Nehra	16	14	3	0
Extras	(b 1, lb 5, w 14, nb 1)		21			
Total	(all out, 23 overs, 123 mins)		109			

Fall of wickets: 1-2 (Atapattu, 1.3 ov), 2-2 (Mubarak, 1.5 ov), 3-3 (Jayawardene, 2.4 ov), 4-15 (de Silva, 3.4 ov), 5-40 (Jayasuriya, 7.6 ov), 6-59 (Sangakkara, 14.5 ov), 7-75 (Arnold, 17.2 ov), 8-78 (Vaas, 18.4 ov), 9-78 (Nissanka, 18.6 ov), 10-109 (Muralitharan, 22.6 ov).

Bowling	O	M	R	W	
Khan	7	0	33	2	(1nb, 5w)
Srinath	9	1	35	4	(2w)
Nehra	7	1	35	4	(1w)

SUPER SIX
Australia v New Zealand

At St. George's Park, Port Elizabeth, 11 March 2003 (50-overs)
Result: Australia won by 96 runs. Points: Australia 4, New Zealand 0.
Toss: New Zealand. Umpires: SA Bucknor (WI) and EAR de Silva (SL).
TV Umpire: BG Jerling. Match Referee: RS Madugalle (SL).
Man of the Match: SE Bond.

Australia innings (50 overs maximum)			R	B	4	6
+AC Gilchrist	lbw	b Bond	18	20	2	0
ML Hayden	c McCullum	b Bond	1	4	0	0
*RT Ponting	c Fleming	b Bond	6	20	0	0
DR Martyn	c McCullum	b Bond	31	53	3	0
DS Lehmann	c Astle	b Adams	4	9	1	0
MG Bevan	c Vincent	b Oram	56	94	4	1
GB Hogg	lbw	b Bond	0	1	0	0
IJ Harvey		b Bond	2	11	0	0
AJ Bichel	c Cairns	b Oram	64	83	7	1
B Lee	not out		15	6	0	2
GD McGrath	not out		3	2	0	0
Extras	(lb 1, w 4, nb 3)		8			
Total	(9 wickets, 50 overs, 212 mins)		208			

Fall of wickets: 1-17 (Hayden, 2.2 ov), 2-24 (Gilchrist, 4.5 ov), 3-31 (Ponting, 8.4 ov), 4-47 (Lehmann, 12.3 ov), 5-80 (Martyn, 24.1 ov), 6-80 (Hogg, 24.2 ov), 7-84 (Harvey, 26.3 ov), 8-181 (Bevan, 47.5 ov), 9-192 (Bichel, 49.1 ov).

Bowling	O	M	R	W	
Bond	10	2	23	6	(1nb, 1w)
Adams	9	0	46	1	(1nb, 1w)
Vettori	10	1	40	0	
Oram	7	0	48	2	(1nb)
Harris	10	1	24	0	
Styris	3	0	18	0	(1w)
Astle	1	0	8	0	

New Zealand innings (target: 209 runs from 50 overs)			R	B	4	6
DL Vettori	c Gilchrist	b McGrath	10	9	1	0
*SP Fleming	c Gilchrist	b Lee	48	70	7	0
NJ Astle	c Ponting	b McGrath	0	3	0	0
SB Styris	lbw	b McGrath	3	6	0	0
CL Cairns	c Lee	b Bichel	16	25	2	1
L Vincent	c Martyn	b Harvey	7	20	1	0
CZ Harris	not out		15	24	0	0
+BB McCullum	lbw	b Lee	1	7	0	0
JDP Oram		b Lee	0	1	0	0
AR Adams		b Lee	0	6	0	0
SE Bond		c & b Lee	3	10	0	0
Extras	(lb 4, w 5)		9			
Total	(all out, 30.1 overs, 147 mins)		112			

Fall of wickets: 1-14 (Vettori, 2.3 ov), 2-14 (Astle, 2.6 ov), 3-33 (Styris, 6.1 ov), 4-66 (Cairns, 14.1 ov), 5-84 (Vincent, 19.5 ov), 6-102 (Fleming, 24.5 ov), 7-104 (McCullum, 26.5 ov), 8-104 (Oram, 26.6 ov), 9-108 (Adams, 28.2 ov), 10-112 (Bond, 30.1 ov).

Bowling	O	M	R	W	
McGrath	6	1	29	3	(3w)
Lee	9.1	2	42	5	(1w)
Harvey	6	3	11	1	
Bichel	5	0	15	1	(1w)
Hogg	4	0	11	0	

SUPER SIX
Kenya v Zimbabwe

At Goodyear Park, Bloemfontein, 12 March 2003 (50-overs)
Result: Kenya won by 7 wickets. Points: Kenya 4, Zimbabwe 0.
Toss: Zimbabwe. Umpires: Aleem Dar (Pak) and S Venkataraghavan (Ind).
TV Umpire: BF Bowden (NZ). Match Referee: Wasim Raja (Pak).
Man of the Match: MA Suji.

Zimbabwe innings (50 overs maximum)			R	B	4	6
CB Wishart	c Otieno	b MA Suji	5	7	0	0
ADR Campbell	lbw	b MA Suji	7	25	0	0
A Flower		b Odoyo	63	101	5	0
GW Flower	c Otieno	b MA Suji	7	15	1	0
+T Taibu	c Otieno	b Obuya	3	18	0	0
DD Ebrahim	st Otieno	b Obuya	13	24	1	0
AM Blignaut	run out (Odumbe/Otieno)		4	8	0	0
*HH Streak	c Shah	b Obuya	0	4	0	0
DA Marillier		b Tikolo	21	39	2	0
HK Olonga	c Odumbe	b Tikolo	3	12	0	0
DT Hondo	not out		0	14	0	0
Extras	(lb 1, w 4, nb 2)		7			
Total	(all out, 44.1 overs, 190 mins)		133			

Fall of wickets: 1-8 (Wishart, 2.2 ov), 2-26 (Campbell, 8.1 ov), 3-45 (GW Flower, 14.4 ov), 4-66 (Taibu, 20.5 ov), 5-85 (Ebrahim, 26.2 ov), 6-95 (Blignaut, 29.2 ov), 7-97 (Streak, 30.5 ov), 8-114 (A Flower, 35.2 ov), 9-129 (Olonga, 40.2 ov), 10-133 (Marillier, 44.1 ov).

Bowling	O	M	R	W	
MA Suji	8	2	19	3	(1w)
Odoyo	10	0	43	1	(2nb, 1w)
Ongondo	5	2	16	0	(1w)
Obuya	10	0	32	3	
Karim	9	0	20	0	
Tikolo	2.1	0	2	2	(1w)

Kenya innings (target: 134 runs from 50 overs)			R	B	4	6
+KO Otieno	lbw	b Olonga	19	50	2	0
RD Shah	run out (Blignaut)		14	27	2	0
*SO Tikolo	c Streak	b Blignaut	2	7	0	0
TM Odoyo	not out		43	60	9	0
MO Odumbe	not out		38	20	8	0
Extras	(lb 4, w 6, nb 9)		19			
Total	(3 wickets, 26 overs, 133 mins)		135			

DNB: HS Modi, CO Obuya, AO Suji, MA Suji, PJ Ongondo, AY Karim.
Fall of wickets: 1-24 (Shah, 7.3 ov), 2-33 (Tikolo, 9.4 ov), 3-62 (Otieno, 16.6 ov).

Bowling	O	M	R	W	
Streak	6	0	24	0	(1w)
Blignaut	9	1	36	1	(4w)
Olonga	4	0	21	1	(8nb, 1w)
Hondo	3	1	14	0	
GW Flower	3	0	27	0	
Marillier	1	0	9	0	

SUPER SIX
India v New Zealand

At SuperSport Park, Centurion, 14 March 2003 (50-overs)
Result: India won by 7 wickets. Points: India 4, New Zealand 0.
Toss: India. Umpires: DJ Harper (Aus) and P Willey (Eng).
TV Umpire: DB Hair (Aus). Match Referee: RS Madugalle (SL).
Man of the Match: Z Khan.

New Zealand innings (50 overs maximum)			R	B	4	6
CD McMillan	c Harbhajan Singh	b Khan	0	2	0	0
*SP Fleming	c Tendulkar	b Srinath	30	59	4	0
NJ Astle	lbw	b Khan	0	1	0	0
SB Styris	c Dravid	b Nehra	15	21	1	0
+BB McCullum		b Khan	4	16	0	0
CL Cairns	c Khan	b Harbhajan Singh	20	26	1	0
CZ Harris	lbw	b Khan	17	37	2	0
JDP Oram		b Sehwag	23	54	1	0
DL Vettori	c Ganguly	b Harbhajan Singh	13	40	2	0
DR Tuffey		c & b Mongia	11	13	2	0
SE Bond	not out		0	6	0	0
Extras	(lb 5, w 4, nb 4)		13			
Total	(all out, 45.1 overs, 187 mins)		146			

Fall of wickets: 1-0 (McMillan, 0.2 ov), 2-0 (Astle, 0.3 ov), 3-38 (Styris, 8.1 ov), 4-47 (McCullum, 13.4 ov), 5-60 (Fleming, 17.3 ov), 6-88 (Cairns, 25.3 ov), 7-96 (Harris, 28.2 ov), 8-129 (Vettori, 39.6 ov), 9-144 (Oram, 43.2 ov), 10-146 (Tuffey, 45.1 ov).

Bowling	O	M	R	W	
Khan	8	0	42	4	(2nb, 1w)
Srinath	8	0	20	1	(3w)
Nehra	10	3	24	1	(1nb)
Harbhajan Singh	10	2	28	2	
Ganguly	2	0	4	0	
Tendulkar	5	0	20	0	(1nb)
Sehwag	2	1	3	1	
Mongia	0.1	0	1	1	

India innings (target: 147 runs from 50 overs)			R	B	4	6
V Sehwag	c Styris	b Bond	1	6	0	0
SR Tendulkar	c Oram	b Tuffey	15	16	3	0
*SC Ganguly		b Bond	3	6	0	0
M Kaif	not out		68	129	8	0
+R Dravid	not out		53	89	7	0
Extras	(w 8, nb 2)		10			
Total	(3 wickets, 40.4 overs, 168 mins)		150			

DNB: Yuvraj Singh, D Mongia, J Srinath, A Nehra, Z Khan, Harbhajan Singh.
Fall of wickets: 1-4 (Sehwag, 1.6 ov), 2-9 (Ganguly, 3.5 ov), 3-21 (Tendulkar, 4.5 ov).

Bowling	O	M	R	W	
Tuffey	10	1	41	1	(1nb, 4w)
Bond	8	2	23	2	(1nb, 2w)
Oram	5	0	20	0	
Vettori	5	0	18	0	
McMillan	2	1	4	0	
Styris	6.4	0	29	0	(1w)
Harris	4	1	15	0	

SUPER SIX
Sri Lanka v Zimbabwe

At Buffalo Park, East London, 15 March 2003 (50-overs)
Result: Sri Lanka won by 74 runs. Points: Sri Lanka 4, Zimbabwe 0.
Toss: Sri Lanka. Umpires: BG Jerling and RE Koertzen.
TV Umpire: S Venkataraghavan (Ind). Match Referee: CH Lloyd (WI).
Man of the Match: MS Atapattu.

Sri Lanka innings (50 overs maximum)			R	B	4	6
MS Atapattu	not out		103	127	7	0
*ST Jayasuriya	c Taibu	b Streak	22	44	2	0
DA Gunawardene		c & b Marillier	41	62	2	0
PA de Silva	c Taibu	b Ervine	25	31	2	0
+KC Sangakkara	c GW Flower	b Streak	35	25	4	0
RP Arnold	c GW Flower	b Hondo	1	3	0	0
WPUJC Vaas	not out		11	8	1	0
Extras	(lb 3, w 15)		18			
Total	(5 wickets, 50 overs, 208 mins)		256			

DNB: HP Tillakaratne, M Muralitharan, CRD Fernando, PW Gunaratne.

Fall of wickets: 1-41 (Jayasuriya, 12.2 ov), 2-124 (Gunawardene, 30.2 ov), 3-175 (de Silva, 40.2 ov), 4-227 (Sangakkara, 46.4 ov), 5-233 (Arnold, 47.4 ov).

Bowling	O	M	R	W	
Streak	10	0	40	2	
Blignaut	8	0	40	0	(4w)
Friend	2	0	13	0	(1w)
Hondo	5	0	36	1	(2w)
GW Flower	10	0	44	0	(1w)
Marillier	10	0	43	1	
Matsikenyeri	2	0	13	0	(1w)
Ervine	3	0	24	1	(2w)

Zimbabwe innings (target: 257 runs from 50 overs)			R	B	4	6
CB Wishart		b Jayasuriya	43	71	4	0
DA Marillier	c Jayasuriya	b Gunaratne	19	14	2	0
TJ Friend		b Gunaratne	21	20	4	0
A Flower	lbw	b de Silva	38	51	1	0
GW Flower		c & b Jayasuriya	31	52	4	0
+T Taibu		b Muralitharan	2	10	0	0
AM Blignaut	c de Silva	b Fernando	1	5	0	0
SM Ervine		b Vaas	12	19	1	0
*HH Streak	c Atapattu	b Jayasuriya	2	7	0	0
S Matsikenyeri	not out		1	3	0	0
DT Hondo		b Vaas	0	2	0	0
Extras	(lb 5, w 4, nb 3)		12			
Total	(all out, 41.5 overs, 172 mins)		182			

Fall of wickets: 1-36 (Marillier, 5.2 ov), 2-68 (Friend, 11.3 ov), 3-111 (Wishart, 21.3 ov), 4-140 (A Flower, 28.3 ov), 5-150 (Taibu, 32.1 ov), 6-151 (Blignaut, 33.2 ov), 7-178 (Ervine, 39.2 ov), 8-181 (Streak, 40.4 ov), 9-181 (GW Flower, 40.6 ov), 10-182 (Hondo, 41.5 ov).

Bowling	O	M	R	W	
Vaas	9.5	0	46	2	(3nb)
Gunaratne	7	0	33	2	
de Silva	9	1	36	1	(1w)
Muralitharan	7	0	22	1	
Jayasuriya	6	0	30	3	(1w)
Fernando	3	0	10	1	

SUPER SIX
Australia v Kenya

At Kingsmead, Durban (day/night), 15 March 2003 (50-overs)
Result: Australia won by 5 wickets. Points: Australia 4, Kenya 0.
Toss: Australia. Umpires: BF Bowden (NZ) and SA Bucknor (WI).
TV Umpire: EAR de Silva (SL). Match Referee: MJ Procter.
Man of the Match: AY Karim.

Kenya innings (50 overs maximum)			R	B	4	6
+KO Otieno		b Lee	1	12	0	0
RD Shah	c sub (NM Hauritz)	b Hogg	46	83	6	0
BJ Patel	c Ponting	b Lee	0	1	0	0
DO Obuya		b Lee	0	1	0	0
*SO Tikolo	c Bichel	b Lehmann	51	100	5	0
HS Modi	not out		39	74	2	0
CO Obuya	c Gilchrist	b Bichel	3	6	0	0
PJ Ongondo	c Gilchrist	b Bichel	1	3	0	0
AO Suji	c Ponting	b Lehmann	1	2	0	0
MA Suji	not out		15	19	0	1
Extras	(lb 10, w 6, nb 1)		17			
Total	(8 wickets, 50 overs, 212 mins)		174			

DNB: AY Karim.

Fall of wickets: 1-3 (Otieno, 3.4 ov), 2-3 (Patel, 3.5 ov), 3-3 (DO Obuya, 3.6 ov), 4-82 (Shah, 26.1 ov), 5-131 (Tikolo, 39.6 ov), 6-139 (CO Obuya, 42.2 ov), 7-141 (Ongondo, 42.6 ov), 8-144 (AO Suji, 43.5 ov).

Bowling	O	M	R	W	
McGrath	10	1	32	0	(3w)
Lee	8	3	14	3	(1nb)
Bichel	9	1	42	2	(2w)
Hogg	10	1	31	1	
Harvey	7	0	23	0	(1w)
Lehmann	6	0	22	2	

NB: Lee took hat-trick (KO Otieno, BJ Patel, DO Obuya).

Australia innings (target: 175 runs from 50 overs)			R	B	4	6
+AC Gilchrist	c DO Obuya	b Ongondo	67	43	9	3
ML Hayden	c sub (JO Angara)	b Ongondo	20	14	5	0
*RT Ponting	lbw	b Karim	18	30	2	0
A Symonds	not out		33	49	5	1
DS Lehmann	c DO Obuya	b Karim	2	7	0	0
GB Hogg		c & b Karim	0	3	0	0
IJ Harvey	not out		28	43	5	0
Extras	(b 4, lb 1, w 4, nb 1)		10			
Total	(5 wickets, 31.2 overs, 134 mins)		178			

DNB: DR Martyn, AJ Bichel, B Lee, GD McGrath.

Fall of wickets: 1-50 (Hayden, 5.5 ov), 2-98 (Gilchrist, 11.3 ov), 3-109 (Ponting, 15.5 ov), 4-117 (Lehmann, 17.3 ov), 5-117 (Hogg, 17.6 ov).

Bowling	O	M	R	W	
MA Suji	3	0	36	0	
Ongondo	10	0	44	2	(1nb, 2w)
AO Suji	2	0	24	0	(1w)
CO Obuya	8	0	62	0	
Karim	8.2	6	7	3	

Semi Final
Australia v Sri Lanka
At St. George's Park, Port Elizabeth, 18 March 2003 (50-overs)
Result: Australia won by 48 runs (D/L Method). Australia advances to the final.
Toss: Australia. Umpires: RE Koertzen and DR Shepherd (Eng).
TV Umpire: BF Bowden (NZ). Match Referee: CH Lloyd (WI).
Man of the Match: A Symonds.

Australia innings (50 overs maximum)			R	B	4	6
+AC Gilchrist	c Sangakkara	b de Silva	22	20	2	1
ML Hayden	c Tillakaratne	b Vaas	20	38	2	0
*RT Ponting	c Jayasuriya	b Vaas	2	8	0	0
DS Lehmann		b Jayasuriya	36	66	2	0
A Symonds	not out		91	118	7	1
MG Bevan	c Sangakkara	b Jayasuriya	0	1	0	0
GB Hogg	st Sangakkara	b de Silva	8	19	0	0
IJ Harvey	c Sangakkara	b Vaas	7	10	0	0
AJ Bichel	not out		19	21	0	1
Extras	(lb 3, w 3, nb 1)		7			
Total	(7 wickets, 50 overs, 199 mins)		212			

DNB: B Lee, GD McGrath.
Fall of wickets: 1-34 (Gilchrist, 5.2 ov), 2-37 (Ponting, 6.5 ov), 3-51 (Hayden, 12.2 ov), 4-144 (Lehmann, 34.6 ov), 5-144 (Bevan, 36.1 ov), 6-158 (Hogg, 40.3 ov), 7-175 (Harvey, 43.5 ov).

Bowling	O	M	R	W	
Vaas	10	1	34	3	(1nb, 1w)
Gunaratne	8	0	60	0	(1w)
de Silva	10	0	36	2	(1w)
Muralitharan	10	0	29	0	
Jayasuriya	10	0	42	2	
Arnold	2	0	8	0	

Sri Lanka innings (target: 172 runs from 38.1 overs)			R	B	4	6
MS Atapattu		b Lee	14	17	3	0
*ST Jayasuriya	c Symonds	b McGrath	17	24	0	1
HP Tillakaratne	c Gilchrist	b Lee	3	15	0	0
DA Gunawardene	c Ponting	b Lee	1	4	0	0
PA de Silva	run out (Bichel)		11	16	2	0
+KC Sangakkara	not out		39	70	3	0
DPMD Jayawardene	c Gilchrist	b Hogg	5	8	1	0
RP Arnold	c Lee	b Hogg	3	27	0	0
WPUJC Vaas	not out		21	50	1	1
Extras	(b 4, lb 1, w 2, nb 2)		9			
Total	(7 wickets, 38.1 overs, 167 mins)		123			

DNB: M Muralitharan, PW Gunaratne.
Fall of wickets: 1-21 (Atapattu, 3.6 ov), 2-37 (Jayasuriya, 8.5 ov), 3-37 (Tillakaratne, 9.3 ov), 4-43 (Gunawardene, 11.2 ov), 5-51 (de Silva, 13.1 ov), 6-60 (Jayawardene, 16.1 ov), 7-76 (Arnold, 24.2 ov).

Bowling	O	M	R	W	
McGrath	7	1	20	1	
Lee	8	0	35	3	(2nb, 2w)
Bichel	10	4	18	0	
Hogg	10	1	30	2	
Harvey	2.1	0	11	0	
Lehmann	1	0	4	0	

Semi Final
India v Kenya
At Kingsmead, Durban (day/night), 20 March 2003 (50-overs)
Result: India won by 91 runs. India advances to the final.
Toss: India. Umpires: SA Bucknor (WI) and DJ Harper (Aus).
TV Umpire: SJA Taufel (Aus). Match Referee: MJ Procter.
Man of the Match: SC Ganguly.

India innings (50 overs maximum)			R	B	4	6
V Sehwag	c Odumbe	b Ongondo	33	56	3	0
SR Tendulkar	c DO Obuya	b Tikolo	83	101	5	1
*SC Ganguly	not out		111	114	5	5
M Kaif	run out (CO Obuya)		15	20	0	0
Yuvraj Singh	c DO Obuya	b Odoyo	16	10	1	1
+R Dravid	not out		1	1	0	0
Extras	(w 9, nb 2)		11			
Total	(4 wickets, 50 overs, 222 mins)		270			

DNB: D Mongia, J Srinath, A Nehra, Z Khan, Harbhajan Singh.
Fall of wickets: 1-74 (Sehwag, 18.3 ov), 2-177 (Tendulkar, 37.5 ov), 3-233 (Kaif, 45.5 ov), 4-267 (Yuvraj Singh, 49.3 ov).

Bowling	O	M	R	W	
Suji	10	1	62	0	
Odoyo	10	1	45	1	(2nb, 1w)
Ongondo	10	1	38	1	
Karim	4	0	25	0	(1w)
Tikolo	10	0	60	1	(2w)
CO Obuya	6	0	40	0	(1w)

Kenya innings (target: 271 runs from 50 overs)			R	B	4	6
+KO Otieno	c Dravid	b Srinath	15	43	1	0
RD Shah	lbw	b Khan	1	17	0	0
PJ Ongondo	c Khan	b Nehra	0	5	0	0
TM Odoyo	c Sehwag	b Nehra	7	15	0	0
*SO Tikolo		b Tendulkar	56	83	5	2
MO Odumbe	c Khan	b Yuvraj Singh	19	16	1	1
HS Modi	c Dravid	b Khan	9	25	0	0
DO Obuya	run out (Kaif/Harbhajan Singh)		3	23	0	0
CO Obuya	lbw	b Tendulkar	29	42	1	1
MA Suji		b Khan	1	8	0	0
AY Karim	not out		0	1	0	0
Extras	(b 16, lb 8, w 15)		39			
Total	(all out, 46.2 overs, 190 mins)		179			

Fall of wickets: 1-20 (Shah, 8.2 ov), 2-21 (Ongondo, 10.1 ov), 3-30 (Otieno, 13.1 ov), 4-36 (Odoyo, 14.3 ov), 5-63 (Odumbe, 18.4 ov), 6-92 (Modi, 26.4 ov), 7-104 (DO Obuya, 33.1 ov), 8-161 (Tikolo, 43.4 ov), 9-179 (CO Obuya, 45.4 ov), 10-179 (Suji, 46.2 ov).

Bowling	O	M	R	W	
Khan	9.2	2	14	3	(3w)
Srinath	7	1	11	1	(1w)
Nehra	5	1	11	2	(2w)
Harbhajan Singh	10	1	32	0	
Yuvraj Singh	6	0	43	1	
Sehwag	3	1	16	0	(1w)
Tendulkar	6	0	28	2	(3w)

Final
Australia v India
At New Wanderers Stadium, Johannesburg, 23 March 2003 (50-overs)
Result: Australia won by 125 runs. Australia wins the 2003 ICC World Cup.
Toss: India. Umpires: SA Bucknor (WI) and DR Shepherd (Eng).
TV Umpire: RE Koertzen. Match Referee: RS Madugalle (SL).
Man of the Match: RT Ponting. Player of the Series: SR Tendulkar.

Australia innings (50 overs maximum)			R	B	4	6
+AC Gilchrist	c Sehwag	b Harbhajan Singh	57	48	8	1
ML Hayden	c Dravid	b Harbhajan Singh	37	54	5	0
*RT Ponting	not out		140	121	4	8
DR Martyn	not out		88	84	7	1
Extras	(b 2, lb 12, w 16, nb 7)		37			
Total	(2 wickets, 50 overs, 205 mins)		359			

DNB: DS Lehmann, MG Bevan, A Symonds, GB Hogg, AJ Bichel, B Lee, GD McGrath.
Fall of wickets: 1-105 (Gilchrist, 13.6 ov), 2-125 (Hayden, 19.5 ov).

Bowling	O	M	R	W	
Khan	7	0	67	0	(2nb, 6w)
Srinath	10	0	87	0	(3nb, 2w)
Nehra	10	0	57	0	(3w)
Harbhajan Singh	8	0	49	2	
Sehwag	3	0	14	0	
Tendulkar	3	0	20	0	(1w)
Mongia	7	0	39	0	(2nb)
Yuvraj Singh	2	0	12	0	

India innings (target: 360 runs from 50 overs)			R	B	4	6
SR Tendulkar	c & b McGrath		4	5	1	0
V Sehwag	run out (Lehmann)		82	81	10	3
*SC Ganguly	c Lehmann	b Lee	24	25	3	1
M Kaif	c Gilchrist	b McGrath	0	3	0	0
+R Dravid		b Bichel	47	57	2	0
Yuvraj Singh	c Lee	b Hogg	24	34	1	0
D Mongia	c Martyn	b Symonds	12	11	2	0
Harbhajan Singh	c McGrath	b Symonds	7	8	0	0
Z Khan	c Lehmann	b McGrath	4	8	0	0
J Srinath		b Lee	1	4	0	0
A Nehra	not out		8	4	2	0
Extras	(b 4, lb 4, w 9, nb 4)		21			
Total	(all out, 39.2 overs, 180 mins)		234			

Fall of wickets: 1-4 (Tendulkar, 0.5 ov), 2-58 (Ganguly, 9.5 ov), 3-59 (Kaif, 10.3 ov), 4-147 (Sehwag, 23.5 ov), 5-187 (Dravid, 31.5 ov), 6-208 (Yuvraj Singh, 34.5 ov), 7-209 (Mongia, 35.2 ov), 8-223 (Harbhajan Singh, 37.1 ov), 9-226 (Srinath, 38.2 ov), 10-234 (Khan, 39.2 ov).

Bowling	O	M	R	W	
McGrath	8.2	0	52	3	
Lee	7	1	31	2	(4nb, 2w)
Hogg	10	0	61	1	(2w)
Lehmann	2	0	18	0	
Bichel	10	0	57	1	(4w)
Symonds	2	0	7	2	(1w)

World Cup **2007**

by Tony Cozier

"A great place for the World Cup" was the catchphrase the West Indies Cricket Board used in convincing the International Cricket Council in June 1998 to assign the game's premier event to the Caribbean for the first time, in 2007.

No one doubted the veracity of the WICB boast. The region's rich cricketing history and the natural environment that renders it one of the most desirable holiday spots on earth made it a self-evident truth.

Yet, from the start, there was a lingering scepticism, not only outside but also within the West Indies, summed up by Mike Atherton, the former England captain, in his newspaper column just over a year before the event.

"The West Indies World Cup has the potential to be a terrific celebration of cricket," he wrote. "It also has all the makings of a shambles."

Nowhere is the game more passionately loved or more joyfully followed. Carnival, calypso and cricket are synonymous with the Caribbean but they are counter-balanced by unique complexities.

The entire populations of many of the mini states that embraced the game bequeathed by British colonialism are small enough to be comfortably accommodated in the Melbourne Cricket Ground or Kolkata's Eden Gardens.

Although the West Indies have played as a unified cricket team since their inaugural tour, to Canada and the United States, nearly 150 years ago, there is no such political entity. After more than one failed attempt at integration, the scattered parts all went their separate ways into full independence, all with their own governments, flags, anthems, currencies and, except for cricket, their own individual sporting teams. And, to complicate matters even further, they are separated by water, from Guyana on the south American mainland to Jamaica in the northern Caribbean.

These were some of the hurdles that Chris Dehring, the Jamaican investment banker who, as the WICB's chief marketing officer, had to persuade fellow ICC members could be overcome in mounting what he properly described as "the biggest event that we've ever hosted in the Caribbean in any sphere". In the end, the ICC's vote in favour was unanimous.

The West Indies' turn was long overdue. Each of the other full members of the ICC had hosted the Cup, either separately or on a joint basis. England had held

it four times, India and Pakistan shared it twice. South Africa jumped the queue after its 22 years of isolation was ended by the demise of apartheid and was granted the 2003 tournament.

The ICC made the organisation that much harder by bumping up the number of teams for the 2007 event from 14 to 16 with the addition of two more of its associate members. They were placed into four groups of four each in the first-round, all allocated according to the ICC seedings at the end of April, 2005. The top two from each group move on to the Super Eight round and ultimately to the semi-finals and final.

According to Dehring, who subsequently became chief executive of the regional company formed to plan and oversee the Cup, the estimate of an "economic windfall" of US$500 million was based on ticket sales, sponsorship, broadcasting rights, concessions, merchandising and tourism.

To achieve such a return required heavy financial investment in overall infrastructure, another significant benefit as cities holding the Olympics and other major sporting extravaganzas have discovered. "Legacy" was the buzzword soon firmly affixed to "World Cup".

As much as the event would be judged on its organization and the legacy it leaves, success also hinges on the wholehearted involvement of the people and of the performance of the West Indies team before its own people on its own patch.

The first-round elimination of the hosts diminished the tournaments in Australia in 1992, England in 1999 and South Africa in 2003. Such an early exit would have an even more profound effect on a public yearning for an end to a decade-long decline that has sent the West Indies plunging from top to near bottom in the world game.

Such failure by any other team would be less traumatic for those to whom the game is not everything, those coming to combine a holiday with a rare sporting experience.

As many as 10,000 supporters have followed England to Barbados and Antigua on their recent tours but this time the influx is global and bound to be appreciably higher. While their presence is a boost to the various economies, the strain on accommodation, both in and away from the grounds, was inevitable.

The Queen's Park Oval in Trinidad was originally the only Test venue with a capacity of more than 15,000. Even in islands with well-developed tourist sectors, there were unlikely to be enough rooms to meet the expected demand. For overburdened and much maligned internal airlines, there would be pressure to get fans – and their luggage – to their listed destinations together and on time. And the need to clear immigration and customs and convert currency at every port would, as always, be an annoying and time-consuming process.

In addition, legislation was required for the duration of the tournament to deal with the ICC's strict and specific demands on security and the advertising and promotional intrusion of competitors to its main sponsors, so-called "ambush marketing". That meant the approval of eight different parliaments.

So new and, at the very least, refurbished stadiums with capacity enough to seat the expected invasion were commissioned. New roads were constructed, old ones repaired, flyovers planned. Accommodation was significantly increased and the public urged to open their homes on a bed-and-breakfast basis to the cricket tourists.

An aerial view of how the architects envisage Kensington Oval after its extreme makeover for the Super Eight and Final.

International tour operators were quick to beat the shortage of hotel beds by leasing cruise liners to act as floating hotels. Tenders were advertised for charter aircraft companies to augment the scheduled airlines.

Through their umbrella organisation, Caricom (the Caribbean Community), the governments pledged the temporary regulations stipulated by the ICC, the so-called "sunset legislation", for the duration of the tournament. They included the issuing a "World Cup passport" to players, officials and fans to facilitate easier travel between venues. Teams of volunteers, such a feature of South Africa in 2003, were recruited and trained.

It was daunting and costly yet no self-respecting West Indian country could easily pass up the chance to be part of such a high-profile cricket event. Of the WICB affiliates, only Dominica and the very smallest declined to tender to be one of the eight venues. Claims even came from the Bahamas, Bermuda and the United States (through the city of Lauderhill, Florida), none of them WICB members but all under its ambit by ICC mandate.

The contenders were guided by the Bid Book, a hefty tome such as those used in the Olympics and other major games. Put together by a consortium of technocrats with world games and cricket World Cup know-how, headed by an experienced American, Don Lockerbie, and dubbed the venue assessment team (VAT), it detailed the minimum requirements and standards that had to be met (from stadiums to immigration and customs, from accommodation to political environment, from communications to medical facilities).

When the host territories were announced on July 12, 2004, Barbados, scene of the West Indies' first home Test in 1930 and birthplace of more Test cricketers per square mile than any place on earth, was awarded the final and one of the Super Eight rounds. The semi-finals and a first round went to Jamaica and St. Lucia. Antigua, Grenada and Guyana were assigned Super Eight groups, Trinidad and St. Kitts got first-round matches. St. Kitts (population 36,000) was the surprise in the pack, for it had never previously staged an international match.

Lauderhill, reportedly because of doubts over the U.S. to provide visas for every team, the Bahamas and Bermuda missed out. St. Vincent had to make do with the consolation of warm-up matches, one of which was the plum, Australia against England.

Antigua and Guyana immediately abandoned their traditional, now inadequate, homes of international cricket, at the Antigua Recreation Ground and Bourda, in favour of sizeable, new, modern stadiums. The former was duly dubbed the Sir Viv Richards Stadium.

The West Indies and India inaugurate international cricket's newest venue, Warner Park in Basseterre, St. Kitts, during the 2006 season. It will be the site for the first-round group including champions and top seeds Australia in the 2007 World Cup.

The **Tournament**

OPENING CEREMONY (Trelawney, Jamaica).
Sunday, March 11

GROUP STAGE (all matches have a reserve day)

GROUP A (Warner Park, St. Kitts)
Wednesday, March 14	Australia v Scotland
Friday, March 16	South Africa v Holland
Sunday, March 18	Australia v Holland
Tuesday, March 20	South Africa v Scotland
Thursday, March 22	Scotland v Holland
Saturday, March 24	Australia v South Africa

GROUP B (Queen's Park Oval, Trinidad)
Thursday, March 15	Sri Lanka v Bermuda
Saturday, March 17	India v Bangladesh
Monday, March 19	India v Bermuda
Wednesday, March 21	Sri Lanka v Bangladesh
Friday, March 23	India v Sri Lanka
Sunday, March 25	Bermuda v Bangladesh

GROUP C (Beausejour Stadium, St. Lucia)
Wednesday, March 14	Kenya v Canada
Friday, March 16:	England v New Zealand
Sunday, March 18:	England v Canada
Tuesday, March 20:	New Zealand v Kenya
Thursday, March 22:	New Zealand v Canada
Saturday, March 24:	England v Kenya

GROUP D (Sabina Park, Jamaica)
Tuesday, March 13:	West Indies v Pakistan
Thursday, March 15:	Zimbabwe v Ireland
Saturday, March 17:	Pakistan v Ireland
Monday, March 19:	West Indies v Zimbabwe
Wednesday, March 21:	Zimbabwe v Pakistan
Friday, March 23:	West Indies v Ireland

SUPER EIGHT SERIES

ANTIGUA/BARBUDA (Sir Viv Richards Stadium)
Tuesday, March 27:	Group D 2nd v Group A 1st
Thursday, March 29:	Group D 2nd v Group C 1st
Saturday, March 31:	Group A 1st v Group B 2nd
Monday, April 2:	Group B 2nd v Group C 1st
Wednesday, April 4:	Group C 2nd v Group B 1st
Sunday, April 8:	Group A 1st v Group C 2nd

GUYANA (Esperance Stadium)
Wednesday, March 28:	Group A 2nd v Group B 1st.
Friday, March 30:	Group D 1st v Group C 2nd
Sunday, April 1:	Group D 2nd v Group B 1st
Tuesday, April 3:	Group D 1st v Group A 2nd
Saturday, April 7:	Group B 2nd v Group A 2nd
Monday, April 9:	Group D 1st v Group C 1st

GRENADA (New Queen's Park Stadium)
Tuesday, April 10:	Group D 2nd v Group A 2nd
Thursday, April 12:	Group B 1st v Group C 1st
Saturday, April 14:	Group A 2nd v Group C 1st
Monday, April 16:	Group A 1st v Group B 1st
Wednesday, April 18:	Group D 1st v Group B 1st
Friday, April 20:	Group A 1st v Group C 1st

BARBADOS (Kensington Oval)
Wednesday, April 11:	Group C 2nd v Group B 2nd
Friday, April 13:	Group A 1st v Group D 1st
Sunday, April 15:	Group B 2nd v Group D 1st
Tuesday, April 17:	Group A 2nd v Group C 2nd
Thursday, April 19:	Group D 2nd v Group B 2nd
Saturday, April 21:	Group D 2nd v Group C 2nd

SEMI-FINALS

JAMAICA (Sabina Park)
Tuesday, April 24: Super Eight 2nd v 3rd
ST LUCIA (Beausejour Stadium)
Wednesday, April 25: Super Eight 1st v 4th

FINAL

BARBADOS (Kensington Oval)
Saturday, April 28 (Reserve day, Sunday, April 29)

St. Kitts used Warner Park, the established home of sport on the island, for its 10,000-seat stadium that would host the group including champions Australia, the top seeds aiming to complete a World Cup hat-trick following their triumphs in 1999 and 2003. A one day international and a test against India in 2006 proved successful rehearsals.

For the sake of history and sentiment, Barbados and Jamaica chose to retain the locations of their famous grounds, Kensington Oval and Sabina Park, but planned comprehensive make-overs. At the same time, Jamaica erected a new facility at Trelawney on the north coast to stage the opening ceremony and warm-up matches.

The Queen's Park Oval in Trinidad, always the largest ground in the West Indies and, like Kensington and Sabina, with a background of more than 100 years, required only comparatively limited change, including a new club pavilion.

Queen's Park in Grenada was six years old, Beausejour Stadium in St. Lucia four. Minor alterations were required for both – until Queen's Park was almost totally destroyed by Hurricane Ivan in September 2004. It had to be rebuilt, almost from scratch.

Such work was mainly underwritten by the governments concerned, in most cases undertaken with loans and by construction companies from China (both mainland and Taiwan) and India. Kensington Oval's renovations was the most expensive, estimated at US$70 million. Others varied between US$20 and US$50 million.

They represented the major portion of overall costs provisionally estimated at US$250 million. It is a high price tag for a group of small nations with limited resources to fork out but not more than the "terrific celebration" of a sport that has brought them international recognition and respect is worth.

"They're saying"

Chris Dehring, Cricket World Cup 2007 chief executive officer, in an interview with The Independent, London, February 2006: *"It's going to be a fantastic World Cup; you may stand in line a little longer but you're going to have the best time in that line that you've had in your life, so the fact you have to wait a little longer won't matter much. That is what the experience is, it's what we sell and you buy."*

Owen Arthur, Barbados Prime Minister: *"It is an expression of confidence of who we are and what we can do as a people, that the Caribbean governments no matter how financially strapped maybe our circumstances, should not only act on the belief but pursue the belief that this region should host something as important as a cricket World Cup and a cricket World Cup final."*

Ken Gordon, West Indies Cricket Board president and Cricket World Cup 2007 chairman: *"Every day brings a crisis. The key is that we have a good team managing it, and that is always the essence of it. So far, all of the problems that have arisen, we have been able to deal with them."*

Michael Hall, Cricket World Cup 2007 cricket operations director: *"The plan is also to have chartered, dedicated jet aircraft transportation for teams and officials. Each team will have a baggage master whose specific responsibility is nothing but the team's baggage."*

Reverend Wes Hall, Former WICB president and West Indies fast bowler: *"We do not wish to carry any baggage into the World Cup. The Lord does not wish us to do that. We have to stop the finger-pointing, we have to stop making excuses. How many of you know that an excuse is the skin of a reason stuffed with a lie; that's what it is. Let's communicate optimism to six million West Indians."*

Donald Lockerbie, Cricket World Cup 2007 venue development director: *"I would think that if any country failed at the Cricket World Cup that the government would collapse, and no one would want to see that happen."*

Formats

The number of teams has been bumped up to 16, the most in any tournament. Four teams were divided into four qualifying groups according to seeding, each in a separate venue. Top two teams in each group move on to the 'Super Eight' stage, in four different venues, leading to semis and final. The number of matches, 51, down by three from 2003 but the number of playing days up from 43 to 47.

Innovations

Not finalised but likely to include at least the two, obligatory five-over 'power plays', further fielding restrictions to be used by the bowling side at any time after 10 overs. Also likely is the issuing of 'World Cup passports' to overcome the immigration bottlenecks between the eight independent venue nations and the use of cruise liners as floating hotels to surmount the overall accommodation shortfall.

World Cup Records **1975–2003**

TEAM RESULTS

Team	Tournaments	Matches	Won	Lost	Tied	No results
Australia	8	58	40	17	1	0
West Indies	8	48	31	16	0	1
England	8	50	31	18	0	1
India	8	55	31	23	0	1
Pakistan	8	53	29	22	0	2
New Zealand	8	52	28	23	0	1
South Africa	4	30	19	9	2	0
Sri Lanka	8	46	17	27	1	1
Zimbabwe	6	42	8	31	0	3
Kenya	3	20	5	14	0	1
Bangladesh	2	11	2	8	0	1
United Arab Emirates	1	5	1	4	0	0
Canada	2	9	1	8	0	0
Holland	2	11	1	10	0	0
East Africa	1	3	0	3	0	0
Scotland	1	5	0	5	0	0
Namibia	1	6	0	6	0	0

HIGHEST TOTALS

398-5	(50.0 ov)	Sri Lanka v Kenya at Kandy	1996
373-6	(50.0 ov)	India v Sri Lanka at Taunton	1999
360-4	(50.0 ov)	West Indies v Sri Lanka at Karachi	1987
359-2	(50.0 ov)	Australia v India at Johannesburg	2003
340-2	(50.0 ov)	Zimbabwe v Namibia at Harare	2003
338-5	(60.0 ov)	Pakistan v Sri Lanka at Swansea	1983
334-4	(60.0 ov)	England v India at Lord's	1975
333-9	(60.0 ov)	England v Sri Lanka at Taunton	1983
330-6	(60.0 ov)	Pakistan v Sri Lanka at Nottingham	1975
329-2	(50.0 ov)	India v Kenya at Bristol	1999
328-5	(60.0 ov)	Australia v Sri Lanka at The Oval	1975
328-3	(50.0 ov)	South Africa v Netherlands at Rawalpindi	1996
322-6	(60.0 ov)	England v New Zealand at The Oval	1983
321-2	(50.0 ov)	South Africa v U.A.E. at Rawalpindi	1996
320-9	(60.0 ov)	Australia v India at Nottingham	1983

LOWEST TOTALS

36	(18.4 ov)	Canada v Sri Lanka at Paarl	2003
45	(40.3 ov)	Canada v England at Manchester	1979
45	(14.0 ov)	Namibia v Australia at Potchefstroom	2003
68	(31.3 ov)	Scotland v West Indies at Leicester	1999
74	(40.2 ov)	Pakistan v England at Adelaide	1992
84	(17.4 ov)	Namibia v Pakistan at Kimberley	2003
86	(37.2 ov)	Sri Lanka v West Indies at Manchester	1975
93	(36.2 ov)	England v Australia at Leeds	1975
93	(35.2 ov)	West Indies v Kenya at Poona	1996
94	(52.3 ov)	East Africa v England at Birmingham	1975
103	(41.0 ov)	England v South Africa at The Oval	1999
104	(35.5 ov)	Kenya v West Indies at Kimberley	2003
105	(33.2 ov)	Canada v Australia at Birmingham	1979
108	(35.1 ov)	Bangladesh v South Africa at Bloemfontein	2003
109	(23.0 ov)	Sri Lanka v India at Johannesburg	2003

LEADING SCORERS

Player	Team	Matches	Runs	HS	100s	Average	Strike rate
SR Tendulkar	India	33	1732	152	4	59.72	87.56
Javed Miandad	Pakistan	33	1083	103	1	43.32	67.89
PA de Silva	Sri Lanka	35	1064	145	2	36.68	86.57
IVA Richards	West Indies	23	1013	181	3	63.31	85.05
ME Waugh	Australia	22	1004	130	4	52.84	83.04
RT Ponting	Australia	28	998	140*	3	41.58	74.98
SR Waugh	Australia	33	978	120*	1	48.89	81.02
A Ranatunga	Sri Lanka	30	969	88*	0	46.14	80.95
BC Lara	West Indies	25	956	116	2	43.45	87.70

LEADING SCORERS cont'd

Player	Team	Matches	Runs	HS	100s	Average	Strike rate
Saeed Anwar	Pakistan	21	915	113*	3	53.82	79.08
GA Gooch	England	21	897	115	1	44.85	63.21
MD Crowe	New Zealand	21	880	100*	1	55.00	83.49
DL Haynes	West Indies	25	854	105	1	37.13	57.50
SC Ganguly	India	18	844	183	4	56.26	81.78
M Azharuddin	India	30	826	93	0	39.33	77.19

HIGHEST SCORES

188*	G Kirsten	South Africa v U.A.E. at Rawalpindi	1996
183	SC Ganguly	India v Sri Lanka at Taunton	1999
181	IVA Richards	West Indies v Sri Lanka at Karachi	1987
175*	N Kapil Dev	India v Zimbabwe at Tunbridge Well	1983
172*	CB Wishart	Zimbabwe v Namibia at Harare	2003
171*	GM Turner	New Zealand v East Africa at Birmingham	1975
161	AC Hudson	South Africa v Netherlands at Rawalpindi	1996
152	SR Tendulkar	India v Namibia at Pietermaritzburg	2003
145	PA de Silva	Sri Lanka v Kenya at Kandy	1996
145	R Dravid	India v Sri Lanka at Taunton	1999
143*	A Symonds	Australia v Pakistan at Johannesburg	2003
143	HH Gibbs	South Africa v New Zealand at Johannesburg	2003
142	DL Houghton	Zimbabwe v New Zealand at Hyderabad	1987
141	SB Styris	New Zealand v Sri Lanka at Bloemfontein	2003
140*	SR Tendulkar	India v Kenya at Bristol	1999
140*	RT Ponting	Australia v India at Johannesburg	2003

LEADING WICKET-TAKERS

Player	Team	Matches	Runs	Wickets	Average	BB
Wasim Akram	Pakistan	38	1311	55	23.83	5/28
GD McGrath	Australia	28	935	45	20.77	7/15
J Srinath	India	34	1224	44	27.81	4/30
AA Donald	S.Africa	25	913	38	24.02	4/17
WPUJC Vaas	Sri Lanka	21	754	36	20.94	6/25
Imran Khan	Pakistan	28	655	34	19.26	4/37
CZ Harris	NZ	28	861	32	26.90	4/7
SK Warne	Australia	17	624	32	19.50	4/29
IT Botham	England	22	762	30	25.39	4/31
M Muralitharan	Sri Lanka	21	693	30	23.10	4/28
PAJ DeFreitas	England	22	742	29	25.58	3/28
N Kapil Dev	India	26	892	28	31.85	5/43
A Kumble	India	17	670	28	23.92	4/32
CA Walsh	W.Indies	17	547	27	20.25	4/25
SR Waugh	Australia	33	814	27	30.14	3/36
CJ McDermott	Australia	17	599	27	22.18	5/44
Shoaib Akhtar	Pakistan	16	643	27	23.81	4/46

BEST FIGURES

7-15	GD McGrath	Australia v Namibia at Potchefstroom	2003
7-20	AJ Bichel	Australia v England at Port Elizabeth	2003
7-51	WW Davis	West Indies v Australia at Leeds	1983
6-14	GJ Gilmour	Australia v England at Leeds	1975
6-23	A Nehra	India v England at Durban	2003
6-23	SE Bond	New Zealand v Australia at Port Elizabeth	2003
6-25	WPUJC Vaas	Sri Lanka v Bangladesh at Pietermaritzburg	2003
6-39	KH MacLeay	Australia v India at Nottingham	1983
5-14	GD McGrath	Australia v West Indies at Manchester	1999
5-21	AG Hurst	Australia v Canada at Birmingham	1979
5-21	PA Strang	Zimbabwe v Kenya at Patna	1996
5-21	L Klusener	South Africa v Kenya at Amstelveen	1999
5-24	CO Obuya	Kenya v Sri Lanka at Nairobi	2003
5-25	RJ Hadlee	New Zealand v Sri Lanka at Bristol	1983
5-27	BKV Prasad	India v Pakistan at Manchester	1999
5-27	A Codrington	Canada v Bangladesh at Durban	2003